MASS MEDIA AN

Mass Media and Health: Examining Media Impact on Individuals and the Health Environment covers media health influences from a variety of angles, including the impact on individual and public health, the intentionality of these effects, and the nature of the outcomes. Author Kim Walsh-Childers helps readers understand the influence that mass media has on an individual's health beliefs and, in turn, their behaviors. She explains how public health policy can be affected, altering the environment in which a community's members make choices, and discusses the unintentional health effects of mass media, examining them through the strategic lens of news framing and advocacy campaigns.

Written for students across a variety of disciplines, *Mass Media and Health* will serve as primary reading for courses examining the broader view of mass media and health impacts, as well as providing supplemental reading for courses on health communication, public health campaigns, health journalism and media effects.

Dr. Kim Walsh-Childers is a former newspaper health reporter who teaches courses in mass media and health, along with courses in journalism and media ethics, at the University of Florida College of Journalism and Communications. Her research focuses on news coverage of health issues, the effects of health news coverage on individual health and health policy, cancer communication, and individuals' use of online health information. Her work has been published in *Health Communication, Journalism and Mass Communication Quarterly, Newspaper Research*

Journal, Science Communication, Communication Research, Pediatrics, AIDS Education and Prevention, and the *Journal of Adolescent Health Care,* among others. Her research has been supported by grants from the Kaiser Family Foundation, the Robert Wood Johnson Foundation, the National Cancer Institute and the Department of Defense. She was a Fulbright Scholar in Ireland during the 2004 to 2005 academic year, studying the impact of news coverage on Irish health policy.

MASS MEDIA AND HEALTH
Examining Media Impact on Individuals and the Health Environment

Kim Walsh-Childers

NEW YORK AND LONDON

First published 2017
by Routledge
711 Third Avenue, New York, NY 10017

and by Routledge
2 Park Square, Milton Park, Abingdon, Oxon OX14 4RN

Routledge is an imprint of the Taylor & Francis Group, an informa business

Library of Congress Cataloging in Publication Data
Names: Walsh-Childers, Kim, author.
Title: Mass media and health : examining media impact on individuals and the health environment / Kim Walsh-Childers.
Description: New York : Routledge, 2016.
Identifiers: LCCN 2016024162| ISBN 9781138925595 (hardback) | ISBN 9781138925601 (pbk.) | ISBN 9781315683683 (ebk.)
Subjects: LCSH: Health in mass media–United States.
Classification: LCC P96.H43 W35 2016 | DDC 070.4/49613–dc23
LC record available at https://lccn.loc.gov/2016024162

ISBN: 978-1-138-92559-5 (hbk)
ISBN: 978-1-138-92560-1 (pbk)
ISBN: 978-1-315-68368-3 (ebk)

Typeset in ITC Legacy Serif
by Wearset Ltd, Boldon, Tyne and Wear

DEDICATION

To my parents, John R. and Nina Walsh, whose love gave me roots and wings. I wish I had written this 15 years earlier, so you could have seen it.

To my sons, Ian and Aidan. I have cherished every single moment watching each of you grow to be men – every laugh, every heartbreak, every (fortunately brief) minute of terror, every goofy but still brilliant home-made video, every groan-inducing pun. And every time – and there have been many – that you have made me so proud to say, "That's my son."

And to my husband Hoyt, my Renaissance man, my artist in words and pictures and clay. You are my safe harbor and my favorite adventuring partner.

CONTENTS

FIGURES

PREFACE

More than 25 years ago, Dr. Jane Brown of the University of North Carolina-Chapel Hill was invited to write a chapter for a new edited book, *Media Effects: Advances in Theory and Research*. I was then completing the final year of my doctoral program at UNC under Dr. Brown's guidance, and she invited me to co-author the chapter, which was to review the literature on the impacts of mass media on health. Other authors, we learned, would write chapters focused on the media and violence literature and on the effects of pornography, so we were able to cut those topics from our outline. Nonetheless, when we completed the manuscript – which was supposed to be limited to 30 pages of text – we had 30 pages in references alone. We began talking then about the idea that we should expand the chapter to book length.

In the intervening years, Dr. Brown and I produced two updated editions of the *Media Effects* chapter, recognizing with each version that there were more and more topics that needed to be addressed. The need for the book became increasingly clear, but neither of us really had the time to put it together. So the conversation continued.

In about 1994 I began teaching an annual graduate seminar on mass media and health, one focused on the unintended impacts of mass media. For a while I had students read Dr. Nancy Signorielli's excellent summary text, *Mass Media Images and Impact on Health: A Sourcebook*, but when that book became somewhat dated I turned to assigning sets of more recent journal articles related to each class topic. The growing body of literature on the Internet as a health information source meant that I needed to add that topic to the class. More recently, both student interest in and the volume of research on social media effects added another subject to the syllabus. Every fall, while reviewing the readings for the spring course, I wished there was a textbook I could offer students that would provide a summary of at least the more important studies in each area, including topics we sometimes did not have time to cover in class discussions.

This book, then, is the culmination of that original conversation with Dr. Brown and of my attempts to keep up with the ever-increasing body of research on the health effects mass media can have, both at the level of individual health behavior and through health policy development. My intent is to provide students and fellow scholars with a sense of what we have learned from nearly a century of research on these topics. I certainly would not claim that the chapters summarize every important area of research on mass media health effects, but I have attempted, to the extent possible, to provide a thorough overview of the most critical and heavily studied issues.

A cursory glance at the Contents page will immediately reveal one enormous area of research that is not included: the impact of mass media health communication campaigns. I chose not to cover traditional mass media public health campaigns for one key reason: there are many excellent texts already available that summarize the research in this area, provide guidance in the development of health communication campaigns, and discuss the factors contributing to the success or failure of such campaigns.

This book does address the use of mass media to affect health *policy* change, through media advocacy efforts focusing on influencing news coverage of health and through paid political advertising aimed at building public and policy-making support for (or opposition to) legislation and regulation that has impacted upon the health environment. These important topics have received significantly less attention, at least in book form, and I believe it is important that health communication scholars recognize both the importance of policy in restricting or encouraging specific health behaviors and the ways in which mass media can affect health policy development.

Although the book focuses, for the most part, on unintended impacts of mass media content and use, I believe it will be of significant use not only to those interested in these unintended effects but also to those whose work focuses on using mass media intentionally to influence individual health behavior. The second part of the book, which deals with the health policy effects of mass media, addresses the ways in which the health environment (to which health policy is a key contributor) can influence individual health behavior in both positive and negative ways. In addition, however, I believe it is crucial for those hoping to use mass media to encourage individuals to choose healthier behaviors to understand how the media environment can impinge upon mediated public health campaigns. Mass media messages often compete with those of health promotion campaigns (e.g., anti-smoking PSAs versus $1 billion or more spent each year advertising tobacco products), and the ubiquity of many health-related messages (e.g., those promoting a thin ideal standard of beauty for women) create a huge barrier for health promotion campaigns to overcome.

STRUCTURE OF THE BOOK

Chapter 1 attempts to establish a context for the rest of the content by providing a summary of the current state of mass media use in the United States and of the health status of the country, in comparison to other developed nations. Media use patterns seem to change rapidly; nonetheless, this section of the chapter provides a sense of the media environment surrounding individuals as they make health decisions. The second section, which examines some of the key health issues facing the United States, reveals that – contrary to what people often assume – Americans are far from having the world's best health care system. Nor does the per capita health spending gap between the United States and other countries stem from poorer health among minority groups or higher expenditures on individuals with severe health problems (Woolf & Aron, 2013).

The remainder of this book is divided into two major parts corresponding to the two levels of media effects – on individuals and on public policy relevant to health. Because far more research has focused on individual-level effects, Part I is much more extensive, and it is somewhat easier to categorize the effects, overall, as being primarily positive or primarily negative. Part II focuses on policy-level effects, acknowledging that because relatively little research has been done on these topics it is substantially less clear whether media influences should be viewed as primarily positive or primarily negative. And because health policies are often controversial, the chapters in Part II will discuss the fact that media effects on policy may be viewed, simultaneously, as positive and negative, depending on the viewpoint of the observer.

As noted above, the most obvious type of media message that would be included in the category of positive, intended, individual health impacts would be traditional public health campaigns using PSAs, telenovelas, or other types of mediated messages to raise awareness of a health issue and/or promote the adoption of healthier attitudes and behaviors. However, traditional public health campaigns are not the only form of media that can have positive effects on individual health behaviors. Chapter 2 discusses other types of media content that, as intended by their producers, have been shown to have a positive influence on individual health.

On first consideration, it is difficult to imagine a type of media message that would be intended by its producer to have a negative impact on individual health; after all, who would *want* to make people less healthy? However, Chapter 3 argues that, given that tobacco use has no discernible health benefit and that smoking is the leading cause of preventable illness and death in the United States, it seems reasonable to argue that any media content promoting tobacco use should be viewed as being intended to cause illness. Chapter 4 discusses the question of whether alcohol advertising should be viewed in a similar way.

Chapters 5 to 12 turn to the unintended negative impacts of media messages on individual health, covering topics that have dominated much of the research on media health effects. These chapters review the literature on the potential and documented negative effects of direct-to-consumer prescription drug advertising (Chapter 5), the effects of entertainment content on smoking, alcohol, and drug use and abuse (Chapter 6), media's impact on diet and exercise choices (Chapter 7), the relationship between exposure to the media's thin ideal and harmful body image effects (Chapter 8), the (mostly) negative influences of media exposure on sexual behavior (Chapter 9), and finally, one of the most thoroughly studied areas of media effects, the research on media violence and its effects on aggressive and violent behavior (Chapter 10). Chapter 11 reviews studies examining how news media cover health issues and how exposure to that coverage affects individual health decisions, for better or for worse, and Chapter 12 looks at individuals' use of the Internet, including social media, for health information, and how that use can lead to both positive and negative health outcomes.

Chapters 13 to 15 turn to examinations of the ways in which mass media content may influence the health environment through effects on local, state, and national health policy and corporate decisions that influence health. The research in these areas is far sparser than that on media influences on individual health behavior, but these topics are nonetheless critical to consider because of the substantial impact corporate and government policies can have on individuals' opportunities to live healthier lives. Chapter 13 examines the (usually) unintended impact of news coverage on health policy development, while Chapter 14 describes the research on intended uses of the media, especially news media, to affect corporate or government health policy, a practice generally referred to as "media advocacy." Chapter 15 reviews the research on political or issue advertising and its impact on health policy development

The final chapter of the book attempts to summarize, to the extent possible, what we do *not* yet know about how mass media content and use influence health. The purpose of this chapter is to suggest an agenda for future research on mass media and health. Replication of previous studies is certainly important in solidifying – or challenging – our understanding of media health impacts. However, progress in the field also requires that we address emerging topics, taking advantage of previous research to kick-start the development of both descriptive knowledge and theory that enables us to explain and predict mass media effects on health.

This is certainly not the first book ever written that addresses a broad range of health impacts of mass media. However, my hope is that bringing reviews of the research on many of the major issues together will give students and scholars alike a better sense of the "big picture" of mass media's impact on health. Many themes occur frequently across a variety of media channels and types of content, both in terms of the types of effects media may have and the characteristics of people most likely to be affected. In addition, some of the gaps in the research are relevant to more than one issue (e.g., the impact of problematic media content on adults). Metaphorically, many previous works, including both individual research articles and scholarly books, have helped us to see the individual trees (or groves of trees) in the media/health forest. By discussing the most heavily researched issues in one collection, I hope to offer a better perspective on the forest as a whole.

Finally, a few acknowledgments. First, my deepest gratitude to Linda Bathgate for her constant encouragement and support, and for keeping me from panicking when my deadline was looming. Thanks, too, to Ross Wagenhofer for taking care of all the business details and for tracking me down when I needed reminders. Many thanks to the reviewers who have offered their wisdom and valuable feedback on this book, from the proposal stage to finished product, including Ann King, whose sharp eyes saved me from several embarrassing mistakes, and the unnamed proposal reviewers, whose comments and suggestions helped me refine my decisions about what to include. To my colleagues at the College of Journalism and Communications, thanks for carrying all the loads I dropped while on sabbatical to write this book, and to the CJC and the University of Florida for giving me the time to write.

Perhaps the most important acknowledgment, however, I owe to Dr. Jane Delano Brown, who taught me not only how to do research but how to love research, and who has been my mentor, role model and idol throughout my entire academic career. Jane, your spirit is in every single line in this book. Your belief that I could write it on my own gave me the courage to try.

CHAPTER 1

THE MEDIA ENVIRONMENT, U.S. HEALTH AND THE MEDIA–HEALTH EFFECTS MATRIX

When my alarm clock goes off in the morning, I wake to the sounds of my local National Public Radio station's morning news show. While fixing myself a cup of tea, I frequently turn on my laptop so that I can check my work and home email accounts. If a major news event was breaking the previous night, I may check CNN.com, my local newspaper's website or Twitter to get the latest updates. If my schedule permits, I may check my Facebook page to see what friends have posted. If I go for a run, walk or bike ride, my smartphone comes with me.

On my drive to work, I pick up the print copy of my local newspaper and listen to NPR's "Morning Edition" on the car radio. At the end of the day, I'll tune in again on the way home, or perhaps I'll listen to music – either on the radio or via my iPod. If I stop at the grocery store, I'll have time to read the cover blurbs on the magazines while standing in the check-out line. At home, there are books and magazines to read, or I watch a TV show or stream a movie through my sons' Wii console. After dinner, I'm likely to be back at the computer, checking the news again, making travel reservations or shopping, paying bills electronically, responding to email, searching for information I need either for work or for my family, uploading readings to an e-learning site for my students, perhaps posting to Facebook.

While other individuals' specific interactions with mass media will differ from mine, most of us share this basic reality. In much of the world today, people live media-saturated lives. A 2013 report from the University of Southern California's Institute for Communication Technology

Management predicted that by 2015, average daily media use per person in the United States would equal 15.5 hours per day – *not* including media consumption at work (Short, 2013). Assuming an eight-hour working day for most people and at least six hours' sleep, that figure gives "multimedia" a whole new meaning. Many of us, during at least some part of our day, are interacting simultaneously with multiple media channels.

The notion that the average person will soon spend substantially more than half of every day interacting with some sort of media raises significant questions about how *so* much media consumption affects us, both individually and as a society. Surely we should expect numerous impacts – economic, political, intellectual, sociological. However, the more specific focus of this book is on how interaction with media affects our health, including both media's effects on our individual health behaviors and on the health environments in which we live. To illustrate, let me return for a moment to my daily media routine.

When NPR wakes me up in the morning, I generally turn it off before I'm awake enough to process any news story that may be running at that moment. But as I head downstairs to make tea, I clip my Fitbit to my pajamas to start monitoring my steps for the day. As soon as I sit down in front of my laptop, it will automatically sync to my account, and, if I choose, I can log in to see how well (or poorly) I've met my activity goals for the week. Email may bring updates about recent health or health policy research or events, or a prayer request from my pastor may inform me about a health problem someone in my church is experiencing. Even if there's no health information in the emails themselves, advertising surrounding my home email account encourages me to check out some new supplement described as the "holy grail for weight loss" or to see what "amazing" new discovery Dr. Oz is touting on TV.

A check of CNN.com (in mid-September 2015) offers me the "Restaurant report card grades on antibiotics in meat supply," providing information about how the use of antibiotic-laden meat from restaurants like McDonald's or Denny's may be contributing to the development of antibiotic-resistant bacteria. The entertainment section updates the story of Caitlyn Jenner's gender change. My local newspaper's website reports that my county is part of a pilot program aimed at improving coordination of area mental health services. At home, *National Geographic*'s October 2015 issue includes a story about the health risks its story-tellers often face, from being run over by hippos or elephants, attacked by sharks or abducted by guerilla fighters, to being bitten by venomous snakes or by swarms of sand-flies that carry potentially fatal parasites. In the grocery store check-out line, the cover of *Cosmopolitan* promises to tell me how to have "Sex For One" and "What Works, What Doesn't" in removing cellulite. If my radio station is playing Beyoncé and Jay Z's 2013 song "Drunk in Love," I'll hear lyrics that – according to some critics, at least – make light of domestic violence. If I listen to radio news or turn on the evening TV news broadcast, I'll hear about the latest violence in Israel, Gaza, Ukraine, Iraq, Syria and other troubled places in the world.

If I log in to Facebook, I can see a friend's update reporting her doctor's diagnosis of the cause for her chronic insomnia problem (adrenal fatigue) and another friend's "shared" pictures offering mental health advice, such as "Stop holding on to what hurts and make room for what feels good." Other friends offer updates about their children's health issues, ranging from the minor to the chronic and potentially life-threatening, while yet another, whose husband has early-onset Alzheimer's disease, may have posted a message advocating for more research on improved treatment options.

In short, not only do we live media-saturated lives, but that media saturation exposes us to a steady stream of messages about health. Over the past 40 years, researchers have attempted to determine what impact that river of health messages has on us, both as individuals making health decisions for ourselves and our families, and as communities and societies creating policies and regulations, through our elected and appointed officials, that influence the health opportunities available to us all. This book is intended to review the research on the most important and most thoroughly studied topics related to mass media's impact on health, to offer some conclusions about what we do and do not know about media effects on health, and to identify key areas for future research.

To establish a context for this discussion, this chapter first examines in more detail recent data on individuals' interactions with the media environment, focusing primarily on the United States. The next section summarizes the health environment, drawing on multinational studies to show how the health status of U.S. citizens compares to that of individuals in other developed countries throughout the world. The chapter then introduces a matrix for categorizing health impacts of mass media based on whether the health effect is an intended or unintended outcome of the mass media message, whether the effect is positive or negative, and whether it occurs at the level of individual behavior or public health policy (Brown & Walsh-Childers, 1994).

MEDIA CONSUMPTION

Television

Given the enormous growth of Internet use over the past two decades, we might assume that the Web now dominates media consumption. In fact, however, the average consumer still spends more hours watching television content than in any other media activity, with TV accounting for 40 percent of our annual media consumption hours (Short, 2013). From 2008 to 2012, Nielsen figures show a decline of about 15 minutes a day in viewing time for traditional, over-the-air, satellite and cable TV – from 4 hours and 44 minutes in 2008 to 4 hours and 35 minutes in 2012. However, the average individual's overall weekly time spent with television programming – including viewing television content via DVDs, DVR, video-streaming through the Internet and mobile TV sub-scriptions – increased from slightly more than 38 hours per week in 2008 to nearly 39 hours in 2012, and is projected to increase to nearly 42 hours per week by 2015; the projected increase is attributed primarily to growth in the use of DVRs, along with mobile and Internet TV (Short, 2013). The most recent Nielsen audience report showed that during the first quarter of 2015, American adults spent about 5.5 hours per day (38.5 hours per week) watching TV content, including traditional "live" TV and time-shifted TV content; adding in use of a DVD or Blu-Ray device would boost the total by ten minutes per day for an overall TV use rate of 39.66 hours per week (The Nielsen Company, 2015b).

The dramatic growth in online TV viewing is a particularly important trend, with 106.2 million Americans reporting in a 2013 Belkin-Harris Interactive poll that they watch TV shows online at least once a month. By 2014, the survey projected that more than 50 percent of Americans would watch TV online (Kleinman, 2013). The growth of online TV viewing helps explain another recent phenomenon, called "cord-cutting," which refers to individuals discontinuing their cable or satellite TV subscriptions. A November 2013 *Los Angeles Times* article reported that the pay TV industry lost 113,000 subscribers, overall, during the third quarter of 2013, with the largest losses occurring among cable subscribers, some 687,000, during that period (James, 2013). As of early August 2014, nearly half (47%) of American households subscribed to one of the three top video-streaming services – Netflix, Hulu, or Amazon Prime; the percentage of Netflix subscribers who also used a pay TV service had dropped from 88 percent in 2010 to 80 percent in 2014 (Seitz, 2014). During 2014, 8.2 percent of cable TV subscribers reported dropping that service, compared to 6.9 percent who said they had ditched cable TV in 2013. In addition, 45.2 percent of cable subscribers said they had cut back on their cable service, as they spent more time with streaming services (Perez, 2015).

Radio

In 2014, nearly 92 percent of Americans listened to the radio in some format, with radio reaching nearly 90 percent of individuals in every major demographic group; on average, Americans spend about 2.5 hours per day listening to the radio (Nielsen, 2014). The majority of radio listening continues to occur via traditional AM/FM stations, which reached approximately 243 million Americans in 2012 (Short, 2013), but as with online TV viewing, online radio is growing, reaching nearly three-quarters of all Americans in 2015. The number of individual tracks streamed online grew an astonishing 90 percent between the first half of 2014 and the same months of 2015 (The Nielsen Company, 2015a). AM/FM radio is still used more frequently for in-car listening than any other option, followed by CD players, MP3 players, and satellite radio. However, online radio, once used primarily at home or at work, has begun moving into our cars; in 2014, more than one-quarter of mobile phone owners reported listening to online radio in their cars by connecting their phone to the car's audio system (Edison Research & Triton Digital, 2014). This trend is likely to accelerate as more cars come equipped with wifi hotspot technology, introduced by Audi in 2011; General Motors and Chrysler also now offer built-in wifi (Newcomb, 2014).

Pandora dominates the online radio market, with 31 percent of individuals aged 12 and older reporting that they had used Pandora during the previous month, but iTunes radio, launched in September 2013, had moved into the No. 3 spot, behind Pandora and iHeartRadio, by early

2014. Interestingly, 41 percent of iTunes radio listeners said the platform was increasing their listening time, rather than replacing other online or traditional radio or CD/MP3 listening (Edison Research & Triton Digital, 2014). Across all platforms, country music formats had the greatest share of listeners (14.8 percent of all radio listeners), followed by news/talk stations (11.3%) (Nielsen, 2014).

Music

Music consumption obviously accounts for the vast majority of radio listening, but does radio account for the majority of music consumption? By 2014, the answer was "It depends on the listener." While adults remain most likely to listen to music on the radio, by 2012, Nielsen research showed that teenagers – who listen to music most often and spend the most time, nearly six hours per week, with music (Nielsen, 2013) – were most likely to cite YouTube as their preferred music-listening venue; 64 percent of teens said they listen to music on YouTube, compared to 56 percent who listen on the radio, 53 percent who use iTunes and 50 percent who listen to CDs (Gross, 2012). That preference for YouTube listening may help explain the recent decline in U.S. album sales, which dropped 15 percent from the first half of 2013 to the first half of 2014. According to Nielsen's most recent mid-year SoundScan report, 2014 was only the third year since the studies began in 1991 in which only one album had sold more than a million copies by mid-year; that one album was the soundtrack for the Disney movie *Frozen*. A 15 percent drop in digital song purchases provided further evidence of the shift toward music streaming and away from music ownership (Stassen, 2014). By 2013, the Recording Industry Association of America reported that more than one-fifth of total music industry revenues were coming from streaming services (Joshua Friedlander, n.d.). Similarly, Nielsen's comparison of 2012 to 2013 music industry data showed overall music streaming up by 32 percent, while overall music sales were down 6.3 percent (Nielsen, 2013).

Movies

"Seeing a movie" these days is more likely to involve the couch in people's living rooms than movie theater seats. The number of movie theater tickets sold dropped 11 percent between 2004 and 2013, with a 3 percent drop between 2012 and 2013 (Schwartzel & Fritz, 2014; Motion Picture Association of America, 2013). Sales of movie tickets declined another 6 percent from 2013 to 2014 (Motion Picture Association of America, 2014). Fans who go to the movies once a month or more buy half of all movie tickets; 25- to 39-year-olds are the age group most likely to see movies in the theater more than once a month. Among ethnic groups, Hispanics are the most likely to go to the movies, accounting for 25 percent of all tickets sold in 2013 (Motion Picture Association of America, 2013). The trend toward content streaming is also apparent in the movie industry. Digital movie sales increased 47 percent between 2012 and 2013 (Fritz, 2014), helping to even out the decline in sales and rentals of DVDs, which declined 30 percent between 2004 and 2013 (Dade Hayes, 2013).

Video/Computer Games

According to the Entertainment Software Association, 58 percent of all Americans play video games, and 51 percent of all households own at least one dedicated game console – whether it's a Playstation, Wii, Xbox or some other platform. Somewhat surprisingly, the average player is not a teenage boy. In fact, the average age of gamers is 30, with only 32 percent of gamers 18 or younger, 32 percent 18 to 35 and 36 percent aged 36 or older. Although 55 percent of all gamers are male, boys aged 17 and younger represent only 19 percent of all gamers, while women aged 18 and older account for 31 percent of the gaming population. Again, perhaps belying the stereotype, only 40 percent of online games are action, sports, strategy and role-playing (26%) or "persistent multi-player universe" games (14%); the remainder are classified as puzzle, board game, game show, trivia and card games (34%), as "casual, social games" (19%) or other (8%). Perhaps reflecting the rise of "Candy Crush," "Farmville" and "Words With Friends," these types of games are even more common on mobile devices, with "traditional" action, sports and role-playing games and multi-player universe games accounting for only 17 percent of mobile games (Entertainment Software Association, 2013). Time spent with video games has increased in the past few years, with the average gamer aged 13 or older spending 6.3 hours per week with any gaming platform in 2013, an increase of more than one hour per week from 2011 ("Multi-Platform Gaming," 2014).

Magazines

According to the Association of Magazine Media, in 2012, U.S. magazines reported more than 187 million readers aged 18 and older and total subscription and single copy sales of 311,684,051 magazines. These figures, however, reflected an 11.6 percent drop in total circulation since 2003, although the number of readers aged 18 and older actually increased 4.5 percent from 2004 to 2013 (Association of Magazine Media, 2013). Data from early 2013 suggest that single copy sales of print editions of consumer magazines were 10 percent lower for the first half of 2013 than for the same period in 2012 (Haughney, 2013), and the decline continued into the last half of 2014, with total consumer magazine circulation dropping 2.2 percent (Rondon, 2015). Subscriptions to consumer magazines' digital editions, however, nearly doubled from spring 2012 to spring 2013 – from 5.4 million in 2012 to 10.2 million (Haughney, 2013), increasing to 11.8 million issues industry-wide during the last half of 2014 (Rondon, 2015). However, digital editions represent only a small part of total consumer magazine circulation – about 3.8 percent during the first half of 2014 (Alliance for Audited Media, n.d.).

Newspapers

As almost anyone who pays attention to the media knows, newspaper circulation and readership have declined dramatically over the past two decades. At its peak in 1984, daily newspaper circulation stood at 63.3 million (Seelye, 2006). By 2013, however, daily circulation – including paid digital subscriptions – had dropped by more than 50 percent, to 31.3 million (Guskin, 2014b). Between 2013 and 2014, circulation dropped another 3 percent (Barthel, 2015). At some of the nation's largest newspapers, circulation has actually grown substantially in recent years, in part due to the growth of paid digital subscriptions and use of mobile editions. Between September 2012 and September 2013, *USA Today*'s total circulation for print and digital editions increased an astonishing 68 percent, while the *New York Times* saw nearly an 18 percent increase, the *New York Post*'s circulation grew more than 10 percent and the *Los Angeles Times* increased its circulation by nearly 4.74 percent (Guskin, 2014a). Nonetheless, the percentage of Americans who get their news primarily from newspapers has declined substantially, from 56 percent in 1991 to only 29 percent in 2012 ("Where Americans Get News," 2014). These declines have been relatively consistent across income groups (Wormald, 2014d), age (Wormald, 2014a), education level (Wormald, 2014b) and ethnicity (Wormald, 2014c). As has been true for the past decade or more, whites, older adults, and those with the highest levels of income and education are most likely to read a daily newspaper (Wormald, 2014a–d). Newspapers have experienced the shift toward digital consumption, via websites and mobile news applications, more than any other medium; a 2014 analysis from the Newspaper Association of America showed that only 54.9 percent of daily newspaper circulation (and about three-quarters of Sunday circulation) is in print ("Key Indicators in Media & News," 2014).

The Internet

The Internet, of course, has been a component of every other media category discussed thus far, and its impact on every media type – from newspapers and magazines to music, movies, TV and gaming – seems destined only to grow. Although the Web is changing the way Americans experience every other medium, it also offers a variety of totally new types of content and mediated experiences, and those experiences now reach the overwhelming majority of Americans. In 1995, when the Pew Research Center first surveyed Americans about their access to the Internet, only 14 percent of adults had access. The most recent Pew survey, in 2014, showed that 87 percent of adults use the Internet at least sometimes. Internet use is essentially equal for men and women and nearly equal for the major racial groups; 85 percent of whites, 83 percent of Hispanics and 81 percent of African-Americans report using the Internet. However, substantial differences remain among different age groups and across varying levels of education and income, with younger, more highly educated and higher income Americans most likely to use the Web. Indeed, among 18- to 29-year-olds and those with at least an undergraduate degree, 97 percent use the Internet, and among those with annual household incomes of $75,000 or more, 99 percent use the Web (Fox & Rainie, 2014).

Another important change is the growth in home Web access; on a typical day, 90 percent of Internet users report going online from home, an increase from 76 percent in 2000. It is reasonable to argue, in fact, that home Internet access has driven the increased use of the Web over the past 14 years, given that use of the Internet during a typical work day has not changed much – from 41 percent in 2000 to 44 percent in 2014. However, the most dramatic shift has been the explosion of mobile use of the Web: "68% of U.S. adults now say they access the internet on a cell phone, tablet, or other mobile device, at least occasionally" (Fox & Rainie, 2014). The Pew Research Center's report also demonstrates how thoroughly the Internet has woven itself into our daily lives. Among those who go online, 53 percent (nearly half of all adults) say it would be very hard – or even "impossible" – to give up (Fox & Rainie, 2014).

What makes the Internet so indispensable? Beyond reading the news, watching TV, listening to music, streaming movies and playing games, what do people do online? Perhaps the single most important activity, not surprisingly, is searching for information, which took up 46 percent of all Internet use time by 2012, a substantial increase from 2008, when information searches represented 35 percent of all time spent online (Short, 2013). Another important activity is email, which accounted for nearly a quarter of all time spent online in 2012; however, that reflected a significant drop from 2008, when email accounted for more than 34 percent of all time spent online (Short, 2013). Pew data from 2002 to 2011 confirm that email and information searches are the most popular online activities, with 92 percent of Internet users in 2011 engaging in both activities. In 2011, the other most common online activities were getting news (76%), buying products (71%) and visiting social networking sites (65%) (Purcell, 2011).

By January 2014, social media use had risen to nearly three-quarters of all adult Internet users, according to data from the Pew Internet Project. Although, not surprisingly, the highest use rates were among 18- to 29-year-olds, social media reached very close to half of every age group, with 49 percent of Internet-using seniors (65+) reporting use of social networking sites ("Social Networking Fact Sheet," 2014). Among all the major social networking sites, Facebook remained the most popular, with 57 percent of all U.S. adults and 73 percent of 12- to 17-year-olds using Facebook (Smith, 2014). By way of comparison, 71 percent of online adults used Facebook in 2013, compared to only 22 percent for the next most popular site, LinkedIn. Most Facebook users

(63%), as well as most Instagram users (57%), visit the site at least once a day; for Facebook, 40 percent of users report checking in multiple times every day (Duggan & Smith, 2013).

Summary

Media consumption in the United States (and worldwide, to some extent) is an increasingly complicated phenomenon. People who subscribe to and/or read newspapers and magazines in print form sometimes, but not always, also subscribe to and read articles produced by these media online. "Reading online" may mean consuming content displayed on one's home or office desktop or laptop computer, but, increasingly, it may include reading a mobile version of the story on a smartphone or tablet. In addition, both newspapers' and magazines' online and mobile versions are increasingly likely to include audio and video stories, while online and mobile sites or apps produced by radio and television stations often include text-based content as well as the traditional audio and video. Audiences for audio content may include individuals listening to music, audiobooks, podcasts produced by traditional broadcast outlets or by independent content creators, and a wide variety of specialty satellite radio services; listening may mean turning on one's radio, streaming music or other content from an online service, surfing to a favorite radio station's live-streaming service on one's computer or streaming audio content through a tablet or smartphone. We access the Internet through our computers, our TVs, our game consoles, our phones, and soon through our cars. The bottom line, as noted at the beginning of this chapter, is that we live media-saturated lives, surrounded by and inundated with media content during nearly all of our waking hours (and perhaps, for some people, while we sleep).

HEALTH IN THE UNITED STATES

The focus of this book, of course, is not just media consumption but how that consumption and the media environment itself influence our health. Later chapters will provide more detailed information about the health behaviors and problems associated with specific types of media consumption. However, before we move on to discussing the particular ways media may help improve or damage our health, we first need to

11

understand the overall context of health in the United States. This section, then, will answer the question "How healthy are Americans?"

The answer, in short, is: "Not very healthy compared to people in other similarly wealthy and developed nations." In fact, even in comparison to some significantly less developed nations, some analysts see the United States as falling short. The most recent multi-country comparison from the Social Progress Imperative ranks the U.S.A. sixteenth in overall social progress, but seventieth on the subcomponent of health and wellness; that ranking puts the United States below developed countries like Japan, Switzerland, Sweden and Canada, and less developed countries such as Colombia, Paraguay, Bolivia, Cambodia and Ghana ("Health and Wellness," 2014).

The subtitle of a recent report by the National Research Council and the Institute of Medicine puts it bluntly: "Shorter Lives, Poorer Health." Despite spending more on health care than any other country in the world, Americans are far from being the healthiest. In fact, in the report's comparison of life expectancy rates for citizens of the U.S.A. and 16 other developed nations, the United States ranks last for men and next to last for women. Based on life expectancy at birth, Swiss, Australian and Japanese men live, on average, at least 3.5 years longer than American men. French women live, on average, 3.65 years longer than American women, and Japanese women live more than five years longer. Perhaps even more concerning, these gaps in the life expectancies of Americans versus their counterparts in other developed nations have been growing over the past 30 years, especially among women (Woolf & Aron, 2013).

The NRC/IOM report concludes that Americans of all ages are less healthy, on average, than their peers in other wealthy nations. In fact, research suggests that deaths before the age of 50 account for two-thirds of the life expectancy gap for men and about one-third for women. From the time they're born, people in the United States experience poorer health outcomes in many areas:

- The United States has the highest infant mortality rate of any developed country, in part because U.S. teen pregnancy rates are the highest in the developed countries, contributing to higher rates of premature and low-birth weight infants. American children are more likely to die before their fifth birthday. High infant mortality rates account for much of this disadvantage, but U.S. children also have higher rates of asthma and a greater likelihood of dying from both accidental and intentional injuries, and from neglect (Woolf & Aron, 2013).

- Compared to citizens of other wealthy nations, Americans experience much higher rates of fatal injuries, including automobile and non-transportation-related accidents. In the United States, injuries claimed 53 lives per 100,000 population in 2008; only Finland's rate of 58 deaths per 100,000 population was worse. In France, which ranked just above the United States, the rate was only 38 deaths per 100,000. Fatal traffic crashes have been more common among U.S. adolescents and young adults since the 1950s, and this difference is not due to Americans driving more miles (Woolf & Aron, 2013).

- Americans are more likely to kill each other than are people in other developed countries. A study that compared 23 Organization for Economic Cooperation and Development member countries in 2003 showed that the "United States had a homicide rate 6.9 times higher than those in the other high-income countries, driven by a firearm homicide rate that was 19.5 times higher" (Richardson & Hemenway, 2011, p. 240). In fact, overall, eight out of ten gun deaths in all 23 countries in 2003 occurred in the United States, which had 86 percent of all firearms deaths for women and 87 percent of gun deaths for children aged 0 to 14 (Richardson & Hemenway, 2011). More recently, a study that assessed the links between gun ownership rates, the prevalence of mental illness and gun-related deaths concluded that "the number of guns per capita per country correlated strongly and was an independent predictor of fire-arm-related deaths" (Bangalore & Messerli, 2013, p. 875); mental illness was only of "borderline significance" in the model.

- The United States ranks second in HIV infection overall and highest among 15- to 24-year-olds, and has the highest rates of AIDS compared to the other 16 developed countries. U.S. adolescents are also more likely to contract non-HIV sexually transmitted diseases (Woolf & Aron, 2013).

- Although Americans do not necessarily drink more heavily than citizens of other countries, drug use – especially use of marijuana, cocaine, amphetamines and prescription painkillers – is higher. As a result, Americans are more likely to die of drug- and alcohol-related causes than are those in peer countries, even when drunk-driving crashes are not included (Woolf & Aron, 2013).

- Simply put, we're fatter than people in other countries. Higher rates of obesity begin in childhood and continue throughout all age groups, in part because Americans, on average, consume more calories per day – 3,770 per person per day for 2005 to 2007 – than people in any other country in the world. The prevalence of overweight and obese children, both boys and girls, is higher in the United States than in any other country; in fact, children in America are more than 2.5 times as likely to be obese (35.9% of girls, 35% of boys) as their peers in countries with the lowest obesity rates (Switzerland for girls – 13.1%, Norway for boys – 12.9%) (Woolf & Aron, 2013).

- The high incidence of obesity contributes to the United States having the highest prevalence of diabetes among the 17 nations. On average, based on 2008 data, diabetes killed 15.2 Americans per 100,000 population, compared to 10.2 per 100,000, on average, in the 16 comparison countries (Woolf & Aron, 2013).

- Heart disease, the leading cause of death in the United States, is more common and more often deadly for American adults aged 50 and older than for their peers in the other developed countries. For those younger than age 50, the United States has the second highest rate of heart disease (Woolf & Aron, 2013).

- Chronic lung disease is more common and causes more deaths in the United States, compared to the other countries, although among developed countries smoking rates are now the lowest in the United States. The report concludes, however, that the higher rates of chronic lung disease we experience now may stem from high smoking rates in earlier generations; when U.S. smoking peaked in the 1950s, tobacco use here was higher than in any other country (Woolf & Aron, 2013).

- Finally, arthritis and other activity-limiting disabilities are more common among older adults in the United States than among seniors in the comparison countries (Woolf & Aron, 2013).

What causes the U.S. health disadvantage? The NRC/IOM report found answers in multiple areas, from individual behaviors like drug abuse and not wearing seatbelts to the health care system to the physical and social environments. Socioeconomic factors have a significant influence. Poverty and income inequality are significant problems in the United States compared to the other developed countries, and the United States offers less social mobility – less opportunity to improve one's socio-economic position, relative to one's parents. Somewhat surprisingly, however, even non-minorities at the upper end of the economic spectrum fare worse in the United States than in other countries (Woolf & Aron, 2013).

Physical and social environments also contribute to poorer health outcomes. For instance, the report notes that our love affair with cars has produced an infrastructure designed for automobiles, not pedestrians, which discourages physical activity and creates a dependency on cars that increases our likelihood of being in traffic accidents. Those who grow, process, distribute, market and sell the food we eat make choices that influence our dietary patterns. The easy availability of guns almost certainly increases both accidental and violence-related injury and death in the United States. Civilian gun ownership in the United States stands just short of 89 guns for every 100 persons; the closest competitor among the 16 peer countries is Switzerland, where civilians own 45.7 guns for every 100 persons (Woolf & Aron, 2013).

Of course, another important influence on health outcomes is the health care system and its success or failure. Americans generally believe that the quality of health care in the United States is good. According to a series of Gallup polls, as of November 2013, 54 percent of those surveyed rated the quality of health care overall as excellent or good, while 79 percent said the health care they personally received was excellent or good. Although 52 percent said the health care system has "major problems" and less than one-third said health care coverage overall is excellent or good, 69 percent rated their own health care coverage as excellent or good, and 59 percent were satisfied with the total cost they pay for health care (Newport, 2013).

International comparisons, however, suggest that many in the United States are misinformed about the success of the health care system. A Commonwealth Fund report published in mid-2014 concluded that, based on its comparison of health care systems in 11 developed nations,

the U.S. ranks last, as it did in the 2010, 2007, 2006, and 2004 editions of (the report). Most troubling, the U.S. fails to achieve better health outcomes than the other countries, and as shown in the earlier editions, the U.S. is last or near last on dimensions of access, efficiency, and equity.

(Davis et al., 2014, p. 5)

In fact, despite spending 94 percent more per person on health care than the average for the other ten countries, the U.S. ranked fifth or higher in only four categories considered by the Commonwealth Fund analysts – fifth for timeliness and overall quality of care, fourth for providing "patient-centered care" and third for effectiveness of care. For cost, efficiency, equity and supporting healthy lives, the U.S. ranked last. The authors state that "the most notable way the U.S. differs from other industrialized countries is the absence of universal health insurance coverage" (Davis et al., 2014, p. 6). Even after the implementation of the Affordable Care Act, 13.4 percent of the U.S. population had no insurance, although the percentage of uninsured had dropped from a high of 18 percent during the third quarter of 2013. A Gallup Poll in early 2014 showed that the uninsured rate was dropping most rapidly in states that had implemented state health exchanges and had expanded Medicaid eligibility (Witters, 2014).

The previous two sections have described the prevalence of both exposure to mass media through multiple channels and higher-than-average rates of illness and death in the United States, compared to other similarly well-developed and prosperous nations. The key question of this book, then, is how those two sets of phenomena – high media use and poorer health – are related to each other.

HOW MEDIA CONTRIBUTE TO U.S. HEALTH: FOR BETTER OR WORSE

What roles do mass media play in influencing health at any of these levels? The rest of this book will attempt to answer this question as fully as possible, at least in regard to two of the layers of health influences, but it's worth a brief discussion here. First, mass media may influence individual health behaviors in lifestyles in both positive and negative ways. For instance, advertising that promotes the consumption of unhealthy products, including tobacco, excessive alcohol and calorie-dense, low-nutrition foods certainly influences individual health behaviors to negative effect, even if advertising is not the primary contributor to these poor health choices. On the other hand, mass media may also have positive influences on individual health behaviors, such as when news coverage of a new flu outbreak encourages people to get the flu vaccine, to wash their hands more regularly or to stay at home if they're experiencing flu-like symptoms. Even entertainment programming that addresses serious health topics such as mental illness or sexual respons-ibility in positive ways can influence individuals to alter their behavior, encouraging them to seek treatment for depression or to adopt safer sex practices.

The "Social Factors" level refers to societal characteristics such as income and wealth, income inequality, education, employment, social status, household composition, racial and ethnic factors, migration, and stress. Certainly it is *possible* that mass media have effects on these char-acteristics, both for individuals and at community or population levels. For instance, entertainment programming that denigrates blue-collar occupations and idealizes white-collar careers as a requirement for social status may encourage more young people to attend college. The media could encourage people to accept stress-filled lives as "normal" if they present high-stress work environments as acceptable or even desirable and portray multiple extra-curricular activities for children as necessary for success in life. There is even some evidence that extensive exposure to trauma-focused media can increase symptoms of acute stress, even for those not directly exposed to the original trauma. For instance, researchers studying the aftermath of the Boston Marathon bombings found that controlling for pre-bombing mental health, demographic characteristics and prior cumulative stress exposure, individuals who were exposed daily to six or more hours of media related to the bombing reported higher acute stress than those with direct exposure to the bombing – residents of Boston (Holman et al., 2014).

Some media effects may also occur at the level of the physical and social environment. For instance, bullying has been a health threat for some children and adolescents for probably as long as human beings have existed. In earlier eras, however, home offered a safe haven for most bullying victims because bullying generally occurred at school during school hours. Cyberbullying victims, however, are far more accessible to their tormentors because media technologies – texting, email and social media – mean that bullies can reach their victims virtually anywhere, at any time. Tokunaga concludes that "[t]he persistence of the bullying behaviors may result in even stronger negative outcomes than traditional bullying" (2010, p. 279).

However, in most cases, media effects on social factors and the social or physical environment seem more likely to occur indirectly through the impact of media on health-related policies, such as local or state-wide bans on smoking in public places, taxes on tobacco products, gun control regulations, the availability of publicly funded health insurance coverage, school sex education curricula, etc. Therefore, this book focuses on media effects at two primary levels: individual behavior and policies and social values.

Figure 1.1 illustrates the Media Health Effects Matrix, first introduced by Dr. Jane Brown and myself in 1994 (Brown & Walsh-Childers, 1994). As the matrix illustrates, there are multiple ways in which media effects on health can be categorized. First, as reflected in the columns and as discussed in the previous section, media can have effects on individual behavior, such as when an individual watches a public service ad showing how texting while driving can cause car crashes and subsequently decides not to text while driving (see this anti-texting PSA for a great example: www.facebook.com/photo.php?v=10152359791929200&fref=nf). Media can also have effects at the public policy level, such as when intense coverage of a health problem spurs the passage of legislation designed to correct or control the problem. For instance, Shoemaker and colleagues (1989) argued that intensive media coverage of drugs during the summer of 1986 likely influenced Congress's passage of a $1.7 billion anti-drug program, which some critics argued was hastily constructed and not well-thought out.

These two examples also illustrate two other dimensions of the matrix. First, media effects on health can be intended, as in the case of the positive effects of public service ads, or they can be unintentional, as in the case of news coverage pushing legislators to adopt new legislation meant to control or reduce a health problem. In addition, media effects on either individual health behaviors or public health policy, intended or unintended, can be positive, in the sense that they make individuals and/or society healthier; or negative, when they cause or exacerbate health problems.

As discussed in the Preface, the remainder of this book addresses what research has revealed about media effects on health, first through impacts on individual health knowledge, beliefs and behaviors, and then through influences on the development of public health policy, including, in some cases, corporate decisions that can affect the health environment in which

Figure 1.1: The Media Health Effects Matrix, With Examples

		Individual behavior	Public policy
Intended effects	Positive	Traditional mass media campaigns; Some online health information, such as Healthfinder.gov, FamilyDoctor.org; Inclusion of suicide prevention tips in news coverage of celebrity suicide	Media advocacy campaigns; Social media campaigns supporting health policy improvements
	Negative	Tobacco advertising	"Astro-turf" social media campaigns to block health policy improvements
Unintended effects	Positive	Increased risk awareness – news coverage of celebrity disease diagnoses. Social media conversations about flu	News agenda-setting/framing supports local bans on smoking in public spaces or restrictions on alcohol advertising; Viral social media response to a school shooting encourages passage of gun control measures
	Negative	"Screen-time" displaces exercise; DTC prescription drug advertising promotes newer, more expensive – but not necessarily safer or more effective – drugs	News framing of the economic costs of environmental protection or economic benefits of "fracking" discourage government investment in solar, wind and fuel-cell technologies

we live. More than 50 years' worth of research has demonstrated that mass media content is an important element in a society's health environment and that the use of mass media can have significant health effects, even when those health effects are not intended by those who design the media content. In some cases the effects improve individual and public health, but in other areas, consumption of some types of media content can be considered a health risk behavior in its own right.

REFERENCES

Alliance for Audited Media. (n.d.). *Top 25 U.S. Consumer Magazines for June 2014.* Arlington Heights, IL. Retrieved August 8, 2014 from http://auditedmedia.com/news/research-and-data/top-25-us-consumer-magazines-for-june-2014.aspx.

Association of Magazine Media. (2013). *Magazine Media MPA Factbook 2013/2014.* New York. Retrieved August 13, 2014 from http://browndigital.bpc.com/publication/index.php?i=171192.

Bangalore, S. & Messerli, F.H. (2013). Gun Ownership and Firearm-related Deaths. *The American Journal of Medicine*, *126*(10), 873–876. http://doi.org/10.1016/j. amjmed.2013.04.012.

Barthel, M. (2015, April 29). Newspapers: Fact Sheet. Retrieved September 8, 2015 from www.journalism.org/2015/04/29/newspapers-fact-sheet/.

Brown, J. & Walsh-Childers, K. (1994). Effects of Media on Personal and Public Health. In *Media Effects: Advances in Theory and Research* (1st edn, pp. 389–415). Hillsdale, NJ: Lawrence Erlbaum Associates.

Dade Hayes. (2013, July 8). Six Reasons Why DVDs Still Make Money – And Won't Die Anytime Soon. Retrieved August 13, 2014 from www.forbes.com/sites/dade-hayes/2013/07/08/six-reasons-why-dvds-still-make-money-and-wont-die-anytime-soon/.

Davis, K., Stremikis, K., Squires, D. & Schoen, C. (2014). *Mirror, Mirror on the Wall, 2014 Update: How the U.S. Health Care System Compares Internationally*. Retrieved August 15, 2014 from www.commonwealthfund.org/~/media/files/publications/ fund-report/2014/jun/1755_davis_mirror_mirror_2014_exec_summ.pdf.

Duggan, M. & Smith, A. (2013, December 30). Social Media Update 2013. Retrieved August 14, 2014 from www.pewinternet.org/2013/12/30/social-media-update-2013/.

Edison Research & Triton Digital. (2014). *The Infinite Dial 2014*.

Entertainment Software Association. (2013). *Essential Facts About the Computer and Video Game Industry*. Retrieved August 14, 2014 from www.theesa.com/facts/pdfs/ esa_ef_2013.pdf.

Fox, S. & Rainie, L. (2014, February 27). The Web at 25 in the U.S. Retrieved August 14, 2014 from www.pewinternet.org/2014/02/27/the-web-at-25-in-the-u-s/.

Fritz, B. (2014, January 8). Sales of Digital Movies Surge. *Wall Street Journal*. Retrieved August 13, 2014 from http://online.wsj.com/news/articles/SB1000142405270230 4887104579306440621142958.

Gross, D. (2012, August 15). Teens' First Choice for Music Listening? YouTube. Retrieved August 13, 2014 from www.cnn.com/2012/08/15/tech/web/teens-music-youtube/index.html.

Guskin, E. (2014a, March 26). Average Circulation at the Top 5 U.S. Newspapers Reporting Monday–Friday Averages. Retrieved August 14, 2014 from www. journalism.org/media-indicators/average-circulation-at-the-top-5-u-s-newspapers-reporting-monday-friday-averages/.

Guskin, E. (2014b, March 26). Daily Newspaper Circulation. Retrieved August 14, 2014 from www.journalism.org/media-indicators/daily-newspaper-circulation/.

Haughney, C. (2013, August 6). Magazine Newsstand Sales Plummet, but Digital Editions Thrive. *New York Times*. Retrieved August 14, 2014 from www.nytimes. com/2013/08/07/business/media/magazine-newsstand-sales-plummet-but-digital-editions-thrive.html.

Health and Wellness. (2014). Retrieved August 15, 2014 from www.socialprogressim-perative.org/data/spi#data_table/countries/com7/dim1,dim2,com7,dim3.

Holman, E.A., Garfin, D.R. & Silver, R.C. (2014). Media's Role in Broadcasting Acute Stress Following the Boston Marathon Bombings. *Proceedings of the National Academy of Sciences*, *111*(1), 93–98. http://doi.org/10.1073/pnas.1316265110.

James, M. (2013, November 12). Cord-cutting: Pay-TV Companies Lose 113,000 Customers in Quarter. *Los Angeles Times*. Retrieved August 11, 2014 from http:// articles.latimes.com/2013/nov/12/entertainment/la-et-ct-cord-cutting-continues-companies-lose-113k-customers-20131112.

Joshua Friedlander. (n.d.). *News and Notes on 2013 RIAA Music Industry Shipment and*

Revenue Statistics. Recording Industry Association of America. Retrieved August 13, 2014 from http://76.74.24.142/2463566A-FF96-E0CA-2766-72779A364D01.pdf.

Key Indicators in Media & News. (2014, March 26). Retrieved August 14, 2014 from www.journalism.org/2014/03/26/state-of-the-news-media-2014-key-indicators-in-media-and-news/.

Kleinman, A. (2013, April 2). 30% Of Internet Users In The U.S. Would Consider Becoming Cable Cutters: Survey. Retrieved August 11, 2014, from www.huffington-post.com/2013/04/02/cable-cutters-internet_n_3000576.html?view=print&comm_ref=false.

Motion Picture Association of America. (2013). *Theatrical Market Statistics 2013.* Sherman Oaks, CA. Retrieved September 18, 2015 from www.mpaa.org/wp-content/uploads/2014/03/MPAA-Theatrical-Market-Statistics-2013_032514-v2.pdf.

Motion Picture Association of America. (2014). *Theatrical Market Statistics 2014.* Sherman Oaks, CA. Retrieved September 18, 2015 from www.mpaa.org/wp-content/uploads/2015/03/MPAA-Theatrical-Market-Statistics-2014.pdf.

Multi-Platform Gaming: For the Win! (2014, May 27). Retrieved August 14, 2014 from www.nielsen.com/content/corporate/us/en/insights/news/2014/multi-platform-gaming-for-the-win.html.

Newcomb, D. (2014, December 19). Tapping Into In-car Wifi. Retrieved September 17, 2015 from http://forums.edmunds.com/discussion/embed.

Newport, F. (2013, November 25). Americans' Views of Healthcare Quality, Cost, and Coverage. Retrieved August 15, 2014 from www.gallup.com/poll/165998/americans-views-healthcare-quality-cost-coverage.aspx.

Nielsen. (2013). *U.S. Music Industry Year-end Review 2013.* New York. Retrieved August 13, 2014 from www.nielsen.com/content/dam/corporate/us/en/reports-downloads/2014%20Reports/nielsen-us-music-year-end-report-2013.pdf.

Nielsen. (2014). *State of the Media: Audio Today 2014.*

Perez, S. (2015, June 23). New Study Shows a Rise in Cord Cutting – 8.2 Percent Ditched Pay TV in 2014, Up 1.3% YoY. Retrieved August 11, 2014 from http://social.techcrunch.com/2015/06/23/new-study-shows-a-rise-in-cord-cutting-8-2-percent-ditched-pay-tv-in-2014-up-1-3-yoy/.

Purcell, K. (2011, August 9). Search and Email Still Top the List of Most Popular Online Activities. Retrieved August 14, 2014 from www.pewinternet.org/2011/08/09/search-and-email-still-top-the-list-of-most-popular-online-activities/.

Richardson, E.G. & Hemenway, D. (2011). Homicide, Suicide, and Unintentional Firearm Fatality: Comparing the United States With Other High-income Countries, 2003. *Journal of Trauma: Injury, Infection, and Critical Care, 70*(1), 238–243. http://doi.org/10.1097/TA.0b013e3181dbaddf.

Rondon, M. (2015, February 12). Magazine Circ Continues Downward Spiral. Retrieved September 18, 2015 from www.foliomag.com/2015/magazine-circ-continues-downward-spiral/.

Schwartzel, E. & Fritz, B. (2014, March 25). Fewer Americans Go to the Movies: Theater Owners Consider Cutting Ticket Prices One Day a Week. *Wall Street Journal.* Retrieved August 13, 2014 from http://online.wsj.com/news/articles/SB10001424052702303949704579461813982237426.

Seelye, K.Q. (2006, October 31). Newspaper Circulation Falls Sharply. *New York Times.* Retrieved August 14, 2014 from www.nytimes.com/2006/10/31/business/media/31paper.html.

Seitz, P. (2014, August 6). Signs Point to Pay-TV Cord Cutting Ahead. Retrieved August

11, 2014 from http://news.investors.com/SiteAds/TopInHouseAd.aspx?page=/News AndAnalysis/Article.aspx&position=housetop&identifier=Technology&tile=3&or d=1470826854929328.

Shoemaker, P., Wanta, W. & Leggett, D. (1989). Drug Coverage and Public Opinion, 1972–1986. In *Communication Campaigns About Drugs* (pp. 67–80). Hillsdale, NJ: Lawrence Erlbaum Associates.

Short, J.E. (2013). *How Much Media? Report on American Consumers*. University of Southern California. Retrieved July 22, 2014 from www.marshall.usc.edu/faculty/ centers/ctm/research/how-much-media.

Smith, A. (2014, February 3). 6 New Facts About Facebook. Retrieved January 5, 2015 from www.pewresearch.org/fact-tank/2014/02/03/6-new-facts-about-facebook/.

Social Networking Fact Sheet. 2014. Pew Research Internet Project. www.pewinternet. org/fact-sheets/social-networking-fact-sheet/.

Stassen, M. (2014, July 3). US Album and Digital Song Sales Down in H1 2014. Retrieved August 13, 2014 from www.musicweek.com/news/read/mid-year- numbers-album-digital-song-sales-down/058913.

The Nielsen Company. (2015a). *Nielsen Music 360 Report: 2015 Highlights*. New York. Retrieved September 18, 2015 from www.nielsen.com/content/dam/corporate/us/ en/reports-downloads/2015-reports/music-360-2015-highlights-sept-2015.pdf.

The Nielsen Company. (2015b). *The Total Audience Report Q1 2015*. New York. Retrieved September 18, 2015 from www.nielsen.com/us/en/insights/reports/2015/the-total- audience-report-q1-2015.html.

Tokunaga, R.S. (2010). Following You Home from School: A Critical Review and Synthesis of Research on Cyberbullying Victimization. *Computers in Human Behavior, 26*(3), 277–287. http://doi.org/10.1016/j.chb.2009.11.014.

Where Americans Get News. (2014, March 26). Retrieved August 14, 2014 from www.journalism.org/media-indicators/where-americans-get-news/.

Witters, D. (2014, August 5). Arkansas, Kentucky Report Sharpest Drops in Unin- sured Rate. Retrieved August 18, 2014 from www.gallup.com/poll/174290/ arkansas-kentucky-report-sharpest-drops-uninsured-rate.aspx.

Woolf, S.H. & Aron, L. (2013). *U.S. Health in International Perspective: Shorter Lives, Poorer Health*. Washington, DC: National Academies Press (US). Retrieved August 15, 2014 from www.nap.edu/catalog/13497/us-health-in-international-perspective-shorter- lives-poorer-health.

Wormald, B. (2014a, March 26). Newspaper Readership by Age. Retrieved August 14, 2014 from www.journalism.org/media-indicators/newspaper-readership-by-age/.

Wormald, B. (2014b, March 26). Newspaper Readership by Education Level. Retrieved August 14, 2014 from www.journalism.org/media-indicators/ newspaper-readership-by-education-level/.

Wormald, B. (2014c, March 26). Newspaper Readership by Ethnic Group. Retrieved August 14, 2014 from www.journalism.org/media-indicators/newspaper-readership- by-ethnic-group/.

Wormald, B. (2014d, March 26). Newspaper Readership by Income Level. Retrieved August 14, 2014 from www.journalism.org/media-indicators/newspaper-readership- by-income-level/.

Part I

Media Effects on Individuals and Health

INTRODUCTION

The United States is generally recognized as an individualistic society. In fact, some have argued that individualism is "a quintessentially American thing" (Oyserman et al., 2002, p. 3). One element of this individualism is a focus on individual responsibility for one's own circumstances, implying that "judgment, reasoning, and causal inference are generally oriented toward the person rather than the situation or social context" (Oyserman et al., 2002, p. 5). Thus it is perhaps not surprising that the vast majority of research on media health effects has focused on how exposure to mass media content impacts health knowledge, attitudes and behaviors at the individual level. The same tendency has occurred in research focused on intentional use of mass media to promote public health; the focus of most interventions has been changing individuals' knowledge, attitudes and behavior to support healthier behavior (Flora et al., 1989).

As a consequence, most of the research to be discussed in the following chapters addresses the effects of media health content on individual health behavior. This is certainly not an unreasonable approach; individual decision-making does play a key role in health behavior. Media consumption patterns vary across generations, racial groups, regions, communities and even within families. Similarly, health behaviors may be influenced by the context within which an individual operates, but these behaviors also vary from one individual to the next, even within close-knit communities and families. Thus, it makes sense for researchers to want to know how mass media content affects individual health knowledge, attitudes and behaviors.

REFERENCES

Flora, J.A., Maibach, E.W. & Maccoby, N. (1989). The Role of Media Across Four Levels of Health Promotion Intervention. *Annual Review of Public Health*, *10*(1), 181–201. http://doi.org/10.1146/annurev.pu.10.050189.001145.

Oyserman, D., Coon, H.M. & Kemmelmeier, M. (2002). Rethinking Individualism and Collectivism: Evaluation of Theoretical Assumptions and Meta-analyses. *Psychological Bulletin*, *128*(1), 3–72. http://doi.org/10.1037/0033-2909.128.1.3.

CHAPTER 2

HEALTH INFORMATION ONLINE: BUILDING A WEB TO IMPROVE HEALTH BEHAVIOR

Before my sons started school, I learned a lesson known to nearly all parents. When children are going to spike a fever, complain of nausea, develop a weird-looking rash or come down with some sort of unusual-sounding cough, they inevitably do so at approximately 5.45 p.m. on a Friday afternoon. I wouldn't say that children actually *choose* this specific time to begin manifesting symptoms of some unfamiliar health problem, but in our household, at least, health concerns always seemed to arise at this time – because the pediatrician's office closed at 5.30 p.m. The timing meant that getting a health care professional's assessment of the problem would require a trip to either the emergency room or an urgent care center, staffed by doctors and nurses we had never met before. Visiting either of those places meant, first of all, taking a child who might already be feeling bad into an unknown environment, waiting for an hour (or more, sometimes much more) to see a doctor, and exposing both child and parent to all of the (potentially more serious) viruses *other* patients had brought to the waiting room. In most cases we knew that the rash, cough, fever or upset stomach would turn out to be of no great consequence anyway, but when one's child is ill, most parents experience an intense need for reliable, trustworthy health information. How to balance that need to have questions answered and reassurance provided against the inconvenience, possible discomfort and potential for exposure to other illnesses inherent in taking the child to an urgent care center?

The answer, at least some of the time, was the Internet or, as it's sometimes called, "Dr. Google" (Fox, 2013). While we would never have hesitated to take our boys to a health facility for an injury or a clearly serious illness, there were certainly times when it was helpful to be able to use an online site like Healthfinder.gov or the American Academy of Pediatrics' healthychildren.org to obtain information that would help us decide whether we needed to see a doctor as soon as possible or take a wait-and-see approach.

The Web today gives individuals access to a vast wealth of free health information accessible 24 hours a day from anywhere the individual can connect to the Internet. Of course, that information varies widely in terms of quality, reliability and usefulness, and some of it is far more likely to cause harm (e.g., tobacco advertising, promotions for "miracle" drugs or supplements, pro-anorexia sites) than to help individuals improve their health. However, there are also numerous sites produced by governments, health advocacy organizations, disease-specific patient communities and even corporate entities like hospitals and insurance companies that are intended to help individuals develop and maintain better health. These online health information resources differ from traditional public health campaigns in that they often cover a very wide range of topics rather than focusing on a specific issue, and may be oriented toward helping people improve their overall health rather than encouraging people to adopt one or two specific health-promoting behaviors. For that reason, online health information is categorized here as being focused primarily at the individual level and being intended to produce positive health outcomes. This chapter discusses the research on the availability, quality and use of online health information, and the impact online health information use has on individuals; it focuses on health information provided, usually by a government agency or health-related organization, for use by consumers seeking health information or advice. Chapter 12 addresses the impact of social media, blogs and online forums, which may have either positive or negative effects on individuals' health knowledge, beliefs and behavior but are not necessarily intended to do so.

One obvious question that is, nonetheless, nearly impossible to answer is this: How much health information is available online? Perhaps not surprisingly, there appear to be no official data on the number of organizations, groups or individuals regularly posting health information on the Web. A Google search for the term "health information" returns nearly 29 million hits, but of course, the vast majority of people searching for health information would not use such a generic term; rather, most people seeking health information online will start with terms specific to their concern, such as "rash" or "breast cancer" or "insurance."

In terms of the professional biomedical literature – research articles published by researchers primarily for clinicians or other researchers – an assessment published in 2006 estimated that this literature, much of it fully accessible online, had grown at a "double-exponential pace" over the preceding 20 years. Hunter and Cohen (2006) calculated that MEDLINE, the database used by the National Library of Medicine's PubMed search engine, had "grown at a ~4.2% compounded annual growth rate" (p. 589). Of the 16 million publications indexed in MEDLINE by 2005, three million had been added since 2000, with more than 1,800 publications added to the index per day in 2005 (Hunter & Cohen, 2006). By 2014, PubMed had indexed more than 24 million citations from MEDLINE, other life science journals and e-books (National Library of Medicine, n.d.). PubMed's 24 million citations primarily reflect information intended for use by health professionals or researchers, rather than consumers, and for most individuals a consultation with "Dr. Google" will return very few links, if any, to these scholarly articles. Still, in many cases the information is available for consumers who have the confidence to attempt to understand the technical language.

QUALITY OF ONLINE HEALTH INFORMATION

There are, of course, probably hundreds of thousands of websites that provide some kind of health information which may or may not be based on accurate interpretations of peer-reviewed scientific research. Indeed, the Food and Drug Administration has issued warnings this year to companies marketing "cures" or "treatments" for both autism (U.S. Food and Drug Administration, 2014a) and Ebola (U.S. Food and Drug Administration, 2014b), and other researchers have warned of online quacks selling human growth hormones as an "anti-aging" treatment (Perls, 2004). Another study examining the information provided on crisis pregnancy center websites included in state resource directories found that 80 percent included at least one piece of false or misleading information (Bryant et al., 2014). Similarly, a study of websites providing information about the HPV vaccine found that many provided inaccurate or incomplete information (Madden et al., 2012).

Most studies assessing online health information, like the two mentioned above, have focused on online information relating to a specific issue, such as pregnancy, vaccinations, CPR (Yaylaci et al., 2014), hypertension (Kumar et al., 2014) or concussion (Berg et al., 2014). However, there have also been some systematic reviews of the quality of online health information. In their systematic analysis of research examining online health information quality, Eysenbach and colleagues (2002) found that 70 percent of the studies concluded that online information quality is a problem. Of the seven studies (9%) concluding that that information quality was acceptable, none assessed online information using evidence-based guidelines. The reviewed studies criticized online information as incomplete and inaccurate.

Another study, which assessed the quality of online information related to breast cancer, depression, obesity and childhood asthma identified through English- and Spanish-language search engines, showed that fewer than a quarter of the links that appeared within the first page of search engine results provided relevant information. The researchers found that English-language websites provided more than minimal coverage of only 45 percent of "clinical elements," which were key facts about the specific condition as identified by panels of specialists in that condition; 24 percent of the elements were not covered at all. On Spanish-language websites, only 22 percent of these "clinical elements" received more than minimal coverage, and 53 percent were not discussed at all.

A more recent study, however, suggests that the quality of online information most accessible to consumers may be improving. In 2011, researchers performed Google searches using each of the 2,069 health terms included in the National Library of Medicine's MEDLINEPlus index. The study then assessed the quality, based on domain-level characteristics, of the websites included in the first page of search results for each term, which yielded 5,249 unique domains. Quality was determined based on certification and evaluation by MEDLINEPlus and/or the HON (Health on the Net) Foundation, an independent non-governmental organization that works worldwide to improve the quality of health information available online. The results showed that, overall, more than 50 percent of the domains identified in the first page of search results were considered of high quality, meaning that they had been certified by either the HON Foundation or were referenced by MEDLINEPlus. "Therefore consumers who exhibit common behavior by examining only the first page of search results, or possibly only the first few results returned, will be more likely than not to view results which lead them to high quality information" (Kitchens et al., 2014, p. 457). However, the results also showed variations based on the search terms. Searches for terms specifically related to body systems, disorders or conditions, and diagnosis or therapy returned larger proportions of links to high-quality domains than did searches for terms related to health and wellness, such as "food and nutrition" or "wellness and lifestyle."

As a result of concerns about online health information quality, numerous organizations and researchers have produced instruments designed to help consumers assess the quality of the information they find. In fact, a study reviewing these quality assessment tools identified 273 separate instruments. However, most were either not intended for consumers to use in their own assessments of website quality or required assessment of too many individual elements to be practical for consumers to use. Only 21 existing instruments had ten or fewer specific elements to consider in determining website quality, were focused on content rather than design and provided sufficient information to allow evaluation of their criteria. Of these, 14 included criteria that the researchers deemed too subjective for consumers to use successfully (e.g., content author is qualified). Only one instrument, produced by the Mayo Clinic, included only reliably assessable elements; one other instrument, produced by the World Health Organization, met standards for readability, meaning that the content could be understood by someone reading at the eighth-grade level. The researchers concluded that few of these instruments were likely to be of any use to consumers attempting to evaluate the quality of the online health information they encounter (Bernstam et al., 2005).

Another study that examined 343 unique webpages related to breast cancer identified 41 inaccurate statements on 18 pages, which represented only 5.2 percent of the pages studied. However, none of the 15 quality criteria or the three website criteria normally recommended for judging health information quality, whether used alone or in combination, was significantly associated with the pages containing inaccurate information. Webpages containing information about complementary

29

or alternative medicine were significantly more likely than other pages to include inaccurate statements (Bernstam et al., 2008).

A more recent study developed assessment tools focused on evaluating health websites for their design, information validity, motivational health content and literacy, and then applied these tools to 155 breast cancer websites. The authors concluded that the assessment tools "were useful in evaluating the quality of websites, and could serve as valuable resources for health website developers in the future" (Whitten et al., 2013, p. 366); however, the assessment tools included far more than ten items, meaning that this set of measures would also not likely be of much use to consumers

Consumers' Use of Online Health Information

Despite health professionals' concerns about the inconsistent quality of health information online, consumers regularly take advantage of the Internet as a health information resource (Fox, 2013; Fox & Duggan, n.d.; Pew Internet Project, 2014). In fact, even ten years ago, the Pew Internet Project estimated that six million Americans searched for health information online every day, meaning that consultations with "Dr. Google" outnumbered visits to actual health professionals (Fox & Rainie, 2002). According to the most recent data from the Pew Research Center's Internet Project, 87 percent of U.S. adults used the Internet as of January 2014. In a 2012 Pew Center survey, 72 percent of Internet users said they had looked online for health information within the past year, with 55 percent reporting that they were looking for information about a specific disease or medical problem, 43 percent trying to learn more about a medical treatment or procedure, 27 percent percent looking for weight loss or weight management information, and a quarter seeking information about health insurance, including both private insurance and Medicare/Medicaid. Health information seekers are equally likely to be looking for information for themselves or on behalf of someone else, with 39 percent reporting seeking information for someone else, 39 percent looking for information related to their own health and 15 percent saying the search was for information relevant to both their own and someone else's health; the distribution of searches for oneself or for others has remained consistent since Pew began tracking online health information use in 2000 (Fox & Duggan, 2013c).

Figure 2.1: Most Internet Users Seek Health Information Online
(iStock 80127219)

A study of New York tenth-graders, conducted in May 2000, showed that nearly half (49%) had sought some sort of health information online. Among the students who used the Internet, 42.1 percent said they had sought information about sex, including sexual activities, birth control and pregnancy; 37 percent had looked for information about sexually transmitted diseases. Other commonly searched-for topics included fitness and exercise (41.6%), diet and nutrition (36.5%), alcohol and drug use (24.7%) and dating violence or rape (23%). About one in five had searched for information about other diseases, cancer, tobacco and smoking, and medicines. The teens were asked to rate how "worthwhile" it is to have information about various topics available online, and girls were more likely than boys to give high scores for online information about sexual health topics, including birth control, sexual abuse and dating violence, as well as information about diet and nutrition, fitness and exercise, and physical abuse (Borzekowski & Rickert, 2001).

Research has shown that the significant predictors of online health information seeking include being female and having more education and income (Fox & Duggan, 2013c; Weaver et al., 2010). Similarly, data from the National Cancer Institute's 2012 Health Information National

31

Trends Survey (HINTS) revealed no race or ethnicity differences in the use of online health information, although socioeconomic status and sex did predict online health information seeking (Kontos et al., 2014). Other researchers have found that women search for information on a greater variety of topics than do men, and that women and parents are more likely to search for information about another's health rather than their own (Stern et al., 2012). The 2013 Pew survey showed that whites are more likely than those of other races to search for information about specific diseases, while blacks are more likely to seek information about a drug they had seen advertised; Hispanic/Latino consumers were more likely to report seeking information about pregnancy and childbirth, and both blacks and Hispanics/Latinos were more likely than whites to seek online information about weight loss and management (Fox & Duggan, 2013b).

Adults aged 65 and older were less likely than members of other age groups to seek health information online. In 2012, 58 percent of Internet users in this group had searched the Web for health information during the previous year compared to 76 percent of 18- to 29-year-olds, 75 percent of 30- to 49-year-olds and 71 percent of 50- to 64-year-olds. The likelihood of searching for specific topics also varied significantly among different age groups, with middle-aged consumers more likely than younger or older Internet users to seek information about a specific disease or medical condition or about a specific treatment or procedure. The youngest Internet users (18–29), perhaps not surprisingly, were most likely to look online for information about pregnancy and childbirth. Despite being least likely, overall, to look for health information online, seniors (65+) were more likely than those in other age groups to search for information about specific treatments or procedures, weight loss/management, health insurance, food and drug safety or recalls, medical test results, caring for an aging relative or friend and reducing health care costs, although these differences were not always statistically significant (Fox & Duggan, 2013c).

Using the most recent HINTS data, Kontos et al. (2014) found that individuals with less education were less likely to go online to look for a health care provider, communicate with a doctor through email or another online form, track their diet, weight or physical activity on a website, or to download health information to a phone or other mobile device. The HINTS data also revealed gender differences in web-based health activity, with women being more likely than men to report searching for a health provider or communicating with a provider via the Internet. In addition, women were 1.5 times as likely as men to report searching online for health information on behalf of someone else. Other studies also have supported the idea that women are more likely than men to search for health information online (Atkinson et al., 2009; Lorence et al., 2006). However, another analysis of HINTS data revealed no gender differences in likelihood of seeking health information from the Internet *first*, before attempting to obtain information from a health provider or other source (Koch-Weser et al., 2010).

Another characteristic that influences online health information seeking is health status. Several studies have shown that individuals who have chronic health conditions are more likely than those who are healthy to engage in health information seeking online. Ayers and Kronenfeld (2007) found not only that individuals dealing with chronic illness were more likely to seek health information online but that the number of chronic conditions also influenced Internet health information use. Somewhat counterintuitively, the data suggested that the use of online health information was *lowest* among those who had the greatest number of chronic conditions, a finding that may be explained by the association between age and having more health problems. Those who suffered from two chronic illnesses used online health information more often than any other group. In addition, the nature of the chronic illness played a role, with individuals suffering from allergies, depression and high cholesterol being most likely to report using online health information sometimes or often. These patterns may have changed, however, because the data for this study were collected in 2001.

A more recent study showed that those in poorer health, perhaps not surprisingly, were more likely than those in good health to search for illness information online. However, many health information seekers looked for information about illness *and* about wellness, and those who sought both types of information did not differ significantly from those who sought only illness information in terms of demographic characteristics, health status, health risk behaviors, behaviors, or the perceived value of health information (Weaver et al., 2010).

Bundorf and colleagues (2006) also found that, regardless of health insurance status, individuals who suffered from a chronic condition were more likely than healthier individuals to seek health information online; health insurance status did have an effect, however. Among the privately insured, the chronically ill were 1.4 times as likely as healthy consumers to report searching for health information online at least every two or three months, while among those with public insurance (e.g., Medicare, Medicaid), those with a chronic condition were 2.6 times as likely to conduct frequent online searches for health information. The uninsured with chronic conditions were nearly twice as likely (1.9 times) as those without chronic conditions to make frequent use of the Internet for online health information.

Finally, some early research suggests that individuals who search for health information online may be more health-conscious, in general, than those who do not. Using data from the 1999 Porter Novelli Health-Styles database, Dutta-Bergman (2004) found that online health information seekers were more concerned about health in general, more interested in staying informed about health issues, more likely to engage in healthy activities and more likely to have strong beliefs about the importance of specific health behaviors, such as not smoking, drinking plenty of water and exercising regularly. Overall, having a health information orientation (wanting to stay informed about health issues) was the strongest predictor of Internet health information activities, including searching for medical news, information about medical services, drug/medication information, disease-specific information, healthy lifestyle information and health-focused discussion groups.

WHAT MOTIVATES THE USE OF ONLINE HEALTH INFORMATION?

The most common trigger for an online health information search is learning that someone the consumer knows has been diagnosed with a medical condition; in 2001, 81 percent of respondents to a Pew Internet Project survey said they had gone online to learn more about someone else's diagnosis or condition (Fox & Rainie, 2002). Often, searching for health information on behalf of someone else occurs without prompting; in other words, people try to find information that will help someone else without being asked to do so (Abrahamson et al., 2008). Other significant motivators include being diagnosed oneself with a new health problem (58%) and being prescribed a new medication or treatment protocol (56%). Nearly half of the adults in the Pew survey said they had sought information online because they were dealing with an ongoing medical condition (47%), had unanswered questions following a doctor's visit (47%) or had decided to change their diet or exercise habits (46%). Taking on the role of caregiver to someone else was a factor for 38 percent of those surveyed. For most people, lack of access to a doctor was not a common reason for online health information seeking; only 14 percent said they sought information online because they did not have time to see a doctor, and only 8 percent said they went online because they had been unable to get a referral to or appointment with a specialist (Fox & Rainie, 2002). Rice's (2006) analysis of data from this Pew survey revealed that these motivations influence the frequency of online health information searches. Those who sought health information online more often included consumers who rated their health less positively, had a new or chronic condition or had been prescribed a new treatment, those who had less access to a physician or wanted to diagnose or treat a condition without talking to their doctor and those who needed information about a sensitive health issue they were uncomfortable discussing with their doctor.

A study of individuals' medical help-seeking behavior revealed that one of the primary reasons consumers seek health information online is the perception that it is easy to find useful information. In a study of 819 Americans aged 12 and older who had found health information online during the previous year (Ybarra & Suman, 2006), 40 percent said they had sought the information online because it was easy, and 36 percent cited the availability of a wide range of information. Nearly one-third (31%) went online because they needed information quickly. Fewer individuals reported using the Internet because the health topic was sensitive or embarrassing (4.2%) or because the information would be free or very inexpensive compared to consulting a health care professional (1.7%).

Although few individuals in Ybarra and Suman's (2006) study indicated that they had sought health information online because it would be less expensive than seeing a doctor, a more recent study, using data from the 2009 National Health Interview Survey, showed that barriers to health care access do influence use of the Web for health information. The poll of 27,210 adults revealed that individuals were more likely to look for general health information online if they faced financial barriers to seeing health professionals, had trouble getting timely medical appointments or had scheduling conflicts during regular clinic hours

(Bhandari et al., 2014). In another study, 11 percent of individuals who had used the Internet for health information said they did so instead of consulting their doctors, often seeking "second opinion" information or information about complementary or alternative medicine (Diaz et al., 2002).

Some participants in the study by Diaz et al. (2002) recorded comments suggesting another reason for online health information seeking: frustrations with one's health care provider. Among those who said they had sought information online instead of consulting their doctor, some wrote comments suggesting that the patients felt their doctors wouldn't listen to their suggestions, didn't fully understand their concerns or did not have time to provide as much information as the patient wanted. Other studies offer support for the idea that dissatisfaction with the individual's health provider motivates some to turn to the Internet (Dolce, 2011; Hou & Shim, 2010; Tustin, 2010). Among respondents participating in the National Cancer Institute's 2007 HINTS Survey, those who perceived their interactions with their health provider to be more open and more patient centered were less likely to report using the Internet for health information, to search for a different health care provider, or to help them develop or maintain a healthy diet, weight or exercise routine (Hou & Shim, 2010). Tustin (2010) found that, among cancer listserv users, 35 percent named the Internet as their preferred health information source, while only 19 percent chose their oncologist as their best information source. The study showed that patients who were dissatisfied with their provider's level of empathy and/or the quality of time he or she spent with the patient were more likely to seek and trust online health information.

However, even among patients who perceive their providers to be empathetic and patient centered, online health information seeking is common immediately before or after a medical appointment (Bell et al., 2011; Flynn et al., 2006; Hesse et al., 2005; Li et al., 2014). A survey of participants in a large online support community (www.dailystrength.org) showed that, among those who had visited a doctor during the previous month, most rated the physician they had seen as being "patient centered"; nonetheless, 80.4 percent had looked for health information online following the visit. Curiosity was the most commonly given reason for going online for more health information. However, 30 percent said they looked online because they hadn't received complete information from the doctor, and nearly one in four (22.8%) believed the quality of care they had received was inadequate. About one in seven (14.4%) went online to check the accuracy of something their physician had said. Individuals who rated their doctors as less patient centered were more likely to list concerns about inadequate or inaccurate information as their reason for looking for health information online. Encouragement from the physician (12.8%) or from family members and friends (10.4%) led some to look online for more information about their health condition, and 4.8 percent said they looked online for information about a question they had been embarrassed to ask the doctor (Li et al., 2014).

Researchers have found that individuals in poorer health, especially those with cancer, are more likely to look for online health information following a doctor's visit (Flynn et al., 2006). Increased worry after the visit was positively related to going online to answer questions they had been embarrassed to ask the doctor, believing that their doctor had provided incomplete or inaccurate information and feeling that they had received inadequate care (Li et al., 2014). The results of this study were consistent with those from an earlier study of dailystrength.org users; the earlier study also showed that patients were more likely to seek online information due to the perceived incompleteness of information provided by the doctor, rather than because they believed the doctor's information to be inaccurate (Bell et al., 2011).

Motivations for seeking health information online may be slightly different among adolescents. A study using single-gender focus groups to assess U.S. and U.K. teens' use of the Internet for health information showed that, for many, the Internet is their primary information source, in part because the Internet gives teens 24-hour-a-day access to health information, most often without requiring them to leave home. For these teens, searching for information online was far more convenient than having to schedule and attend a visit with a health care professional, especially given that most teens expected to be using the Internet to gain information about relatively minor ailments. In addition, however, teens believed doing research online before a health visit would empower them to be better able to interact with health professionals and, potentially, would reduce their need to rely on a doctor's advice. The adolescents also liked the interactivity of the Internet and the fact that some websites enabled them to access information they saw as

37

being personalized for them based on their answers to online surveys (Gray et al., 2005).

FROM WHY TO HOW: CONSUMERS' ONLINE HEALTH INFORMATION SEARCH PROCESSES

As the previous section illustrated, individuals have a variety of reasons for going online to seek health information. But once the online health information search has been triggered, how do people go about finding the information they want?

First, most studies show that, regardless of the question they hope to answer, most consumers begin with a general search engine – "Dr. Google" or "Dr. Yahoo" – rather than starting with a specialized health-focused search engine. For instance, in the Pew Research Center's 2013 survey of online health information seeking, 77 percent said they began their searches at a site like Google or Yahoo, and only 13 percent said they would begin the search at a website focused on health information, such as WebMD (Fox & Rainie, 2002). In a review of the early literature about health information searches, Morahan-Martin (2004) noted that research has consistently demonstrated consumers' reliance on general purpose search engines in the United States, Canada, Australia, Germany and across Europe. Most consumers do not ask others for advice about how to find the information they seek. For instance, a 2001 Pew study showed that only 14 percent reported asking for advice about how to search, and those who did were more likely to ask a friend (38% of those who sought advice) or family member (38%) for advice than to ask a doctor or nurse (25%). Even when they sought search advice, fewer than half (49%) followed the advice they received (Fox & Rainie, 2002).

Surprisingly little research has focused on examining the search process consumers use when accessing online health information. An analysis of searches for cancer information using Ask.com revealed that users employed both keyword searches and sentence or question searches, using vocabulary that ranged from simplistic to very sophistic-ated. Misspelled words were common (Bader & Theofanos, 2003). A think-aloud study of adolescents' online health information searches showed that the teenagers' searches were somewhat haphazard, in that they did not read through either results pages or websites in systematic ways; they sometimes missed finding the answers they had been asked to search for, even though they had reached a page containing that answer. After choosing a website to examine, only one of the 12 students included in the study looked past the first page linked from the search results list. Misspelled words were common, and even if the search engine offered a revised search with the correct spelling, students most often stuck with the results produced for the incorrect spelling (Hansen et al., 2003).

The Pew Research Center's "Vital Decisions" study showed that consumers visit two to five sites in a typical search, usually starting at the top of the list of search results and working their way down (45%) or skimming the results list for links that seem most relevant (39%). Only 12 percent choose a link because they recognize the name or the sponsor. Less than one-third (29%) have bookmarked a favorite site for health information to which they return frequently. Among the 14 percent who named a specific favorite site, WebMD was the most popular, but those surveyed also named the Mayo Clinic's site, NIH, InteliHealth, Medline and DrKoop.com (Fox & Rainie, 2002), a site that seems to have been replaced by HealthCentral.com.

A focus group study of Australian consumers' methods for finding drug information online revealed that search skills varied significantly; some users understood the value of using quotation marks around key phrases, while others – most often retirees or full-time homemakers – used less successful approaches, such as typing a question or full sentence into the search engine. Some simply typed the name of the drug into the search engine. Procedures for selecting which links to select from the search results also varied, with some simply starting with the top link on the search page and working their way down, and others assessing the URL to see if it seemed "professional" and to determine if the site came from a government agency, university, not-for-profit organization or a drug company. "It was clear that most participants did not pay conscious attention to how they selected Internet-based information" (Peterson et al., 2003, p. 11).

One widely cited study of consumers' search processes for health information was conducted in Germany in 2001, using focus groups and observation of adult men and women. Only 35 percent of the searches observed included more than one search term, and only 3.5 percent of the searches included the use of phrases enclosed in quotation marks. Most participants chose a result from the first page of results, then redid the search using different terms rather than looking at the second page of results. Virtually all (97.2%) of the links participants selected for further examination came from the first page of search results, and one of the 17 observational study participants thought the first ten pages of results reflected all the information available on that topic. Most webpage visits were brief, lasting only 69 seconds on average (Eysenbach & Kohler, 2002).

The Internet search process may be particularly challenging for low-literacy individuals. For instance, a think-aloud study of adults participating in an adult literacy class showed that participants had difficulty coming up with the search terms they needed to answer the questions they were given unless they copied phrases directly from written versions of the questions. Some did not remember to put spaces between the words in the search phrase. Participants assumed that the first page of search results would provide all the information they needed, and, overall, they had difficulty finding answers to the questions they had been given, in part because they had trouble coming up with a specific search question. The participants often accessed sponsored sites, some of which led to information about commercial products, such as an Asian dietary supplement touted as a cure for cancer or the use of radio frequency treatment to interfere with tumor growth (Birru et al., 2004).

Even for more experienced and well-educated consumers, however, finding complete and accurate information that fully answers their questions may be difficult. Keselman and colleagues (2008) conducted a qualitative study examining consumers' online searches in response to a hypothetical scenario in which they were told to imagine that a relative was experiencing symptoms of "stable angina." The participants discussed what they believed might be causing these symptoms during interviews with the researchers and then searched MedlinePlus for information in a think-aloud session. The results indicated that none of the patients fully understood the condition, even though at least two held Ph.D. degrees. Even though many of the participants eventually ended up on pages that held relevant information or links, none was able to use that information to come to a correct conclusion about the likely cause of the hypothetical relative's symptoms. The problem stemmed in part from the fact that the consumers either began with or quickly developed hypotheses about the situation, then searched for and interpreted information as confirming those hypotheses.

EVALUATION OF ONLINE HEALTH INFORMATION

Despite the problems researchers have identified in consumers' health information search practices, research suggests that most consumers are satisfied with the results of their searches (Eysenbach & Kohler, 2002; Fox, 2006; Fox & Rainie, 2002; Graham et al., 2006; Zeng et al., 2004). Among respondents to one of the earlier Pew Research Center surveys, 82 percent said they had found most or all of the information they were looking for in their most recent search, with younger individuals more likely than older searchers to be satisfied with their success. Although younger consumers were no more likely than older consumers to have a favorite health information site or search strategy, 37 percent of 18- to 29-year-olds said they "always" find the information they sought, compared to only 23 percent of those aged 30 to 49 and 19 percent of individuals aged 50 to 64 (Fox & Rainie, 2002). In a 2011 Harris Poll, 90 percent of those who searched for health information online said their searches were successful; nine out of ten also described the information they found as reliable (Harris Interactive, 2011).

Zeng and colleagues (2004) conducted an observational study of 97 consumers who were instructed to search for any health topic that interested them, starting at the home page of MedlinePlus website, a health information site provided by the National Library of Medicine. The researchers found that participants regularly used the Internet for health information and had positive attitudes about online health information; however, many of their search attempts were unsuccessful. Being unable to find the information they were searching for during the study session seemed to have relatively little effect on participants' evaluations of online health information in general, although it did lead to more negative comments about the site or the information they uncovered. The specific problems included not finding information they had not already known, the information being too generic, the website's organization being confusing, or being overwhelmed with the amount of information uncovered. Some of these failings, the authors concluded, stemmed from poor search strategies – simply browsing what was available or using short queries that inadequately expressed what they hoped to find. Other researchers, too, have noted that consumers often use poor search strategies, relying on trial and error to find the information they seek (Kim et al., 2011).

Another study analyzed the relationships between consumers' perceived quality of health information on a website, the perceived technical adequacy of the site (e.g., page-loading speed, search capability, customization features), the appearance of the site, and overall satisfaction with the information retrieval experience. The results showed that the least important characteristic in determining consumer satisfaction was whether the website included the kind of specific information often recommended by health experts, such as the inclusion of privacy policies, identification of authors, contact information, etc. Interestingly, trust in the content had only a small effect on search satisfaction (Bliemel & Hassanein, 2006).

When consumers see a set of search results or visit a website containing health information, how do they evaluate that information? How do they decide what to trust and what to reject? Researchers have found fairly consistently that consumers do not follow health experts' recommendations about how to verify the quality of health information online (Eysenbach & Kohler, 2002; Fox, 2006; Fox & Rainie, 2002; Kim et al., 2011; Morahan-Martin, 2004). Among respondents to a 2006 survey by the Pew Internet & American Life project, only 15 percent of those who had looked for health information online said they "always" check the source and date of the information they find, while another 10 percent said they check this information "most of the time" (Fox, 2006).

Even if consumers do not fully follow health experts' advice for evaluating online health information, they do not treat all information equally. A 2002 Pew Center report concluded that about a quarter of consumers "are vigilant about verifying a site's information, another quarter are concerned but follow a more casual protocol, and about half mostly avoid the kind of search strategies experts recommend" (Fox & Rainie, 2002, p. 17). The survey results showed that 47 percent of online health information seekers reported turning away from a site that seemed "too commercial," a finding that has been supported by other research (Kim et al., 2011), and 42 percent said they had rejected a site because they could not determine the information's source. More than one-third (37%) had rejected information because they could not tell when it had been updated, and 30 percent said they had done so because the site had not been endorsed by a trusted independent organization. Prior knowledge and beliefs also play a role in consumers' evaluations, with 26 percent saying they had rejected online health information because it conflicted with what they already knew to be true, and 20 percent saying the information conflicted with advice from the consumer's own doctor (Fox & Rainie, 2002).

Focus groups conducted as part of this same study confirmed that consumers are more likely to trust information that fits with what they already believe or have heard from their doctors. In addition, they are more likely to trust information included in multiple sites. The Pew report notes that one flaw in this "confirmation" procedure is that because some health information is syndicated it may appear on multiple sites without representing independent confirmation. "Consumers may think they have verified a piece of information by reading two sources, but in fact may have simply re-read the same material from the same syndicate at two different Web sites" (Fox & Rainie, 2002, pp. 18–19). Interestingly, finding conflicting information did not have a corresponding dampening effect on consumers' trust. Of those who had found conflicting information, only 23 percent said it gave them less confidence in the website.

Although consumers report that they turn away from health information for which they cannot identify the source or that is lacking endorsement by a trusted independent organization, they may not always be so discerning in practice. A 2005 experiment among adults in a city in Ohio tested the impact of source attribution on participants' evaluations of the information's trustworthiness, truthfulness, readability and completeness. Participants were randomly assigned to read information about lung cancer attributed to one of three high-credibility sources – the American Lung Association, the American Cancer Society or the National Cancer Institute – or to a generic "webpage about preventing lung cancer" (Bates et al., 2006, p. 47). The results revealed no differences in participants' ratings of the information's trustworthiness, truthfulness or completeness.

Other research has suggested, however, that source expertise does influence the credibility ratings of online health information. Participants in one experiment were told that the information they read came from an HIV specialist medical doctor, the widow of an AIDS patient or a high school freshman. Regardless of source, all the information was judged more credible than not, suggesting that consumers have a tendency to believe what they read online, regardless of source. However,

43

those who believed what they were reading had been written by a doctor judged the information to be more credible (Eastin, 2001). Similarly, a study by Zulman and colleagues (2011) suggested that providing clear cues about the source and credibility of online health information increased trust among adults aged 65 and older.

Consumers' tendency to make use of online health information of dubious quality was illustrated in an experiment that tested participants' willingness to use less trustworthy websites when they appear at the top of a list of search engine results. In this study, German college students were given the task of searching for information about two competing therapies on behalf of a hypothetical friend who had been diagnosed with an unfamiliar rheumatic disease. Participants in the first study were given mock Google search result pages for each therapy; each result was similarly relevant to the disease and/or therapy, but they varied in trustworthiness. Half of the participants received a list ordered so that the most trustworthy sites appeared at the top of the page, while the other group saw the search results in reverse trustworthiness order. After having time to link to and read any of the pages in the list, the students were asked to list arguments for or against the two therapies. The results showed that when the links were presented from least to most trustworthy, the students were less likely to view, spend time on and use arguments from the most trustworthy sites. The authors concluded that "the ranking position of a result had substantial influence on whether the users selected it" (Kammerer & Gerjets, 2014, p. 183). Trustworthiness was not totally ignored, however, because even when the most trustworthy sites appeared at the bottom of the page of links, participants were equally likely to select the "good" sites as the "bad" sites. Nonetheless, this study, as well as others, supports the idea that consumers often fail to successfully distinguish between high- and low-quality online information, which may lead them to trust and act upon inaccurate and even dangerous information (Benotsch et al., 2004; Kim et al., 2011; McPherson et al., 2014).

Another experimental study suggested that, among college students, message characteristics such as inclusion of statistics, information currency, inclusion of author and reference information and inclusion of testimonial narratives, significantly affected participants' attitudes toward the health topic about which they were reading but had no effect on credibility judgments. Structural characteristics, however, including inclusion of the name of a sponsoring organization, a privacy policy, and links to external websites and images, did impact credibility perceptions (Rains & Karmikel, 2009). The results were consistent with those of an earlier study, which showed that including a street address for the website's sponsoring organization led to higher credibility ratings for articles about diabetes and hepatitis. Although the quantitative results showed no significant association between inclusion of links to an external site and credibility ratings, qualitative analysis of written comments from the participants suggested that the links did have an impact for some participants (Freeman & Spyridakis, 2004).

THE IMPACT OF ONLINE HEALTH INFORMATION

Given that consumers often use online health information sources without carefully checking for markers of quality, health experts would seem to have significant cause for concern about the Internet's impact on health decisions and behaviors. Overall, however, the research does not suggest that using online health information causes most consumers to make worse health choices than they would otherwise make.

Online health information does have an impact on health decisions, according to multiple surveys of consumers (Fox, 2006; Fox & Duggan, 2013c; Fox & Rainie, 2002; Liszka et al., 2006; Rice, 2006; Wolters Kluwer Health, 2012). The Pew Research Center's 2013 survey revealed that more than one-third of U.S. adults (35%) had used the Internet to try to self-diagnose a medical condition, either for themselves or for someone else. Of those "online diagnosers," 46 percent said the information they found online suggested that they should seek medical attention, while 38 percent said the online information led them to conclude that the problem could be managed without a health care professional's advice. More than half (53%) spoke with a health professional about the information they found online. Of all online diagnosers, 18 percent said a clinician from whom they sought advice disagreed with their diagnosis, while 41 percent said the health professional they consulted confirmed the self-diagnosis (Fox & Duggan, 2013b). In another 2012 survey, 63 percent of consumers who had sought health information online said they have never misdiagnosed themselves using online information. However, 77 percent said they would discuss online information with a doctor to verify their diagnosis (Wolters Kluwer Health, 2012).

Having access to online information seems to help assuage people's worries about undiagnosed conditions. In a survey of randomly selected Microsoft employees, White and Horvitz (2009b) found that, on average, the participants searched for information about undiagnosed conditions twice a month. While 38.5 percent of the participants said these searches sometimes made them feel more anxious about the undiagnosed condition, more than half (50.3%) said the searches had made them feel less anxious; nearly 40 percent said online health information searches had led them to behave differently in regard to a medical condition.

Informed Consumers = Empowered Consumers

Numerous studies of adults' online health information use have concluded that access to health information helps consumers prepare themselves for visits to health care professionals and, post-visit, provides them with a source of answers to questions they may have forgotten to ask or which there was insufficient time to discuss during the health appointment. For instance, Iverson and colleagues (2008) found that among patients who reported seeking online health information, 55 percent reported a change in how they think about their health and 46 percent reported making behavior changes. These changes included asking more questions during office visits (66%), changing their diet (54%) and adhering more closely to their doctor's advice (54%); most of them (73%) told their doctor about the changes they were making. Similarly, a survey of patients at a family medicine clinic revealed that of those who sought health information online, 73 percent used the information in making a health decision, but only 50 percent discussed the information with their doctors (Liszka et al., 2006). In a later study of osteopathic patients, 54 percent of those who had sought health information online had changed behaviors as a result; 55 percent of these patients informed their doctors about their behavior changes (Cooley et al., 2011).

As these studies suggest, it appears fairly common for consumers to research a health topic online prior to a doctor's appointment, with the intention of discussing that information with the doctor and/or being better prepared to understand what the doctor has to say (Bass et al., 2006). For instance, a study of breast cancer patients showed that, on average, the patients were most likely to have read information about side effects, diagnosis, prognosis and proven or traditional treatments; the topics they were most likely to report planning to discuss with their doctors included side effects and traditional treatments but also alternative therapies (Maloney et al., 2013). Another study of cancer patients and their caregivers reported several reasons for discussing with their doctors information they had found online, including the desire to educate themselves further, the desire to be proactive in improving their treatment or health, wanting to take advantage of the doctor's expertise to determine what to believe. Some patients, and especially caregivers, used online information to "test" the doctor's knowledge and currency on the latest research. For the most part, patients and caregivers reported feeling comfortable in these discussions with their doctor (Bylund et al., 2009).

In a survey of participants in the online support group DailyStrength. org, 91.7 percent reported using a search engine to obtain more information prior to a doctor's appointment. Other online health information-seeking activities were also common, including reading DailyStrength forum posts (89.5%), visiting another authoritative health site (78.8%), reading medical articles online (72.7%), visiting a medical association's website (69.1%) and posting questions in the DailyStrength forum's treatment section (63%). In fact, the only offline information activity reported by a majority of those surveyed was reading printed patient education materials (65.3%). The research suggested that those who spent more time using online resources before the doctor's visit were more likely to perceive themselves as having personal control over their illness. "Presumably, information and support have more utility for those who have self-efficacy and can act upon what they learn online" (Hu et al., 2012, p. 974). Other researchers have also documented this link between the use of online health information and greater health self-efficacy (Bass et al., 2006).

One concern about access to online health information is that it may turn some people into "cyberchondriacs" who overuse health care resources, convinced that they have developed every new disease or condition they saw discussed on the Internet. Some research suggests that online health information use increases anxiety among some but decreases anxiety among others (Baumgartner & Hartmann, 2011; Sabel et al., 2005). Among those who are already anxious about their health, frequent online health information searches are associated with more doctor visits (Eastin & Guinsler, 2006; White & Horvitz, 2009a). The opposite effect holds for those who are only mildly or not concerned about their health; for these individuals, online health information seeking *decreases* the frequency of doctor visits (Eastin & Guinsler, 2006).

As noted earlier in this chapter, patients also often seek online health information following a visit to their doctor or another health professional. Bell and colleagues (2011) reported that 68.2 percent of their survey respondents searched for health information online following their appointments, most often seeking information that had already been posted online rather than seeking further interaction with health providers or other patients. They note that curiosity was the primary motivator, and those who were dissatisfied with information given during their visit to the doctor most often felt they needed more information, rather than questioning the validity of the doctor's information. Nonetheless, post-visit information seeking was higher among those who did not fully trust their doctor.

This finding raises a question that is among the most studied and commented upon of any issue related to online health information: How does the Internet affect the doctor–patient relationship? One review of studies examining this issue concluded that consumers' use of online health information can have advantages, including the following:

- making patients better informed, producing better outcomes and reducing inappropriate use of health services;
- allowing patients and physicians to "share the burden of responsibility for knowledge" (Wald et al., 2007, p. 220), creating a sense of teamwork and cooperation between the consumer and his or her doctor (Bass et al., 2006);
- increasing the efficiency of the appointment time due to patients coming to the visit with a better base of knowledge and more prepared to make decisions;
- improved patient satisfaction with the treatment decisions (Wald et al., 2007).

The more interactive aspects of the Web 2.0 environment, including patients' access to their electronic health records, social networking communities surrounding specific health issues or conditions, and sites that post patient ratings of drugs and other medical products, doctors and health facilities, offer additional benefits. These may include more individually tailored health information, improved quality of care and the psychosocial benefits patients gain from interacting with others who share similar experiences (Lo & Parham, 2010).

However, there are downsides as well. The wide variation in quality of online health information may lead to doctors having to spend significant appointment time correcting consumers' inaccurate beliefs and/or discouraging them from requesting inappropriate treatments. In addition, if the use of online health information creates unnecessary worry among patients, it could lead to unnecessary appointments or otherwise disrupt the relationships among health professionals and patients by fostering mistrust (Wald et al., 2007). Some research suggests that frequent use of online health information is associated with poorer compliance with the doctor's instructions (Bass et al., 2006; Weaver III et al., 2009). Patients who control access to and the content of their electronic health records could enter inaccurate or misleading information or block their physicians from accessing relevant information. In addition, online interactions that involve sharing patients' medical records present privacy risks (Lo & Parham, 2010). Finally, although most physicians today seem willing to discuss the information their patients have found online, some still do not respond positively to such information, especially if it challenges something they have told the patient (Broom, 2005; Helft et al., 2003; Lo & Parham, 2010; McMullan, 2006; Murray et al., 2003; Wald et al., 2007).

BEYOND THE DOCTOR–PATIENT RELATIONSHIP

Consumers often report that the health information they find online has an impact on their own health or their care for someone else. More than half of the health information seekers in a 2006 Pew Center poll said the information they found online affected their own health care or the way they cared for someone else, with 11 percent characterizing this impact as "major" and 42 percent saying the impact was "minor." Among those who reported an impact, more than half said the online information affected a decision about treating an illness or condition (58%), changed their overall approach to their own health or their care for someone else (55%), or led them to ask a doctor new questions or to seek a second opinion from another doctor (54%). Others said the online information changed the way they thought about diet, exercise or stress management (44%), or the way they coped with a chronic condition or managed pain (39%), or influenced a decision about seeing a doctor (35%) (Fox, 2006). In another study, more than three-quarters (77.3%) of online health information seekers said that "the Internet had influenced the improvement of their health or medical information and services" (Lorence et al., 2006, p. 255).

Online information appears to have an impact on consumers' health decisions throughout their lives. Several studies have documented the frequency of online information seeking among pregnant women (Bernhardt & Felter, 2004; Lagan et al., 2006, 2010, 2011; Larsson, 2009; Lewallen & Côté-Arsenault, 2014). In addition to seeking social support from other pregnant women, the research suggests that pregnant women seek information about specific pregnancy- or childbirth-related problems and home remedies for maintaining their health (Lagan et al., 2006). In a recent qualitative study of pregnant women in the United States, Lewallen and Côté-Arsenault (2014) summarized the women's primary reasons for searching the Internet into four categories: help with decision-making, anticipatory guidance (understanding what is happening to the woman herself and her baby), connecting with others to compare experiences and finding general information.

As the beginning of this chapter might suggest, as children grow up, parents continue to use online health information to help them understand and respond to their children's health needs and problems. A review of research on parents' Internet use showed that "the majority of today's parents search for both information and social support on the internet" (Plantin & Daneback, 2009, p. 1), in part because fewer parents have the necessary child-rearing support from their own parents and other relatives or friends. In some cases, parents have used the Internet to help them diagnose rare diseases in their children (Bouwman et al., 2010). A study of Australian parents showed that they were more likely to use online information to help them understand their child's medical issues or treatments than to diagnose the child's illness or make decisions about treatment; nevertheless, parents did use online information for diagnosis and treatment decision-making (Walsh et al., 2012). A survey of parents whose children received outpatient care in a hospital's pediatric surgery unit showed that parents were most likely to report using the Internet to look for information about the surgeon (60 percent of those who searched online for health information) or for information about their child's treatment. Slightly more or fewer than one-third reported looking for information about the surgical procedure (37%), the risks (34%) or other (32%) health information, and more than half (52%) said the online information they found influenced their decisions at least partly (Semere et al., 2003). Another study, focused on parents whose children required cardiac surgery, did not ask specifically about influences on treatment decisions, but showed that the majority of parents who had looked for cardiology information online characterized the information as helpful in improving their understanding of the child's heart defect; two-thirds said the online information was "very helpful," and 29 percent said it was helpful (Ikemba et al., 2002). Similarly, a study of parents whose children were scheduled for head, neck or throat surgery revealed that nearly half of those who had Internet access searched online for information about their child's diagnosis, and of those who did so, 93 percent rated the information as understandable and helpful. A large majority (84%) said the online information influenced their decision-making regarding their children's treatment; less than half (43%) discussed the information they had found with the child's surgeon (Boston et al., 2005).

In some cases, research shows that parents' use of online information can interfere with positive medical decision-making. A recent study linking parents' use of various vaccine information sources with their decisions about childhood vaccinations showed that parents who used online vaccine information were more likely to perceive vaccines as being unsafe and ineffective and less concerned about their child's susceptibility to the diseases. In addition, their children were more likely to have non-medical exemptions from school vaccination requirements. This was a cross-sectional study, however, so it is not clear whether use of online information influenced parents' decisions or whether their pre-existing distrust of vaccines prompted online searches for vaccine information (Jones et al., 2012). On the other hand, a North Carolina study showed that parents' use of the Internet for information about the HPV vaccine was positively associated with willingness to have their daughters vaccinated, along with lower perceived vaccine harms and uncertainty about the vaccine. The study showed that among boys' parents, perceived barriers to HPV vaccination were *higher* among those

51

who found their information online, compared to those who used other sources for HPV information, but Internet use was unrelated to willingness to have their sons vaccinated (McRee et al., 2012).

By the time children reach adolescence, they have begun to conduct their own health information searches online (Gray et al., 2005). Often, these searches focus on obtaining sexual health information and on attempts to reassure themselves that various aspects of their anatomy, behaviors and experiences are "normal" (Harvey et al., 2007). At least one focus group study of adolescents suggested that the information they find online does lead to action, including personal behavior change; however, teens in this study also noted that online health information searches can be frustrating, leading to information overload without producing answers to the teens' specific questions (Skinner et al., 2003). Other studies have confirmed that teens use online health information but seem to have paid relatively little attention to what young people do with the information once they have found it. A recent review of the research on teens' online health information use concluded that adolescents are using the Internet for health information more than ever but identified no "seminal work exploring how adolescents translate online health information into behavioral changes" (Jain & Bickham, 2014, p. 437).

Among adults, there is evidence of some specific ways in which online information affects health-related behavior, beyond self-diagnosis, improved understanding and anxiety reduction. For instance, adults who used a North Carolina health information website reported that the information they had found had emotional, cognitive and physical effects, including leading to a lifestyle change such as quitting smoking (Abrahamson et al., 2008). Another study, which linked the volume of online searches for information about H1N1 ("swine") flu and HPV vaccines, found that there was a positive association of search activity and uptake of the vaccines within states; although the cross-sectional study did not allow conclusions about causality, the authors suggest that the search activity could encourage vaccination, especially if public health officials attempt to ensure that accurate, reliable information is more prevalent online than inaccurate information that may discourage vaccination (Kalichman & Kegler, 2014).

In a study of individuals with chronic illnesses, Ayers and Kronenfeld (2007) found that use of online health information was positively related to making changes in one's health care, with those who use the Internet often more than twice as likely to change their behavior as those who do not. The specific behaviors considered included taking an over-the-counter medicine or supplement, starting alternative or complementary treatment, asking the doctor for a prescription drug, making an appointment for a check-up, requesting preventive care, changing doctor, hospital or other health care provider, and talking to a health professional about health concerns. Of course, these behaviors are not necessarily inherently positive; alternative therapies could be ineffective and even dangerous, as could some supplements, and some health screenings can lead to over-diagnosis and over-treatment. In addition, this study did not assess lifestyle behavior changes that can have important health benefits, such as improving one's diet and exercise or stopping smoking. Nonetheless, the research does seem to support the authors' conclusion that "[u]sing the Internet increases patients' participation in management of their own health problems and increases their ability to make informed decisions about health" (Ayers & Kronenfeld, 2007, p. 343).

Hundreds of papers have now been published examining multiple aspects of the content, use and impact of online health information. Naturally, the results of those studies have not been entirely consistent, but it is possible to draw a few conclusions from the research:

- The quality and usefulness of online health information vary widely. The Internet offers high-quality, accurate and readable information that could benefit consumers, but it also provides access to the electronic equivalent of snake oil.
- Consumers turn increasingly to the Internet to seek more information about their health and health care. Although they express concerns about the trustworthiness of online health information, they rarely engage in systematic or careful evaluation of the information they find.
- Consumers share some, but not all, of the results of their health information searches with their health care providers.
- Online health information has an impact on consumers' health decisions and behaviors. For some consumers that impact can be harmful, leading to unnecessary worry and potentially to overuse of medical services. However, for the majority of consumers, access to

online health information seems to have an overall positive effect, although more research remains to be done to confirm that this is true.

Because online health information can be useful and accurate (but is sometimes dangerously wrong or misleading), and because consumers look for and want trustworthy information (but don't always know how to find it or take the steps to critically evaluate it), and because online information influences health decisions and behaviors (but may not always lead to better decisions and healthier behaviors), most health experts seem to be cautiously optimistic about the role the Internet can play in encouraging better health. One of the most common refrains, however, is the need for health experts – from researchers to advocacy organizations to medical specialty groups to the government – to create more high-quality content that is easily accessible and readily understandable for lay audiences. In addition, because the vast majority of people continue to view their health care providers as the most trustworthy source of health information (Chaudhuri et al., 2013; Rains, 2007; Shahrokni et al., 2014), a number of experts have begun to advise doctors to provide "information prescriptions" for their patients. In other words, rather than sending patients away with diagnoses, drug prescriptions and orders for further testing, knowing that patients are likely to search online – more or less effectively – for more information on these topics, health professionals could help their patients to use online health information more successfully by steering them to high-quality resources (D'Alessandro et al., 2004; McMullan, 2006; Ritterband et al., 2005; Siegel et al., 2006). However, several studies have suggested that leading consumers to access better quality health information may not be as easy as handing out URLs or emailing links to good information (Coberly et al., 2010; D'Alessandro et al., 2004; Siegel et al., 2006). For instance, Coberly and her colleagues (2010) found that among patients who received a "physician-directed, condition-specific email prescription incorporating MedlinePlus," 68 percent reported receiving the prescription, and 74 percent expressed interest in receiving information prescriptions in the future. However, of those who "filled" their information prescription, only 35 percent said it had improved their understanding of an illness or health problem, and only 55 percent thought the information was more valuable because their doctor had prescribed it.

The information prescription, then, may not solve the problem, such as it is, of consumers accessing and using online health information of questionable quality. First of all, as the research discussed here illustrates, many online health information searches occur entirely outside the context of a medical visit, as consumers look to satisfy their curiosity about an issue or look for information that ultimately leads them to conclude that they have no need to seek professional medical advice. Second, in at least some cases, consumers are actively seeking information because they distrust or reject the information their physicians have provided. In addition, because the majority of online health information searches are actually conducted on behalf of someone else, the individual who receives an information prescription from his or her doctor may also be receiving Internet-sourced health information from others who have not seen the doctor's "information prescription."

It may make more sense, then, to focus on efforts to improve consumers' ability to find and evaluate online health information on their own. That perspective has led to a growing body of research on how to promote "eHealth literacy," which has been defined as "the ability to seek, find, understand, and appraise health information from electronic sources and apply the knowledge gained to addressing or solving a health problem" (Norman & Skinner, 2006, para. 6). Discussion of the research on eHealth literacy is beyond the scope of this chapter. The concept, however, makes intuitive sense: regardless of the intentions of those producing online health content, if consumers are to achieve the most benefit (and most successfully avoid any potential harm) from online health information, they must know how to find information that is trustworthy, how to determine whether the information they find is relevant to their own or their loved ones' health situations, and how to incorporate the knowledge they gain from that information into their own health practices and/or their care for others. Given that, a key research area for the future will focus on discovering how best to promote consumers' acquisition of those eHealth skills.

REFERENCES

Abrahamson, J.A., Fisher, K.E., Turner, A.G., Durrance, J.C. & Turner, T.C. (2008). Lay Information Mediary Behavior Uncovered: Exploring How Nonprofessionals Seek Health Information for Themselves and Others Online. *Journal of the Medical Library Association : JMLA, 96*(4), 310–323. http://doi.org/10.3163/1536-5050.96.4.006.

Atkinson, N.L., Saperstein, S.L. & Pleis, J. (2009). Using the Internet for Health-related Activities: Findings from a National Probability Sample. *Journal of Medical Internet Research, 11*(1), e4. http://doi.org/10.2196/jmir.1035.

Ayers, S.L. & Kronenfeld, J.J. (2007). Chronic Illness and Health-seeking Information on the Internet. *Health, 11*(3), 327–347. http://doi.org/10.1177/1363459307077547.

Bader, J.L. & Theofanos, M.F. (2003). Searching for Cancer Information on the Internet: Analyzing Natural Language Search Queries. *Journal of Medical Internet Research, 5*(4), e31. http://doi.org/10.2196/jmir.5.4.e31.

Bass, S.B., Ruzek, S.B., Gordon, T.F., Fleisher, L., McKeown-Conn, N. & Moore, D. (2006). Relationship of Internet Health Information Use With Patient Behavior and Self-efficacy: Experiences of Newly Diagnosed Cancer Patients Who Contact the National Cancer Institute's Cancer Information Service. *Journal of Health Communication, 11*(2), 219–236. http://doi.org/10.1080/10810730500526794.

Bates, B.R., Romina, S., Ahmed, R. & Hopson, D. (2006). The Effect of Source Credibility on Consumers' Perceptions of the Quality of Health Information on the Internet. *Informatics for Health and Social Care, 31*(1), 45–52. http://doi.org/10.1080/14639230600552601.

Baumgartner, S.E. & Hartmann, T. (2011). The Role of Health Anxiety in Online Health Information Search. *Cyberpsychology, Behavior, and Social Networking, 14*(10), 613–618. http://doi.org/10.1089/cyber.2010.0425.

Bell, R.A., Hu, X., Orrange, S.E. & Kravitz, R.L. (2011). Lingering Questions and Doubts: Online Information-seeking of Support Forum Members Following Their Medical Visits. *Patient Education and Counseling, 85*(3), 525–528. http://doi.org/10.1016/j.pec.2011.01.015.

Benotsch, E.G., Kalichman, S. & Weinhardt, L.S. (2004). HIV-AIDS Patients' Evaluation of Health Information on the Internet: The Digital Divide and Vulnerability to Fraudulent Claims. *Journal of Consulting and Clinical Psychology, 72*(6), 1004.

Berg, G.M., Hervey, A.M., Atterbury, D., Cook, R., Mosley, M., Grundmeyer, R. & Acuna, D. (2014). Evaluating the Quality of Online Information About Concussions. *JAAPA: Official Journal of the American Academy of Physician Assistants, 27*(2), 1–8. http://doi.org/10.1097/01.JAA.0000442712.05009.b1.

Bernhardt, J.M. & Felter, E.M. (2004). Online Pediatric Information Seeking among Mothers of Young Children: Results from a Qualitative Study Using Focus Groups. *Journal of Medical Internet Research, 6*(1), e7. http://doi.org/10.2196/jmir.6.1.e7.

Bernstam, E.V., Shelton, D.M., Walji, M. & Meric-Bernstam, F. (2005). Instruments to Assess the Quality of Health Information on the World Wide Web: What Can Our Patients Actually Use? *International Journal of Medical Informatics, 74*(1), 13–19.

Bernstam, E.V., Walji, M.F., Sagaram, S., Sagaram, D., Johnson, C.W. & Meric-Bernstam, F. (2008). Commonly Cited Website Quality Criteria Are Not Effective at Identifying Inaccurate Online Information About Breast Cancer. *Cancer, 112*(6), 1206–1213. http://doi.org/10.1002/cncr.23308.

Bhandari, N., Shi, Y. & Jung, K. (2014). Seeking Health Information Online: Does Limited Healthcare Access Matter? *Journal of the American Medical Informatics Association: JAMIA.* http://doi.org/10.1136/amiajnl-2013-002350.

Birru, M.S., Monaco, V.M., Charles, L., Drew, H., Njie, V., Bierria, T. & Steinman, R.A. (2004). Internet Usage by Low-literacy Adults Seeking Health Information: An Observational Analysis. *Journal of Medical Internet Research, 6*(3). http://doi.org/10.2196/jmir.6.3.e25.

Bliemel, M. & Hassanein, K. (2006). Consumer Satisfaction with Online Health Information Retrieval: A Model and Empirical Study. *E-Service Journal, 5*(2), 53–83.

Borzekowski, D.L. & Rickert, V.I. (2001). Adolescent Cybersurfing for Health Information: A New Resource that Crosses Barriers. *Archives of Pediatrics & Adolescent Medicine, 155*(7), 813–817.

Boston, M., Ruwe, E., Duggins, A. & Willging, J. (2005). Internet Use by Parents of Children Undergoing Outpatient Otolaryngology Procedures. *Archives of Otolaryngology–Head & Neck Surgery, 131*(8), 719–722. http://doi.org/10.1001/archotol. 131.8.719.

Bouwman, M.G., Teunissen, Q.G.A., Wijburg, F.A. & Linthorst, G.E. (2010). "Doctor Google" Ending the Diagnostic Odyssey in Lysosomal Storage Disorders: Parents Using Internet Search Engines as an Efficient Diagnostic Strategy in Rare Diseases. *Archives of Disease in Childhood, 95*(8), 642–644. http://doi.org/10.1136/ adc.2009.171827.

Broom, A. (2005). Virtually He@lthy: The Impact of Internet Use on Disease Experience and the Doctor–Patient Relationship. *Qualitative Health Research, 15*(3), 325–345. http://doi.org/10.1177/1049732304272916.

Bryant, A.G., Narasimhan, S., Bryant-Comstock, K. & Levi, E.E. (2014). Crisis Pregnancy Center Websites: Information, Misinformation and Disinformation. *Contraception.* http://doi.org/10.1016/j.contraception.2014.07.003.

Bundorf, M.K., Wagner, T.H., Singer, S.J. & Baker, L.C. (2006). Who Searches the Internet for Health Information? *Health Services Research, 41*(3p1), 819–836. http:// doi.org/10.1111/j.1475-6773.2006.00510.x.

Bylund, C.L., Gueguen, J.A., D'Agostino, T.A., Imes, R.S. & Sonet, E. (2009). Cancer Patients' Decisions About Discussing Internet Information With Their Doctors. *Psycho-Oncology, 18*(11), 1139–1146. http://doi.org/10.1002/pon.1511.

Chaudhuri, S., Le, T., White, C., Thompson, H. & Demiris, G. (2013). Examining Health Information-seeking Behaviors of Older Adults. *Computers, Informatics, Nursing: CIN, 31*(11), 547–553. http://doi.org/10.1097/01.NCN.0000432131.92020.42.

Coberly, E., Boren, S.A., Davis, J.W., McConnell, A.L., Chitima-Matsiga, R., Ge, B. & Hodge, R.H. (2010). Linking Clinic Patients to Internet-based, Condition-specific Information Prescriptions. *Journal of the Medical Library Association: JMLA, 98*(2), 160–164. http://doi.org/10.3163/1536-5050.98.2.009.

Cooley, D.L., Mancuso, A.M., Weiss, L.B. & Coren, J.S. (2011). Health-related Internet Use Among Patients of Osteopathic Physicians. *The Journal of the American Osteopathic Association, 111*(8), 473–482.

D'Alessandro, D.M., Kreiter, C.D., Kinzer, S.L. & Peterson, M.W. (2004). A Randomized Controlled Trial of an Information Prescription for Pediatric Patient Education on the Internet. *Archives of Pediatrics & Adolescent Medicine, 158*(9), 857–862.

Diaz, J.A., Griffith, R.A., Ng, J.J., Reinert, S.E., Friedmann, P.D. & Moulton, A.W. (2002). Patients' Use of the Internet for Medical Information. *Journal of General Internal Medicine, 17*(3), 180–185. http://doi.org/10.1046/j.1525-1497.2002.10603.x.

Dolce, M.C. (2011). The Internet as a Source of Health Information: Experiences of Cancer Survivors and Caregivers with Healthcare Providers. *Oncology Nursing Forum, 38*(3), 353–359. http://doi.org/10.1188/11.ONF.353-359.

Dutta-Bergman, M.J. (2004). Health Attitudes, Health Cognitions, and Health Behaviors among Internet Health Information Seekers: Population-based Survey. *Journal of Medical Internet Research, 6*(2). http://doi.org/10.2196/jmir.6.2.e15.

Eastin, M.S. (2001). Credibility Assessments of Online Health Information: The Effects of Source Expertise and Knowledge of Content. *Journal of Computer-Mediated Communication, 6*(4). doi: 10.1111/j.1083-6101.2001.tb00126.x.

57

Eastin, M.S. & Guinsler, N.M. (2006). Worried and Wired: Effects of Health Anxiety on Information-seeking and Health Care Utilization Behaviors. *CyberPsychology & Behavior, 9*(4), 494–498. http://doi.org/10.1089/cpb.2006.9.494.

Eysenbach, G. & Kohler, C. (2002). How Do Consumers Search For and Appraise Health Information on the World Wide Web? Qualitative Study Using Focus Groups, Usability Tests, and In-depth Interviews. *BMJ: British Medical Journal, 324*(7337), 573–577.

Eysenbach, G., Powell, J., Kuss, O. & Sa, E.-R. (2002). Empirical Studies Assessing the Quality of Health Information for Consumers on the World Wide Web: A Systematic Review. *JAMA, 287*(20), 2691–2700.

Flynn, K.E., Smith, M.A. & Freese, J. (2006). When Do Older Adults Turn to the Internet for Health Information? Findings from the Wisconsin Longitudinal Study. *Journal of General Internal Medicine, 21*(12), 1295–1301. http://doi.org/10.1111/j.1525-1497.2006.00622.x.

Fox, S. (2006). *Online Health Search 2006*. Washington, DC: Pew Internet & American Life Project. Retrieved October 16, 2014 from www.pewinternet.org/files/old-media//Files/Reports/2006/PIP_Online_Health_2006.pdf.pdf.

Fox, S. (2013, December 17). What Ails America? Dr. Google Can Tell You. Retrieved October 2, 2014 from www.google.com/trends/topcharts.

Fox, S. & Duggan, M. (2013a, January 15). Health Online 2013. Retrieved from www.pewinternet.org/2013/01/15/health-online-2013/.

Fox, S. & Duggan, M. (2013b, January 15). Information Triage. Retrieved October 6, 2014 from www.pewinternet.org/2013/01/15/information-triage/.

Fox, S. & Duggan, M. (2013, January 15). Health Online 2013. Retrieved October 10, 2014, from http://www.pewinternet.org/2013/01/15/health-online-2013/.

Fox, S. & Duggan, M. (n.d.). Tracking for Health. Retrieved October 2, 2014 from www.pewinternet.org/2013/01/28/tracking-for-health/.

Fox, S. & Rainie, L. (2002, May 22). Vital Decisions: A Pew Internet Health Report. Retrieved October 9, 2014 from www.pewinternet.org/2002/05/22/vital-decisions-a-pew-internet-health-report/.

Freeman, K.S. & Spyridakis, J.H. (2004). An Examination of Factors That Affect the Credibility of Online Health Information. *Technical Communication, 51*(2), 239–263.

Graham, L., Tse, T. & Keselman, A. (2006). Exploring User Navigation during Online Health Information Seeking. *AMIA Annual Symposium Proceedings, 2006*, 299–303.

Gray, N.J., Klein, J.D., Noyce, P.R., Sesselberg, T.S. & Cantrill, J.A. (2005). Health Information-seeking Behaviour in Adolescence: The Place of the Internet. *Social Science & Medicine, 60*(7), 1467–1478.

Hansen, D.L., Derry, H.A., Resnick, P.J. & Richardson, C.R. (2003). Adolescents Searching for Health Information on the Internet: An Observational Study. *Journal of Medical Internet Research, 5*(4). http://doi.org/10.2196/jmir.5.4.e25.

Harris Interactive. (2011, September 15). The Growing Influence and Use of Health Care Information Obtained Online. Retrieved October 16, 2014 from www.harris-interactive.com/vault/HI-Harris-Poll-Cyberchondriacs-2011-09-15.pdf.

Harvey, K.J., Brown, B., Crawford, P., Macfarlane, A. & McPherson, A. (2007). "Am I Normal?" Teenagers, Sexual Health and the Internet. *Social Science & Medicine, 65*(4), 771–781. http://doi.org/10.1016/j.socscimed.2007.04.005.

Helft, P.R., Hlubocky, F. & Daugherty, C.K. (2003). American Oncologists' Views of Internet Use by Cancer Patients: A Mail Survey of American Society of Clinical Oncology Members. *Journal of Clinical Oncology, 21*(5), 942–947.

Hesse, B.W., Nelson, D.E., Kreps, G.L., Croyle, R.T., Arora, N.K., Rimer, B.K. & Viswanath, K. (2005). Trust and Sources of Health Information: The Impact of the Internet and its Implications for Health Care Providers: Findings from the First Health Information National Trends Survey. *Archives of Internal Medicine, 165*(22), 2618–2624. http://doi.org/10.1001/archinte.165.22.2618.

Hou, J. & Shim, M. (2010). The Role of Provider–Patient Communication and Trust in Online Sources in Internet Use for Health-related Activities. *Journal of Health Communication, 15*(sup3), 186–199. http://doi.org/10.1080/10810730.2010.522691.

Hu, X., Bell, R.A., Kravitz, R.L. & Orrange, S. (2012). The Prepared Patient: Information Seeking of Online Support Group Members Before Their Medical Appointments. *Journal of Health Communication, 17*(8), 960–978. http://doi.org/10.1080/10810730.2011.650828.

Hunter, L. & Cohen, K.B. (2006). Biomedical Language Processing: Perspective What's Beyond PubMed? *Molecular Cell, 21*(5), 589–594. http://doi.org/10.1016/j.molcel.2006.02.012.

Ikemba, C.M., Kozinetz, C.A., Feltes, T.F., Fraser, C.D., McKenzie, E.D., Shah, N. & Mott, A.R. (2002). Internet Use in Families With Children Requiring Cardiac Surgery for Congenital Heart Disease. *Pediatrics, 109*(3), 419–422. http://doi.org/10.1542/peds.109.3.419.

Iverson, S.A., Howard, K.B. & Penney, B.K. (2008). Impact of Internet Use on Health-related Behaviors and the Patient–Physician Relationship: A Survey-based Study and Review. *The Journal of the American Osteopathic Association, 108*(12), 699–711.

Jain, A.V. & Bickham, D. (2014). Adolescent Health Literacy and the Internet: Challenges and Opportunities. *Current Opinion in Pediatrics, 26*(4), 435–439. http://doi.org/10.1097/MOP.0000000000000119.

Jones, A.M., Omer, S.B., Bednarczyk, R.A., Halsey, N.A., Moulton, L.H., & Salmon, D.A. (2012). Parents' source of vaccine information and impact on vaccine attitudes, beliefs, and nonmedical exemptions. *Advances in Preventive Pedicine, 2012,* e932741. http://doi.org/10.1155/2012/932741.

Kalichman, S.C. & Kegler, C. (2014). Vaccine-related Internet Search Activity Predicts H1N1 and HPV Vaccine Coverage: Implications for Vaccine Acceptance. *Journal of Health Communication,* 1–7. http://doi.org/10.1080/10810730.2013.852274.

Kammerer, Y. & Gerjets, P. (2014). The Role of Search Result Position and Source Trustworthiness in the Selection of Web Search Results When Using a List or a Grid Interface. *International Journal of Human–Computer Interaction, 30*(3), 177–191. http://doi.org/10.1080/10447318.2013.846790.

Keselman, A., Browne, A.C. & Kaufman, D.R. (2008). Consumer Health Information Seeking as Hypothesis Testing. *Journal of the American Medical Informatics Association, 15*(4), 484–495. http://doi.org/10.1197/jamia.M2449.

Kim, H., Park, S-Y. & Bozeman, I. (2011). Online Health Information Search and Evaluation: Observations and Semi-structured Interviews with College Students and Maternal Health Experts. *Health Information & Libraries Journal, 28*(3), 188–199. http://doi.org/10.1111/j.1471-1842.2011.00948.x.

Kitchens, B., Harle, C.A. & Li, S. (2014). Quality of Health-related Online Search Results. *Decision Support Systems, 57,* 454–462. http://doi.org/10.1016/j.dss.2012.10.050.

Koch-Weser, S., Bradshaw, Y.S., Gualtieri, L. & Gallagher, S.S. (2010). The Internet as a Health Information Source: Findings from the 2007 Health Information National Trends Survey and Implications for Health Communication. *Journal of Health Communication, 15*(sup3), 279–293. http://doi.org/10.1080/10810730.2010.522700.

Kontos, E., Blake, K.D., Chou, W-Y.S. & Prestin, A. (2014). Predictors of eHealth Usage: Insights on the Digital Divide from the Health Information National Trends Survey 2012. *Journal of Medical Internet Research*, *16*(7), e172. http://doi.org/10.2196/jmir.3117.

Kumar, N., Pandey, A., Venkatraman, A. & Garg, N. (2014). Are Video Sharing Web Sites a Useful Source of Information on Hypertension? *Journal of the American Society of Hypertension: JASH*, *8*(7), 481–490. http://doi.org/10.1016/j.jash.2014.05.001.

Lagan, B.M., Sinclair, M. & Kernohan, W.G. (2006). Pregnant Women's Use of the Internet: A Review of Published and Unpublished Evidence. *Evidence Based Midwifery*, *4*(1), 17–23.

Lagan, B.M., Sinclair, M. & Kernohan, W.G. (2010). Internet Use in Pregnancy Informs Women's Decision Making: A Web-based Survey. *Birth (Berkeley, Calif.)*, *37*(2), 106–115. http://doi.org/10.1111/j.1523-536X.2010.00390.x.

Lagan, B.M., Sinclair, M. & Kernohan, W.G. (2011). What is the Impact of the Internet on Decision-making in Pregnancy? A Global Study. *Birth (Berkeley, Calif.)*, *38*(4), 336–345. http://doi.org/10.1111/j.1523-536X.2011.00488.x.

Larsson, M. (2009). A Descriptive Study of the Use of the Internet by Women Seeking Pregnancy-related Information. *Midwifery*, *25*(1), 14–20. http://doi.org/10.1016/j.midw.2007.01.010.

Lewallen, L.P. & Côté-Arsenault, D.Y. (2014). Implications for Nurses and Researchers of Internet Use by Childbearing Women. *Nursing for Women's Health*, *18*(5), 392–400. http://doi.org/10.1111/1751-486X.12147.

Li, N., Orrange, S., Kravitz, R.L. & Bell, R.A. (2014). Reasons for and Predictors of Patients' Online Health Information Seeking Following a Medical Appointment. *Family Practice*. http://doi.org/10.1093/fampra/cmu034.

Liszka, H.A., Steyer, T.E. & Hueston, W.J. (2006). Virtual Medical Care: How Are Our Patients Using Online Health Information? *Journal of Community Health*, *31*(5), 368–378.

Lo, B. & Parham, L. (2010). The Impact of Web 2.0 on the Doctor–Patient Relationship. *The Journal of Law, Medicine & Ethics*, *38*(1), 17–26. http://doi.org/10.1111/j.1748-720X.2010.00462.x.

Lorence, D.P., Park, H. & Fox, S. (2006). Assessing Health Consumerism on the Web: A Demographic Profile of Information-seeking Behaviors. *Journal of Medical Systems*, *30*(4), 251–258.

Madden, K., Nan, X., Briones, R. & Waks, L. (2012). Sorting Through Search Results: A Content Analysis of HPV Vaccine Information Online. *Vaccine*, *30*(25), 3741–3746. http://doi.org/10.1016/j.vaccine.2011.10.025.

Maloney, E.K., D'Agostino, T.A., Heerdt, A., Dickler, M., Li, Y., Ostroff, J.S. & Bylund, C.L. (2013). Sources and Types of Online Information that Breast Cancer Patients Read and Discuss with Their Doctors. *Palliative & Supportive Care*, *FirstView*, 1–8. http://doi.org/10.1017/S1478951513000862.

McMullan, M. (2006). Patients Using the Internet to Obtain Health Information: How This Affects the Patient–Health Professional Relationship. *Patient Education and Counseling*, *63*(1), 24–28.

McPherson, A.C., Gofine, M.L. & Stinson, J. (2014). Seeing is Believing? A Mixed-methods Study Exploring the Quality and Perceived Trustworthiness of Online Information About Chronic Conditions Aimed at Children and Young People. *Health Communication*, *29*(5), 473–482. http://doi.org/10.1080/10410236.2013.768325.

McRee, A.-L., Reiter, P.L. & Brewer, N.T. (2012). Parents' Internet Use for Information About HPV Vaccine. *Vaccine*, *30*(25), 3757–3762. http://doi.org/10.1016/j.vaccine.2011.11.113.

Morahan-Martin, J.M. (2004). How Internet Users Find, Evaluate, and Use Online Health Information: A Cross-cultural Review. *CyberPsychology & Behavior*, *7*(5), 497–510.

Murray, E., Lo, B., Pollack, L., Donelan, K., Catania, J., Lee, K. & Turner, R. (2003). The Impact of Health Information on the Internet on Health Care and the Physician–Patient Relationship: National US Survey Among 1.050 US Physicians. *Journal of Medical Internet Research*, *5*(3). Retrieved October 20, 2014 from www.ncbi.nlm.nih.gov/pmc/articles/PMC1550564/.

National Library of Medicine. (n.d.). PubMed. Retrieved October 2, 2014 from www.ncbi.nlm.nih.gov/pubmed.

Norman, C.D. & Skinner, H.A. (2006). eHealth Literacy: Essential Skills for Consumer Health in a Networked World. *Journal of Medical Internet Research*, *8*(2). http://doi.org/10.2196/jmir.8.2.e9.

Perls, T.T. (2004). Anti-aging Medicine: The Legal Issues of Anti-aging Quackery: Human Growth Hormone and Tricks of the Trade – More Dangerous Than Ever. *The Journals of Gerontology Series A: Biological Sciences and Medical Sciences*, *59*(7), B682–B691. http://doi.org/10.1093/gerona/59.7.B682.

Peterson, G., Aslani, P. & Williams, K.A. (2003). How Do Consumers Search for and Appraise Information on Medicines on the Internet? A Qualitative Study Using Focus Groups. *Journal of Medical Internet Research*, *5*(4). http://doi.org/10.2196/jmir.5.4.e33.

Pew Internet Project. (2014). Health Fact Sheet. Retrieved October 6, 2014 from www.pewinternet.org/fact-sheets/health-fact-sheet/.

Plantin, L. & Daneback, K. (2009). Parenthood, Information and Support on the Internet. A Literature Review of Research on Parents and Professionals Online. *BMC Family Practice*, *10*(34). http://doi.org/10.1186/1471-2296-10-34.

Rains, S.A. (2007). Perceptions of Traditional Information Sources and Use of the World Wide Web to Seek Health Information: Findings From the Health Information National Trends Survey. *Journal of Health Communication*, *12*(7), 667–680. http://doi.org/10.1080/10810730701619992.

Rains, S.A. & Karmikel, C.D. (2009). Health Information-seeking and Perceptions of Website Credibility: Examining Web-use Orientation, Message Characteristics, and Structural Features of Websites. *Computers in Human Behavior*, *25*(2), 544–553. http://doi.org/10.1016/j.chb.2008.11.005.

Rice, R.E. (2006). Influences, Usage, and Outcomes of Internet Health Information Searching: Multivariate Results from the Pew Surveys. *International Journal of Medical Informatics*, *75*(1), 8–28.

Ritterband, L.M., Borowitz, S., Cox, D.J., Kovatchev, B., Walker, L.S., Lucas, V. & Sutphen, J. (2005). Using the Internet to Provide Information Prescriptions. *Pediatrics*, *116*(5), e643–e647. http://doi.org/10.1542/peds.2005-0404.

Sabel, M.S., Strecher, V.J., Schwartz, J.L., Wang, T.S., Karimipour, D.J., Orringer, J.S. & Bichakjian, C.K. (2005). Patterns of Internet Use and Impact on Patients with Melanoma. *Journal of the American Academy of Dermatology*, *52*(5), 779–785. http://doi.org/10.1016/j.jaad.2004.10.874.

Semere, W., Karamanoukian, H.L., Levitt, M., Edwards, T., Murero, M., D'Ancona, G. & Glick, P.L. (2003). A Pediatric Surgery Study: Parent Usage of the internet for Medical Information. *Journal of Pediatric Surgery*, *38*(4), 560–564. http://doi.org/10.1053/jpsu.2003.50122.

Shahrokni, A., Mahmoudzadeh, S. & Lu, B.T. (2014). In Whom Do Cancer Survivors Trust Online and Offline? *Asian Pacific Journal of Cancer Prevention: APJCP, 15*(15), 6171–6176.

Siegel, E.R., Logan, R.A., Harnsberger, R.L., Cravedi, K., Krause, J.A., Lyon, B. & Lindberg, D.A. (2006). Information Rx: Evaluation of a New Informatics Tool for Physicians, Patients, and Libraries. *Information Services and Use, 26*(1), 1–10.

Skinner, H., Biscope, S., Poland, B. & Goldberg, E. (2003). How Adolescents Use Technology for Health Information: Implications for Health Professionals from Focus Group Studies. *Journal of Medical Internet Research, 5*(4). http://doi.org/10.2196/jmir.5.4.e32.

Stern, M.J., Cotten, S.R. & Drentea, P. (2012). The Separate Spheres of Online Health Gender, Parenting, and Online Health Information Searching in the Information Age. *Journal of Family Issues, 33*(10), 1324–1350. http://doi.org/10.1177/0192513X11425459.

Tustin, N. (2010). The Role of Patient Satisfaction in Online Health Information Seeking. *Journal of Health Communication, 15*(1), 3–17. http://doi.org/10.1080/10810730903465491.

U.S. Food and Drug Administration. (2014a, April 25). Beware of False or Misleading Claims for Treating Autism [WebContent]. Retrieved October 3, 2014 from www.fda.gov/ForConsumers/ConsumerUpdates/ucm394757.htm#cracks.

U.S. Food and Drug Administration. (2014b, August 14). FDA Warns Consumers About Fraudulent Ebola Treatment Products [WebContent]. Retrieved October 3, 2014 from www.fda.gov/newsevents/newsroom/pressannouncements/ucm410086.htm.

Wald, H.S., Dube, C.E. & Anthony, D.C. (2007). Untangling the Web – The Impact of Internet Use on Health Care and the Physician–Patient Relationship. *Patient Education and Counseling, 68*(3), 218–224. http://doi.org/10.1016/j.pec.2007.05.016.

Walsh, A.M., Hyde, M.K., Hamilton, K. & White, K.M. (2012). Predictive Modelling: Parents' Decision Making to Use Online Child Health Information to Increase Their Understanding and/or Diagnose or Treat Their Child's Health. *BMC Medical Informatics and Decision Making, 12*(1), 144. http://doi.org/10.1186/1472-6947-12-144.

Weaver III, J.B., Thompson, N.J., Weaver, S.S. & Hopkins, G.L. (2009). Healthcare Non-adherence Decisions and Internet Health Information. *Computers in Human Behavior, 25*(6), 1373–1380. http://doi.org/10.1016/j.chb.2009.05.011.

Weaver, J.B., Mays, D., Weaver, S.S., Hopkins, G.L., Eroglu, D. & Bernhardt, J.M. (2010). Health Information-seeking Behaviors, Health Indicators, and Health Risks. *American Journal of Public Health, 100*(8), 1520–1525. http://doi.org/10.2105/AJPH.2009.180521.

White, R.W. & Horvitz, E. (2009a). Cyberchondria: Studies of the Escalation of Medical Concerns in Web Search. *ACM Trans. Inf. Syst., 27*(4), 23:1–23:37. http://doi.org/10.1145/1629096.1629101.

White, R.W. & Horvitz, E. (2009b). Experiences with Web Search on Medical Concerns and Self Diagnosis. *AMIA Annual Symposium Proceedings, 2009*, 696–700.

Whitten, P., Nazione, S. & Lauckner, C. (2013). Tools for Assessing the Quality and Accessibility of Online Health Information: Initial Testing among Breast Cancer Websites. *Informatics for Health & Social Care, 38*(4), 366–381. http://doi.org/10.3109/17538157.2013.812644.

Wolters Kluwer Health. (2012, May 16). Survey: Consumers Show High Degree of Trust in Online Health Information, Report Success in Self-diagnosis. Retrieved October 20, 2014 from www.wolterskluwerhealth.com/News/Pages/Survey-

Consumers-Show-High-Degree-of-Trust-in-Online-Health-Information,-Report-Success-in-Self-Diagnosis-.aspx.

Yaylaci, S., Serinken, M., Eken, C., Karcioglu, O., Yilmaz, A., Elicabuk, H. & Dal, O. (2014). Are YouTube Videos Accurate and Reliable on Basic Life Support and Cardiopulmonary Resuscitation? *Emergency Medicine Australasia: EMA, 26*(5), 474–477. http://doi.org/10.1111/1742-6723.12274.

Ybarra, M.L. & Suman, M. (2006). Help Seeking Behavior and the Internet: A National Survey. *International Journal of Medical Informatics, 75*(1), 29–41. http://doi.org/10.1016/j.ijmedinf.2005.07.029.

Zeng, Q.T., Kogan, S., Plovnick, R.M., Crowell, J., Lacroix, E-M. & Greenes, R.A. (2004). Positive Attitudes and Failed Queries: An Exploration of the Conundrums of Consumer Health Information Retrieval. *International Journal of Medical Informatics, 73*(1), 45–55. http://doi.org/10.1016/j.ijmedinf.2003.12.015.

Zulman, D.M., Kirch, M., Zheng, K. & An, L.C. (2011). Trust in the Internet as a Health Resource Among Older Adults: Analysis of Data From a Nationally Representative Survey. *Journal of Medical Internet Research, 13*(1). http://doi.org/10.2196/jmir.1552.

CHAPTER 3

TOBACCO ADVERTISING: THE PARADOX OF MARKETING TO SHORTEN CUSTOMERS' LIVES

Figure 3.1: The "Be Marlboro" Campaign Targets Teens (source: From the collection of Stanford Research Into the Impact of Tobacco Advertising (tobacco.stanford.edu))

"Maybe Never Wrote a Song," says the headline on one ad, accompanying a black and white photo of a young woman, smiling as she looks away from the camera, a guitar in her lap and a smoking cigarette in her hand. "Maybe Never Fell in Love," says another, showing a young couple kissing on a dark city street. "Don't Be A Maybe," advises a third version of the ad, which shows a young man leaping into the air above the stage at a rock concert, guitar in hand. "Maybe Never Feels Free," proclaims another, next to a photo of a young woman, standing up through the sunroof of a car, smiling as the wind ruffles her hair. What's the alternative to "Maybe," according to the ad campaign? "Be Marlboro."

The campaign, which Philip Morris is running in 50 low- and medium-income countries worldwide, was intended to replace the brand's iconic "Marlboro Man" image. In a report on the campaign, an alliance of anti-smoking organizations argue that the campaign's themes, featuring young people partying, traveling to exciting places and reveling in their freedom, "exploits adolescents' search for identity by suggesting that – in the face of uncertainty – they should BE a Marlboro smoker" (Alliance for the Control of Tobacco Use (ACT Brazil), Campaign for Tobacco-Free Kids, Corporate Accountability International, Framework Convention Alliance, InterAmerican Heart Foundation, Southeast Asia Tobacco Control Alliance, 2014, p. 3).

Phillip Morris's global campaign to promote Marlboro cigarettes, decried in numerous countries worldwide for clearly targeting teenagers, is not officially in use in the United States because U.S. law prohibits targeting children in tobacco advertising. And yet, the headlines in many of the campaign ads are in English. The song used in a campaign video, which shows young people dancing at a club, swimming in a lake, cavorting around a beach bonfire, and engaging in other fun, adventurous and social activities, is also in English. Both static and video versions of the ads are easily found online, and, ironically, it's possible that U.S. news coverage of complaints about the campaign may have raised awareness – and reach – of the campaign in the United States.

The "Don't Be A Maybe" campaign illustrates many of the themes common in research on the ways in which tobacco companies have targeted smokers and potential smokers. From the iconic "Marlboro Man" to Newport's "Alive with Pleasure" campaigns to Camel's pool-playing, motorcycle-riding "Joe Camel" cartoon to Virginia's Slims' reminders that women have "come a long way, baby," cigarette manufacturers have promoted the idea that smoking cigarettes (and using tobacco in other ways) symbolizes independence, self-reliance, willingness to take risks and, if necessary, flout social convention. These themes have helped tobacco manufacturers ensure a steady stream of new customers, which is critical to an industry whose product regularly kills off its existing users.

This chapter reviews the research on tobacco advertising and its effects, making the case for including tobacco advertising as the one type of media message that is actually intended to have a negative health impact at the level of individual behavior. This argument is bolstered by the findings of a recent Campaign for Tobacco-Free Kids report explaining how tobacco companies have changed cigarette formulations to make them "more addictive, more attractive to kids and even more deadly" (Campaign for Tobacco-Free Kids, 2014, p. 1). The report documents how tobacco manufacturers have increased addictiveness by increasing nicotine levels and adding ammonia compounds and sugars. Today's cigarettes are also more appealing to adolescents and adult smokers because they contain additives that reduce the harshness of nicotine and expand the lung's airways so that smoke passes into the lungs more easily. In addition, flavors, such as chocolate, make cigarettes taste sweeter and more appealing to youth, and menthol "cools and numbs the throat to reduce throat irritation and makes the smoke feel smoother" (Campaign for Tobacco-Free Kids, 2014, p. 5). These changes, however, have also made cigarettes more deadly, with higher levels of cancer-causing tobacco-specific nitrosamines and ventilation holes in the filters that have reduced tar and nicotine levels, as measured by machines, but increased the frequency and depth of smoke inhalation among smokers. The result is that even though smokers today smoke fewer cigarettes than they did in 1964, when the first Surgeon General's report was released, they face greater risks of developing lung cancer and chronic obstructive pulmonary disease (National Center for Chronic Disease Prevention and Health Promotion (US) Office on Smoking and Health, 2014).

These changes, as well as increased efforts to market tobacco products worldwide, may have stemmed, in part, from the general downward trend in the use of cigarettes and other tobacco products in the United States. According to the most recent data from the Centers for Disease Control (CDC), the percentage of smokers in the United States has dropped from 42.4 percent in 1965 to 18.1 percent in 2012 (Centers for Disease Control and Prevention, 2013, 2014). Similarly, smoking among students (aged younger than 18) dropped from a high of 36.4 percent in 1997 to 14 percent of high school students in 2012 (CDC's Office on Smoking and Health, 2014; Centers for Disease Control and Prevention, 2014a). Unfortunately, these figures are misleadingly low; when all tobacco products, including smokeless tobacco, cigars, hookahs, pipes, electronic cigarettes, snus, etc. are considered, the percentage of high school users rises to more than one in five (23.3%) and almost 7 percent of middle school students currently use some kind of tobacco product. Among adult users, 21.3 percent reported using some kind of tobacco product "every day" or "some days" in 2012 to 2013 (Agaku et al., 2014b). While traditional cigarette use has declined, "electronic cigarette use doubled among middle and high school students" between 2011 and 2012 (CDC's Office on Smoking and Health, 2014b, para. 6).

One particularly troubling trend is the increased use of tobacco in newer forms, especially electronic cigarettes (or vaping) and hookah. Hookah (or water pipe) smoking began in ancient Persia and India (American Lung Association, 2011), and for decades, at least, hookah parlors or lounges have existed in the larger cities in the United States, where they were patronized primarily by men of Egyptian, Lebanese and Syrian descent ("Hookah Bars Find a Place in America," 2006). However, in the past decade, the number of hookah bars has grown, especially in college towns; rather than catering to older men from Middle Eastern countries, their customers are primarily younger, white and male. Although some are also cigarette smokers, one recent study showed that higher percentages of college students reported ever using hookah (46.4% vs. 42.1% for cigarettes) and using hookah in the preceding year (28.4% for hookah, 19.6% for cigarettes). In this college student population, Hispanic students were most likely to report current hookah use (Barnett et al., 2013b). Studies of knowledge and attitudes about hookah smoking suggest that college students view hookah as a healthier alternative to cigarette smoking (Holtzman et al., 2013) and see it as more socially acceptable (Barnett et al., 2013a; Sidani et al., 2014).

Similarly, electronic cigarettes (e-cigarettes) are becoming increasingly popular in the United States, with the percentage of middle and high school students who had ever used e-cigarettes increasing from 3.1 percent in 2011 to 6.8 percent in 2012. Among students, about one in ten e-cigarette users said they had never smoked a regular cigarette (CDC's Office on Smoking and Health, 2014d). Health officials suspect, however, that "vaping" may prove to be a gateway behavior, in part because researchers have found that students who have ever used any kind of tobacco product, including e-cigarettes, have higher adjusted odds of intending to smoke traditional cigarettes (Bunnell et al., 2014; Dutra & Glantz, 2014).

On the other hand, e-cigarettes may offer a less damaging alternative to conventional cigarettes (Gualano et al., 2014; Polosa et al., 2014), and some researchers argue that vaping may help smokers kick the habit entirely (Bullen et al., 2013; Hajek et al., 2014). Others, however, note that no longitudinal studies have examined the long-term effects of electronic cigarettes, meaning that it is too soon to conclude that e-cigarettes offer a healthy alternative to smoking or an effective route to smoking cessation (Grana et al., 2014; Odum et al., 2012). In August, the American Heart Association released a policy statement recommending that the Food and Drug Administration (FDA) regulate electronic cigarettes as it does all other tobacco products and that physicians should not counsel their patients to use e-cigarettes as a primary tool for smoking cessation (Bhatnagar et al., 2014).

HEALTH EFFECTS OF TOBACCO USE

Smoking cigarettes, of course, is the most common use of tobacco. This one behavior causes nearly half a million deaths each year in the United States alone, accounting for about one in every five deaths. The CDC notes that smoking has killed more Americans than have died in all the wars in U.S. history, and that its annual death toll is higher than the combined fatalities from HIV, drug and alcohol use, automobile accidents and gun-related deaths. Smokers have two to four times the risk of developing heart disease and stroke, and 25 to 26 times the risk of developing lung cancer. In addition, smoking can cause cervical, colorectal, esophageal, liver, stomach, bladder and pancreatic cancers, as well as acute myeloid leukemia and cancers of the larynx, throat, tongue, soft palate, tonsils and trachea (National Center for Chronic Disease Prevention and Health Promotion (US) Office on Smoking and Health, 2014)

In addition to these life-threatening diseases, smoking can decrease both men's and women's fertility and increases the risk of ectopic pregnancies, miscarriages, stillbirth, pre-term delivery, low birth weight, sudden infant death syndrome (SIDS) and birth defects in infants. Individuals who smoke are 30 to 40 percent more likely to develop Type 2 diabetes and are more likely than non-smokers to develop cataracts and macular degeneration. Smokers are at greater risk of developing rheumatoid arthritis, and post-menopausal women who smoke are at greater risk of broken bones due to lower bone density. Smoking also makes gum disease and tooth loss more likely and can reduce immune system function (National Center for Chronic Disease Prevention and Health Promotion (US) Office on Smoking and Health, 2014).

Smoking also has negative health consequences for non-smokers. In fact, in the 50 years since the U.S. Surgeon General's first report on the dangers of smoking, published in 1964, government health officials estimate that 2.5 million *non-smokers* have died as a result of breathing secondhand smoke, which includes the smoke from the burning tip of a cigarette and that exhaled by smokers. Children exposed to secondhand smoke are more susceptible to asthma, respiratory and ear infections and SIDS. Among non-smoking adults, secondhand smoke exposure at home or at work increases the risk of heart disease and stroke and lung cancer by 20 to 30 percent (CDC's Office on Smoking and Health, 2014c).

As noted earlier, the percentage of Americans who smoke has declined over the past four decades, although the rate of decline has slowed during recent years (National Center for Chronic Disease Prevention and Health Promotion (US) Office on Smoking and Health, 2014). At least one study suggests, however, that rates of smokeless tobacco use have remained stable (Agaku et al., 2013b) or have actually increased, from 4.9 percent of those aged 12 and older in 2002 to 5.4 percent in 2011 (Fix et al., 2014). Data from the Youth Risk Behavior Surveillance System survey from 2012 to 2013 showed that 8.8 percent of ninth- to twelfth-graders reported using smokeless tobacco, which includes chewing tobacco, snuff and snus, during the 30 days before the survey. Use of smokeless tobacco, especially among youth, is concerning because there is some evidence that chewing tobacco can be a precursor to smoking and because use of smokeless tobacco itself has serious negative health effects. These effects can include cancer of the mouth, tongue, cheek, gum, throat, esophagus, stomach and pancreas; some evidence suggests that smokeless tobacco may also increase the user's risks of heart disease and stroke (American Cancer Society, 2013).

Few conclusive data are available about the health effects of electronic cigarettes. The research suggests that although e-cigarettes are pro-moted as "safer" alternatives to traditional cigarettes, the currently avail-able information does not support such a conclusion. Recent reviews of the research have concluded that there are too little data on short-term health effects, no adequate data on long-term effects and little definitive evidence that e-cigarette use promotes smoking cessation (Callahan-Lyon, 2014; Gualano et al., 2014; Hajek et al., 2014).

Although fewer studies have examined the health effects of water pipe smoking, health officials warn that it is not, as many hookah users believe, a safer alternative to smoking. A recent review of research on the health effects of hookah use concluded that the practice produces outcomes similar to cigarette smoking, including cancer, impaired lung function, and reproductive problems, including infertility among male water pipe users and low birth weight babies among female users (Knishkowy & Amitai, 2005). Cobb and colleagues (2010, p. 275) note that, "depending on the toxicant measured, a single waterpipe session produces the equivalent of at least 1 and as many as 50 cigarettes." However, many hookah smokers believe the practice is less risky than smoking cigarettes, which may encourage greater frequency of and length of time in hookah use (Barnett et al., 2013a; Braun et al., 2012; Holtzman et al., 2013; Rezk-Hanna et al., 2014; Sidani et al., 2014).

The bottom line, then, is that regardless of the form or delivery device, human consumption of tobacco is harmful. Given that, any activity that promotes the consumption of tobacco should be viewed as being intended to have harmful effects on human health. It is worth noting that the intended harm applies to encouraging people to continue tobacco use, as well as encouraging initiation of tobacco use. Thus, even if it was true, as the tobacco companies typically claim, that advertising and other promotions are designed only to attract existing users to a company's brand or to build brand loyalty among existing users (as opposed to encouraging new individuals to *start* smoking, vaping or using smokeless tobacco), such promotions would still have an intended negative effect.

This leads to the primary question of this chapter: How important *is* tobacco advertising in the initiation and maintenance of tobacco use? Does exposure to tobacco advertising increase an individual's likelihood of starting to smoke or use chewing tobacco? And how does that effect compare to the influence of other factors, such as parental tobacco use?

WHAT INCREASES THE LIKELIHOOD OF TOBACCO USE?

Researchers have identified numerous factors that influence the likelihood that a particular individual will start smoking; for 90 percent of smokers the habit begins before the age of 18. Not surprisingly, one important factor is whether the individual's parents smoke, although a review of 87 studies assessing familial effects on smoking initiation revealed inconsistent findings, leading the authors to conclude that "parental influence may be relatively modest" (Avenevoli & Merikangas, 2003, p. 12). More recent studies, however, suggest that parent smoking does increase the likelihood of adolescents becoming daily smokers – even when the parents have negative attitudes toward teen smoking (Hill et al., 2005). Other studies have shown that parents' and older siblings' smoking also increases the progression of smoking, from experimentation to monthly to daily smoking (Bricker et al., 2006, 2007; Peterson Jr. et al., 2006). Family or household use of smokeless tobacco is also associated with adolescents' use of these products (Agaku et al., 2013b).

Peers also play a significant role in both initiation and progression of cigarette smoking. For instance, in one Canadian study, 9- to 12-year-olds who had friends who smoked were 2.3 times as likely to begin smoking within a year (O'Loughlin et al., 1998). Another study of seventh- to ninth-graders in the United States showed that peer smoking had a greater effect than parental smoking, especially among youth who initially were not smokers, and the relative strength of peers' influence increased over time, especially among girls (Hu et al., 1995). Although adolescents who smoke are more likely to choose friends who also smoke, several studies have shown that the effects of selection (choosing friends with similar behaviors) are less important than peer influence (adopting the behaviors of friends who smoke) (Ali & Dwyer, 2009; Hoffman et al., 2007). Other studies have produced results suggesting a greater impact of selection (Go et al., 2010).

Not surprisingly, researchers have found similar influences of peers and parents on adolescents' use of smokeless tobacco products. In the United States, the most important predictor of smokeless tobacco use is gender; according to Centers for Disease Control data, 4.8 percent of adult men use smokeless tobacco, compared to 0.3 percent of women (Agaku et al., 2014b). Among adolescent males, most studies seem to suggest that peer use has the greatest effect. In a study of 846 teenage boys, Ary (1989) found that peer use of smokeless tobacco was related to trying smokeless tobacco and to advancing to daily use of these products, as well as to the use of cigarettes, marijuana and alcohol. A more recent study, which followed a cohort of students from fifth- to eighth-grade in 96 schools in California, Louisiana, Minnesota and Texas, showed that eighth-graders with a parent who smokes were about 1.5 times more likely to have used smokeless tobacco in the preceding 30 days, while those whose best friend smoked were nearly five times as likely to have used smokeless tobacco in the past month (Johnson et al., 2002). However, other researchers have found parents' approval to be more important than peer influences in predicting adolescent boys' use of smokeless tobacco. Biglan and colleagues (1995) found that a father's approval of smokeless tobacco was positively related to the use of these products; interestingly, boys who perceived their mothers to approve of smokeless tobacco were *less* likely to use it. A more recent study of fifth-, eighth- and eleventh-grade boys in West Virginia showed that smokeless tobacco was more common among boys who had a friend who used smokeless tobacco, a family member living outside the home who used it, who played football and who had parents who allowed smokeless tobacco use at home (Goebel et al., 2000). Data from the 2011 National Youth Tobacco survey also confirm that peer and parent/sibling use of smokeless tobacco increases adolescents' likelihood of using these products (Agaku et al., 2013).

Research on smokeless tobacco use among college students demonstrates that peers also have a significant impact among young adults. For instance, a study of students at 13 four-year Texas colleges and universities revealed that participation in intercollegiate sports, peer smoking and peer smokeless tobacco use predicted both ever having used smokeless tobacco and current use; membership in a fraternity or sorority also predicted lifetime use of smokeless tobacco but not current use (Morrell et al., 2005).

The Intent of Tobacco Advertising

Parents and peers play important roles in encouraging teens to smoke and use other forms of tobacco. However, the most recent report from the U.S. Surgeon General points to another key influence: tobacco advertising. The report states, "The evidence is sufficient to conclude that advertising and promotional activities by the tobacco companies cause the onset and continuation of smoking among adolescents and young adults" (National Center for Chronic Disease Prevention and

Health Promotion (US) Office on Smoking and Health, 2014, p. 12). Similarly, a recent analysis of data from several years of the National Consumer Survey produced "consistent and robust evidence that exposure to ST (smokeless tobacco) ads in magazines raises ST use, especially among males" (Dave & Saffer, 2013, p. 682).

Of course, marketing cigarettes or smokeless tobacco to people younger than age 18 violates FDA regulations. Representatives of the tobacco companies insist that they abide by this law, making no attempt to encourage under-age adolescents to use tobacco. For instance, R.J. Reynolds' website insists that "Reynolds's American and its operating companies are guided by the belief that minors should never use tobacco products" ("Youth Tobacco Prevention," n.d.). The Philip Morris website states that the company "identifies and adheres to applicable laws, principles and/or policies for marketing its products with the goal of responsibly marketing to the respective intended audience and limiting reach to underage audiences" ("Helping Reduce Underage Tobacco Use," n.d.). However, analyses of internal tobacco company documents make it clear that this "determination" to discourage teenagers from developing the smoking habit is, at best, a recent development and, at worst, a claim that remains in conflict with industry practices. For instance, Cheryl Perry, who served as an expert witness for the State of Minnesota in its suit against the tobacco companies, wrote that her systematic review of internal company documents produced the following conclusions:

- Tobacco company executives recognized – and still do – that under-age smokers are critical to the success of the industry, in large part because only about 18 percent of smokers begin at age 18 or older. Perry argues that tobacco companies realized that teens are more likely than adults to begin smoking because younger teenagers, especially, do not have the cognitive capability to fully understand the health risks of smoking, and even if they do, "the long-term consequences of smoking are mostly remote and irrelevant to adolescents" (Perry, 1999, p. 935).
- Industry documents explicitly describe declines in the number of teen smokers as *negative* trends. Perry cites a 1982 R.J. Reynolds marketing department report stating that "the loss of younger adult males and teenagers is more important in the long term, drying up

the supply of new smokers to replace the old" (Burrows, 1982, cited in Perry, 1999, p. 936). Another RJR document lamented a decline in the percentage of 14- to 17-year-olds who smoked RJR brands but pointed to planned marketing activities that might "correct" that trend (Perry, 1999, p. 937).

- Tobacco industry research was explicitly designed to help them understand the "young adult" market, which internal company documents described as including 14- to 24-year-olds. One RJR document recommended reviewing high school American history textbooks and other materials to help them find potential brand names and images appealing to teenagers. A document from Brown & Williamson, maker of KOOL cigarettes, referred to the need to focus its advertising efforts in magazines that would reach the 16- to 25-year-old population. A Philip Morris document crowed about the success of its Marlboro Man campaign among baby boom teenagers (Perry, 1999).

Given this history, Perry argues,

> tobacco industry promises and actions concerning youth smoking should be closely scrutinized and monitored because the industry's survival depends on underage smokers to be "replacement smokers" for those smokers who quit or die. Their actions, including their advertising and promotional activities in this country and overseas, may likely continue to contradict their promises.
>
> (Perry, 1999, p. 940)

CHILDREN'S AND ADOLESCENTS' EXPOSURE TO TOBACCO ADVERTISING

U.S. regulations, including the provisions of the 1998 Master Settlement Agreement (MSA) between the four largest tobacco companies and 46 states' attorneys general and the Family Smoking Prevention and Tobacco Control Act, which took effect in 2009, are intended to prevent tobacco companies from advertising or marketing their products to adolescents and children at all. Subsection III(a) of the MSA states:

> No Participating Manufacturer may take any action, directly or indirectly, to target Youth within any Settling State in the advertising,

promotion or marketing of Tobacco Products, or take any action the primary purpose of which is to initiate, maintain or increase the incidence of Youth smoking within any Settling State.

The specific effects of the MSA included:

- prohibiting billboards and outdoor advertising, except for up to 14-square-foot signs outside a tobacco retail seller, an adult-only facility or a tobacco manufacturing facility;
- banning the use of cartoon characters – such as the highly successful "Joe Camel" – in any advertising, promotion or packaging;
- outlawing product placements and endorsements (Kline & Davidson, 1999).

The MSA included no specific provisions regarding magazine advertising, and in May 2000 the Massachusetts Department of Public Health released data showing dramatic increases in cigarette advertising in magazines popular with young readers (Hamilton et al., 2002). Soon after, Philip Morris announced plans to suspend advertising in magazines likely to reach youth. Brown & Williamson and R.J. Reynolds stated that they were already committed to advertising that did not target youth. However, one year later, an analysis of advertising expenditures in youth-oriented magazines – those for which young readers constituted at least 15 percent of the readership or that reached at least two million young readers – showed that the tobacco companies' advertising spending in youth-oriented magazines was higher for youth-oriented brands (e.g., Camel, Marlboro and Newport) than for adult brands. During the two years after the MSA, advertising spending in youth magazines increased by 53.8 percent for Camel, 8 percent for Marlboro and 13.2 percent for Newport. The researchers determined that ads for youth brands of cigarettes reached 81.9 percent of all young people, with an average of 17 exposures per person during 2000 (King & Siegel, 2001).

Research shows that the combination of the MSA and of public pressure on tobacco companies, resulting in part from widespread publicity about the continued targeting of youth through magazine advertising, eventually did have an effect. Hamilton et al. (2002) analyzed cigarette

Figure 3.2: Joe Camel Was as Recognizable as Mickey Mouse (source: From the collection of Stanford Research Into the Impact of Tobacco Advertising (tobacco.stanford.edu))

advertising before the MSA (January to November 1998), immediately after the MSA (December 1998 to June 2000) and after the release of the Massachusetts Public Health Department data on cigarette advertising in youth magazines (July to November 2000). Their data showed that the proportion of advertising spending in youth magazines declined slightly after the MSA took effect, from 39 percent of all ad spending in magazines to 34 percent. However, in response to the public pressure that began in May 2000, youth magazine spending fell to only 20 percent of all magazine ad spending; however, these changes varied by company. There were significant reductions in spending allocated to youth magazines for Philip Morris, Brown & Williamson and Lorillard, but R.J. Reynolds maintained allocation to youth magazines at 40 percent of its overall magazine ad budget (Hamilton et al., 2002).

By 2006, magazine advertising budgets for the four major tobacco companies had fallen to $91.9 million, down from a high of $552 million in 1999, the year after the MSA was signed. Philip Morris, in fact, had eliminated all magazine advertising in 2004. However, the percentage of ad spending allocated to menthol brands – which are more popular with younger smokers than with those aged 18 and older – rose from 13 percent of all expenditures in 1998 to 76 percent of all magazine ad spending in 2006. Between 2002 and 2006, smoking of menthol cigarettes increased 8 percent per year. Overall magazine advertising for smokeless tobacco products also increased, from $18.7 million in 1998 to $34 million in 2004, then declined to $26.6 million in 2006. Advertising in magazines with high youth readership (more than 15 percent of readers or more than two million readers younger than age 18) fell significantly, and by 2006 at least three of the four major tobacco companies had discontinued advertising in magazines popular with young people. The researchers studying these trends concluded that "[t]he period following the MSA can therefore be characterized by gradual compliance within a narrow definition of the MSA's intent to cease targeting youth with magazine advertising, but not by a complete cessation of youth targeting or exposure" (Alpert et al., 2008, p. w509).

When it took effect in 2009, the Tobacco Control Act further restricted tobacco promotions, banning tobacco company sponsorship of sports or entertainment events, prohibiting give-aways of free samples of tobacco products or tobacco-branded goods such as hats and T-shirts, barring the use of language suggesting FDA or government "approval" of tobacco products, and disallowing the use of "reduced harm" terms such as "light," "low" or "mild" without specific FDA approval. The law originally included limits on the color and design of ads and packaging, requiring the use of only black and white text and prominent graphic warnings about the health risks of tobacco use – in color – on cigarette packages and advertising ("FDA Regulation of Tobacco," n.d.). However, the tobacco companies appealed this graphic warning requirement, and in 2012 the U.S. Court of Appeals ruled that this requirement violated the tobacco companies' First Amendment free speech rights. In March 2013, U.S. Attorney General Eric Holder announced that the government would not appeal that decision to the U.S. Supreme Court and would, instead, direct the FDA to propose new labels (CBS/AP, 2013).

Despite all these additional restrictions, the tobacco industry continues to reach non-smokers, especially adolescents, with its promotional messages. Data from the 2000 to 2012 National Youth Tobacco Survey, a biennial, school-based poll of U.S. middle and high school students, show that measures of students' exposure to tobacco ads online, in newspapers and magazines and in retail stores were higher than the targets set in the Healthy People, 2020 report. The survey results show that the percentage of middle and high school students who reported seeing tobacco ads in newspapers and magazines declined significantly from 2000 to 2012; even so, the overall exposure percentage for 2012 was 36.9 percent. Considering only those students who said they actually read newspapers or magazines, 46.4 percent reported exposure to tobacco ads. Within the group reporting reading newspapers and magazines, more than half of current smokers (51.7%) and nearly half of all high school students (48.9%) were exposed to tobacco advertising in these media. White (47%), black (47%) and Hispanic (46%) adolescent newspaper and magazine readers were more likely to report seeing tobacco ads than were Asians (37.7%) (Agaku et al., 2014a).

The vast majority of adolescents are also regularly exposed to tobacco product advertisements in retail stores, although that exposure has also declined somewhat from 2000 levels. In the 2000 survey, 87.8 percent of middle and high school students reported seeing tobacco ads at least sometimes in convenience stores, supermarkets or gas stations. By 2012 the overall exposure figure had declined to 76.2 percent, but non-smokers (75.8%) were only somewhat less likely than smokers (81.5%) to report seeing retail store tobacco advertising. (Agaku et al., 2014a).

Declines in exposure to printed ads – those in retail stores and those in newspapers and magazines – were offset by increases in exposure to online ads. The NYTS figures show that online exposure to tobacco ads nearly doubled over the 12-year period. In 2000, 22.3 percent of the students reported seeing tobacco product ads online, but by 2012 that percentage had grown to 43 percent. The increases were consistently high among smokers and non-smokers, middle and high school students, and boys and girls; overall, girls reported the highest exposure, with 46.7 percent saying they had seen tobacco ads online in 2012 (Agaku et al., 2014a). Another study using data from the New Jersey Adult Tobacco Survey documented a significant increase in recall of tobacco ads online between 2001 (6.9 percent of adults with Internet access) and 2005 (17.8%). The researchers estimated that 12.2 percent of all New Jersey adults had seen online tobacco advertising in 2005.

Agaku and colleagues (2014a) suggest that adolescents' increased exposure to online advertising may result from increasingly frequent use of social media websites. In the United States, at least, restrictions stemming from the MSA and the Tobacco Control Act mean that such sites (e.g., brand sites on Facebook, Twitter or YouTube) are not likely to have been created by the tobacco companies themselves. However, such pages can attract significant attention on social media. For instance, Camel cigarettes has a Facebook page that features the cartoon images of Joe Camel and numerous vintage Camel advertisements. In September 2014, the page had 40,842 "likes" – not an especially large number for a Facebook page, but enough to make the Camel cartoon logo easily accessible to Facebook users today. Facebook does not accept advertising for tobacco products; however, it will accept ads for blogs or groups intended to "connect people whose interests are related to these products ... as long as the service does not lead to the sale of any tobacco or tobacco-related products" (Facebook.com, 2014, para. 3).

In addition, Facebook now boasts more than 1,000 pages that include the word "e-cigarettes," including pages for numerous e-cigarette retailers. One of those pages touts "e-HealthCigarettes.com" and includes links to YouTube videos explaining "Why You Should Switch to the New Advance E-HealthCigarette" ("E-HealthCigarettes.com," 2013). Others offer discounts, coupon codes and other price promotions. Thus, while Facebook may not *sell* advertising for tobacco products, it is clearly possible for tobacco products, especially electronic cigarettes, to be advertised within Facebook via the establishment of Facebook pages for specific brands and/or retailers.

Because the FDA does not regulate advertising for electronic cigarettes as it does for other tobacco products, the past decade has seen tremendous growth in e-cigarette advertising, including television ads, resulting in a 251 percent increase in exposure to televised e-cigarette ads between 2011 and 2013 among 12- to 17-year-olds and a 321 percent increase over the same period among 18- to 24-year-olds. Most of that exposure (76%) occurred via cable television, and 81.7 percent of exposure was accounted for by one brand (Duke et al., 2014). The researchers note that many of these ads include celebrity endorsements, show e-cigarettes producing vapor that is visually indistinguishable from regular cigarette smoke and often emphasize that vaping is an adult behavior – "creating new social norms around e-cigarettes and increasing the desirability of e-cigarettes" (Duke et al., 2014, p. e34).

TOBACCO ADVERTISING CONTENT

What messages are conveyed through tobacco advertising? The answer to that question has changed, to some extent, from the earliest days of tobacco advertising up until today, although e-cigarette advertising seems to be repeating many of the earlier cigarette ad themes (Stanford School of Medicine, n.d.a). During the 1940s it was not uncommon for tobacco companies to promote cigarettes using health-related imagery, suggesting, for instance, that "More Doctors Smoke Camels than any other cigarette," as a 1946 Camel ad claimed. Another common claim was that the specific brand of cigarettes was "medically proven" not to cause throat irritation; these ads often used "throat specialist" doctors to tout their products. The ads, used extensively in the 1930s through 1950, included campaigns touting "scientific" studies showing that throat specialists preferred to smoke Old Gold cigarettes or that doctors had found "not one single case of throat irritation due to smoking Camels." Ads for menthol cigarettes focused on their "coolness" and, in some cases, suggested that this cooling effect made menthol cigarettes healthier than traditional cigarettes. For instance, a 1937 ad for Kool cigarettes used the brand's mascot, Willie the penguin, dressed as an otolaryngologist (ear, nose and throat specialist) and advising "Tell him to switch to Kools and he'll be all right."

An analysis of 1,135 magazine cigarette ads from 1954 to 2003 demonstrated that implicit health messages have been and continue to be common. Before 1971, when broadcast ads for cigarettes were banned, 92 percent of the ads were for regular or "medium" cigarettes, rather than for "mild," "light" or "ultralight" cigarettes – a type that was supposed to contain less tar and nicotine. However, as health concerns about cigarettes increased, the percentage of ads promoting lower tar/nicotine varieties increased, from 8.2 percent in the pre-broadcast ban era to 34.4 percent of ads published following the signing of the MSA. Other markers associated with health or with less risk also varied over time. The inclusion of "factual" health claims (e.g., "low tar" or "no additives") were included in nearly a quarter of all ads prior to the broadcast ban, but appeared in only 8.2 percent of ads during the post-MSA era (1999–2003). Across the entire sample, 45 percent of the ads contained some type of verbal health message, whether factual (5.6%), impressionistic (e.g., "mild" or "natural" – 27.7%) or both (11.7%). The ads also frequently included visual health cues, such as depictions of pristine outdoor scenes (mountains, rivers, fields), which were present in 58 percent of all ads (Paek et al., 2010).

Their results were consistent with those of other studies. For instance, Warner (1985) found that the tobacco industry used advertising to respond to negative publicity about the health impacts of smoking, emphasizing technological "solutions" such as filters and low-tar cigarettes. Similarly, Pollay and Dewhirst's (2002) analysis of internal tobacco company documents and ads revealed that cigarette ads touted – falsely – the notion that filtered cigarettes were safe and that low-tar and menthol cigarettes were healthier, in addition to using active, athletic-looking models, slogans like "Alive with Pleasure" and virtuous brand names (e.g., Life, Merit, True, Vantage).

Analysis of tobacco advertising and promotions reviewed by the Federal Trade Commission between the 1960s and late 1980s identified three common themes: tobacco products are satisfying, especially in terms of taste; tobacco users need not worry about negative health effects; and using tobacco products is associated with positive outcomes. The taste theme, exemplified by Marlboro's "Come to where the flavor is" tagline, continues to be popular; for instance, a 2007 American Spirit ad claims "Natural tastes better" and stresses that the cigarettes contain only "100% additive free natural tobacco." Ads for Salem menthol cigarettes called the flavor "springtime fresh," while Newport ads from the 1960s claimed that the brand was "fresher than any other menthol cigarette" (Stanford School of Medicine, n.d.b). As noted earlier, many cigarette brands used brand names and ad copy designed to reassure smokers that choosing menthol and/or lower tar and lower nicotine cigarettes reduced the health risks of smoking. For instance, a campaign for True cigarettes often showed individuals looking concerned, serious or thoughtful, with headline copy such as "All the fuss about smoking got me thinking I'd either quit or smoke True. I smoke True" (Stanford School of Medicine, n.d.c). Finally, tobacco ads often have been designed to associate use of the product with positive or popular individuals, including singers, television and movie stars and other celebrities, with positive personal characteristics, places (e.g., Marlboro Country), activities, and social, sexual and financial success. For instance, a Camel ad running in *Popular Science* in 2014 tells readers they can be "inspired," "passionate" and "original," and that smoking Camels will enable them to "taste it all." A Skoal tobacco ad in the same magazine shows two young men, covered in mud and dirt, riding ATVs. A recent Newport ad shows a young couple in swimsuits relaxing in a hammock at the beach, and a Winston ad from 2010 shows a couple embracing, apparently in the front seat of a convertible. The woman, her arms around the man's neck and a cigarette in her mouth, looks defiantly at the camera, above the ad's headline: "At least you can still smoke in your car" (Campaign for Tobacco-Free Kids, 2010).

More recently, Sung and Hennink-Kaminski (2008) examined ads in the youth-oriented magazines *Sports Illustrated* and *Rolling Stone*, comparing ads run before and after the signing of the MSA. They found that nearly half of the human models appearing in post-MSA ads (49%) appeared to be 18 to 29 years old. The most common themes in the ads were adventure, individualism, erotic or romantic scenes, humor and sociability or peer approval. The researchers concluded that, in terms of visual imagery, the MSA changed little in how cigarettes were advertised in youth-oriented magazines, with the ads in *Sports Illustrated* and *Rolling Stone* continuing "to emphasize the visual, to use models matched to readership, and to associate smoking with adventurous lifestyles and rewards of sociability and now sex" (Sung & Hennink-Kaminski, 2008, p. 346). Baek and Mayer (2010) also confirmed an increase in the use of sexual imagery in cigarette advertising post-MSA, based on an analysis of cigarette ads in these same two magazines, as well as *Cosmopolitan*. Their analysis of 657 unduplicated ads published from 1994 to 2003 revealed a significant increase in the percentage of ads showing suggestively or partially clad women, from 16 percent before the MSA to nearly one in four (24.9%) post-MSA. Overall, they identified a statistically significant increase in the sexual explicitness of cigarette ads.

THE ORIGINAL TARGET AUDIENCE: MEN

In the early 1900s, cigarette ads were targeted almost exclusively to men, and white men in particular, because smoking was deemed unseemly and inappropriate for women. Even today, men continue to be the primary audience for tobacco companies because, while smoking rates are comparable for men and women, the use of smokeless tobacco products, along with cigars and pipe tobacco, is almost exclusively a male activity. In 2012/2013, about one in five adult men smoked cigarettes (20%) and 4.8 percent used smokeless tobacco, compared to 14.5 percent of adult women who smoked and fewer than 1 percent who used smokeless tobacco (Agaku et al., 2014b). The Marlboro Man, in many ways, epitomizes the image most often used to encourage men to smoke; the smoking man, according to cigarette advertising, is strong, rugged, handsome, independent and virile. Advertising for both cigarettes and smokeless tobacco products historically has featured men working or adventuring outdoors, often in wild or challenging locations (Davis et al., 1998).

In particular, tobacco advertising and promotion has targeted military personnel and working-class men. Promotions aimed at men in the military often focused on price discounts – and even free distribution of cigarettes to soldiers. Throughout advertising and other promotions to soldiers, the themes have focused on "freedom, independence, success with women, adventure and virility" (Davis et al., 1998, p. 153). To reach working-class men, who smoke at higher rates than men in white-collar professions, the tobacco companies used advertising in magazines focused on outdoor activities like hunting (e.g., *Field & Stream*), automobiles (e.g., *Car and Driver, Road & Track, Hot Rod, Motor Trend, Popular Mechanics*) as well as in newspaper sports sections. The ads portray smokers as rugged, self-reliant, athletic men engaged in typically male activities – logging, construction, auto and motorcycle racing, hunting, working on oil rigs, rodeo and so on. To reach younger men, ads – especially for menthol products – focus on showing men having fun, enjoying "cool" lifestyles; ad campaigns that might seem to feature a more traditional world, such as the Marlboro Man ads, portray themes important to adolescents, including independence and freedom from authority (Davis et al., 1998).

TARGETING WOMEN

According to the CDC, tobacco companies began marketing cigarettes directly to women in the 1920s, and by the 1930s, cigarette ads aimed at women were commonplace (CDC's Office on Smoking and Health, 2001). The Stanford School of Medicine's website on the impact of tobacco advertising shows numerous early examples of mass marketing of cigarettes to women, including Chesterfield's late 1920s "Blow some my way" campaign, which used images suggesting that although women might coyly refuse a man's offer to share his cigarette, they still enjoyed the tobacco smoke. Lucky Strike's 1928 "Cream of the Crop" campaign featured celebrity testimonials, including singers, models, and even Amelia Earhart, who told campaign audiences that she carried Lucky Strikes on her airplane, the "Friendship," when she crossed the Atlantic Ocean.

The following year, Lucky Strike began taking advantage of women's fears of becoming overweight, urging them to "Reach for a Lucky instead of a Sweet" (Stanford School of Medicine, n.d.d). One of these ads, for instance, shows a slender woman in a swimsuit leaning out from the end of a diving board. Behind her is what appears to be her shadow – but the shadow appears 75 pounds heavier. The headline asks ominously, "Is this you five years from now?" The campaign boosted Lucky Strike's market share by 200 percent or more and helped push Lucky sales ahead of all other brands for two years (Amos & Haglund, 2000). Since that time, cigarette companies have promoted the idea that smoking helps women remain slim, athletic and attractive by using models with these characteristics (CDC's Office on Smoking and Health, 2001). Such ads continue today; for instance, one ad in the new Virginia Slims "It's a woman thing" campaign shows an attractive blonde wearing a swimsuit with a towel around her shoulders and looking back toward the camera. The copy line reads, "When we're wearing a swimsuit, there is no such thing as 'constructive criticism'" (Boyd et al., 2003, p. 275).

Other ads aimed to ease women's fears about the health impacts of smoking by touting "low" tar and nicotine content or using pristine outdoor settings or models engaged in sports or other vigorous activities. Other themes used to encourage women to smoke include the idea that smoking is sexy and glamorous, that smoking together helps women bond with their female friends, and – perhaps best exemplified in Virginia Slims' "You've come a long way, baby" campaign – that smoking reflects women's independence and equality with men (Stanford School of Medicine, n.d.d).

Tying smoking to women's empowerment was not a new idea in the late 1960s, when Virginia Slims was introduced, but the brand capitalized, perhaps more successfully than any other, on tying smoking to the women's liberation movement. Early television and magazine ads for the brand compared the women of the past, downtrodden and controlled by the men in their lives, to the "modern" woman, who could reasonably do and have whatever she wanted – even a brand of cigarettes designed especially for her. For instance, one Virginia Slims ad informed TV viewers and magazine readers:

> In 1910, Pamela Benjamin was caught smoking in the gazebo. She got a severe scolding and no supper that night. In 1915, Mrs. Cynthia Robinson was caught smoking in the cellar behind the preserves. Although she was 34, her husband sent her straight to her room. Then, in 1920, women won their rights.
>
> (O'Keefe & Pollay, 1996, p. 68)

A more recent analysis of tobacco industry documents relating to marketing to women and of ad campaigns that targeted women, either exclusively or in addition to men, showed that campaigns are typically designed to appeal to women's psychological, social and emotional needs and interests. For instance, during the early to mid-1980s, ads for Lorillard's Satin brand cigarettes showed women relaxing in the bathtub or on the sofa, encouraging women to pamper themselves, to escape briefly from others' demands on their time and energy by taking a cigarette break. Later, in the 1980s, Philip Morris' Benson & Hedges brand used the "For People Who Like to Smoke" campaign to reassure smokers that, even in an increasingly anti-smoking world, one could smoke and still be socially accepted; ads often showed smokers and non-smokers interacting in casual social situations to emphasize that smokers should not think of themselves as social outcasts. For its Capri cigarettes,

Brown & Williamson created a campaign using scenes of exotic, romantic and generally foreign locations, such as the Mediterranean, to associate the cigarettes with relaxing, indulgent escapes from the woman's day-to-day life. During this same period, Philip Morris altered its traditional Marlboro Man ads to appeal to young adult women, whom the company dubbed "Mavericks": women who valued their independence and sought exciting lifestyles but who nonetheless wanted to fit in with their peers and to be liked. Instead of focusing on the solitary, super-masculine Marlboro Man, these new ads showed groups of cowboys working, talking and laughing together. Virginia Slims, with its "It's a woman thing" campaign, downplayed women's concerns about feminism and instead appealed to women's desire for a sense of belonging. The researchers conclude that the ads "offer visuals that suggest needs satisfaction, and only by association do they introduce the brand of cigarettes as the means of satisfying needs" (Anderson et al., 2005, p. 132).

Targeting Minority Groups

African Americans and Hispanics also have been key target groups for the tobacco companies, with studies of advertising prior to the MSA showing disproportionately common cigarette advertising via billboards and retail store advertising in African American neighborhoods. For instance, a study of outdoor advertising in Los Angeles showed a greater density of tobacco billboards in minority neighborhoods, although this difference declined between 1990 and 1994. However, billboards in African American neighborhoods were more likely to be ethnically targeted, with a greater proportion of billboards showing youthful African American models (Stoddard et al., 1998). Similarly, a study in Boston, MA, showed that low-income and minority communities had larger cigarette ads, which were more likely to promote menthol cigarettes and more likely to be located within 1,000 feet of a school (Seidenberg et al., 2010). Analysis of billboard advertising in St. Louis, MO, in 1998 produced similar results, with tobacco billboards more likely to be located in low-income and African American neighborhoods (Luke et al., 2000). In general, researchers have found that African Americans are exposed to proportionately more tobacco advertising compared to whites (Barbeau et al., 2005; Primack et al., 2007).

Studies of advertising content have also revealed different approaches to targeting African Americans. For instance, a study of cigarette ads from *Life* and *Ebony* magazines from 1950 to 1965 showed that ads in *Ebony* were more likely to feature black athletes and musicians, and these celebrities, even though well known among white audiences, never appeared in *Life* ads. "For 1950–1965, endorsements from athletes were about five times more common in *Ebony* than in *Life*" (Pollay et al., 1992, p. 51). A more recent analysis of tobacco industry documents and magazine ads from 1989 to 1990 and 1999 to 2000 showed that ads aimed at African Americans were designed to make cigarettes seem classy, to associate smoking with social and financial success – the "good life"; ads in three African American magazines (*Ebony*, *Essence* and *Jet*) were more likely than ads in *People Weekly* to feature fantasy/escape themes and nightlife themes, to include images of expensive objects and to promote menthol cigarettes (Balbach et al., 2003). Another study that examined advertising for menthol cigarettes via magazine and online ads, direct mail and email in 2012/2013 concluded that these ads disproportionately target African Americans, as well as younger consumers, often featuring themes of sociability and sexuality (Richardson et al., 2014b).

The rapidly growing Hispanic/Latino population in the United States also has been a desirable target for the tobacco companies, who have built advertising campaigns for this group around Hispanic cultural values, including "pride, loyalty, courage, challenge, family, friends, honesty, satisfaction and reward, accomplishment and dreams" (R.J. Reynolds Tobacco Company, 1986, p. 3). Hispanic-focused ads for Newport cigarettes emphasized sociability and fun, while the recent Virginia Slims "Find Your Voice" campaign, including ads in Spanish, focused on encouraging Hispanic/Latina women to express themselves in their own unique ways (Davis et al., 1998).

ADVERTISING THE SMOKING ALTERNATIVES: "SMOKELESS" TOBACCO

Because smoking has been and remains so much more common than the use of smokeless tobacco, it is not surprising that relatively little research has examined smokeless tobacco advertising. The studies that have done so suggest that such advertising may be increasing in the United States as smoking becomes less socially acceptable, in part due to concerns about secondhand smoke (Morrison et al., 2008; Richardson et al., 2014c). For instance, a study of smokeless tobacco ads in six general interest adult magazines and 11 men's magazines from 1998 to 1999 and 2005 to 2006 showed that nearly two-thirds of the ads appeared during the later period, with the number of smokeless tobacco ads per magazine issue doubling over time. Almost all of the models shown in the ads were white (94.2%), and only 9.3 percent of ads included female models; these female characters appeared in the background rather than serving as the focus of attention. The data revealed an increase over time in ads for flavored products and ads with indoor settings; the prevalence of alternative-to-cigarettes messages also increased (Curry et al., 2011). Another study suggests that many of these ads are tailored to white men aged 35 and older, with masculinity as the primary theme (Richardson et al., 2014c). Analysis of Camel snus ads and R.J. Reynolds internal documents suggested, however, that the company has designed messages for recent Camel snus campaigns to appeal to a more diverse group (Timberlake et al., 2011), including those who want to use tobacco in situations where smoking is prohibited, for individuals who enjoy trendy, popular, urban activities and "for adventurous women and young men concerned with their image" (Mejia & Ling, 2010, p. 84). Recent Camel snus ads, for instance, describe the product as a way to circumvent smoking restrictions. For instance, one ad, which shows only black text on a blue background with a slightly darker silhouette of the brand's camel logo, recommends: "Just say no to people saying no."

E-CIGARETTE ADVERTISING

Because electronic cigarettes represent a new type of product, they are not yet subject to the same kinds of marketing regulations that apply to cigarettes and smokeless tobacco; however, several health and government organizations, including the American Heart Association, the American Lung Association and the National Association of Attorneys General, have urged the FDA to subject e-cigarettes to the same restrictions as other tobacco products. In April 2014, the FDA announced its intentions to regulate e-cigarettes, as well as cigars, pipe tobacco and hookahs. The new rules would prohibit e-cigarette manufacturers from giving away samples or making health-related claims without providing research-based evidence, require health warnings and the disclosure of ingredients, and impose age restrictions on e-cigarette purchase. The

FDA is not, at this point, banning television advertising or sales of e-cigarette flavorings intended to appeal to youth (Dennis, 2014). Thus, e-cigarette manufacturers remain free from the advertising and marketing restrictions enforced for other tobacco products through the MSA and the Tobacco Control Act.

Studies of e-cigarette advertising suggest that the manufacturers are taking advantage of this freedom and, as noted earlier, exposure to e-cigarette advertising among children and adolescents has grown rapidly in recent years (Duke et al., 2014). Among adults, a national study conducted in 2013 showed that 86 percent had heard of e-cigarettes, a dramatic increase since 2009, when fewer than 20 percent of U.S. adults were aware of e-cigarettes. Most often they had learned about e-cigarettes from another person, with 48 percent of current smokers, 39 percent of former smokers and 34 percent of never-smokers learning about e-cigarettes this way. However, television advertising was also a significant source of information, with 40 percent of current smokers, 35 percent of former smokers and 31 percent of never-smokers hearing about e-cigarettes through TV ads. The percentages of adults who had learned about e-cigarettes online ranged from 12 percent of never-smokers to 28 percent of current smokers, but adults younger than age 30 were more likely than older respondents to cite the Internet as a source of information about e-cigarettes (Pepper et al., 2014a).

A study examining all online tobacco advertising on U.S. and Canadian websites between April 2012 and April 2013 revealed that tobacco companies spent $2 million for online advertising during this period. The researchers identified tobacco and e-cigarette ads on 180 of the 250 websites monitored by the advertising tracking firm they hired, with 24 of 37 product ads promoting e-cigarettes. Ads for e-cigarettes appeared regularly on websites with significant youth audiences, with the average site advertising e-cigarettes reporting about 10.5 percent of its audience to be younger than age 18; one site advertising e-cigarettes reported that 35 percent of its audience was younger than age 18. Often the ads appeared on sites focused on music and/or entertainment. One of the most common themes for e-cigarette ads was harm reduction; 37 percent advertised the product as being healthier than cigarettes. About one in five (20.8%) of the ads suggested e-cigarettes as a smoking cessation aid, but of the ads that, when clicked, led to a landing page for the brand, none offered information about how to quit smoking. E-cigarette ads were significantly more likely (33.3%) to promote e-cigarettes as an alternative the individual could use when he or she could not smoke regular cigarettes. More than half of the ads (54.2%) claimed that e-cigarettes were more environmentally friendly than regular cigarettes. The researchers note that these themes may be especially appealing to young people, including those who have never smoked traditional cigarettes, raising concerns that, far from reducing the number of people who smoke, e-cigarette advertising may encourage young people to initiate tobacco use that will eventually lead to addiction to regular cigarettes (Richardson et al., 2014a).

Another study examining online promotion of e-cigarettes identified 466 unique brands advertised or promoted via brand websites in January 2014. The study compared the claims made about e-cigarettes that had been marketed online in May to August 2012 and those added in December 2013 to January 2014, and found that the older brands promoted their e-cigarettes as being healthier and less expensive than traditional cigarettes and usable in places where smoking is banned; six in ten claimed indirectly that the product was an effective smoking cessation aid. Newer brands, however, tended to focus more on offering multiple flavors; the average number of flavors for older brands was 32, compared to 49 for newer brands (Zhu et al., 2014).

Comparison of e-cigarette ads with those promoting traditional cigarettes shows that many of the same themes are being used. For instance, e-cigarette ads often include images of doctors emphasizing the health benefits of switching to e-cigarettes. Ads aimed at African Americans often include images of musicians or wealthy-looking models. Ads aimed at men use images of masculinity and rugged, capable-looking models. Celebrities, such as actor Stephen Dorff and model Jenny McCarthy, appear in ads for blu e-cigarettes. Women appearing in e-cigarette ads often appear in sexy or glamorous poses, wearing beautiful evening gowns, or looking athletic in swimwear or sports attire (Stanford School of Medicine, n.d.a). Sex is often used to promote the product. For instance, a blu e-cigarette ad in the 2014 swimsuit issue of *Sports Illustrated* shows the brand logo printed on the very skimpy bikini bottom worn by a slender model above the headline "Slim. Charged. Ready To Go" ("An e-Cigarette Ad," 2014). The Campaign for Tobacco-Free Kids also argues that e-cigarettes appeal to children and teenagers by advertising candy-like flavors and using cartoon characters, and that,

Figures 3.3a and 3.3b: E-cigarette Ads Echo Traditional Cigarette Ad Themes (source: From the collection of Stanford Research Into the Impact of Tobacco Advertising (tobacco.stanford.edu))

like ads for low-tar and nicotine cigarettes, many ads aimed at smokers promote switching to e-cigarettes rather than quitting smoking entirely ("7 Ways," 2013).

TOBACCO ADVERTISING EFFECTS

As noted earlier in this chapter, the U.S. Surgeon General has concluded that tobacco advertising does contribute to both the initiation and continuance of smoking, as well as the use of "smokeless" tobacco products like chewing tobacco and snus (National Center for Chronic Disease Prevention and Health Promotion (US) Office on Smoking and Health, 2014). How, specifically, does this influence occur?

First, even at very early ages while they are still in elementary school, children are exposed to advertising for tobacco products and can recognize tobacco brands and logos. In a systematic review conducted in 2005, DiFranza et al. (2006) identified 16 different studies that have demonstrated that children are exposed to tobacco advertising before they begin using any tobacco product. In one of the best-known studies, conducted before the FDA banned the use of cartoon characters (such as Joe Camel) in cigarette advertising, researchers found that 30 percent of three-year-olds and 91.3 percent of six-year-olds could match Joe Camel with Camel cigarettes, and this percentage was not significantly lower than the percentage who could match the Mickey Mouse logo with the Disney Channel. In addition, the ability to match cigarette logos with cigarettes did not differ significantly according to whether or not there was a smoker in the household (Fischer et al., 1991). Other studies have produced similar findings (Henke, 1995; Mizerski, 1995). Several studies have documented that children and adolescents who have never smoked are familiar with cigarette brand promotions, can name favorite cigarette ads and own cigarette promotional materials (Altman et al., 1996; Coeytaux et al., 1995; Evans et al., 1995; Feighery et al., 1998; Gilpin et al., 1997; Sargent et al., 2000).

In addition to promoting awareness, tobacco advertising promotes curiosity about tobacco use. Analysis of data from the 2012 National Youth Tobacco Survey showed that exposure to advertising in magazines was positively related to curiosity about smokeless tobacco, while exposure to point-of-sale advertising and receptivity to tobacco advertising was associated with greater curiosity about cigarettes, cigars and smokeless tobacco (Portnoy et al., 2014). This impact on curiosity is important because research suggests that curiosity about smoking increases susceptibility to smoking initiation among teens who have never smoked, and susceptibility increases the likelihood of experimentation with cigarettes. Thus, advertising seems to increase curiosity, which increases susceptibility, which increases smoking initiation among teens (Pierce et al., 2005). Among adult smokers, exposure to e-cigarette ads increased interest in trying e-cigarettes, especially when the ads emphasize the differences between e-cigarettes and regular cigarettes and when they showed someone using an e-cigarette (Pepper et al., 2014b).

Exposure to tobacco advertising is also linked to attitudes toward smoking. A meta-analysis of 51 studies concluded that exposure to tobacco marketing messages increases teenagers' odds of having positive attitudes toward tobacco use; youth who were exposed to pro-tobacco messages were 50 percent more likely to have positive attitudes toward tobacco or to express intentions to use tobacco in the future (Wellman et al., 2006). More recently, Kim and colleagues (2013) found that, among non-smoking New York state youth living outside New York

City, exposure to advertising was associated with significantly more positive attitudes toward smoking. Another study showed that, among fifth-, seventh- and ninth-graders who had tried cigarettes even once or twice, exposure to magazine cigarette ads led to more positive attitudes toward smoking, although there was no similar effect on youth who had never tried smoking (Turco, 1997). Arnett and Terhanian (1998) found that teenagers liked ads for Marlboro and Camel – the most popular youth brands of tobacco at the time – better than ads for other brands, and saw Joe Camel and Marlboro Man ads as making smoking seem more appealing; this trend was even stronger among adolescents who were already smoking. The authors concluded that the Camel and Marlboro Man ads "have succeeded in promoting not only a widespread awareness of these advertisements among adolescents but also a positive affect toward these brands and toward smoking" (Arnett & Terhanian, 1998, p. 132).

The most important question, of course, is whether exposure to tobacco advertising actually causes young people to begin using tobacco or makes those who have experimented with tobacco use more likely to progress to regular use. Again, numerous studies – including a number of systematic reviews and/or meta-analyses of the research – have concluded that advertising does have these effects (Hanewinkel et al., 2010, 2011; Lovato et al., 2011; Pierce et al., 1991, 1994; Voorhees et al., 2011; Wellman et al., 2006). In a systematic review of 51 studies, Wellman et al. (2006) concluded that exposure to pro-tobacco marketing more than doubles the likelihood that young people will begin using tobacco products. Another analysis examined the findings of nine longitudinal studies involving a total of 12,000 young people (aged 18 or younger at baseline) who were non-smokers when the study began. In all nine studies, teens who expressed greater awareness of or receptivity to tobacco advertising were more likely to experiment with smoking or become regular smokers. The authors conclude that the studies "consistently suggest that exposure to tobacco advertising and promotion is associated with the likelihood that adolescents will start to smoke" (Lovato et al., 2011, p. 10).

Even when parents are working to discourage their children from starting to smoke, advertising can undermine those efforts. Pierce et al. (2002) found that adolescents with more authoritative parents were significantly less likely to initiate smoking during the study period

(1996–1999); however, receptivity to tobacco advertising had a much greater influence on the transition to smoking among this group, in comparison with adolescents with less authoritative parents. Pierce et al. (2002) argue that the independence, freedom and excitement themes the tobacco industry uses, especially with youth-oriented brands such as Camel, are particularly salient to adolescents whose parents are more authoritative, such that tobacco advertising can undercut authoritative parents' otherwise effective parenting practices.

Ultimately, DiFranza et al. (2006) concluded that a systematic review of the research on advertising effects leads to one conclusion: tobacco advertising causes the initiation of tobacco use. Although advertising is not the only contributor, it does promote positive attitudes toward tobacco use and leads young people to expect positive outcomes from tobacco use, increasing intentions to use tobacco and ultimately making young people more likely to experiment with tobacco. There is a dose-response relationship such that the more youth are exposed to tobacco advertising and promotion, the greater the likelihood that they will initiate tobacco use. These findings have proven robust across multiple cultures and among different groups within cultures, and persists even after controlling for other contributors, such as the influence of parent and peer smoking. "Causality is the only plausible scientific explanation for the observed data" (DiFranza et al., 2006, p. e1237).

Once an individual has begun smoking, other research suggests that advertising both encourages progression to established-smoker status and interferes with smokers' attempts to quit. For instance, in a study of 529 Massachusetts teens, Biener and Siegel (2000) found that being highly receptive to tobacco advertising in 1993 more than doubled the likelihood of being an established smoker by 1997, compared to those with low receptivity to tobacco advertising. A more recent study of German sixth- to eighth-graders who had never smoked at baseline revealed that for every ten additional contacts with tobacco advertising, the relative risk of being an established smoker increased 38 percent, and the risk of being a daily smoker increased 30 percent; the study controlled for age, gender, socioeconomic status, school performance, time spent watching TV, personality characteristics, and peer and parent smoking (Morgenstern et al., 2013). In the United States, a study of 17,287 13- to 19-year-olds showed that the predictors of progression to more established smoking included exposure to others smoking and poor school performance, but owning or willingness to own a tobacco promotional product and having a favorite cigarette advertisement also increased the likelihood of progressing to regular smoking (Kaufman et al., 2002).

Tobacco advertising also may interfere with users' attempts to break their tobacco habits. For instance, Salgado-Garcia and colleagues (2013) found that pro-smoking images, such as a picture of a young man smoking or a cigarette in an ashtray, accompanied by a cup of coffee or a beer, induced more tobacco cravings among light and intermittent smokers than did anti-smoking or neutral stimuli. Another study compared the neuronal cue reactions and subjective craving experiences of moderately and highly dependent smokers and non-smokers exposed to tobacco ads. The researchers found the strongest effects among moderately dependent smokers, who experienced greater cravings as the experiment progressed (Vollstädt-Klein et al., 2011). Analyses of tobacco industry documents suggest that the manufacturers have put considerable effort into discouraging smokers from quitting, especially through their promotion of low-tar/low-nicotine cigarettes, and have also developed strategies to "recapture" former smokers who have quit (Ling & Glantz, 2004). Thus, tobacco advertising may be designed, in part, to capitalize on the fact that seeing these ads induces cigarette cravings in smokers and former smokers, thus reducing their likelihood of successfully kicking the tobacco habit.

TOBACCO ADVERTISING: NEGATIVE EFFECTS INTENDED?

To summarize: tobacco use in any form has negative health impacts. While some forms of tobacco, such as smokeless tobacco and e-cigarettes, may not be *as* harmful as traditional cigarette smoking, their use nonetheless produces harmful outcomes, including leading users to be more likely to take up cigarette smoking. Tobacco advertising has been carefully designed to encourage use of the product, including use among children and adolescents to whom the products cannot be sold legally. It has been tailored to expand tobacco's appeal to specific demographic groups, including women and minorities, and often has included content intended to make tobacco use appear less harmful than it is and to discourage smokers from quitting. Researchers have even determined that tobacco advertising expenditures are increased in January and February to counter smokers' New Year's resolutions to quit (Basil et al., 2000). Despite agreeing not to market their products to children and adolescents, tobacco companies have continued to push youth-oriented brands such as Camel and Newport in magazines with high percentages or numbers of readers younger than age 18 and have increased the amount of online advertising to reach smokers and potential smokers. Finally, the preponderance of evidence demonstrates that this advertising is effective. Although it may not be the only cause of tobacco use, it is an important cause (Biener & Siegel, 2000; DiFranza et al., 2006). In 1999, Emery and colleagues (1999) estimated that between 1988 and 1998, tobacco advertising was responsible for an additional 193,000 adult smokers who picked up the habit as teenagers, resulting in 46,400 deaths due to smoking and costing $21.7 billion to $33.3 billion in health care and mortality-related costs and lost productivity. The most recent Surgeon General's report on smoking estimates that, unless tobacco use is further reduced, "5.6 million youth currently aged 0–17 years of age will die prematurely of a smoking-related illness" (National Center for Chronic Disease Prevention and Health Promotion (US) Office on Smoking and Health, 2014, p. 667).

The final piece of evidence needed to put tobacco advertising firmly into the category of intentional negative effects on individuals is documentation that tobacco manufacturers knew smoking was harmful and purposely misled consumers into underestimating the risks of smoking. That evidence was provided in January 2014 when the major tobacco companies reached an agreement with the federal government to publish corrective statements acknowledging that the companies had lied about cigarettes' deadly effects. That agreement was developed in response to a 2006 U.S. District Court ruling in which Judge Gladys Kessler found that Philip Morris USA, R.J. Reynolds Tobacco and Lorillard, the Top three U.S. cigarette manufacturers, had known for decades that smoking causes disease and death but deliberately hid that information from consumers. For one year, each of the companies must publish full-page ads in the print and online Sunday editions of 35 newspapers covering 33 states and the District of Columbia. In addition, they must broadcast "corrective statement" ads, in prime time, five times a week on one of the major networks: ABC, NBC or CBS; the companies have the option of airing up to one-third of the broadcast ads on channels other than the three major networks so long as that station reaches an overall audience that is at least as large as the smallest audience on the major networks during that time slot. The companies also must publish the statements on their own websites and attach them to a specified number of cigarette packages for two years (Felberbaum, 2014; Troutman Sanders Tobacco Practice, n.d.).

After signing the agreement in January 2014, the tobacco companies' lawyers announced plans to appeal the required wording of the statements; however, in June 2014, the United States District Court for the District of Columbia approved an agreement that included the wording of the "corrective statements," which must begin with an acknowledgment that Philip Morris USA, its owner Altria, R.J. Reynolds Tobacco and Lorillard "deliberately deceived the American public about" the five topics the statements address: the adverse health effects of smoking, the health effects of secondhand smoke, the addictiveness of smoking and nicotine, the fact that "low-tar," "light," "ultra light," "mild" and "natural" cigarettes are no less harmful than regular cigarettes, and that cigarettes are designed to make them more addictive ("Text," n.d.).

One question that remains is why the U.S. government has not banned all tobacco advertising, as several other countries have done. After all, by 2013, 16 other countries, with a population of more than half a billion people, had instituted complete bans on all tobacco advertising, promotion and sponsorship (World Health Organization, 2013). These bans are effective in reducing smoking (Saffer & Chaloupka, 2000; World Health Organization, 2013). In particular, the bans have proven effective in reducing teen smoking initiation, in part because they lead to declines in adolescents' perceptions of the prevalence of smoking (Burton et al., 2010; Moodie et al., 2008). The World Health Organization concluded that tobacco consumption can be reduced by about 7 percent through total bans on tobacco advertising, including bans on promotions and displays of brand names and logos, even without any other tobacco control interventions, such as increasing prices or running anti-smoking ad campaigns (Blecher, 2008; Galduróz et al., 2007; World Health Organization, 2013). Although Blecher (2008) concluded that even limited bans on advertising can have some benefit, other researchers have concluded that partial bans are not effective because tobacco companies continue to find ways of encouraging young people to pick up the tobacco habit and of discouraging current smokers from quitting (Centers for Disease Control and Prevention (CDC), 2012; Harris et al., 2006; Henriksen, 2012; Kasza et al., 2011).

Many countries that have initiated limitations or bans on tobacco advertising and promotion have done so following the World Health Organization's Framework Convention on Tobacco Control, which requires countries signing the agreement to prohibit all forms of tobacco promotion, including advertising and sponsorship. The United States signed the treaty in 2004 but has yet to ratify it (Centers for Disease Control and Prevention (CDC), 2012), although analysis of worldwide implementation of FCTC requirements has demonstrated that total "bans on advertising and information dissemination activities would also be cost effective in most countries" (Shibuya, 2003, p. 157).

In the United States, however, First Amendment protection of the right to free speech, including commercial speech such as advertising for a legal product, may make full implementation of the FCTC problematic. Because a complete ban on advertising for tobacco would likely violate the First Amendment, the CDC recommends that state and local governments counter tobacco marketing by putting more effort and resources into changing the public's knowledge, attitudes and practices related to tobacco use through anti-tobacco advertising campaigns (CDC's Office on Smoking and Health, 2014a), which have been at least somewhat effective in reducing smoking initiation among young people and helping former smokers avoid relapsing (Davis et al., 1998; Durkin et al., 2012; McAfee et al., 2013; Wakefield et al., 2011, 2013). The challenge for such anti-tobacco marketing campaigns, however, is that government budgets for such campaigns almost always will be limited, and they must compete against an industry that spends millions of dollars every year ($451.7 million in 2011) on tobacco advertising and promotion, and even more ($7 billion in 2011) on coupons and other price discounts that are highly effective in encouraging tobacco consumption. It remains to be seen whether any tobacco education efforts, no matter how widespread in schools, communities and the mass media, can effectively compete against tobacco industry promotions which, in 2011, amounted to $24 million every day.

References

7 Ways E-cigarette Companies are Copying Big Tobacco's Playbook: (or 7 Reasons FDA Should Quickly Regulate e-cigarettes. (2013, October 2)). Retrieved September 22, 2014 from www.tobaccofreekids.org/tobacco_unfiltered/post/2013_10_02_ecigarettes.

Agaku, I.T., Ayo-Yusuf, O.A., Vardavas, C.I., Alpert, H.R. & Connolly, G.N. (2013a). Use of Conventional and Novel Smokeless Tobacco Products among US Adolescents. *Pediatrics, 132*(3), e578–e586. http://doi.org/10.1542/peds.2013-0843.

Agaku, I.T., Vardavas, C.I., Ayo-Yusuf, O.A., Alpert, H.R. & Connolly, G.N. (2013b). Temporal Trends in Smokeless Tobacco Use among US Middle and High School Students, 2000–2011. *JAMA, 309*(19), 1992–1994. http://doi.org/10.1001/jama.2013.4412.

Agaku, I.T., King, B.A. & Dube, S.R. (2014a). Trends in Exposure to Pro-tobacco Advertisements over the Internet, in Newspapers/Magazines, and at Retail Stores among U.S. Middle and High School Students, 2000–2012. *Preventive Medicine, 58*, 45–52. http://doi.org/10.1016/j.ypmed.2013.10.012.

Agaku, I.T., King, B.A., Husten, C.G., Bunnell, R., Ambrose, B.K., Hu, S.S. et al., Centers for Disease Control and Prevention (CDC). (2014b). Tobacco Product Use among Adults – United States, 2012–2013. *MMWR. Morbidity and Mortality Weekly Report, 63*(25), 542–547.

Ali, M.M. & Dwyer, D.S. (2009). Estimating Peer Effects in Adolescent Smoking Behavior: A Longitudinal Analysis. *Journal of Adolescent Health, 45*(4), 402–408. http://doi.org/10.1016/j.jadohealth.2009.02.004.

Alliance for the Control of Tobacco Use (ACT Brazil), Campaign for Tobacco-Free Kids, Corporate Accountability International, Framework Convention Alliance, InterAmerican Heart Foundation, Southeast Asia Tobacco Control Alliance. (2014). *Maybe You're the Target.* Retrieved August 25, 2014 from http://global.tobaccofreekids.org/content/what_we_do/industry_watch/yourethetarget_report.pdf.

Alpert, H.R., Koh, H.K. & Connolly, G.N. (2008). After the Master Settlement Agreement: Targeting and Exposure of Youth to Magazine Tobacco Advertising. *Health Affairs, 27*(6), w503–w512. http://doi.org/10.1377/hlthaff.27.6.w503.

Altman, D.G., Levine, D.W., Coeytaux, R., Slade, J. & Jaffe, R. (1996). Tobacco Promotion and Susceptibility to Tobacco Use among Adolescents Aged 12 Through 17 Years in a Nationally Representative Sample. *American Journal of Public Health, 86*(11), 1590–1593. http://doi.org/10.2105/AJPH.86.11.1590.

American Cancer Society. (2013, December 3). Smokeless Tobacco. Retrieved August 27, 2014 from www.cancer.org/cancer/cancercauses/tobaccocancer/smokeless-tobacco.

American Lung Association. (2011). *Hookah Smoking: A Growing Threat to Public Health.* Washington, DC: American Lung Association. Retrieved August 26, 2014 from www.lung.org/stop-smoking/tobacco-control-advocacy/reports-resources/cessation-economic-benefits/reports/hookah-policy-brief.pdf.

Amos, A. & Haglund, M. (2000). From Social Taboo to "Torch of Freedom": The Marketing of Cigarettes to Women. *Tobacco Control, 9*(1), 3–8.

Anderson, S.J., Glantz, S.A. & Ling, P.M. (2005). Emotions for Sale: Cigarette Advertising and Women's Psychosocial Needs. *Tobacco Control, 14*(2), 127–135. http://doi.org/10.1136/tc.2004.009076.

An E-Cigarette Ad on an Itsy, Bitsy Bikini – Campaign for Tobacco Free Kids: Teens Sure to be Attracted by Ad in *Sports Illustrated* Swimsuit Issue. (2014, February 24). Retrieved August 25, 2014 from www.tobaccofreekids.org/tobacco_unfiltered/post/2014_02_24_si.

Arnett, J.J. & Terhanian, G. (1998). Adolescents' Responses to Cigarette Advertisements: Links between Exposure, Liking, and the Appeal of Smoking. *Tobacco Control, 7*(2), 129–133. http://doi.org/10.1136/tc.7.2.129.

Ary, D.V. (1989). Use of Smokeless Tobacco among Male Adolescents: Concurrent and Prospective Relationships. *NCI Monographs: A Publication of the National Cancer Institute, 8*, 49–55.

Avenevoli, S. & Merikangas, K.R. (2003). Familial Influences on Adolescent Smoking. *Addiction, 98*, 1–20. http://doi.org/10.1046/j.1360-0443.98.s1.2.x.

Baek, T.H. & Mayer, M. (2010). Sexual Imagery in Cigarette Advertising Before and After the Master Settlement Agreement. *Health Communication, 25*(8), 747–757. http://doi.org/10.1080/10410236.2010.521917.

Balbach, E.D., Gasior, R.J. & Barbeau, E.M. (2003). R.J. Reynolds' Targeting of African Americans: 1988–2000. *American Journal of Public Health, 93*(5), 822–827.

Barbeau, E.M., Wolin, K.Y., Naumova, E.N. & Balbach, E. (2005). Tobacco Advertising in Communities: Associations with Race and Class. *Preventive Medicine, 40*(1), 16–22. http://doi.org/10.1016/j.ypmed.2004.04.056.

Barnett, T.E., Shensa, A., Kim, K.H., Cook, R.L., Nuzzo, E. & Primack, B.A. (2013a). The Predictive Utility of Attitudes Toward Hookah Tobacco Smoking. *American Journal of Health Behavior, 37*(4), 433–439. http://doi.org/10.5993/AJHB.37.4.1.

Barnett, T.E., Smith, T., He, Y., Soule, E.K., Curbow, B.A., Tomar, S.L. & McCarty, C. (2013b). Evidence of Emerging Hookah Use among University Students: A Cross-sectional Comparison between Hookah and Cigarette Use. *BMC Public Health, 13*, 302. http://doi.org/10.1186/1471-2458-13-302.

Basil, M.D., Basil, D.Z. & Cobb, C. (2000). Cigarette Advertising to Counter New Years Resolutions. *Journal of Health Communication, 5*(2), 161–174. http://doi.org/10.1080/108107300406875.

Bhatnagar, A., Whitsel, L.P., Ribisl, K.M., Bullen, C., Chaloupka, F., Piano, M.R. & Benowitz, N. (2014). Electronic Cigarettes A Policy Statement From the American Heart Association. *Circulation*, CIR.0000000000000107. http://doi.org/10.1161/CIR.0000000000000107.

Biener, L. & Siegel, M. (2000). Tobacco Marketing and Adolescent Smoking: More Support for a Causal Inference. *American Journal of Public Health, 90*(3), 407–411.

Biglan, A., Duncan, T.E., Ary, D.V. & Smolkowski, K. (1995). Peer and Parental Influences on Adolescent Tobacco Use. *Journal of Behavioral Medicine, 18*(4), 315–330.

Blecher, E. (2008). The Impact of Tobacco Advertising Bans on Consumption in Developing Countries. *Journal of Health Economics, 27*(4), 930–942. http://doi.org/10.1016/j.jhealeco.2008.02.010.

Boyd, T.C., Boyd, C.J. & Greenlee, T.B. (2003). A Means to an End: Slim Hopes and Cigarette Advertising. *Health Promotion Practice, 4*(3), 266–277.

Braun, R.E., Glassman, T., Wohlwend, J., Whewell, A. & Reindl, D.M. (2012). Hookah Use among College Students from a Midwest University. *Journal of Community Health, 37*(2), 294–298. http://doi.org/10.1007/s10900-011-9444-9.

Bricker, J.B., Peterson Jr., A.V., Sarason, I.G., Andersen, M.R. & Rajan, K.B. (2007). Changes in the Influence of Parents' and Close Friends' Smoking on Adolescent Smoking Transitions. *Addictive Behaviors, 32*(4), 740–757. http://doi.org/10.1016/j.addbeh.2006.06.020.

Bricker, J.B., Peterson, A.V., Andersen, M.R., Leroux, B.G., Rajan, K.B. & Sarason, I.G. (2006). Close Friends', Parents', and Older Siblings' Smoking: Reevaluating Their Influence on Children's Smoking. *Nicotine & Tobacco Research, 8*(2), 217–226. http://doi.org/10.1080/14622200600576339.

Bullen, C., Howe, C., Laugesen, M., McRobbie, H., Parag, V., Williman, J. & Walker, N. (2013). Electronic Cigarettes for Smoking Cessation: A Randomised Controlled Trial. *Lancet, 382*(9905), 1629–1637. http://doi.org/10.1016/S0140-6736(13)61842-5.

Bunnell, R.E., Agaku, I.T., Arrazola, R., Apelberg, B.J., Caraballo, R.S., Corey, C.G. & King, B.A. (2014). Intentions to Smoke Cigarettes among Never-smoking U.S. Middle and High School Electronic Cigarette Users, National Youth Tobacco Survey, 2011–2013. *Nicotine & Tobacco Research: Official Journal of the Society for Research on Nicotine and Tobacco.* http://doi.org/10.1093/ntr/ntu166.

Burrows, D.S. (1982). *NBER Models of Price Sensitivity by Age/Sex, Memo to J.R. Moore* (No. RJR Bates No. 50301 1370).

Burton, D., Graham, J.W., Johnson, C.A., Uutela, A., Vartiainen, E. & Palmer, R.F. (2010). Perceptions of Smoking Prevalence by Youth in Countries With and Without a Tobacco Advertising Ban. *Journal of Health Communication, 15*(6), 656–664. http://doi.org/10.1080/10810730.2010.499595.

Callahan-Lyon, P. (2014). Electronic Cigarettes: Human Health Effects. *Tobacco Control, 23 Suppl 2*, ii36–40. http://doi.org/10.1136/tobaccocontrol-2013-051470.

Campaign for Tobacco-Free Kids. (2010, November 26). "No Bull" Campaign. Retrieved September 18, 2014 from www.tobaccofreekids.org/ad_gallery/ad/no_bull_campaign.

Campaign for Tobacco-Free Kids. (2014). *Designed for Addiction: How the Tobacco Industry Has Made Cigarettes More Addictive, More Attractive to Kids and Even More Deadly.* Washington, DC. Retrieved August 25, 2014 from www.tobaccofreekids.org/content/what_we_do/industry_watch/product_manipulation/2014_06_19_DesignedforAddiction_web.pdf.

CBS/AP. (2013, March 19). FDA's Graphic Cigarette Labels Rule Goes Up in Smoke after U.S. Abandons Appeal. Retrieved September 11, 2014 from www.cbsnews.com/news/fdas-graphic-cigarette-labels-rule-goes-up-in-smoke-after-us-abandons-appeal/.

CDC's Office on Smoking and Health. (2001, March 27). Smoking and Tobacco Use; Surgeon General's Reports; 2001; Marketing Cigarettes to Women. Retrieved September 16, 2014 from www.cdc.gov/tobacco/data_statistics/sgr/2001/highlights/marketing/.

CDC's Office on Smoking and Health. (2014a). *Best Practices for Comprehensive Tobacco Control Programs – 2014.* Retrieved August 25, 2014 from www.cdc.gov/tobacco/stateandcommunity/best_practices/.

CDC's Office on Smoking and Health. (2014b, February 14). Youth and Tobacco Use. Retrieved August 26, 2014 from www.cdc.gov/tobacco/data_statistics/fact_sheets/youth_data/tobacco_use/.

CDC's Office on Smoking and Health. (2014c, March 5). Health Effects of Second-hand Smoke. Retrieved August 27, 2014 from www.cdc.gov/tobacco/data_statistics/fact_sheets/secondhand_smoke/health_effects/.

CDC's Office on Smoking and Health. (2014d, March 10). Electronic Cigarette Use Among Middle and High School Students – Smoking & Tobacco Use. Retrieved August 26, 2014 from www.cdc.gov/tobacco/data_statistics/mmwrs/byyear/2013/mm6235a6/highlights.htm.

Centers for Disease Control and Prevention (CDC). (2012). Adult Awareness of Tobacco Advertising, Promotion, and Sponsorship – 14 countries. *MMWR. Morbidity and Mortality Weekly Report, 61*(20), 365–369.

Centers for Disease Control and Prevention. (2013, November 14). Trends in Current Cigarette Smoking. Retrieved August 26, 2014 from www.cdc.gov/tobacco/data_statistics/tables/trends/cig_smoking/.

Centers for Disease Control and Prevention (CDC). (2014, February 14). Adult Cigarette Smoking in the United States; Retrieved August 26, 2014 from www.cdc.gov/tobacco/data_statistics/fact_sheets/adult_data/cig_smoking/.

Cobb, C., Ward, K.D., Maziak, W., Shihadeh, A.L. & Eissenberg, T. (2010). Waterpipe Tobacco Smoking: An Emerging Health Crisis in the United States. *American Journal of Health Behavior, 34*(3), 275–285.

Coeytaux, R.R., Altman, D.G. & Slade, J. (1995). Tobacco Promotions in the Hands of Youth. *Tobacco Control, 4*(3), 253–257.

Curry, L.E., Pederson, L.L. & Stryker, J.E. (2011). The Changing Marketing of Smokeless Tobacco in Magazine Advertisements. *Nicotine & Tobacco Research: Official Journal of the Society for Research on Nicotine and Tobacco, 13*(7), 540–547. http://doi.org/10.1093/ntr/ntr038.

Dave, D. & Saffer, H. (2013). Demand for Smokeless Tobacco: Role of Advertising. *Journal of Health Economics, 32*(4), 682–697. http://doi.org/10.1016/j.jhealeco.2013.03.007.

Davis, R.M., Gilpin, E.A., Loken, B., Viswanath, K. & Wakefield, M.A. (1998). The Role of the Media in Promoting and Reducing Tobacco Use. *Health, 98*, 4302.

Dennis, B. (2014, April 23). FDA Outlines Plan to Regulate e-cigarettes. *Washington Post.* Retrieved September 19, 2014 from www.washingtonpost.com/national/health-science/fda-outlines-plan-to-regulate-e-cigarettes/2014/04/23/4e7c8684-ca39-11e3-93eb-6c0037dde2ad_story.html.

DiFranza, J.R., Wellman, R.J., Sargent, J.D., Weitzman, M., Hipple, B.J. & Winickoff, J.P. (2006). Tobacco Promotion and the Initiation of Tobacco Use: Assessing the Evidence for Causality. *Pediatrics, 117*(6), e1237–e1248. http://doi.org/10.1542/peds.2005-1817.

Duke, J.C., Lee, Y.O., Kim, A.E., Watson, K.A., Arnold, K.Y., Nonnemaker, J.M. & Porter, L. (2014). Exposure to Electronic Cigarette Television Advertisements Among Youth and Young Adults. *Pediatrics, 134*(1), e29–e36. http://doi.org/10.1542/peds.2014-0269.

Durkin, S., Brennan, E. & Wakefield, M. (2012). Mass Media Campaigns to Promote Smoking Cessation among Adults: An Integrative Review. *Tobacco Control, 21*(2), 127–138. http://doi.org/10.1136/tobaccocontrol-2011-050345.

Dutra, L.M. & Glantz, S.A. (2014). Electronic Cigarettes and Conventional Cigarette Use among US Adolescents: A Cross-sectional Study. *JAMA Pediatrics, 168*(7), 610–617. http://doi.org/10.1001/jamapediatrics.2013.5488.

E-HealthCigarettes.com. (2013). Retrieved September 15, 2014 from https://www.facebook.com/healthecigs.

Emery, S., Choi, W.S. & Pierce, J.P. (1999). The Social Costs of Tobacco Advertising and Promotions. *Nicotine & Tobacco Research, 1*(Suppl. 2), S83–S91. http://doi.org/10.1080/14622299050011871.

Evans, N., Farkas, A., Gilpin, E., Berry, C. & Pierce, J.P. (1995). Influence of Tobacco Marketing and Exposure to Smokers on Adolescent Susceptibility to Smoking. *Journal of the National Cancer Institute, 87*(20), 1538–1545.

Facebook.com. (2014). Prohibited Content. Retrieved September 15, 2014 from https://www.facebook.com/help/174908809241578.

FDA Regulation of Tobacco. (n.d.). Retrieved September 11, 2014 from http://tobaccopolicycenter.org/tobacco-control/recent-cases/fda-regulation-of-tobacco/.

Feighery, E., Borzekowski, D.L.G., Schooler, C. & Flora, J. (1998). Seeing, Wanting, Owning: The Relationship between Receptivity to Tobacco Marketing and Smoking Susceptibility in Young People. *Tobacco Control, 7*(2), 123–128. http://doi.org/10.1136/tc.7.2.123.

Felberbaum, M. (2014, January 10). Deal Reached on Tobacco Firm Corrective Statements. *Washington Post.* Retrieved September 24, 2014 from www.washingtonpost.

com/business/economy/deal-reached-on-tobacco-firm-corrective-statements/2014/01/10/bc960eca-7a47-11e3-8963-b4b654bcc9b2_story.html.

Fischer, P.M., Schwartz, M.P., Richards, J.W. Jr., Goldstein, A.O. & Rojas, T.H. (1991). Brand Logo Recognition by Children Aged 3 to 6 Years: Mickey Mouse and Old Joe the Camel. *JAMA, 266*(22), 3145-3148. http://doi.org/10.1001/jama.1991.03470220061027.

Fix, B.V., O'Connor, R.J., Vogl, L., Smith, D., Bansal-Travers, M., Conway, K.P. & Hyland, A. (2014). Patterns and Correlates of Polytobacco Use in the United States Over a Decade: NSDUH 2002-2011. *Addictive Behaviors, 39*(4), 768-781. http://doi.org/10.1016/j.addbeh.2013.12.015.

Galdurόz, J.C.F., Fonseca, A.M., Noto, A.R. & Carlini, E.A. (2007). Decrease in Tobacco Use among Brazilian Students: A Possible Consequence of the Ban on Cigarette Advertising? *Addictive Behaviors, 32*(6), 1309-1313. http://doi.org/10.1016/j.addbeh.2006.09.004.

Gilpin, E.A., Pierce, J.P. & Rosbrook, B. (1997). Are Adolescents Receptive to Current Sales Promotion Practices of the Tobacco Industry? *Preventive Medicine, 26*(1), 14-21. http://doi.org/10.1006/pmed.1996.9980.

Go, M-H., Green Jr., H.D., Kennedy, D.P., Pollard, M. & Tucker, J.S. (2010). Peer Influence and Selection Effects on Adolescent Smoking. *Drug and Alcohol Dependence, 109*(1-3), 239-242. http://doi.org/10.1016/j.drugalcdep.2009.12.017.

Goebel, L.J., Crespo, R.D., Abraham, R.T., Masho, S.W. & Glover, E.D. (2000). Correlates of Youth Smokeless Tobacco Use. *Nicotine & Tobacco Research, 2*(4), 319-325.

Grana, R., Benowitz, N. & Glantz, S.A. (2014). E-Cigarettes. *Circulation, 129*(19), 1972-1986. http://doi.org/10.1161/CIRCULATIONAHA.114.007667.

Gualano, M.R., Passi, S., Bert, F., Torre, G.L., Scaioli, G. & Siliquini, R. (2014). Electronic Cigarettes: Assessing the Efficacy and the Adverse Effects Through a Systematic Review of Published Studies. *Journal of Public Health*, fdu055. http://doi.org/10.1093/pubmed/fdu055.

Hajek, P., Etter, J-F., Benowitz, N., Eissenberg, T. & McRobbie, H. (2014). Electronic Cigarettes: Review of Use, Content, Safety, Effects on Smokers and Potential for Harm and Benefit. *Addiction (Abingdon, England)*. http://doi.org/10.1111/add.12659.

Hamilton, W.L., Turner-Bowker, D.M., Celebucki, C.C. & Connolly, G.N. (2002). Cigarette Advertising in Magazines: The Tobacco Industry Response to the Master Settlement Agreement and to Public Pressure. *Tobacco Control, 11*(Suppl. 2), ii54-ii58. http://doi.org/10.1136/tc.11.suppl_2.ii54.

Hanewinkel, R., Isensee, B., Sargent, J.D. & Morgenstern, M. (2010). Cigarette Advertising and Adolescent Smoking. *American Journal of Preventive Medicine, 38*(4), 359-366. http://doi.org/10.1016/j.amepre.2009.12.036.

Hanewinkel, R., Isensee, B., Sargent, J.D. & Morgenstern, M. (2011). Cigarette Advertising and Teen Smoking Initiation. *Pediatrics, 127*(2), e271-278. http://doi.org/10.1542/peds.2010-2934.

Harris, F., MacKintosh, A.M., Anderson, S., Hastings, G., Borland, R., Fong, G.T., ITC Collaboration. (2006). Effects of the 2003 Advertising/Promotion Ban in the United Kingdom on Awareness of Tobacco Marketing: Findings from the International Tobacco Control (ITC) Four Country Survey. *Tobacco Control, 15*(Suppl. 3), iii26-33. http://doi.org/10.1136/tc.2005.013110.

Helping Reduce Underage Tobacco Use. (n.d.). Retrieved September 11, 2014 from www.philipmorrisusa.com/en/cms/Responsibility/Helping_Nav/Helping_Reduce_Underage_Tobacco_Use/default.aspx?src=search&q=Youth%20tobacco%20use.

Henke, L.L. (1995). Young Children's Perceptions of Cigarette Brand Advertising

Symbols: Awareness, Affect, and Target Market Identification. *Journal of Advertising, 24*(4), 13–28.

Henriksen, L. (2012). Comprehensive Tobacco Marketing Restrictions: Promotion, Packaging, Price and Place. *Tobacco Control, 21*(2), 147–153. http://doi.org/10.1136/tobaccocontrol-2011-050416.

Hill, K.G., Hawkins, J.D., Catalano, R.F., Abbott, R.D. & Guo, J. (2005). Family Influences on the Risk of Daily Smoking Initiation. *The Journal of Adolescent Health: Official Publication of the Society for Adolescent Medicine, 37*(3), 202–210. http://doi.org/10.1016/j.jadohealth.2004.08.014.

Hoffman, B.R., Monge, P.R., Chou, C-P. & Valente, T.W. (2007). Perceived Peer Influence and Peer Selection on Adolescent Smoking. *Addictive Behaviors, 32*(8), 1546–1554. http://doi.org/10.1016/j.addbeh.2006.11.016.

Holtzman, A.L., Babinski, D. & Merlo, L.J. (2013). Knowledge and Attitudes Toward Hookah Usage among University Students. *Journal of American College Health: J of ACH, 61*(6), 362–370. http://doi.org/10.1080/07448481.2013.818000.

Hookah Bars Find a Place in America. (2006, January 2). Retrieved August 26, 2014 from www.nbcnews.com/id/10620103/ns/business-small_business/t/hookah-bars-find-place-america/.

Hu, F.B., Flay, B.R., Hedeker, D., Siddiqui, O. & Day, L.E. (1995). The Influences of Friends' and Parental Smoking on Adolescent Smoking Behavior: The Effects of Time and Prior Smoking 1. *Journal of Applied Social Psychology, 25*(22), 2018–2047. http://doi.org/10.1111/j.1559-1816.1995.tb01829.x.

Johnson, C.C., Li, D., Perry, C.L., Elder, J.P., Feldman, H.A., Kelder, S.H. & Stone, E.J. (2002). Fifth Through Eighth Grade Longitudinal Predictors of Tobacco Use among a Racially Diverse Cohort: CATCH. *The Journal of School Health, 72*(2), 58–64.

Kasza, K.A., Hyland, A.J., Brown, A., Siahpush, M., Yong, H-H., McNeill, A.D. & Cummings, K.M. (2011). The Effectiveness of Tobacco Marketing Regulations on Reducing Smokers' Exposure to Advertising and Promotion: Findings from the International Tobacco Control (ITC) Four Country Survey. *International Journal of Environmental Research and Public Health, 8*(2), 321–340. http://doi.org/10.3390/ijerph8020321.

Kaufman, N.J., Castrucci, B.C., Mowery, P.D., Gerlach, K.K., Emont, S. & Orleans, C.T. (2002). Predictors of Change on the Smoking Uptake Continuum among Adolescents. *Archives of Pediatrics & Adolescent Medicine, 156*(6), 581–587.

Kim, A.E., Loomis, B.R., Busey, A.H., Farrelly, M.C., Willett, J.G. & Juster, H.R. (2013). Influence of Retail Cigarette Advertising, Price Promotions, and Retailer Compliance on Youth Smoking-related Attitudes and Behaviors. *Journal of Public Health Management and Practice: JPHMP, 19*(6), E1–9. http://doi.org/10.1097/PHH.0b013e3182980c47.

King, C. & Siegel, M. (2001). The Master Settlement Agreement with the Tobacco Industry and Cigarette Advertising in Magazines. *New England Journal of Medicine, 345*(7), 504–511. http://doi.org/10.1056/NEJMsa003149.

Kline, R. & Davidson, P. (1999). Advertising Restrictions. In *The multistate Master Settlement Agreement and the Future of State and Local Tobacco Control: An analysis of selected topics and provisions of the multistate Master Settlement Agreement of November 23, 1998*. Boston, MA: Tobacco Control Resource Center, Inc. at Northeastern University School of Law.

Knishkowy, B. & Amitai, Y. (2005). Water-pipe (Narghile) Smoking: An Emerging Health Risk Behavior. *Pediatrics, 116*(1), e113–e119. http://doi.org/10.1542/peds.2004-2173.

Ling, P.M. & Glantz, S.A. (2004). Tobacco Industry Research on Smoking Cessation. Recapturing Young Adults and Other Recent Quitters. *Journal of General Internal Medicine*, 19(5, Part 1), 419–426. http://doi.org/10.1111/j.1525-1497.2004.30358.x.

Lovato, C., Watts, A. & Stead, L.F. (2011). Impact of Tobacco Advertising and Promotion on Increasing Adolescent Smoking Behaviours. *The Cochrane Database of Systematic Reviews*, (10), CD003439. http://doi.org/10.1002/14651858.CD003439.pub2.

Luke, D., Esmundo, E. & Bloom, Y. (2000). Smoke Signs: Patterns of Tobacco Billboard Advertising in a Metropolitan Region. *Tobacco Control*, 9(1), 16–23. http://doi.org/10.1136/tc.9.1.16.

McAfee, T., Davis, K.C., Alexander, R.L., Pechacek, T.F. & Bunnell, R. (2013). Effect of the First Federally Funded US Antismoking National Media Campaign. *The Lancet*, 382(9909), 2003–2011. http://doi.org/10.1016/S0140-6736(13)61686-4.

Mejia, A.B. & Ling, P.M. (2010). Tobacco Industry Consumer Research on Smokeless Tobacco Users and Product Development. *American Journal of Public Health*, 100(1), 78–87. http://doi.org/10.2105/AJPH.2008.152603.

Mizerski, R. (1995). The Relationship between Cartoon Trade Character Recognition and Attitude Toward Product Category in Young Children. *The Journal of Marketing*, 58–70.

Moodie, C., MacKintosh, A.M., Brown, A. & Hastings, G.B. (2008). Tobacco Marketing Awareness on Youth Smoking Susceptibility and Perceived Prevalence Before and After an Advertising Ban. *European Journal of Public Health*, 18(5), 484–490. http://doi.org/10.1093/eurpub/ckn016.

Morgenstern, M., Sargent, J.D., Isensee, B. & Hanewinkel, R. (2013). From Never to Daily Smoking in 30 Months: The Predictive Value of Tobacco and Non-tobacco Advertising Exposure. *BMJ Open*, 3(6). http://doi.org/10.1136/bmjopen-2013-002907.

Morrell, H.E.R., Cohen, L.M., Bacchi, D. & West, J. (2005). Predictors of Smoking and Smokeless Tobacco Use in College Students: A Preliminary Study Using Web-based Survey Methodology. *Journal of American College Health*, 54(2), 108–115. http://doi.org/10.3200/JACH.54.2.108-115.

Morrison, M.A., Krugman, D.M. & Park, P. (2008). Under the Radar: Smokeless Tobacco Advertising in Magazines with Substantial Youth Readership. *American Journal of Public Health*, 98(3), 543–548. http://doi.org/10.2105/AJPH.2006.092775.

National Center for Chronic Disease Prevention and Health Promotion (US) Office on Smoking and Health. (2014). *The Health Consequences of Smoking – 50 Years of Progress: A Report of the Surgeon General*. Atlanta, GA: Centers for Disease Control and Prevention (US). Retrieved August 27, 2014 from www.ncbi.nlm.nih.gov/books/NBK179276/.

Odum, L.E., O'Dell, K.A. & Schepers, J.S. (2012). Electronic Cigarettes: Do They Have a Role in Smoking Cessation? *Journal of Pharmacy Practice*, 25(6), 611–614. http://doi.org/10.1177/0897190012451909.

O'Keefe, A.M. & Pollay, R.W. (1996). Deadly Targeting of Women in Promoting Cigarettes. *Journal of the American Medical Women's Association (1972)*, 51(1–2), 67–69.

O'Loughlin, J., Paradis, G., Renaud, L. & Gomez, L.S. (1998). One-year Predictors of Smoking Initiation and of Continued Smoking among Elementary Schoolchildren in Multiethnic, Low-income, Inner-city Neighbourhoods. *Tobacco Control*, 7(3), 268–275. http://doi.org/10.1136/tc.7.3.268.

Paek, H-J., Reid, L.N., Choi, H. & Jeong, H.J. (2010). Promoting Health (Implicitly)? A Longitudinal Content Analysis of Implicit Health Information in Cigarette

Advertising, 1954–2003. *Journal of Health Communication, 15*(7), 769–787. http://doi.org/10.1080/10810730.2010.514033.

Pepper, J.K., Emery, S.L., Ribisl, K.M. & Brewer, N.T. (2014a). How U.S. Adults Find Out About Electronic Cigarettes: Implications for Public Health Messages. *Nicotine & Tobacco Research: Official Journal of the Society for Research on Nicotine and Tobacco, 16*(8), 1140–1144. http://doi.org/10.1093/ntr/ntu060.

Pepper, J.K., Emery, S.L., Ribisl, K.M., Southwell, B.G. & Brewer, N.T. (2014b). Effects of Advertisements on Smokers' Interest in Trying E-cigarettes: The Roles of Product Comparison and Visual Cues. *Tobacco Control, 23*(Suppl. 3), iii31–36. http://doi.org/10.1136/tobaccocontrol-2014-051718.

Perry, C.L. (1999). The Tobacco Industry and Underage Youth Smoking: Tobacco Industry Documents from the Minnesota Litigation. *Archives of Pediatrics & Adolescent Medicine, 153*(9), 935–941. http://doi.org/10.1001/archpedi.153.9.935.

Peterson Jr., A.V., Leroux, B.G., Bricker, J., Kealey, K.A., Marek, P.M., Sarason, I.G. & Andersen, M.R. (2006). Nine-year Prediction of Adolescent Smoking by Number of Smoking Parents. *Addictive Behaviors, 31*(5), 788–801. http://doi.org/10.1016/j.addbeh.2005.06.003.

Pierce, J.P., Lee, L. & Gilpin, E.A. (1994). Smoking Initiation by Adolescent Girls, 1944 through 1988: An Association with Targeted Advertising. *JAMA, 271*(8), 608–611.

Pierce, J.P., Distefan, J.M., Kaplan, R.M. & Gilpin, E.A. (2005). The Role of Curiosity in Smoking Initiation. *Addictive Behaviors, 30*(4), 685–696. http://doi.org/10.1016/j.addbeh.2004.08.014.

Pierce, J.P., Distefan, J.M., Jackson, C., White, M.M. & Gilpin, E.A. (2002). Does Tobacco Marketing Undermine the Influence of Recommended Parenting in Discouraging Adolescents from Smoking? *American Journal of Preventive Medicine, 23*(2), 73–81. http://doi.org/10.1016/S0749-3797(02)00459-2.

Pierce, J.P., Gilpin, E., Burns, D.M., Whalen, E., Rosbrook, B., Shopland, D. & Johnson, M. (1991). Does Tobacco Advertising Target Young People to Start Smoking? Evidence from California. *JAMA, 266*(22), 3154–3158.

Pollay, R.W. & Dewhirst, T. (2002). The Dark Side of Marketing Seemingly "Light" Cigarettes: Successful Images and Failed Fact. *Tobacco Control, 11*(Suppl. 1), i18–i31. http://doi.org/10.1136/tc.11.suppl_1.i18.

Pollay, R.W., Lee, J.S. & Carter-Whitney, D. (1992). Separate, but Not Equal: Racial Segmentation in Cigarette Advertising. *Journal of Advertising, 21*(1), 45–57. http://doi.org/10.1080/00913367.1992.10673359.

Polosa, R., Morjaria, J.B., Caponnetto, P., Campagna, D., Russo, C., Alamo, A. & Fisichella, A. (2014). Effectiveness and Tolerability of Electronic Cigarette in Real-life: A 24-month Prospective Observational Study. *Internal and Emergency Medicine, 9*(5), 537–546. http://doi.org/10.1007/s11739-013-0977-z.

Portnoy, D.B., Wu, C.C., Tworek, C., Chen, J. & Borek, N. (2014). Youth Curiosity about Cigarettes, Smokeless Tobacco, and Cigars: Prevalence and Associations with Advertising. *American Journal of Preventive Medicine, 47*(2, Suppl. 1), S76–S86. http://doi.org/10.1016/j.amepre.2014.04.012.

Primack, B.A., Bost, J.E., Land, S.R. & Fine, M.J. (2007). Volume of Tobacco Advertising in African American Markets: Systematic Review and Meta-Analysis. *Public Health Reports, 122*(5), 607–615.

Rezk-Hanna, M., Macabasco-O'Connell, A. & Woo, M. (2014). Hookah Smoking among Young Adults in Southern California. *Nursing Research, 63*(4), 300–306. http://doi.org/10.1097/NNR.0000000000000038.

Richardson, A., Ganz, O. & Vallone, D. (2014a). Tobacco on the Web: Surveillance and Characterisation of Online Tobacco and E-cigarette Advertising. *Tobacco Control.* http://doi.org/10.1136/tobaccocontrol-2013-051246.

Richardson, A., Ganz, O., Pearson, J., Celcis, N., Vallone, D. & Villanti, A.C. (2014b). How the Industry is Marketing Menthol Cigarettes: The Audience, the Message and the Medium. *Tobacco Control.* http://doi.org/10.1136/tobaccocontrol-2014-051657.

Richardson, A., Ganz, O., Stalgaitis, C., Abrams, D. & Vallone, D. (2014c). Noncombustible Tobacco Product Advertising: How Companies Are Selling the New Face of Tobacco. *Nicotine & Tobacco Research: Official Journal of the Society for Research on Nicotine and Tobacco, 16*(5), 606–614. http://doi.org/10.1093/ntr/ntt200.

R.J. Reynolds Tobacco Company. (1986). *Winston "Real People" Campaign* (Bates no. 506749165/9169.). Retrieved September 18, 2014 from http://legacy.library.ucsf.edu/tid/irf28c00/pdf;jsessionid=7CAB4725535A8578963F86ACEA18A882.tobacco04.

Saffer, H. & Chaloupka, F. (2000). The Effect of Tobacco Advertising Bans on Tobacco Consumption. *Journal of Health Economics, 19*(6), 1117–1137.

Salgado-García, F.I., Cooper, T.V. & Taylor, T. (2013). Craving Effect of Smoking Cues in Smoking and Antismoking Stimuli in Light Smokers. *Addictive Behaviors, 38*(10), 2492–2499. http://doi.org/10.1016/j.addbeh.2013.04.008.

Sargent, J.D., Dalton, M., Beach, M., Bernhardt, A., Heatherton, T. & Stevens, M. (2000). Effect of Cigarette Promotions on Smoking Uptake among Adolescents. *Preventive Medicine, 30*(4), 320–327. http://doi.org/10.1006/pmed.1999.0629.

Seidenberg, A.B., Caughey, R.W., Rees, V.W. & Connolly, G.N. (2010). Storefront Cigarette Advertising Differs by Community Demographic Profile. *American Journal of Health Promotion: AJHP, 24*(6), e26–e31. http://doi.org/10.4278/ajhp.090618-QUAN-196.

Shibuya, K. (2003). WHO Framework Convention on Tobacco Control: Development of an Evidence Based Global Public Health Treaty. *BMJ, 327*(7407), 154–157. http://doi.org/10.1136/bmj.327.7407.154.

Sidani, J.E., Shensa, A., Barnett, T.E., Cook, R.L. & Primack, B.A. (2014). Knowledge, Attitudes, and Normative Beliefs as Predictors of Hookah Smoking Initiation: A Longitudinal Study of University Students. *Nicotine & Tobacco Research: Official Journal of the Society for Research on Nicotine and Tobacco, 16*(6), 647–654. http://doi.org/10.1093/ntr/ntt201.

Stanford School of Medicine. (n.d.a). Comparisons: Cigs vs. eCigs. Retrieved September 17, 2014 from http://tobacco.stanford.edu/tobacco_main/subtheme.php?token=fm_tn_mt035.php.

Stanford School of Medicine. (n.d.b). Fresh, Pure, Natural. Retrieved September 17, 2014 from http://tobacco.stanford.edu/tobacco_main/images.php?token2=fm_st125.php&token1=fm_img3612.php&theme_file=fm_mt010.php&theme_name=Fresh,%20Pure,%20Natural%20&%20Toasted&subtheme_name=No%20Additives.

Stanford School of Medicine. (n.d.c). Reassuring Brand Names. Retrieved September 17, 2014 from http://tobacco.stanford.edu/tobacco_main/images.php?token2=fm_st107.php&token1=fm_img3290.php&theme_file=fm_mt008.php&theme_name=Reassuring%20Brand%20Names&subtheme_name=True.

Stanford School of Medicine. (n.d.d). Targeting Women. Retrieved September 17, 2014 from http://tobacco.stanford.edu/tobacco_main/subtheme.php?token=fm_mt012.php.

107

Stoddard, J.L., Johnson, C.A., Sussman, S., Dent, C. & Boley-Cruz, T. (1998). Tailoring Outdoor Tobacco Advertising to Minorities in Los Angeles County. *Journal of Health Communication, 3*(2), 137–146. http://doi.org/10.1080/108107398127427.

Sung, Y. & Hennink-Kaminski, H.J. (2008). The Master Settlement Agreement and Visual Imagery of Cigarette Advertising in Two Popular Youth Magazines. *Journalism & Mass Communication Quarterly, 85*(2), 331–352. http://doi.org/10.1177/107769900808500207.

Text of Corrective Statements. (n.d.). Campaign for Tobacco-Free Kids. Retrieved September 24, 2014 from www.tobaccofreekids.org/content/what_we_do/industry_watch/doj/corrective_statements/Text%20of%20corrective%20statements%20Jan%202014.pdf.

Timberlake, D.S., Pechmann, C., Tran, S.Y. & Au, V. (2011). A Content Analysis of Camel Snus Advertisements in Print Media. *Nicotine & Tobacco Research: Official Journal of the Society for Research on Nicotine and Tobacco, 13*(6), 431–439. http://doi.org/10.1093/ntr/ntr020.

Troutman Sanders Tobacco Practice. (n.d.). Federal Government and Major Tobacco Companies Agree on Corrective Statements. Retrieved September 24, 2014 from www.tobaccolawblog.com/2014/06/federal-government-and-major-tobacco-companies-agree-on-corrective-statements/.

Turco, R.M. (1997). Effects of Exposure to Cigarette Advertisements on Adolescents' Attitudes Toward Smoking. *Journal of Applied Social Psychology, 27*(13), 1115–1130.

Vollstädt-Klein, S., Kobiella, A., Bühler, M., Graf, C., Fehr, C., Mann, K. & Smolka, M.N. (2011). Severity of Dependence Modulates Smokers' Neuronal Cue Reactivity and Cigarette Craving Elicited by Tobacco Advertisement. *Addiction Biology, 16*(1), 166–175. http://doi.org/10.1111/j.1369-1600.2010.00207.x.

Voorhees, C.C., Ye, C., Carter-Pokras, O., MacPherson, L., Kanamori, M., Zhang, G. & Fiedler, R. (2011). Peers, Tobacco Advertising, and Secondhand Smoke Exposure Influences Smoking Initiation in Diverse Adolescents. *American Journal of Health Promotion: AJHP, 25*(3), e1–e11. http://doi.org/10.4278/ajhp.090604-QUAN-180.

Wakefield, M.A., Spittal, M.J., Yong, H-H., Durkin, S.J. & Borland, R. (2011). Effects of Mass Media Campaign Exposure Intensity and Durability on Quit Attempts in a Population-based Cohort Study. *Health Education Research, 26*(6), 988–997. http://doi.org/10.1093/her/cyr054.

Wakefield, M.A., Bowe, S.J., Durkin, S.J., Yong, H-H., Spittal, M.J., Simpson, J.A. & Borland, R. (2013). Does Tobacco-control Mass Media Campaign Exposure Prevent Relapse among Recent Quitters? *Nicotine & Tobacco Research: Official Journal of the Society for Research on Nicotine and Tobacco, 15*(2), 385–392. http://doi.org/10.1093/ntr/nts134.

Warner, K.E. (1985). Tobacco Industry Response to Public Health Concern: A Content Analysis of Cigarette Ads. *Health Education Quarterly, 12*(2), 115–127.

Wellman, R.J., Sugarman, D.B., DiFranza, J.R. & Winickoff, J.P. (2006). The Extent to Which Tobacco Marketing and Tobacco Use in Films Contribute to Children's Use of Tobacco: A Meta-analysis. *Archives of Pediatrics & Adolescent Medicine, 160*(12), 1285–1296. http://doi.org/10.1001/archpedi.160.12.1285.

World Health Organization. (2013). WHO Report on the Global Tobacco Epidemic, 2013: Enforcing Bans on Tobacco Advertising, Promotion and Sponsorship. Retrieved September 25, 2014 from www.who.int/tobacco/global_report/en/.

Youth Tobacco Prevention. (n.d.). Retrieved September 11, 2014 from http://reynoldsamerican.com/youth-tobacco-prevention.cfm.

Zhu, S.-H., Sun, J.Y., Bonnevie, E., Cummins, S.E., Gamst, A., Yin, L. & Lee, M. (2014). Four Hundred and Sixty Brands of E-cigarettes and Counting: Implications for Product Regulation. *Tobacco Control*, *23*(Suppl. 3), iii3–iii9. http://doi. org/10.1136/tobaccocontrol-2014-051670.

CHAPTER 4

PREDICTABLE NEGATIVE EFFECTS: MARKETING ALCOHOL MISUSE AND ABUSE

Fleetwood Mac's song "Landslide" plays in the background as a young farmer looks through the barred top of a stall door, admiring the newborn Clydesdale lying in wood shavings on the floor. The song continues to play as we watch the young farmer bottle-feeding the foal, leading the young horse, being playfully nudged by the yearling, playing with the young gelding in a paddock, sleeping in the stall until the Clydesdale nudges him awake. We see the horse racing along the fence line as his owner drives his pick-up on the other side, then the farmer riding in a cart pulled by the Clydesdale. As Stevie Nicks sings, "Well, I've been afraid of changes 'cause I've built my life around you," we see the horse being led into a horse trailer. As it drives away, the farmer waving, we see the Budweiser logo on the back. Looking wistful, the farmer loops the lead rope in his hands.

Three years later, according to the text on the screen, we see the same young farmer reading a newspaper, a Budweiser bottle on the table in front of him. The camera angle switches so that we can see the story he has been reading: "Budweiser Clydesdales Coming to Chicago." We see him driving into the city, squeezing through the crowd at a parade to catch a glimpse of the Budweiser wagon. He spots and recognizes one of the lead horses. He watches it walk past, but it doesn't look at him. He looks disappointed as he turns and heads back to his truck.

And then we see the Clydesdale's harness being removed. Immediately, it turns and looks down the street to where the farmer is walking away. The young farmer gets into his truck, still looking a little sad. He glances in his side mirror to see the horse cantering around the corner and down the now-empty street toward him. The man gets out of his truck and jogs toward the horse, his arms outstretched to calm the runaway. As the horse nears, it slows, then stops. The farmer wraps his arms around the Clydesdale's neck and lays his face against its shoulder, smiling.

So what exactly does this (somewhat exaggerated) story of the bond between a horse and his trainer have to do with beer? Perhaps not much, other than the fact that the huge draft horses have been an iconic symbol of the Budweiser brand since 1933, when Anheuser-Busch arranged to have a six-horse Clydesdale hitch pulling a beer wagon through New York City during an event celebrating the end of Prohibition ("Budweiser Clydesdales," n.d.). But the ad certainly did not represent wasted money for Anheuser-Busch. Within 24 hours of its first showing during the 2013 Super Bowl, the "Brotherhood" ad had become the most shared of that year's Super Bowl commercials. Within six days, it was rated the third most shared Super Bowl commercial of all time, with 1.8 million shares and 6.5 million views. The reason, analysts said, was that while it may say little about beer, the ad produces strong positive emotions in viewers (Sanburn, 2013). In addition to sharing the ad, consumers remembered it and took action, using the company's Twitter hashtag #clydesdales to participate in a contest to name a Clydesdale foal (Vozza, 2013). Consumers rated it the most effective of all the Super Bowl 2013 ads, according to the marketing analysis company Ace Metrics ("Budweiser Produces," 2013).

Is there anything *wrong* with a beer commercial producing strong, positive emotions? Some research suggests that moderate consumption of alcohol – including beer – is linked to lower rates of cardiovascular disease. Beer's anti-oxidant content is equivalent to that of wine, and beer contains more protein and Vitamin B. ("Moderate" consumption means one drink per day for women, two for men.) Therefore, Denke argues that doctors "should be aware of the growing evidence supporting the nutritional and health benefits of moderate consumption" of beer (2000, p. 320). In addition, beer is the primary source of human exposure to the flavonoid xanthohumol, described in laboratory studies as a broad-spectrum cancer preventative, and a related compound, 8-prenylnaringenin, which is "the most potent phytoestrogen known to date" (Stevens & Page, 2004, p. 1317), and could be useful in cancer prevention and treatment of menopausal "hot flashes" and osteoporosis.

But beer is also the type of alcoholic beverage that is most strongly associated with binge drinking. Among adult bingers who completed questionnaires related to binge drinking in the Behavioral Risk Factor Surveillance System surveys from 2003 and 2004, nearly three-quarters drank beer either exclusively or predominantly; those who drank beer at least sometimes represented eight of every ten binge-drinking adults. The analysis revealed that beer made up two-thirds (67.1%) of the drinks consumed by bingers. In addition, beer accounted for the majority of drinks consumed by those who engaged in the riskiest activities. Among those who binged at least three times a month, 70.7 percent of their drinks were beer. Beer accounted for seven of every ten drinks consumed by those who had eight or more drinks per binge episode and more than two-thirds of all drinks for those who drank and drove (Naimi et al., 2007).

Unlike tobacco, alcohol consumption does seem to have some potential health benefits when used in moderation. However, the Centers for Disease Control classifies excessive alcohol consumption as the third or fourth leading preventable cause of death in the United States, estimating that excessive drinking caused one in every ten deaths among adults of working age from 2006 through 2010. During that period, an average of 87,798 individuals died per year as a result of excessive alcohol use (Stahre et al., 2014). Perhaps even more shocking, however, is that 5,000 alcohol-related deaths occur each year among people younger than age 21 – individuals who, in the United States, are not legally allowed to drink alcohol (National Institute on Alcohol Abuse and Alcoholism, n.d.b).

In this chapter, the focus is on how advertising alcoholic beverages may contribute to these grim statistics and to the non-fatal harms associated with alcohol consumption. Unlike tobacco companies, alcohol manufacturers have a reasonable claim that promotion of their product does not necessarily lead to harm because, as noted above, consumption of small or moderate amounts of alcohol can be benign or even beneficial to health; thus, alcohol advertising does not fall as squarely into the "intended negative effects" category as does tobacco advertising.

Nonetheless, there *is* evidence that alcohol advertising encourages young people, including those legally too young to drink, to consume alcohol, and the research also suggests that young drinkers are more likely to engage in binge or excessive drinking compared to those who are older. Thus, while alcohol advertising may not inherently cause negative health effects to the extent that such ads promote under-age and excessive drinking, they may be regarded as having easily predictable negative effects. Some would even argue that by using advertising approaches that encourage under-age and/or excessive alcohol consumption, alcohol manufacturers knowingly and perhaps even inevitably contribute to the health problems that inappropriate alcohol consumption can cause (Smith, 2011). This is especially true given that alcohol manufacturers' advertising practices do not comply with their own voluntary restrictions on advertising placement, so that "youth are disproportionately exposed to messages about alcohol in popular media outlets" (Centers for Disease Control and Prevention, 2011, para. 19).

EXCESSIVE ALCOHOL CONSUMPTION

According to a Gallup Poll conducted in July 2013, 60 percent of American adults aged 18 and older drink alcoholic beverages at least occasionally, which is fairly consistent with the historical average of 63 percent who drink alcohol. Approximately equal percentages prefer beer (36%) or wine (35%), while 23 percent prefer to drink whiskey, vodka or some other "hard" liquor. Americans aged 50 or older prefer wine over beer, and the percentage of 18- to 29-year-olds who prefer beer has dropped from 71 percent in 1992 to 1994 to 41 percent in 2013; for those in the middle age range, the decline in preference for beer has been smaller (-5%) and accompanied by an uptick in preference for liquor (+7%). On average, people who drink report consuming about four drinks each week (Jones, 2013).

In the same Gallup survey, 21 percent of drinkers admitted that they sometimes drink to excess, consistent with averages ranging from 17 percent to 25 percent in the past decade. Nearly one-third (29%) say their family has experienced problems related to alcohol consumption (Jones, 2013). In 2009, the most recent year for which CDC data are available, 5.1 percent of the total U.S. population engaged in "heavy" drinking, defined as consuming more than two drinks per day for men and more than one drink per day for women, and 15.7 percent of the population engaged in binge drinking (CDC, 2014). Binge drinkers, who are most likely to be male, white and 18 to 34 years old, down eight drinks per bingeing episode, accounting for more than half of all alcohol

113

consumed by U.S. adults (Office of Juvenile Justice and Delinquency Prevention, 2005). Somewhat surprisingly, most binge drinkers are *not* alcoholics (Centers for Disease Control and Prevention, 2014a).

Binge drinking is particularly problematic among those who are legally too young to drink alcohol at all. Drinking alcohol is less frequent for under-age individuals than for adults, but when young people do drink, they consume greater quantities; on average, under-age drinkers consume five drinks per drinking occasion, meaning that binge drinking is very common (National Institute on Alcohol Abuse and Alcoholism, n.d.b). Binge drinking among under-age youth has been declining more or less steadily since its peak in 1979, when more than 40 percent of twelfth-graders reported binging (Johnston et al., 2013). Nonetheless in 2012, 23.7 percent of high school seniors participating in the Monitoring the Future survey reported having binged at least once during the preceding two weeks; 7.7 percent reported having binged three or more times in the previous two weeks (Bachman et al., 2014).

Excessive alcohol use tends to begin in adolescence, but it continues through the young adult years. According to the CDC, both the prevalence and intensity of binge drinking are highest among 18- to 24-year-olds and 25- to 34-year-olds; in 2010, CDC data showed that 28.2 percent and 27.9 percent of people in these age groups, respectively, reported binge drinking, with an average frequency of 5.5 times per month. The younger group (18–24) reported consuming, on average, 9.3 drinks per binge episode; among those aged 25 to 34, the average was 8.4 drinks per occasion (Centers for Disease Control and Prevention, 2012).

Alcohol use also can be a problem among those at the other end of the age spectrum. Researchers have found that 14.5 percent of adults aged 65 and older who consume alcohol exceed the recommended limits of no more than seven drinks per week and no more than three per day. However, when the individuals' health status was taken into account, more than half engaged in drinking patterns considered at least "hazardous," and more than one-third (37.4%) reported drinking patterns considered "harmful," given their other health risks (Wilson et al., 2014). A 20-year study of older adult drinkers showed a decline in the percentages who consumed three or more drinks per day or 14 or more drinks per week, from 26.1 percent of women and 49.2 percent of men at age 55 to 65 to 11.8 percent of women and 31.8 percent of men at age 75 to 85. Still, the results showed that nearly one-third of men and more than one in every ten women who drank any alcohol during late middle age drank excessively, even in their seventies and eighties (Moos et al., 2010).

Regardless of one's age, excessive drinking has very negative health effects. According to the CDC, excessive alcohol use causes 79,000 deaths annually in the United States. On average, every alcohol-related death results in 30 years of lost life, and when this lost productivity is added to the costs of health care and criminal justice services attributable to excessive alcohol use, the total averages $185 billion annually. The negative effects of excessive alcohol use include 32 deaths per day in automobile crashes involving someone driving drunk or impaired; in addition, about two-thirds of all instances of intimate partner violence involve alcohol use (Centers for Disease Control and Prevention, 2011).

Because the body's ability to process alcohol can decline as people age, older adults may be affected by alcohol more quickly, putting them at greater risk for alcohol-related accidents, including car crashes and other injuries. In addition, because older adults are more likely to be taking prescription or non-prescription drugs, they are more vulnerable to negative drug–alcohol interactions; dangerous interactions can occur when alcohol is mixed with the use of painkillers, including those available over the counter, cold or allergy remedies or cough syrup, sleeping pills and anti-depressants or anti-anxiety drugs (National Institute on Alcohol Abuse and Alcoholism, n.d.a).

Another practice that can make alcohol consumption particularly risky is drinking alcohol in combination with high caffeine or "energy" drinks, such as Red Bull or Monster. These "energy" drinks contain caffeine, along with other stimulants and sugars. They have no effect on the body's metabolism of alcohol but can make the user *feel* less intoxicated. Research shows that individuals who consume alcohol mixed with energy drinks are more likely to binge drink, drive while intoxicated, ride with someone who is drunk, engage in risky sexual behavior and develop alcohol dependence (Marczinski & Fillmore, 2014).

For both men and women, alcohol intoxication is associated with a higher risk of suicide, especially through violent means such as a self-inflicted gunshot, hanging or falling (Kaplan et al., 2013). In addition, heavy drinking increases women's risk of being sexually assaulted and men's likelihood of engaging in sexual assault (Abbey, 2002; Abbey et al., 2004; Benson et al., 2007; Marx et al., 1999), in part due to beliefs among both men and women that drinking increases sexual arousal and willingness to have sex (Davis, 2010; Palmer et al., 2010; Pumphrey-Gordon & Gross, 2007).

The association of drinking with sexual arousal is ironic, given that high alcohol consumption can reduce men's ability to achieve an erection (George et al, 2006). Excessive drinking also reduces testosterone levels in the blood and can impair testicular function and the production of hormones critical to reproduction (Emanuele & Emanuele, 2001). Men who drink to excess also have increased risks of developing cancer of the mouth, throat, esophagus, liver and colon (Centers for Disease Control and Prevention, 2014d). Heavy drinking is also associated with a higher risk of chronic diseases such as cirrhosis of the liver, pancreatitis, high blood pressure, and, of course, alcoholism (Centers for Disease Control and Prevention, 2014c).

Women also face negative reproductive consequences for excessive drinking, including a greater risk of unprotected sex, potentially leading to sexually transmitted infections and/or unintended pregnancies. In addition, excessive drinking is associated with higher risks of infertility, miscarriage or stillbirth and giving birth prematurely. Any level of drinking during pregnancy – let alone excessive drinking – puts a woman's baby at risk of fetal alcohol spectrum disorder (FASD), a condition characterized by symptoms such as poor coordination, hyperactivity, difficulty with attention and memory, learning disabilities (especially for math), poor reasoning and judgment, and problems with vision, hearing, cardiac and kidney functions and bone development ("Facts About FASDs," 2014).

Like men, women who drink excessively have a higher risk of developing cancers of the colon, liver, mouth, throat, larynx and esophagus; in addition, excessive drinking increases women's risk of breast cancer. Women are more likely than men to suffer memory loss and brain shrinkage due to alcohol use, and these effects occur after shorter periods of excessive drinking among women compared to men. Excessive alcohol use, even at lower drinking levels, is also more likely to cause damage to the heart muscle in women than in men (Centers for Disease Control and Prevention, 2014b, 2014c).

RISK FACTORS FOR EXCESSIVE DRINKING

Although excessive drinking is a problem for males and females of every ethnic group, nearly all age groups and at every level of socioeconomic status, alcohol abuse is more common among certain types of people. Males are more likely to drink excessively than are females, and whites are more likely to abuse alcohol than non-whites, beginning in adolescence (Centers for Disease Control and Prevention, 2011; Swendsen et al., 2012). Individuals living in urban and rural areas are more likely to drink to excess than are suburban dwellers, except in the South, where those living in rural areas were *least* likely to exceed recommended daily alcohol limits (Borders & Booth, 2007).

Alcohol use typically begins during adolescence. As noted earlier, alcohol use among students in middle and high school has declined since the mid- to late 1970s, but under-age drinking is still common; according to the 2011 Monitoring the Future study, half of high school sophomores and nearly two-thirds of high school seniors said they had drunk alcohol during the previous month. This early use of alcohol is important because early drinking is a predictor of adult alcohol abuse, especially among teens who drink while under-age for social and recreational reasons (e.g., to have a good time with friends, to relieve boredom), to cope with negative emotions (e.g., to escape problems or due to anger and frustration) or to increase the effects of other drugs (Patrick et al., 2011).

Figure 4.1: Drinking Alcohol is Common among Teenagers
(Getty Images Creative 84491791)

Several parental behaviors are associated with greater alcohol use among adolescents. The frequency of parents' drinking has been shown to predict teen alcohol use; however, some research suggests that even among parents who drink excessively, good family management practices (careful monitoring of children's behavior, consistent rewards for positive behavior, and appropriate and consistent punishment for unwanted behavior) reduce the effect of parental drinking. In addition, refraining from involving children in the parents' alcohol use (e.g., not having children get or pour drinks for the parent) mitigates the effect of parental drinking on teen alcohol use (Peterson et al., 1994).

Other researchers have found that, compared to parental alcohol use, sibling and peer alcohol use are stronger predictors of adolescent drinking (Allen et al. 2003; Windle, 2000). For instance, Mrug and McKay (2013) found that, not surprisingly, parents disapproved of adolescents drinking more than peers did, and this gap widened as teens grew older; in addition, peer disapproval had a greater impact on teens' drinking behavior than did parents' disapproval. In addition, a meta-analysis by Allen et al. (2003) revealed that the relative size of parental and peer influence changed with increases in age; interestingly, this analysis showed that parents' influence over teen alcohol use increased with age, while the influence of peers remained fairly stable.

Peer influence becomes even more important during late adolescence and early adulthood when adolescents leave home and start college or careers, where they are likely to be separated geographically from their parents. This influence is especially important, given that the incidence of alcohol abuse is highest among 18- to 29-year-olds (Grant et al., 2004). Among individuals who had ever been alcohol dependent, 15 percent were diagnosable before age 18, but two-thirds were diagnosable by age 25 (Hingson et al., 2006). Among college students, one study showed that students who had a close network of friends who drank more heavily were ten times as likely to engage in hazardous drinking behavior compared to students with low-risk friend networks (Mason et al., 2014). In another study comparing the influence of perceived drinking norms among college students and non-college age peers, researchers found that descriptive norms – perceptions of the number of drinks their same-gendered social group members consumed in a typical week – had a significantly greater effect on college students' drinking than for non-college respondents (Quinn & Fromme, 2011).

ALCOHOL ADVERTISING REGULATION

Simply put, alcohol advertising does affect alcohol consumption, at least among adolescents (Anderson et al., 2009); surprisingly little research has examined the impact of alcohol ads on adult consumption. Before discussing the research on the impact of alcohol advertising, however, it makes sense to establish the context in which that advertising occurs. In the United States, no federal regulations prohibit or limit alcohol advertising. Alcoholic beverage containers are required to include a warning label, but no such warnings are required in alcohol marketing content. The Federal Alcohol Administration Act (FAAA), passed soon after the repeal of Prohibition in the United States, gives the federal government some limited control over alcohol advertising; enforcement of the FAAA is primarily the responsibility of the Alcohol and Tobacco Tax and Trade Bureau (TTB), although the Federal Trade Commission (FTC), which regulates advertising for other products, also has authority over alcohol marketing.

The alcohol industry does impose self-regulatory standards regarding alcohol advertising content and placement, primarily through three trade associations: the Distilled Spirits Council of the United States (DISCUS), the Beer Institute (BI) and the Wine Institute (WI). Each of these organizations has adopted codes intended to "reduce the likelihood that alcohol advertising will, by its content or placement, target consumers below the legal drinking age" (FTC, 2014, p. 1).

For members of all three trade associations, these codes include requiring manufacturers to advertise only in venues for which 71.6 percent or more of the audience is age 21 or older; this very specific percentage was selected because 2010 census data showed that 71.6 percent of the U.S. population is of legal drinking age. The Beer Institute and DISCUS codes also tell members what sorts of demographic data they should consider before placing ads in a particular advertising outlet and how they should audit exposure to the ads after they run (FTC, 2014).

FTC "Special Orders," issued periodically, require the industry associations and individual alcohol companies to answer questions about how they ensure compliance with these guidelines. For the most recent FTC report, companies were required to collect and report a variety of information, including audience demographic characteristics, for each ad placed in a newspaper, magazine, on television or radio or online between January 1 and June 30, 2011. The FTC also assessed the codes' provisions for how alcohol industry media buyers should assess the audience demographics for a potential ad placement before the purchase is made (FTC, 2014).

For January to June 2011, the FTC's assessment concluded that about 93.1 percent of all alcohol industry ads were placed in channels for which at least 70 percent of the audience was age 21 or older. The FTC also assessed alcohol ads according to the percentage of overall impressions among people aged 21 or older; in other words, if each time a person sees a particular ad is considered one impression, what percentage of those impressions occurred among people of legal drinking age? For early 2011, the FTC calculated that percentage at 97.3 percent. Ultimately, the FTC concluded that alcohol manufacturers have "substantially improved in self-regulation" since the FTC's initial assessment in 1999, when the Commission review revealed poor industry compliance with its own much less stringent placement standards (FTC, 2014, p. 34).

While that glowing report may suggest that alcohol manufacturers are doing everything they can to avoid targeting youth, some critics argue that the steps the industry has taken "fall far short of recommendations from the National Academy of Sciences, state attorneys general, and other scientific and advocacy organizations" (Center on Alcohol Marketing and Youth, 2012a, para. 3). In its 2012 report on state laws regulating alcohol marketing, CAMY noted that although adolescents' exposure to alcohol advertising in magazines had declined substantially since 2002, exposure via television advertising grew significantly, so that between 2001 and 2009, TV alcohol ad exposure for those younger than age 21 increased more rapidly than exposure for those of legal drinking age (Center on Alcohol Marketing and Youth, 2012b).

In some cases, individual states have enacted legislation that allows further control of alcohol advertising. As of 2010, 26 states had adopted regulations that (1) prohibit false advertising; (2) prohibit misleading advertising, which can include advertising that creates a false impression, even if the specific information is not false, and/or (3) applies to all alcohol advertising in the state; 11 states had enacted all three of these provisions. Some states had also adopted regulations prohibiting the "targeting" of minors in alcohol advertising, but CAMY noted that these laws are often ineffective because they include language requiring proof that the advertiser intended to encourage people younger than age 21 to buy alcohol or prohibit only specific child-oriented content, like Santa Claus or the Easter Bunny (Center on Alcohol Marketing and Youth, 2012b).

Some states give their Alcoholic Beverage Control agencies authority to set limits on television and radio alcohol advertising originating within the state (e.g., from local TV and radio stations), and some states limit either the content or the placement of outdoor advertising (billboards) for alcohol. Additional state-level marketing regulations include limiting the use of alcohol advertising in the windows of retail stores, such as liquor stores, prohibiting any alcohol advertising on college campuses, restricting alcohol company sponsorship of civic events held on public property or where a substantial percentage of participants will be younger than age 21, and limiting alcohol manufacturer or retailer give-aways or contests (Center on Alcohol Marketing and Youth, 2012b).

Exposure to Alcohol Advertising

Despite industry self-regulation and state legislation, youth younger than 21 years old continue to have high rates of exposure to alcohol advertising; this is perhaps not surprising, considering the amount of money the alcohol industry spends on ads. In 2013, the beer, wine and liquor industry collectively spent more than $2 billion for advertising in all media. Cable TV received the greatest share of that spending, accounting for $698 million, while approximately $507 million went to broadcast TV advertising, $255 million to magazine advertising and more than $55 million to Internet advertising ("Alcohol Industry," 2014).

Spending for alcohol advertising has been growing. For instance, in 2012, beer manufacturers spent more than $1 billion on television ads alone. Distilled spirits makers' TV ad expenditures increased more than $100 million between 2009 and 2012, from $144 million to more than $243 million; for makers of bourbon, vodka and other hard liquors, the money has gone primarily into cable TV advertising (Steinberg, 2013).

As a result, the likelihood of adolescents seeing or hearing alcohol companies' advertising messages remains high, especially on television. Youth exposure to alcohol advertising on television actually increased dramatically between 2001 and 2009. A CAMY analysis revealed that youth exposure increased 71 percent between 2001 and 2009. In 2001, 90 percent of 12- to 20-year-olds saw TV ads for alcohol, at an average rate of 217 ads per youth; by 2009, 91 percent of youth were seeing an average of 366 alcohol ads on TV. The change could be attributed primarily to increased exposure to beer/ale and hard liquor ads. In 2001, 89 percent of 12- to 20-year-olds were exposed to an average of 181.5 beer/ale ads, but hard liquor ads reached only 58 percent of youth, at a rate of about 5.6 ads for the year. By 2009, 90 percent of youth saw beer/ale ads, at an average rate of 238 per person, and hard liquor ads were reaching 87 percent of youth, with an average of 113.5 exposures per person (Center on Alcohol Marketing and Youth, 2010b).

A more recent CAMY analysis of youth exposure to alcohol ads in 25 local television markets, using Nielsen data from 2010, showed that of 196,494 alcohol ads that ran in these TV markets, nearly a quarter (23.7%) aired during programs for which more than 30 percent of the audience was under-age, thereby violating the alcohol industry's self-imposed standard. The analysis also estimated the percentage of ads that would violate a more stringent standard, proposed in 2003 by the National Research Council/Institute of Medicine, which would prohibit alcohol advertising during programs for which more than 15 percent of the audience was under-age. Using this stricter standard, more than one-third of all ads in these 25 markets (35.4%) ran during programs exceeding the 15 percent threshold for youth viewership (Centers for Disease Control and Prevention, 2013).

Although adolescents' exposure to magazine alcohol ads has declined, these ads continue to be a significant source of youth contact with alcohol-promotion messages. Between 2001 and 2008, youth exposure to magazine ads for alcohol dropped by 48 percent, compared to declines of 29 percent for all adults aged 21 and older and 31 percent for 21- to 34-year-olds (Center on Alcohol Marketing and Youth, 2010a). However, a comparison of national magazine advertising exposure per capita in 2008 showed that 12- to 20-year-olds still had substantially greater exposure to beer/ale and "alcopops" (highly sweetened liquor-based drinks marketed primarily to young people) than did those aged 21 and older; ads for hard liquor (whiskey, vodka, etc.) had only slightly greater exposure per capita among those aged 21 and older, compared to the younger group. Only in the case of wine ads did those of legal drinking age have substantially greater exposure per capita than did 12- to 20-year-olds (Center on Alcohol Marketing and Youth, 2010a).

Targeting Under-age Drinkers

Of course, the fact that teens are exposed to alcohol advertising, in itself, does not mean that the alcohol industry is targeting under-age drinkers. After all, the types of magazines, websites, and broadcast or cable programming that appeal to young adults are fairly likely to appeal to those in the 16- to 20-year-old age group too, and under-age youth cannot be prevented from consuming content aimed at those who are legally old enough to consume alcohol.

Critics have argued, however, that both the content and placement of alcohol advertising often provide evidence that, in fact, alcohol manufacturers have chosen to create messages that will appeal to individuals younger than age 21 and to place them in media where under-age individuals are likely to see or hear them (Austin & Hust, 2005; Rhoades & Jernigan, 2013; Ross et al., 2014a; Smith & Geller, 2009). First, as noted in the preceding section, adolescents continue to be exposed to many alcohol ads every year, and their exposure to TV alcohol advertising has increased, even as the alcohol industry has, according to the FTC, adhered more closely to its voluntary standards for avoiding youth exposure to advertising. In addition, however, analysis of exposure data indicates that under-age youth are, in some cases, *more* likely than adults to be exposed to alcohol ads. For instance, a CAMY analysis of alcohol advertising in 2009 showed that more than one of every five alcohol ad placements (21.4%) reached a youth audience that was, in terms of percentage, larger than the percentage of youth in the population. In other words, youth aged two to 20 represent about 13 percent of the U.S. population. Thus, when ads are placed in TV programs for which youth account for 14 percent or more of the audience, this constitutes disproportionate youth exposure to the ads. CAMY notes that, in reality, more than half of the instances of overexposure came from shows in which youth comprised between 15 and 30 percent of the audience (Center on Alcohol Marketing and Youth, 2010b).

In a recent study, researchers attempted to explain why youth exposure to alcohol advertising has been increasing more rapidly than adult exposure, to establish whether evidence showed that the alcohol industry chooses advertising venues that have as much reach and frequency among youth (per capita) as among adults, and to determine whether alcohol manufacturers could develop different advertising strategies that would maintain the same levels of adult exposure but simultaneously reduce youth exposure. Using data on TV alcohol advertising from 2005 to 2011, they revealed that the increase in youth exposure could be attributed to increased spending for cable TV ads reaching 18- to 20-year-olds. The data showed that, on cable TV, alcohol ad exposure among 18- to 20-year-olds increased faster than among any other age group between 2005 and 2011. "Of particular note, exposure of viewers ages 18–20 (grew) faster than that of viewers ages 21–24, suggesting that this result was not incidental 'spillover' of advertising to young legal-age adults" (Ross et al., 2014a, p. 115).

During most of these years, cable TV ads for "alcopops," beer and hard liquor achieved essentially the same levels of exposure among 18- to 20-year-olds as they did among viewers aged 21 and older. Exposure to wine advertising, however, was generally significantly lower among 18- to 20-year-olds, compared to those in the older age groups. Further, the analysis demonstrated that different advertising strategies would have enabled alcohol manufacturers to maintain the same levels of advertising exposure among those aged 21 and older while significantly reducing exposure among those just younger than the legal drinking age (Ross et al., 2014a). Comparing their analysis to the standards a California appellate court had used to determine that R.J. Reynolds was targeting teenagers with tobacco advertising, the researchers concluded that "there is evidence of targeting of 18–20-years olds (*sic*) relative to 21–24-year olds with alcopops, beer, and spirits advertisers in each year from 2008 through 2011" (Ross et al., 2014a, p. 115).

Further evidence that alcohol companies may be deliberately marketing their products to under-age youth comes from the content of many alcohol ads. In a study of magazine and video ads between November 1999 and April 2000, Austin and Hust (2005) found that, compared to ads for non-alcoholic beverages, alcohol ads were more likely to stereotype women and often portrayed themes of romance, flirting and sex. However, many other features of the two types of ads were quite similar, which may "increase youths' receptivity to alcohol ads" (Austin & Hust, 2005, pp. 782–783). The research team's expert coders concluded that one of every six magazine ads and one of every 14 TV ads seemed designed to appeal to *under-age* drinkers, often using appeals that have been shown to be effective with teenagers (Austin & Hust, 2005).

A more recent study of magazine alcohol ads examined the content of ads appearing in youth-oriented magazines between 2003 and 2007. The research demonstrated that ads including content that violated alcohol industry voluntary guidelines were most likely to appear in magazines with the highest percentage of under-age youth in the audience, "suggesting that the industry is more likely to be 'edgy' in content when it is also being 'edgy' in terms of its placement practices" (Rhoades & Jernigan, 2013, p. 121). In addition, the brands most likely to include content that violated industry guidelines or included suggestions about addiction (e.g., showing consumption at inappropriate times, including references to excuses for drinking, etc.) were also most likely to be placed in magazines for which per capita youth exposure was as high or higher than per capita adult exposure (Rhoades & Jernigan, 2013).

On the other hand, an analysis of magazine ads published between 2008 and 2010 led another team of researchers to conclude that the ads, for the most part, were consistent with existing federal regulations and the industry's voluntary codes. Of the 1,795 ads analyzed, only 23 were coded as violating federal regulations, and 38 were deemed to violate industry standards. However, many ads included content likely to convey positive messages about alcohol use to naïve youth. For instance, ads often included associations between alcohol consumption and positive personality traits or lifestyles, such as a beer ads suggesting that an individual who consumed only four ounces of beer would be seen as a clown, whereas someone who consumed 25.4 ounces would be a secret agent. Many ads depicted sexualized situations or portrayed women in scanty clothes or being objectified, suggesting that consumption of the alcohol would be associated with sexual success. Some ads associated alcohol consumption, particularly of lower calorie beers, with weight loss, weight maintenance or healthy, active lifestyles (Clegg-Smith et al., 2014). While many of these themes would appeal to young adults, they are also likely to convey to under-age youth very positive – and misleading – messages about alcohol use.

Other Issues in Alcohol Advertising Content

Some problematic characteristics of alcohol advertising would remain problematic even if no under-age viewers ever saw the ads. In particular,

Figure 4.2: Ads Often Associate Beer with Sexual Success

as noted in the previous paragraph, alcohol advertising often associates the consumption of alcohol with sexual interaction and/or with behaviors that should not be undertaken in conjunction with alcohol consumption. The association of sex with beer consumption, for instance, has been called "virtually inseparable" (Chambers, 2006, p. 161), but sex and alcohol consumption are often connected in ads for other types of alcohol as well. Clegg-Smith and colleagues (2014) found that about 30 percent of the alcohol ads they examined included depictions of people. Of the ads that included people, 17 percent included depictions of sex or had sexual connotations. Sexual connotations were slightly less common in the magazine ads Rhoades and Jernigan (2013) examined; 8.26 percent of the ads included depictions showing sexism or objectification of women, and 12.47 percent depicted situations or language with sexual connotations. Sexism and sexual connotations appeared more often in beer and spirits ads than in those for wine or alcopops.

In an earlier study of magazine and TV alcohol ads, Austin and Hust (2005) found that when women appeared in magazine alcohol ads, the focus was on their sexual appeal; sex appeal was emphasized in 70 percent of magazine alcohol ads that included women, compared to 28 percent of non-alcohol beverage ads that depicted women. Women in video ads were more likely to be portrayed as product users (54%) than as sex objects (30%). Men were never shown as sex objects in video ads and in only 12 percent of the magazine ads. Another study, examining television beer commercials aired during the early 1990s, found that beer commercials are less likely to include women as characters but were far more likely to depict women, rather than men, in swimwear and to include female, rather than male, "body-shots" – those focused on the individual's chest, buttocks, legs or crotch. The authors note that the inclusion of these body-shots promotes the idea "that women are 'bodies' rather than 'somebodies' (personalities)" (Hall & Crum, 1994, p. 335).

Rhoades and Jernigan (2013) found that magazine alcohol ads were relatively unlikely to include messages or images promoting alcohol use in association with activities that could lead to injury (e.g., driving), encouraging overconsumption or normalizing alcohol addiction; however, these types of messages did exist. About 4 percent of the ads they coded violated industry guidelines by associating alcohol consumption with risky activities such as snorkeling, highlighting the alcohol content of the product, seeming to target under-age drinkers or including inappropriate sexual content. Just under 3 percent of ads were coded as promoting overconsumption, and fewer than 2 percent seemed to promote or normalize addiction and/or excuses for drinking, such as in a Stolichnaya vodka campaign that included the tagline, "Is there anything not worth drinking to?" Although instances of this kind of content were not common, they did exist, suggesting that alcohol manufacturers do not consistently avoid including problematic messages in their ads.

Austin and Hust's (2005) earlier study of magazine and video alcohol ads found a substantially greater prevalence of depictions of risky activities in video ads. Among the video ads they examined, 15 percent portrayed risky situations, including dangerous driving or hazardous work conditions. This study identified only 2 percent of magazine ads as portraying risky activities, suggesting that TV alcohol ads (which reach larger audiences) are more likely to include messages associating alcohol consumption with risky activities.

THE IMPACT OF ALCOHOL ADVERTISING

Perhaps the most important, and most troubling, of the effects of alcohol advertising is that exposure to these ads increases the likelihood that adolescents will begin drinking before they turn 21. Numerous individual studies and at least three systematic reviews of the literature have confirmed that exposure to alcohol advertising does, in fact, increase underage drinking. For instance, Hastings and colleagues' (2005) review of the literature noted that econometric studies often touted by the alcohol industry tend to show that advertising has limited effects, if any, on overall consumption of alcohol. On the other hand, Saffer and Dave's (2002) study of the impact of alcohol advertising bans in 20 countries demonstrated that such bans reduce overall alcohol consumption. Based on their review of research with young consumers, Hastings et al. concluded that "the more aware, familiar and appreciative young people are of alcohol advertising, the more likely they are to drink both now and in the future" (2005, p. 303).

Another study focused only on the impact of alcohol advertising and portrayals in media, as demonstrated in seven longitudinal studies that followed more than 13,000 youth aged ten to 26 years old. The researchers noted that the studies varied in their incorporation of potential confounding factors and did not account adequately for the effects of peer drinking or parental attitudes and drinking behavior; nonetheless, the review concluded that exposure to alcohol advertising is significantly related to subsequent drinking (Smith & Foxcroft, 2009). One especially important finding came from two studies that examined the impacts of advertising on both youth who were already drinkers and those who had not begun drinking alcohol. Both showed that alcohol advertising had significant effects on the initiation of drinking. In one, baseline drinkers' exposure to magazines that contained alcohol ads was positively associated with drinking frequency at follow-up (Ellickson et al., 2005). In the other study, researchers found a significant association between the number of alcohol ads participants remembered seeing and the number of drinks they consumed per month; for each additional alcohol ad recalled, drink consumption rose 1 percent among both young adults and under-age drinkers (Snyder et al., 2006).

Another review, also published in 2009 but incorporating studies published through September 2008, assessed the findings of 13 longitudinal studies linking exposure to alcohol advertising or marketing communication to subsequent drinking behaviors. The review, which included nine studies conducted in the United States, involved only studies that examined impacts on under-age drinkers, including several cited in the Smith and Foxcroft (2009) review. Of the 13 studies, all but one found evidence that adolescents' exposure to alcohol advertising and promotional materials increased the likelihood of drinking onset and the levels of alcohol consumption for those who were already drinkers (Anderson et al., 2009). The one study that did not show an impact of ad exposure on drinking behavior did demonstrate a link between exposure to outdoor alcohol advertising and intentions to drink in the next month (Pasch et al., 2007).

Since the most recent review was published, at least four more U.S. studies have linked exposure to alcohol advertising with alcohol consumption and its consequences among under-age youth. Ross and his colleagues (Ross et al., 2014b) investigated the association between exposure to brand-specific alcohol ads on TV and teenagers' consumption of those brands. Controlling for individual participant and brand-related variables, the data showed that teens who had had any exposure to advertising for a specific alcohol brand during the previous 12 months were three times as likely to have consumed that brand in the preceding month. Using exposure as a continuous variable, the researchers found that "the odds of consumption increased dramatically at lower levels of exposure and then reached a point where subsequent increases in exposure resulted in smaller increases in the odds of consumption" (Ross et al., 2014b, p. 2237).

The results of another study suggest that adolescents' self-control influences the impact alcohol advertising may have on them. For adolescents with low self-control, attention to and liking for alcohol and tobacco advertising were associated with a sharp and significant increase in willingness to use these substances; however, there was no significant relationship between attention to or attitudes about the ads and willingness to use alcohol or tobacco among those who scored high on self-control. The researchers argued that good self-control may disrupt the pathway between expectancies and substance use; alcohol ads still may create positive expectancies for alcohol use, but for teens with stronger self-control, those expectancies are less likely to lead to actual use (Wills et al., 2010).

A longitudinal study that tracked 3,890 students from seventh through tenth grades provided evidence that exposure to alcohol advertising not only increases the likelihood of under-age drinking but also contributes to adolescents' alcohol-related problems, including failure to get home-work done, getting into fights, neglecting their responsibilities, or causing someone shame or embarrassment. For the seventh-graders, level of alcohol ad exposure had the greatest effect among those who reported liking the ads. Among girls, seventh-grade exposure to alcohol ads had a direct effect on increased alcohol use, and, through alcohol use, an indi-rect effect on alcohol-related problems by the time they reached tenth grade. Among boys, the interaction between exposure to and liking of alcohol ads in seventh grade was significantly related to alcohol-related problems in tenth grade (Grenard et al., 2013).

Finally, Smith and Geller (2009) used traffic crash data from 2003 to compare the outcomes in states with and without state laws prohibiting any alcohol advertising that targets minors. The study focused on traffic crashes involving 15- to 20-year-old drivers who died in single-vehicle accidents, such as collisions with trees, road signs, etc. At the time of the study, 24 states and the District of Columbia had laws prohibiting alcohol advertising that targeted minors. These laws include restrictions on the placement of alcohol advertising (e.g., near schools and churches) and on the use of symbols, characters or events that are particularly rel-evant to children (such as toys or holidays); in addition, some laws pro-hibit advertising that "encourages" under-age drinking or "makes a special appeal" to minors. The analysis showed that those states had 32.9 percent fewer young drivers killed in alcohol-related, single-vehicle crashes per million youth in this age bracket, compared to states with no ban on alcohol advertising to minors; the relationship held even when controlling for factors such as roadway safety features, traffic con-ditions and the number of licensed drivers in the state. In addition, there was no significant difference in traffic fatalities the police had cate-gorized as being unrelated to alcohol use. Based on the study's results, the authors estimate that 400 fewer young people would die each year if all states enacted bans on advertising to minors, in addition to saving billions of dollars.

ADVERTISING EFFECTS AMONG LEGAL-AGE DRINKERS

While much concern about the impact of alcohol advertising has focused on under-age alcohol use, it is important to note that the negative impacts of excessive alcohol use are not confined to people younger than 21 years old. As noted earlier, the highest prevalence, frequency and intensity of binge drinking occurs among individuals 18 to 24 and 25 to 34 years old (Centers for Disease Control and Prevention, 2012). Much of the impact of alcohol advertising on young adults may actually stem from advertising encountered during adolescence, given that exposure to alcohol advertising encourages earlier initiation of drinking (Collins et al., 2007; Ellickson et al., 2005; Henriksen et al., 2008; Smith & Foxcroft, 2009), and earlier initiation is linked to a greater likelihood of alcohol abuse in young adulthood (DeWit et al., 2000; Gruber et al., 1996; Hawkins et al., 1997; Warner et al., 2007).

Relatively little U.S. research seems to have directly examined the impact of alcohol advertising on drinking patterns among adults aged 21 and older; in fact, in a recent article proposing a "new agenda" for alcohol marketing research, Meier (2011) argued that most marketing is, in fact, intended to influence current consumers, so more research is needed on how alcohol advertising affects individuals past the point of initiation, including during adulthood. An experiment in the Netherlands examined the drinking behaviors of young men who watched a movie that either did or did not include alcohol consumption and either alcohol ads or neutral ads. The data showed that the young men who saw alcohol ads consumed more alcoholic beverages during the movie, as did those who saw a movie in which the characters drank alcohol (Engels et al., 2009).

Two earlier studies in New Zealand also provided support for the link between alcohol advertising and adult alcohol consumption. One study of 1,012 randomly selected 18- to 29-year-olds found that one in four of the men said seeing alcohol ads on TV sometimes made them want to go get an alcoholic beverage to drink. More importantly, the study showed that individuals who reported liking the alcohol ads they saw on TV also had more positive beliefs about alcohol consumption, consumed greater quantities of alcohol, and were subsequently more likely to experience alcohol-related problems. The researchers used structural equation modeling to demonstrate that the reverse relationships were not significant – neither having positive beliefs about alcohol nor consuming more alcohol predicted favorable attitudes about the ads (Wyllie et al., 1998). The second study revealed that liking alcohol ads at age 18 was positively related to beer consumption at age 21, after controlling for beer consumption at age 18; liking alcohol advertising at age 18 was a better predictor of consumption at 21 than either consumption or brand allegiance at age 18. There was also a strong, positive relationship between the amount of beer consumed at age 21 and involvement in alcohol-related aggression. The authors concluded that "advertising may be reinforcing the consumption of high volumes of beer, which in turn are associated with alcohol-related aggression" (Casswell & Zhang, 1998, p. 1216).

In the United States, research has produced inconsistent findings about the links between young adults' exposure to alcohol advertising and their drinking behaviors. Some studies have shown no effect of alcohol advertising on young adults' alcohol consumption. In an experimental study, Koordeman and colleagues (2012) found that college students who saw alcohol ads while watching a television program consumed no more alcohol while watching the show than those who saw no alcohol ads, and Fleming and colleagues (2004) found that exposure to alcohol ads and positive expectancies about alcohol use were related to under-age students' intentions to drink; however, the relationship with alcohol ad exposure was not significant for 21- to 29-year-olds.

However, other researchers have found links between exposure to alcohol advertising and alcohol consumption. For instance, in an experimental study, McCarty and Ewing (1983) found that college students who watched alcohol ads after first drinking an alcoholic beverage consumed more alcohol and reached higher blood alcohol concentrations than did students who saw the ads first, then consumed an alcoholic drink. The authors concluded that hard liquor advertising may encourage those who have already had a drink or two to continue drinking.

In addition, Atkin and Block (1984) conducted research showing that exposure to hard liquor ads was associated with a greater likelihood of recent drinking of hard liquor and including hard liquor in one's typical drinking patterns. Exposure to beer advertising was also positively related to beer consumption, with those who were highly exposed to beer and wine advertising reporting consumption of twice as much beer as those who had low advertising exposure (30 vs. 15 beers over the previous month); those with high advertising exposure consumed about 5.7 beers per week, compared to 3.2 beers per week among those with low ad exposure. Based on their data, the authors state, it is clear that "advertising exerts an influence on the frequency and quantity of adult alcohol consumption," with advertising accounting for as much as 10 to 30 percent of overall alcohol consumption (Atkin & Block, 1984, p. 681). Moreover, the research showed that alcohol advertising exposure was positively related to excessive drinking. Individuals who had low alcohol ad exposure reported consuming about 2.9 drinks during a visit to a bar or a party, while those with high ad exposure consumed an average of 4.5 drinks in these situations, and one-third of those with high alcohol ad exposure said they consumed five or six drinks in a sitting at least once a week, compared to only 16 percent of those who had low alcohol ad exposure (Atkin & Block, 1984).

At least one recent study has documented effects of digital alcohol marketing on the drinking behaviors of U.S. college students. Hoffman and colleagues (2014) used online surveys to gather data about college students' use of alcohol marketing social media and their engagement in risky drinking behaviors. They found that the use of social media marketing applications for alcohol was significantly related to problem drinking and alcohol use frequency during the preceding 30 days; general social media use was unrelated to any alcohol consumption variables.

Another important consideration is the impact of local advertising for alcohol, as opposed to national-level brand advertising. Research examining the volume and impact of alcohol advertising and promotions around 119 U.S. college campuses showed that among off-premise alcohol outlets (e.g., liquor stores, convenience stores) surrounding the campuses, 22.7 percent had interior alcohol advertising outside the alcohol section of the outlet, and an additional 15 percent had alcohol ads covering all available interior ad space. In addition, 22.7 percent had moderate exterior alcohol advertising, and 18 percent had exterior alcohol advertising everywhere. Surveys of students from the nearby college campuses showed that binge-drinking rates were significantly and positively related to the extent of both interior and exterior alcohol advertising (Kuo et al., 2003).

Sexual Risk-taking and Sexual Violence

Alcohol consumption itself is a well-established predictor of involvement in risky sexual behavior, including unprotected sex and sexual violence (Cooper, 2002; Hingson et al., 2009; Nolen-Hoeksema, 2004). Thus, it is reasonable to argue that alcohol advertising is at least indirectly related to the likelihood of engaging in risky sex as well as to both sexual victimization and being the perpetrator of sexual assault. However, is there a more direct relationship?

Somewhat surprisingly, given the alcohol industry's often controversial use of sexual images and innuendo in its advertising, there appears to have been little published research specifically linking exposure to sexualized alcohol advertising with either male or female attitudes toward alcohol and sex. One early study did find that individuals who were heavily exposed to alcohol advertising were more likely, compared to less-exposed individuals, to say that "drinking alcohol improves one's chances of sexual success" (Atkin & Block, 1984, p. 693). In addition, researchers have found that college students associate alcohol consumption with a greater likelihood of sexual interaction (Morr & Mongeau, 2004) and that men who see ads in which women appear as sex objects subsequently report greater acceptance of rape-supportive attitudes (Lanis & Covell, 1995).

Such attitudes, unfortunately, are relatively common among college men. In one study, more than one-third of college men (35%) said their friends approve of getting a woman drunk in order to have sex, and one in five said they have a friend who had done so. More than one in every ten males in this study (12%) acknowledged using alcohol to persuade a woman to have sex, and 15 percent reported being sexually aggressive when they had been drinking (Carr & VanDeusen, 2004). Thus, if exposure to alcohol advertising increases alcohol consumption, if alcohol advertising often portrays women as sex objects and if sex object advertising promotes sexual aggression, it seems reasonable to conclude that men who are exposed to sexual objectification of women in alcohol advertising are more likely to connect alcohol use with sex and therefore more likely to be sexually coercive in drinking situations.

In addition, it is clear that alcohol consumption is strongly related to drinking and engaging in risky sexual behaviors, even when they are consensual. In a review of studies linking alcohol use to sexual behavior among adolescents and college students, Cooper (2002) found that consuming alcohol was consistently correlated not only with the decision to have sex but also with engaging in multiple types of risky sex, including having multiple casual partners; it was less strongly related to failure to use condoms. However, no studies seem to have investigated whether alcohol advertising directly influences either attitudes about sexual risk-taking or the behaviors themselves.

Promotion of Risky Behavior

As with sexual risk behavior, little research seems to have attempted to link exposure to alcohol advertising directly to acceptance of or engaging in risky behaviors, such as driving a car or engaging in sports activities while or after drinking. However, one early study did make these connections. The researchers found that those who are highly exposed to ads are more likely to drive after drinking, drink while riding, drink while sitting in a parked car, drive while intoxicated, and to feel that they can consume more alcohol without affecting their ability to drive (Atkin & Block, 1984, p. 692). Individuals who were highly exposed to alcohol advertising also said that it was acceptable for people to have more alcoholic drinks (3) before driving, compared to individuals with lower alcohol advertising exposure (2.4). Surprisingly, it appears that no subsequent published studies have re-examined these questions.

Interfering with Alcohol Abuse Recovery

One final problem worth mentioning is the impact alcohol advertising can have on individuals who are attempting to recover from alcohol abuse. Although it is not clear that alcohol companies have developed ads specifically intended to interfere with alcoholics' attempts to stop drinking, at least two studies have provided evidence that alcohol ads sometimes have this effect. First, Wolburg and colleagues (1999) found that beer ads consistently show their products as one used by "popular fun-seekers who spend their time enjoying life, expressing emotions, celebrating occasions and performing at high levels of skill ... the very qualities and experiences most elusive to those addicted to alcohol" (p. 35). The ads contained both verbal and visual cues suggesting that people who drink do not experience the problems alcoholics struggle with, including intense (usually negative) feelings, a disrupted experience of time, alienation from themselves and others, and a lack of self-efficacy or the ability to self-regulate. Compared to non-beer ads, beer commercials more frequently included both verbal and visual expressions of emotion, references to an action-packed life and special moments, effortless social and sexual interaction, and depictions of beer drinkers succeeding at whatever they tried to do.

In another study, researchers conducted in-depth interviews with recovering alcoholics and found that, especially for those in the early stages of recovery, the images and techniques used in alcohol ads could trigger the desire to drink. In particular, alcohol ads that focused on the rituals associated with drinking (e.g., watching sports, socializing with friends) were problematic for those attempting to learn how to engage in those activities without consuming alcohol (Treise et al., 1995).

The Alcohol Industry's "Drink Responsibly" Campaigns

The preponderance of research suggests that alcohol advertising does, in fact, have negative impacts. Although the relationships between alcohol advertising exposure and problem behaviors – including drunk driving, binge drinking and risky or coercive sexual behavior – have not been fully explored, alcohol ads clearly do encourage under-age drinking. Given the significant contribution of under-age alcohol consumption to national consumption totals, and the alcohol companies' revenues, it is somewhat difficult to imagine that alcohol manufacturers *truly* want to avoid using advertising techniques that lead to earlier initiation of alcohol use or that discourage individuals in any age group from drinking more than one beer, glass of wine or hard liquor shot per day. After all, according to an analysis of the cash value of problematic U.S. alcohol consumption in 2001, the complete cessation of alcohol use by adolescents in the United States would have cost the alcohol industry, in the short term, $22.5 billion, which amounted to 17.5 percent of all consumer spending for alcohol. The researchers estimated that under-age drinking, combined with abusive or dependent alcohol consumption by adults, accounted for 37.5 percent of all alcoholic beverage consumption in 2001, putting the value to the industry at no less than $48.3 billion (Foster et al., 2006). The authors note that some other ways of calculating the impact of under-age and abusive drinking would put these totals as high as 48.8 percent of consumer spending for alcohol, or $62.9 billion, in 2001.

Still, one must acknowledge that beer and spirits manufacturers do often include in their advertising messages that encourage their customers to "drink responsibly." In fact, one recent study determined that

87 percent of ads for beer, hard liquor and alcopops included some sort of message encouraging consumers to "drink responsibly" (Clegg-Smith et al., 2014). But what impact do these messages actually have? Do they discourage inappropriate use of alcohol?

Textual analysis of all "responsible drinking" messages included in major U.S. magazine ads for beer, spirits or alcopops between 2008 and 2010 revealed that, perhaps not surprisingly, the ad's tagline was more prominent than the "drink responsibly" message. These messages did not define what it means to drink responsibly, nor did they ever recommend not drinking. The researchers categorize 88 percent of these messages as being intended primarily to promote the product, rather than discouraging alcohol misuse or abuse (Clegg-Smith et al., 2014). An earlier analysis of manufacturers' responsibility-promotion messages noted that one major problem with these messages is that they place responsibility for "responsible" alcohol use on the individual, rather than on the product. They also imply that heavy drinking is fine, so long as the drinker is not under-age and is not driving. Wolburg argues that these messages encourage "the drinker to shift responsibility to others" (2005, p. 177).

Smith and colleagues (2006) studied teenagers' and young adults' responses to two major beer company campaigns promoting "responsible" drinking: Anheuser-Busch's "Know When to Say When" campaign and Coors' "Not Now" campaign. The former campaign focused on discouraging driving after drinking, while the latter showed individuals drinking Coors beer in a variety of settings (a party, around a campfire, at sporting events), with "not now" labels attached to intercut scenes showing especially risky situations. The researchers found that teen and young adult viewers reported numerous and varied interpretations of the meaning of these messages and generally rated both the messages and the sponsors of the ads positively. They concluded that there is little evidence that such sponsor-produced messages actually encourage more responsible drinking behaviors or benefit public health. Rather, they suggest that the messages may be intended primarily to "preempt more persuasive campaign efforts from government agencies and prevention organizations" (Smith et al., 2006, p. 10).

Overall, then, the evidence strongly suggests that alcohol advertising – including ads promoting "responsible drinking" messages – encourages more drinking, including under-age and binge drinking. Thus, alcohol advertising escapes categorization as having intended negative health effects at the individual level only because alcohol can be used in moderation without negative health effects and, for many people, alcohol use is not addictive. Nonetheless, the negative impacts of alcohol advertising are easily predictable, suggesting that public policy to reduce the pervasiveness of such advertising would benefit public health.

REFERENCES

Abbey, A. (2002). Alcohol-related Sexual Assault: A Common Problem among College Students. *Journal of Studies on Alcohol and Drugs, Sup*(14), 118.

Abbey, A., Zawacki, T., Buck, P.O., Clinton, A.M. & McAuslan, P. (2004). Sexual Assault and Alcohol Consumption: What Do We Know About Their Relationship and What Types of Research are Still Needed? *Aggression and Violent Behavior, 9*(3), 271–303. http://doi.org/10.1016/S1359-1789(03)00011-9.

Alcohol Industry: U.S. Ad Spend by Medium 2013. (2014). Retrieved November 7, 2014 from www.statista.com/statistics/245318/advertising-spending-of-the-alcohol-industry-in-the-us-by-medium/.

Allen, M., Donohue, W.A., Griffin, A., Ryan, D. & Turner, M.M.M. (2003). Comparing the Influence of Parents and Peers on the Choice to Use Drugs: A Meta-analytic Summary of the Literature. *Criminal Justice and Behavior, 30*(2), 163–186. http://doi.org/10.1177/0093854802251002.

Anderson, P., de Bruijn, A., Angus, K., Gordon, R. & Hastings, G. (2009). Impact of Alcohol Advertising and Media Exposure on Adolescent Alcohol Use: A Systematic Review of Longitudinal Studies. *Alcohol and Alcoholism (Oxford, Oxfordshire), 44*(3), 229–243. http://doi.org/10.1093/alcalc/agn115.

Atkin, C.K. & Block, M. (1984). The Effects of Alcohol Advertising. *Advances in Consumer Research, 11*(1), 688–693.

Austin, E.W. & Hust, S.J.T. (2005). Targeting Adolescents? The Content and Frequency of Alcoholic and Nonalcoholic Beverage Ads in Magazine and Video Formats November 1999–April 2000. *Journal of Health Communication, 10*(8), 769–785. http://doi.org/10.1080/10810730500326757.

Bachman, J.G., Johnston, L.D. & O'Malley, P.M. (2014). Monitoring the Future: Questionnaire Responses From the Nation's High School Seniors 2012. Institute for Social Research, University of Michigan. Retrieved October 30, 2014 from www.monitoringthefuture.org/datavolumes/2012/2012dv.pdf.

Benson, B.J., Gohm, C.L. & Gross, A.M. (2007). College Women and Sexual Assault: The Role of Sex-related Alcohol Expectancies. *Journal of Family Violence, 22*(6), 341–351. http://doi.org/10.1007/s10896-007-9085-z.

Borders, T.F. & Booth, B.M. (2007). Rural, Suburban, and Urban Variations in Alcohol Consumption in the United States: Findings From the National Epidemiologic Survey on Alcohol and Related Conditions. *The Journal of Rural Health, 23*(4), 314–321. http://doi.org/10.1111/j.1748-0361.2007.00109.x.

Budweiser Clydesdales. (n.d.). Retrieved October 28, 2014 from http://anheuser-busch.com/index.php/our-heritage/budweiser-clydesdales/.

Budweiser Produces Most Effective Ad of the Super Bowl | Ace Metrix. (2013, February 4). Retrieved October 28, 2014 from www.acemetrix.com/news/press-releases/budweiser-produces-most-effective-ad-of-the-super-bowl/.

Carr, J.L. & VanDeusen, K.M. (2004). Risk Factors for Male Sexual Aggression on College Campuses. *Journal of Family Violence*, *19*(5), 279–289. http://doi. org/10.1023/B:JOFV.0000042078.55308.4d.

Casswell, S. & Zhang, J.-F. (1998). Impact of Liking for Advertising and Brand Allegiance on Drinking and Alcohol-related Aggression: A Longitudinal Study. *Addiction*, *93*(8), 1209–1217. http://doi.org/10.1046/j.1360-0443.1998.93812099.x.

CDC. (2014, March 24). Text Description for Graph Trends) Data, Trends and Maps Page. Retrieved October 30, 2014 from www.cdc.gov/alcohol/data-table. htm.

Center on Alcohol Marketing and Youth. (2010a). *Youth Exposure to Alcohol Advertising in National Magazines, 2001–2008*. Baltimore, MD: Johns Hopkins Bloomberg School of Public Health. Retrieved November 6, 2014 from www.camy.org/ research/Youth_Exposure_to_Alcohol_Advertising_in_National_Magazines_ 2001-2008/_includes/execsum.pdf.

Center on Alcohol Marketing and Youth. (2010b). *Youth Exposure to Alcohol Advertising on Television, 2001–2009*. Baltimore, MD: Johns Hopkins Bloomberg School of Public Health. Retrieved November 6, 2014 from www.camy.org/research/Youth_ Exposure_to_Alcohol_Ads_on_TV_Growing_Faster_Than_Adults/_includes/ TVReport01-09_Revised_7-12.pdf.

Center on Alcohol Marketing and Youth. (2012a). State Laws to Reduce the Impact of Alcohol Marketing on Youth: Current Status and Model Policies. Retrieved November 6, 2014 from www.camy.org/action/legal_resources/state ad laws/ state_alcohol_advertising_laws_2012.

Center on Alcohol Marketing and Youth. (2012b, May 1). State Laws to Reduce the Impact of Alcohol Marketing on Youth: Current Status and Model Policies. Retrieved November 5, 2014 from www.camy.org/action/Legal_Resources/ State%20Ad%20Laws/CAMY_State_Alcohol_Ads_Report_2012.pdf.

Centers for Disease Control and Prevention. (2011, April 12). Excessive Alcohol Use: Addressing a Leading Risk for Death, Chronic Disease, and Injury. Retrieved October 29, 2014 from www.cdc.gov/chronicdisease/resources/publications/aag/ alcohol.htm.

Centers for Disease Control and Prevention. (2012, January 13). Vital Signs: Binge Drinking Prevalence, Frequency, and Intensity Among Adults – United States, 2010. Retrieved November 3, 2014 from www.cdc.gov/mmwr/preview/mmwrhtml/ mm6101a4.htm?s_cid=mm6101a4_w.

Centers for Disease Control and Prevention. (2013). Youth Exposure to Alcohol Advertising on Television – 25 Markets, United States, 2010. *MMWR. Morbidity and Mortality Weekly Report*, *62*(44), 877–880.

Centers for Disease Control and Prevention. (2014a, January 16). Binge Drinking. Retrieved October 28, 2014 from www.cdc.gov/alcohol/fact-sheets/binge-drinking. htm.

Centers for Disease Control and Prevention. (2014b, January 16). Excessive Alcohol Use and Risks to Women's Health. Retrieved October 28, 2014 from www.cdc.gov/ alcohol/fact-sheets/womens-health.htm.

Centers for Disease Control and Prevention. (2014c, March 14). Frequently Asked Questions – Alcohol. Retrieved November 3, 2014 from www.cdc.gov/alcohol/ faqs.htm#healthProb.

Centers for Disease Control and Prevention. (2014d, September 23). Excessive Alcohol Use and Risks to Men's Health. Retrieved October 28, 2014 from www. cdc.gov/alcohol/fact-sheets/mens-health.htm.

Chambers, J. (2006). Taste Matters: Bikinis, Twins, and Catfights in Sexually Oriented Beer Advertising. *Sex in Consumer Culture: The Erotic Content of Media and Marketing*, 159–177.

Clegg-Smith, K., Cukier, S. & Jernigan, D.H. (2014). Defining Strategies for Promoting Product Through "Drink Responsibly" Messages in Magazine Ads for Beer, Spirits and Alcopops. *Drug & Alcohol Dependence, 142*, 168–173. http://doi.org/10.1016/j.drugalcdep. 2014.06.007.

Collins, R.L., Ellickson, P.L., McCaffrey, D. & Hambarsoomians, K. (2007). Early Adolescent Exposure to Alcohol Advertising and Its Relationship to Underage Drinking. *Journal of Adolescent Health, 40*(6), 527–534. http://doi.org/10.1016/j.jadohealth.2007.01.002.

Cooper, M.L. (2002). Alcohol Use and Risky Sexual Behavior among College Students and Youth: Evaluating the Evidence. *Journal of Studies on Alcohol. Suppl.*(14), 101–117.

Davis, K.C. (2010). The Influence of Alcohol Expectancies and Intoxication on Men's Aggressive Unprotected Sexual Intentions. *Experimental and Clinical Psychopharmacology, 18*(5), 418–428. http://doi.org/10.1037/a0020510.

Denke, M. (2000). Nutritional and Health Benefits of Beer. *The American Journal of the Medical Sciences, 329*(5), 320–326.

DeWit, D.J., Adlaf, E.M., Offord, D.R. & Ogborne, A.C. (2000). Age at First Alcohol Use: A Risk Factor for the Development of Alcohol Disorders. *American Journal of Psychiatry, 157*(5), 745–750. http://doi.org/10.1176/appi.ajp. 157.5.745.

Ellickson, P.L., Collins, R.L., Hambarsoomians, K. & McCaffrey, D.F. (2005). Does Alcohol Advertising Promote Adolescent Drinking? Results from a Longitudinal Assessment. *Addiction (Abingdon, England), 100*(2), 235–246. http://doi.org/10.1111/j.1360-0443.2005.00974.x.

Emanuele, M.A. & Emanuele, N. (2001). Alcohol and the Male Reproductive System. *Alcohol Research & Health: The Journal of the National Institute on Alcohol Abuse and Alcoholism, 25*(4), 282–287.

Engels, R.C.M.E., Hermans, R., van Baaren, R.B., Hollenstein, T. & Bot, S.M. (2009). Alcohol Portrayal on Television Affects Actual Drinking Behaviour. *Alcohol and Alcoholism, 44*(3), 244–249. http://doi.org/10.1093/alcalc/agp003.

Facts About FASDs. (2014, September 3). Retrieved November 3, 2014 from www.cdc.gov/ncbddd/fasd/facts.html.

Fleming, K., Thorson, E. & Atkin, C.K. (2004). Alcohol Advertising Exposure and Perceptions: Links with Alcohol Expectancies and Intentions to Drink or Drinking in Underaged Youth and Young Adults. *Journal of Health Communication, 9*(1), 3–29. http://doi.org/10.1080/10810730490271665.

Foster, S.E., Vaughan, R.D., Foster, W.H. & Califano, J.A. (2006). Estimate of the Commercial Value of Underage Drinking and Adult Abusive and Dependent Drinking to the Alcohol Industry. *Archives of Pediatrics & Adolescent Medicine, 160*(5), 473–478. http://doi.org/10.1001/archpedi.160.5.473.

FTC. (2014). *Self-regulation in the Alcohol Industry: Report of the Federal Trade Commission*. Washington, DC: Federal Trade Commission. Retrieved November 5, 2014 from www.ftc.gov/system/files/documents/reports/self-regulation-alcohol-industry-report-federal-trade-commission/140320alcoholreport.pdf.

George, W.H., Davis, K.C., Norris, J., Heiman, J.R., Schacht, R.L., Stoner, S.A. & Kajumulo, K.F. (2006). Alcohol and Erectile Response: The Effects of High Dosage in the Context of Demands to Maximize Sexual Arousal. *Experimental and Clinical Psychopharmacology, 14*(4), 461.

Grant, B.F., Dawson, D.A., Stinson, F.S., Chou, S.P., Dufour, M.C. & Pickering, R.P. (2004). The 12-month Prevalence and Trends in DSM-IV Alcohol Abuse and Dependence: United States, 1991–1992 and 2001–2002. *Drug and Alcohol Dependence*, 74(3), 223–234. http://doi.org/10.1016/j.drugalcdep. 2004.02.004.

Grenard, J.L., Dent, C.W. & Stacy, A.W. (2013). Exposure to Alcohol Advertisements and Teenage Alcohol-related Problems. *Pediatrics*, 131(2), e369–379. http://doi.org/10.1542/peds.2012-1480.

Gruber, E., DiClemente, R.J., Anderson, M.M. & Lodico, M. (1996). Early Drinking Onset and its Association with Alcohol Use and Problem Behavior in Late Adolescence. *Preventive Medicine*, 25(3), 293–300. http://doi.org/10.1006/pmed.1996.0059.

Hall, C.C.I. & Crum, M.J. (1994). Women and "Body-isms" in Television Beer Commercials. *Sex Roles*, 31(5–6), 329–337. http://doi.org/10.1007/BF01544592.

Hastings, G., Anderson, S., Cooke, E. & Gordon, R. (2005). Alcohol Marketing and Young People's Drinking: A Review of the Research. *Journal of Public Health Policy*, 26(3), 296–311. http://doi.org/10.1057/palgrave.jphp. 3200039.

Hawkins, J.D., Graham, J.W., Maguin, E., Abbott, R.D., Hill, K.G. & Catalano, R.F. (1997). Exploring the Effects of Age of Alcohol Use Initiation and Psychosocial Risk Factors on Subsequent Alcohol Misuse. *Journal of Studies on Alcohol*, 58(3), 280–290.

Henriksen, L., Feighery, E.C., Schleicher, N.C. & Fortmann, S.P. (2008). Receptivity to Alcohol Marketing Predicts Initiation of Alcohol Use. *The Journal of Adolescent Health: Official Publication of the Society for Adolescent Medicine*, 42(1), 28–35. http://doi.org/10.1016/j.jadohealth.2007.07.005.

Hingson, R.W., Heeren, T. & Winter, M.R. (2006). Age of Alcohol-dependence Onset: Associations With Severity of Dependence and Seeking Treatment. *Pediatrics*, 118(3), e755–e763. http://doi.org/10.1542/peds.2006-0223.

Hingson, R.W., Zha, W. & Weitzman, E.R. (2009). Magnitude of and Trends in Alcohol-related Mortality and Morbidity Among U.S. College Students Ages 18–24, 1998–2005. *Journal of Studies on Alcohol and Drugs*, Suppl.(16), 12–20.

Hoffman, E.W., Pinkleton, B.E., Weintraub Austin, E. & Reyes-Velázquez, W. (2014). Exploring College Students' Use of General and Alcohol-related Social Media and Their Associations with Alcohol-related Behaviors. *Journal of American College Health: Journal of ACH*, 62(5), 328–335. http://doi.org/10.1080/07448481.2014.902837.

Johnston, L.D., O'Malley, P.M., Miech, R.A., Bachman, J.G. & Schulenberg, J.E. (2013). Monitoring the Future: 2013 Overview. National Institute on Drug Abuse. Retrieved November 5, 2014 from www.monitoringthefuture.org//pubs/monographs/mtf-overview2013.pdf.

Jones, J. (2013, August 1). U.S. Drinkers Divide Between Beer and Wine as Favorite: Younger Drinkers Most Likely to Have Shifted Preferences Away from Beer. Retrieved October 30, 2014 from www.gallup.com/poll/163787/drinkers-divide-beer-wine-favorite.aspx.

Kaplan, M.S., McFarland, B.H., Huguet, N., Conner, K., Caetano, R., Giesbrecht, N. & Nolte, K.B. (2013). Acute Alcohol Intoxication and Suicide: A Gender-stratified Analysis of the National Violent Death Reporting System. *Injury Prevention: Journal of the International Society for Child and Adolescent Injury Prevention*, 19(1), 38–43. http://doi.org/10.1136/injuryprev-2012-040317.

Koordeman, R., Anschutz, D.J. & Engels, R.C.M.E. (2012). The Effect of Alcohol Advertising on Immediate Alcohol Consumption in College Students: An Experimental Study. *Alcoholism, Clinical and Experimental Research*, 36(5), 874–880. http://doi.org/10.1111/j.1530-0277.2011.01655.x.

Kuo, M., Wechsler, H., Greenberg, P. & Lee, H. (2003). The Marketing of Alcohol to College Students: The Role of Low Prices and Special Promotions. *American Journal of Preventive Medicine, 25*(3), 204–211. http://doi.org/10.1016/S0749-3797(03)00200-9.

Lanis, K. & Covell, K. (1995). Images of Women in Advertisements: Effects on Attitudes Related to Sexual Aggression. *Sex Roles, 32*(9–10), 639–649. http://doi.org/10.1007/BF01544216.

Marczinski, C.A. & Fillmore, M.T. (2014). Energy Drinks Mixed With Alcohol: What Are the Risks? *Nutrition Reviews, 72 Suppl. 1*, 98–107. http://doi.org/10.1111/nure.12127.

Marx, B.P., Gross, A.M. & Adams, H.E. (1999). The Effect of Alcohol on the Responses of Sexually Coercive and Noncoercive Men to an Experimental Rape Analogue. *Sexual Abuse: A Journal of Research and Treatment, 11*(2), 131–145. http://doi.org/10.1007/BF02658843.

Mason, M.J., Zaharakis, N. & Benotsch, E.G. (2014). Social Networks, Substance Use, and Mental Health in College Students. *Journal of American College Health: Journal of ACH, 62*(7), 470–477. http://doi.org/10.1080/07448481.2014.923428.

McCarty, D. & Ewing, J.A. (1983). Alcohol Consumption While Viewing Alcoholic Beverage Advertising. *Substance Use & Misuse, 18*(7), 1011–1018. http://doi.org/10.3109/10826088309033067.

Meier, P.S. (2011). Alcohol Marketing Research: The Need for a New Agenda. *Addiction (Abingdon, England), 106*(3), 466–471. http://doi.org/10.1111/j.1360-0443.2010.03160.x.

Moos, R.H., Schutte, K.K., Brennan, P.L. & Moos, B.S. (2010). Late-life and Life History Predictors of Older Adults' High-risk Alcohol Consumption and Drinking Problems. *Drug and Alcohol Dependence, 108*(1-2), 13–20. http://doi.org/10.1016/j.drugalcdep.2009.11.005.

Morr, M.C. & Mongeau, P.A. (2004). First-date Expectations: The Impact of Sex of Initiator, Alcohol Consumption, and Relationship Type. *Communication Research, 31*(1), 3–35. http://doi.org/10.1177/0093650203260202.

Mrug, S. & McCay, R. (2013). Parental and Peer Disapproval of Alcohol Use and its Relationship to Adolescent Drinking: Age, Gender, and Racial Differences. *Psychology of Addictive Behaviors: Journal of the Society of Psychologists in Addictive Behaviors, 27*(3), 604–614. http://doi.org/10.1037/a0031064.

Naimi, T.S., Brewer, R.D., Miller, J.W., Okoro, C. & Mehrotra, C. (2007). What Do Binge Drinkers Drink? Implications for Alcohol Control Policy. *American Journal of Preventive Medicine, 33*(3), 188–193. http://doi.org/10.1016/j.amepre.2007.04.026.

National Institute on Alcohol Abuse and Alcoholism. (n.d.a). Older Adults. Retrieved October 30, 2014 from www.niaaa.nih.gov/alcohol-health/special-populations-co-occurring-disorders/older-adults.

National Institute on Alcohol Abuse and Alcoholism. (n.d.b). Underage Drinking. Retrieved October 30, 2014 from www.niaaa.nih.gov/alcohol-health/special-populations-co-occurring-disorders/underage-drinking.

Nolen-Hoeksema, S. (2004). Gender Differences in Risk Factors and Consequences for Alcohol Use and Problems. *Clinical Psychology Review, 24*(8), 981–1010. http://doi.org/10.1016/j.cpr.2004.08.003.

Office of Juvenile Justice and Delinquency Prevention. (2005). *Drinking in America: Myths, Realities, and Prevention Policy.* U.S. Department of Justice, Office of Justice Programs, Office of Juvenile Justice and Delinquency Prevention.

Palmer, R.S., McMahon, T.J., Rounsaville, B.J. & Ball, S.A. (2010). Coercive Sexual Experiences, Protective Behavioral Strategies, Alcohol Expectancies and Consumption among Male and Female College Students. *Journal of Interpersonal Violence, 25*(9), 1563–1578. http://doi.org/10.1177/0886260509354581.

Pasch, K.E., Komro, K.A., Perry, C.L., Hearst, M.O. & Farbakhsh, K. (2007). Outdoor Alcohol Advertising Near Schools: What Does it Advertise and How is it Related to Intentions and Use of Alcohol Among Young Adolescents? *Journal of Studies on Alcohol and Drugs, 68*(4), 587.

Patrick, M.E., Schulenberg, J.E., O'Malley, P.M., Johnston, L.D. & Bachman, J.G. (2011). Adolescents' Reported Reasons for Alcohol and Marijuana Use as Predictors of Substance Use and Problems in Adulthood. *Journal of Studies on Alcohol and Drugs, 72*(1), 106–116.

Peterson, P.L., Hawkins, J.D., Abbott, R.D. & Catalano, R.F. (1994). Disentangling the Effects of Parental Drinking, Family Management, and Parental Alcohol Norms on Current Drinking by Black and White Adolescents. *Journal of Research on Adolescence, 4*(2), 203–227. http://doi.org/10.1207/s15327795jra0402_3.

Pumphrey-Gordon, J.E. & Gross, A.M. (2007). Alcohol Consumption and Females' Recognition in Response to Date Rape Risk: The Role of Sex-related Alcohol Expectancies. *Journal of Family Violence, 22*(6), 475–485. http://doi.org/10.1007/s10896-007-9104-0.

Quinn, P.D. & Fromme, K. (2011). Alcohol Use and Related Problems Among College Students and Their Noncollege Peers: The Competing Roles of Personality and Peer Influence. *Journal of Studies on Alcohol and Drugs, 72*(4), 622–632.

Rhoades, E. & Jernigan, D.H. (2013). Risky Messages in Alcohol Advertising, 2003–2007: Results From Content Analysis. *Journal of Adolescent Health, 52*(1), 116–121. http://doi.org/10.1016/j.jadohealth.2012.04.013.

Ross, C.S., Ostroff, J. & Jernigan, D.H. (2014a). Evidence of Underage Targeting of Alcohol Advertising on Television in the United States: Lessons From the Lockyer v. Reynolds Decisions. *Journal of Public Health Policy, 35*(1), 105–118. http://doi.org/10.1057/jphp. 2013.52.

Ross, C.S., Maple, E., Siegel, M., DeJong, W., Naimi, T.S., Ostroff, J. & Jernigan, D.H. (2014b). The Relationship Between Brand-specific Alcohol Advertising on Television and Brand-specific Consumption among Underage Youth. *Alcoholism, Clinical and Experimental Research, 38*(8), 2234–2242. http://doi.org/10.1111/acer.12488.

Saffer, H. & Dave, D. (2002). Alcohol Consumption and Alcohol Advertising Bans. *Applied Economics, 34*(11), 1325–1334. http://doi.org/10.1080/00036840110102743.

Sanburn, J. (2013, February 5). Super Bowl 2013's 6 Most Shared Commercials (And Why They Went Viral). *Time*. Retrieved October 28, 2014 from http://business.time.com/2013/02/05/super-bowl-2013s-6-most-shared-commercials-and-why-they-went-viral/.

Smith, K.C., Cukier, S. & Jernigan, D.H. (2014). Regulating Alcohol Advertising: Content Analysis of the Adequacy of Federal and Self-regulation of Magazine Advertisements, 2008–2010. *American Journal of Public Health, 104*(10), 1901–1911. http://doi.org/10.2105/AJPH.2013.301483.

Smith, L.A. & Foxcroft, D.R. (2009). The Effect of Alcohol Advertising, Marketing and Portrayal on Drinking Behaviour in Young People: Systematic Review of Prospective Cohort Studies. *BMC Public Health, 9*, 51. http://doi.org/10.1186/1471-2458-9-51.

Smith, R. (2011, August 9). Are Alcohol Companies Doomed to Cause Harm? Retrieved October 29, 2014 from http://blogs.bmj.com/bmj/2011/08/09/richard-smith-are-alcohol-companies-doomed-to-cause-harm/.

Smith, R.C. & Geller, E.S. (2009). Marketing and Alcohol-related Traffic Fatalities: Impact of Alcohol Advertising Targeting Minors. *Journal of Safety Research, 40*(5), 359–364. http://doi.org/10.1016/j.jsr.2009.08.001.

Smith, S.W., Atkin, C.K. & Roznowski, J. (2006). Are "Drink Responsibly" Alcohol Campaigns Strategically Ambiguous? *Health Communication*, *20*(1), 1–11. http://doi.org/10.1207/s15327027hc2001_1.

Snyder, L.B., Milici, F.F., Slater, M., Sun, H. & Strizhakova, Y. (2006). Effects of Alcohol Advertising Exposure on Drinking among Youth. *Archives of Pediatrics & Adolescent Medicine*, *160*(1), 18–24. http://doi.org/10.1001/archpedi.160.1.18.

Stahre, M., Roeber, J., Kanny, D., Brewer, R.D. & Zhang, X. (2014). Contribution of Excessive Alcohol Consumption to Deaths and Years of Potential Life Lost in the United States. *Preventing Chronic Disease*, *11*. http://doi.org/10.5888/pcd11.130293.

Steinberg, B. (2013, October 10). Increased Ad Spending on Tap for Beer, Liquor Makers. Retrieved November 7, 2014 from http://variety.com/2013/biz/news/increased-ad-spending-on-tap-for-beer-liquor-makers-1200709329/.

Stevens, J.F. & Page, J.E. (2004). Xanthohumol and Related Prenylflavonoids From Hops and Beer: To Your Good Health! *Phytochemistry*, *65*(10), 1317–1330. http://doi.org/10.1016/j.phytochem.2004.04.025.

Swendsen, J., Burstein, M., Case, B. et al. (2012). Use and Abuse of Alcohol and Illicit Drugs in US Adolescents: Results of the National Comorbidity Survey – Adolescent Supplement. *Archives of General Psychiatry*, *69*(4), 390–398. http://doi.org/10.1001/archgenpsychiatry.2011.1503.

Treise, D.M., Taylor, R.E. & Wells, L.G. (1995). How Recovering Alcoholics Interpret Alcoholic-beverage Advertising. *Health Marketing Quarterly*, *12*(2), 125–139. http://doi.org/10.1300/J026v12n02_10.

Vozza, S. (2013, February 4). 5 Marketing Lessons From the Super Bowl's Most Popular Commercials. Retrieved October 28, 2014 from www.entrepreneur.com/blog/225667.

Warner, L.A., White, H.R. & Johnson, V. (2007). Alcohol Initiation Experiences and Family History of Alcoholism as Predictors of Problem-drinking Trajectories. *Journal of Studies on Alcohol and Drugs*, *68*(1), 56.

Wills, T.A., Gibbons, F.X., Sargent, J.D., Gerrard, M., Lee, H.-R. & Dal Cin, S. (2010). Good Self-control Moderates the Effect of Mass Media on Adolescent Tobacco and Alcohol Use: Tests with Studies of Children and Adolescents. *Health Psychology: Official Journal of the Division of Health Psychology, American Psychological Association*, *29*(5), 539–549. http://doi.org/10.1037/a0020818.

Wilson, S.R., Knowles, S.B., Huang, Q. & Fink, A. (2014). The Prevalence of Harmful and Hazardous Alcohol Consumption in Older U.S. Adults: Data from the 2005–2008 National Health and Nutrition Examination Survey (NHANES). *Journal of General Internal Medicine*, *29*(2), 312–319. http://doi.org/10.1007/s11606-013-2577-z.

Windle, M. (2000). Parental, Sibling, and Peer Influences on Adolescent Substance Use and Alcohol Problems. *Applied Developmental Science*, *4*(2), 98–110. http://doi.org/10.1207/S1532480XADS0402_5.

Wolburg, J.M. (2005). How Responsible Are "Responsible" Drinking Campaigns for Preventing Alcohol Abuse? Null. *Journal of Consumer Marketing*, *22*(4), 176–177. http://doi.org/10.1108/07363760510605281.

Wolburg, J.M., Hovland, R. & Hopson, R.E. (1999). Cognitive Restructuring as a Relapse Prevention Strategy. *Alcoholism Treatment Quarterly*, *17*(4), 29–51. http://doi.org/10.1300/J020v17n04_03.

Wyllie, A., Zhang, J.F. & Casswell, S. (1998). Positive Responses to Televised Beer Advertisements Associated with Drinking and Problems Reported by 18 to 29-year-olds. *Addiction*, *93*(5), 749–760. http://doi.org/10.1046/j.1360-0443.1998.93574911.x.

CHAPTER 5

TAKE A PILL FOR "BETTER HEALTH": DIRECT-TO-CONSUMER PRESCRIPTION DRUG ADVERTISING

Heart disease is the Number 1 cause of death in the United States, accounting for one in every four deaths and killing 600,000 people annually. In addition to high blood pressure and smoking, one of the key risk factors for heart disease is having high low-density lipoprotein (LDL) cholesterol (Centers for Disease Control and Prevention (CDC), 2014). Given this fact, along with statistics showing that more than 25 percent of adults aged 40 to 74 have high LDL cholesterol, it may be difficult to see any downside to advertising that encourages consumers to start taking drugs that lower their cholesterol.

There is certainly little indication of any downside in the consumer-directed television ads for Crestor (rosuvastatin), which was the single most frequently prescribed drug in the United States for 2013 (Lowes, 2013). The ads for Crestor, prescribed for 23.7 million Americans in 2013, show middle-aged adults, most of them appearing to be somewhat overweight, celebrating as a white-coated "doctor" spokesman explains that studies show Crestor to be more effective than its competitor, Lipitor, in helping patients achieve their LDL cholesterol "goal". One ad, called "SuperFan," portrays a man reacting to a TV news announcement of this comparison the way one might expect a sports fan to respond when his favorite football team wins the Super Bowl – dancing around his living room in celebration, wearing an oversized, Crestor-labeled foam "thumbs-up," while his wife and teenage son look on, shaking their heads. The man's celebration continues in the ad's visuals as the voice-over runs through the required list of potential negative side effects.

The use of statins, including Crestor and its competitors, does indeed appear to have contributed to lower cholesterol levels among American adults. In a study of trends in cholesterol levels among adults 20 to 74, Ford and Capewell (2013) found that total cholesterol levels (LDL and HDL – high-density lipoprotein, or "good cholesterol") declined about 4 percent from 1988 through 2008; their analysis suggested that about 46 percent of the decline could be attributed to increasing use of cholesterol-lowering drugs. The study showed no significant impact of dietary changes that would lead to lower cholesterol levels, largely because the data revealed no significant changes in intake of total fat, saturated fat, polyunsaturated fat or dietary cholesterol. Based on these results alone, DTC advertising for statins, at least, seems to be a public health winner.

However, like the SuperFan's wife and son, we may do well to temper our own celebration of DTC advertising, even for cholesterol-lowering drugs. Additional research suggests that DTC advertising for statins does indeed increase demand for these drugs, one reason Crestor and its competitors are so profitable (Niederdeppe et al., 2013). In the United States alone, Crestor earned $4.4 billion for its manufacturer, Astra-Zeneca, in 2011; its chief competitor, Lipitor, brought in $7.7 billion for Pfizer that year (Moyer, 2012). The problem is that exposure to DTC advertising appears to increase diagnoses of high cholesterol and, subsequently, prescribed statin use almost exclusively among men and women at *low risk* of having a heart attack or other negative cardiac event in the future. In fact, among women at high risk for future heart attacks, exposure to DTC statin ads was associated with *lower* statin use. Thus, more frequent exposure to DTC ads for drugs like Lipitor and Crestor seems to increase statin use among those for whom the drugs are least valuable and to be associated with lower use among women most likely to benefit from the drugs (Niederdeppe et al., 2013).

Direct-to-consumer advertising of prescription drugs has been controversial since it began in the United States (one of only two developed nations to allow it) in the 1980s. Proponents argue that DTC advertising provides consumers with important information about drugs that may benefit them, helps raise awareness and build concern about under-treated health issues, empowers consumers to be more involved in their health care decisions, facilitates conversations between patients and their physicians, reduces the stigma and embarrassment associated with such problems as erectile dysfunction and mental illness, leads to increased compliance with drug prescriptions and ultimately improves the cost-effectiveness of the health care system (Atherly & Rubin, 2009; Gilbody et al., 2005; Kelly, 2004; Rubin, 1985). Critics, on the other hand, contend that DTC advertising provides one-sided information, misleads consumers to overestimate the benefits and underestimate the risks of prescription drugs, promotes use of newer and costlier drugs rather than less expensive generics whose potential for harmful side effects is better understood, increases consumers' likelihood of taking drugs that may have harmful side effects, creates pressure on doctors to prescribe drugs when over-the-counter medicines or lifestyle changes might be as effective or even more beneficial, leads to unnecessary doctor visits, and ultimately pushes health system costs higher through overuse and over-prescription (Almasi et al., 2006; Frosch & Grande, 2010; Frosch et al., 2011; Gilbody et al., 2005; Lexchin & Mintzes, 2002; Mintzes, 2012; Spence et al., 2005). This chapter will discuss the available evidence for both sides of the argument. In regard to our matrix of media health effects, that evidence suggests that while DTC advertising is certainly *intended* to benefit consumers by encouraging them to seek and adhere to treatment for health problems, the concurrent goal of building profits for the pharmaceutical companies often leads to unintended negative consequences for consumers, physicians and the health care system.

DTC Advertising History

For many media consumers today, it may seem that our TV viewing and magazine reading always has included frequent exposure to ads for Lipitor, Lunesta, Abilify and Cialis, urging us, respectively, to lower our cholesterol levels, sleep more soundly, battle depression and re-invigorate our sex lives. In fact, however, the first DTC prescription drug ads appeared in the early 1980s, including a *Reader's Digest* ad for Mercke's pneumonia vaccine, Pneumovax®, and the first television ad, produced by British-based Boots Pharmaceuticals and comparing the price of its prescription ibuprofen, Rufen, with that of Motrin (Greene & Herzberg, 2010). Pines (1999) reports that physicians working for the Food and Drug Administration, which regulates prescription drug advertising, viewed the vaccine ad as potentially beneficial but were more concerned about the appropriateness of the Rufen advertising, even though the initial ad contained no product claims.

The following year, in a speech to the Pharmaceutical Advertising Council, then-FDA Commissioner Arthur Hull Hayes, Jr. predicted dramatic growth in DTC advertising for prescription drugs. Although the comment was not meant to indicate FDA approval or tolerance of DTC advertising, Pines (1999) states, the drug manufacturers interpreted it as such, leading them to submit a raft of proposed DTC ads to the FDA's Division of Drug Advertising and Labeling.

In September 1983, the FDA requested and the pharmaceutical companies agreed to a voluntary moratorium on DTC advertising. Only price comparison ads were allowed for the next two years while the FDA and the industry studied the implications of DTC advertising. FDA and industry research revealed, however, that consumers found value in DTC advertising because it provided information about prescription drugs they might otherwise not have (Pines, 1999). In fact, Donohue argues that consumers' increasing desire to be more informed about and involved in health decision-making was a key factor in the rise of DTC advertising; "the pharmaceutical promotion of prescription drugs to consumers was made possible by the rise of consumer-oriented medicine following the social movements for patients' and consumers' rights" (Donohue, 2006, p. 661). Ultimately, in September 1985, the FDA issued a ruling stating that DTC advertisements were allowable but must meet the same standards as ads directed at physicians, which were required to include a balance of benefit and risk information and a "brief summary" of the risks of taking the advertised drug (Pines, 1999). Because buying enough broadcast time to include the full "brief summary" was prohibitively expensive, radio and TV ads were initially limited to help-seeking ads, which could discuss a disease or medical condition but could not name a specific drug, or reminder ads, which could include the drug name but could not mention the condition the drug was intended to treat (Greene & Herzberg, 2010).

Concerned that consumers were confused by the choppy nature of broadcast DTC advertising, the FDA convened a 1995 hearing on the putative risks and benefits of easing its regulation. Two years later, in 1997, the FDA issued a draft guidance on DTC advertising, followed by a final guidance in 1999 that redefined "adequate provision" of risks and benefits to include reference to a toll-free number or Web site. This opened the door for federally regulated DTC advertising over broadcast media, and the industry responded quickly.

(Greene & Herzberg, 2010, p. 800)

The FDA's 1985 ruling, Pines contends, was "not intended to open the floodgates for DTC advertising" (1999, p. 493). Nonetheless, the gates had been opened. Pharmaceutical company spending on advertising to consumers grew from $0 in 1979 to $791 million in 1996 (Vogt, 2005). The flood of DTC advertising increased dramatically following the FDA's 1997/1999 modification of the regulations. Spending on DTC advertising grew from $1.2 billion in 1998 to a whopping $5.4 billion in the peak year, 2006 (Ventola, 2011). Since that time, spending on DTC has declined somewhat, dropping to $3.4 billion in 2012 but then growing again to $3.8 billion in 2013 (Statista, 2014c). As Figure 5.1 shows, that growth trend continued through 2015, when pharmaceutical companies spent $5.2 billion advertising their products directly to consumers. Perhaps not surprisingly, the majority of DTC advertising spending goes to television, which claims 65 percent of all DTC advertising dollars (Statista, 2014c). Interestingly, spending on online DTC advertising actually declined 14.4 percent between 2012 and 2013 (Dobrow, 2014).

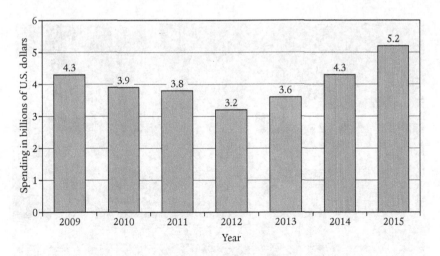

Figure 5.1: Pharmaceutical Industry Direct to Consumer Media Spending in the United States (source: Figures supplied by Nielsen)

THE VOLUME OF DTC ADVERTISING

The result of those billions of dollars' worth of advertising is that the average American consumer may see "nine drug ads a day, totaling 16 hours per year, which far exceeds the amount of time the average individual spends with a primary care physician" (Ventola, 2011, p. 671). In 2001, when data show that pharmaceutical companies spent $2.7 billion on DTC drug advertising (Ventola, 2011), researchers logged 428 prescription drug ads on network television over the course of one week, with more than two-thirds of the ads (68.4%) appearing during news programming or soap operas (Brownfield et al., 2004); it's worth noting that these figures would not include cable, syndicated or spot TV ads, which accounted for almost a quarter (23.2%) of pharmaceutical advertising in 2010 (Ad Age, 2011). Nielsen data show that the average monthly exposure of TV audiences to prescription drug advertising declined by about 24 percent between 2008 and 2012 (Statista, 2014a). Nonetheless, a 2010 survey commissioned by *The AARP Bulletin* showed that 91 percent of the survey respondents (adults aged 18 or older) reported having seen or heard at least one prescription drug ad; 78 percent reported having seen a television ad for prescription drugs (Brown, 2010).

Of course, DTC ad spending is not evenly divided among all brand name drugs or even all drugs that are advertised directly to consumers.

Figure 5.2: "Lifestyle" Drug Ads Are Common

In 2013, for instance, the top 20 brands, in terms of dollars spent on DTC advertising, included four drugs (including the two most-advertised drugs) used to treat sexual dysfunction in men (Cialis, Viagra and two topical treatments for low testosterone), five brands used to treat arthritis, two asthma drugs, two blood thinners, and two anti-depressants, as well as drugs used to treat dry eyes and nicotine addiction. Two drugs make it into the top 20 twice: Lyrica as a treatment for diabetes and fibromyalgia, and Humira as a treatment for arthritis and psoriasis (Statista, 2014b).

The Content of DTC Advertising

Given that DTC advertising is intended to promote drugs to prevent or treat many different health conditions, the content of the ads naturally varies. However, researchers have identified a number of consistent themes and similarities in DTC advertising. Perhaps the most frequently identified (and unsurprising) finding is that DTC ads tend to over-emphasize the benefits of the drugs they're touting while simultaneously downplaying potentially harmful side effects (Avery et al., 2011; Faerber & Kreling, 2014; Frosch et al., 2007; Kaphingst & DeJong, 2004; Macias et al., 2010; Macias et al., 2007; Woloshin et al., 2001). For instance, in a study of 23 DTC television ads broadcast on the major networks in 2001, Kaphingst and DeJong (2004) found that ads were designed to facilitate easier processing of benefit information than risk information, in that risk facts were presented more rapidly and, in 83 percent of the ads, in one continuous segment, while benefit information was presented more slowly and was interspersed throughout the commercial. In addition, during the voice-over presentations of risk information, the visual images were always either positive or neutral, never negative.

A more recent study of 106 network and cable TV ads for prescription drugs showed that the average 60-second commercial spent only 8 seconds disclosing information about side effects, limitations on the drug's effectiveness and contraindications that would make use of the drug unwise or even harmful. Thus, on average, 13 percent of each ad was devoted to risks (Macias et al., 2007). Another study, which examined both magazine ads and television commercials for anti-depressant medications between 1995 and January 2007, revealed that when mentioning side effects, the ads more often than not listed more prevalent and less severe side effects first. Television commercials were nine times as likely to present side effects in prevalence order as they were to list them in order of severity, and magazine ads were nearly twice as likely to use prevalence-ordered rather than severity-ordered listings of side effects. In addition, when risk information was being presented through voice-overs in the television ads, the on-screen images were positive, rather than negative or neutral, 99 percent of the time, and of the television ads aired in 2006 or January 2007, 44.1 percent included statements that discounted the risk of severe or serious side effects from use of the drug. The authors concluded that the ads, in general, were

> not necessarily consistent with FDA guidelines for fair balance. Drug benefit information occupied more than 85% of all print copy and greater than 67% of all air time for television commercials. Furthermore, the more creative aspects of ad copy heavily emphasized benefits over risks.
>
> (Avery et al., 2011, p. 272)

While the majority of any given DTC ad focuses on the drug's benefits, the ads rarely present benefit information in quantitative terms. For instance, in their examination of magazine DTC ads from 1998 and 1999, Woloshin et al. (2001) found that 87 percent of the ads used vague qualitative terms to describe benefits, while only 13 percent presented data about benefits. About one in four ads (24%) used phrases such as "clinically proven" or "proven relief" in their presentations of the drug's benefits. Visuals included in DTC ads virtually always show individuals who are happy and who appear healthy after using the touted drug. One early study showed that of magazine ads that included a human model, 91.8 percent depicted healthy-looking individuals (Welch Cline & Young, 2004), and an analysis of more recent television ads showed that more than half (52.7%) portrayed the primary character engaging in some physical activity (Frosch et al., 2007). Researchers have also found that one of the most commonly touted benefits is that the advertised drug will enable users to "get back to normal" or to regain control lost due to a medical condition (Frosch et al., 2007; Macias et al., 2007; Woloshin et al., 2001). "DTCA often presents best-case scenarios that can distort and inflate consumers' expectations about what prescription drugs can accomplish" (Frosch et al., 2007, p. 12).

Another element commonly missing in DTC advertising is information that would help to educate consumers about their likelihood of experiencing the disease or condition the drugs are meant to treat. For instance, Kaphingst and DeJong's (2004) study of network TV DTC ads showed that 70 percent of the TV ads they analyzed included no information about risk factors for or symptoms of the condition the drug was meant to treat. In addition, although more than four out of five ads advised consumers to "talk to your doctor" about the *drug*, only one ad encouraged consumers to seek further information about the condition. Two-thirds of the ads failed to note that the drug might not work for everyone.

A related problem, identified in several studies, is that DTC advertising often fails to include information about the prevalence of the disease the drug treats, potentially suggesting to consumers that virtually everyone is a likely candidate for use of the drug (Byrne et al., 2013; Kaphingst & DeJong, 2004; Woloshin et al., 2001). Some studies have shown that DTC ads often make reference to common symptoms that many consumers could manage on their own without medical advice or drug use and encourage consumers to view lifestyle changes as likely to be ineffective responses when medical problems do arise. For example, one drug ad asked consumers, "Is it just forgetfulness, or is it Alzheimer's?" Another ad cautioned that consumers who experience heartburn symptoms more than once a week "may have a potentially serious condition called acid reflux disease" (Woloshin et al., 2001, p. 1144).

In another study, focused specifically on drugs to treat high cholesterol, 80.1 percent of magazine ads and 74 percent of television ads included statements specifically warning that dietary changes and increased exercise might not be enough to enable consumers to achieve healthy cholesterol levels. The authors found that the ads often included mixed messages. For instance, 65.3 percent of magazine ads and 48.4 percent of television ads mentioned that exercise could help reduce cholesterol, but of those ads, 96.7 percent specifically stated that exercise alone might not solve the problem. Similarly, nearly three-quarters of TV ads mentioned the link between diet and cholesterol reduction, but of those, 88.6 percent said diet alone might not be effective. "Images of food and exercise were almost always portrayed in ads that cast doubt on the efficacy of lifestyle solutions. Therefore, DTC ads may provide images to attract attention to more detailed claims about the inefficacy

153

of diet and exercise" (Byrne et al., 2013, p. 811). Similarly, Frosch et al. (2007) found that none of the ads related to conditions that could be treated with lifestyle change mentioned behavior change as an altern-ative to drug use, and 18 percent of the ads specifically suggested that lifestyle change alone would not be effective.

Finally, most of the studies note that DTC ads use emotional appeals, rather than rational arguments, to promote their products. Although the drugs are intended to treat illness, virtually all use images of friendly, healthy-looking people often engaged in vigorous physical activity – especially, the ads imply, *after* using the drug (Frosch et al., 2007; Welch Cline & Young, 2004). For instance, in one study of DTC television ads from 2004, 95 percent of product claim ads and 100 percent of reminder ads used positive emotional appeals, and 69 percent showed someone in a fearful or negative state before using the advertised drug. Welch Cline and Young (2004) concluded that DTC advertising's message is that using prescription drugs will make consumers healthy, lively, attractive and socially appealing, even when the ads are promoting drugs for serious health conditions such as cancer, HIV/AIDS and severe arthritis.

The bottom line, according to a recent study, is that the content of many DTC drug ads is potentially misleading. Faerber and Kreling (2014) analyzed a sample of prescription drug ads aired between 2008 and 2010, comparing each ad's most emphasized claim to objective medical evidence and categorizing each claim as objectively true, poten-tially misleading or false. They defined "potentially misleading" as any claims that omitted important information, exaggerated information, expressed unsupported opinions about the drug or associated use of the drug with a desirable lifestyle or subgroup (e.g., "on-the-go women"). Their analysis identified 23 percent of the most emphasized claims in DTC ads as objectively true, while 61 percent were categorized as poten-tially misleading, and 17 percent were rated as factually false. Among the claims deemed potentially misleading, the most common problem was the inclusion of non-facts expressing opinions or associated the drug with a desirable lifestyle or group. The authors note that while some critics may say that such ads do not violate regulations prohibiting mis-leading advertising, "a high level of misleading information may be affecting the quality of decision-making about drug use" (Faerber & Kreling, 2014, p. 116).

CONSUMERS' VS. DOCTORS' PERSPECTIVES ON DTC ADVERTISING

As noted earlier, one of the reasons the FDA initially agreed to allow DTC advertising of prescription drugs was that, as consumers became more active participants in health care decision-making, they wanted and needed more information about all sorts of medical interventions, including prescription drugs (Donohue, 2006). Some early studies showed that consumers overall held fairly neutral views toward DTC advertising, although attitudes were significantly more positive among individuals who believed, wrongly, that the FDA had to give prior approval of the ads or that the FDA only allowed marketing of drugs that were "completely safe," had no serious side effects and/or were "extremely effective." Attitude toward DTC advertising was also positively associated with awareness of such ads (Bell et al., 1999a). In another 1999 survey, consumers who had been exposed to at least one DTC ad rated the ads' utility at 2.5 on a 4-point scale, reflecting a generally positive view of such ads (Deshpande et al., 2004).

Another early study, conducted in 2001 by the Kaiser Family Foundation, revealed that 64 percent of respondents who had just been shown an ad said they would put "some" or "a lot" of trust in the information the ad provided about the relevant health condition, but only 33 percent of those who had not seen an ad said that, in general, they would trust information about health conditions included in DTC advertising. When asked about the trustworthiness of information about the drug they had seen advertised, 62 percent said they would trust that information, while only 46 percent who had not viewed an ad said they trusted drug information provided in DTC ads. In addition, regardless of which ad they had seen or what drug it advertised, at least two-thirds of those who viewed an ad

> said that the ad did an excellent or good job telling them about the condition the medicine is designed to treat (84%), the potential benefits of the medicine (72%), and who should take the drug (66%). Respondents were more divided about whether the ad they saw did an excellent or good job communicating who should *not* take the medicine (55%), the questions to ask a doctor about the medicine (55%), and the potential side effects (52%).
>
> (Kaiser Family Foundation, 2001, p. 11, emphasis in original)

However, individuals who had not just viewed an ad were far less positive in judging DTC ads they had seen in the past. The most positive assessment was for providing information about potential benefits; 60 percent said prescription drug ads are excellent or good in this regard. When asked about DTC ads in general, the percentages of respondents giving "excellent" or "good" ratings were 58 percent for information about the medical condition the drug treats, 47 percent for who should take the medicine, 41 percent for who should *not* take the medicine, 34 percent for questions to ask a doctor about the medicine, and only 30 percent for potential side effects (Kaiser Family Foundation, 2001).

Another survey conducted in 2001 revealed that 47 percent of consumers viewed DTC advertising as "good" or "very good." More specifically, 88 percent said that DTC advertisements give patients the confidence to talk to doctors about their concerns, 81 percent said the ads encourage people to follow treatment advice, 72 percent said they improve people's understanding of medical conditions and treatments, and 69 percent said they help patients get treatments they wouldn't otherwise receive. Although the majority also said that DTC ads drive up the cost of prescription drugs (76%) and promote unnecessary fear of side effects (54%), fewer than half of the respondents agreed that DTC ads promote unnecessary doctor visits (48%), cause patients to use more of their doctors' time (38%) or interfere in patient–physician relationships (30%) (Murray et al., 2004).

A somewhat later study of pharmacy customers in the southern United States showed that the respondents agreed with nearly all statements about the utility of DTC advertising, including statements that such advertising "accurately portrays side effects and risks," presents accurate information, and facilitates a more equal patient–physician relationship. In addition, the participants generally agreed that they would ask their doctor and had asked their doctor for a specific drug they had seen advertised, and that they have gone to the doctor because they believed their symptoms were similar to what was portrayed in a drug ad. They disagreed that DTC ads had reminded them to take or refill their prescriptions or that the ads had convinced them that a brand name drug was better than a generic. One concern was that lower income individuals were more likely to have found DTC advertising persuasive; they were more likely to report that they would ask their doctor about an advertised drug, that DTC advertising had prompted them to visit a doctor and that an ad had persuaded them to prefer a brand name drug over a generic (Mathew et al., 2008).

At least one more recent study also suggested that consumers have fairly positive opinions about DTC advertising. In a 2008 study of public opinion about prescription drugs and the pharmaceutical industry, 53 percent agreed that prescription drug advertising is "mostly a good thing, and two-thirds (67%) agree that these ads educate people about treatments and encourage them to get help" (USA Today, Kaiser Family Foundation & Harvard School of Public Health, 2008, p. 3). However, some studies have shown consumers to be more skeptical about DTC ads. For instance, a study of Colorado residents showed that fewer than one-third agreed that the growth of DTC advertising was a positive trend (29%) or that the ads enabled them to make more informed health decisions (28.6%); only 10.5 percent said the ads motivated them to seek medical care (Robinson et al., 2004). Another survey of American adults, conducted via email in 2005, showed that 90 percent of respondents said DTC advertising makes consumers aware of new medications, and two-thirds agreed that advertising increases consumers' knowledge about new drugs and their availability. However, one-third of respondents said prescription drug ads confuse consumers, and about half believed the ads make consumers worry unnecessarily about negative side effects (Polen et al., 2009).

Wood and Cronley (2013) compared consumers' attitudes from surveys conducted in 2003 and 2012 and found that attitudes toward DTC advertising have grown "significantly more negative" (p. 814). In 2003, on average, consumers rated DTC advertising above the mid-point (3.5 on a 7-point scale) on seven semantic differential measures, indicating that they found the ads useful, interesting, helpful, informative, easy to understand and beneficial. The only term for which the rating was less than 4 was "enjoyable" (3.61), and the overall rating of consumer attitudes about DTC ads was 4.32. By 2012, however, that overall rating had dropped to 3.96, and consumers rated the ads as significantly less useful, helpful, informative and beneficial (Wood & Cronley, 2013).

Doctors, in general, have been far more critical of DTC advertising since its inception. For instance, a 1997 survey of family physicians showed that the majority agreed that DTC advertising encourages patients' active involvement in their care (60%), encourages them to seek care when they might not otherwise do so (56%) and makes patients more aware of new products (73%). However, 75 percent said that DTC advertising leads to higher drug prices, 71 percent said the ads create pressure for physicians to prescribe drugs they otherwise might not choose for their patients, and 89 percent strongly disagreed that DTC advertising improves relationships between doctors and their patients (Lipsky & Taylor, 1997). Similarly, a survey of 535 American physicians conducted in 2000/2001 showed that although 83 percent agreed that DTC advertising encourages patients to share concerns with their doctors and 72 percent said that ads encourage people to adhere to their doctors' treatment advice, most doctors also perceived significant disadvantages to DTC advertising: 81 percent said the ads increase prescription drug costs, 59 percent said they create unnecessary fear of side effects, and 53 percent said they lead to patient questions that take up more of the physician's time. Substantial percentages expressed concern that DTC advertising promotes unnecessary doctor visits (45%) and interferes with doctor–physician relationships (39%). Most physicians (78%) said their patients were fair or poor at judging whether the information in a DTC ad was relevant to them (Murray et al., 2003).

Murray et al.'s (2004) survey of Colorado doctors and consumers showed that physicians viewed DTC advertising negatively. Virtually all of the doctors (98.7%) said the ads provide too little information about drug costs, and 94.9 percent said the ads do not provide enough information about alternative treatment options. In addition, the majority (54.8%) said DTC ads provide too little information about harmful side effects. The doctors said DTC advertising encourages patients to request specific drugs (80.7%), changes patients' expectations about what the doctor will prescribe (67%) and requires them to spend more time in visits with patients (55.9%). Physicians were significantly less likely than consumers to believe that DTC advertising is a positive trend in health care.

A survey of Arizona primary care doctors and physician assistants showed that health providers responded more negatively to hypothetical situations in which a patient asked for information about a drug if DTC advertising prompted the request versus a scenario in which the patient had seen something about the drug in the *Physicians' Desk Reference* (PDR), a commonly used drug reference text. In comparison to clinicians asked about a patient query prompted by the PDR, those responding to the DTC advertising scenario were significantly more likely to say that they would be annoyed with the patient asking for more information and would attempt to change the subject rather than discuss the drug and less likely to say they would answer the patient's questions about the drug or provide additional written information. If the patient asked to try the medication, clinicians in the DTC advertising scenario said they would be more frustrated and annoyed with the patient and more likely to prescribe a different drug to discourage future DTC advertising-prompted medication requests; in comparison to clinicians responding to the PDR scenario, those dealing with a hypothetical patient requesting a drug they had seen advertised were less likely to provide samples of the drug or to write a prescription for the drug if they had no samples available (Zachry et al., 2003).

In summary, although consumers have become somewhat more skeptical about DTC advertising, they have always been and remain more likely than physicians to see DTC advertising as beneficial and useful. Which group is correct? What benefits does DTC advertising offer? What negative impacts does it have? And does the evidence show that, overall, the benefits outweigh the harms?

Benefits of DTC Advertising

Proponents of DTC advertising contend that it produces a number of benefits, including raising consumers' awareness of diseases and treatment options they may not know about otherwise, empowering them to seek treatment and ask questions of their health care providers, reminding them to take drugs their doctors have already prescribed, reducing the stigma associated with certain diseases, and ultimately, improving health outcomes. There is some evidence that DTC advertising may prompt consumers to seek additional information about health concerns. FDA surveys in 1999 and 2002 showed that exposure to DTC advertising was an important influence on seeking additional information, with 43 percent of the 2002 respondents saying that exposure to an ad encouraged them to seek more information either about the advertised drug or about a health issue. Among those who looked for more information, the most common sources were doctors (89%) and pharmacists (51%). Nearly two-thirds sought information about side effects (61%), while only 10 percent sought more information about the drug's benefits. While only 4 percent of FDA survey respondents said

DTC advertising was primarily responsible for a doctor visit, about one-third said a DTC ad had prompted them to question their doctor about something, and nearly one-third (32%) reported asking their doctor if there was a prescription drug to treat their condition or symptoms (Aikin et al., 2004).

Research also suggests that exposure to DTC advertising encourages at least some consumers to seek treatment for health concerns they otherwise might not have recognized. Becker and Huh (2005) found that exposure to DTC advertising was a good predictor of consumers' likelihood of seeking more information about the advertised drug, feeling "primed" to talk to a doctor about the drug and actually communicating with a doctor. Similarly, in a survey of consumers who participated in a Harris Interactive survey between July 2001 and January 2002, 35 percent reported that a DTC ad had given them reason to discuss with their doctor a drug or a health concern. Of those people, about 45 percent said that the ad was one of the primary information sources leading them to discuss the issue with their doctor, and about 20 percent had discussed a new health issue, rather than simply discussing the drug or the possibility of changing their treatment for a previously diagnosed condition. About one in five (20.1%) were told they did *not* have the condition mentioned in the ad.

However, among those whose doctor visits were influenced at least in part by DTC advertising, almost one in four (24.7%) received a new diagnosis, and 43 percent of these new diagnoses were considered "high-priority" conditions. The most common new diagnoses were allergies, high cholesterol, arthritis, hypertension, diabetes, depression, and diseases of the stomach, esophagus and duodenum (Weissman et al., 2004).

Among those receiving a new diagnosis, 80 percent received a drug prescription, with more than half of those (44.7%) for the advertised drug; in addition, 35.7 percent were referred to a specialist, and 58.3 percent were encouraged to make lifestyle changes. Among those prescribed a drug who took it as prescribed, about 80 percent "reported that they felt much better or somewhat better overall after taking the drug, and similar numbers reported that their symptoms improved" (Weissman et al., 2003, pp. W3-90). The authors note that they "found that DTCA visits resulted in health care actions taken on behalf of patients that went beyond the expected prescribing of drugs, both advertised and not" (pp. W3-91). Most visits were for clinically important rather than "lifestyle" problems, and the research did not show any significant negative health effects among these patients.

Another benefit proponents often claim for DTC advertising is improved compliance with drug prescriptions; in other words, they argue, seeing DTC advertising can help remind patients to take a drug their doctor has prescribed. For instance, a study focused specifically on DTC advertising for anti-depressants showed that, following periods of high spending for such ads, larger numbers of individuals diagnosed with depression began taking an anti-depressant, and ad spending had a small positive impact on the likelihood of diagnosed individuals continuing anti-depressant treatment for at least four months (Donohue et al., 2004). On the other hand, a more recent study found that only promotion to physicians was associated with patients' adherence to anti-depressant prescriptions; DTC advertising of anti-depressants had no effect (Hansen et al., 2010).

Another study, focused on compliance with the use of cholesterol-lowering drugs, showed that overall levels of advertising for such drugs increases compliance – but not necessarily among users of the advertised brand. The study showed that higher levels of DTC advertising for statins increased compliance rates among patients taking other drugs in the category. Somewhat surprisingly, for one statin brand – Lipitor – increased levels of advertising were actually associated with *lower* compliance among Lipitor-using patients, which may have been attributable to the discussion of negative side effects in Lipitor advertising. Wosinska (2005) suggests that this may mean that Lipitor's ads may have included negative side effect information more prominently than did ads for Zocor or Pravachol, or that Lipitor users responded more negatively to the side effect information than did Zocor or Pravachol users. The data suggested that the volume of Lipitor advertising negatively affected compliance only among patients who had been taking Lipitor before the company began running television ads, including the required negative side effect information.

Another potential benefit of direct-to-consumer advertising is a reduction in the stigma associated with certain health conditions, especially mental illnesses, sexual dysfunction and other embarrassing health conditions. Some studies have shown that exposure to DTC advertising may reduce stigma associated with some health problems, although that impact may be limited primarily to those who suffer from those health problems. For instance, one study in which individuals watched an ad for the anti-depressant Cymbalta and two ads for non-pharmaceutical products showed that, after watching the ad, individuals who self-identified with mental illness reacted more positively toward a hypothetical man identified as having major depression, feeling that he was less to blame and less dangerous, and reporting greater pity, less desire to avoid that sort of person and a greater willingness to help; they were also more likely to believe he could recover (Corrigan et al., 2014). However, among those who did not identify as having mental illness the impact was the opposite; they were less likely to offer help, to believe that the depressed man would recover or to agree that he would be able to determine what happens to him (e.g., that he could earn a college degree). On the other hand, An and colleagues (2009) found that among individuals who had not experienced depression symptoms, greater exposure to DTC anti-depressant ads was associated with more positive evaluations of anti-depressant treatment; however, the same pattern did not hold among those who had themselves experienced symptoms of depression.

Another study, which used data from an online survey, revealed that greater familiarity with DTC advertising for erectile dysfunction drugs was a significant predictor of having used the ED drug Viagra with a prescription; there was no effect of DTC advertising attitudes or familiarity in having used Viagra without a prescription. The authors concluded that their data show that DTC encourages men to seek medical advice before obtaining Viagra (Myers et al., 2011).

Of course, the most important potential benefit of DTC advertising would be improved health outcomes, which could result if DTC advertising prompts individuals with a serious and untreated medical condition to seek, obtain and adhere to a treatment regimen that controls the original condition without causing significant negative side effects. For instance, Block (2007) calculated that for each depressed individual prompted to begin taking anti-depressants in response to DTC advertising, the value of the economic benefit to society was 63 times the cost of the treatment. Block concluded that this results in a net gain to society, even though his analysis suggested that 94 percent of those who begin taking anti-depressants in response to DTC advertising are actually not depressed. His argument assumes that the only costs for anti-depressant treatment – whether necessary or not – is the cost of the drug and the initial doctor visit, and that the net economic outcome is positive because those who were depressed benefit so much from the relief of their symptoms through anti-depressant use. Other researchers have also found that DTC advertising helps avert undertreatment of depression because requests for anti-depressants, either in general or by brand name, increased physicians' likelihood of providing acceptable initial care to those demonstrating symptoms of major depression (Kravitz et al., 2005).

Some proponents argue that DTC advertising may create positive expectancies for treatment with a particular drug, and these positive expectancies produce a placebo effect that enhances the effectiveness of the drug "beyond that which is expected from their purely biological mechanisms" (Almasi et al., 2006, p. e146). Unfortunately, it appears that no studies have specifically examined this potential effect, and, in fact, little research has produced clear and direct evidence of health outcome benefits caused by DTC advertising. Some authors have suggested that DTC advertising may produce benefits primarily when health professionals have "ample evidence that a particular therapy works ... and underuse exists" (Dubois, 2003, pp. W3-101). When that is not the case, patients may receive no benefit or may receive some benefit but at a higher cost than is necessary.

THE NEGATIVE EFFECTS OF DTC DRUG ADVERTISING

Critics argue that DTC advertising of prescription drugs has the potential to cause harm in a number of ways, many of which stand in direct contradiction to the benefits claimed by DTC advertising's proponents. For instance, rather than educating consumers about medical conditions and treatments, some scholars have argued that DTC advertising misleads and confuses consumers, particularly leading consumers to overestimate the benefits and underestimate the potential risks of prescription drug use. As noted earlier, analyses of DTC advertising content show that the ads often fail to present clear numerical information about either benefits or risks (Avery et al., 2011; Faerber & Kreling, 2014; Frosch et al., 2007; Kaphingst & DeJong, 2004; Macias et al., 2010; Macias et al., 2007; Woloshin et al., 2001).

In addition, some studies with consumers suggest that DTC ads are not as educational as their proponents claim. For instance, the majority of participants in a U.S.-based online depression forum rated the quality of information provided in anti-depressant ads as only fair or poor. The respondents, most of whom had been diagnosed with depression, were particularly critical of the ads' provision of information about the causes of depression, rated poor by 54.7 percent and fair by another 24.3 percent, and information about medication effectiveness, rated poor by nearly one-third and fair by 42.6 percent. Less than half (46.7%) rated the ads' information about depression symptoms as being good or excellent, and less than one-third (29.1%) gave high ratings to the information about drug risks and side effects (Bell et al., 2010).

A Kaiser Family Foundation study examined consumers' responses to DTC ads for Nexium (for acid reflux), Lipitor (for high cholesterol) and Singulair (an asthma drug). Comparisons of those who watched the ads to those who did not suggested that the ads did not necessarily provide new information about acid reflux disease or cholesterol. Some people gained new information about the specific medicine, but others did not. For instance, a minority of individuals who saw the Lipitor ad did not know already what it had said about Lipitor's effectiveness in preventing future heart attacks. People who viewed the Singulair ad were more likely than those who did not to know that there are drugs which people with asthma can take to prevent asthma attacks; however, a quarter of those who saw the Singulair ad reported the mistaken belief that the drug could be used in place of an inhaler *during* an asthma attack. Ad viewers often could not recall what kind of side effects the drug might cause, even immediately after watching the ad, although they were more likely than those who hadn't watched the ads to perceive the potential side effects as serious. In addition, few of those who watched the ads could remember where they had been directed to go for further information (Kaiser Family Foundation, 2001).

A more recent study examining comprehension of DTC ad information among low-literacy adults showed that although more than three-quarters of the participants rated the ads they viewed as "very" or "somewhat" clear, the average participant answered correctly only 59 percent of 35 true-false knowledge questions asked about information from the ads. For some information, especially about side effects or risks of taking the drug, the percentages answering correctly were substantially below 50 percent; for instance, only 26 percent understood that taking Singulair can cause ear infections (Kaphingst et al., 2005). In another study, 67 African American teenage girls participated in focus groups about the human papillomavirus (HPV) vaccine and DTC advertising for it. The study demonstrated that although nearly all of the girls reported having seen one of the ads and some could even recite its tag line, "I want to be one less," few could understand the central message of the ad. The girls often said that the spoken information in the ad ran too quickly for them to understand what was being said, even to the point that they did not understand that HPV was a disease. The information teens were most likely to have understood was that vaccine users could experience side effects and that it was not approved for use by pregnant women. They emphasized that, for teens like them to understand the ad's message, the voice-over needed to be spoken more slowly and the text information needed to be in a larger font and/or left on the screen for longer. Some teens also suggested that the ad needed to provide more information about HPV to help teens understand why young people might need the vaccine (Leader et al., 2011).

If DTC advertising confuses consumers regarding the risks and/or benefits of the advertised drugs, critics charge, such confusion could lead to several undesirable effects. First, the ads' required inclusion of information about potential side effects may, in some cases, raise unnecessary concerns among consumers, possibly even leading some individuals to discontinue taking prescribed drugs without consulting their doctor. Indeed, in one survey, nearly one in five respondents (17.8%) said they had stopped taking a medication because they were worried about serious side effects mentioned in a DTC ad (Polen et al., 2009). Exposure to ads that include side effects warnings may be more likely to lead to discontinuance of a prescription if the patient had been taking the drug before seeing the ads (Wosinska, 2005).

On the other hand, DTC ads' overemphasis of a medication's benefits may tend to reduce consumers' motivation to adopt lifestyle changes that would benefit them. At least one study has suggested that ads for cholesterol-reducing medications include content that seems likely to discourage consumers from seeing increased exercise and/or a healthier diet as effective ways of lowering their cholesterol (Byrne et al., 2013). In addition, in-depth interviews with participants who watched ads for heart disease prevention or treatment drugs (e.g., Lipitor, Plavix, etc.) revealed that although some consumers expressed willingness to make whatever lifestyle changes were necessary to avoid taking a prescription drug, the most common responses reflected a "Negotiator" stance, characterized by willingness to take prescription drugs if, after a period of time, lifestyle changes hadn't been effective. Those who were uninsured and senior participants were most likely to be "Embracers," those who would immediately opt for the prescription drug and would not make any attempt to improve their health through lifestyle changes. Several consumers noted that the ads often presented taking the drug as the only viable choice, rather than as an alternative or supplement to healthy lifestyle change. The researchers concluded that these ads may present heart disease as a condition beyond individuals' control, suggesting that one could take the advertised drug without needing to feel any guilt about not adopting lifestyle changes (Frosch et al., 2011). Similarly, Bell and colleagues (2010) found that exposure to anti-depressant ads may discourage depressed individuals from seeking treatment via psychotherapy and could even lead some individuals to switch doctors if their request for an advertised anti-depressant was denied. Payton and Thoits (2011) found that exposure to DTC anti-depressant ads led non-depressed consumers to view prescription drugs as the most appropriate treatment for depression.

Another complaint critics charge against DTC advertising is that it promotes "medicalization" of normal life changes or minor problems, leading people to take prescription drugs with potentially serious negative side effects and little significant benefit. For instance, Conrad (2005) argues that DTC advertising helped transform Viagra from a drug intended primarily for older men who experienced erectile problems due to diabetes, prostate cancer or other medical problems into a "solution" that might be deemed appropriate for virtually any man who views himself as having sexual performance difficulties. "The drug industry has expanded the notion of ED and has even subtly encouraged the use of Viagra-like drugs as an enhancement to sexual pleasure and relationships" (Conrad, 2005, p. 6). Similarly, he contends, manufacturers of drugs that treat social anxiety disorder and generalized anxiety disorder have succeeded in selling these originally obscure diagnoses as common but also abnormal conditions that should be treated with medication; "it is clear that GlaxoSmithKline's campaign for Paxil increased the medicalization of anxiety, inferring that shyness and worrying may be medical problems, with Paxil as the proper treatment" (Conrad, 2005, p. 7).

There is little question that many consumers follow the advice often included in DTC drug ads to "talk to your doctor" about the drug (Aikin et al., 2004; Becker & Huh, 2005; Js et al., 2003; Weissman et al., 2003). However, the opponents of DTC advertising warn that these conversations may lead to consumers taking drugs that offer little benefit and potentially significant risks. For instance, a study linking exposure to DTC advertising to prescriptions for COX-2 inhibitors showed that individuals who had asked their doctor about a COX-2 drug they had seen advertised were more likely than any other patients to receive a prescription for a COX-2 drug, though not necessarily the one about which they had asked. For some patients this would be beneficial; however, the effect held even for patients who should instead have been prescribed a non-steroidal anti-inflammatory drug due to gastrointestinal risk factors (Spence et al., 2005). Similarly, Block (2007) determined that 94 percent of individuals who receive new prescriptions for anti-depressants are, in fact, not clinically depressed and therefore should not be taking anti-depressants.

Another study of physicians and patients in the United States and Canada showed that physicians usually gave patients prescriptions for drugs they had requested after seeing the drugs advertised, even though the doctors viewed half of those new prescriptions as only "possible" or "unlikely" choices for similar patients; in comparison, doctors gave similar ratings only 12.4 percent of the time in relation to new prescriptions patients had not requested (Mintzes et al., 2003). In addition, Murray et al. (2003) found that even when physicians regarded patients' DTC-influenced requests (for tests, specialist referrals or changes in medication) as clinically *inappropriate*, they nonetheless agreed to the requests 69 percent of the time.

In addition to influencing prescribing practices, DTC advertising also has the potential to affect the doctor–patient relationship in negative ways (Bell et al., 1999b; Blose & Mack, 2009; Cline & Young, 2005; Murray et al., 2003; Robinson et al., 2004). Consumers predict that they would generally react negatively in situations in which their doctor refused to prescribe a drug the patient had requested based on the information he or she had seen in a DTC ad. In a survey of California adults, Bell et al. (1999b) found that 46 percent said they would be disappointed if their doctor denied their request for an advertised drug, and a quarter said they would try to persuade the doctor to change his or her mind. One in four said they would seek the prescription from another doctor, and 15 percent predicted that they would consider switching doctors entirely.

A later experimental study showed that participants would rate their satisfaction with physicians lower if they were denied a requested DTC-advertised drug, although the manner in which the physician com-municated the denial had a significant impact on satisfaction (Shah et al., 2006). Such scenarios are likely to be relatively commonplace, given that nearly half (49%) of the physicians in one survey viewed patients' DTC advertising-prompted requests as clinically inappropriate (Murray et al., 2003). That survey, as well as others, has shown that physicians see DTC advertising as causing longer and/or less efficient patient visits and changing patients' expectations about what their doctor will prescribe (Murray et al., 2003; Robinson et al., 2004).

Although impacts on the physician–patient relationship are certainly important, arguably the most important question about DTC advert-ising is whether it contributes to better or worse health outcomes. As noted earlier, some proponents of DTC advertising argue that it leads to a net improvement in health-related quality of life at the population level, even when most new prescriptions prompted by DTC advertising go to individuals who do not have the relevant condition (Block, 2007). However, at least two systematic analyses of the health outcomes associ-ated with DTC advertising concluded that no evidence exists of benefits to health outcomes, and some research suggests significant negative effects. Gilbody and colleagues (2005) reviewed studies that were rigor-ous enough to assess the impact of DTC advertising on outcomes and found that such ads influenced patient demand for drugs and changed doctors' prescribing behavior, but had no impact on improving health outcomes. In addition, at least one of the studies reviewed documented a significant impact of DTC advertising on the use of the Novartis drug Lamisil (terbinafine) to treat toenail fungus. The fungus itself is never a significant health threat, causing only cosmetically unappealing discol-oration and thickening of the nails. However, terbinafine's common side effects include diarrhea, stomach upset and temporary loss of taste, and the drug can cause severe liver damage (Cunha, n.d.).

A more recent systematic review of the literature suggests other negative impacts. A re-analysis of the data Block (2007) used to argue in favor of DTC advertising of anti-depressants suggests that the original analysis overstated benefits and underestimated health harms (Jureidini et al., 2008). Commenting on that re-analysis, Mintzes notes that including data on harmful effects of anti-depressant use "predicts that serious adverse events would occur 2–7 times as often as depression remission, and common adverse events such as sexual dysfunction 35 to 78 times as often" (Mintzes, 2012, p. 268). Even when the negative effects of a given drug are not serious, DTC advertising-prompted increases in the number of different prescriptions an individual takes can increase the risk of adverse drug interactions, especially among seniors who are more likely to be taking other prescription drugs already (Datti & Carter, 2006).

Other researchers have also suggested that exposure to DTC advertising may actually contribute to consumers engaging in less healthy and/or more risky behaviors. For instance, one small study of HIV-positive homosexual men in San Francisco showed that those who had greater exposure to DTC advertising for HIV drugs perceived AIDS as a less serious disease and were more likely to engage in unprotected anal sex (Klausner et al., 2002). Early reports about the study led the FDA to send warning letters to the makers of anti-retroviral drugs, insisting that they discontinue the use of sexy, athletic-looking models, often shown in the ads engaging in unrealistically rigorous activity such as sailing, mountain-climbing and riding bikes (Josefson, 2001). Another study linking DTC advertising exposure to health behaviors showed that greater exposure to DTC advertising for drugs related to diabetes, hypertension, high cholesterol and overweight was associated with a reduced likelihood of engaging in moderate exercise (Iizuka & Jin, 2005).

Overall, systematic reviews of the research conclude that DTC advertising increases consumers' likelihood of talking to their doctors about the drugs they've seen advertised but does not improve health outcomes (Gilbody et al., 2005; Lexchin & Mintzes, 2002; Mintzes, 2012). As Mintzes notes in the discussion of her more recent review, "more medicine use is not necessarily better" (2012, p. 271).

This finding that DTC advertising does not lead to improvements in public health is particularly disturbing, given that there is very good evidence that the advertising increases overall spending on prescription drugs and may, in fact, increase the costs of specific drugs. This occurs, in part, because the drugs advertised to consumers are those for which drug manufacturers still hold the patent; that is, they are newer drugs for which there are no generic alternatives, meaning manufacturers can charge more per unit without worrying about losing patients to cheaper generic equivalents. For instance, researchers who studied Medicaid spending for clopidogrel (Plavix), a drug used to prevent heart attacks and strokes, found that the cost of the drug increased by 40 cents per unit soon after DTC advertising for the drug had begun, resulting in a total increased cost of $207 million in Medicaid pharmacy spending (Law et al., 2009). Another study, which examined overall spending for arthritis, cholesterol, acid reflux and insomnia drugs between 1994 and 2005, concluded that DTC advertising – especially broadcast advertising – has a significant impact on both overall spending driven by increased demand for the drugs and on spending caused by higher drug prices. The authors concluded that the expansion of broadcast DTC advertising after 1998 accounted for 17 to 20 percent of the overall increase in spending on these drugs (Dave & Saffer, 2012). This influence on increased drug spending is significant, given that total U.S. spending for prescription drugs totaled $329.2 billion in 2013, a 3.2 percent increase from 2012 (IMS Institute for Healthcare Informatics, 2014).

EMERGING DTC ADVERTISING ISSUES

Most of the research thus far has focused on direct-to-consumer promotion of prescription drugs. However, increasingly, scholars are examining the content and effects of advertising for other medical products and services; in particular, there is great interest in and concern about DTC advertising of genetic testing. Public health experts and physicians generally take a negative view of this sort of advertising, on the grounds that the tests identify genetic mutations that are quite rare in the population, meaning that for the vast majority of people who would be tested, there would be little or no benefit. Advertising for cancer-related genetic testing is more likely to reach those at low risk, rather than those at high risk, and subsequently creates increased demand for both the tests and genetic counseling. In addition, false positive test results can elevate psychological and emotional stress, and use of genetic testing by low-risk individuals "increases health care costs and challenges the genetic counselling system, which is already inundated with high-risk patients" (Kontos & Viswanath, 2011, p. 144).

The 2002 DTC advertising campaign run by Myriad, a Canadian biotechnology company, illustrates some of the pitfalls of direct-to-consumer promotion of genetic testing. The 2002 campaign, which encouraged women to use Myriad's test for the BRCA1 and BRCA2 genes linked to breast cancer, ran intensively for five months in Atlanta and Denver. Myriad's direct-to-consumer advertising campaign significantly increased wait times for genetic counseling, prompted a significant increase in genetic testing of *low-risk* women, and led to a 30 percent decrease in genetic testing referrals for *high-risk* women during the advertising campaign (Tracy, 2008).

One of the most serious problems with DTC advertising for genetic testing is that test kits, unlike prescription drugs, can be purchased and used by consumers without any interaction with a health care professional. Consumers who use these at-home genetic testing kits may receive and process test results without ever interacting directly with a health professional, relying instead on the information provided by the genetic testing companies, usually via their websites, which may provide misleading, scientifically unsupported content and advice. For instance, the Federal Trade Commission warns that some genetic testing companies suggest that their test results can predict whether or not an individual will develop a specific disease or condition, or how the individual will react to environmental toxins or cigarette smoke; others suggest that, based on the genetic test results, they can offer consumers "personalized" diets or supplements that will protect them against serious diseases. None of these claims is supported by valid scientific studies (Federal Trade Commission, 2014).

Health professionals are also increasingly concerned about DTC advertising for medical interventions and products such as hip replacement products or stents used in heart surgery. Mitka (2008) notes that spending on DTC advertising of medical devices grew from $116 million in 2005 to $193 million in 2007. That advertising has consequences potentially even more significant than those for DTC advertising of drugs, in that medical devices are generally much more expensive than drugs and require significant training on the part of the surgeon to be used successfully. Thus, a change in device or technique can lead to more surgical or medical complications for the patient. In addition, because many medical devices are surgically implanted and thus more or less permanent, the potential adverse consequences to the patient and the surgeon are considerable if an inappropriate or unfamiliar implant or surgical technique is used, and the choice of implant or procedure cannot be easily substituted if the result of surgery is unfavorable.

(Bozic et al., 2007)

For these reasons, nearly three-quarters of orthopedic surgeons said DTC advertising for medical devices negatively affected their practice, and 77 percent said DTC advertising often led their patients to be misinformed or confused about how their condition should be treated.

RESHAPING DTC ADVERTISING TO BENEFIT CONSUMERS

Direct-to-consumer advertising of medical products, including drugs, medical devices and testing, is a type of commercial speech protected in the United States by the First Amendment. Thus, it seems relatively unlikely that the U.S. government will ever enforce a complete ban on DTC advertising, despite evidence that its harms may outweigh its benefits (Gilbody et al., 2005; Lexchin & Mintzes, 2002; Mintzes, 2012). Given this reality, some scholars have suggested changes to the FDA's requirements for content in DTC ads. For instance, one approach would be to differentiate among three categories of ads: those for products targeting asymptomatic patients who have not been diagnosed with the relevant disease or condition, those for products targeting undiagnosed patients who are experiencing symptoms, and those targeting previously diagnosed conditions. This framework would require different types of ad content depending on the category, so that advertising would give consumers clearer information about whether the advertised product is appropriate for them; in addition, ads would be required to provide specific quantitative information about the benefits of using the product as well as specific and accurate information about potential risks (Frosch et al., 2010).

Consumers today, for the most part, want increased access to information they can use to make health decisions, and despite some increasing skepticism about DTC advertising (Wood & Cronley, 2013), the public considers DTC advertising to offer at least some useful health information (Deshpande et al., 2004; Donohue, 2006; Weissman et al., 2003). Thus, increasing the ratio of beneficial to harmful effects of DTC advertising may require both increased regulatory guidance in terms of DTC advertising content (Frosch et al., 2010), as well as greater efforts toward improving consumers' health literacy so that they are better able to understand and to critically assess the information DTC ads provide.

References

Ad Age. (2011). *Pharmaceutical Marketing*. Chicago, IL. Retrieved December 3, 2014 from http://adage.com/images/bin/pdf/WPpharmmarketing_revise.pdf.

Aikin, K.J., Swasy, J.L. & Braman, A.C. (2004). Patient and Physician Attitudes and Behaviors Associated with DTC Promotion of Prescription Drugs – Summary of FDA Survey Research Results. *Food and Drug Administration. Center for Drug Evaluation and Research, 19.*

Almasi, E.A., Stafford, R.S., Kravitz, R.L. & Mansfield, P.R. (2006). What Are the Public Health Effects of Direct-to-consumer Drug Advertising? *PLoS Medicine, 3*(3), e145. http://doi.org/10.1371/journal.pmed.0030145.

An, S., Jin, H.S. & Brown, J.D. (2009). Direct-to-consumer Antidepressant Ads and Young Adults' Beliefs About Depression. *Health Marketing Quarterly, 26*(4), 259–278. http://doi.org/10.1080/07359680903303981.

Atherly, A. & Rubin, P.H. (2009, December). The Cost-effectiveness of Direct-to-consumer Advertising for Prescription Drugs. *Medical Care Research and Review, 66*(6), 639–657. doi: 10.1177/1077558709335362. Epub 2009 May 7.

Avery, R.J., Eisenberg, M. & Simon, K.I. (2011). Fair Balance in Direct-to-consumer Antidepressant Print and Television Advertising, 1995–2007. *Journal of Health Communication, 17*(3), 250–277. http://doi.org/10.1080/10810730.2011.585698.

Becker, L.B., & Huh, J. (2005). Direct-to-consumer Prescription Drug Advertising: Understanding its Consequences. *International Journal of Advertising, 24*(4), 441–466.

Bell, R.A., Kravitz, R.L. & Wilkes, M.S. (1999a). Direct-to-consumer Prescription Drug Advertising and the Public. *Journal of General Internal Medicine, 14*(11), 651–657.

Bell, R.A., Taylor, L.D. & Kravitz, R.L. (2010). Do Antidepressant Advertisements Educate Consumers and Promote Communication between Patients with Depression and Their Physicians? *Patient Education and Counseling, 81*(2), 245–250. http://doi.org/10.1016/j.pec.2010.01.014.

Bell, R.A., Wilkes, M.S. & Kravitz, R.L. (1999b). Advertisement-induced Prescription Drug Requests: Patients' Anticipated Reactions to a Physician Who Refuses. *The Journal of Family Practice, 48*(6), 446–452.

Block, A.E. (2007). Costs and Benefits of Direct-to-consumer Advertising: The Case of Depression. *PharmacoEconomics, 25*(6), 511–521.

Blose, J.E. & Mack, R.W. (2009). The Impact of Denying a Direct-to-consumer Advertised Drug Request on the Patient/Physician Relationship. *Health Marketing Quarterly, 26*(4), 315–332. http://doi.org/10.1080/07359680903304294.

Bozic, K.J., Smith, A.R., Hariri, S., Adeoye, S., Gourville, J., Maloney, W.J. & Rubash, H.E. (2007). THE 2007 ABJS MARSHALL URIST AWARD: *Clinical Orthopaedics and Related Research, PAP.* http://doi.org/10.1097/BLO.0b013e31804fdd02.

Brown, H. (2010). *Direct-to-consumer Advertising of Prescription Drugs: Exposure and Response.* Washington, DC: AARP. Retrieved December 2, 2014 from http://assets.aarp.org/rgcenter/general/prescription-drug-advertising-10.pdf.

Brownfield, E.D., Bernhardt, J.M., Phan, J.L., Williams, M.V. & Parker, R.M. (2004). Direct-to-consumer Drug Advertisements on Network Television: An Exploration of Quantity, Frequency, and Placement. *Journal of Health Communication, 9*(6), 491–497. http://doi.org/10.1080/10810730490523115.

Byrne, S., Niederdeppe, J., Avery, R.J. & Cantor, J. (2013). "When Diet and Exercise are not Enough": An Examination of Lifestyle Change Inefficacy Claims in Direct-to-consumer Advertising. *Health Communication, 28*(8), 800–813. http://doi.org/10.1080/10410236.2012.725125.

Centers for Disease Control and Prevention (CDC). (2014, October 29). Heart Disease Facts. Retrieved December 1, 2014 from www.cdc.gov/heartdisease/facts.htm.

Cline, R.J.W. & Young, H.J. (2005). Direct-to-consumer Print Ads for Drugs: Do They Undermine the Physician–Patient Relationship? *The Journal of Family Practice, 54*(12), 1049–1057.

Conrad, P. (2005). The Shifting Engines of Medicalization. *Journal of Health and Social Behavior, 46*(1), 3–14. http://doi.org/10.1177/002214650504600102.

Corrigan, P.W., Kosyluk, K.A., Fokuo, J.K. & Park, J.H. (2014). How Does Direct to Consumer Advertising Affect the Stigma of Mental Illness? *Community Mental Health Journal, 50*(7), 792–799. http://doi.org/10.1007/s10597-014-9698-7.

Cunha, J.P. (n.d.). Side Effects of Lamisil (Terbinafine) Drug Center. Retrieved December 16, 2014 from www.rxlist.com/lamisil-side-effects-drug-center.htm.

Datti, B. & Carter, M.W. (2006). The Effect of Direct-to-consumer Advertising on Prescription Drug Use By Older Adults. *Drugs & Aging, 23*(1), 71–81.

Dave, D. & Saffer, H. (2012). Impact of Direct-to-consumer Advertising on Pharmaceutical Prices and Demand. *Southern Economic Journal, 79*(1), 97–126. http://doi.org/10.4284/0038-4038-79.1.97.

Deshpande, A.D., Menon, A.M., Perri III, M. & Zinkhan, G.M. (2004). Direct-to-consumer Advertising and its Utility in Health Care Decision Making: A Consumer Perspective. *Journal of Health Communication, 9*(6), 499–513. http://doi.org/10.1080/10810730490523197.

Dobrow, L. (2014, April 1). DTC Report: DTC Gets Smart. Retrieved December 2, 2014 from www.mmm-online.com/dtc-report-dtc-gets-smart/article/339357/.

Donohue, J. (2006). A History of Drug Advertising: The Evolving Roles of Consumers and Consumer Protection. *The Milbank Quarterly, 84*(4), 659–699. http://doi.org/10.1111/j.1468-0009.2006.00464.x.

Donohue, J.M., Berndt, E.R., Rosenthal, M., Epstein, A.M. & Frank, R.G. (2004). Effects of Pharmaceutical Promotion on Adherence to the Treatment Guidelines for Depression. *Medical Care, 42*(12), 1176–1185.

Dubois, R.W. (2003). Pharmaceutical Promotion: Don't Throw the Baby Out With the Bathwater. *Health Affairs.* http://doi.org/10.1377/hlthaff.w3.96.

Faerber, A.E. & Kreling, D.H. (2014). Content Analysis of False and Misleading Claims in Television Advertising for Prescription and Nonprescription Drugs. *Journal of General Internal Medicine, 29*(1), 110–118. http://doi.org/10.1007/s11606-013-2604-0.

Federal Trade Commission. (2014, January). Direct-to-consumer Genetic Tests. Retrieved December 17, 2014 from www.consumer.ftc.gov/articles/0166-direct-consumer-genetic-tests.

Ford, E.S. & Capewell, S. (2013). Trends in Total and Low-density Lipoprotein Cholesterol among U.S. Adults: Contributions of Changes in Dietary Fat Intake and Use of Cholesterol-lowering Medications. *PLoS ONE, 8*(5). http://doi.org/10.1371/journal.pone.0065228.

Frosch, D.L. & Grande, D. (2010). Direct-to-consumer Advertising of Prescription Drugs. *LDI Issue Brief, 15*(3), 1–4.

Frosch, D.L., Grande, D., Tarn, D.M. & Kravitz, R.L. (2010). A Decade of Controversy: Balancing Policy with Evidence in the Regulation of Prescription Drug Advertising. *American Journal of Public Health, 100*(1), 24–32. http://doi.org/10.2105/AJPH.2008.153767.

Frosch, D.L., May, S.G., Tietbohl, C. & Pagán, J.A. (2011). Living in the "land of no"? Consumer perceptions of healthy lifestyle portrayals in direct-to-consumer advertisements of prescription drugs. *Social Science & Medicine (1982), 73*(7), 995–1002. http://doi.org/10.1016/j.socscimed.2011.06.064.

Frosch, D.L., Krueger, P.M., Hornik, R.C., Cronholm, P.F. & Barg, F.K. (2007). Creating Demand for Prescription Drugs: A Content Analysis of Television Direct-to-consumer Advertising. *The Annals of Family Medicine, 5*(1), 6–13. http://doi.org/10.1370/afm.611.

Gilbody, S., Wilson, P. & Watt, I. (2005). Benefits and Harms of Direct to Consumer Advertising: A Systematic Review. *Quality and Safety in Health Care, 14*(4), 246–250. http://doi.org/10.1136/qshc.2004.012781.

Greene, J.A. & Herzberg, D. (2010). Hidden in Plain Sight: Marketing Prescription Drugs to Consumers in the Twentieth Century. *American Journal of Public Health, 100*(5), 793–803. http://doi.org/10.2105/AJPH.2009.181255.

Hansen, R.A., Chen, S.-Y., Gaynes, B.N. & Maciejewski, M.L. (2010). Relationship of Pharmaceutical Promotion to Antidepressant Switching and Adherence: A Retrospective Cohort Study. *Psychiatric Services (Washington, D.C.), 61*(12), 1232–1238. http://doi.org/10.1176/appi.ps.61.12.1232.

Iizuka, T., & Jin, G. Z. (2005). The Effect of Prescription Drug Advertising on Doctor Visits. *Journal of Economics & Management Strategy,* 14(3), 701–727. http://dx.doi.org/10.1111/j.1530-9134.2005.00079.xx

Institute for Healthcare Informatics (IMS). (2014). *Medicine Use and Shifting Costs of Healthcare: A Review of the Use of Medicines in the U.S. in 2013.* Parsippany, NJ: IMS Institute for Healthcare Informatics. Retrieved December 16, 2014 from www.imshealth.com/portal/site/imshealth/menuitem.762a961826aad98f53c753c71ad8c22a/?vgnextoid=2684d47626745410VgnVCM10000076192ca2RCRD.

Josefson, D. (2001). FDA Warning to Manufacturers of AIDS Drugs. *BMJ: British Medical Journal, 322*(7295), 1143.

Js, W., D, B., Aj, S., M, N., K, Z., R, L. & S, F. (2003). Physicians Report on Patient Encounters Involving Direct-to-consumer Advertising. *Health Affairs (Project Hope), Suppl Web Exclusives,* W4–219–233.

Jureidini, J., Mintzes, B. & Raven, M. (2008). Does Direct-to-consumer Advertising of Antidepressants Lead to a Net Social Benefit? *PharmacoEconomics, 26*(7), 557–566; discussion 567–568.

Kaiser Family Foundation. (2001). *Understanding the Effects of Direct-to-consumer Prescription Drug Advertising.* Menlo Park, CA. Retrieved December 5, 2014 from http://kaiserfamilyfoundation.files.wordpress.com/2013/01/understanding-the-effects-of-direct-to-consumer-prescription-drug-advertising-report.pdf.

Kaphingst, K.A. & DeJong, W. (2004). The Educational Potential Of Direct-to-consumer Prescription Drug Advertising. *Health Affairs, 23*(4), 143–150. http://doi.org/10.1377/hlthaff.23.4.143.

Kaphingst, K.A., Rudd, R.E., DeJong, W. & Daltroy, L.H. (2005). Comprehension of Information in Three Direct-to-consumer Television Prescription Drug Advertisements among Adults with Limited Literacy. *Journal of Health Communication, 10*(7), 609–619.

Kelly, P. (2004, April 28). DTC Advertising's Benefits Far Outweigh Its Imperfections. *Health Affairs*, W4-246–248.

Klausner, J.D., Kim, A. & Kent, C. (2002). Are HIV Drug Advertisements Contributing to Increases in Risk Behavior among Men in San Francisco, 2001? *AIDS*, *16*(17), 2349–2350.

Kontos, E.Z. & Viswanath, K. (2011). Cancer-related Direct-to-consumer Advertising: A Critical Review. *Nature Reviews. Cancer*, *11*(2), 142–150. http://doi.org/10.1038/nrc2999.

Kravitz, R.L., Epstein, R.M., Feldman, M.D., Franz, C.E., Azari, R., Wilkes, M.S. & Franks, P. (2005). Influence of Patients' Requests for Direct-to-consumer Advertised Antidepressants – A Randomized Controlled Trial. *JAMA – Journal of the American Medical Association*, *293*(16), 1995–2002. http://doi.org/10.1001/jama.293.16.1995.

Law, M.R., Soumerai, S.B., Adams, A.S. & Majumdar, S.R. (2009). Costs and Consequences of Direct-to-consumer Advertising for Clopidogrel in Medicaid. *Archives of Internal Medicine*, *169*(21), 1969–1974. http://doi.org/10.1001/archinternmed.2009.320.

Leader, A.E., Cashman, R., Voytek, C.D., Baker, J.L., Brawner, B.M. & Frank, I. (2011). An Exploratory Study of Adolescent Female Reactions to Direct-to-consumer Advertising: The Case of the Human Papillomavirus (HPV) Vaccine. *Health Marketing Quarterly*, *28*(4), 372–385. http://doi.org/10.1080/07359683.2011.630289.

Lexchin, J. & Mintzes, B. (2002). Direct-to-consumer Advertising of Prescription Drugs: The Evidence Says No. *Journal of Public Policy & Marketing*, *21*(2), 194–201. http://doi.org/10.1509/jppm.21.2.194.17595.

Lipsky, M.S. & Taylor, C.A. (1997). The Opinions and Experiences of Family Physicians Regarding Direct-to-consumer Advertising. *The Journal of Family Practice*, *45*(6), 495–499.

Lowes, R. (2013, November 1). Crestor Tops List of Best-selling Drugs. Retrieved December 1, 2014 from www.webmd.com/cholesterol-management/news/20131101/crestor-is-top-selling-drug.

Macias, D.W., Lewis, L.S. & Baek, T.H. (2010). The Changing Face of Direct-to-consumer Print Advertising. *Pharmaceutical Medicine*, *24*(3), 165–177. http://doi.org/10.1007/BF03256813.

Macias, W., Pashupati, K. & Lewis, L.S. (2007). A Wonderful Life or Diarrhea and Dry Mouth? Policy Issues of Direct-to-consumer Drug Advertising on Television. *Health Communication*, *22*(3), 241–252. http://doi.org/10.1080/10410230701626893.

Mathew, J., Spake, D.F. & Finney, Z. (2008). Consumer Attitudes Toward Pharmaceutical Direct-to-consumer Advertising: An Empirical Study and the Role of Income. *International Journal of Pharmaceutical and Healthcare Marketing*, *2*(2), 117–133. http://doi.org/http://dx.doi.org/10.1108/17506120810887916.

Mintzes, B. (2012). Advertising of Prescription-only Medicines to the Public: Does Evidence of Benefit Counterbalance Harm? *Annual Review of Public Health*, *33*, 259–277. http://doi.org/10.1146/annurev-publhealth-031811-124540.

Mintzes, B., Barer, M.L., Kravitz, R.L., Bassett, K., Lexchin, J., Kazanjian, A. & Marion, S.A. (2003). How Does Direct-to-consumer Advertising (DTCA) Affect Prescribing? A Survey in Primary Care Environments With and Without Legal DTCA. *CMAJ: Canadian Medical Association Journal = Journal de l'Association Medicale Canadienne*, *169*(5), 405–412.

Mitka M. (2008). Direct-to-consumer Advertising of Medical Devices Under Scrutiny. *JAMA*, *300*(17), 1985–1986. http://doi.org/10.1001/jama.2008.528.

Moyer, M.W. (2012, May 21). The Stats On Statins: Should Healthy Adults Over 50 Take Them? *Scientific American*. Retrieved December 1, 2014 from: www.scientific american.com/article/statins-should-healthy-adults-over-50-take-them/.

Murray, E., Lo, B., Pollack, L., Donelan, K. & Lee, K. (2003). Direct-to-consumer Advertising: Physicians' Views of Its Effects on Quality of Care and the Doctor–Patient Relationship. *The Journal of the American Board of Family Practice, 16*(6), 513–524. http://doi.org/10.3122/jabfm.16.6.513.

Murray, E., Lo, B., Pollack, L., Donelan, K. & Lee, K. (2004). Direct-to-consumer Advertising: Public Perceptions of Its Effects on Health Behaviors, Health Care, and the Doctor–Patient Relationship. *The Journal of the American Board of Family Practice, 17*(1), 6–18. http://doi.org/10.3122/jabfm.17.1.6.

Myers, S.D., Royne, M.B. & Deitz, G.D. (2011). Direct-to-consumer Advertising: Exposure, Behavior, and Policy Implications. *Journal of Public Policy & Marketing, 30*(1), 110–118. http://doi.org/10.1509/jppm.30.1.110.

Niederdeppe, J., Byrne, S., Avery, R.J. & Cantor, J. (2013). Direct-To-consumer Television Advertising Exposure, Diagnosis with High Cholesterol, and Statin Use. *Journal of General Internal Medicine, 28*(7), 886–893. http://doi.org/10.1007/s11606-013-2379-3.

Payton, A.R. & Thoits, P.A. (2011). Medicalization, Direct-to-consumer Advertising, and Mental Illness Stigma. *Society and Mental Health, 1*(1), 55–70. http://doi.org/10.1177/2156869310397959.

Pines, W.L. (1999). History and Perspective on Direct-to-consumer Promotion, A. *Food and Drug Law Journal, 54*, 489–518.

Polen, H.H., Khanfar, N.M. & Clauson, K.A. (2009). Impact of Direct-to-consumer Advertising (DTCA) on Patient Health-related Behaviors and Issues. *Health Marketing Quarterly, 26*(1), 42–55. http://doi.org/10.1080/07359680802473521.

Robinson, A.R., Hohmann, K.B., Rifkin, J.I., Topp, D., Gilroy, C.M., Pickard, J.A. & Anderson, R.J. (2004). Direct-to-consumer Pharmaceutical Advertising: Physician and Public Opinion and Potential Effects on the Physician–Patient Relationship. *Archives of Internal Medicine, 164*(4), 427–432. http://doi.org/10.1001/archinte.164.4.427.

Rubin, P.H. (1985). Matching Prescription Drugs and Consumers: The Benefits of Direct Advertising. *New England Journal of Medicine, 313*, 513–515.

Shah, M.B., Bentley, J.P. & McCaffrey, D.J. (2006). Evaluations of Care by Adults Following a Denial of an Advertisement-related Prescription Drug Request: The Role of Expectations, Symptom Severity, and Physician Communication Style. *Social Science & Medicine (1982), 62*(4), 888–899. http://doi.org/10.1016/j.socscimed.2005.06.053.

Spence, M.M., Teleki, S.S., Cheetham, T.C., Schweitzer, S.O. & Millares, M. (2005). Direct-to-consumer Advertising of COX-2 Inhibitors: Effect on Appropriateness of Prescribing. *Medical Care Research and Review: MCRR, 62*(5), 544–559. http://doi.org/10.1177/1077558705279314.

Statista. (2014a). GRPs on Prescription Drugs in U.S. Television 2012. Retrieved December 2, 2014 from www.statista.com/statistics/307213/grps-on-prescription-drugs-in-us-television/.

Statista. (2014b). Leading Pharmaceutical Brands in the U.S. by DTC 2013. Retrieved December 3, 2014 from www.statista.com/statistics/317800/dtc-leading-pharmaceutical-brands-usa/.

Statista. (2014c). Pharmaceutical Industry DTC Media Spending in the U.S. 2013. Retrieved December 2, 2014 from www.statista.com/statistics/317819/pharmaceutical-industry-dtc-media-spending-usa/.

Tracy, E.E. (2008). Prospects and Problems of Direct-to-public Genetic Tests. *Personalized Medicine*, 5(5), 511+.

USA Today, Kaiser Family Foundation & Harvard School of Public Health. (2008). *The Public On Prescription Drugs and Pharmaceutical Companies*. Menlo Park, CA: USA Today/Kaiser Family Foundation/Harvard School of Public Health. Retrieved December 5, 2014 from http://kaiserfamilyfoundation.files.wordpress.com/2013/01/7748.pdf.

Ventola, C.L. (2011). Direct-to-consumer Pharmaceutical Advertising. *Pharmacy and Therapeutics*, 36(10), 669–684.

Vogt, D.U. (2005). Direct-to-consumer Advertising of Prescription Drugs. Congressional Research Service, The Library of Congress.

Weissman, J.S., Blumenthal, D., Silk, A.J., Zapert, K., Newman, M. & Leitman, R. (2003). Consumers' Reports on the Health Effects of Direct-to-consumer Drug Advertising. *Health Affairs (Project Hope), Suppl Web Exclusives*, W3-82–95.

Welch Cline, R.J. & Young, H.N. (2004). Marketing Drugs, Marketing Health Care Relationships: A Content Analysis of Visual Cues in Direct-to-consumer Prescription Drug Advertising. *Health Communication*, 16(2), 131–157. http://doi.org/10.1207/S15327027HC1602_1.

Woloshin, S., Schwartz, L.M., Tremmel, J. & Welch, H.G. (2001). Direct-to-consumer Advertisements for Prescription Drugs: What Are Americans Being Sold? *The Lancet*, 358(9288), 1141–1146. http://doi.org/10.1016/S0140-6736(01)06254-7.

Wood, K.S. & Cronley, M.L. (2013). Then and Now: Examining How Consumer Communication and Attitudes of Direct-to-consumer Pharmaceutical Advertising Have Changed in the Last Decade. *Health Communication*, 29(8), 814–825. http://doi.org/10.1080/10410236.2013.803437.

Wosinska, M. (2005). Direct-to-consumer Advertising and Drug Therapy Compliance. *Journal of Marketing Research*, 42(3), 323–332. http://doi.org/10.1509/jmkr.2005.42.3.323.

Zachry III, W.M., Dalen, J.E. & Jackson, T.R. (2003). Clinicians' Responses to Direct-to-consumer Advertising of Prescription Medications. *Archives of Internal Medicine*, 163(15), 1808–1812. http://doi.org/10.1001/archinte.163.15.1808.

CHAPTER 6

FUN AND GLAMOR THROUGH SMOKING, DRINKING AND DRUGS: ENTERTAINMENT MEDIA PORTRAYALS OF SUBSTANCE USE

The 2014 season finale of the popular NBC show *The Blacklist* shows its main character, Raymond Reddington, sharing a bottle of vodka with his long-standing enemy, Berlin, while the two discuss the death of another character earlier in the episode. As the Russian villain downs the last drop, Reddington takes out a gun and shoots him dead.

Most episodes of the AMC show *Mad Men* feature characters drinking cocktails, which are so common on the show that its official website offers a "cocktail guide" ("Cocktail Guide," n.d.); some analysts believe the show has contributed significantly to a resurgence of the "cocktail culture" in the United States (Olmsted, 2012). *Mad Men* characters are also among the most popular of the declining share of TV characters who smoke cigarettes (Dealer, 2014).

In the 2014 movie *Lucy*, Scarlett Johansson plays the title character, a woman forced by a drug lord to have a bag containing a dangerous synthetic drug surgically implanted into her abdomen; the plan is that she will serve as a "mule," delivering the drug to Europe. But when the drug leaks into her system, Lucy gains enhanced mental and physical capabilities, essentially becoming superhuman.

A 2009 episode of the animated program *Family Guy* features Brian, a talking dog, getting caught in possession of marijuana and becoming an activist for legalization. The show features a musical number called

Figure 6.1: Mad Men *Reinvigorated "Cocktail Culture" (AMC)*

"Everything's Better With a Bag of Weed." Marijuana, once associated primarily with rock and rap music, is now mentioned with increasing frequency through casual and mostly positive references in country-western music (Maddux, 2013).

Beyond the depiction of both negative and positive characters using tobacco, alcohol, marijuana and other drugs, what these examples have in common is that (with the exception of *Lucy,* perhaps) none is especially dramatic. The visual or verbal references to substance use appear, for the most part, in passing; they are not necessarily central to the narrative or presented as being unusual in any way. In entertainment media, the use of alcohol and other substances is often presented as normal or, at the very least, to be expected.

Even the most critical observers of these depictions do not argue that the writers and producers of entertainment media *intend* to encourage substance use or abuse by making the behaviors seem more common or normative. However, the research shows that these depictions can have unintended consequences; when substance use is portrayed more frequently among media characters, real-life substance use tends to increase (Engels et al., 2009; Jamieson & Romer, 2014; Koordeman et al., 2012; Primack et al., 2009; Sargent, 2005). This chapter examines the research documenting those effects.

SUBSTANCE USE IN THE UNITED STATES

Earlier chapters have already discussed the prevalence and health consequences of the use of legally obtainable substances, including alcohol, tobacco, and prescription and over-the-counter drugs. Illegal drugs, of course, also have significant negative health consequences; in general, that is why the law prohibits their use or severely limits the circumstances under which they may be prescribed. Nonetheless, the use of illegal ("street") drugs continues to be a significant public health problem in the United States, even if one considers only their health impacts and ignores consequences related to the criminal justice system.

Despite more than 40 years of the "war on drugs" initiated in 1971 by then-President Richard Nixon, illegal drug use in the United States has continued to increase (National Institute on Drug Abuse, 2014a). According to the 2013 National Survey on Drug Use and Health, 8.8 percent of adolescents aged 12 to 17 years reported any illicit drug use, including marijuana and non-medical use of prescription drugs; that rate represented a decline from rates reported from 2002 to 2012, which ranged from 9.5 to 11.6 percent during that period. Among 18- to 25-year-olds, illicit drug use (19.1%) remained about the same as from 2009 to 2012, but was higher than during 2002 to 2008, when rates ranged from 16.1 to 17.3 percent. Among adults 26 and older, 7.3 percent reported any illicit drug use, reflecting an increase from rates of 5.5 to 6.6 percent reported from 2002 to 2011. Overall, nearly one in ten Americans (9.4%) – approximately 24.6 million people aged 12 and older – reported having used at least one illicit drug during the month before the survey (Substance Abuse and Mental Health Services Administration, 2014).

Perhaps not surprisingly, the most commonly used illegal drug was marijuana. Among those aged 12 and older who reported any illicit drug use, 80.6 percent had used marijuana in the preceding month; for nearly two-thirds of those individuals (64.7%), marijuana was the only illegal drug they had used. About one in five drug users (19.4%) reported taking other drugs but not using marijuana, while 15.9 percent said they used marijuana and other drugs. Among those aged 12 and older, individuals were three times as likely to report using marijuana as to report non-medical use of psychotherapeutics (19.8%), including prescription pain relievers, tranquilizers, sedatives or stimulants. Use of cocaine (1.5%), hallucinogens (1.3%), inhalants (0.5%) and heroin (0.3%) were much less common (Substance Abuse and Mental Health Services Administration, 2014).

The illegal use of drugs can obviously result in several types of crimes, including possession or sale of the drug itself; theft, prostitution and other crimes related to obtaining drugs (e.g., stealing money or goods to exchange for drugs); violent behaviors influenced by drug use (e.g., sexual assault, domestic violence), and crimes related to driving a vehicle while under the influence of drugs (National Institute on Drug Abuse, 2014b). Some of these crimes have health implications, including injuries and death related to violent behaviors and crashes due to drugged driving, as well as the spread of sexually transmitted diseases through prostitution. However, even if that was not the case, misuse of drugs would have negative health consequences.

Marijuana

In the past five years, the legal status of marijuana use has changed dramatically in many U.S. states. As of January 2015, recreational use was legal in Colorado and Washington and will be legal in Oregon and Alaska as of 2016; in addition, 27 states and the District of Columbia had decriminalized possession of marijuana, allowed its use for medical purposes, or both. In other states, however, possession of as little as an eighth of an ounce of marijuana can lead to a prison sentence and significant fines (Boyette & Wilson, 2015).

The trend toward more relaxed laws regulating marijuana use may lead some to believe that the drug has no significant health consequences. That is incorrect. Like tobacco, alcohol and other legally obtainable drugs, marijuana use can cause significant adverse health effects. Reviews of research on marijuana's health effects conclude that use can cause anxiety and panic, especially in those not accustomed to using the drug. In addition, laboratory studies have shown that marijuana use impairs reaction time, information processing, motor performance, attention and tracking, and a loss of perceptual–motor coordination. This impairment means that individuals who attempt to drive or operate other equipment while high are at increased risk of being involved in accidents; however, the effect is less severe than that caused by alcohol intoxication because people driving under the influence of marijuana tend to drive more slowly and take fewer risks than do drunk drivers. Some studies have suggested that children born to women who smoked marijuana during pregnancy have lower birth weights and other negative outcomes (Hall & Degenhardt, 2009). In addition, chronic marijuana use, defined as daily or near-daily use continued over years, increases an individual's risk of marijuana dependence, respiratory damage, cardiovascular disease and cognitive impairment, as well as having negative effects on adolescents' psychosocial development and mental health (Hall & Degenhardt, 2014).

Cocaine

According to the 2013 NSDUH survey, only about 1.5 percent of the population aged 12 and older reported past-month cocaine use. Cocaine increases heart rate and blood pressure and can lead to a potentially fatal heart attack or stroke. Snorting cocaine can damage the nasal passages, causing a loss of the sense of smell, nosebleeds and a chronic runny nose as well as damage to the throat, while oral use can restrict blood flow to the bowels, causing gangrene. Those who use cocaine repeatedly can build up a tolerance so that they require higher doses to feel the same high; attempting to prolong that high through cocaine bingeing increases the risk for addiction, as well as irritability, anxiousness and even severe paranoia that may include losing touch with reality and having auditory hallucinations (National Institute on Drug Abuse, 2013).

Hallucinogens

These drugs, including LSD, peyote, psilocybin (found in mushrooms) and PCP, cause users to "see images, hear sounds, and feel sensations that seem real but are not. Some hallucinogens also produce rapid, intense emotional swings;" these effects can last as long as 12 hours (National Institute on Drug Abuse, 2014d, para. 11). The specific health effects of various hallucinogens differ, but in addition to the risk of a "bad trip," during which the user experiences frightening or emotionally negative delusions or hallucinations, hallucinogen use can lead to flashbacks during which the hallucinations are re-experienced despite no drug being ingested. PCP users who take higher doses of the drug may suffer a significant drop in blood pressure, pulse and breathing as well as nausea and vomiting. Dizziness and loss of muscle coordination makes PCP users more prone to accidental injury and death. Some PCP users become suicidal, while others become violent toward others (National Institute on Drug Abuse, 2014d).

Inhalants

These substances – the only type of substance more likely to be abused by younger vs. older adolescents – include solvents, aerosols and gases found in common household or work environment products such as cleaning fluids, glues, spray paint, markers, hair spray, vegetable oil spray and butane lighters. They also include nitrites called "poppers" and are used most often to enhance sex. Inhalants can lead to convulsions or seizures, asphyxiation when the fumes displace oxygen in the lungs, and accidental death related to inhalant intoxication. Chronic use leads to brain damage as well as significant and in many cases permanent harm to the heart, lungs, liver and kidneys. Inhalant use also has been linked to disordered eating and to earlier initiation and a greater likelihood of lifetime use of cigarettes, alcohol and most other drugs (National Institute on Drug Abuse, 2012).

Heroin

Past-month use of heroin declined between 2012 and 2013; however, use of heroin at least once in the preceding year has been climbing in the United States since 2007, increasing from 373,000 past-year users in 2007 to 681,000 in 2013 (Substance Abuse and Mental Health Services Administration, 2014). Nearly one in every four individuals (23%) who use heroin will become addicted. Because heroin is usually injected, users have a higher risk of contracting infectious diseases such as HIV and hepatitis; in addition, abusers are at increased risk of fatal overdoses stemming from the drug's suppression of breathing. Collapsed veins, infections of the heart lining and valves, and diseases of the liver and kidney are also more common among heroin users. A woman who uses heroin while pregnant faces a higher risk of miscarriage and is more likely to have a low birth weight baby; abuse can lead to the baby being born addicted to heroin, so that the baby will suffer withdrawal symptoms requiring hospitalization (National Institute on Drug Abuse, 2014c). A Centers for Disease Control analysis of data from 28 states showed that although heroin overdoses now occur less than half as often as those caused by prescription pain relievers (2.1 vs. 5.6 deaths per 100,000 population in 2012), heroin overdose deaths increased by nearly 102 percent between 2010 and 2012, while deaths due to prescription pain-killer overdoses declined by 6.6 percent (Rudd et al., 2014). The most likely reason is that while states have enacted laws making it tougher – and more expensive – for abusers to obtain prescription painkillers for non-medical use, heroin has become comparatively easier to obtain and is less expensive (Gray, 2014).

LINKING ENTERTAINMENT MEDIA TO SUBSTANCE USE AND ABUSE

As is true of smoking, excessive alcohol use and non-medical use of pre-scription drugs, use of illegal drugs is influenced by numerous factors, including peer group pressure, drug availability, low self-esteem, having a parent with mental illness or who died early, and prior use of legal drugs such as cigarettes and alcohol (von Sydow et al., 2002). Adoles-cents from low-income families, those who start using marijuana before late adolescence and those with prior use of three or more legal drugs are more likely to become dependent on marijuana soon after they begin using (Chen et al., 2005). Perhaps not surprisingly, college-bound ado-lescents are less likely to use illegal drugs during high school than are teens who do not plan to attend college. More surprising is that while low family socioeconomic status (SES) predicts drug use among eighth-graders, most of these differences have disappeared by the time students reach tenth or twelfth grade, although low SES continues to predict use of marijuana, synthetic marijuana, heroin, crack and powder cocaine (Bachman et al., 2014). Among adults, childhood adversity, family members' drug addiction, smoking, alcohol abuse or dependence and having a pre-existing mood or personality disorder are associated with illegal drug use (Harrington et al., 2011).

Previous chapters have established that advertising for tobacco, alcohol and prescription drugs plays a significant role in the use and abuse of these substances. Because marijuana legalization is recent and advertising is severely restricted, even in states where recreational use is legal (Ingold, 2014; Tremoglie, 2014), no published studies have examined the impact of marijuana advertising, and, of course, no advertising is allowed for other illegal drugs. However, researchers have examined the impact of entertainment media portrayals of many of these substances. These studies have provided evidence that exposure to these portrayals can have the unintended consequence of making substance use more attractive, especially to adolescent and young adult audiences (Dalton et al., 2003; Denniston et al., 2011; Engels et al., 2009; Sargent, 2005; Stoolmiller et al., 2012; Wingood et al., 2003).

SUBSTANCE USE CONTENT IN ENTERTAINMENT MEDIA

Television

The most recent comprehensive examination of television's portrayals of cigarettes, alcohol and other drugs was completed more than a decade ago and examined 42 top-rated programs from the fall 1998/1999 season (Christenson et al., 2000). This study showed that alcohol was either shown or mentioned in 77 percent of all episodes, with 71 percent of the episodes showing someone actually consuming alcohol. Alcohol portrayals were four times as likely to suggest that drinking was a positive (40%) vs. a negative (10%) experience; and 45 percent of episodes showing alcohol associated drinking with humor. Although few episodes showed under-age characters drinking, 65 percent of the episodes of teen-favorite programs showed a character consuming alcohol, compared to 71 percent of shows most popular with adults. Less than a quarter of the episodes portraying alcohol use (23%) showed any negative consequences for alcohol (Christenson et al., 2000)

Although only 3 percent of the episodes showed illicit drug use, the topic was seen or mentioned in one in every five episodes, appearing only slightly less often than tobacco (22%). Nearly a quarter (23%) of episodes portraying tobacco use included a negative statement about smoking; 13 percent of the episodes included positive statements about smoking. However, only two episodes showing smoking included a portrayal of its negative consequences. Among the episodes mentioning or showing illicit drugs, 41 percent included at least one negative statement about drugs, and two-thirds of the episodes showing drug use mentioned negative consequences (Christenson et al., 2000).

Another study of prime-time shows from the late 1990s produced contrasting results, comparing the prevalence of characters using alcohol, tobacco and illicit drugs to the actual rates of U.S. use. That study showed that 11 percent of characters drank alcohol, compared to 51 percent of the population, while 2.5 percent of characters smoked, compared to 28.9 percent of the population at the time. Fewer than 1 percent of TV characters used illicit drugs, compared to 6.1 percent of the population. The researchers concluded that, in fact, the use of these substances was less common in prime-time TV than in the real world (Long et al., 2002).

A more recent analysis of popular shows from the 2003 season showed that alcoholic drinks were shown or referenced, on average, at the rate of 2.3 alcoholic drinks per hour in prime-time shows and 2.4 drinks per hour in shows aimed at tweens. "Thus, drinking alcohol was as common on the subset of shows favored by tweens as it was in adult shows" (Greenberg et al., 2009, p. 301). In prime time, more than a quarter of incidents involving alcohol (27%) were associated with celebration or social motives; non-alcoholic beverages were never associated with celebration or social motives. Neither positive nor negative outcomes of alcohol use were portrayed frequently enough to allow statistical analysis.

Tobacco portrayals in popular prime-time television dramas declined between 1955 and 2010, dropping from 2.89 instances per episode hour in 1955 to 1964 to .31 instances per hour from 2001 to 2010 (Jamieson & Romer, 2014). That does not necessarily mean, however, that TV watchers never saw tobacco use. A study of movie trailers televised between August 2001 and July 2002 showed that 24 percent of trailers for R-rated films and 7.8 percent of those for PG-13- and PG-rated movies included tobacco use content (Healton et al., 2006). In addition, a study of the top-rated U.S. television shows among 12- to 17-year-olds in fall 2007 showed that 40 percent of TV episodes included at least one depiction of tobacco use. Such depictions appeared *more* often in shows rated TV-PG (50 percent for cigarettes only, 60 percent when cigars are included) than in those rated TV-14 (26.4 percent for cigarettes only, 32.1 percent including cigars), "indicating that exposure to tobacco use may skew toward youth of younger ages, resulting in earlier exposure to this behavior" (Cullen et al., 2011, p. 150).

There appear to have been no recent studies comprehensively assessing television content related to illicit drug use. One study focused specifically on the reality TV show *The Osbournes*, which followed the lives of former Black Sabbath lead singer Ozzy Osbourne, his wife and two children from 2002 to 2005. The first season won an Emmy for non-fiction programming, and in April 2002, the show's audience of 7.8 million Americans made it MTV's all-time highest rated series up to that point. Analysis of shows from the first season showed that references to or depictions of alcohol, tobacco and drug use appeared 9.1 times per episode, with alcohol references most common; references to drug use were more common than references to tobacco. The researchers coded most drug use references as negative (rejections of drug use); however, most references to tobacco and alcohol use "implied endorsements" (Blair et al., 2005, p. 1518). Rejections were generally verbal; however, endorsements – which often included showing one of the characters using the substance – were generally visual.

Music/Music Videos

Given that Ozzy Osbourne is an acknowledged former drug addict, the trend toward the rejection of illicit drug use in a reality show about his family may not be surprising. However, analyses of music and music video content show that both alcohol and illicit drug use are more likely to be presented positively than negatively in these media types. For instance, a study of songs ranked in the Billboard top 100 from 1968, 1978, 1988, 1998 and 2008 revealed a "substantial increase" in references to drug and alcohol use, especially between 1988 and 2008. The percentages of references to either alcohol or drugs increased from 8 percent of top-100 songs in 1968 to 30 percent of top-100 songs in 2008. References to alcohol were somewhat more common than references to drugs (e.g., 19 percent vs. 12 percent of songs, respectively, in 2008). Marijuana was the most commonly mentioned drug, appearing in 3.4 percent of all songs in the sample. "Through 1988, only three songs mentioned drugs (1%); in the last two decades 25 of the 200 songs (12.5%) referred to some type of drug" (Christenson et al., 2012, p. 125).

Over the entire sample, only six songs (1.2%) mentioned some sort of negative consequence of alcohol use, although 40 percent of the 1968 to 1988 songs and 20 percent of the 1988 to 2008 songs mentioned being drunk. Of the 25 songs that mentioned drug use, 20 percent mentioned negative consequences. Overall, the authors concluded that alcohol was much more likely to be portrayed positively rather than negatively (57 percent vs. 14 percent of references, respectively), and the trend toward positivity grew during the later period, when 64 percent of songs including alcohol references were judged as positive and only one song (3%) referred to alcohol use negatively. The same was true for references to drug use; 61 percent presented drugs in a positive light, while 14 percent referenced drugs negatively; among the 1998 to 2008 songs, 68 percent of drug references were rated as positive, compared to 12 percent rated negative. "Substance use is almost never condemned, and potential negative consequences of alcohol and drug use are seldom mentioned, especially in songs from 1998 and 2008" (Christenson et al., 2012, p. 127). Other studies have produced similar results (Herd, 2014; Primack et al., 2008; Siegel et al., 2013). Another relatively recent study of alcohol references in popular music showed that in the 793 songs that were most popular with adolescents from 2005 to 2007, 21.3 percent included some reference to alcohol, and for nearly a quarter of those songs (24.3%), a specific alcohol brand name was included in the lyrics. Brand name inclusion was most common in the lyrics of rap and hip-hop/R&B songs. Name brand alcohol was associated with wealth and luxury objects, sex, partying, weapons, other drugs and vehicles (Primack et al., 2012).

Not surprisingly, substance use is also common in music videos, which combine the songs with visual depictions or interpretations of the lyrics. For instance, a study of music videos broadcast in 2001 showed that 43 percent of the videos contained some visual reference to the use of tobacco, alcohol or other drugs, with depictions of alcohol most common; more than one-third of the videos (34.5%) included alcohol depictions, and one in every ten videos showed alcohol consumption. References to illicit drugs, either in the lyrics or in the visuals, appeared in 13 percent of the sample, while tobacco references were included in 10 percent of the videos. Rap and hip-hop videos were more likely than those for other music genres to include substance use references or depictions, and this was especially true for illicit drugs. The analysis showed that videos including tobacco, alcohol or other drug portrayals were 2.5 times as likely to have humorous elements, in comparison to videos that did not include any reference to substance use (Gruber et al., 2005). A more recent study, which examined YouTube music videos on the United Kingdom's Top 40 list from 2013 to 2014,

189

showed that 45 percent of all videos included alcohol imagery and 22 percent included tobacco images. A survey of British adolescents showed that 81 percent had seen at least one of the 32 most popular videos that included alcohol or tobacco content (Cranwell et al., 2014).

Movies

Movies offer another important venue through which audiences are exposed to messages about tobacco, alcohol and other drugs. Analysis of movie content related to tobacco, alcohol and other drugs has demonstrated that illegal drug use portrayals are relatively rare, while portrayals of alcohol and tobacco use are more common, especially in films that include violence (Bleakley, Romer & Jamieson, 2014). Perhaps more importantly, however, the research has shown that portrayals tend to be more positive than negative and rarely include depictions of any negative consequences (Gunaseker et al., 2005; Stern & Morr, 2013; Stern, 2005). For instance, in an analysis of 87 top box-office movies released between 1983 and 2003 (excluding animated movies, G- and PG-rated movies, films about non-humans and those set in a time before 1983) researchers found seven movies that depicted use of marijuana. Of 27 episodes of marijuana use in these movies, 14 depicted marijuana positively, and the remainder of the depictions were neutral; none portrayed marijuana use negatively. Six of the movies showed characters using illicit drugs that were not injected, and, of the 13 specific episodes, none showed drug use in a negative light. Fifty-nine (68%) of the movies showed at least one character smoking, and about one-third (32%) showed at least one character intoxicated (Gunasekera et al., 2005).

Another study focused on alcohol use in top-100 box-office hits from 1998 to 2002, as well as 34 top movies from 2003. The researchers found that the majority of movies (83%) showed characters drinking alcohol, including more than half (56.6%) of movies rated G or PG, 88.2 percent of PG-13 movies and 89.8 percent of R-rated movies. More than half of the movies (52%) included reference to a specific brand of alcohol. Hard liquor was more likely to be shown than beer or wine. Perhaps counterintuitively, characters were most likely to be shown as intoxicated in PG-13 movies (42.3%), although such depictions occurred almost as often in R-rated movies (40%). Overall, a little more than one-third of the movies (36.3%) showed at least one character becoming intoxicated.

Through a survey of adolescents' exposure to these 534 movies, the researchers estimated that adolescents who were between ten and 14 years old at the time of the survey had been exposed, in total, to 5.1 billion instances and 334.7 minutes of movie alcohol use; a greater percentage of this exposure came from PG-13 movies than from R-rated movies, in part because young adolescents were more likely to have seen PG-13 movies than R movies (Dal Cin et al., 2008).

An analysis of teen movie characters' use of tobacco, alcohol and drugs in top-grossing movies from 1999 to 2001 showed that two of every five teens drank alcohol. Only six characters – about one in ten – were portrayed as being regretful at all about their use of alcohol, and of 26 teen characters who were offered alcohol, only one refused the drink. Among teen characters shown drinking alcohol, 14.3 percent experienced only positive short-term consequences, while 35.7 percent experienced negative short-term consequences. For more than two-thirds of these characters (69.6%), there were no long-term consequences at all. Drinking teens did not differ significantly from non-drinking teen characters in terms of apparent wealth, virtuousness or physical appearance. Tobacco and drug use were less common, with 17.1 percent of the major teen characters shown smoking, often more than once. About one in every seven major teen characters (15.1%) was shown using illegal drugs, most often (63.6%) more than once. Although drug-using teen characters were portrayed as less "good" than those who didn't use drugs, there were no statistically significant differences in gender, socioeconomic status or physical attractiveness. Based on these findings, Stern (2005, p. 340) concluded, "the world portrayed in recent teen-centered movies is one in which substance use is relatively common and mostly risk-free."

Two more recent studies of substance use in top-grossing movies show that while substance use has become less common, the portrayals remain problematic. A study examining the most popular teen-centered films from 1980 to 2007 showed that the highest percentage of portrayals of substance use came from movies released during the 1990s, which accounted for nearly half (49%) of all substance use depictions coded; in comparison, only 11 percent came from movies released in 2000 or later. Relatively few incidents showed substances being offered, but when that did occur, characters accepted the offered substance two-thirds of the time; only 1.2 percent of all depictions of substance use showed a character refusing an offered substance (Callister et al., 2012). Another more recent study analyzing teen characters in top-rated films from 2007 to 2009 also showed that substance use among teen characters had declined from the levels documented by Stern (2005). Only eight teen characters – one in every 20 – smoked cigarettes, and most of those depictions came from only two movies. About one in five characters were shown drinking alcohol. Of those shown drinking, about one-third appeared to be drunk; none was depicted as driving under the influence. On the other hand, only one in five of the characters shown drinking experienced any negative short-term consequences, and none experienced long-term harm from drinking. Of 19 characters offered alcohol in the movies, only two declined, and of the 56 teen characters shown drinking, only one expressed regret about having done so. Comedies were more likely than other genres to include teen drinking. Two movies, one of them R-rated, accounted for six of the seven characters shown using drugs. Four of the seven characters experienced negative short-term consequences, but only one experienced long-term negative consequences. The authors note that, although substance use by teen characters declined, the remaining portrayals may still send harmful messages by suggesting that teens who are offered alcohol or drugs usually accept, that teen drinkers experience few negative consequences and that, when they do, those consequences are funny. The later movies contained more depictions of negative short-term consequences of drug use but still showed only one drug-using character experiencing long-term negative consequences (Stern & Morr, 2013).

Video Games

Most research on video games has focused on their violent content and gender role depictions, and only a handful appear to have assessed content related to substance use and abuse. One study of teen-rated games available in the United States in 2001 showed that 15 percent of the 81 sampled games included depiction of alcohol, tobacco or drugs, although none of the ESRB content descriptors for those games mentioned drug use and only one had warned about tobacco or alcohol-related content (Haninger & Thompson, 2004). Another study analyzed 147 M-rated games (for mature audiences) available for the major game consoles in April 2004 and found depictions of alcohol use in 47 percent, depictions of tobacco use in 22 percent and depictions of illicit drugs in 14 percent of the games. As was true of the teen-rated games, the frequency of warnings about substance use content in the ESRB descriptors for these games was far lower than the actual percentage of games including substance use content. For all 147 games, only 4 percent had descriptors related to substance use (Thompson et al., 2006).

Internet/Social Media

As nearly all media scholars now recognize, perhaps the single most dramatic change in the use of media for entertainment over the past decade has been the rise in use of social media, especially among adolescents and young adults. Researchers have only begun to examine the types of substance-related content audiences are likely to encounter via social networking sites such as Facebook, YouTube, Instagram and so on, but these studies do suggest that visual and verbal references to substance use are commonly included in social media profiles, especially for young people. For instance, one study of 400 MySpace profiles for 17- to 20-year-olds from Washington showed that more than half (56.3%) included alcohol references; white males were most likely to refer to alcohol use in their profiles (Moreno et al., 2010). In another study, which focused on the MySpace profiles of 18- to 20-year-olds from a low-income urban area, 85.3 percent included some verbal or visual mention of smoking, drinking alcohol and other substance use (Moreno et al., 2009). An examination of images from young adults' MySpace, Facebook and YouTube profiles showed that images and videos showing alcohol consumption were usually of women in social gatherings, but marijuana use images and videos generally showed males by themselves. Many of the videos had been viewed numerous times and had been rated positively by viewers (Morgan et al., 2010). Similarly, an analysis of YouTube videos related to smokeless tobacco use showed that the average video had been viewed 15,422 times, and the average viewer rating was 4.6 out of 5 stars. Descriptions of the flavor or smell of the tobacco were included in nearly half (48.8%) of the videos, and almost two-thirds (63.4%) included references to social interactions. However, only 12.2 percent mentioned the effects of the nicotine contained in the tobacco, and about one in ten (9.8%) contained any sort of public health information. Only one of the 41 videos

193

Figure 6.2: Adderall Tweets Increase During Final Exams

examined mentioned addiction to smokeless tobacco, and none mentioned quitting (Seidenberg et al., 2012). The personal and social nature of the substance use content from social networking sites may make them particularly influential, in that they not only model substance use behavior but may suggest to viewers that such behaviors are the norm among their peer groups (Egan & Moreno, 2011).

Social media also may encourage non-medical use of prescription drugs by making such use seem normative and/or by suggesting functional reasons for their use. For instance, a study of college students' Twitter status messages mentioning the attention deficit disorder drug Adderall showed that such tweets grew more frequent during college final exam periods. Although almost 10 percent of the tweets mentioned some side effect from Adderall use or abuse, a higher percentage (12.9%) mentioned an alternative motive for taking the drug other than its normal medical use (e.g., taking it as a study aid), which may communicate to readers that the benefits of use outweigh any negative side effects (Hanson et al., 2013b).

ENTERTAINMENT MEDIA EFFECTS ON SUBSTANCE USE

The majority of the research examining the impact of substance use depictions in entertainment media has focused on effects on adolescents and young adults, who are presumed to be more likely to be affected by media depictions than would older adults. The results of these studies suggest that exposure to substance use in media is associated with a higher frequency of substance use among media audiences, and at least some researchers have concluded that media exposure does increase the likelihood of substance use, although the impacts vary depending on media type and substance.

Tobacco

Although tobacco use in prime-time television programming has declined significantly (Jamieson & Romer, 2014), audiences remain likely to see characters smoking on screen. The 2004 National Youth Tobacco Survey showed that more than three-quarters of middle school students (77.9%) and 86.5 percent of high school students had seen actors using tobacco either on television or in movies (Centers for Disease Control and Prevention (CDC), 2005). Data from the 2011 survey showed a median percentage of 75.7 percent of middle school students and 81.7 percent of high school students reporting that they had seen actors using tobacco in movies or on TV. Those portrayals of tobacco use do seem to have an effect: a review of studies of exposure to movie portrayals of smoking revealed "strong empirical evidence" of an effect on adolescent smoking initiation (Charlesworth & Glantz, 2005, p. 1516).

A 2002 study of exposure to tobacco use in movies showed that middle school students who had never smoked had been exposed, on average, to 80 instances of tobacco use by movie characters but this figure was much higher for some students. Exposure to more instances of movie tobacco use was associated with more positive expectancies about smoking and with believing that most adults smoke – attitudes that predict a greater likelihood of smoking initiation (Sargent et al., 2002). Data from that same study showed that smoking initiation was more common among students who had more exposure to depictions of smoking among movie characters (Sargent et al., 2001). A number of other studies have documented associations between viewing movies, especially R-rated movies, and smoking among teenagers. Dalton et al. (2002) compared smoking among fifth- through eighth-graders whose parents did or did not restrict their viewing of R-rated movies. Controlling for grade, peer and family members' smoking, parental disapproval of smoking, maternal supervision and other factors, students who were allowed to watch R-rated movies without any restrictions were significantly more likely to smoke than were their peers who were never allowed to watch R-rated movies. A longitudinal study that followed 6,522 U.S. 10- to 14-year-olds for two years found that the extent of exposure to smoking in hit movies released during the five years before the initial survey predicted the youths' likelihood of having become established smokers by the two-year follow-up measurement (Sargent et al., 2007).

A systematic review of research linking exposure to non-advertising media with substance use identified 24 studies that met the review criteria and included tobacco use as an outcome measure. Twenty-one of the studies, including all ten longitudinal studies, reported statistically significant associations between exposure to media and increased smoking behaviors. Three studies found no association between media use and smoking, and one study revealed that more time spent reading health magazines predicted a lower likelihood of smoking. The authors concluded that the "evidence supporting the relationship between media and tobacco use was the strongest" (Nunez-Smith et al., 2010, p. 189).

Alcohol

As noted earlier, television, movie and music video characters often are shown drinking alcohol, and references to specific alcohol brands are common, especially in rap or hip-hop music or music videos. Evidence of the impact of these depictions is not as strong as that for tobacco (Nunez-Smith et al., 2010); nonetheless, the research shows that exposure to alcohol-related content in entertainment media increases the likelihood of drinking, especially among adolescents (Denniston et al., 2011; Koordeman et al., 2012; Tucker et al., 2013). For instance, a survey of American teenagers revealed that "the more TV adolescents were exposed to, the less they believed that heavy episodic drinking was risky and the more they intended to drink in the future" (Russell et al., 2014, p. 12). Another TV-focused study examined college students' responses to a youth-oriented series *The O.C.*, a program set in Southern California that was, for a time after its 2003 debut, the most-watched drama among teens (12–17) and young adults (18–34). Viewers saw the program's alcohol-related messages as showing both positive and negative outcomes. While overall exposure to the program was associated with recall of negative outcomes, feeling connected to the program was associated with perceiving positive outcomes of alcohol use. Believing that the show conveyed more messages about negative outcomes was associated with having negative expectancies for alcohol use in real life, and perceptions of messages about positive outcomes were associated with having positive expectancies for alcohol use in real life, especially among those who felt more connected to the program (Russell et al., 2009).

Movie viewing also has been found to influence alcohol-related attitudes and behaviors (Sargent et al., 2002, 2006). Dalton et al. (2002) found that among fifth- to eighth-grade students whose parents placed no restrictions on their viewing of R-rated movies, 46 percent had tried alcohol. In comparison, 16 percent of students whose parents imposed some restrictions on R-rated movie viewing and only 4 percent of those whose parents banned R-rated movies had tried alcohol; the association remained significant after controlling for grade, maternal supervision and child personality characteristics. Another study, which followed 6,522 U.S. adolescents over two years, found that parents' drinking, parenting style and availability of alcohol at home were significantly related to earlier initiation of drinking among adolescents. However, exposure to movies containing alcohol messages was the third strongest predictor of early onset of alcohol use, behind older age and having many peers who drank alcohol. The strongest predictors of progression to binge drinking were, again, high peer alcohol use and age, along with being white (rather than African American or Hispanic) and having a high exposure to alcohol messages in movies. In fact, movie alcohol exposure was a more important predictor of both early onset drinking and binge drinking than was receptivity to alcohol marketing. "After control for multiple covariates, MAE (movie alcohol exposure) accounted for 28% of the alcohol onset and 20% of the binge drinking transitions observed in this cohort, making it a risk factor with important public health implications" (Stoolmiller et al., 2012, p. 7). Perhaps not surprisingly, researchers also have found that exposure to alcohol messages in movies is associated with increases over time in teen alcohol use, in use of alcohol among their friends, and, indirectly, with alcohol-related problems such as being suspended from school due to drinking or vandalizing property, fighting, being hurt, being arrested or riding in a car while drinking (Wills et al., 2009).

In addition to the longer term effects of exposure to alcohol use in movies, Dutch researchers have demonstrated that exposure to alcohol portrayals in movies led young adult males to drink more alcohol in the short term. Participants in this study watched one-hour movie clips that contained either many or few alcohol portrayals; the movie clips were interrupted twice, showing either alcohol commercials or ads for a car and a video camera. While watching, the men were allowed to get free beer, wine or soft drinks from a nearby refrigerator. Those who watched the movie containing many alcohol depictions but saw no alcohol commercials consumed, on average, 1.86 drinks, while those who watched the low-alcohol movie consumed only 1.51 drinks. Those who watched the movie with alcohol portrayals *and* alcohol ads drank, on average, 2.98 alcoholic drinks during the hour (Engels et al., 2009).

Fewer studies have assessed the impact of music on alcohol consumption, but the studies that have focused on music or music videos have provided evidence of some effects. A study of ninth-graders in California showed that those who spent more hours watching music videos were more likely to begin drinking, although there was no association with continued drinking (Robinson et al., 1998). British researchers showed that exposure to popular music increased the rate at which young adult women consumed alcohol. In addition, listening to music disrupted the relationship between negative mood and enjoyment of the drink, suggesting that "music altered the relationship between sensory and affective systems, which influence the rate of alcohol consumption" (Stafford & Dodd, 2013, p. 413). Although the British study suggested that the tempo of the music did not influence results, Dutch researchers have found evidence that the inclusion of alcohol-related lyrics does affect alcohol consumption. The researchers persuaded bartenders in three bars to play songs from a set containing references to alcohol or, in the control condition, from a set matched for artist, tempo and energy levels but containing no references to alcohol. Regardless of which bar they visited or how busy the bar was, customers who were listening to songs containing alcohol messages spent significantly more money (€18 more per bar per night, on average) on alcoholic drinks, compared to patrons listening to similar music that contained no alcohol references. The authors concluded that the study provides "preliminary evidence that playing music with alcohol infused lyrics actually leads to more drinking in public places" (Engels et al., 2011, p. 532).

Illegal Drugs

Because references to illegal drug use are somewhat less common in media than are references to tobacco and alcohol and perhaps because illegal drug use is less common, fewer scholars seem to have attempted to assess the impact of mass media on the use of illegal drugs. However, some studies have linked media use activity to the use of illegal drugs. For instance, Denniston et al. (2011) used data from the 2007 Youth Risk Behavior Survey to test for associations between television viewing and video game use and drug use. Controlling for sex, ethnicity and grade in school, frequent television use was significantly and positively associated with using marijuana on school property and lifetime heroin use. In addition, frequent video game playing was significantly associated with several types of drug use, including using marijuana on school property, current cocaine use and lifetime use of inhalants, heroin or other illegal injection drugs.

Another study, based on a survey of primarily white, middle-income high school students, showed no significant relationship between television viewing and marijuana use; however, music use was a significant predictor. After controlling for numerous demographic, socioeconomic and family variables, the data showed that students who spent an average of three to four hours per day listening to music were nearly twice as likely, and those who spent more than four hours per day with music were nearly three times as likely to have used marijuana, as were students who spent less than an hour a day listening to music. The researchers also found that video game playing was negatively related to marijuana use, with teens who spent at least 90 minutes a day, on average, playing computer games being significantly less likely to have used marijuana. No other types of media use were significantly related to marijuana use (Primack et al., 2009).

Adults' video game-playing frequency was associated with problematic use of alcohol, tobacco and caffeine-containing substances among those who played games while using those substances, but no similar relationship was found for marijuana use. However, adults who acknowledged problem video game playing – meaning that they had tried to control their playing time or often spent more time playing than they had intended – were also likely to report problem use of marijuana, as well as the other substances. Socioeconomic stressors, such as being unemployed, were strongly associated with problem video game playing as well as substance abuse (Ream et al., 2011). In addition, a study of fourth- and fifth-grade students from 31 Kentucky elementary schools showed that spending more than three hours a day watching TV and playing video games was significantly associated with both marijuana use and sniffing solvents; unfortunately, study limitations prevented the researchers from distinguishing between TV effects vs. video game effects (Armstrong et al., 2010).

In addition to Primack et al. (2009), several other teams of researchers have identified relationships between music use and illegal drug use. One study of 14- to 18-year-old African American girls showed that those who spent more time watching rap music videos at baseline were 1.5 times as likely as those with less exposure to have used illegal drugs and alcohol during the 12-month follow-up period (Wingood et al., 2003). Similarly, a study of 15- to 25-year-olds in California revealed that, controlling for gender, race/ethnicity and sensation seeking, listening to rap music was a significant and positive predictor of marijuana use, as well as use and abuse of alcohol and aggressive behavior; frequently listening to reggae music also was related significantly to marijuana use (Chen et al., 2006). Slater and Henry (2013) found that music-related media exposure (including seeking music-related magazine and Internet content) was related to marijuana use; however, in this case the effect was indirect, operating through the relationship of music exposure with having peers who used marijuana. That is, adolescents who reported greater music exposure during the first wave of data collection were more likely to report having friends who used marijuana, and those with more marijuana-using friends at each wave were more likely to have initiated marijuana use before the subsequent wave of data collection. The authors conclude:

> it seems likely that modeling of behaviors by exemplars in media content may lead to adoption of attitudes and perceptions of norms consistent with those behaviors. Such attitudes and normative perceptions would be likely to both support association with

substance-using peers and adopting substance-use behaviors characterizing that peer group.

(Slater & Henry, 2013, p. 302)

The important influence of peer relationships and norms on drug use makes online social networks a particularly interesting – and potentially problematic – type of media content, although researchers are just beginning to investigate the relationships between social media use and drug use. One study of 3,448 18- to 24-year-olds revealed no relationship between marijuana use and having more positive attitudes about posting alcohol and drug-related pictures and comments on social media sites (Stoddard et al., 2012). However, another study analyzed the links between online peer ties (a measure of the connections between members of an individual's online social network) and drug use among 2,153 U.S. young adults. The data revealed that having more peer ties was significantly and positively related to illegal drug use, as were reporting more discussion of and greater acceptance of drug use among one's online network members, especially among men (Cook et al., 2012). Similarly, Hanson and colleagues (2013a) analyzed the tweets by Twitter users belonging to the social circles of individuals who had posted tweets suggesting that they abused prescription drugs. The data revealed that index users and those in their social circles tended to post tweets about the same drugs, and that the amount of Twitter interaction related to prescription drugs was strongly correlated with the number of tweets indicative of prescription drug abuse (e.g., those mentioning simultaneous use of multiple drugs or making reference to drug dependence). The researchers noted that although tweets suggesting drug abuse may not reflect actual behavior, "the simple act of discussing the behavior within a social circle can impact the social norms of those within that circle" (Hanson et al., 2013b, p. 24). Clearly, more research will be needed to determine how social media influences, and perhaps facilitates, substance use behaviors.

SUMMARY

Although depictions of tobacco use in entertainment programming have declined, audiences remain likely to encounter portrayals of tobacco use, especially in movies. Portrayals of alcohol use are common across all types of media, including television programs and movies oriented toward teens and even younger children. Alcohol references are also common in music and music videos, and references to drug use are especially common in rap and hip-hop music. Users of social media sites, including Facebook and YouTube, are increasingly likely to see references to alcohol, tobacco and drugs. These portrayals are, in general, more likely to be positive or at least neutral than negative, and substance-using characters rarely suffer any negative consequences. Reviews of the research linking exposure to these portrayals with effects on viewers conclude that such exposure is strongly linked to the use of tobacco, and while the evidence for media effects on alcohol and drug use is not as strong, it is substantial. Thus, while the producers of entertainment content do not intend to promote the use of these substances, the research suggests that the portrayals do have an effect. Because portrayals often put substance use in the context of humor and rarely include negative short- or long-term consequences, exposure to substance use in the media increases the likelihood that audience members will themselves consume tobacco, alcohol and, increasingly, illegal drugs. While media portrayals of substance use may have less impact than other risk factors (e.g., socioeconomic status, peer group norms), these portrayals nonetheless appear to contribute to substance use and abuse, and to the resulting negative social and health consequences.

REFERENCES

Armstrong, K.E., Bush, H.M. & Jones, J. (2010). Television and Video Game Viewing and its Association with Substance Use by Kentucky Elementary School Students, 2006. *Public Health Reports (Washington, D.C.: 1974)*, *125*(3), 433–440.

Bachman, J.G., Johnston, L.D. & O'Malley, P.M. (2014). Monitoring the Future: Questionnaire Responses From the Nation's High School Seniors 2012. Institute for Social Research, University of Michigan. Retrieved October 30, 2014 from www.monitoringthefuture.org/datavolumes/2012/2012dv.pdf.

Blair, N.A., Yue, S.K., Singh, R. & Bernhardt, J.M. (2005). Depictions of Substance Use in Reality Television: A Content Analysis of The Osbournes. *BMJ*, *331*(7531), 1517–1519. http://doi.org/10.1136/bmj.331.7531.1517.

Bleakley, A., Romer, D. & Jamieson, P.E. (2014). Violent Film Characters' Portrayal of Alcohol, Sex, and Tobacco-related Behaviors. *Pediatrics*, *133*(1), 71–77. http://doi.org/10.1542/peds.2013-1922.

Boyette, C. & Wilson, J. (2015, January 7). It's 2015: Is Weed Legal in Your State? Retrieved January 8, 2015 from www.cnn.com/2015/01/07/us/recreational-marijuana-laws/index.html.

Callister, M., Coyne, S.M., Robinson, T., Davies, J.J., Near, C., Van Valkenburg, L. &

Gillespie, J. (2012). "Three Sheets to the Wind": Substance Use in Teen-centered Film from 1980 to 2007. *Addiction Research & Theory, 20*(1), 30–41. http://doi.org/10.3109/16066359.2011.552818.

Centers for Disease Control and Prevention (CDC). (2005). Tobacco Use, Access, and Exposure to Tobacco in Media among Middle and High School Students – United States, 2004. *MMWR. Morbidity and Mortality Weekly Report, 54*(12), 297–301.

Charlesworth, A. & Glantz, S.A. (2005). Smoking in the Movies Increases Adolescent Smoking: A Review. *Pediatrics, 116*(6), 1516–1528. http://doi.org/10.1542/peds.2005-0141.

Chen, C.-Y., O'Brien, M.S. & Anthony, J.C. (2005). Who Becomes Cannabis Dependent Soon After Onset of Use? Epidemiological Evidence from the United States: 2000–2001. *Drug and Alcohol Dependence, 79*(1), 11–22. http://doi.org/10.1016/j.drugalcdep. 2004.11.014.

Chen, M.-J., Miller, B.A., Grube, J.W. & Waiters, E.D. (2006). Music, Substance Use, and Aggression. *Journal of Studies on Alcohol and Drugs, 67*(3), 373.

Christenson, P., Roberts, D.F. & Bjork, N. (2012). Booze, Drugs, and Pop Music: Trends in Substance Portrayals in the Billboard Top 100 – 1968–2008. *Substance Use & Misuse, 47*(2), 121–129. http://doi.org/10.3109/10826084.2012.637433.

Christenson, P.G., Henriksen, L., Roberts, D.F. et al. (2000). *Substance Use in Popular Prime-time Television.* The Office. Retrieved January 12, 2015 from http://library.stmarytx.edu/acadlib/edocs/supptt.pdf.

Cocktail Guide. (n.d.). Retrieved December 31, 2014 from www.amctv.com/shows/mad-men/cocktail-guide.

Cook, S.H., Bauermeister, J.A., Gordon-Messer, D. & Zimmerman, M.A. (2012). Online Network Influences on Emerging Adults' Alcohol and Drug Use. *Journal of Youth and Adolescence, 42*(11), 1674–1686. http://doi.org/10.1007/s10964-012-9869-1.

Cranwell, J., Murray, R., Lewis, S., Leonardi-Bee, J., Dockrell, M. & Britton, J. (2014). Adolescents' Exposure to Tobacco and Alcohol Content in YouTube Music Videos. *Addiction (Abingdon, England).* http://doi.org/10.1111/add.12835.

Cullen, J., Sokol, N.A., Slawek, D., Allen, J.A., Vallone, D. & Healton, C. (2011). Depictions of Tobacco Use in 2007 Broadcast Television Programming Popular among US Youth. *Archives of Pediatrics & Adolescent Medicine, 165*(2), 147–151. http://doi.org/10.1001/archpediatrics.2010.276.

Dal Cin, S., Worth, K.A., Dalton, M.A. & Sargent, J.D. (2008). Youth Exposure to Alcohol Use and Brand Appearances in Popular Contemporary Movies. *Addiction, 103*(12), 1925–1932. http://doi.org/10.1111/j.1360-0443.2008.02304.x.

Dalton, M.A., Ahrens, M.B., Sargent, J.D., Mott, L.A., Beach, M.L., Tickle, J.J. & Heatherton, T.F. (2002). Relation Between Parental Restrictions on Movies and Adolescent Use of Tobacco and Alcohol. *Effective Clinical Practice: ECP, 5*(1), 1–10.

Dalton, M.A., Sargent, J.D., Beach, M.L., Titus-Ernstoff, L., Gibson, J.J., Ahrens, M.B. & Heatherton, T.F. (2003). Effect of Viewing Smoking in Movies on Adolescent Smoking Initiation: A Cohort Study. *The Lancet, 362*(9380), 281–285. http://doi.org/10.1016/S0140-6736(03)13970-0.

Dealer, A.T. The Plain. (2014, April 4). Tobacco Less Visible on Prime Time TV; Study Links Trend to Drop in U.S. Smoking Rates. Retrieved January 7, 2015 from www.cleveland.com/healthfit/index.ssf/2014/04/tobacco_less_visible_on_prime.html.

Denniston, M.M., Swahn, M.H., Hertz, M.F. & Romero, L.M. (2011). Associations between Electronic Media Use and Involvement in Violence, Alcohol and Drug

Use among United States High School Students. *The Western Journal of Emergency Medicine, 12*(3), 310–315.

Egan, K.G. & Moreno, M.A. (2011). Alcohol References on Undergraduate Males' Facebook Profiles. *American Journal of Men's Health*, 1557988310394341. http://doi.org/10.1177/1557988310394341.

Engels, R.C.M.E., Slettenhaar, G., Bogt, T. ter & Scholte, R.H.J. (2011). Effect of Alcohol References in Music on Alcohol Consumption in Public Drinking Places. *The American Journal on Addictions/American Academy of Psychiatrists in Alcoholism and Addictions, 20*(6), 530–534. http://doi.org/10.1111/j.1521-0391.2011.00182.x.

Engels, R.C.M.E., Hermans, R., van Baaren, R.B., Hollenstein, T. & Bot, S.M. (2009). Alcohol Portrayal on Television Affects Actual Drinking Behaviour. *Alcohol and Alcoholism, 44*(3), 244–249. http://doi.org/10.1093/alcalc/agp003.

Gray, E. (2014, February 4). Heroin Gains Popularity as Cheap Doses Flood the U.S. *Time*. Retrieved January 9, 2015 from http://time.com/4505/heroin-gains-popularity-as-cheap-doses-flood-the-u-s/.

Greenberg, B.S., Rosaen, S.F., Worrell, T.R., Salmon, C.T. & Volkman, J.E. (2009). A Portrait of Food and Drink in Commercial TV Series. *Health Communication, 24*(4), 295–303. http://doi.org/10.1080/10410230902889233.

Gruber, E.L., Thau, H.M., Hill, D.L., Fisher, D.A. & Grube, J.W. (2005). Alcohol, Tobacco and Illicit Substances in Music Videos: A Content Analysis of Prevalence and Genre. *Journal of Adolescent Health, 37*(1), 81–83. http://doi.org/10.1016/j.jadohealth.2004.02.034.

Gunasekera, H., Chapman, S. & Campbell, S. (2005). Sex and Drugs in Popular Movies: An Analysis of the Top 200 Films. *Journal of the Royal Society of Medicine, 98*(10), 464–470.

Hall, W. & Degenhardt, L. (2009). Adverse Health Effects of Non-medical Cannabis Use. *The Lancet, 374*(9698), 1383–1391. http://doi.org/10.1016/S0140-6736(09)61037-0.

Hall, W. & Degenhardt, L. (2014). The Adverse Health Effects of Chronic Cannabis Use. *Drug Testing and Analysis, 6*(1–2), 39–45. http://doi.org/10.1002/dta.1506.

Haninger, K. & Thompson, K.M. (2004). Content and Ratings of Teen-rated Video Games. *JAMA, 291*(7), 856–865. http://doi.org/10.1001/jama.291.7.856.

Hanson, C.L., Cannon, B., Burton, S. & Giraud-Carrier, C. (2013a). An Exploration of Social Circles and Prescription Drug Abuse Through Twitter. *Journal of Medical Internet Research, 15*(9). http://doi.org/10.2196/jmir.2741.

Hanson, C.L., Burton, S.H., Giraud-Carrier, C., West, J.H., Barnes, M.D. & Hansen, B. (2013b). Tweaking and Tweeting: Exploring Twitter for Nonmedical Use of a Psychostimulant Drug (Adderall) Among College Students. *Journal of Medical Internet Research, 15*(4), e62. http://doi.org/10.2196/jmir.2503.

Harrington, M., Robinson, J., Bolton, S.L., Sareen, J. & Bolton, J. (2011). A Longitudinal Study of Risk Factors for Incident Drug Use in Adults: Findings from a Representative Sample of the US Population. *Canadian Journal of Psychiatry. Revue Canadienne de Psychiatrie, 56*(11), 686–695.

Healton, C.G., Watson-Stryker, E.S., Allen, J.A., Vallone, D.M., Messeri, P.A., Graham, P.R. & Glantz, S.A. (2006). Televised Movie Trailers: Undermining Restrictions on Advertising Tobacco to Youth. *Archives of Pediatrics & Adolescent Medicine, 160*(9), 885–888. http://doi.org/10.1001/archpedi.160.9.885.

Herd, D. (2014). Changes in the Prevalence of Alcohol in Rap Music Lyrics 1979–2009. *Substance Use & Misuse, 49*(3), 333–342. http://doi.org/10.3109/10826084.2013.840003.

Ingold, J. (2014, February 11). Magazines Sue Colorado Over Marijuana Advertising Restrictions. Retrieved January 12, 2015 from www.denverpost.com/news/ci_25117594/magazines-sue-colorado-over-marijuana-advertising-restrictions.

Jamieson, P.E. & Romer, D. (2014). Portrayal of Tobacco Use in Prime-time TV Dramas: Trends and Associations with Adult Cigarette Consumption – USA, 1955–2010. *Tobacco Control*. http://doi.org/10.1136/tobaccocontrol-2012-050896.

Koordeman, R., Anschutz, D.J. & Engels, R.C.M.E. (2012). Alcohol Portrayals in Movies, Music Videos and Soap Operas and Alcohol Use of Young People: Current Status and Future Challenges. *Alcohol and Alcoholism (Oxford, Oxfordshire)*, 47(5), 612–623. http://doi.org/10.1093/alcalc/ags073.

Long, J.A., O'Connor, P.G., Gerbner, G. & Concato, J. (2002). Use of Alcohol, Illicit Drugs, and Tobacco among Characters on Prime-time Television. *Substance Abuse*, 23(2), 95–103. http://doi.org/10.1080/08897070209511479.

Maddux, R. (2013, May 15). Hashville Skyline. *Slate*. Retrieved December 31, 2015 from www.slate.com/articles/arts/culturebox/2013/05/marijuana_and_country_music_kacey_musgraves_pistol_annies_and_other_weed.html.

Moreno, M.A., Briner, L.R., Williams, A., Brockman, L., Walker, L. & Christakis, D.A. (2010). A Content Analysis of Displayed Alcohol References on a Social Networking Web Site. *Journal of Adolescent Health*, 47(2), 168–175. http://doi.org/10.1016/j.jadohealth.2010.01.001.

Moreno, M.A., VanderStoep, A., Parks, M.R., Zimmerman, F.J., Kurth, A. & Christakis, D.A. (2009). Reducing At-risk Adolescents' Display of Risk Behavior on a Social Networking Web Site: A Randomized Controlled Pilot Intervention Trial. *Archives of Pediatrics & Adolescent Medicine*, 163(1), 35–41. http://doi.org/10.1001/archpediatrics.2008.502.

Morgan, E.M., Snelson, C. & Elison-Bowers, P. (2010). Image and Video Disclosure of Substance Use on Social Media Websites. *Computers in Human Behavior*, 26(6), 1405–1411. http://doi.org/10.1016/j.chb.2010.04.017.

National Institute on Drug Abuse. (2012). *Inhalants* (NIH Publication No. 12–3818). Washington, DC. Retrieved January 8, 2015 from www.drugabuse.gov/sites/default/files/inhalantsrrs.pdf.

National Institute on Drug Abuse. (2013, April). DrugFacts: Cocaine. Retrieved January 8, 2015 from www.drugabuse.gov/publications/drugfacts/cocaine.

National Institute on Drug Abuse. (2014a, January). DrugFacts: Nationwide Trends. Retrieved January 8, 2015 from www.drugabuse.gov/publications/drugfacts/nationwide-trends.

National Institute on Drug Abuse. (2014b, April). Drug Addiction Treatment in the Criminal Justice System. Retrieved January 8, 2015 from www.drugabuse.gov/related-topics/criminal-justice/drug-addiction-treatment-in-criminal-justice-system.

National Institute on Drug Abuse. (2014c, October). DrugFacts: Heroin. Retrieved January 8, 2015 from www.drugabuse.gov/publications/drugfacts/heroin.

National Institute on Drug Abuse. (2014d, December). DrugFacts: Hallucinogens – LSD, Peyote, Psilocybin, and PCP. Retrieved January 8, 2015 from www.drugabuse.gov/publications/drugfacts/hallucinogens-lsd-peyote-psilocybin-pcp.

Nunez-Smith, M., Wolf, E., Huang, H.M., Chen, P.G., Lee, L., Emanuel, E.J. & Gross, C.P. (2010). Media Exposure and Tobacco, Illicit Drugs, and Alcohol Use among Children and Adolescents: A Systematic Review. *Substance Abuse*, 31(3), 174–192. http://doi.org/10.1080/08897077.2010.495648.

Olmsted, L. (2012, May 2). Gin And The Classic Cocktail Resurgence. Retrieved

December 31, 2014 from www.forbes.com/sites/larryolmsted/2012/05/02/gin-and-the-classic-cocktail-resurgence/.

Primack, B.A., Kraemer, K.L., Fine, M.J. & Dalton, M.A. (2009). Media Exposure and Marijuana and Alcohol Use among Adolescents. *Substance Use & Misuse, 44*(5), 722-739. http://doi.org/10.1080/10826080802490097.

Primack, B.A., Nuzzo, E., Rice, K.R. & Sargent, J.D. (2012). Alcohol Brand Appearances in US Popular Music. *Addiction, 107*(3), 557-566. http://doi.org/10.1111/j.1360-0443.2011.03649.x.

Primack, B.A., Dalton, M.A., Carroll, M.V., Agarwal, A.A. & Fine, M.J. (2008). Content Analysis of Tobacco, Alcohol, and Other Drugs in Popular Music. *Archives of Pediatrics & Adolescent Medicine, 162*(2), 169-175. http://doi.org/10.1001/archpediatrics.2007.27.

Ream, G.L., Elliott, L.C. & Dunlap, E. (2011). Playing Video Games While Using or Feeling the Effects of Substances: Associations with Substance Use Problems. *International Journal of Environmental Research and Public Health, 8*(10), 3979-3998. http://doi.org/10.3390/ijerph8103979.

Robinson, T.N., Chen, H.L. & Killen, J.D. (1998). Television and Music Video Exposure and Risk of Adolescent Alcohol Use. *Pediatrics, 102*(5), e54-e59.

Rudd, R.A., Paulozzi, L.J., Bauer, M.J., Burleson, R.W., Carlson, R.E., Dao, D. and Centers for Disease Control and Prevention (CDC). (2014). Increases in Heroin Overdose Deaths – 28 States, 2010 to 2012. *MMWR. Morbidity and Mortality Weekly Report, 63*(39), 849-854.

Russell, C.A., Russell, D.W. & Grube, J.W. (2009). Nature and Impact of Alcohol Messages in a Youth-oriented Television Series. *Journal of Advertising, 38*(3), 97-112. http://doi.org/10.2753/JOA0091-3367380307.

Russell, C.A., Russell, D.W., Boland, W.A. & Grube, J.W. (2014). Television's Cultivation of American Adolescents' Beliefs about Alcohol and the Moderating Role of Trait Reactance. *Journal of Children and Media, 8*(1), 5-22. http://doi.org/10.1080/17482798.2014.863475.

Sargent, J.D. (2005). Smoking in Movies: Impact on Adolescent Smoking. *Adolescent Medicine Clinics, 16*(2), 345-370, ix. http://doi.org/10.1016/j.admecli.2005.02.003.

Sargent, J.D., Wills, T.A., Stoolmiller, M., Gibson, J. & Gibbons, F.X. (2006). Alcohol Use in Motion Pictures and its Relation with Early-onset Teen Drinking. *Journal of Studies on Alcohol, 67*(1), 54-65.

Sargent, J.D., Beach, M.L., Dalton, M.A., Mott, L.A., Tickle, J.J., Ahrens, M.B. & Heatherton, T.F. (2001). Effect of Seeing Tobacco Use in Films on Trying Smoking among Adolescents: Cross Sectional Study. *BMJ, 323*(7326), 1394. http://doi.org/10.1136/bmj.323.7326.1394.

Sargent, J.D., Dalton, M.A., Beach, M.L., Mott, L.A., Tickle, J.J., Ahrens, M.B. & Heatherton, T.F. (2002). Viewing Tobacco Use in Movies: Does it Shape Attitudes That Mediate Adolescent Smoking? *American Journal of Preventive Medicine, 22*(3), 137-145.

Sargent, J.D., Stoolmiller, M., Worth, K.A. et al. (2007). Exposure to Smoking Depictions in Movies: Its Association with Established Adolescent Smoking. *Archives of Pediatrics & Adolescent Medicine, 161*(9), 849-856. http://doi.org/10.1001/archpedi.161.9.849.

Seidenberg, A.B., Rodgers, E.J., Rees, V.W. & Connolly, G.N. (2012). Youth Access, Creation, and Content of Smokeless Tobacco ("Dip") Videos in Social Media. *Journal of Adolescent Health, 50*(4), 334-338. http://doi.org/10.1016/j.jadohealth.2011.09.003.

Siegel, M., Johnson, R.M., Tyagi, K., Power, K., Lohsen, M.C., Ayers, A.J. & Jernigan, D.H. (2013). Alcohol Brand References in U.S. Popular Music, 2009–2011. *Substance Use & Misuse*, 48(14), 1475–1484. http://doi.org/10.3109/10826084.2013.79 3716.

Slater, M.D. & Henry, K.L. (2013). Prospective Influence of Music-related Media Exposure on Adolescent Substance-use Initiation: A Peer Group Mediation Model. *Journal of Health Communication*, 18(3), 291–305. http://doi.org/10.1080/10810730. 2012.727959.

Stafford, L.D. & Dodd, H. (2013). Music Increases Alcohol Consumption Rate in Young Females. *Experimental and Clinical Psychopharmacology*, 21(5), 408–415. http://doi.org/10.1037/a0034020.

Stern, S.R. (2005). Messages from Teens on the Big Screen: Smoking, Drinking, and Drug Use in Teen-centered Films. *Journal of Health Communication*, 10(4), 331–346. http://doi.org/10.1080/10810730590950057.

Stern, S. & Morr, L. (2013). Portrayals of Teen Smoking, Drinking, and Drug Use in Recent Popular Movies. *Journal of Health Communication*, 18(2), 179–191. http://doi.org/10.1080/10810730.2012.688251.

Stoddard, S.A., Bauermeister, J.A., Gordon-Messer, D., Johns, M. & Zimmerman, M.A. (2012). Permissive Norms and Young Adults' Alcohol and Marijuana Use: The Role of Online Communities. *Journal of Studies on Alcohol and Drugs*, 73(6), 968.

Stoolmiller, M., Wills, T.A., McClure, A.C., Tanski, S.E., Worth, K.A., Gerrard, M. & Sargent, J.D. (2012). Comparing Media and Family Predictors of Alcohol Use: A Cohort Study of US Adolescents. *BMJ Open*, 2(1), e000543. http://doi.org/10.1136/bmjopen-2011-000543.

Substance Abuse and Mental Health Services Administration. (2014). *Results from the 2013 National Survey on Drug Use and Health: Summary of National Findings* (No. HHS Publication No. (SMA) 14–4863). Rockville, MD: Substance Abuse and Mental Health Services Administration.

Thompson, K.M., Tepichin, K. & Haninger, K. (2006). Content and Ratings of Mature-rated Video Games. *Archives of Pediatrics & Adolescent Medicine*, 160(4), 402–410. http://doi.org/10.1001/archpedi.160.4.402.

Tremoglie, M.P. (2014, April 17). These Roadblocks Are Killing Marijuana Advertising's Vibes. Retrieved January 12, 2015 from www.businessinsider.com/roadblocks-to-marijuana-advertising-2014-4.

Tucker, J.S., Miles, J.N.V. & D'Amico, E.J. (2013). Cross-lagged Associations between Substance Use-related Media Exposure and Alcohol Use during Middle School. *Journal of Adolescent Health*, 53(4), 460–464. http://doi.org/10.1016/j.jadohealth.2013.05.005.

von Sydow, K., Lieb, R., Pfister, H., Höfler, M. & Wittchen, H.-U. (2002). What Predicts Incident Use of Cannabis and Progression to Abuse and Dependence? A 4-year Prospective Examination of Risk Factors in a Community Sample of Adolescents and Young Adults. *Drug and Alcohol Dependence*, 68(1), 49–64.

Wills, T.A., Sargent, J.D., Gibbons, F.X., Gerrard, M. & Stoolmiller, M. (2009). Movie Exposure to Alcohol Cues and Adolescent Alcohol Problems: A Longitudinal Analysis in a National Sample. *Psychology of Addictive Behaviors*, 23(1), 23–35. http://doi.org/10.1037/a0014137.

Wingood, G.M., DiClemente, R.J., Bernhardt, J.M., Harrington, K., Davies, S.L., Robillard, A. & Hook, E.W. (2003). A Prospective Study of Exposure to Rap Music Videos and African American Female Adolescents' Health. *American Journal of Public Health*, 93(3), 437–439. http://doi.org/10.2105/AJPH.93.3.437.

CHAPTER 7

DO THE MEDIA MAKE US FAT?: ADVERTISING AND ENTERTAINMENT PORTRAYALS OF FOOD, NUTRITION AND EXERCISE

Let's follow a typical American family – we'll call them the Smiths – through an average day of food and beverage consumption. Emma Smith, aged ten, starts her day with a big bowl of Cinnamon Toast Crunch while her 14-year-old brother, Jacob, prefers Kellogg's Apple Jacks. Their mom, Janice Smith, aged 44, is sometimes too busy getting everyone out of the door to have breakfast herself, but when she does sit down she tries to eat something she thinks is a little healthier, such as Chobani yogurt and a Nature Valley granola bar. Tom Smith, aged 45, has a cup of Folgers coffee before leaving home, then goes through the Starbucks drive-thru on his way to work to grab a white chocolate mocha and a slice of banana bread.

Eating school cafeteria food is "not cool," so both of the Smith kids take lunches from home. Emma loves Lunchables, the ones that come with a package of Reese's Peanut Butter Cups and a Capri Sun. When work is especially busy, Janice and Tom sometimes give in and buy the Lunchables, but generally they insist on making Emma "real" peanut butter and jelly or cheese and ham sandwiches. Janice adds in a box of raisins, but the box is often returned unopened, unless she puts in yogurt-covered raisins. Jacob makes his own sandwich, slapping several pieces of ham and American cheese singles between two pieces of Nature's Own Whitewheat®. A bag of Lay's potato chips, another of

Oreos and a Gatorade fill up the rest of his lunch bag. Most days, Janice takes along a Lean Cuisine, unless she's planning a lunch with colleagues. She keeps a box or two of granola bars in her desk for snacks. Coffee (with Splenda and low-fat non-dairy creamer) keeps her going during the mornings. For the afternoon slump, she perks herself up with diet Coke. Tom and his co-workers usually hit the Subway near their office for lunch, unless they have a big meeting, in which case the boss will order pizza or sandwiches from a nearby deli.

Tom and Emma are hungry and thirsty when they get home from school. If either parent is home, they encourage the children to have an apple or a banana, but on the days when Tom and Janice are both still at work, the kids often open another bag (or two) of cookies, chips or crackers, or munch on Snickers bars or Reese's Peanut Butter Cups from the convenience store they pass on the way home. A convenience store stop usually means that Tom and Emma's afternoon snack will include a Pepsi or Mountain Dew.

When they get home early enough – and when no one has an evening activity or meeting – Tom and Janice cook dinner, taking advantage of items such as prepackaged salads, frozen grilled chicken or beef strips and canned or frozen vegetables, when necessary, to speed up the process. When they're rushed, they pick up pizza, barbecue or some other type of take-out, or perhaps heat up a frozen pizza or frozen lasagna. Dessert is likely to be some flavor of Blue Bell ice cream. Soccer practice for Emma or a chess club meeting for Jacob generally means stopping at McDonald's or Burger King for dinner on the way.

Overall, on a typical day, Emma Smith's diet means she's consuming about 1,700 calories – not bad on the soccer practice days, but 100 to 300 calories more than she needs on less active days. For Jacob, who isn't involved in any sports, daily calorie intake is about 2,100 calories, which is actually within the normal range for boys of his age (2,000 to 2,400 for those who are inactive). But because Jacob spends most of his free time reading, watching TV or playing video games, he's overweight. So is his father, whose daily food intake totals nearly 2,500 calories – 100 to 300 more per day than he needs, given that he rarely has time for exercise. Janice's calorie intake typically hovers around 1,800 per day, which would be fine if she could figure out how to go to the gym regularly. Unfortunately, she finds little time to work out between managing housework, office work she often brings home with her, and chauffeuring the children to extracurricular activities. When she does have free time, she tends to spend it watching TV with the kids, checking in with her friends on Facebook or shopping online.

The Smiths are obviously a fictional family, but their diet and exercise habits are, in fact, typical for Americans. The research suggests that the epidemic of obesity and overweight currently facing the United States is not only a function of over-consumption of calories; rather, too little exercise, combined with too many calories *and* the low nutritional value of much of the food we consume, has tipped the national scales in a decidedly unhealthy direction. The question this chapter explores is this: What role do mass media play in our diet and exercise choices? Or, stated more bluntly, are mass media making us fat? The answer, of course, is complicated, given that weight status results from a complex interplay of genetics, diet and dieting, and environment. However, much of the research suggests that mass media may contribute to the problem in at least three ways: through advertising promotion of high-calorie, low-nutrition foods, through modeling of unhealthy eating behavior and through displacement of calorie-burning activity.

HOW FAT ARE AMERICANS?

"Fat" may seem a harsh description, but there's really no other way to characterize the United States' current weight status. More than one-third of Americans aged 20 and older (35.1%) are obese, defined as having a body mass index (BMI) of 30 or higher. For an individual 5'9" tall, that means a weight of 203 pounds or more (Centers for Disease Control and Prevention, 2012, 2014, n.d.b). Add in those who are over-weight but not obese – individuals with a BMI between 25 and 29.9 – and the total is a staggering 69 percent of all U.S. adults (Centers for Disease Control and Prevention, 2014). Cross-national comparison data from the Organization for Economic Cooperation and Development (OECD) show that although adult obesity rates are rising in many countries worldwide, the U.S. adult population is still heavier than people in all other high-income countries (Finucane et al., 2011). For instance, the prevalence of obesity among American men is nine times the rate in Korea (Sassi et al., 2009). One study concluded that if obesity rates continue to climb at current rates, by 2030, more than half of the U.S. adult population will be obese (Wang et al., 2011).

Even more disturbing than the grim statistics for adult overweight and obesity are the corresponding figures for U.S. children and adolescents. CDC figures show that the percentage of obese six- to 11-year-olds in the United States more than doubled between 1980 and 2012, from 7 percent to almost 18 percent. During that same time period, the percentage of obese teenagers (12 to 19 years old) more than quadrupled, from 5 percent in 1980 to 21 percent in 2012 (Centers for Disease Control and Prevention, n.d.a). When overweight youth are included, the percentage totals more than one-third of children six to 19 years old; even among very young children – two to five years old – more than one in five (22.8%) is overweight or obese (Ogden et al., 2014). Data from the 2001/2002 *Health Behavior in School-aged Children Study* revealed that the United States had the highest percentages of overweight and obese children of any of the 34 participating countries, with the exception of Malta (Janssen et al., 2005).

Weight gain occurs when an individual consumes more calories over time than he or she burns, and therein lies one of the most obvious explanations for our growing national girth: many, if not most, people consume more calories than they use up through exertion. For instance, an analysis of energy intake studies from 1971 through 2010 showed that the average number of calories per day increased from 1,955 in 1971 to 1975 to 2,269 in 2003 to 2004; calorie intake had declined to 2,195 per day by 2009/2010 (Ford & Dietz, 2013). However, a decline in calorie intake, by itself, does not lead to weight loss or even prevent weight gain if individuals continue to take in more calories than they burn. Although CDC data show some increase in the percentage of American adults who met the government's recommended guidelines for both aerobic and muscle-strengthening activity – from 14.3 percent in 1998 to 20.8 percent in 2012 – the vast majority of Americans still aren't getting enough exercise. The data show that, in 2012, nearly half the adult population (46.6%) met neither guideline (National Center for Health Statistics, 2014). Thus, despite some decrease in calorie intake and some increase in exercise, Americans still don't burn enough of the calories they consume. Recent analysis of changes in Americans' "energy imbalance gap" (EIG – the difference between calories consumed and calories expended) showed that while the gap has been shrinking since about 2003/2004 for non-Hispanic whites and non-Hispanic blacks, "none of these groups showed a negative or zero EIG, suggesting that obesity continues to increase, albeit at a slower rate" (Fallah-Fini et al.,

2014, p. 1233); for Hispanic Americans, the EIG is continuing to increase, leading to even higher rates of overweight and obesity.

Being overweight or obese may be the most significant outcome of poor dietary habits, but it is not the only indicator. Surveys of Americans' eating habits "demonstrate that adults continue to fall short in meeting the *Dietary Guidelines for Americans 2005* recommendations," established by the U.S. Department of Agriculture's Center for Nutrition Policy and Promotion (CNPP). Specifically, analysis of data from the 2003/2004 National Health and Nutrition Examination Survey (NHANES) revealed that adults met the recommended guidelines in only two categories: all grains and meat and beans. The worst scores were for under-consumption of dark green and orange vegetables and legumes and whole grains and over-consumption of sodium and calories from solid fats, alcoholic beverages and added sugars. Women scored slightly better than men, consuming more fruits, vegetables and legumes and healthy oils and taking in fewer calories from solid fats, alcoholic beverages and added sugars (Ervin et al., 2011). Data from the NHANES studies show that added sugars accounted for approximately 14.9 percent of daily calorie consumption intake among adults in 2005 to 2010, a significant decline from 16.8 percent of daily calories in 1999 to 2004; however, for one in ten individuals, added sugars continued to account for a quarter (or more) of their daily calories (Yang et al., 2014).

Research on the eating habits of children and adolescents presents a similarly gloomy picture. Analysis of children's data from the 2003 to 2010 NHANES studies showed an increase of 12 percent per year in the consumption of whole fruits, but 60 percent of children still consume less fruit than health officials recommend. Vegetable consumption did not change, with 93 percent of children consuming fewer servings of vegetables than recommended. White potatoes accounted for nearly one-third (30%) of all vegetable calories consumed, and even that occurred primarily via the consumption of potato chips and fried potatoes. "No sociodemographic group met the HP2020 (Health People 2020) total vegetable target and only children aged 2–5 met the total fruit target" (Kim et al., 2014). Another analysis of NHANES data showed that, on average, solid fats and added sugars accounted for one-third of all daily calories consumed by children two to 18 years old, with solid fats accounting for 19 percent and sugars accounting for 14 percent of the calories (Slining & Popkin, 2013); in comparison, the

Department of Agriculture's Dietary Guidelines for Americans 2010 state that no more than 5 to 15 percent of daily calories should come from added sugars and solid fats combined (Ahmed & Blumberg, 2009). The analysis suggested that although calorie intake from solid fats and added sugars has declined, the declines leveled off after 2007/2008 (Slining & Popkin, 2013).

As noted earlier, the most obvious consequence of unhealthy eating and exercise patterns is the growing percentage of adults and children who are overweight or obese. That outcome alone – being overweight or obese – has significant psychological, emotional and social consequences, especially for children and adolescents. Overweight children are substantially more likely than their non-overweight peers to report being teased. For instance, in one study, 78 percent of overweight children aged ten to 14, compared to 37.2 percent of non-overweight children in the same age group, reported that they had been teased. Less than one-third of non-overweight children had been teased about their weight, compared to 89.1 percent of overweight children. Overweight children were more than twice as likely to say the teasing was moderately to extremely upsetting (56.6 percent vs. 22 percent for non-overweight children), and they were more likely to report being teased by peers in general, while non-overweight children were most likely to have been teased by one specific peer. The more weight-related teasing the overweight children had experienced, the more likely they were to report weight concerns, loneliness and a preference for solitary or sedentary activities; weight-related teasing was also associated with lower perceived social abilities competence and lower self-confidence about the child's physical appearance (Hayden-Wade et al., 2005). Other studies have produced similar results, and some have even linked weight-related teasing to disordered eating behaviors (Dave & Rashad, 2009; Swahn et al., 2009) and thoughts of suicide.

Overweight and obese adults also report exposure to many stigmatizing situations, especially having other people make negative assumptions about the individual, hearing nasty comments from children, having to deal with physical barriers and obstacles (such as too-small seats in public places), and hearing inappropriate or negative comments from doctors and family members (Puhl & Brownell, 2006). Depression is more common among obese adults (Vogelzangs et al., 2010; Xiang & An, 2014). Overweight or obese adults may face discrimination when they seek employment (Larkin & Pines, 1979; Pingitore et al., 1994; Rothblum et al., 1990). For women, being overweight has even been linked to lower net worth among those at or near retirement age (Fonda et al., 2004).

Of course, physical health concerns are the primary focus of most efforts to encourage people to reach and maintain acceptable weight levels. Being overweight or obese increases individuals' risk of numerous diseases and conditions, including heart disease (the No. 1 cause of death in the United States), stroke, Type 2 diabetes, osteoarthritis, high blood pressure, high "bad" cholesterol and lower "good" cholesterol, liver and gallbladder disease, sleep apnea and other respiratory problems, abnormal menstrual periods and infertility, and endometrial, breast and colon cancers (Panel et al., 1998). There is also growing evidence that obesity contributes to the risk of Alzheimer's disease and other types of cognitive decline and dementia (Nguyen et al., 2014). A recent analysis of causes of death in the United States concluded that obesity "accounts for a rising share of older adult deaths across successive birth cohorts" and caused nearly one in five (18%) of all deaths among 40- to 85-year-olds between 1986 and 2006. (Masters et al., 2013, p. 1900). The researchers concluded that obesity is likely to cause an even greater share of U.S. deaths in the near future owing to the increasing prevalence of obesity in younger age cohorts. Similarly, Stewart and colleagues (2009) predicted that increasing obesity in the United States may well produce enough negative health effects by 2020 to outweigh the positive health effects being achieved through declines in smoking. They concluded that failure to maintain declines in smoking and to stabilize or reverse the trend toward increasing obesity "could result in an erosion of the pattern of steady gains in health observed in the United States since the early 20th century" (Stewart et al., 2009, p. 2259).

WHAT CAUSES POOR DIET AND EXERCISE HABITS?

The simplest explanation of the growing overweight/obesity epidemic in the United States is that, in general, people consume too many calories, eat too many calorie-dense but nutrient-poor foods and do not get enough exercise. But why is that? And are those who are overweight or obese entirely responsible for their own poor diet and exercise habits, or are there contributing factors beyond individual control?

One potential contributor is a lack of knowledge, in that people may make bad food and exercise choices because they don't understand how food consumption relates to good health. Some studies suggest that most adults do know that food and beverage choices affect people's risks of developing major diseases. For instance, in a study comparing nutrition knowledge among Swiss and American adults, 100 percent of the Americans agreed that dietary choices affect an individual's health. Strong majorities of the U.S. respondents said better health was associated with avoiding salt (76%), avoiding sugar (76%), lowering cholesterol (70%) and avoiding being overweight (61%); however, Swiss respondents were significantly more likely to recognize the importance of avoiding salt (82%), sugar (89%) and being overweight (86%). All U.S. respondents were aware that dietary fiber was an issue, but only 23 percent believed they personally consumed high-fiber diets. Only 11 percent said their diets were high in fat. Overall, BMI was not associated with any of the knowledge measures, suggesting that diet and nutrition knowledge may be of somewhat limited importance in determining people's food choices.

Other researchers have found that, in making food choices, Americans are generally more concerned about taste and cost than they are about nutrition. In rating the importance of five food characteristics – taste, cost, nutrition, convenience and contribution to weight control – Americans of all ethnic groups rated weight control as least important (Glanz et al., 1998). A more recent study, which focused on food consumption away from home, also emphasized the importance of convenience and an enjoyable dining experience as influences on people's decisions about which restaurants to visit and what foods to order. Participants in a 2006 survey ranked taste as the most important characteristic of restaurant food, followed by nutrition and convenience (Stewart et al., 2006). However, a review of studies linking out-of-home eating with dietary intake found that eating out more frequently was associated with higher total calorie intake, a higher percentage of fat calories and lower intake of micronutrients (Lachat et al., 2012).

Other researchers have found that cost – both real and perceived – plays an important role in determining what foods people consume. In general, low-income individuals are more likely to be overweight or obese than are their higher income peers, although the relationship between income and obesity varies for different age and ethnic groups

(Beydoun & Wang, 2007; Chang & Lauderdale, 2005; Wang et al., 2011; Wang & Zhang, 2006). One explanation for this link is that energy-dense foods tend to be less expensive as well as tasting good and being convenient (e.g., highly processed, so little or no preparation is required), while nutrient-dense, lower calorie foods, such as lean meats, fish, fresh vegetables and fruit, tend to cost more. In addition, however, the lower cost, energy-dense foods seem to be less effective at satiating hunger, leading people to overeat (Drewnowski, 2004; Drewnowski & Darmon, 2005). Researchers comparing food prices in the United States have found, in fact, that the cost disparity is growing, such that healthier foods which offer high nutrition with fewer calories are becoming even more expensive compared to low-nutrient, high-calorie foods (Monsivais et al., 2010).

Socioeconomic status also influences exercise habits. For instance, one review of studies linking the physical environment to individuals' likelihood of exercising showed that living in an unsafe neighborhood was a significant barrier to physical activity, while access to attractive environments such as a park or beach and having in-home exercise equipment or gym memberships were associated with greater physical activity (Humpel et al., 2002). Another review identified "convincing" evidence of an association between having access to exercise equipment and being involved in vigorous physical activity; however, the research-ers concluded that there was less consistent evidence of a relationship between physical activity and availability of and convenient access to recreational facilities. The authors concluded that having social support for physical activity and having someone to exercise with were important determinants of numerous types of activity, including walking, biking, sports, walking or biking to work, and physical activity in general (Wendel-Vos et al., 2007). Among youth, family income, mother's educa-tional status and living in a low-crime area have been associated consist-ently with more physical activity (Ferreira et al., 2007).

Other studies have identified a number of important barriers to phys-ical activity. For instance, a study of students from middle school through the first year in college revealed that intrapersonal and institu-tional barriers were reported most often. Among students at every level except the first year in college, the most commonly mentioned barriers were intrapersonal factors, such as a lack of motivation to exercise, not having the money for costs associated with the physical activity, and the belief that the individual didn't have the skills needed for physical activity. Institutional barriers were most important for college students and the second most important for other students; for younger students, the primary issue in this category was having competing interests, while university students said their school workloads left them too little time for physical activity (Gyurcsik et al., 2006). A study of Canadian high school students also identified time constraints related to school work, competing interests and family activities as the most important barriers to physical activity (Allison et al., 1999). A study of sedentary adolescent girls in the United States similarly identified lack of time as the most common barrier to physical activity (Kimm et al., 2006).

Having too little time and being more concerned with work, family commitments and other priorities are also associated with a lack of physical activity among adults (Salmon et al., 2003). A review of studies examining the correlates of physical activity participation published between 1998 and 2000 concluded that researchers have repeatedly documented an association between perceived lack of time to exercise and physical inactivity. Interestingly, the review also found a documented lack of association between attitudes toward physical activity and participation in such activity; in other words, believing that physical activity is desirable and/or enjoyable does not seem to have much influence on actually being involved in exercise (Trost et al., 2002). Among older adults (age 60 and over), a systematic review of the research revealed that the key barriers to physical activity participation included a lack of social support for exercise, being stuck in sedentary habits, having competing priorities (such as caring for grandchildren or an elderly partner), lacking access to suitable facilities and equipment, and being disinterested in physical activity. Some older people were disinterested in physical activity because they believed it would not improve their health, while others believed exercise could actually be harmful to them (Franco et al., 2015).

As the previous section has demonstrated, researchers have identified numerous intrapersonal, societal and environmental factors that contribute to poor dietary and exercise habits. The remainder of this chapter will attempt to explain how mass media consumption fits into that complex interplay of personal, social, institutional and environmental influences on the behaviors that lead to overweight and obesity.

MASS MEDIA INFLUENCES ON DIET AND EXERCISE

Screen Time Effects

Research on the potential effects of mass media on a particular health behavior often begins with an analysis of mass media content related to that behavior. In the case of media contributions to unhealthy weight, however, some of the most important effects may be unrelated to the specific content of the media being consumed. In other words, media use in and of itself – regardless of the content we are consuming – may be a significant contributor to the growth in overweight and obesity. In this case, the problem is that interacting with mass media, which is generally a sedentary activity, now consumes more and more of our free time, leaving us with less time to engage in calorie-burning physical activity and potentially displacing time that may otherwise have been spent shopping for and preparing healthier foods. According to an eMarketer.com study from April 2014, the average U.S. adult now spends five hours and 46 minutes per day with digital media, up from three hours and 11 minutes daily in 2010. Time spent watching TV, which was surpassed by time spent with digital media in 2013, still totaled four hours and 28 minutes daily in 2014, and adding in use of radio, print media and other media consumption brings the total to 12 hours and 14 minutes per day. Thus, time spent with media has increased by nearly 14 percent since 2010 ("Mobile Continues," 2014).

For those concerned about the obesity epidemic, a key issue is whether more time spent with media equates to less time spent in physical activity. Research suggests that the relationship between screen time and engagement in physical activity varies across age and gender groups. For instance, analysis of data from the 2003 National Survey of Children's Health showed that, for both boys and girls aged six to 17, spending more time each day with screen-based leisure activities, including computer and television use, was associated with a reduced likelihood of daily physical activity. In addition, the study showed that children whose daily routines included little physical activity but high levels of screen-based leisure activities were almost twice as likely to be overweight, compared to children with high physical activity and low screen-based activity (Sisson et al., 2010).

Similarly, an analysis of health behaviors among 11-, 13- and 15-year-olds from 39 different European and North American countries revealed that spending more than two hours a day watching television was associated with less time in moderate physical activity for both boys and girls and with less vigorous activity for girls. Boys who spent more time playing computer games had lower levels of moderate and vigorous physical activity, but vigorous activity was *positively* related to non-gaming computer use for both boys and girls. In addition, the relationship between screen-based activity and physical activity varied across countries, such that the strongest evidence for displacement effects of screen time occurred in countries where, overall, physical activity was fairly high (Melkevik et al., 2010).

Researchers who assessed physical activity and screen time effects on overweight among U.S. children aged seven to 12 found that both behaviors significantly influenced the likelihood of a child being categorized as overweight. Children who spent more than two hours daily in screen-based activity and who also failed to meet the American Academy of Pediatrics' recommendations for daily physical activity were three to four times as likely to be overweight, compared to children who got the recommended amount of exercise and spent less than two hours a day with television, computer use and video games. However, the researchers found no statistically significant relationship between physical activity and screen-based activity (Laurson et al., 2008).

One study of screen time and physical activity among college students showed that those who reported low levels of physical activity spent more time with screen-based activity. However, the authors concluded that time spent watching television did not displace physical activity, in part because male students reported more physical activity and more TV time than did females (Fountaine et al., 2011). However, Ballard and colleagues (2009) found that, among male undergraduates, time spent exercising decreased significantly as frequency of video game play increased, and frequency of exercise was negatively correlated with length of video game play during a single sitting, especially among those who played online games.

The data seem to suggest that playing video games may be more problematic than TV viewing in terms of displacing physical activity. However, the effects of playing video games may depend, to some extent, on what type of game the individual plays. The popularity of "exer-games" – those that use some sort of monitor to track the players' physical movements – has led researchers to investigate whether these video games might actually encourage more energy expenditure. Although these games were introduced in the late 1980s, their popularity began to grow dramatically after 1999, when video game maker Konami Digital Entertainment introduced Dance Dance Revolution, followed a few years later by Nintendo's Wii console and Wii Fit software and X-Box's Kinect system (Raymond, 2013). Numerous studies have shown that using exergames produced significant improvements in a variety of physical and mental health outcomes for assisted living residents (Chao et al., 2014b), heart failure patients (Klompstra et al., 2014), women with low back pain (Kim, 2014), older adults (Chao et al., 2014a), children (Lamboglia et al., 2013), and in adolescents, young and older adults (Graves et al., 2010). A review of research analyzing the impacts of exergames concluded that "exergaming is a potentially major strategy to help improve physical activity levels and reduce obesity among Americans" (Sween et al., 2014, p. 7). However, another review, which focused on studies involving youth (aged 21 or younger), noted that games that required only upper body movement (e.g., bowling, tennis) produced significantly lower energy expenditure than those that required upper and lower body movement (e.g., boxing, dance). The review authors also noted that participation in active game play frequently declines over time, meaning that the long-term efficacy of such games remains unclear (Biddiss & Irwin, 2010).

Another concern about screen time, regardless of content, stems from research showing that the more time individuals spend watching TV, playing sedentary video games and using computers, the more calories they tend to consume. A review of ten studies assessing the link between non-advertising screen time and dietary intake concluded that screen-based activities in general, even without the effects of advertising, stimulate greater consumption, especially of energy-dense foods. This effect may stem from the fact that screen time distracts the individual from regular food habits and/or interferes with recognition of the physiological cues to satiation. Another is simply that sedentary activity, regardless of content, serves as a cue to eat and, in particular, to eat calorie-dense foods; in other words, we tend to associate sitting in front of the TV or the computer with junk food consumption. Yet another explanation is that screen use can interfere with our memory of having eaten, such that while watching TV or sitting in front of a computer screen, we simply forget how many cookies, chips or sodas we've consumed already.

Finally, some evidence suggests that screen time activities produce a type of stress reaction, leading to increased food consumption in the absence of hunger (Marsh et al., 2013).

Food and Beverage Advertising

Another important mechanism through which mass media may influence diet and exercise behaviors is exposure to advertising for food, beverages and products or services related to exercise or weight loss. Food and beverage marketing to children and adolescents has become such a concern in the United States that, in 2006, the Council of Better Business Bureaus created a voluntary initiative whose members agreed to change their advertising practices to encourage children younger than age 12 to choose healthier diets. However, after initial reports on the impact of the Children's Food and Beverage Advertising Initiative (CFBAI) showed it had produced only minimal improvements, the Federal Trade Commission conducted a follow-up study, using 2009 data on food marketing expenditures. This study showed that although there had been a 19.5 percent inflation-adjusted decline in spending for food marketing to youth, the biggest chunk of that reduction (38.7%) was due to fast food restaurants distributing fewer and less expensive toys with children's meals.

Children's exposure to TV ads for foods and beverages declined between 2003 and 2009, dropping 17.8 percent for children aged two to five and by 6.9 percent for children aged six to 11. However, between 2009 and 2011, exposure increased again, by 8.3 percent and 4.7 percent, respectively for the two age groups, erasing much of the ground gained in reduced exposure. Another problem is that more than half of the advertising children see appears in the context of general interest programming and therefore was not affected at all by any changes in marketing. In addition, at the same time that spending on TV advertising to youth was declining, food companies increased their levels of spending in other venues, such as through product placements, athletic sponsorships, celebrity fees and other types of promotions. Even with the reduced spending for advertising in programs targeted to youth, children and adolescents see 12 to 16 TV ads per day for unhealthy food and beverage products. The FTC's analysis showed little improvement in the nutritional quality of the products advertised to youth on television.

In addition, the food companies' and fast food restaurants' increased spending on digital advertising – often disguised via "advergames" or social media messages – may render irrelevant any progress in relation to TV advertising (Powell et al., 2013a).

Although advertising through other venues is increasing, children are still most likely to see foods and beverages advertised on television, whether they are watching programming targeted at children or more general audience programs. Nearly half of all broadcast and cable advertising during children's programs is for food products (Stitt & Kunkel, 2008). The research shows that the majority of the food and beverage ads children and adolescents see promote unhealthy foods (Batada et al., 2008; Batada & Wootan, 2007; Powell et al., 2007b, 2013b; Stitt & Kunkel, 2008; Warren et al., 2008). For instance, one recent study of televised cereal advertisements targeted to children showed that the average child would see 1.7 cereal ads per day, with 87 percent of the ads promoting high-sugar cereals (LoDolce et al., 2013). Another recent study of TV food and beverage ads used TV ratings data to analyze the types of foods and drinks likely to be seen by children aged two to five and six to 11 during 2009. The study revealed that 95.8 percent of the ads younger children would see and 97.3 percent of the ads older children would see during children's programming were for products containing high levels of saturated fat, trans-fat, sugar and/or sodium. Ironically, the ads produced by companies belonging to the Children's Food and Beverage Advertising Initiative were substantially *more* likely than ads from non-CFBAI-member companies to be promoting high fat, sugar or salt products; during children's programming, 97.8 percent of CFBAI-member ads seen by two- to five-year-olds and 98.1 percent of ads seen by six- to 11-year-olds were for unhealthy foods. The researchers concluded that "self-regulation has not been successful at protecting children from exposure to advertising for unhealthy foods" (Powell et al., 2013b, p. 530). This conclusion seems to be something of an understatement, given that advertising from companies participating in the "self-regulation" was worse than that of non-member companies.

Despite the unhealthy nature of most of the food and beverage products marketed to children, researchers have found that such ads often suggest that the foods promoted have health benefits or associate the foods with healthy people or healthy lifestyles. For instance, a study of food ads appearing during children's broadcast programming and on the cable networks with the largest child audiences (Nickelodeon, Cartoon Network) showed that 72 percent of the ads promoted low-nutrition products, but 53 percent included cues associating the product with a health benefit; about one in five ads (20.6%) made a health claim about the food (e.g., "low-fat" or "heart-healthy"), 17.7 percent included characters engaged in healthy physical activity and nearly one-third (32.8%) associated the food with fruit. The researchers suggest that the use of such health messages can mislead children into thinking that the promoted product is healthier than it is (Castonguay et al., 2013).

Another area of concern is the idea that manufacturers of unhealthy foods and fast food restaurants target minority audiences more heavily than white audiences. For instance, a study of food advertising in general audience and African American-targeted television programming showed that programs aimed at African Americans included more food ads. In comparison to the ads in general audience programming, the African American-targeted ads were more likely to promote fast food, candy, soda and meat, and less likely to promote cereal, grains and pasta, or fruits and vegetables. One positive point was that they were also less likely to promote desserts or alcohol (Henderson & Kelly, 2005). Similarly, a study of adolescent exposure to TV food ads showed that food-related ads, including ads for fast food restaurants, made up 14 percent of all advertising content seen by adolescents in 2003/2004. However, food ads, including those for food products and for both fast food and non-fast food restaurants, accounted for higher percentages of ads seen by African American teens, compared to the ads seen by white teens (Powell et al., 2007a). Analysis of geographically targeted television ads also demonstrates that food-related advertising, especially ads promoting sugar-sweetened drinks and fast food, disproportionately targets black and low-income youth (Powell et al., 2014). Black teens are more likely than white teens to recall seeing or hearing ads for (highly sweetened) fruit and sports drinks (Kumar et al., 2014). Another study compared the ads shown during after-school programming on three channels – Black Entertainment Television (BET), The WB (Warner Brothers) and the Disney Channel – during July 2005. BET ads were significantly more likely to be for food and beverages and were less likely to include health-related content or physical activity-related content (Outley & Taddese, 2006). A review of studies on differential promotion of foods to African Americans versus whites concluded that African

Americans are disproportionately targeted with marketing for unhealthy foods (Grier & Kumanyika, 2008).

On the other hand, at least some research suggests that food advertising on Spanish-language TV in the United States provides more information about nutrition and health than do mainstream TV food ads. Compared to ads in mainstream prime-time programming, food-related ads in Spanish-language prime-time programs were less likely to promote restaurants, but restaurant ads were more likely to be for fast food places than for casual dining establishments. Celebrity spokespersons were common in both sets of ads, but especially those in Spanish-language programs. The authors suggest that the greater focus on nutritional claims in Spanish-language ads may help explain why Hispanics who spend less time with general audience TV tend to have healthier diets than those who are more acculturated into the mainstream (Abbatangelo-Gray et al., 2008).

In the past decade, health advocates have become increasingly concerned about the use of online food and beverage marketing, particularly that aimed at youth and often disguised in the form of entertainment (e.g., advergames). Analyses of online food and beverage marketing to children show that virtually all of the promoted products are of low nutritional quality (Culp et al., 2010; Henry & Story, 2009; Lee et al., 2009; Moore & Rideout, 2007; Paek Hye-Jin et al., 2014). These websites and games often provide mixed messages about health, with some offering information or making statements about nutrition or a healthy lifestyle while simultaneously making health claims about unhealthy products, such as stating that a cereal provides 100 percent of children's daily recommended dose of Vitamin C or more general claims such as "great for kids" (Moore & Rideout, 2007; Paek Hye-Jin et al., 2014). Lee et al. (2009) found that only 2.7 percent of the advergames they analyzed provided information that would actually educate children about nutrition or health.

For instance, Thomson (2011) analyzed the content of General Mills' Millsberry.com website, which promotes GM's child-targeted cereal brands. Children playing on the Millsberry.com site create a "Buddy" avatar and care for its health by feeding it and having it participate in various activities. The site will not allow children to continue to feed their Buddy after it is "full" and encourages players to give their Buddy a variety of types of foods (e.g., grains, dairy, fruits, etc.); however, the site makes no distinction between sugary cereals and a piece of whole wheat toast, both of which are considered "grains." In addition, some of the games earn players virtual boxes of cereal that the Buddy can consume in one bite.

Moore and Rideout (2007) found that few food marketing websites aimed at children include ad-break disclosures, which are posted messages or banners intended to remind players of the advertising purpose of the material. In addition, they found that most food marketers encourage children to recruit their friends to visit the websites, with 64 percent of websites inviting children to email their friends brand-related messages about the site. On the most heavily visited sites, visitors could challenge friends to play a game with them or send personalized brand message birthday or holiday greetings. More than half of the sites included video links that enable children to watch and rewatch TV commercials for the brands.

Health advocates are concerned about the content and messages of food advertising and food advergames because research shows that exposure to advertising and advergames has a significant – and unhealthy – impact on children's food preferences and behavior. Although the impact of gender and other characteristics has varied from study to study, researchers have found consistently that exposure to

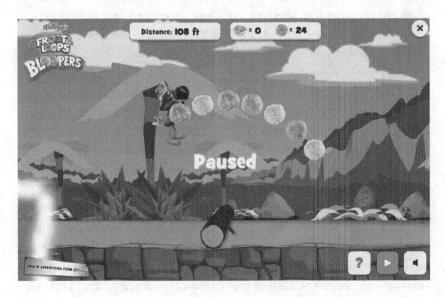

Figure 7.1: Advergames Encourage Low-nutrition Food Consumption

225

food and beverage advertising is associated with greater desire for and consumption of low-nutrition foods and less consumption of fruits and vegetables among children (Anderson et al., 2014; Andreyeva et al., 2011; Halford et al., 2008a, 2008b; Mallinckrodt & Mizerski, 2007; Panic et al., 2013), adolescents (Boynton-Jarrett et al., 2003; Falbe et al., 2013, 2014) and adults (Wonderlich-Tierney et al., 2013; Zimmerman & Shimoga, 2014). For instance, one study showed that adolescents who spent more time watching TV and DVDs and playing electronic games drank more sugar-sweetened beverages and ate more fast food, sweets and salty snacks and fewer servings of fruit and vegetables. Time spent watching TV had the most consistent association with increased consumption of low-nutrient foods (Falbe et al., 2014). A systematic review of randomized controlled trial studies linking food advertising with children's dietary behavior concluded that all "showed an association between TV advertising and energy intake" (Gregori et al., 2014, p. 572).

Although children may be exposed to food-related advertising more often via TV viewing, playing food-related advergames seems to have a particularly troublesome effect because, when playing games, even understanding the marketing intent of the games did not interfere with the games' persuasive power. For instance, a study that compared the effects of TV food advertising with an advergame showed that Belgian children who had a better understanding of the persuasive intent of these media were less likely to ask their parents to buy the advertised food when they saw it advertised in a TV commercial. However, persuasion knowledge had no significant effect on purchase requests when children were playing an advergame associated with the food – even when the children received a cue reminding them about the game's commercial intent. The study showed that "in a gaming context, children's defense mechanisms simply do not influence behavioral outcomes" (Panic et al., 2013, p. 270). Similarly, a study of U.S. five- to ten-year-olds showed that understanding the persuasive intent of advergames did not significantly moderate effects on children's perceptions of how healthy the cereal was or how likely they were to ask a parent to buy it (Rifon et al., 2014). Such findings have led some food industry critics to call for stronger government policy to protect youth from food and beverage advertising that may be considered inherently misleading because children lack the cognitive development necessary to understand and resist these messages (Cheyne et al., 2014; Graff et al., 2012).

226

Adults understand more fully the commercial purpose of food advertising, but research shows that they, too, are influenced by watching food ads. In one study, men and women high in "transportability" – the tendency to become absorbed in a narrative so that one temporarily loses touch with reality – ate more cookies while watching a situation comedy embedded with food-related ads, compared to the same show containing non-food-related ads or no ads. Among women, the key variable appeared to be transportability; women who scored high in transportability consumed more cookies than did low-transportability women, regardless of which type of ads they saw (Wonderlich-Tierney et al., 2013). Another study of adults tested college students' snack consumption while watching a TV show segment containing food ads versus non-food advertising. Watching food ads significantly increased the total number of calories consumed, but only for students exposed to the ads under a high cognitive load condition, meaning that these participants had been told to remember a seven-digit number they had been shown just before watching the TV show; in addition, they had been asked to count the number of times a specific word was spoken by any of the actors in the show. For those in the high cognitive load condition, those who saw food ads consumed 94 more calories, on average, than the group watching non-food ads; they also chose different types of snacks, consuming 107 more calories from unhealthy snacks than those who saw non-food ads. The authors note that many people now watch television while multi-tasking, thereby increasing their cognitive load, and this may exacerbate the impact of advertising on their food consumption (Zimmerman & Shimoga, 2014).

Clearly, for both children and adults, the relationship between exposure to food advertising and food choices is complex, and no health advocate is likely to argue that food advertising – on its own – has caused the U.S. (and increasingly worldwide) obesity epidemic. However, Hoek and Gendall (2006) argue that advertising helps reinforce and normalize the consumption of an unhealthy diet, encouraging people to see low-nutrition, high-calorie foods as appropriate and regular elements of a healthy diet.

BEYOND ADVERTISING EFFECTS

The vast majority of research investigating media portrayals of foods and non-alcoholic beverages has focused on advertising – distinct and usually separate messages that are clearly intended to promote a specific product. But, of course, audiences are often exposed to messages about food and beverages that do not come from advertising. Unfortunately, few studies have examined these messages about food and beverages specifically in relation to physical activity and food choices, although a large body of work (to be discussed in Chapter 8) has examined portrayals of weight and body shape and their impacts on audience attitudes and behaviors related to thinness.

One of the few analyses of eating behaviors and food messages outside the context of advertising was published 25 years ago. Story and Faulkner (1990) examined references to food and eating behavior in both prime-time programming and the commercials embedded in those programs. Their research showed that an average 30 minutes of prime-time programming contained 4.8 references to food or beverages, excluding commercials. The most common food category mentioned was low-nutrient beverages, which were referenced, on average, twice per half hour; coffee appeared most often (.93 references per half hour), followed by alcohol (.64 references per half hour) and soft drinks (.43 references per hour). The second most commonly referenced food category was sweets, which were mentioned .86 times per half hour of programming. Meats were mentioned more often than fruit and vegetables, and dairy products were referenced least often of all the food categories. One of the most interesting findings was that 72 percent of all episodes showing food consumption portrayed between-meal snacking rather than regular meals (Story & Faulkner, 1990).

A more recent examination of food and beverage references in 2008 prime-time programming focused on food, beverage and restaurant brand appearances or mentions. The researchers found that 60 percent of these paid "product placements" were for soft drinks, traditional (not fast food) restaurants and energy or sports drinks (e.g., Gatorade). The data showed that children and adolescents would have seen relatively few of these appearances – fewer than one per day for children and 1.2 per day for adolescents, with soft drinks, especially Coca-Cola products, accounting for 70 percent of all brand appearances seen by children and 61 percent of brand appearances seen by teenagers. For teenagers, 94 percent of Coke brand appearances occurred during the popular talent show *American Idol* (Speers et al., 2011).

Unfortunately, no recent research appears to have examined non-branded references to food and beverage consumption in any media the way the Story and Faulkner (1990) study did, and no research could be identified that has examined the impact of these portrayals on media audiences' beliefs about food and nutrition or their eating behaviors. Thus, it is difficult to know whether or how watching non-advertising portrayals of food and beverage consumption or of physical activity influences audiences' eating and physical activity behaviors. However, given that research on the portrayals of alcohol and smoking in mass media has linked exposure to non-advertising portrayals with increased consumption (See Chapters 3 and 4), it seems very likely that audiences are also influenced by media portrayals of non-alcoholic beverage and food consumption.

There is a similar dearth of information about the relationship, if any, between consumption of media related to physical activity and the audience members' involvement in physical activity. One might suspect, for instance, that regularly watching sports on television or reading sports magazines would increase the likelihood of personal involvement in sports, or at least in some sort of physical activity. However, relatively little research seems to support that idea. One study showed that among middle-class white boys, interest in sports media was positively related to physical activity (DiLorenzo et al., 1998). Another showed that adolescents who reported wanting to look like same-sex figures in the media were more physically active, but the study did not differentiate between what types of media figures (e.g., athletes, actors, models) the adolescents wanted to emulate (Taveras et al., 2004). On the other hand, a study of 14- to 18-year-old women showed that while participation in organized sports increased physical activity, following sports through mass media was associated with significantly *lower* levels of physical activity (Bungum & Vincent, 1996). In addition, a review of 18 published systematic reviews of the correlates of physical activity in children and adolescents concluded that exposure to sports media had no significant impact on child or adolescent physical activity (de Vet et al., 2011); however, only two of the studies they examined had included a question about exposure to or interest in sports media.

While there are gaps in the research linking media use to dietary choices and physical activity levels, the research that does exist supports a clear conclusion: use of mass media currently contributes to both poor eating habits and reduced involvement in physical activity. Thus, although the current national and international epidemics of overweight and obesity cannot be blamed on any one factor, it is clear that the impact of traditional mass media use should be viewed as substantially more negative than positive.

The increasing popularity of diet and fitness apps has the potential to tip the scale back toward the positive end, although it's probably too early to draw any definitive conclusion about these apps and the websites associated with them. A content analysis of smartphone applications available in the "health and fitness" category of the U.S. Apple App Store in September 2011 analyzed 3,336 paid English-language applications promoting health or intended to prevent disease or injury. The researchers categorized one-third of the apps (33.2%) as promoting physical activity, making this the most common type of app; 19.5 percent of the apps promoted healthy eating, the third most common category. Nearly two-thirds of the apps (65.4%) included some sort of "enabling" function, such as teaching a skill, providing a service or tracking behavior, but less than one in ten included any sort of reinforcing function, which public health professionals view as critical to successful behavior change (West et al., 2012). More detailed analyses of diet/weight loss applications and physical activity-only apps have concluded that few use theory to guide behavior change, suggesting that many may have limited effectiveness (Azar et al., 2013; Cowan et al., 2012; Middelweerd et al., 2014).

Research suggests that electronic activity monitors (e.g., Fitbit, Jawbone) may be more effective, in that they generally provide not only monitoring but goal-setting tools and help users recognize the discrepancy between their current behaviors and their goals. An evaluation of 13 types of monitors available for retail purchase in 2013 found that these monitors include many behavior change techniques that have proven effective in weight loss and/or physical activity promotion. The researchers concluded that these monitors could provide more cost-effective ways of helping people learn to balance their energy intake and expenditures (Lyons et al., 2014). Thus far, little published research has tested the real-world effectiveness of these monitors and their associated applications or websites in helping people improve their diets or physical activity levels. One small study using 18 sedentary adult volunteers showed that wearing an activity monitor produced significant reductions in sedentary time and significant increases in light-, moderate- and vigorous-intensity physical activity. The volunteers' energy expenditures were significantly higher at the end of the four-week program than they had been at baseline (Barwais & Cuddihy, 2015). However, another study of 102 Dutch office workers, which combined the use of a physical activity monitor with a tailored online advice, showed that the intervention did not improve physical activity (Slootmaker et al., 2009). More research will be needed to determine whether online and mobile applications, with or without the use of electronic activity monitors, can produce enough positive results to balance the otherwise negative impact of media on diet and physical activity.

REFERENCES

Abbatangelo-Gray, J., Byrd-Bredbenner, C. & Austin, S.B. (2008). Health and Nutrient Content Claims in Food Advertisements on Hispanic and Mainstream Prime-time Television. *Journal of Nutrition Education and Behavior, 40*(6), 348–354. http://doi.org/10.1016/j.jneb.2008.01.003.

Ahmed, S. & Blumberg, J. (2009). Dietary Guidelines for Americans 2010. *Nutrition Reviews, 67*, 615–623.

Allison, K.R., Dwyer, J.J.M. & Makin, S. (1999). Perceived Barriers to Physical Activity among High School Students. *Preventive Medicine, 28*(6), 608–615. http://doi.org/10.1006/pmed.1999.0489.

Anderson, G.H., Khodabandeh, S., Patel, B., Luhovyy, B.L., Bellissimo, N. & Mollard, R.C. (2014). Mealtime Exposure to Food Advertisements While Watching Television Increases Food Intake in Overweight and Obese Girls But Has a Paradoxical Effect in Boys. *Applied Physiology, Nutrition, and Metabolism = Physiologie Appliquee, Nutrition Et Metabolisme*, 1–6. http://doi.org/10.1139/apnm-2014-0249.

Andreyeva, T., Kelly, I.R. & Harris, J.L. (2011). Exposure to Food Advertising on Television: Associations with Children's Fast Food and Soft Drink Consumption and Obesity. *Economics & Human Biology, 9*(3), 221–233. http://doi.org/10.1016/j.ehb.2011.02.004.

Azar, K.M.J., Lesser, L.I., Laing, B.Y., Stephens, J., Aurora, M.S., Burke, L.E. & Palaniappan, L.P. (2013). Mobile Applications for Weight Management: Theory-based Content Analysis. *American Journal of Preventive Medicine, 45*(5), 583–589. http://doi.org/10.1016/j.amepre.2013.07.005.

Ballard, M., Gray, M., Reilly, J. & Noggle, M. (2009). Correlates of Video Game Screen Time among Males: Body Mass, Physical Activity, and Other Media Use. *Eating Behaviors, 10*(3), 161–167. http://doi.org/10.1016/j.eatbeh.2009.05.001.

Barwais, F.A. & Cuddihy, T.F. (2015). Empowering Sedentary Adults to Reduce Sedentary Behavior and Increase Physical Activity Levels and Energy Expenditure: A Pilot Study. *International Journal of Environmental Research and Public Health, 12*(1), 414–427. http://doi.org/10.3390/ijerph120100414.

Batada, A. & Wootan, M.G. (2007). Nickelodeon Markets Nutrition-poor Foods to Children. *American Journal of Preventive Medicine, 33*(1), 48–50. http://doi.org/10.1016/j.amepre.2007.02.035.

Batada, A., Seitz, M.D., Wootan, M.G. & Story, M. (2008). Nine out of 10 Food Advertisements Shown during Saturday Morning Children's Television Programming are for Foods High in Fat, Sodium, or Added Sugars, or Low in Nutrients.

Journal of the American Dietetic Association, 108(4), 673–678. http://doi.org/10.1016/j. jada.2008.01.015.

Beydoun, M.A. & Wang, Y. (2007). How Do Socio-economic Status, Perceived Economic Barriers and Nutritional Benefits Affect Quality of Dietary Intake among US Adults? *European Journal of Clinical Nutrition, 62*(3), 303–313. http://doi. org/10.1038/sj.ejcn.1602700.

Biddiss, E. & Irwin, J. (2010). Active Video Games to Promote Physical Activity in Children and Youth: A Systematic Review. *Archives of Pediatrics & Adolescent Medicine, 164*(7), 664–672. http://doi.org/10.1001/archpediatrics.2010.104.

Boynton-Jarrett, R., Thomas, T.N., Peterson, K.E., Wiecha, J., Sobol, A.M. & Gortmaker, S.L. (2003). Impact of Television Viewing Patterns on Fruit and Vegetable Consumption among Adolescents. *Pediatrics, 112*(6 Pt. 1), 1321–1326.

Bungum, T. & Vincent, V. (1996). Determinants of Physical Activity among Female Adolescents. *American Journal of Preventive Medicine, 13*(2), 115–122.

Castonguay, J., Kunkel, D., Wright, P. & Duff, C. (2013). Healthy Characters? An Investigation of Marketing Practices in Children's Food Advertising. *Journal of Nutrition Education and Behavior, 45*(6), 571–577. http://doi.org/10.1016/j. jneb.2013.03.007.

Centers for Disease Control and Prevention. (2012, April 27). Defining Overweight and Obesity. Retrieved February 3, 2015 from www.cdc.gov/obesity/adult/ defining.html.

Centers for Disease Control and Prevention. (2014, January 21). Obesity and Overweight. Retrieved February 3, 2015 from www.cdc.gov/nchs/fastats/obesity-overweight.htm.

Centers for Disease Control and Prevention. (n.d.a). Adolescent and School Health. Retrieved February 3, 2015 from www.cdc.gov/healthyyouth/obesity/facts.htm.

Centers for Disease Control and Prevention. (n.d.b). Adult Obesity Facts: Obesity is Common, Serious and Costly. Retrieved February 3, 2015 from www.cdc.gov/ obesity/data/adult.html.

Chang, V.W. & Lauderdale, D.S. (2005). Income Disparities in Body Mass Index and Obesity in the United States, 1971–2002. *Archives of Internal Medicine, 165*(18), 2122–2128. http://doi.org/10.1001/archinte.165.18.2122.

Chao, Y.-Y., Scherer, Y.K. & Montgomery, C.A. (2014a). Effects of Using Nintendo WiiTM Exergames in Older Adults: A Review of the Literature. *Journal of Aging and Health.* http://doi.org/10.1177/0898264314551171.

Chao, Y.-Y., Scherer, Y.K., Montgomery, C.A., Wu, Y.-W. & Lucke, K.T. (2014b). Physical and Psychosocial Effects of Wii Fit Exergames Use in Assisted Living Residents: A Pilot Study. *Clinical Nursing Research.* http://doi.org/10.1177/1054773814562880.

Cheyne, A., Mejia, P., Nixon, L. & Dorfman, L. (2014). Food and Beverage Marketing to Youth. *Current Obesity Reports, 3*(4), 440–450. http://doi.org/10.1007/s13679-014-0122-y.

Cowan, L.T., Wagenen, S.A.V., Brown, B.A., Hedin, R.J., Seino-Stephan, Y., Hall, P.C. & West, J.H. (2012). Apps of Steel: Are Exercise Apps Providing Consumers With Realistic Expectations? A Content Analysis of Exercise Apps for Presence of Behavior Change Theory. *Health Education & Behavior*, 1090198112452126. http://doi. org/10.1177/1090198112452126.

Culp, J., Bell, R.A. & Cassady, D. (2010). Characteristics of Food Industry Web Sites and "Advergames" Targeting Children. *Journal of Nutrition Education and Behavior, 42*(3), 197–201. http://doi.org/10.1016/j.jneb.2009.07.008.

Dave, D. & Rashad, I. (2009). Overweight Status, Self-perception, and Suicidal

Behaviors among Adolescents. *Social Science & Medicine, 68*(9), 1685–1691. http://doi.org/10.1016/j.socscimed.2009.02.015.

de Vet, E., de Ridder, D.T.D. & de Wit, J.B.F. (2011). Environmental Correlates of Physical Activity and Dietary Behaviours among Young People: A Systematic Review of Reviews. *Obesity Reviews, 12*(5), e130–e142. http://doi.org/10.1111/j.1467-789X.2010.00784.x.

DiLorenzo, T.M., Stucky-Ropp, R.C., Vander Wal, J.S. & Gotham, H.J. (1998). Determinants of Exercise among Children. II. A Longitudinal Analysis. *Preventive Medicine, 27*(3), 470–477. http://doi.org/10.1006/pmed.1998.0307.

Drewnowski, A. (2004). Obesity and the Food Environment: Dietary Energy Density and Diet Costs. *American Journal of Preventive Medicine, 27*(Supp. 3), 154–162. http://doi.org/10.1016/j.amepre.2004.06.011.

Drewnowski, A. & Darmon, N. (2005). Food Choices and Diet Costs: An Economic Analysis. *The Journal of Nutrition, 135*(4), 900–904.

Ervin, R.B. et al. (2011). Healthy Eating Index – 2005 Total and Component Scores for Adults Aged 20 and Over: National Health and Nutrition Examination Survey, 2003–2004. *National Health Statistics Report, 44.* Retrieved February 4, 2015 from http://198.246.124.22/nchs/data/nhsr/nhsr044.pdf.

Falbe, J., Rosner, B., Willett, W.C., Sonneville, K.R., Hu, F.B. & Field, A.E. (2013). Adiposity and Different Types of Screen Time. *Pediatrics, 132*(6), e1497–e1505. http://doi.org/10.1542/peds.2013-0887.

Falbe, J., Willett, W.C., Rosner, B., Gortmaker, S.L., Sonneville, K.R. & Field, A.E. (2014). Longitudinal Relations of Television, Electronic Games, and Digital Versatile Discs with Changes in Diet in Adolescents. *The American Journal of Clinical Nutrition, 100*(4), 1173–1181. http://doi.org/10.3945/ajcn.114.088500.

Fallah-Fini, S., Rahmandad, H., Huang, T.T.-K., Bures, R.M., & Glass, T.A. (2014). Modeling US adult obesity trends: a system dynamics model for estimating energy imbalance gap. *American Journal of Public Health, 104*(7), 1230–1239. http://doi.org/10.2105/AJPH.2014.301882.

Ferreira, I., van der Horst, K., Wendel-Vos, W., Kremers, S., van Lenthe, F.J. & Brug, J. (2007). Environmental Correlates of Physical Activity in Youth – A Review and Update. *Obesity Reviews: An Official Journal of the International Association for the Study of Obesity, 8*(2), 129–154. http://doi.org/10.1111/j.1467-789X.2006.00264.x.

Finucane, M.M., Stevens, G.A., Cowan, M.J., Danaei, G., Lin, J.K., Paciorek, C.J. & Ezzati, M. (2011). National, Regional, and Global Trends in Body-mass Index since 1980: Systematic Analysis of Health Examination Surveys and Epidemiological Studies with 960 Country-years and 9.1 Million Participants. *The Lancet, 377*(9765), 557–567.

Fonda, S.J., Fultz, N.H., Jenkins, K.R., Wheeler, L.M. & Wray, L.A. (2004). Relationship of Body Mass and Net Worth for Retirement-aged Men and Women. *Research on Aging, 26*(1), 153–176. http://doi.org/10.1177/0164027503258739.

Ford, E.S. & Dietz, W.H. (2013). Trends in Energy Intake among Adults in the United States: Findings from NHANES. *The American Journal of Clinical Nutrition, 97*(4), 848–853. http://doi.org/10.3945/ajcn.112.052662.

Fountaine, C., Liguori, G., Mozumdar, A. & Schuna, J. (2011). Physical Activity and Screen Time Sedentary Behaviors in College Students. *International Journal of Exercise Science, 4*(2). Retrieved February 10, 2015 from http://digitalcommons.wku.edu/ijes/vol. 4/iss2/3.

Franco, M.R., Tong, A., Howard, K., Sherrington, C., Ferreira, P.H., Pinto, R.Z. & Ferreira, M.L. (2015). Older People's Perspectives on Participation in Physical

Activity: A Systematic Review and Thematic Synthesis of Qualitative Literature. *British Journal of Sports Medicine.* http://doi.org/10.1136/bjsports-2014-094015.

Glanz, K., Basil, M., Maibach, E., Goldberg, J. & Snyder, D. (1998). Why Americans Eat What They Do: Taste, Nutrition, Cost, Convenience, and Weight Control Concerns as Influences on Food Consumption. *Journal of the American Dietetic Association, 98*(10), 1118–1126. http://doi.org/10.1016/S0002-8223(98)00260-0.

Graff, S., Kunkel, D. & Mermin, S.E. (2012). Government Can Regulate Food Advertising to Children Because Cognitive Research Shows That it is Inherently Misleading. *Health Affairs, 31*(2), 392–398. http://doi.org/10.1377/hlthaff.2011.0609.

Graves, L.E.F., Ridgers, N.D., Williams, K., Stratton, G., Atkinson, G. & Cable, N.T. (2010). The Physiological Cost and Enjoyment of Wii Fit in Adolescents, Young Adults, and Older Adults. *Journal of Physical Activity & Health, 7*(3), 393–401.

Gregori, D., Ballali, S., Vecchio, M.G., Sciré, A.S., Foltran, F. & Berchialla, P. (2014). Randomized Controlled Trials Evaluating Effect of Television Advertising on Food Intake in Children: Why Such a Sensitive Topic is Lacking Top-level Evidence? *Ecology of Food and Nutrition, 53*(5), 562–577. http://doi.org/10.1080/036702 44.2014.883976.

Grier, S.A. & Kumanyika, S.K. (2008). The Context for Choice: Health Implications of Targeted Food and Beverage Marketing to African Americans. *American Journal of Public Health, 98*(9), 1616–1629. http://doi.org/10.2105/AJPH.2007.115626.

Gyurcsik, N.C., Spink, K.S., Bray, S.R., Chad, K. & Kwan, M. (2006). An Ecologically Based Examination of Barriers to Physical Activity in Students from Grade Seven Through First-year University. *Journal of Adolescent Health, 38*(6), 704–711. http://doi.org/10.1016/j.jadohealth.2005.06.007.

Halford, J.C., Boyland, E.J., Hughes, G.M., Stacey, L., McKean, S. & Dovey, T.M. (2008a). Beyond-brand Effect of Television Food Advertisements on Food Choice in Children: The Effects of Weight Status. *Public Health Nutrition, 11*(9), 897–904. http://doi.org/10.1017/S1368980007001231.

Halford, J.C.G., Boyland, E.J., Cooper, G.D., Dovey, T.M., Smith, C.J., Williams, N. & Blundell, J.E. (2008b). Children's Food Preferences: Effects of Weight Status, Food Type, Branding and Television Food Advertisements (Commercials). *International Journal of Pediatric Obesity: IJPO: An Official Journal of the International Association for the Study of Obesity, 3*(1), 31–38. http://doi.org/10.1080/17477160701645152.

Hayden-Wade, H.A., Stein, R.I., Ghaderi, A., Saelens, B.E., Zabinski, M.F. & Wilfley, D.E. (2005). Prevalence, Characteristics, and Correlates of Teasing Experiences among Overweight Children vs. Non-overweight Peers. *Obesity Research, 13*(8), 1381–1392. http://doi.org/10.1038/oby.2005.167.

Henderson, V.R. & Kelly, B. (2005). Food Advertising in the Age of Obesity: Content Analysis of Food Advertising on General Market and African American Television. *Journal of Nutrition Education and Behavior, 37*(4), 191–196. http://doi.org/10.1016/ S1499-4046(06)60245-5.

Henry, A.E. & Story, M. (2009). Food and Beverage Brands that Market to Children and Adolescents on the Internet: A Content Analysis of Branded Web Sites. *Journal of Nutrition Education and Behavior, 41*(5), 353–359. http://doi.org/10.1016/j. jneb.2008.08.004.

Hoek, J. & Gendall, P. (2006). Advertising and Obesity: A Behavioral Perspective. *Journal of Health Communication, 11*(4), 409–423. http://doi.org/10.1080/10810730600671888.

Humpel, N., Owen, N. & Leslie, E. (2002). Environmental Factors Associated with Adults' Participation in Physical Activity: A Review. *American Journal of Preventive Medicine, 22*(3), 188–199. http://doi.org/10.1016/S0749-3797(01)00426-3.

Janssen, I., Katzmarzyk, P.T., Boyce, W.F., Vereecken, C., Mulvihill, C., Roberts, C. & the Health Behaviour in School-aged Children Obesity Working Group. (2005). Comparison of Overweight and Obesity Prevalence in School-aged Youth from 34 Countries and Their Relationships with Physical Activity and Dietary Patterns. *Obesity Reviews, 6*(2), 123–132. http://doi.org/10.1111/j.1467-789X.2005.00176.x.

Kim, S.A., Moore, L.V., Galuska, D., Wright, A.P., Harris, D., Grummer-Strawn, L.M. & the Division of Nutrition, Physical Activity, and Obesity, National Center for Chronic Disease Prevention and Health Promotion, CDC. (2014). Vital Signs: Fruit and Vegetable Intake among Children – United States, 2003–2010. *MMWR. Morbidity and Mortality Weekly Report, 63*(31), 671–676.

Kim, S.-S., Min, W.-K., Kim, J.-H. & Lee, B.-H. (2014). The Effects of VR-based Wii Fit Yoga on Physical Function in Middle-aged Female LBP Patients. *Journal of Physical Therapy Science, 26*(4), 549–552. http://doi.org/10.1589/jpts.26.549.

Kimm, S.Y.S., Glynn, N.W., Mcmahon, R.P., Voorhees, C.C., Striegel-Moore, R.H. & Daniels, S.R. (2006). Self-perceived Barriers to Activity Participation among Sedentary Adolescent Girls. *Medicine & Science in Sports & Exercise, 38*(3), 534–540. http://doi.org/10.1249/01.mss.0000189316.71784.dc.

Klompstra, L., Jaarsma, T. & Strömberg, A. (2014). Exergaming to Increase the Exercise Capacity and Daily Physical Activity in Heart Failure Patients: A Pilot Study. *BMC Geriatrics, 14*, 119. http://doi.org/10.1186/1471-2318-14-119.

Kumar, G., Onufrak, S., Zytnick, D., Kingsley, B. & Park, S. (2014). Self-reported Advertising Exposure to Sugar-sweetened Beverages among US Youth. *Public Health Nutrition*, 1–7. http://doi.org/10.1017/S1368980014001785.

Lachat, C., Nago, E., Verstraeten, R., Roberfroid, D., Van Camp, J. & Kolsteren, P. (2012). Eating Out of Home and its Association with Dietary Intake: A Systematic Review of the Evidence. *Obesity Reviews: An Official Journal of the International Association for the Study of Obesity, 13*(4), 329–346. http://doi.org/10.1111/j.1467-789X.2011.00953.x.

Lamboglia, C.M.G.F., da Silva, V.T.B.L., de Vasconcelos Filho, J.E., Pinheiro, M.H.N.P., Munguba, M.C. da S., Silva Júnior, F.V.I. & da Silva, C.A.B. (2013). Exergaming as a Strategic Tool in the Fight against Childhood Obesity: A Systematic Review. *Journal of Obesity, 2013*, 438364. http://doi.org/10.1155/2013/438364.

Larkin, J.C. & Pines, H.A. (1979). No Fat Persons Need Apply: Experimental Studies of the Overweight Stereotype and Hiring Preference. *Work and Occupations, 6*(3), 312–327. http://doi.org/10.1177/073088847900600303.

Laurson, K.R., Eisenmann, J.C., Welk, G.J., Wickel, E.E., Gentile, D.A. & Walsh, D.A. (2008). Combined Influence of Physical Activity and Screen Time Recommendations on Childhood Overweight. *The Journal of Pediatrics, 153*(2), 209–214. http://doi.org/10.1016/j.jpeds.2008.02.042.

Lee, M., Choi, Y., Quilliam, E.T. & Cole, R.T. (2009). Playing With Food: Content Analysis of Food Advergames. *Journal of Consumer Affairs, 43*(1), 129–154. http://doi.org/10.1111/j.1745-6606.2008.01130.x.

LoDolce, M.E., Harris, J.L. & Schwartz, M.B. (2013). Sugar as Part of a Balanced Breakfast? What Cereal Advertisements Teach Children about Healthy Eating. *Journal of Health Communication, 18*(11), 1293–1309. http://doi.org/10.1080/10810730.2013.778366.

Lyons, E.J., Lewis, Z.H., Mayrsohn, B.G. & Rowland, J.L. (2014). Behavior Change Techniques Implemented in Electronic Lifestyle Activity Monitors: A Systematic Content Analysis. *Journal of Medical Internet Research, 16*(8), e192. http://doi.org/10.2196/jmir.3469.

Mallinckrodt, V. & Mizerski, D. (2007). The Effects of Playing an Advergame on

Young Children's Perceptions, Preferences, and Requests. *Journal of Advertising*, 36(2), 87–100. http://doi.org/10.2753/JOA0091-3367360206.

Marsh, S., Ni Mhurchu, C. & Maddison, R. (2013). The Non-advertising Effects of Screen-based Sedentary Activities on Acute Eating Behaviours in Children, Adolescents, and Young Adults. A Systematic Review. *Appetite*, 71, 259–273. http://doi.org/10.1016/j.appet.2013.08.017.

Masters, R.K., Reither, E.N., Powers, D.A., Yang, Y.C., Burger, A.E. & Link, B.G. (2013). The Impact of Obesity on US Mortality Levels: The Importance of Age and Cohort Factors in Population Estimates. *American Journal of Public Health*, 103(10), 1895–1901. http://doi.org/10.2105/AJPH.2013.301379.

Melkevik, O., Torsheim, T., Iannotti, R.J. & Wold, B. (2010). Is Spending Time in Screen-based Sedentary Behaviors Associated with Less Physical Activity: A Cross National Investigation. *The International Journal of Behavioral Nutrition and Physical Activity*, 7, 46. http://doi.org/10.1186/1479-5868-7-46.

Middelweerd, A., Mollee, J.S., van der Wal, C.N., Brug, J. & Velde, S.J.Te. (2014). Apps to Promote Physical Activity among Adults: A Review and Content Analysis. *The International Journal of Behavioral Nutrition and Physical Activity*, 11, 97. http://doi.org/10.1186/s12966-014-0097-9.

Mobile Continues to Steal Share of US Adults' Daily Time Spent with Media – eMarketer. (2014, April 22). Retrieved February 10, 2015 from www.emarketer.com/Article/Mobile-Continues-Steal-Share-of-US-Adults-Daily-Time-Spent-with-Media/1010782.

Monsivais, P., Mclain, J. & Drewnowski, A. (2010). The Rising Disparity in the Price of Healthful Foods: 2004–2008. *Food Policy*, 35(6), 514–520. http://doi.org/10.1016/j.foodpol.2010.06.004.

Moore, E.S. & Rideout, V.J. (2007). The Online Marketing of Food to Children: Is it Just Fun and Games? *Journal of Public Policy & Marketing*, 26(2), 202–220.

National Center for Health Statistics. (2014). *Health, United States, 2013: With Special Feature on Prescription Drugs*. Hyattsville, MD: National Center for Health Statistics. Retrieved February 5, 2015 from www.cdc.gov/nchs/data/hus/hus13.pdf.

Nguyen, J.C.D., Killcross, A.S. & Jenkins, T.A. (2014). Obesity and Cognitive Decline: Role of Inflammation and Vascular Changes. *Frontiers in Neuroscience*, 8, 375. http://doi.org/10.3389/fnins.2014.00375.

Ogden, C.L., Carroll, M.D., Kit, B.K. & Flegal, K.M. (2014). Prevalence of Childhood and Adult Obesity in the United States, 2011–2012. *JAMA*, 311(8), 806–814. http://doi.org/10.1001/jama.2014.732.

Outley, C.W. & Taddese, A. (2006). A Content Analysis of Health and Physical Activity Messages Marketed to African American Children during After-school Television Programming. *Archives of Pediatrics & Adolescent Medicine*, 160(4), 432–435.

Paek Hye-Jin, Taylor Quilliam, E., Kim Sookyong, J., Weatherspoon, L.J., Rifon, N. & Lee, M. (2014). Characteristics of Food Advergames that Reach Children and the Nutrient Quality of the Foods They Advertise. *Internet Research*, 24(1), 63–81. http://doi.org/10.1108/IntR-02-2013-0018.

Panel, N.O.E.I.E. et al. (1998). Clinical Guidelines on the Identification, Evaluation, and Treatment of Overweight and Obesity in Adults. Retrieved February 5, 2015 from www.ncbi.nlm.nih.gov/books/NBK2003.

Panic, K., Cauberghe, V. & De Pelsmacker, P. (2013). Comparing TV Ads and Advergames Targeting Children: The Impact of Persuasion Knowledge on Behavioral Responses. *Journal of Advertising*, 42(2–3), 264–273.

Pingitore, R., Dugoni, B.L., Scott, R. & Spring, B. (1994). Bias Against Overweight

Job Applicants in a Simulated Employment Interview. *Journal of Applied Psychology*, 79(6), 909–917. http://doi.org/10.1037/0021-9010.79.6.909.

Powell, L.M., Harris, J.L. & Fox, T. (2013a). Food Marketing Expenditures Aimed At Youth: Putting the Numbers in Context. *American Journal of Preventive Medicine*, 45(4), 453–461. http://doi.org/10.1016/j.amepre.2013.06.003.

Powell, L.M., Schermbeck, R.M. & Chaloupka, F.J. (2013b). Nutritional Content of Food and Beverage Products in Television Advertisements Seen on Children's Programming. *Childhood Obesity (Print)*, 9(6), 524–531. http://doi.org/10.1089/chi.2013.0072.

Powell, L.M., Szczypka, G. & Chaloupka, F.J. (2007a). Adolescent Exposure to Food Advertising on Television. *American Journal of Preventive Medicine*, 33(Supp. 4), S251–S256. http://doi.org/10.1016/j.amepre.2007.07.009.

Powell, L.M., Wada, R. & Kumanyika, S.K. (2014). Racial/Ethnic and Income Disparities in Child and Adolescent Exposure to Food and Beverage Television Ads Across the U.S. Media Markets. *Health & Place*, 29, 124–131. http://doi.org/10.1016/j.healthplace.2014.06.006.

Powell, L.M., Szczypka, G., Chaloupka, F.J. & Braunschweig, C.L. (2007b). Nutritional Content of Television Food Advertisements Seen by Children and Adolescents in the United States. *Pediatrics*, 120(3), 576–583. http://doi.org/10.1542/peds.2006-3595.

Puhl, R.M. & Brownell, K.D. (2006). Confronting and Coping with Weight Stigma: An Investigation of Overweight and Obese Adults. *Obesity*, 14(10), 1802–1815. http://doi.org/10.1038/oby.2006.208.

Raymond, S. (2013, February 26). Exergaming as Physical Activity: How Effective Are Exergames at Increasing Physical Activity in Youth? Retrieved February 11, 2015 from http://altarum.org/health-policy-blog/exergaming-as-physical-activity-how-effective-are-exergames-at-increasing-physical-activity-in-youth.

Rifon, N.J., Taylor Quilliam, E., Paek, H.-J., Weatherspoon, L.J., Kim, S.-K. & Smreker, K.C. (2014). Age-dependent Effects of Food Advergame Brand Integration and Interactivity. *International Journal of Advertising*, 33(3), 475–508. http://doi.org/10.2501/IJA-33-3-475-508.

Rothblum, E.D., Brand, P.A., Miller, C.T. & Oetjen, H.A. (1990). The Relationship between Obesity, Employment Discrimination, and Employment-related Victimization. *Journal of Vocational Behavior*, 37(3), 251–266. http://doi.org/10.1016/0001-8791(90)90044-3.

Salmon, J., Owen, N., Crawford, D., Bauman, A. & Sallis, J.F. (2003). Physical Activity and Sedentary Behavior: A Population-based Study of Barriers, Enjoyment, and Preference. *Health Psychology*, 22(2), 178–188. http://doi.org/10.1037/0278-6133.22.2.178.

Sassi, F., Devaux, M., Cecchini, M. & Rusticelli, E. (2009). *The Obesity Epidemic: Analysis of Past and Projected Future Trends in Selected OECD Countries* (OECD Health Working Papers). Paris: Organisation for Economic Co-operation and Development. Retrieved February 4, 2015 from www.oecd-ilibrary.org/content/working paper/225215402672.

Sisson, S.B., Broyles, S.T., Baker, B.L. & Katzmarzyk, P.T. (2010). Screen Time, Physical Activity, and Overweight in U.S. Youth: National Survey of Children's Health 2003. *Journal of Adolescent Health*, 47(3), 309–311. http://doi.org/10.1016/j.jadohealth.2010.02.016.

Slining, M.M. & Popkin, B.M. (2013). Trends in Intakes and Sources of Solid Fats and Added Sugars among U.S. Children and Adolescents: 1994–2010. *Pediatric Obesity*, 8(4), 307–324. http://doi.org/10.1111/j.2047-6310.2013.00156.x.

Slootmaker, S.M., Chinapaw, M.J.M., Schuit, A.J., Seidell, J.C. & Van Mechelen, W. (2009). Feasibility and Effectiveness of Online Physical Activity Advice Based on a Personal Activity Monitor: Randomized Controlled Trial. *Journal of Medical Internet Research, 11*(3), e27. http://doi.org/10.2196/jmir.1139.

Speers, S.E., Harris, J.L. & Schwartz, M.B. (2011). Child and Adolescent Exposure to Food and Beverage Brand Appearances During Prime-time Television Programming. *American Journal of Preventive Medicine, 41*(3), 291–296. http://doi.org/10.1016/j.amepre.2011.04.018.

Stewart, H., Blisard, N. & Jolliffe, D. (2006). *Let's Eat Out: Americans Weigh Taste, Convenience, and Nutrition* (Economic Information Bulletin No. 59411). United States Department of Agriculture, Economic Research Service. Retrieved February 9, 2015 from https://ideas.repec.org/p/ags/uersib/59411.html.

Stewart, S.T., Cutler, D.M. & Rosen, A.B. (2009). Forecasting the Effects of Obesity and Smoking on U.S. Life Expectancy. *New England Journal of Medicine, 361*(23), 2252–2260. http://doi.org/10.1056/NEJMsa0900459.

Stitt, C. & Kunkel, D. (2008). Food Advertising During Children's Television Programming on Broadcast and Cable Channels. *Health Communication, 23*(6), 573–584. http://doi.org/10.1080/10410230802465258.

Story, M. & Faulkner, P. (1990). The Prime Time Diet: A Content Analysis of Eating Behavior and Food Messages in Television Program Content and Commercials. *American Journal of Public Health, 80*(6), 738–740. http://doi.org/10.2105/AJPH.80.6.738.

Swahn, M.H., Reynolds, M.R., Tice, M., Miranda-Pierangeli, M.C., Jones, C.R. & Jones, I.R. (2009). Perceived Overweight, BMI, and Risk for Suicide Attempts: Findings from the 2007 Youth Risk Behavior Survey. *Journal of Adolescent Health, 45*(3), 292–295. http://doi.org/10.1016/j.jadohealth.2009.03.006.

Sween, J., Wallington, S.F., Sheppard, V., Taylor, T., Llanos, A.A. & Adams-Campbell, L.L. (2014). The Role of Exergaming in Improving Physical Activity: A Review. *Journal of Physical Activity & Health, 11*(4), 864–870. http://doi.org/10.1123/jpah.2011-0425.

Taveras, E.M., Rifas-Shiman, S.L., Field, A.E., Frazier, A.L., Colditz, G.A. & Gillman, M.W. (2004). The Influence of Wanting to Look Like Media Figures on Adolescent Physical Activity. *Journal of Adolescent Health, 35*(1), 41–50. http://doi.org/10.1016/j.jadohealth.2003.09.005.

Thomson, D.M. (2011). The Mixed Health Messages of Millsberry: A Critical Study of Online Child-targeted Food Advergaming. *Health Communication, 26*(4), 323–331. http://doi.org/10.1080/10410236.2010.549817.

Trost, S.G., Owen, N., Bauman, A.E., Sallis, J.F. & Brown, W. (2002). Correlates of Adults' Participation in Physical Activity: Review and Update. *Medicine and Science in Sports and Exercise, 34*(12), 1996–2001. http://doi.org/10.1249/01.MSS.0000038974.76900.92.

Vogelzangs, N., Kritchevsky, S.B., Beekman, A.T.F., Brenes, G.A., Newman, A.B., Satterfield, S. & the Health ABC Study. (2010). Obesity and Onset of Significant Depressive Symptoms: Results from a Prospective Community-based Cohort Study of Older Men and Women. *The Journal of Clinical Psychiatry, 71*(4), 391–399. http://doi.org/10.4088/JCP.08m04743blu.

Wang, Y. & Zhang, Q. (2006). Are American Children and Adolescents of Low Socioeconomic Status at Increased Risk of Obesity? Changes in the Association between Overweight and Family Income between 1971 and 2002. *The American Journal of Clinical Nutrition, 84*(4), 707–716.

Wang, Y.C., McPherson, K., Marsh, T., Gortmaker, S.L. & Brown, M. (2011). Health and Economic Burden of the Projected Obesity Trends in the USA and the UK. *The Lancet, 378*(9793), 815–825. http://doi.org/10.1016/S0140-6736(11)60814-3.

Warren, R., Wicks, R.H., Wicks, J.L., Fosu, I. & Chung, D. (2008). Food and Beverage Advertising on U.S. Television: A Comparison of Child-targeted Versus General Audience Commercials. *Journal of Broadcasting & Electronic Media, 52*(2), 231–246. http://doi.org/10.1080/08838150801992037.

West, J.H., Hall, P.C., Hanson, C.L., Barnes, M.D., Giraud-Carrier, C. & Barrett, J. (2012). There's an App for That: Content Analysis of Paid Health and Fitness Apps. *Journal of Medical Internet Research, 14*(3), e72.

Wonderlich-Tierney, A.L., Wenzel, K.R., Vander Wal, J.S. & Wang-Hall, J. (2013). Food-related Advertisements and Food Intake among Adult Men and Women. *Appetite, 71*, 57–62. http://doi.org/10.1016/j.appet.2013.07.009.

Xiang, X. & An, R. (2014). Obesity and Onset of Depression among U.S. Middle-aged and Older Adults. *Journal of Psychosomatic Research.* http://doi.org/10.1016/j.jpsychores.2014.12.008.

Yang, Q., Zhang, Z., Gregg, E.W., Flanders, W., Merritt, R. & Hu, F.B. (2014). Added Sugar Intake and Cardiovascular Diseases Mortality among US Adults. *JAMA Internal Medicine, 174*(4), 516–524. http://doi.org/10.1001/jamainternmed.2013.13563.

Zimmerman, F.J. & Shimoga, S.V. (2014). The Effects of Food Advertising and Cognitive Load on Food Choices. *BMC Public Health, 14*, 342. http://doi.org/10.1186/1471-2458-14-342.

CHAPTER 8

SHOWING US WHAT WE SHOULD (AND CANNOT) BE: THE MASS MEDIA MIRROR AND BODY IMAGE

In February 2015, social media nationwide filled up with responses to the online leak of a photograph of 48-year-old supermodel Cindy Crawford, even though there was nothing especially controversial about what Crawford was wearing, or doing, in the photo. In it, Crawford wears a black bra and panties, topped by what appears to be a black fur coat, and sports a black hat.

What was remarkable about the photo, originally shot to accompany a 2013 cover story in the Mexican/Latin American version of *Marie Claire* magazine but never actually published, is that it appeared unretouched. Unlike the flawless, perfectly toned bodies we have come to expect in fashion magazines, this photo not only showed Crawford's tan lines but also revealed – *gasp* – that her stomach was not utterly flat, her skin not completely smooth, her thighs not totally free of any bulges or dimples.

In other words, she looked like a normal 48-year-old woman who has maintained a healthy weight and reasonably good muscle tone.

The photo itself, and audience reactions to it, went viral on social media, with many commentators initially praising Crawford for being "brave" enough to show the global audience what "real" women look like. However, after it became clear that Crawford had not authorized the release of the photo, the media discussion turned toward how the photo's release had violated Crawford's privacy (Cameron, 2015). Although Crawford herself never responded to the controversy, the photographer who shot the original photo later stated that, in fact, it had been altered – to make Crawford appear less slender and fit than she actually is.

The hoopla surrounding the Crawford photo illustrates a common complaint about mass media portrayals, especially of women. The people we see pictured in the pages of magazines, on TV, in the movies and in celebrity-focused websites bear little resemblance to the vast majority of people we would encounter in the real world. In short, they are simply too perfect. The women are tall and slender, with perfect muscle tone, full breasts, unblemished complexions, white teeth and glossy hair. The men, too, are tall, with wide shoulders, narrow hips, muscular arms, legs and shoulders, six-pack abdominals, clear skin, straight white teeth and enviable hair. Of course, there are individuals in the real world who fit these descriptions, but, let's face it, they are the exception rather than the rule, while in the media these nearly perfect figures represent the norm.

It isn't simply that only the most beautiful women and the most handsome men achieve success as models, actors and singers. Rather, it's that in many cases – especially in magazines – images of these naturally attractive models, actresses and singers are digitally edited to make them even more "perfect" than they already are (Kee & Farid, 2011). Even supermodel Cindy Crawford has said, "I wish I looked like Cindy Crawford," a reflection of the fact that the images audiences see in advertisements, billboards and magazine covers often represent an individual who does not exist in real life at all (Jhally & Kilbourne, 2010).

This chapter focuses on the impact of our constant exposure to these digitally edited images and their presentation as the cultural standard of beauty. This impact, research suggests, manifests itself in widespread body image dissatisfaction, damage to our self-esteem and, for some people, damaging behavioral responses, including eating disorders and other types of unhealthy dieting.

Diet, Dieting and Eating Disordered Behavior

At the outset, it is important to make a distinction between diet and dieting. Dieting generally focuses on strictly limiting the amounts or types of foods one consumes and on the attempt to lose weight. Maintaining a healthy diet, on the other hand, focuses more often on achieving a balance in food consumption, ensuring that one eats *enough* of the right types of foods to meet the nutritional needs of that individual's lifestyle, and the purpose of those food choices is to help the individual achieve and maintain good health (Jacobsen, 2011). While maintaining a healthy diet, in combination with good exercise habits, should enable the individual to achieve and maintain an acceptable weight, the goal is not to reach a specific number on the scale.

The previous chapter discussed in some detail the ways in which many Americans (and many people worldwide) are failing to follow healthy dietary practices and the resulting epidemic of overweight and obesity. Being overweight or obese certainly creates or exacerbates many types of health risks, but that is also true of many of the behaviors people adopt in their attempts to avoid becoming overweight or to lose excessive weight. Critics have argued that much of our cultural obsession with maintaining the "perfect" weight and body shape is at least encouraged, if not driven, by our exposure to mass-mediated images (Bair et al., 2012; Chan et al., 2010; Hausenblas et al., 2013; Jhally & Kilbourne, 2010; Nouri et al., 2011; van den Berg et al., 2007).

Although recent research by the U.S. Department of Agriculture suggests that Americans may be making healthier dietary choices (Todd, 2014), dieting remains a common practice. A report by The NPD Group, which has tracked Americans' dieting behaviors since 1980, showed that about one in five adults reported being on a diet in 2012, compared to nearly one-third (31%) in 1991. At the beginning of every year, the number of dieters increases, however, leading the NPD to estimate that in January 2013, 50 million Americans were on some sort of diet (NPD Group, 2013).

The percentages of dieters differ significantly within certain age and demographic groups. Women have always been more likely than men to diet. Data from the National Health and Nutrition Examination Surveys (NHANES) show significantly higher percentages of women dieting from 1950 through 2008; in 2008, 57 percent of women and 40 percent of men reported having been on a diet during the previous year (Montani et al., 2015).

These gender differences begin early. A longitudinal study of adolescents through young adulthood showed that when first surveyed in 1994/1995, 21 percent of girls (grades 7–12) reported dieting, along with 5.6 percent of boys. By the third wave, when the participants were 18 to 26 years old, 27.3 percent of women and 11.3 percent of men reported dieting (Liechty & Lee, 2013). Another analysis, which tracked weight control behaviors among adolescents and young adults between 1999 and 2010, showed that among younger adolescent girls the percentages reporting that they had been on a diet during the preceding year remained steady at about 55 percent (55.3 percent in 1999, 54.6 percent in 2010); among young adult women there was a non-significant increase, from 57.5 percent in 1999 to 59 percent in 2010. Although the figures showed no significant changes, they do show that more than half of all adolescent and young adult women reported having been on a diet at least once during the preceding year. Among teenage boys in the same study, the percentages who reported dieting declined from 28.6 percent in 1999 to 25.6 percent in 2010, but among young adult men there was a significant increase, from just over one in five (21.9%) in 1999 to more than one-third (34.5%) in 2010 (Neumark-Sztainer et al., 2011).

Ironically, one of the reasons dieting prevalence is so important is that regular dieting is a significant predictor of weight *gain* rather than weight loss (Lowe et al., 2013; Montani et al., 2015; Neumark-Sztainer et al., 2007). This seems to be especially true for people who start dieting even though their weight is within the normal range. Lowe and colleagues (2013) reviewed 25 studies that had tracked non-obese participants' weight gain or loss over time; the average age of participants was at least 12 for all studies. Only one study (of post-menopausal women) found no significant weight change, and in the other 24 studies, researchers found significant weight gain over time. Three-quarters (75%) of the analyses testing the impact of dieting revealed that dieters were significantly more likely than non-dieters to gain weight. Similarly, Lowe and another set of colleagues determined that female college freshmen who said they were dieting to lose weight actually gained twice as much weight as women who reported dieting in the past and three times as much as women who said they had never been on a diet (Lowe et al., 2006).

Dieting may be more effective among individuals who are already overweight or obese when they begin the diet. For instance, one comparison of the impacts of dietary fat restriction and exercise among participants with an average starting BMI of 33.6 (obese) showed that fat intake restriction was more effective than exercise for men, although both the dietary changes and exercise led to some weight loss. Among women there was an interaction effect, such that all levels of fat intake restriction enhanced the effects of exercise, but only moderate and greater increases in exercise enhanced the effect of fat intake restriction (Dunn et al., 2006). Another study compared long-term (two-year) adherence to low-fat, Mediterranean and low-carbohydrate diets, and found that long-term compliance was highest among obese individuals randomly assigned to the low-fat diet. Weight loss within the first six months of the diet was the best predictor of long-term adherence to the diet and to successful weight loss, but women and smokers had a harder time sticking to their diets, especially around holidays (Greenberg et al., 2009). Other studies have produced different results, especially in terms of the comparative success of low-carbohydrate versus low-fat diets. A review of 13 randomized controlled trials compared the two types of diets with obese participants and concluded that low-carb/high-protein diets were more effective than low-fat diets in producing weight loss in the first six months and as effective for up to one year (Hession et al., 2009). Another meta-analysis comparing the two types of diets showed that low-carbohydrate diets were more effective for the first six months, but there was no significant difference in weight loss after one year. However, individuals on low-fat diets had better results in terms of improving their cholesterol levels (Nordmann et al., 2006).

Thus, dieting may be effective in reducing weight and improving other health measures among those who are overweight or obese when they begin dieting. However, these types of diets generally require significant changes in diet and exercise over long periods of time, leading some individuals to turn to extreme weight loss behaviors such as diet pills, laxatives or vomiting. Such behaviors increase in prevalence during adolescence and young adulthood. One study that followed a cohort of adolescents from 1994/1995 through 2007/2008 showed that the prevalence of extreme weight loss behaviors grew from less than 1% in the first wave, when the participants were in seventh to twelfth grade (1.5 percent of girls, 0.3 percent of boys) to 3.56 percent by the time the group reached young adulthood (ages 18–26), with one in every 17 young adult women engaging in extreme weight loss behaviors. Girls who reported dieting during the first wave of the study were 1.6 times as likely to have begun engaging in extreme weight loss behaviors by the third wave. Dieting during adolescence also was associated with a greater risk of binge eating in young adulthood, but only for women (Liechty & Lee, 2013).

The most extreme of all extreme weight loss behaviors, categorized as eating disorders, include anorexia nervosa and bulimia nervosa. Anorexia nervosa, characterized as severe food restriction, obsession with having a thin figure and an irrational fear of weight gain, affects fewer than one of every 100 women (0.9%) and about one-third as many men (0.3%) in the United States. Bulimia nervosa, which involves binging on food during a short period of time and then purging through vomiting or the use of laxatives, diuretics or excessive exercise, has a lifetime prevalence of 1.5 percent in women and 0.5 percent in men in the United States (Hudson et al., 2007). Some sources put prevalence rates for anorexia and bulimia significantly higher, with combined rates between 3 and 10 percent of females aged 15 to 29. At least twice as many people display disordered eating behaviors without reaching the level of having full-blown anorexia or bulimia (Polivy & Herman, 2002). Within the U.S. population, the most common eating-related mental illness is binge eating disorder, characterized by binge eating without subsequent purging; lifetime prevalence of binge eating disorder is 3.5 percent among women and 2 percent among men (Hudson et al., 2007).

Each of these disorders has significant negative health effects. Individuals with anorexia nervosa experience numerous mental and physical health problems, including mood disorders and memory problems, anemia and other blood disorders, weak muscles, swollen joints, bone loss and increased risk for fractures, a higher likelihood of developing kidney stones, dry and easily bruised skin, brittle nails and hair, and hormonal problems, including cessation of menstrual periods and a greater risk of having a miscarriage or low birth weight baby among women who are anorexic during pregnancy. In the long term, anorexia can lead to kidney and heart failure, and death (Office on Women's Health, 2012b). Bulimia can produce many of the same effects, including anemia, irregular heartbeat and heart failure, irregular or absent periods, and dry skin. In addition, bulimics may have kidney problems related to abuse of diuretics, constipation or diarrhea, gum disease and tooth decay caused by frequent vomiting; damage to the esophagus and the stomach can increase the risk of ulcers, tearing and rupture (Office on Women's Health, 2012c). Although researchers have found that 74 percent of bulimics and 33 percent of anorexics recover fully within about seven or eight years of treatment (Herzog et al., 1999), mortality rates, including deaths from suicide, have been estimated at .51 percent of anorexics and .17 percent of bulimics per year (Smink et al., 2012). A meta-analysis comparing mortality associated with mental illnesses concluded that the highest risk of premature death occurred among those with eating disorders. The all-cause death rate for those with ano-rexia nervosa was five times what would be expected for a comparable population, and the risk of suicidal death was 32 times the expected rate (Harris & Barraclough, 1998).

Unlike individuals with anorexia or bulimia nervosa, those with binge eating disorders make no attempt to control their food intake, to purge food after binging. However, like bulimics, they may have episodes in which they eat until they are uncomfortably full, eating more quickly than usual and when they are not hungry. They often feel out of control while they're eating and then feel disgusted or guilty after overeating. In addition to increasing the likelihood of obesity – and the associated risks of diabetes, high blood pressure, high cholesterol, gallbladder disease, heart disease and some types of cancer – individuals with binge eating disorder are often depressed and experience higher than normal levels of stress, sleep disturbance and suicidal thoughts, as well as low self-esteem (Office on Women's Health, 2012a).

Although eating disorders such as anorexia and bulimia nervosa may be most familiar to the public, related body image disorders lead some individuals – usually men – to focus obsessively on becoming larger and more muscular, rather than thinner. Muscle dysmorphia, sometimes called "reverse anorexia" or "bigorexia," refers to a condition in which the individual perceives himself as lacking sufficient size, strength and/ or muscularity. These individuals spend excessive amounts of time lifting weights, often to the extent that they forgo other career and social opportunities to spend more time attempting to build muscle mass. In addition, they may waste money on ineffective and even dan-gerous "performance-enhancing" substances, including steroids, even when they understand the risks these substances create (Labre, 2002). Although prevalence rates remain unclear, some research suggests that the desire to be larger and more muscular has become increasingly common, even among adolescent and pre-adolescent boys (Cafri et al., 2006; Leone et al., 2005; Tiggemann et al., 2007).

What Causes Eating Disorders?

Numerous factors, from family relationships, individual experiences and characteristics, biological traits, and, of course, the sociocultural environment, have been linked to increased risk of eating disorders. Recent research suggests that genetics may play a role; relatives of eating disorder patients are seven to 12 times as likely to develop an eating disorder as are individuals who have no eating disordered relative (Campbell & Peebles, 2014). Evidence also suggests that a serotonin imbalance may contribute to eating disorders, although a review of these studies suggests that serotonin is more likely to play a role in bulimia than in anorexia. Another biological factor may be a deficiency in the ability to identify physiological states, such as hunger, and emotional states, leading anorexics to be unable to identify hunger when they are hungry and bulimics to perceive hunger even when they really are not. However, much of the research on biological characteristics associated with eating disorders has been unable to determine whether these characteristics should be considered causes or consequences of the eating disorder (Polivy & Herman, 2002).

A similar criticism may be made of much of the research linking eating disorders with cognitive problems, including the tendency toward obsessive and rigid thinking, perfectionism, impulsivity (in the case of bulimics), and an inability to accurately judge one's own weight/body shape. Obsessive thoughts contribute to eating disorders in the sense that most eating disorder patients spend more than three hours every day thinking about eating or food, weight or shape and related issues; some report having these types of thoughts, to some extent, 24 hours a day. Anorexic patients, in particular, tend to score high on perfectionism, and these tendencies persist even among those who have recovered from the eating disorder, suggesting that perfectionism may indeed create a predisposition to eating disorders. Finally, research suggests that those with eating disorders tend toward all-or-nothing thinking, such that they see even minor mistakes as proof of failure (Polivy & Herman, 2002).

Individual risk factors that seem to contribute to the development of eating disorders include traumatic experiences, such as being a victim of childhood emotional or sexual abuse, stressful life events and being teased about one's weight, shape or appearance. Women with eating disorders tend to report more self-directed hostility, guilt and anger, and they are also more likely to be depressed, both before and after the onset of the eating disorder symptoms. Low self-esteem and body dissatisfaction, which may become increasingly problematic among those who are dieting (and failing), are common among both anorexic and bulimic patients. In particular, body dissatisfaction often leads initially to dieting and subsequently, in some women, to the development of eating disorders. Polivy and Herman (2002) note, however, that while many individuals experience body dissatisfaction, most do not develop eating disorders, leading them to conclude that body dissatisfaction is a necessary but not sufficient factor in the onset of an eating disorder:

> Why is it that of two dissatisfied people, one throws herself into (usually futile) attempts to achieve a satisfactory body, whereas the other remains dissatisfied but does not diet/starve, binge, or purge? The determining factor, we suggest, is whether or not the individual seizes upon weight and shape as the answer to the problems of identity and control. Some young women become invested in achieving a "perfect" body as an existential project (i.e., as a way of giving their lives meaning, coherence, and emotional fulfillment that are otherwise lacking). Some become invested in achieving complete control over their eating, weight, and shape, believing that control in these domains is possible even though such control is not possible elsewhere in their lives. For many with EDs, these two goals overlap. In the final analysis, BD (body dissatisfaction) may contribute to EDs primarily by conferring purpose: The narrow ambitions of the ED patient – in particular, the exclusive focus on weight – may make her life simpler, more certain, and more efficacious.
>
> (Polivy & Herman, 2002, p. 199)

Family characteristics commonly described by eating disorder patients include poor communication, low perceived parental caring and expectations, maternal invasion of privacy, jealousy and competitiveness, and little encouragement of the child's autonomy. Girls and women with eating disorders are more likely than their non-eating disordered peers to have mothers who believe their daughters should lose weight, criticize their daughters' attractiveness and exhibit disordered eating patterns themselves (Polivy & Herman, 2002). Individuals with eating disorders are more likely than those without to have had dysfunctional families and negative food-related experiences in the family environment (Kluck, 2008). In addition, both eating disordered teens and their mothers react to stress using maladaptive coping strategies (Lantzouni et al., 2015).

Not surprisingly, peers also seem to play a substantial role in eating disorders, although research has produced sometimes conflicting findings about the levels and mechanisms of peer influence. For instance, a study of Australian female high school students identified no significant association between friends' influence and disordered eating (Rayner et al., 2013). However, a study of peer influences on body dissatisfaction among Israeli women aged 18 to 42 revealed that the single most damaging factor, in terms of the woman's body dissatisfaction, was the woman's belief that her best friend was thinner than herself; both direct and indirect comparisons to best friends and to sisters also significantly influenced drive for thinness and body dissatisfaction (Lev-Ari et al., 2014). Other researchers have identified having poor-quality female friendships (Schutz & Paxton, 2007; Sharpe et al., 2014) and peers' criticism of one's appearance (Jones et al., 2004) as predictors of body dissatisfaction, leading to disordered eating.

In general, less research has investigated the predictors of male body dissatisfaction, in part because boys and men seem to be less likely than women to experience body dissatisfaction. In addition, because males are more likely than women to want to be larger and more muscular rather than thinner, health advocates initially did not view the behaviors associated with male body dissatisfaction – primarily weight-lifting and other exercise routines – as unhealthy or negative. As noted earlier, however, male body dissatisfaction and especially an internalized drive for muscularity *can* lead to unhealthy behaviors, including excessive time spent exercising, negative diet practices, use of muscle-building supplements that can have negative side effects and, in some cases, use of anabolic steroids (Cafri et al., 2006; McCabe & Ricciardelli, 2004; Neumark-Sztainer et al., 2006; Smolak et al., 2005; Striegel-Moore et al., 2009).

As is the case with girls and women, numerous factors are associated with male body dissatisfaction. Cognitive/personality factors that seem to be associated with male body dissatisfaction include low self-esteem, internalization of societal body ideals, and both self-oriented and socially prescribed perfectionism, which refer, respectively, to the tendency to constantly self-appraise and to hold oneself to extremely high standards and to the perception that others expect the individual to be perfect (Grammas & Schwartz, 2009; Grieve, 2007). In addition, a greater focus on appearance is also associated with drive for muscularity (Davis et al., 2005), as is a greater tendency to engage in social comparison (Karazsia & Crowther, 2009).

Among adolescent boys, body image dissatisfaction has also been associated with family and peer influences (Jones et al., 2004; Paxton et al., 2006; Schaefer & Blodgett Salafia, 2014; Smolak et al., 2005; Vincent & McCabe, 2000). Interviews with Australian adolescent boys suggest that, in particular, the feedback boys receive from their male friends and their fathers focuses on the need to exercise to gain muscle mass or grow stronger (Ricciardelli et al., 2000). Another study showed that boys who had less parental support and perceived more family and peer pressure to be muscular scored higher on a measure of disordered eating attitudes (Ata et al., 2006). A review of the literature concluded that parents are more likely to influence boys' body image concerns through their comments than through modeling effects (Rodgers & Chabrol, 2009).

MASS MEDIA'S ROLE

In addition to these influences, research supports the contention that exposure to mass media images increases females' desire to be thinner and males' desire to be more muscular (Barlett et al., 2008; Grabe et al., 2008; Groesz et al., 2002; Hausenblas et al., 2013; Levine & Murnen, 2009; McCabe & Ricciardelli, 2004). The remaining sections of the chapter will discuss this research in more detail, considering media effects on females and males separately.

Somewhat surprisingly, the most recent published analysis of the portrayal of women's body shapes in U.S. mass media is now nearly ten years old. This study examined the female models used in advertising appearing in the June 2007 issues of five fitness and health magazines and five beauty/fashion magazines. That analysis revealed that most models (81%) appeared to be 21 to 30 years old, with fashion magazine models appearing younger than those in fitness magazines. In terms of body shape, 95 percent of the fashion magazine models were classified as ectomorphic (lean or thin), compared to 55 percent of fitness magazine models; more than one-third (36.3%) of the models in fitness magazines were classified as mesomorphic (muscular). Across both types of magazines, only 6.1 percent of the models were classified as endomorphic (soft, round). The researchers judged the body ideals presented in

Figure 8.1: The "Thin Ideal" Increases Body Dissatisfaction

both types of magazines as unattainable for most people (Wasylkiw et al., 2009).

Another relatively recent study examined written content and cover model images in the two most popular magazines targeted to teenage girls – *Seventeen* and *YM* – from 1956 through 2005. The analysis showed that, over time, *YM* included an increasing amount of material related to dieting, while dieting-related content in *Seventeen* peaked during the early 1980s. Content related to exercise increased in both magazines over time, as did the average body size of *YM* cover models; however, the authors caution that this may be an artifact reflecting the magazine's 1964 switch from drawn illustrations to photographs (Luff & Gray, 2009).

Overall, researchers have documented that the majority of media models are dramatically thinner than the average American woman. Body weight ideals, as depicted in the media, declined significantly over the last half of the twentieth century (Garner et al., 1980; Seifert, 2005; Spitzer et al., 1999; Sypeck et al., 2004); at one point, a study of Miss America contestants and *Playboy* magazine centerfolds showed that more than two-thirds (69%) met the criteria for anorexia nervosa based on their weight-to-height ratios (Wiseman et al., 1992). A more recent analysis of *Playboy* centerfold models from 1979 to 1999 suggests that although the average models' size is no longer declining and may actually have begun to increase slightly, their weights remained 10 to 15

251

percent below the norm for their age group. In addition, the study documented a significant increase in the centerfold models' average bust size, while their hip sizes remained unchanged (Sypeck et al., 2006).

One exception to this trend seems to occur in magazines aimed at African American audiences. For instance, an analysis of images of African American women on the cover of *Ebony* magazine from 1969 to 2008 showed that the cover models had actually increased somewhat in size over time, although the majority of women were in the normal weight category (76.4%). Overweight women were more likely to be shown in groups than were normal weight women, and the number of articles about diet and exercise peaked at about 35.9 percent of all articles listed in the table of contents during the 1990s; during the 2000s, about 30 percent of articles dealt with diet and exercise. The authors suggest that the findings may reflect – but also influence – greater acceptance of larger body sizes within the African American community (Thompson-Brenner et al., 2011). Another study produced similar results in a content analysis of African American women pictured in *Jet* magazine's Beauty of the Week feature (Dawson-Andoh et al., 2011).

In addition to showing women how they are supposed to look through images of models, actresses and celebrities, research shows that the verbal content of many types of media reinforces the idea that women, especially Caucasian women, must be thin to be considered attractive. For instance, an analysis of body-shaping content in five top women's health and fitness magazines from 2010 showed that the magazines were more likely to address appearance motivations, instead of health motivations, in discussions of exercise and diet; overall, body-shaping messages accounted for one-fifth of all content in these magazines (Willis & Knobloch-Westerwick, 2014). Another study of magazine editorial content examined body-shape-related articles in eight popular women's magazines between January 1989 and April 2007. The data showed that the number of articles about exercise and diet for weight loss declined, although diet articles increased again somewhat from 2003 to 2007. Over the same time period, however, the number of articles about cosmetic surgery increased, suggesting that magazines are increasingly likely to present surgery as a reasonable alternative to diet and exercise for women who want to improve their body shape (Saraceni & Russell-Mayhew, 2007).

In the past decade in particular, health advocates have become increasingly concerned about online content that may promote the thin ideal, either unintentionally or, in some cases, intentionally. In particular, this concern stems from the growth of so-called "pro-ana" or "pro-mia" websites, which often encourage users to view eating disordered behavior not as a health problem but as a lifestyle choice to be supported, praised and admired. Although no study to date seems to have assessed the prevalence of exposure to these websites, one study determined that Google users search for pro-eating disorder terms more than 13 million times a year, with more than 100,000 searches per month for the terms "pro ana," "thinspiration" and "thinspo" (Lewis & Arbuthnott, 2012).

Those searching for such terms are likely to find what they seek. One content analysis of 180 active pro-eating disorders websites showed that 91 percent were open to the public, and the majority (84%) provided pro-anorexia content and/or pro-bulimia content (64%). Large majorities (85% and 83% respectively) included "thinspiration" material (e.g., photos of extremely thin models, athletes or other celebrities) and how-to tips to motivate and help others follow eating disordered practices. Although only 4 percent explicitly claimed to be "pro-recovery," 31 percent provided what the researchers deemed "substantial" amounts of pro-recovery content. About 40 percent included a warning that the site's content could be distressing or even dangerous, and 27 percent included a disclaimer that the site could not be held responsible if the materials it provided spurred users to engage in dangerous behavior. Nearly one-third (32%) included statements discouraging the site's use by "wannabes" who might be trying to develop an eating disorder without having already done so. One site, for example, put it this way:

> IF YOU WANT TO LOSE WEIGHT, GO ON A DIET FATTY. ONE IS EITHER ANA/MIA, OR NOT. IT IS A GIFT AND YOU CANNOT DECIDE TO HAVE AN EATING DISORDER. SO IF YOU ARE LOOKING FOR A WAY TO LOSE WEIGHT, S-S-S-SORRY JUNIOR!! MOVE ON, TRY JENNY CRAIG.
>
> (Borzekowski et al., 2010, p. 1528)

Following up on a qualitative analysis of pro-eating disorders websites (Norris et al., 2006), the content analysis monitored the same themes

253

identified in the earlier study and found that the most common were success, control, perfection and solidarity. In terms of control, some sites offered an eating disorder "creed" or a set of "Thin Commandments," including either severely self-deprecating statements about the user's failures and lack of worth or rules one must follow, such as "Thou shalt not eat without feeling guilty" or "Being thin is more important than being healthy" (Borzekowski et al., 2010, p. 1530). The most problematic aspects of the sites, the authors suggest, are the "thinspiration" images along with provision of always-available support for engaging in extreme weight loss behavior.

Researchers also have begun to explore the unintended impact of social media sites, such as YouTube, Twitter and Facebook, on attitudes or behaviors related to weight control or eating disorders. Among the studies that have examined social media impacts, whether the effects are positive or negative appears to be related to the outcome under consideration. For instance, both correlational (Fardouly et al., 2015a; Meier & Gray, 2014; Tiggemann & Miller, 2010; Tiggemann & Slater, 2013, 2014) and experimental research (Fardouly et al., 2015b; Mabe et al., 2014) has provided evidence of harmful associations between social media use and body image. In many ways, this seems especially interesting in that the photographs posted on Facebook will generally depict peers – real-life "friends" – while traditional media sources primarily contain (often digitally altered) photos of models, actresses and other celebrities. It may be, however, that these peer photos have even greater impact because the models they provide may seem more attainable (Fardouly et al., 2015a).

The way in which individuals use social media may influence the impact of social media. Kim and Chock (2015) found no significant correlation between time spent on Facebook and body image dissatisfaction. However, for both men and women, use of Facebook for "social grooming" – viewing and commenting on peers' profiles – was positively related to a drive for thinness; the relationship was mediated by appearance comparison, with individuals who compared their own appearance to that of their friends reporting a greater drive for thinness.

Social media's impact may not always be negative, however. One study of individuals who discussed their weight loss attempts on Twitter showed that these participants rated their interactions on Twitter and weight loss-specific social networks as offering more positive social support and less negative social influence than did their offline contacts or their Facebook "friends." In addition, those who reported more social network support through Twitter and Facebook lost more weight (Pagoto et al., 2014).

While the media's body ideal for men generally does not include being underweight or thin, it does include a significant degree of muscularity and low body fat. Evaluations of *Playgirl* magazine centerfolds between 1973 and 1997 showed significant increases in muscularity; the most muscular models, most of whom appeared in 1994 or later, were so heavily muscled that the researchers concluded they would likely have had to use steroids to achieve that shape (Leit et al., 2001). Another study, which examined images of men in *GQ*, *Rolling Stone* and *Sports Illustrated* from 1967 to 1997 showed that the lean, V-shaped ideal became more common between the 1960s and the 1980s, then became somewhat less dominant during the 1990s. Muscularity, however, continued to increase through the 1990s, so that from 1991 to 1997, 35 percent of the images in these three magazines were coded as "very muscular," compared to only 9 percent in 1967 to 1979 (Law & Labre, 2002).

Similarly, a study of both images and editorial content in *Men's Health* and *Men's Fitness* magazines from 1999 to 2003 showed that 96.2 percent of the images of men displayed low body fat. Only 3.1 percent of the images showed males who were not muscular, while 82.2 percent were of very muscular men; 2.9 percent of the images were coded as "unnaturally muscular." Editorial content also focused on leanness and muscularity, with one in every four articles (25.2%) focused on this topic, and more than one-third of the articles (34.4%) included muscularitiy and/or leanness as one of the major benefits discussed, regardless of the article's main topic (Labre, 2005).

Comparison of male models from the women's magazine *Cosmopolitan* and men's magazines *Men's Health*, *Men's Fitness* and *Muscle and Fitness* from 2001 through August 2004 showed that men's magazines portrayed the ideal body as significantly more muscular than did *Cosmopolitan*. Indeed, there were significant differences between each of the magazines, with the level of muscularity increasing from *Cosmopolitan* to *Men's Health* to *Men's Fitness*; *Muscle and Fitness*, which is a body-building magazine, had by far the most muscular depictions (Frederick et al., 2005). Magazines targeted to gay men portray the ideal male body shape as thinner than magazines targeted to men in general; however, both types of men's magazines include more muscular male images than do magazines aimed at general audiences (Lanzieri & Cook, 2013).

Magazines are not alone, of course, in portraying muscularity as a key requirement of masculine attractiveness. An analysis of male characters in top-grossing action movies from 1980 to 2006 revealed that more than three-quarters (76.1%) of male characters were muscular, and nearly two-thirds (65.4%) had low body fat. Over time, the characters became more muscular, with less body fat (Morrison & Halton, 2009). Male "reality TV" cast members are also significantly more muscular and have lower body fat than the average American man (Dallesasse & Kluck, 2013). Even in the virtual worlds of video games, male characters are larger than real-world men, although researchers have found that the most realistically rendered characters are not hypermuscular, nor do they reflect the V-shaped ideal common in other media. Less realistic and detailed figures, which tend to appear in games aimed at children rather than at adults, are so hypermuscular that they appear cartoonish and also do not match the V-shaped ideal (Martins et al., 2011). Researchers also have found that even the action figures marketed to children have become dramatically more muscular over recent decades (Baghurst et al., 2006; Pope et al., 1999).

Media also include messages about the personality characteristics associated with weight and the likely outcomes of being thin versus being overweight or obese. For instance, a study of television characters from the ten highest rated fictional television programs from the 1999/2000 season showed that nearly one-third of all female television characters were underweight, and adding in normal weight female characters accounted for 87 percent of all women depicted in these programs. For TV characters, a larger body size was associated with having fewer interactions with friends and less positive interactions with others generally. Larger characters were portrayed as less helpful, more likely to be the object of humor and more likely to be portrayed as unemployed (Greenberg et al., 2003).

Similarly, Klein and Shiffman (2013) analyzed the portrayal of characters in animated cartoons from 1930 through the mid-1990s and found that, overwhelmingly, the cartoons included increasing percentages of underweight characters and overwhelmingly positive messages about being thin, while overweight characters were more likely to engage in antisocial behavior, to be less intelligent, and, in general, were more likely to be classified as "bad guys." Another study of children's animated movies also showed that nearly two-thirds (64%) linked obesity with negative character traits, including being evil, unattractive, cruel and unfriendly (Herbozo et al., 2004). One exception to these findings was provided by a content analysis of characters in children's situation comedies, which showed that weight status was not related to characters being portrayed in positive ways (Robinson et al., 2008).

Characters who achieve the thin and/or muscular ideal are also more likely to have romantic or sexual success in the media. For instance, the study of male action movie characters showed that muscular characters were more likely to be romantically involved and more likely to engage in sexual interactions (Morrison & Halton, 2009). Similarly, researchers have found that thinner television characters are more romantically successful (Greenberg et al., 2003).

THE IMPACT OF THIN-IDEAL MEDIA

Researchers to date have conducted hundreds, perhaps thousands, of studies investigating the impact of thin-ideal media portrayals on audiences of both genders and nearly all age groups. Although the types of studies (cross-sectional, longitudinal, experimental) and the results have varied, the consensus among researchers is that the media's thin ideal does have an important impact on audiences, especially women and girls. One meta-analysis that combined both experimental and correlational studies concluded that media exposure plays only a minor role in women's body image. The analysis, which examined 34 studies, showed that studies comparing women's reactions to images of thin models versus images of average-weight models produced small effect sizes. However, when the comparison photos showed overweight models, the effect sizes were significantly larger, falling into the medium range (Holmstrom, 2004).

However, five other meta-analyses have concluded that media exposure does, in fact, have important impacts on women's body dissatisfaction and related attitudes and behaviors. For instance, Grabe and colleagues' (2008) meta-analysis of 77 studies linking media exposure to negative outcomes in women found small to moderate effects of media exposure on women's body dissatisfaction, internalization of the thin ideal, and disordered eating-related beliefs and behaviors. The analysis, the authors conclude, showed that "overall, thin-ideal media exposure is related to higher levels of body dissatisfaction, stronger internalization of the thin ideal, and more frequent bulimic and anorexic attitudes and behaviors" (Grabe et al., 2008, p. 470). The results suggest that these effects are actually somewhat stronger for adults (aged 19–32) than for adolescents and when media use in general is considered, as compared to the impacts of magazines or television alone.

An earlier meta-analysis, which included only experimental studies, produced similar findings. Data from 25 studies revealed 38 comparisons in which exposure to thin models led to more negative body satisfaction levels compared to control images, while five comparisons showed the opposite effects: viewing thin models actually improved body satisfaction. Overall, then, the researchers concluded that viewing thin-ideal images significantly reduces body satisfaction. The analysis also revealed that participants with pre-existing body disturbance concerns were affected more negatively by such images than were individuals with no prior body dissatisfaction problems. However, unlike the later meta-analysis (Grabe et al., 2008), the experimental studies suggested that women younger than age 19 were affected more negatively by exposure to the thin ideal than were women age 19 and older (Groesz et al., 2002).

The most recent meta-analysis also included only experimental studies but examined a variety of outcomes related to eating disorders, including body dissatisfaction, positive or negative emotion, depression, anxiety, anger and self-esteem. The results showed that viewing thin-ideal images increases depression and anger and decreases self-esteem. Similar to previous studies, this analysis demonstrated that media have especially harmful effects for those who are already at risk for eating disorders, including those who are overweight or obese or who have low self-esteem. In addition, media effects are larger for those who have internalized the thin-ideal standard of beauty, who self-objectify (viewing their appearance as their most or only important characteristic), or those who already engage in some degree of disordered eating (Hausenblas et al., 2013).

Want (2009) investigated how pre-existing appearance concerns and the instructions given to experiment participants influenced the effects of thin-image exposure on women. His meta-analysis of 25 studies revealed that, of the 75 independent effects examined, 67 were negative and eight were positive, meaning that 89 percent of the comparisons showed harmful effects of media exposure. As expected, the effects were greatest among participants who had reported pre-existing body image concerns.

Contrary to expectations, however, the analysis showed that experimental exposure to thin images had the greatest effect when participants were instructed to pay close attention to something *other* than the model's appearance, leading Want (2009) to conclude that social comparison effects often occur automatically and subconsciously. He argues that women who are instructed to pay attention to others' appearance may be able to "undo" their initial automatic social comparison with the images because, as a defensive reaction, they can consciously generate reasons to discount the comparison. Other researchers have confirmed that negative media effects are reduced when women are reminded that the images they are viewing represent models whose appearance has been artificially improved through make-up, lighting and digital editing (Knobloch-Westerwick & Crane, 2012; Posavac et al., 2001; Yamamiya et al., 2005). Negative impacts also are reduced when women are encouraged to compare themselves to thin models on non-appearance-related dimensions such as personal relationships, intellectual and academic abilities, personalities, sports or arts-related talents, or physical and mental health (Lew et al., 2007).

On the other hand, other researchers have suggested an alternative explanation for the body satisfaction-improving impacts of induced social comparison with idealized media images. Knobloch-Westerwick and Crane (2012) found that women exposed to thin-ideal images over a five-day period reported greater positive change in body satisfaction than did women exposed to control images; however, all of this improvement in body satisfaction was explained by a significant difference in dieting among the women in the experimental condition. Unfortunately, as noted earlier, most dieters, in the long run, gain weight rather than losing weight and maintaining the reduced weight (Juhaeri et al., 2001; Neumark-Sztainer et al., 2007). "Thus media exposure may contribute to a vicious cycle of greater thin-ideal internalization, engaging in dieting that often entails unhealthy eating behaviors, and long-term weight gain" (Knobloch-Westerwick & Crane, 2012, p. 97).

The research showing that reminding women about the unrealistic nature of media images decreases the negative impact of these images has led some to suggest that magazine ads should include disclaimers or warning labels notifying viewers that the images have been digitally edited. However, experimental studies suggest that this effect not only does not improve outcomes but could actually cause more harm. Several studies have shown that including warning labels did not decrease negative impacts on body satisfaction (Ata et al., 2013; Tiggemann et al., 2014), and could actually increase body dissatisfaction among women with strong tendencies to compare their appearance with that of others (Tiggemann et al., 2013).

One of the more recent reviews of body image research identified five major gaps in our understanding of the media's role as a potential cause of body dissatisfaction and eating disordered attitudes and behaviors. These included the need for longitudinal research that clarifies the extent to which media exposure precedes and predicts body image dissatisfaction, as well as assessing individuals' subjective perceptions of media influence. A second gap is that we do not fully understand what types of media content have the most negative effects. Are audiences most affected simply by viewing thin-ideal images or by some other type of media content, such as articles encouraging dieting and/or exercise, or TV programs in which overweight or obese characters are disparaged and criticized? Third, additional research is needed to determine what sorts of interventions might reduce media effects (Levine & Murnen, 2009), especially given that the warning label approach does not seem to be effective.

In addition, the review's authors argue that we need a more complete understanding of indirect media effects; that is, how does media exposure affect the types of family and peer behaviors, such as weight teasing, that have been shown to influence the development of body image disturbance and disordered eating? Finally, more research is needed to determine how the mechanisms of media influence change over time, given that the correlates of negative body image appear to differ among younger children, older adolescents and young adults, and older adults (Levine & Murnen, 2009).

Thus far, there appears to have been no systematic review of research linking exposure to pro-eating disorders websites or other online materials to body dissatisfaction or related behaviors. However, a number of individual studies have provided evidence that exposure to websites and social media can have impacts on weight-related attitudes and behaviors.

For instance, a survey of 1,575 women assessed the characteristics associated with viewing pro-eating disorder websites and professional websites providing information about eating disorders. Of the complete sample, 13 percent of the women reported visiting one or more of the eating disorders-related websites. Women who said they only visited pro-ana sites had higher levels of body image and eating disturbance than did women who visited none of the eating-disorder-related sites; however, they did not differ significantly from women who visited the professional eating disorder information sites. The authors note, however, that it is possible for people to obtain information about eating disorder behaviors from professional sites that do not intend to promote such behaviors, and the small number of women in each group (pro-ED only, professional sites only) limited their ability to identify significant differences in the two groups (Harper et al., 2008).

One experimental study compared affect, beliefs and behavioral expectations among undergraduate women assigned to view a pro-anorexia website, a fashion website using average-weight models or a home decorating website. After spending 25 minutes viewing the assigned website, women exposed to the pro-ana website reported more negative affect, lower social self-esteem and perceived themselves as heavier than the women who had seen the home décor website. In comparison to women who saw the fashion website, women exposed to the pro-ana site also reported more negative affect, lower appearance self-efficacy and were more likely to have thought about their appearance and compared themselves to the images they saw. In addition, they reported a greater likelihood of exercising and thinking about their weight (Bardone-Cone & Cass, 2006).

Another experimental study exposed women of normal or higher BMI with no history of eating disorders to two 45-minute sessions viewing tourism websites, healthy exercise websites or pro-eating disorders websites. Before and after the website sessions, participants completed week-long food diaries. In the week after the viewing sessions, those who had viewed the two pro-eating disorder websites reduced their weekly calorie intake, on average, by 2,470 calories; 84 percent of these participants reduced their calorie consumption, and one-third reduced consumption by 4,000 calories or more. In comparison, the women who were exposed to the healthy exercise websites reduced their calorie intake, on average, by only 176 calories, while those exposed to the tourism sites increased their calorie consumption by 411. However, all of these women reported negative opinions of the pro-ED websites, and none reported returning to the websites after the study was over (Jett et al., 2010).

IMPACT OF THE MUSCULAR MALE IDEAL

These reviews of the literature, along with most of the studies included in the meta-analyses, have been focused on the unintended impacts of mass media on women and girls and their attitudes and behaviors related to weight and body shape. However, researchers also have investigated how the media's muscular ideal for men influences body image attitudes and behaviors among male audiences. Meta-analyses of these studies have documented that media images of the ideal male body can have negative impacts on boys and men, just as media images of ideal female bodies negatively affect girls and women. For instance, Blond (2008) reviewed 15 studies of media effects on male body image, which collectively produced 35 measures of effects; 30 of those effects showed positive associations between media exposure and body dissatisfaction, while five showed negative associations. Overall, then, 86 percent of the tests supported the idea that exposure to idealized images of the male body increases body dissatisfaction among male audiences. The studies demonstrated that negative media effects were more likely to occur among males with pre-existing body dissatisfaction, muscle dissatisfaction, an internalized muscular ideal and poor exercise habits. Having high body satisfaction and a regular muscle-building routine tended to protect male audiences from the effects of viewing idealized images of muscular men. In fact, at least one study has suggested that adolescent boys who are satisfied with their appearance and/or who have a regular exercise routine feel *lower* body dissatisfaction after viewing idealized images, perhaps because they are more likely to view the ideal body depicted in those images as attainable (Humphreys & Paxton, 2004).

Another set of meta-analyses, which examined 25 studies describing 93 measures of media effects, considered correlational and experimental studies separately. Meta-analysis of the correlational studies confirmed a significant negative association between exposure to mediated male ideal images and body satisfaction among males. The negative impact of mediated images was stronger among college-aged men, in comparison to adolescents. A second meta-analysis, which included only experimental studies, also confirmed that exposure to muscular media images led to significant declines in both body satisfaction and body esteem and increases in negative psychological outcomes such as feeling depressed. The authors emphasize that they "are not arguing that the mass media is the only variable that influences body image; however, these results suggest that the mass media is an important factor in how males think and feel about their bodies" (Barlett et al., 2008, p. 302).

BEYOND THINNESS AND MUSCULARITY

While the majority of research on media impacts on body image has focused on thinness for women and muscularity for men, body image includes more than one's perceptions of one's weight and muscle tone. In today's society, body shaping also can go beyond diet/dieting and exercise to include cosmetic surgery to alter body shape and facial features. According to the most recent report from the American Society for Aesthetic Plastic Surgery, the number of cosmetic surgery procedures increased by 6.5 percent between 2012 and 2013; liposuction, the most popular surgical procedure, increased by 16 percent during the year, while breast augmentation, the second most popular, declined by 5.2 percent. Surgeons performed 11,527 buttock-augmentation procedures, an increase of 58 percent over 2012, and labiaplasties – surgeries to reduce and/or reshape the labia minora, the folds of skin covering the clitoris and vaginal opening – accounted for the second largest increase: 44 percent. Overall, 1.9 million cosmetic surgery procedures were performed in the United States during 2013 (American Society for Aesthetic Plastic Surgery, n.d.).

Research suggests that mass media, especially plastic surgery-focused reality television shows and pornographic media, may be among the factors driving the increase in cosmetic surgery. Studies of the factors influencing college women's attitudes toward and consideration of cosmetic surgery have shown that internalization of media ideals increases interest in cosmetic surgery (Markey & Markey, 2009; Sarwer et al., 2005; Swami, 2009). Similarly, Slevec and Tiggemann (2010) found that media exposure positively influenced social motivations for and consideration of plastic surgery among older women (aged 35–55). Other researchers have found that adolescents and young adults who had more positive opinions of reality TV programs featuring cosmetic surgery (e.g., *The Swan, Extreme Makeover*) were more likely to say they would be interested in having cosmetic surgery. The same researchers demonstrated that participants who watched a segment of *Extreme Makeover* were subsequently more likely to say they would like to alter their own appearance than were participants who had watched a neutral television program (Markey & Markey, 2010). Another study showed that perceived realism of cosmetic surgery-focused reality television was linked to more positive attitudes toward having cosmetic surgery (Fogel & King, 2014).

Although thus far there seems to be no research specifically linking mass media use with the increase in female genital cosmetic surgery, such as labioplasty, at least two studies have suggested that the increasing availability of explicit mass media images may play a role. First, Placik and Arkins (2014) demonstrated through a content analysis of *Playboy* magazine centerfolds that the positioning of centerfold photos now puts greater emphasis on the vaginal area and is more likely to fully expose the models' vaginal area; of centerfold photos published from 2010 through 2013, the majority (78.6%) fully exposed the vaginal area. Another study showed that women exposed to images of surgically modified vulvas were more likely to rate these images as looking "more normal" and representing the societal ideal than were women who had previously been exposed to images of unmodified vulva or no images (Moran & Lee, 2014). Taken together, the studies suggest that greater exposure to explicit "crotch shot" photos, either in magazines or online, may encourage women (and, potentially, their sexual partners) to view surgically altered genitalia as more normal and more desirable than unmodified genitals, leading even healthy women with no medical reasons for pursuing labial surgery to seek surgical alteration. If confirmed, this may represent, in some ways, the ultimate in media effects on body image, given that a woman's genital area is arguably the part of her body least likely to be visible to anyone, including the woman herself, during the vast majority of her life.

SUMMARY

The research provides convincing evidence that mass media images of women and men are generally unrealistic. The "ideal" woman portrayed in mass media is thin, often to the point of being unhealthy, and this thin physique is often paired with large breasts, a combination most likely to exist in the real world only through surgical enhancement. The "ideal" male body is slender and well muscled – not an unhealthy image on its own, but one that seems to encourage some adolescents and young men to engage in obsessive exercise, use of muscle-building supplements and other unhealthy behaviors. Of course, these effects are not uniform among all members of the media audience. Some individuals are able to resist media promotion of the "ideal" body, and further research is needed to uncover the mechanisms that enable some individuals to maintain a healthy body image despite regular exposure to the media ideal.

REFERENCES

American Society for Aesthetic Plastic Surgery. (n.d.). *Quick Facts: Highlights of the ASAPS 2013 Statistics on Cosmetic Surgery*. American Society for Aesthetic Plastic Surgery. Retrieved March 25, 2015 from www.surgery.org/sites/default/files/2013-quick-facts_0.pdf.

Ata, R.N., Ludden, A.B. & Lally, M.M. (2006). The Effects of Gender and Family, Friend, and Media Influences on Eating Behaviors and Body Image During Adolescence. *Journal of Youth and Adolescence, 36*(8), 1024–1037. http://doi.org/10.1007/s10964-006-9159-x.

Ata, R.N., Thompson, J.K. & Small, B.J. (2013). Effects of Exposure to Thin-ideal Media Images on Body Dissatisfaction: Testing the Inclusion of a Disclaimer versus Warning Label. *Body Image, 10*(4), 472–480. http://doi.org/10.1016/j.bodyim.2013.04.004.

Baghurst, T., Hollander, D.B., Nardella, B. & Haff, G.G. (2006). Change in Sociocultural Ideal Male Physique: An Examination of Past and Present Action Figures. *Body Image, 3*(1), 87–91. http://doi.org/10.1016/j.bodyim.2005.11.001.

Bair, C.E., Kelly, N.R., Serdar, K.L. & Mazzeo, S.E. (2012). Does the Internet Function Like Magazines? An Exploration of Image-focused Media, Eating Pathology, and Body Dissatisfaction. *Eating Behaviors, 13*(4), 398–401. http://doi.org/10.1016/j.eatbeh.2012.06.003.

Bardone-Cone, A.M. & Cass, K.M. (2006). Investigating the Impact of Pro-anorexia Websites: A Pilot Study. *European Eating Disorders Review, 14*(4), 256–262.

Barlett, C.P., Vowels, C.L. & Saucier, D.A. (2008). Meta-analyses of the Effects of Media Images on Men's Body-image Concerns. *Journal of Social and Clinical Psychology, 27*(3), 279–310. http://doi.org/10.1521/jscp. 2008.27.3.279.

Blond, A. (2008). Impacts of Exposure to Images of Ideal Bodies on Male Body Dissatisfaction: A Review. *Body Image, 5*(3), 244–250. http://doi.org/10.1016/j.bodyim.2008.02.003.

Borzekowski, D.L.G., Schenk, S., Wilson, J.L. & Peebles, R. (2010). e-Ana and e-Mia: A Content Analysis of Pro-eating Disorder Web Sites. *American Journal of Public Health, 100*(8), 1526–1534. http://doi.org/10.2105/AJPH.2009.172700.

Cafri, G., van den Berg, P. & Thompson, J.K. (2006). Pursuit of Muscularity in Adolescent Boys: Relations Among Biopsychosocial Variables and Clinical Outcomes. *Journal of Clinical Child & Adolescent Psychology, 35*(2), 283–291. http://doi.org/10.1207/s15374424jccp3502_12.

Cameron, B. (2015, February 18). Cindy Crawford Photos Cause Online Debate. Retrieved February 20, 2015 from www.bbc.com/news/blogs-trending-31512922.

Campbell, K. & Peebles, R. (2014). Eating Disorders in Children and Adolescents: State of the Art Review. *Pediatrics, 134*(3), 582–592. http://doi.org/10.1542/peds.2014-0194.

Chan, P., Dipper, A., Kelsey, P. & Harrison, J. (2010). Newspaper Reporting of Meticillin-resistant *Staphylococcus Aureus* and "the Dirty Hospital." *The Journal of Hospital Infection, 75*(4), 318–322. http://doi.org/10.1016/j.jhin.2010.01.027.

Dallesasse, S.L. & Kluck, A.S. (2013). Reality Television and the Muscular Male Ideal. *Body Image, 10*(3), 309–315. http://doi.org/10.1016/j.bodyim.2013.02.004.

Davis, C., Karvinen, K. & McCreary, D.R. (2005). Personality Correlates of a Drive for Muscularity in Young Men. *Personality and Individual Differences, 39*(2), 349–359. http://doi.org/10.1016/j.paid.2005.01.013.

Dawson-Andoh, N.A., Gray, J.J., Soto, J.A. & Parker, S. (2011). Body Shape and Size Depictions of African American Women in JET Magazine, 1953–2006. *Body Image, 8*(1), 86–89. http://doi.org/10.1016/j.bodyim.2010.09.006.

Dunn, C.L., Hannan, P.J., Jeffery, R.W., Sherwood, N.E., Pronk, N.P. & Boyle, R. (2006). The Comparative and Cumulative Effects of a Dietary Restriction and Exercise on Weight Loss. *International Journal of Obesity (2005), 30*(1), 112–121. http://doi.org/10.1038/sj.ijo.0803046.

Fardouly, J., Diedrichs, P.C., Vartanian, L.R. & Halliwell, E. (2015a). Social Comparisons on Social Media: The Impact of Facebook on Young Women's Body Image Concerns and Mood. *Body Image, 13*, 38–45. http://doi.org/10.1016/j.bodyim.2014.12.002.

Fardouly, J., Diedrichs, P.C., Vartanian, L.R., & Halliwell, E. (2015b). Social Comparisons on Social Media: The Impact of Facebook on Young Women's Body Image Concerns and Mood. *Body Image, 13C*, 38–45. http://doi.org/10.1016/j.bodyim.2014.12.002.

Fogel, J. & King, K. (2014). Perceived Realism and Twitter Use are Associated with Increased Acceptance of Cosmetic Surgery among Those Watching Reality Television Cosmetic Surgery Programs. *Plastic and Reconstructive Surgery, 134*(2), 233–238. http://doi.org/10.1097/PRS.0000000000000322.

Frederick, D.A., Fessler, D.M.T. & Haselton, M.G. (2005). Do Representations of Male Muscularity Differ in Men's and Women's Magazines? *Body Image, 2*(1), 81–86. http://doi.org/10.1016/j.bodyim.2004.12.002.

Garner, D.M., Garfinkel, P.E., Schwartz, D. & Thompson, M. (1980). Cultural Expectations of Thinness in Women. *Psychological Reports, 47*(2), 483–491. http://doi.org/10.2466/pr0.1980.47.2.483.

Grabe, S., Ward, L.M. & Hyde, J.S. (2008). The Role of the Media in Body Image Concerns among Women: A Meta-analysis of Experimental and Correlational Studies. *Psychological Bulletin, 134*(3), 460–476. http://doi.org/10.1037/0033-2909.134.3.460.

Grammas, D.L. & Schwartz, J.P. (2009). Internalization of Messages from Society and Perfectionism as Predictors of Male Body Image. *Body Image, 6*(1), 31–36. http://doi.org/10.1016/j.bodyim.2008.10.002.

Greenberg, B.S., Eastin, M., Hofschire, L., Lachlan, K. & Brownell, K.D. (2003). Portrayals of Overweight and Obese Individuals on Commercial Television. *American Journal of Public Health, 93*(8), 1342–1348.

Greenberg, I., Stampfer, M.J., Schwarzfuchs, D., Shai, I. & DIRECT Group. (2009).

Adherence and Success in Long-term Weight Loss Diets: The Dietary Intervention Randomized Controlled Trial (DIRECT). *Journal of the American College of Nutrition*, 28(2), 159–168.

Grieve, F.G. (2007). A Conceptual Model of Factors Contributing to the Development of Muscle Dysmorphia. *Eating Disorders*, 15(1), 63–80.

Groesz, L.M., Levine, M.P. & Murnen, S.K. (2002). The Effect of Experimental Presentation of Thin Media Images on Body Satisfaction: A Meta-analytic Review. *International Journal of Eating Disorders*, 31(1), 1–16. http://doi.org/10.1002/eat.10005.

Harper, K., Sperry, S. & Thompson, J.K. (2008). Viewership of Pro-eating Disorder Websites: Association with Body Image and Eating Disturbances. *International Journal of Eating Disorders*, 41(1), 92–95.

Harris, E.C. & Barraclough, B. (1998). Excess Mortality of Mental Disorder. *The British Journal of Psychiatry*, 173(1), 11–53.

Hausenblas, H.A., Campbell, A., Menzel, J.E., Doughty, J., Levine, M. & Thompson, J.K. (2013). Media Effects of Experimental Presentation of the Ideal Physique on Eating Disorder Symptoms: A Meta-analysis of Laboratory Studies. *Clinical Psychology Review*, 33(1), 168–181. http://doi.org/10.1016/j.cpr.2012.10.011.

Herbozo, S., Tantleff-Dunn, S., Gokee-Larose, J. & Thompson, J.K. (2004). Beauty and Thinness Messages in Children's Media: A Content Analysis. *Eating Disorders*, 12(1), 21–34. http://doi.org/10.1080/10640260490267742.

Herzog, D.B., Dorer, D.J., Keel, P.K., Selwyn, S.E., Ekeblad, E.R., Flores, A.T. & Keller, M.B. (1999). Recovery and Relapse in Anorexia and Bulimia Nervosa: A 7.5-year Follow-up Study. *Journal of the American Academy of Child & Adolescent Psychiatry*, 38(7), 829–837.

Hession, M., Rolland, C., Kulkarni, U., Wise, A. & Broom, J. (2009). Systematic Review of Randomized Controlled Trials of Low-carbohydrate vs. Low-fat/Low-calorie Diets in the Management of Obesity and its Comorbidities. *Obesity Reviews: An Official Journal of the International Association for the Study of Obesity*, 10(1), 36–50. http://doi.org/10.1111/j.1467-789X.2008.00518.x.

Holmstrom, A.J. (2004). The Effects of the Media on Body Image: A Meta-analysis. *Journal of Broadcasting & Electronic Media*, 48(2), 196–217. http://doi.org/10.1207/s15506878jobem4802_3.

Hudson, J.I., Hiripi, E., Pope Jr., H.G. & Kessler, R.C. (2007). The Prevalence and Correlates of Eating Disorders in the National Comorbidity Survey Replication. *Biological Psychiatry*, 61(3), 348–358. http://doi.org/10.1016/j.biopsych.2006.03.040.

Humphreys, P. & Paxton, S.J. (2004). Impact of Exposure to Idealised Male Images on Adolescent Boys' Body Image. *Body Image*, 1(3), 253–266. http://doi.org/10.1016/j.bodyim.2004.05.001.

Jacobsen, M.T. (2011, October 12). Dieting vs. Healthy Habits – What's the Difference? Food and Fitness. Retrieved February 23, 2015 from http://blogs.webmd.com/food-and-nutrition/2011/10/dieting-vs-healthy-habits-whats-the-difference.html.

Jett, S., LaPorte, D.J. & Wanchisn, J. (2010). Impact of Exposure to Pro-eating Disorder Websites on Eating Behaviour in College Women. *European Eating Disorders Review: The Journal of the Eating Disorders Association*, 18(5), 410–416. http://doi.org/10.1002/erv.1009.

Jhally, S. & Kilbourne, J. (2010). *Killing Us Softly 4: Advertising's Image of Women*. Media Education Foundation.

Jones, D.C., Vigfusdottir, T.H. & Lee, Y. (2004). Body Image and the Appearance Culture among Adolescent Girls and Boys: An Examination of Friend Conversations, Peer

Criticism, Appearance Magazines, and the Internalization of Appearance Ideals. *Journal of Adolescent Research*, *19*(3), 323–339. http://doi.org/10.1177/07435584 03258847.

Juhaeri, Stevens, J., Chambless, L.E., Tyroler, H.A., Harp, J., Jones, D. & Arnett, D. (2001). Weight Change among Self-reported Dieters and Non-dieters in White and African American Men and Women. *European Journal of Epidemiology*, *17*(10), 917–923. http://doi.org/10.1023/A:1016270128624.

Karazsia, B.T. & Crowther, J.H. (2009). Social Body Comparison and Internalization: Mediators of Social Influences on Men's Muscularity-oriented Body Dissatisfaction. *Body Image*, *6*(2), 105–112. http://doi.org/10.1016/j.bodyim.2008.12.003.

Kee, E. & Farid, H. (2011). A Perceptual Metric for Photo Retouching. *Proceedings of the National Academy of Sciences*, *108*(50), 19907–19912. http://doi.org/10.1073/pnas.1110747108.

Kim, J.W. & Chock, T.M. (2015). Body Image 2.0: Associations between Social Grooming on Facebook and Body Image Concerns. *Computers in Human Behavior*, *48*, 331–339. http://doi.org/10.1016/j.chb.2015.01.009.

Klein, H. & Shiffman, K.S. (2013). Thin is "In" and Stout is "Out": What Animated Cartoons Tell Viewers about Body Weight. *Eating and Weight Disorders – Studies on Anorexia, Bulimia and Obesity*, *10*(2), 107–116. http://doi.org/10.1007/BF03327532.

Kluck, A.S. (2008). Family Factors in the Development of Disordered Eating: Integrating Dynamic and Behavioral Explanations. *Eating Behaviors*, *9*(4), 471–483. http://doi.org/10.1016/j.eatbeh.2008.07.006.

Knobloch-Westerwick, S. & Crane, J. (2012). A Losing Battle: Effects of Prolonged Exposure to Thin-ideal Images on Dieting and Body Satisfaction. *Communication Research*, *39*(1), 79–102. http://doi.org/10.1177/0093650211400596.

Labre, M.P. (2002). Adolescent Boys and the Muscular Male Body Ideal. *Journal of Adolescent Health*, *30*(4), 233–242. http://doi.org/10.1016/S1054-139X(01)00413-X.

Labre, M.P. (2005). Burn Fat, Build Muscle: A Content Analysis of Men's Health and Men's Fitness. *International Journal of Men's Health*, *4*(2), 187–200.

Lantzouni, E., Cox, M.H., Salvator, A. & Crosby, R.D. (2015). Mother–Daughter Coping and Disordered Eating. *European Eating Disorders Review: The Journal of the Eating Disorders Association*, *23*(2), 126–132. http://doi.org/10.1002/erv.2343.

Lanzieri, N. & Cook, B.J. (2013). Examination of Muscularity and Body Fat Depictions in Magazines that Target Heterosexual and Gay Men. *Body Image*, *10*(2), 251–254. http://doi.org/10.1016/j.bodyim.2012.12.003.

Law, C. & Labre, M.P. (2002). Cultural Standards of Attractiveness: A Thirty-year Look at Changes in Male Images in Magazines. *Journalism & Mass Communication Quarterly*, *79*(3), 697–711. http://doi.org/10.1177/107769900207900310.

Leit, R.A., Pope, H.G. & Gray, J.J. (2001). Cultural Expectations of Muscularity in Men: The Evolution of Playgirl Centerfolds. *International Journal of Eating Disorders*, *29*(1), 90–93.

Leone, J.E., Sedory, E.J. & Gray, K.A. (2005). Recognition and Treatment of Muscle Dysmorphia and Related Body Image Disorders. *Journal of Athletic Training*, *40*(4), 352–359.

Lev-Ari, L., Baumgarten-Katz, I. & Zohar, A.H. (2014). Show Me Your Friends, and I Shall Show You Who You Are: The Way Attachment and Social Comparisons Influence Body Dissatisfaction. *European Eating Disorders Review*, *22*(6), 463–469. http://doi.org/10.1002/erv.2325.

Levine, M.P. & Murnen, S.K. (2009). "Everybody Knows That Mass Media Are/Are Not [Pick One] a Cause of Eating Disorders": A Critical Review of Evidence for a

Causal Link Between Media, Negative Body Image, and Disordered Eating in Females. *Journal of Social and Clinical Psychology, 28*(1), 9–42. http://doi.org/10.1521/jscp. 2009.28.1.9.

Lew, A.-M., Mann, T., Myers, H., Taylor, S. & Bower, J. (2007). Thin-ideal Media and Women's Body Dissatisfaction: Prevention using Downward Social Comparisons on Non-appearance Dimensions. *Sex Roles, 57*(7–8), 543–556. http://doi.org/10.1007/s11199-007-9274-5.

Lewis, S.P. & Arbuthnott, A.E. (2012). Searching for Thinspiration: The Nature of Internet Searches for Pro-eating Disorder Websites. *CyberPsychology, Behavior & Social Networking, 15*(4), 200–204. http://doi.org/10.1089/cyber.2011.0453.

Liechty, J.M. & Lee, M.-J. (2013). Longitudinal Predictors of Dieting and Disordered Eating among Young Adults in the U.S. *International Journal of Eating Disorders, 46*(8), 790–800. http://doi.org/10.1002/eat.22174.

Lowe, M.R., Doshi, S.D., Katterman, S.N. & Feig, E.H. (2013). Dieting and Restrained Eating as Prospective Predictors of Weight Gain. *Frontiers in Psychology, 4,* 577. http://doi.org/10.3389/fpsyg.2013.00577.

Lowe, M.R., Annunziato, R.A., Markowitz, J.T., Didie, E., Bellace, D.L., Riddell, L. & Stice, E. (2006). Multiple Types of Dieting Prospectively Predict Weight Gain during the Freshman Year of College. *Appetite, 47*(1), 83–90. http://doi.org/10.1016/j.appet.2006.03.160.

Luff, G.M. & Gray, J.J. (2009). Complex Messages Regarding a Thin Ideal Appearing in Teenage Girls' Magazines from 1956 to 2005. *Body Image, 6*(2), 133–136. http://doi.org/10.1016/j.bodyim.2009.01.004.

Mabe, A.G., Forney, K.J. & Keel, P.K. (2014). Do You "Like" my Photo? Facebook Use Maintains Eating Disorder Risk. *The International Journal of Eating Disorders, 47*(5), 516–523.

Markey, C.N. & Markey, P.M. (2009). Correlates of Young Women's Interest in Obtaining Cosmetic Surgery. *Sex Roles, 61*(3–4), 158–166. http://doi.org/10.1007/s11199-009-9625-5.

Markey, C.N. & Markey, P.M. (2010). A Correlational and Experimental Examination of Reality Television Viewing and Interest in Cosmetic Surgery. *Body Image, 7*(2), 165–171. http://doi.org/10.1016/j.bodyim.2009.10.006.

Martins, N., Williams, D.C., Ratan, R.A. & Harrison, K. (2011). Virtual Muscularity: A Content Analysis of Male Video Game Characters. *Body Image, 8*(1), 43–51. http://doi.org/10.1016/j.bodyim.2010.10.002.

McCabe, M.P. & Ricciardelli, L.A. (2004). Body Image Dissatisfaction among Males across the Lifespan: A Review of Past Literature. *Journal of Psychosomatic Research, 56*(6), 675–685. http://doi.org/10.1016/S0022-3999(03)00129-6.

Meier, E.P. & Gray, J. (2014). Facebook Photo Activity Associated with Body Image Disturbance in Adolescent Girls. *Cyberpsychology, Behavior and Social Networking, 17*(4), 199–206. http://doi.org/10.1089/cyber.2013.0305.

Montani, J-P., Schutz, Y. & Dulloo, A.G. (2015). Dieting and Weight Cycling as Risk Factors for Cardiometabolic Diseases: Who is Really at Risk? *Obesity Reviews, 16,* 7–18. http://doi.org/10.1111/obr.12251.

Moran, C. & Lee, C. (2014). What's Normal? Influencing Women's Perceptions of Normal Genitalia: An Experiment Involving Exposure to Modified and Nonmodified Images. *BJOG: An International Journal of Obstetrics & Gynaecology, 121*(6), 761–766. http://doi.org/10.1111/1471-0528.12578.

Morrison, T.G. & Halton, M. (2009). Buff, Tough, and Rough: Representations of Muscularity in Action Motion Pictures. *The Journal of Men's Studies, 17*(1), 57–74.

Neumark-Sztainer, D., Paxton, S.J., Hannan, P.J., Haines, J. & Story, M. (2006). Does Body Satisfaction Matter? Five-year Longitudinal Associations between Body Satisfaction and Health Behaviors in Adolescent Females and Males. *Journal of Adolescent Health*, *39*(2), 244–251. http://doi.org/10.1016/j.jadohealth.2005.12.001.

Neumark-Sztainer, D., Wall, M., Haines, J., Story, M. & Eisenberg, M.E. (2007). Why Does Dieting Predict Weight Gain in Adolescents? Findings from Project EAT-II: A 5-year Longitudinal Study. *Journal of the American Dietetic Association*, *107*(3), 448–455. http://doi.org/10.1016/j.jada.2006.12.013.

Neumark-Sztainer, D., Wall, M., Larson, N.I., Eisenberg, M.E. & Loth, K. (2011). Dieting and Disordered Eating Behaviors from Adolescence to Young Adulthood: Findings from a 10-year Longitudinal Study. *Journal of the American Dietetic Association*, *111*(7), 1004–1011. http://doi.org/10.1016/j.jada.2011.04.012.

Nordmann, A.J., Nordmann, A., Briel, M., Keller, U., Yancy, W.S., Brehm, B.J. & Bucher, H.C. (2006). Effects of Low-carbohydrate vs Low-fat Diets on Weight Loss and Cardiovascular Risk Factors: A Meta-analysis of Randomized Controlled Trials. *Archives of Internal Medicine*, *166*(3), 285–293. http://doi.org/10.1001/archinte.166.3.285.

Norris, M.L., Boydell, K.M., Pinhas, L. & Katzman, D.K. (2006). Ana and the Internet: A Review of Pro-anorexia Websites. *The International Journal of Eating Disorders*, *39*(6), 443–447. http://doi.org/10.1002/eat.20305.

Nouri, M., Hill, L.G. & Orrell-Valente, J.K. (2011). Media Exposure, Internalization of the Thin Ideal, and Body Dissatisfaction: Comparing Asian American and European American College Females. *Body Image*, *8*(4), 366–372. http://doi.org/10.1016/j.bodyim.2011.05.008.

NPD Group. (2013, January 7). The NPD Group Reports Dieting is at an All Time Low. Retrieved February 23, 2015 from www.npd.com/wps/portal/npd/us/news/press-releases/the-npd-group-reports-dieting-is-at-an-all-time-low-dieting-season-has-begun-but-its-not-what-it-used-to-be/.

Office on Women's Health. (2012a, July 16). Binge Eating Disorder Fact Sheet. Retrieved February 25, 2015 from www.womenshealth.gov/publications/our-publications/fact-sheet/binge-eating-disorder.html#c.

Office on Women's Health. (2012b, July 16). Bulimia Nervosa Fact Sheet. Retrieved February 25, 2015 from www.womenshealth.gov/publications/our-publications/fact-sheet/bulimia-nervosa.html.

Office on Women's Health. (2012c, July 16). Bulimia Nervosa Fact Sheet. Retrieved February 25, 2015 from www.womenshealth.gov/publications/our-publications/fact-sheet/bulimia-nervosa.html#e.

Pagoto, S., Schneider, K.L., Evans, M., Waring, M.E., Appelhans, B., Busch, A.M. & Ziedonis, M. (2014). Tweeting It Off: Characteristics of Adults Who Tweet about a Weight Loss Attempt. *Journal of the American Medical Informatics Association: JAMIA*, *21*(6), 1032–1037. http://doi.org/10.1136/amiajnl-2014-002652.

Paxton, S.J., Eisenberg, M.E. & Neumark-Sztainer, D. (2006). Prospective Predictors of Body Dissatisfaction in Adolescent Girls and Boys: A Five-year Longitudinal Study. *Developmental Psychology*, *42*(5), 888–899. http://doi.org/10.1037/0012-1649.42.5.888.

Placik, O.J. & Arkins, J.P. (2014). Plastic Surgery Trends Parallel Playboy Magazine: The Pudenda Preoccupation. *Aesthetic Surgery Journal/the American Society for Aesthetic Plastic Surgery*, *34*(7), 1083–1090. http://doi.org/10.1177/1090820X14543514.

Polivy, J. & Herman, C.P. (2002). Causes of Eating Disorders. *Annual Review of Psychology*, *53*(1), 187–213. http://doi.org/10.1146/annurev.psych.53.100901.135103.

Pope, H.G., Olivardia, R., Gruber, A. & Ackerman, J. (1999). Evolving Ideals of Male Body Image as Seen Through Action Toys. *The International Journal of Eating Disorders, 26*(1), 65–72.

Posavac, H.D., Posavac, S.S. & Weigel, R.G. (2001). Reducing the Impact of Media Images on Women At Risk For Body Image Disturbance: Three Targeted Interventions. *Journal of Social and Clinical Psychology, 20*(3), 324–340. http://doi.org/10.1521/jscp. 20.3.324.22308.

Rayner, K.E., Schniering, C.A., Rapee, R.M. & Hutchinson, D.M. (2013). A Longitudinal Investigation of Perceived Friend Influence on Adolescent Girls' Body Dissatisfaction and Disordered Eating. *Journal of Clinical Child and Adolescent Psychology: The Official Journal for the Society of Clinical Child and Adolescent Psychology, American Psychological Association, Division 53, 42*(5), 643–656. http://doi.org/10.1080/153744 16.2012.743103.

Ricciardelli, L.A., McCabe, M.P. & Banfield, S. (2000). Body Image and Body Change Methods in Adolescent Boys: Role of Parents, Friends and the Media. *Journal of Psychosomatic Research, 49*(3), 189–197. http://doi.org/10.1016/S0022-3999(00)00159-8.

Robinson, T., Callister, M. & Jankoski, T. (2008). Portrayal of Body Weight on Children's Television Sitcoms: A Content Analysis. *Body Image, 5*(2), 141–151. http://doi.org/10.1016/j.bodyim.2007.11.004.

Rodgers, R. & Chabrol, H. (2009). Parental Attitudes, Body Image Disturbance and Disordered Eating amongst Adolescents and Young Adults: A Review. *European Eating Disorders Review, 17*(2), 137–151. http://doi.org/10.1002/erv.907.

Saraceni, R. & Russell-Mayhew, S. (2007). Cultural Expectations of Thinness in Women: A Partial Replication and Update of Magazine Content. *Eating and Weight Disorders: EWD, 12*(3), e68–e74.

Sarwer, D.B., Cash, T.F., Magee, L., Williams, E.F., Thompson, J.K., Roehrig, M. & Romanofski, M. (2005). Female College Students and Cosmetic Surgery: An Investigation of Experiences, Attitudes, and Body Image. *Plastic and Reconstructive Surgery, 115*(3), 931–938. http://doi.org/10.1097/01.PRS.0000153204.37065.D3.

Schaefer, M.K. & Blodgett Salafia, E.H. (2014). The Connection of Teasing by Parents, Siblings, and Peers with Girls' Body Dissatisfaction and Boys' Drive for Muscularity: The Role of Social Comparison as a Mediator. *Eating Behaviors, 15*(4), 599–608. http://doi.org/10.1016/j.eatbeh.2014.08.018.

Schutz, H.K. & Paxton, S.J. (2007). Friendship Quality, Body Dissatisfaction, Dieting and Disordered Eating in Adolescent Girls. *The British Journal of Clinical Psychology/ the British Psychological Society, 46*(Part 1), 67–83.

Seifert, T. (2005). Anthropomorphic Characteristics of Centerfold Models: Trends Towards Slender Figures over Time. *The International Journal of Eating Disorders, 37*(3), 271–274. http://doi.org/10.1002/eat.20086.

Sharpe, H., Schober, I., Treasure, J. & Schmidt, U. (2014). The Role of High-quality Friendships in Female Adolescents' Eating Pathology and Body Dissatisfaction. *Eating and Weight Disorders – Studies on Anorexia, Bulimia and Obesity, 19*(2), 159–168. http://doi.org/10.1007/s40519-014-0113-8.

Slevec, J. & Tiggemann, M. (2010). Attitudes Toward Cosmetic Surgery in Middle-aged Women: Body Image, Aging Anxiety, and the Media. *Psychology of Women Quarterly, 34*(1), 65–74. http://doi.org/10.1111/j.1471-6402.2009.01542.x.

Smink, F.R.E., van Hoeken, D. & Hoek, H.W. (2012). Epidemiology of Eating Disorders: Incidence, Prevalence and Mortality Rates. *Current Psychiatry Reports, 14*(4), 406–414. http://doi.org/10.1007/s11920-012-0282-y.

Smolak, L., Murnen, S.K. & Kevin, J. (2005). Sociocultural Influences and Muscle

271

Building in Adolescent Boys. *Psychology of Men & Masculinity*, 6(4), 227–239. http://doi.org/10.1037/1524-9220.6.4.227.

Spitzer, B.L., Henderson, K.A. & Zivian, M.T. (1999). Gender Differences in Population Versus Media Body Sizes: A Comparison over Four Decades. *Sex Roles*, 40(7–8), 545–565. http://doi.org/10.1023/A:1018836029738.

Striegel-Moore, R.H., Rosselli, F., Perrin, N., DeBar, L., Wilson, G.T., May, A. & Kraemer, H.C. (2009). Gender Difference in the Prevalence of Eating Disorder Symptoms. *International Journal of Eating Disorders*, 42(5), 471–474. http://doi.org/10.1002/eat.20625.

Swami, V. (2009). Body Appreciation, Media Influence, and Weight Status Predict Consideration of Cosmetic Surgery among Female Undergraduates. *Body Image*, 6(4), 315–317. http://doi.org/10.1016/j.bodyim.2009.07.001.

Sypeck, M.F., Gray, J.J. & Ahrens, A.H. (2004). No Longer Just a Pretty Face: Fashion Magazines' Depictions of Ideal Female Beauty from 1959 to 1999. *International Journal of Eating Disorders*, 36(3), 342–347. http://doi.org/10.1002/eat.20039.

Sypeck, M.F., Gray, J.J., Etu, S.F., Ahrens, A.H., Mosimann, J.E. & Wiseman, C.V. (2006). Cultural Representations of Thinness in Women, Redux: Playboy Magazine's Depiction of Beauty from 1979 to 1999. *Body Image*, 3(3), 229–235. http://doi.org/10.1016/j.bodyim.2006.07.001.

Thompson-Brenner, H., Boisseau, C.L. & St. Paul, M.S. (2011). Representation of Ideal Figure Size in Ebony Magazine: A Content Analysis. *Body Image*, 8(4), 373–378. http://doi.org/10.1016/j.bodyim.2011.05.005.

Tiggemann, M. & Miller, J. (2010). The Internet and Adolescent Girls' Weight Satisfaction and Drive for Thinness. *Sex Roles*, 63(1–2), 79–90. http://doi.org/10.1007/s11199-010-9789-z.

Tiggemann, M. & Slater, A. (2013). NetGirls: The Internet, Facebook, and Body Image Concern in Adolescent Girls. *The International Journal of Eating Disorders*, 46(6), 630–633. http://doi.org/10.1002/eat.22141.

Tiggemann, M. & Slater, A. (2014). NetTweens The Internet and Body Image Concerns in Preteenage Girls. *The Journal of Early Adolescence*, 34(5), 606–620. http://doi.org/10.1177/0272431613501083.

Tiggemann, M., Martins, Y. & Kirkbride, A. (2007). Oh to be Lean and Muscular: Body Image Ideals in Gay and Heterosexual Men. *Psychology of Men & Masculinity*, 8(1), 15–24. http://doi.org/10.1037/1524-9220.8.1.15.

Tiggemann, M., Slater, A. & Smyth, V. (2014). "Retouch Free": The Effect of Labelling Media Images as not Digitally Altered on Women's Body Dissatisfaction. *Body Image*, 11(1), 85–88. http://doi.org/10.1016/j.bodyim.2013.08.005.

Tiggemann, M., Slater, A., Bury, B., Hawkins, K. & Firth, B. (2013). Disclaimer Labels on Fashion Magazine Advertisements: Effects on Social Comparison and Body Dissatisfaction. *Body Image*, 10(1), 45–53. http://doi.org/10.1016/j.bodyim.2012.08.001.

Todd, J.E. (2014). Changes in Eating Patterns and Diet Quality among Working-age Adults, 2005–2010. *Economic Research Report, 161*. Retrieved February 23, 2015 from http://162.79.45.209/media/1259670/err161.pdf.

van den Berg, P., Paxton, S.J., Keery, H., Wall, M., Guo, J. & Neumark-Sztainer, D. (2007). Body Dissatisfaction and Body Comparison with Media Images in Males and Females. *Body Image*, 4(3), 257–268. http://doi.org/10.1016/j.bodyim.2007.04.003.

Vincent, M.A. & McCabe, M.P. (2000). Gender Differences among Adolescents in Family, and Peer Influences on Body Dissatisfaction, Weight Loss, and Binge Eating Behaviors. *Journal of Youth and Adolescence*, 29(2), 205–221. http://doi.org/10.1023/A:1005156616173.

Want, S.C. (2009). Meta-analytic Moderators of Experimental Exposure to Media Portrayals of Women on Female Appearance Satisfaction: Social Comparisons as Automatic Processes. *Body Image*, *6*(4), 257–269. http://doi.org/10.1016/j.bodyim. 2009.07.008.

Wasylkiw, L., Emms, A.A., Meuse, R. & Poirier, K.F. (2009). Are All Models Created Equal? A Content Analysis of Women in Advertisements of Fitness versus Fashion Magazines. *Body Image*, *6*(2), 137–140. http://doi.org/10.1016/j.bodyim.2009.01.005.

Willis, L.E. & Knobloch-Westerwick, S. (2014). Weighing Women Down: Messages on Weight Loss and Body Shaping in Editorial Content in Popular Women's Health and Fitness Magazines. *Health Communication*, *29*(4), 323–331. http://doi.or g/10.1080/10410236.2012.755602.

Wiseman, C.V., Gray, J.J., Mosimann, J.E. & Ahrens, A.H. (1992). Cultural Expectations of Thinness in Women: An Update. *International Journal of Eating Disorders*, *11*(1), 85–89. http://doi.org/10.1002/1098-108X(199201)11:185::AID-EAT22601101123.0.CO;2-T.

Yamamiya, Y., Cash, T.F., Melnyk, S.E., Posavac, H.D. & Posavac, S.S. (2005). Women's Exposure to Thin-and-beautiful Media Images: Body Image Effects of Media-ideal Internalization and Impact-reduction Interventions. *Body Image*, *2*(1), 74–80. http://doi.org/10.1016/j.bodyim.2004.11.001.

CHAPTER 9

LUST, LOVE AND ROMANCE WITH FEW CONSEQUENCES: MEDIA PORTRAYALS OF SEX

By February 26, 2014, the "erotic romance" novel trilogy *Fifty Shades of Grey* had sold more than 100 million copies worldwide, making it "one of the best-selling series in publishing history" (Bosman, 2014, para. 1). A year later, the movie version of *Fifty Shades of Grey* broke the box-office record for movies opening during Presidents' Day weekend, earning $85 million dollars for Universal (Alter, 2015; McNary, 2015). The movie's focus on the sadomasochistic relationship between innocent and naïve college student Anastasia Steele and charismatic but controlling and often violent billionaire Christian Grey spurred controversy and protests from both religious groups and domestic violence activists, who argued that the film glamorizes and condones stalking, emotional abuse and sexual violence (Beaumont-Thomas, 2015).

Barely a week after the movie opened in the United States, a University of Illinois-Chicago freshman was arrested and charged with rape after he allegedly took a female classmate back to his dorm room, used multiple belts to restrain her, stuffed a tie in her mouth, and beat her with another belt and his hands while sexually assaulting her. The alleged rapist, a 19-year-old freshman whose attorney said he had participated in several UIC leadership programs and the university's triathlon team, told police he was acting out scenes from *Fifty Shades of Grey*. Although the woman cried and told him to stop during the assault, he claimed that the sexual interaction was consensual (Holley, 2015; Saul, 2015).

The links between mass media's sexual content and real-world sexual attitudes and behaviors are not usually so clear as they appear to be in

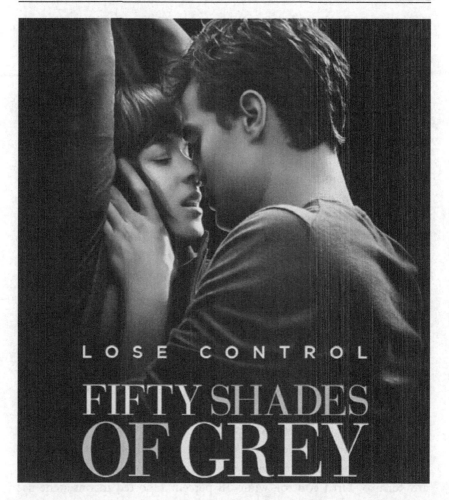

Figure 9.1: Critics Claim *Fifty Shades of Grey* Glamorized Sexual Coerciveness

this rape case. Nonetheless, many researchers have argued that media messages about sex and sexuality do have a significant influence on sex-related attitudes and behaviors, particularly among adolescents; research has documented media effects on sexual initiation, attitudes toward and use of contraception and rape myth acceptance (Bleakley et al., 2008; Brown et al., 2006; Collins et al., 2004; Hust et al., 2008; Kahlor & Eastin, 2011).

Whether and how the media influence sexual attitudes and behaviors is an important health issue. While changing public attitudes toward premarital/extramarital sex, homosexuality, abortion, out-of-wedlock births and even sexually transmitted diseases (STDs) such as HIV/AIDS may be good or bad, depending on one's religious and moral views, it seems difficult to argue that current sexual practices in the United States consistently lead to positive health outcomes. More than half of all U.S. pregnancies today are unintended, with one in five unwanted, more than three in five mistimed and only 49 percent intended. Among sexually active teenagers, the rate of unintended pregnancies is twice that of the comparable rate among women in general. Annual rates of unintended pregnancies declined from 59 per 1,000 women aged 15 to 44 in 1981 to 49 per 1,000 women in 1994, but rates then began increasing again, to 54 per 1,000 in 2008, meaning that approximately one in every 20 U.S. women had an unintended pregnancy that year (Alan Guttmacher Institute, 2015). In 2011, U.S. women underwent 730,322 legal induced abortions; there were 219 abortions for every 1,000 live births, which, fortunately, represents a 5 percent decline from the number and rate in 2010 ("Reproductive Health," 2015).

One reason U.S. women experience so many unintended pregnancies is the inconsistent use of contraceptives. According to data from the most recent National Survey of Family Growth, 38.3 percent of women aged 15 to 44 were not using any contraceptive method, although only 6.9 percent were fertile, sexually active and not pregnant, trying to get pregnant or in the first few months after having a baby (Jones et al., 2012). However, other researchers have found that women often do not use contraception correctly; in 2008, 14 percent of women reported either not using contraceptives or going for long periods without using any form of birth control, while 18 percent reported inconsistent use ("Fact Sheet," 2014).

Consistent contraceptive use is less common among teenagers than among older women. Although teens' contraceptive use has increased, significant percentages of teens still report having sex without using any birth control method. Between 2006 and 2010, 14 percent of teenage girls and 7 percent of teenage boys reported using no contraceptive method during their most recent sexual intercourse. Teens are also increasingly likely to use a contraceptive method the first time they have sex, with 78 percent of girls and 85 percent of boys saying they used birth control the first time they had sex. Teens who begin having sex early (at age 14 or younger) are less likely to use a contraceptive method during their first sexual intercourse and take longer to begin using contraceptives compared to teens who initiate sexual intercourse later.

Although rates of sexual activity among American teens are similar to those of European teens, American teenagers use contraceptives less consistently and are less likely to use the most effective contraceptive methods, leading to higher teen pregnancy rates in the United States ("American Teens," 2014). In 2010 – a record low year for adolescent pregnancies in the United States – nearly 6 percent of 15- to 19-year-olds became pregnant; less than 1 percent of girls aged 14 or younger became pregnant. Despite the decline in teen pregnancy, the teenage pregnancy rate remains dramatically higher in the United States than in other developed countries. For instance, a comparison of 2011 adolescent pregnancy rates in 21 countries showed that the United States had the highest rate, with 57 pregnancies per 1,000 girls 15 to 19 years old; the rate in England and Wales was 47 per 1,000 girls, whereas Canada reported 28, the Netherlands only 14 and Switzerland only eight pregnancies per 1,000 girls (Sedgh et al., 2015).

Teenage pregnancy is a particular concern to health advocates due to its adverse effects on the health of both the mother and her baby. More than one in four teen pregnancies (26%) ends in induced abortion and another 15 percent result in miscarriages ("American Teens," 2014). Teen mothers are more likely to have pre-term and low birth weight babies and to have infants who die before their first birthday. Even among non-smoking, non-drinking married white girls with an age-appropriate educational background and adequate prenatal care, infants born to teen mothers still have worse outcomes (Chen et al., 2007). Children born to teen mothers have more problems in education, behavior and long-term health, compared to those born to older mothers. Having a baby before the age of 20 also has negative health impacts for the girl, who is less likely to finish high school and more likely to be poor as an adult, increasing the likelihood that she and her baby will be dependent on public assistance (Office of Adolescent Health, 2015).

Sexually transmitted diseases constitute another important sexual health issue in the United States. According to the Centers for Disease Control, Americans contract approximately 20 million new STDs every year; half of these occur among people 15 to 24 years old. CDC data for 2013 show that these infections included 1,401,906 cases of chlamydia, 333,004 cases of gonorrhea and 17,375 cases of syphilis. Rates of chlamydia and gonorrhea are either stable or have declined slightly, but the rate of syphilis infections increased by 10 percent between 2012 and

2013, primarily reflecting increased incidence among gay and bisexual men. The increase in syphilis infections is particularly troubling because, left untreated, the disease can cause blindness and stroke, as well as increasing susceptibility to HIV infection (Centers for Disease Control and Prevention, 2014a).

HIV also continues to be a problem in the United States, with the number of new infections each year remaining stable at about 50,000 rather than declining. Because those infected with HIV now live longer, the number of infected individuals is increasing; the CDC estimates HIV prevalence at 1,201,100 individuals age 13 and older, including about 14 percent who do not know that they're infected. Although HIV and AIDS continues to disproportionately affect men who have sex with men, women accounted for two in every ten new infections in 2010; the majority (84%) were infected through heterosexual sex with an infected male partner (Centers for Disease Control and Prevention, 2014c).

Unlike HIV, the herpes simplex-2 virus (HSV-2) is not likely to be life-threatening for the infected individual. However, HSV-2 – the second most common STD in the United States – can result in painful chronic infections and, among women, can lead to miscarriage or premature delivery and can be fatal for a newborn infant. The CDC estimates that more than 24 million new HSV-2 infections occur each year in the United States (Centers for Disease Control and Prevention, 2013).

The most common STD in the United States is the human papillo-mavirus (HPV), which is also the only STD currently that can be prevented through vaccination. According to the CDC, nearly all sexually active individuals will contract HPV during their lifetime, and while some types of HPV infection will resolve on their own without causing health problems, other types of HPV cause genital warts, while still others can cause cancers of the cervix, vulva, vagina, penis or anus, as well as oral and throat cancers (Centers for Disease Control and Prevention, 2014b). The National Cancer Institute estimates that HPV infections are responsible for 5 percent of all cancers worldwide, including virtually all cervical cancers, about 85 percent of anal cancers and more than half of all cancers involving the middle part of the throat (oropharyngeal cancer – the soft palate, base of the tongue and tonsils). Recent data suggest that these HPV-caused oropharyngeal cancers have increased during the past two decades and by 2020 will be more common than cervical cancer ("HPV and Cancer," 2012). Although the death rate from cervical cancer has declined by more than half during the past 30 years, the American Cancer Society predicts that, during 2015, the disease will kill about 4,100 women in the United States ("What Are," 2014).

In addition to the suffering they cause to those infected, STDs represent a costly health problem for the United States. The CDC estimates that the 20 million new infections each year account for almost $16 billion in direct medical costs (Centers for Disease Control and Prevention, 2013).

As troubling as they may be, most unwanted or ill-timed pregnancies and most sexually transmitted infections occur as a result of consensual sex. But non-consensual sex, including both sexual violence toward adults and the sexual abuse of children, also constitutes a significant problem in the United States. In fact, spurred in part by a White House Council on Women and Girls paper released in January 2014 (White House Council on Women, 2014), the past few years have seen significant discussion of whether a "rape culture" exists in the United States (Hamblin, 2014; Kitchens, 2014; Maxwell, 2014; Steinhauer, 2014); "rape culture" refers to the idea that society views sexual assault as inevitable, even normal, leading to policies and systems that provide inadequate support for victims or even contribute to their victimization (Hamblin, 2014).

Whether or not the problem stems from "rape culture," sexual assault is a serious problem in the United States. The White House Council paper noted that nearly one in every five women in the United States will be a victim of attempted or completed sexual assault at some point during her life; in addition, 1.6 million men and boys have been raped. Nearly 98 percent of those who commit sexual assault are male. Despite the stereotype of the rapist lurking in the dark alley, only 14 percent of sexual assaults of women and 15 percent of sexual assaults of men are committed by strangers (White House Council on Women, 2014).

The short- and long-term results of these assaults can include injury during the assault, STDs and unwanted pregnancy, as well as chronic pain and headaches, asthma, irritable bowel syndrome and, not surprisingly, difficulty sleeping. Survivors also face an increased risk of anxiety and post-traumatic stress disorder; sexual assault victims are five times as likely as those who have not been assaulted to experience major depressive disorder episodes. They are more likely, after the assault, to engage in risky behavior, including drug and alcohol abuse, to develop eating disorders and to attempt or consider suicide. The report notes that having either perpetrators or others sharing details of the assault on social media can further traumatize sexual assault victims (White House Council on Women, 2014).

In summary, then, it seems reasonable to argue that sexual behavior in the United States is often problematic, frequently including unsafe sexual practices that lead to unwanted pregnancies and sexually transmitted diseases and far too often occurring without mutual consent. The remainder of this chapter will attempt to explain how mass media portrayals of sex contribute to problematic sexual attitudes and behaviors, as well as addressing research suggesting that some media content actually can promote sexual health.

Media Sexual Content

Mass media scholars and those concerned about adolescent health have long been interested in the ways in which the media depict sexual interactions. In an excellent summary of content analyses of media sexual content, Wright (2009) concludes that the majority of TV sexual interactions involve young, attractive, heterosexual couples, with interactions initiated primarily by the male partner, although soap operas are more gender-egalitarian in terms of initiation of sexual interaction. TV programs most popular among adolescents are more likely than entertainment TV overall to include depictions of casual sex, but also even less likely than other TV programs to provide information about sexual risks and responsibilities (Wright, 2009). For instance, a study of television programs from the 2004/2005 season showed that, overall, entertainment programs included an average of five sexual scenes per hour, while the average for programs most popular with teenagers was 6.7 scenes per hour. This study also showed that only 10 percent of teen-favorite programs included risk/responsibility messages, compared to 14 percent of all shows (Kunkel et al., 2005). In a more recent study of the prime-time programs most popular with teens, researchers found that male and female characters were equally likely to interact sexually and equally likely to experience positive and negative consequences. Negative consequences were more common than positive consequences, but only in relation to sexual talk. Portrayals of sexual behavior resulted only in positive consequences (Ortiz & Brooks, 2014).

Another study specifically examined teen drama stories focused on a character's virginity loss. This study, which examined stories included in ten teen-focused dramas broadcast in the 2003/2004 or 2004/2005 seasons, showed that these virginity-loss narratives were common: approximately one in every four main characters had sex for the first time during the two seasons, most often at age 16. Each of the virginity-loss storylines featured a dominant theme: abstinence as the right choice, virginity loss as an inevitable occurrence that simply needed to be managed correctly (e.g., to include condom use), or virginity as a stigmatizing condition a teenager would be anxious, even desperate, to end. Virginity loss generally occurred within the context of monogamous romantic relationships, and only two of the characters lost their virginity in storylines that did not explicitly include condom use (Kelly, 2010).

These findings contrast significantly with those of a more comprehensive study of sexual content in television, movies, magazines and music popular among American teenagers. This study showed that less than half of 1 percent of content in these media either portrayed or provided information about sexually healthy behavior. Qualitative analysis of the sexual health content showed that the media often offered ambiguous or inaccurate information about sexual health, reinforcing the notion that girls and women must protect themselves from pregnancy while boys and men push for sex; the media often present contraceptive use as embarrassing (Hust et al., 2008).

Other studies of sexual content on television have revealed that sexual intercourse is typically portrayed without reference to risks or responsibilities; only 4 percent of sexual intercourse depictions included the use of any sort of sexual precautions. Nearly one-third of sexual intercourse portrayals (32%) involve characters with no previously established sexual relationship, although intercourse is almost as common (29% of portrayals) among unmarried couples with a previously existing sexual relationship. Sexual intercourse among people who have just met (14%) is nearly as common as sex involving married couples (15%). Relationship status was not associated with portrayals of either risks or sexual responsibility. The majority of characters involved in sexual intercourse are attractive, although this is more often true for females (84%) than for males (78%). Emotional outcomes are most commonly positive (73%); slightly more than a quarter (27%) of sexual intercourse portrayals result in negative emotional consequences. Overall, however, sexual

Figure 9.2: Rap and Hip-hop Music Often Depicts Women Negatively

intercourse was often portrayed as having few lasting consequences of any kind (Eyal & Finnerty, 2007, 2009).

Sexual content is an element in the majority of music videos, although the frequency and nature of sexual content varies depending

282

on the genre of music and the channel on which the videos appear (Ward, 2003; Wright, 2009). Content analyses have shown that as many as three-quarters of all music videos include sexual imagery (Ward, 2003). This finding should not be surprising, given that comparative content analysis has shown that music contains more sexual content than any other medium popular among adolescents (Pardun et al., 2005). A review of multiple studies concludes that the portrayals of sex included in music videos is hedonistically oriented, heterosexual and often sexist (Wright, 2009). Rap and hip-hop music videos have been identified as particularly likely to contain misogynistic sexual portrayals (Aubrey & Frisby, 2011), a fact that in 2005 led *Essence* magazine to launch a campaign against the sexist and degrading portrayals of black women in rap and hip-hop music and videos (Reid-Brinkley, 2007; Weitzer & Kubrin, 2009). A study of the most popular rap music videos aired on the three major music video TV channels (MTV, VH1 and BET) in 2006 revealed that the most common themes of these videos were materialism and misogyny. Female characters were commonly objectified and were more likely to appear in rap videos with these negative themes than in those containing community-oriented (positive) themes (Conrad et al., 2009).

Other than these analyses of music video content, little recent research appears to have examined the portrayals of misogynistic behavior or sexual violence on television, perhaps in part because some studies have suggested that depictions of non-consensual sex are rare (Bufkin & Eschholz, 2000; Eyal & Finnerty, 2009); others, however, have found that references to sex crime account for 10 percent of all sex-related television dialogue (Kunkel et al., 2003). Earlier research suggested that TV portrayals of rape often imply that victims invite sexual assault through their behavior or dress. Rapists are typically portrayed as brutal, depraved believers in sexist stereotypes; this portrayal generally contrasts with that of the male protagonists (e.g., detectives) who comfort and support the victim (Cuklanz, 2000).

Earlier studies have suggested that movies portray sexual violence in a similarly unrealistic way. For instance, an analysis of sexual violence content in the 50 top-grossing movies of 1996 showed that the movies contained 30 sex scenes, of which three were heterosexual rape and two depicted homosexual rape. All of the rapes were violent, with the rapists portrayed as cruel, deranged, lower class individuals (Bufkin & Eschholz,

2000). A more recent analysis, which examined 15 of the most popular movies from 1985 to 2010, showed that 62.8 percent of the movies depicted a violent character who was also shown at some point involved in sexual interaction, with more than a quarter of the movies including violent characters who were depicted in sexually explicit scenes; this was true for 41.2 percent of R-rated movies. Overall, movies depicted sex and violence within the same segment 1.61 times, on average, with sex and violence co-occurring 1.86 times per R-rated movie. It is important to note, here, however, that sexual and violent characters were not necessarily portrayed as rapists or even as "bad" characters (Bleakley et al., 2014).

Sex and graphic violence are often linked in "slasher" films, a type of horror film containing numerous scenes of gore and sadistic violence. Researchers have noted that women are victimized in these movies more often than are men, but female characters who do *not* engage in sexual behavior in the film are more likely to survive. However, male characters' survival was not related to their sexual behavior. Male characters who were killed died just as quickly whether or not they had engaged in sexual behavior, whereas female characters who had been sexually active were shown to take longer to die, meaning that they suffered more (Welsh, 2010).

Video games represent another type of media content in which sex and violence are often linked. Video games typically either underrepresent women or portray them in highly stereotypical and sexualized ways (Beasley & Collins Standley, 2002). An analysis of the top 20 PC video games from 1999 revealed that 12 of the games featured violence as a major theme, and of the violent games, 17 percent included "some aspects of sexualized violence" (Dill, 2009, p. 123); the article does not explain what constituted "sexualized violence," although it mentions the *Grand Theft Auto* series, in which players are rewarded for having sex with a prostitute and then killing her to get their money back.

Ironically, given that many defenders of such antisocial game content justify its inclusion on the grounds that these are "just games," many women in the gaming industry, including developers, reviewers and professional gamers, have been subjected to torrents of online abuse, including often-graphic threats of being raped and killed; these attacks typically begin after the women criticize sexist game content or sexist behavior by men in the gaming industry (Cross, 2014). These threats, which now routinely include bomb threats against venues that have invited prominent female gaming critics to speak, are recognized as a semi-organized "campaign to discredit or intimidate outspoken critics of the male-dominated gaming industry and its culture" (Wingfield, 2014, para. 4).

Sexist and objectifying portrayals of women are also common in men's magazines, including not only "soft" pornography magazines such as *Playboy* and *Penthouse* but also the so-called "lad" magazines like *Maxim, Stuff, FHM (For Him Magazine)* and *Gear*. An analysis of sex-focused articles published in *Maxim, Stuff* and *FHM* in the late 1990s and early 2000s revealed that the most common topics were women's sexual preferences, non-traditional sexual behaviors or positions and improving the reader's sex life. These topics often overlapped, so that articles focused on pleasing women sexually suggested that men should do so primarily to make women more willing to have sex more often and/or to engage in specific sexual behaviors the man desires, such as oral sex. Every article in the study sample included a photograph, virtually all of which (98%) depicted a woman partially nude, beginning to take her clothes off or looking suggestive; more than one-third of the photographs showed multiple women (Taylor, 2005).

One topic rarely addressed in these men's magazines was sexual health, which was coded as a primary topic for only one of the 91 articles, and in this case the article was about trivia related to sexual functioning. Only two articles mentioned HIV/AIDS, and only five mentioned other STDs; condoms were mentioned in 11 articles, but pregnancy in only four. Male homosexuality was mentioned in only three articles, although lesbian women were mentioned in 17 (Taylor, 2006).

Discussion of sexual health topics is far more common in magazines aimed at women and teenage girls. An analysis of sex-related articles published in top-selling women's and teen magazines from 1986 to 1996 showed that 68.8 percent of teen magazine articles and 59.8 percent of women's magazine articles dealing with a sexual topic made some mention of a sexual health issue, with contraception the most commonly mentioned topic for both magazine categories, followed by AIDS/HIV in women's magazines and non-AIDS STDs in teen magazines. Although inclusion of sexual health information was common in both teen and women's magazines, women's magazines especially were even more likely to discuss sex in the context of attracting sex partners and improving sexual performance. Over the ten-year study period, the amount of space women's magazines devoted to non-health sex topics increased significantly, while space devoted to sexual health topics declined. In teen magazines, space devoted to sexual health topics increased slightly, but that devoted to sexual attractiveness or sexual performance increased far more. Both magazine types, then, effectively de-emphasized sexual health as an issue about which their readers should be concerned (Walsh-Childers et al., 2002).

A more recent analysis of the portrayal of sexuality and sexual health in magazines aimed at teenage girls and at middle-aged women revealed that neither type of magazine paid much attention to women's sexual desire. Teen magazines attributed to girls responsibility for avoiding sex, avoiding pregnancy and STDs and warned them that male partners would be untrustworthy. Magazines for adult women linked sex to women's responsibility to preserve their marriages and fulfilling their responsibilities as mothers; this responsibility included monitoring their daughters' sexual behavior (Clarke, 2009).

Another study analyzed women's and men's magazine articles that claimed to tell readers how to achieve "better" sex; the analysis revealed that the magazines related having "great sex" to technical, mechanical and physical factors such as sexual positions and being in good physical shape; to variety, including using pornography for inspiration and engaging in "rough" sex; to sexual communication and having a stronger emotional connection; to psychological improvements such as being more relaxed during sex and understanding more fully one's own sexual preferences; and to pre-sex preparation, which included personal grooming and scene-setting. For four of the five magazines studied, the focus of more than half of the articles was physical or technical techniques or variety. The magazines also communicated numerous sexual stereotypes, such as the idea that men are supposed to be "wild, aggressive and animalistic in their sexuality" (Ménard & Kleinplatz, 2007, p. 13); women, however, were primarily given advice meant to increase their partners' pleasure, not their own. Women's magazines often seemed to promise that use of the sex tips provided would lead to marriage proposals, while men were assured that their success in performing sexually would guarantee that the women experiencing this sexual prowess would never leave them. Men's magazines, unlike women's magazines, offered little sex advice, supporting the stereotype that men already know everything they need to know about sex (Ménard & Klein-platz, 2007).

Although traditional media continue to be important sources of sexual information, the Internet now accounts for a substantial amount of media use among both teenagers and adults. Given the vastness of online content, it is perhaps not surprising that relatively few studies have attempted to analyze its sexual content. Nonetheless, research has offered some insights into the types of sexual information and portrayals which the Web provides. For instance, two recent studies of online pornography produced somewhat differing views of the depiction of sex. One analysis of 400 popular videos from the most-visited online porn sites showed that men and women were portrayed as relatively equal in terms of social or professional status, but women were more likely to be portrayed as submissive, while men were more likely to be dominant. Women were far more likely than men to be the recipients of violence, with violence toward women – most often spanking or gagging – appearing in 37.2 percent of all sex scenes. Although the authors of the paper excluded gagging from what they categorized as "extreme violence," they note that "gagging" included scenes in which the man's penis was inserted so far into the woman's mouth that she would gag. In addition, women were far more likely to respond in positive or neutral (unaffected) ways to either spanking or gagging than to respond negatively. Videos produced by amateurs were more likely than those professionally produced to portray women in unequal and dehumanizing ways (Klaassen & Peter, 2014).

Another recent study examined free, easily accessible pornographic videos identified as featuring either "teens" or "MILFs," a term that refers to sexy women in their forties and fifties. The majority of videos showed either vaginal intercourse (88%), fellatio (86%) or both. Condom use was rare, appearing in only 2 percent of either type of video. Men were the primary initiators in teen videos, while women were more likely to be the initiators in the MILF videos. Male actors were more likely to be portrayed as controlling the pace and direction of the sexual interactions, and women were more likely to be portrayed as exploitation victims; however, the researchers concluded that coercion, exploitation and power differentials were not as common as other research has suggested (Vannier et al., 2014).

The results of these studies of online pornography contrast with earlier studies of rented or purchased pornographic video tapes or discs, which have found that female characters are not only more likely to be portrayed as submissive but are also often subjected to degrading acts, such as having the man ejaculate on the woman's face. One recent study of top-selling pornographic DVDs from 2004/2005 showed that the most commonly depicted act was female-to-male oral sex, which appeared in 90.1 percent of the coded scenes; vaginal intercourse was the second most common sexual act, included in 86.2 percent of the scenes. Non-normative sex acts were also common, with 41.1 percent showing women performing oral sex on a man immediately after he had penetrated her anally, and nearly one in five scenes showing the woman being subjected to simultaneous penetration (anal and vaginal) by two men. Verbal aggression, including insulting, threatening and coercive language, appeared in nearly half of the scenes coded (48.7%), and physical aggression, including gagging, choking, spanking, hair-pulling, slapping with an open hand and bondage, appeared in the vast majority of the scenes (88.2%). The researchers argue that the levels of aggression they identified in these videos present a more realistic picture than many earlier studies, in which researchers classified as aggression only those acts the target attempts to avoid: "by relying on definitions that emphasize consent, these previous studies are (perhaps inadvertently) complicit with naturalizing the presence of violence and aggression" (Bridges et al., 2010, p. 1079). While these videos did not include rape myth depictions, in which women initially resist but then enjoy being forced to have sex, the videos were dominated by scenes in which women willingly subjected themselves to verbal and physical assault.

Of course, the Internet offers far more than pornography, and at least some of the research on online sexual health information suggests that teenagers (and others) searching online for sexual health information should be able to find accurate information. For instance, one study examining information provided through 177 sexual health websites determined that most of the information provided was accurate. However, websites providing technically complex information (e.g., information about contraception and STDs) and those dealing with controversial topics (e.g., abortion, emergency contraception) were most likely to be inaccurate, with nearly half (46.2%) of the websites providing contraceptive information containing at least one inaccuracy; more than a quarter (26.2%) of the websites providing information about STDs or HIV included at least one inaccuracy. The authors also assessed whether the websites met 15 criteria commonly used to judge website quality (e.g., date of last update identified, providing clear information about information sources), and found that the average score across all 177 websites was only 6.8, meaning that most websites met fewer than half of the quality criteria. Website quality and accuracy were not significantly related (Buhi et al., 2010).

A more recent review of 29 websites dedicated specifically to educating teens about health or sexual health revealed that all of the sites had deficiencies related to usability, authority and interactivity. A privately funded site, Scarleteen.com, had the highest score for educational content, followed by the Planned Parenthood site, but many of the sites that scored highly on educational content had lower interactivity scores, and vice versa. Only two of the 29 sites were mobile phone compatible. Nonetheless, the authors concluded that the available content "has the potential to make a positive and beneficial impact on adolescent health" (Whiteley et al., 2012, p. 212). This finding is encouraging, given that one in five young adults (21%) who use the Internet at all report that they search online for sexual health information. Similar percentages of teens (22%) say they use the Internet to look for information on topics that are difficult to discuss, including sexual health, depression and drug use (Lenhart et al., 2009).

THE EFFECTS OF EXPOSURE TO SEXUAL MEDIA CONTENT

Given the frequency and problematic nature of the sexual content to which adolescents (and adults) are exposed through many media channels, it's not surprising that health advocates, researchers and parents have been keenly interested in understanding the impact of this exposure on sex-related attitudes and behaviors, especially among adolescents. Numerous studies have examined these potential relationships, with particular attention to the impacts of television (Aubrey, 2007; Chandra et al., 2008; Gottfried et al., 2013; Tolman et al., 2007; Ward & Friedman, 2006), movies (O'Hara et al., 2012) and music or music videos (Aubrey et al., 2011; DiClemente et al., 2013; Kaestle et al., 2007; Kistler & Lee, 2009; Martino et al., 2006). Some studies have examined the impacts of multiple types of media simultaneously (Bleakley et al., 2008; Brown et al., 2006; Pardun et al., 2005; Steinberg & Monahan, 2011), and several researchers have conducted systematic reviews of the literature (Brown et al., 2005; L'Engle et al., 2006; Ward, 2003; Wright, 2011). While the strength of effects has varied and some studies have examined the relationships between media exposure and attitudes, rather than sexual behavior, only one of the articles listed above has concluded that exposure to mass media has no impact on the early initiation of sexual intercourse (Steinberg & Monahan, 2011).

The most recent systematic analysis of the media and sex research focused on answering the question of whether the data justify the conclusion that exposure to mass media's sexual content has a *causal* effect on youth sexual behavior (Wright, 2011). In other words, it is not enough to know that a correlation exists between exposure to mass-mediated sexual content and sexual behaviors because a correlation could reflect selection of more sexual content among sexually active youth or the impact of some external factor that drives both exposure to sexual content and sexual behavior. Wright (2011) therefore examined the research for evidence of covariation, temporal sequencing (media exposure precedes the behavior in question) and nonspuriousness, which requires that alternative explanations for the relationship between media exposure and sexual behavior are systematically tested and rejected.

In his review, Wright identified five themes or types of outcome variables that have been linked to exposure to media sexual content: coital status (whether or not the individual had ever had sexual intercourse), sexual experience including but not limited to sexual intercourse, non-coital sexual experience, number of sexual partners and experiences with contraceptive use, STDs and pregnancy. The studies reviewed included nine longitudinal surveys and 12 cross-sectional surveys, with 16 of the studies involving adolescents and the remaining studies focused on young adults. Of the eight studies for which coital status was the key outcome variable, all five longitudinal studies confirmed a main or moderated effect for mass media exposure.

For instance, one study using a national sample of 1,792 teenagers interviewed in 2001 and 2002 showed that Time 1 exposure to sexual television content was a significant predictor of having had intercourse for the first time, as well as the likelihood of engaging in more "advanced" non-intercourse sexual behavior, by the second wave of the survey; these effects held even after controlling for baseline sexual behavior, age, having older friends, parental education and monitoring, household structure, academic achievement, religiosity, mental health, sensation seeking and involvement in deviant behavior. The authors of this study found that teens whose consumption of sexual content on TV was one standard deviation higher than average "behaved sexually like youths who were 9 to 17 months older but watched average amounts of sex on TV"; they concluded that "a moderate shift in the average sexual content of adolescent TV viewing could have substantial effects on sexual behavior at the population level" (Collins et al., 2004, p. 287).

Another longitudinal study, involving 1,107 North Carolina youth surveyed at ages 12 to 14 and again at ages 14 to 16 tested the associations between the teens' sexual behaviors and their "sexual media diets," a measure that reflects not only how frequently teens are exposed to television, music, movies and magazines but also the sexual content of the specific media they use. Exposure to media sexual content predicted intercourse initiation by Time 2 for white teens, even after controlling for numerous other variables, including baseline sexual behavior, socioeconomic status, parental education, parents' disapproval of sex and perceived permissiveness of peer sexual norms. Compared to white teens in the lowest quintile for exposure to sexual media content, white teens in the highest quintile were 2.2 times more likely to have initiated sexual intercourse by the second wave of the study. The authors note, too, that one of the strongest predictors of sexual initiation for both black and white teens was believing that one's peers are having sex – a factor that also may be influenced by media exposure (Brown et al., 2006).

A third longitudinal study, based on two waves of an online survey of teens aged 14 to 16 when first recruited, collected complete data from 501 teens. The data analysis revealed that exposure to sexual media content is both a cause and an effect of sexual behavior. The more sexually active the teens were, the more likely they were to be exposed to sexual content in the media, and greater exposure to sex in the media – controlling for previous sexual activity – increased their likelihood of sexual activity progression. The authors conclude that their findings are "consistent with others in the literature that demonstrate a causal effect of sexual content on sexual behavior" (Bleakley et al., 2008, p. 458). Interestingly, the research team found a positive relationship between parental disapproval of teen sex and teens' exposure to media sexual content. Parental disapproval of sexual behavior was associated (non-significantly) with less sexual behavior, but it was also associated with *greater* exposure to sexual media content, which, in turn, led to more involvement in sexual activity.

In addition to documenting the relationships between exposure to media sexual content and initiation of sexual intercourse, researchers have established that consumption of "sexy" media is also linked to non-intercourse sexual behaviors, including kissing, petting and oral sex (Brown et al., 2006; Brown & L'Engle, 2009; Collins et al., 2004; Pardun et al., 2005). These non-coital behaviors are important because they may lead to sexual intercourse but also because oral sex, which is more common than sexual intercourse among teenagers (Halpern-Felsher et al., 2005) and college students (Chambers, 2007), can lead to STD transmission (Edwards & Carne, 1998).

Adolescents' consumption of sexual media content is also associated with an increased likelihood of having multiple sex partners, another behavior that increases the risk of STDs (Kelley et al., 2003; Rosenberg et al., 1999) and involvement in an unwanted pregnancy (Lau et al., 2015). Greater exposure to rap music videos was linked to a greater likelihood of having multiple sex partners among black female adolescents (14 to 18 years old); girls who spent more time watching rap videos during the first wave of the study were twice as likely to report multiple sex partners during the second wave, compared to girls who had lower levels of rap music video exposure (Wingood et al., 2003). Cross-sectional studies also have linked exposure to and attitudes toward media portrayals of sex with an increased likelihood of having multiple sex partners, with increased risk of multiple partners related to television use (Fabes & Strouse, 1987; Strouse & Buerkel-Rothfuss, 1987), exposure to men's magazines (Ward et al., 2011), mainstream movies (Ward et al., 2011), X-rated movies (Wingood et al., 2001) and sexually explicit websites (Braun-Courville & Rojas, 2009; Wright & Randall, 2012).

Given the rarity of mass media providing realistic portrayals of contraceptive use, efforts to protect against STDs or the consequences of unsafe sex, it should not be surprising that some research suggests that exposure to sexual content in the media has been linked to a decreased likelihood of using condoms or other contraceptives consistently and an increased risk of contracting an STD or being involved in an unintended pregnancy. As early as 1988, Solderman and colleagues (1988) found that pregnant teen girls reported greater exposure to soap operas, prime-time TV and R-rated movies containing sexual content than did non-pregnant girls. Another cross-sectional study revealed that among 2,307 youth aged 16 to 20, those who more frequently watched professional wrestling were more likely to engage in a variety of risk behaviors, including having sexual intercourse without using a contraceptive method (DuRant et al., 2008).

Strong evidence of a link between mass media exposure and unsafe sex and its consequences also have come from the lone longitudinal study to have examined these relationships. Using data collected from youth in 2001, 2002 and 2004, Chandra et al. (2008) examined the impact of TV sexual content on the likelihood of becoming pregnant. The data showed that, after controlling for age, school performance, race, education goals, intentions to have a child before age 22, parent education, household structure and involvement in deviant behaviors, youth with the highest levels of exposure to sexy media content were twice as likely as those with the lowest levels of media exposure to have become pregnant or to have impregnated someone.

Based on his systematic review of the research linking exposure to mass media content with problematic sexual behavior among youth, Wright (2011) concluded that "the mass media almost certainly exerts a causal influence on youths' sexual behavior" because "[t]he research to date clearly met the covariation and temporal-sequencing criteria and passed the threshold of substantiation for the nonspuriousness requirement" (p. 373). He argues that researchers are unlikely to identify an external variable that would completely account for the media exposure–sexual behavior link because researchers already have addressed and rejected an extremely wide array of potential confounders drawn from an extensive literature on the biological and environmental drivers of adolescents' sexual behavior. Existing theory, supported by extensive research, provides a strong conceptual explanation for the mechanisms by which mass media may influence sexual behavior, including recognizing experimentally documented impacts of sexy media content on sex-related attitudes and intentions. In addition, he notes that many studies of media effects have produced substantial effect sizes, even when controlling for numerous other relevant variables, meaning that it is unlikely that some other variable that was not included would have enough impact to nullify the impact of media exposure.

Perhaps one of the best arguments, however, is simply that the preponderance of published research supports the claim that exposure to the sexual content in mass media does have an influence on sexual attitudes and beliefs, and subsequently on behaviors. Studies examining the impact of mass media sexual content have employed large, geographically and racially diverse samples, and have adhered to rigorous standards for data collection and analysis. Wright (2011) argues, therefore, that whether exposure to mainstream media sexual content influences sexual behavior – at least among youth – is no longer in question.

Given the strong association between exposure to mainstream media sexual content and sexual behavior, it seems likely that exposure to sexually explicit content, either via traditional pornography channels such as magazines and videos or through online pornography, also would affect sexual health behavior. Researchers have indeed documented an association between the use of pornography and sexual risk behaviors among both heterosexuals and homosexuals (Braithwaite et al., 2015; Eaton et al., 2012; Morgan, 2011; Peter & Valkenburg, 2011; Wright & Randall, 2012). A recent systematic review of the research on this topic identified significant links between use of both online and general pornography and the likelihood of engaging in unsafe sex practices, including having more sex partners (Harkness et al., 2015); the review noted, however, that limitations in the quality of this body of research mean that additional replication, using more rigorous methods, is needed.

MEDIA EFFECTS ON SEXUAL AGGRESSION AND SEXUAL VIOLENCE

Two characteristics are worth noting in relation to the research described in the previous section. One is that the vast majority of these studies have focused on media effects on youth; with the exception of the research on pornography, the oldest participants included in these studies have been college students or other "emerging adults" – no older than their early twenties. Another is that these studies have focused almost exclusively on consensual sexual behavior. The assumption of much of the research, it seems, is that mainstream media portrayals of sex are far more likely to affect adolescents than adults, presumably because adults generally have more real-world sexual experience to which they can compare the media portrayals. In addition, many, if not most, of these studies seem to make the assumption that adolescents and young adults have limited exposure to media portrayals of sexual violence.

However, as noted earlier, researchers have identified both mainstream and pornographic media content that objectifies women, presents male sexual desires and fantasies as more important than women's needs, and even, in some cases, includes portrayals that normalize male sexual aggression and violence (Aubrey & Frisby, 2011; Beasley & Collins Standley, 2002; Klaassen & Peter, 2014; Vannier et al., 2014; Weitzer & Kubrin, 2009). Do these media influence consumers' sexual attitudes and behaviors, especially those related to sexual violence?

Several studies have examined the impact of exposure to sexually aggressive music lyrics and/or images on audience attitudes related to sexual violence and gender stereotypes. For instance, an experimental study of college undergraduates showed that male participants who watched highly sexual content in hip-hop videos subsequently expressed attitudes reflecting more objectification of women and rape myth acceptance, compared to men who had seen less sexualized hip-hop videos (Kistler & Lee, 2009). Another experimental study among male undergraduates showed that those who saw videos in which female artists were portrayed in highly objectified ways subsequently reported more adversarial sexual beliefs and acceptance of interpersonal violence, compared to men who watched the same artists in non-objectifying videos (Aubrey et al., 2011). Among middle school boys, researchers found that frequency of watching music videos was associated with reporting more rape acceptance; after controlling for weekly TV exposure, parenting style and demographic characteristics, boys who watched music videos at least once per week were 10 percent less likely than those who watched no music videos to agree that it is never acceptable to force a romantic partner to have sex (Kaestle et al., 2007). Finally, in a longitudinal study of youth who were 10 to 15 years old when first surveyed, Ybarra and colleagues (2014) found that greater exposure to sexual media during the previous year was associated with greater likelihood of having been sexually victimized.

Because content analysis of pornography has shown such a high prevalence of scenes objectifying women, researchers have investigated the links between exposure to pornography and sexually coercive attitudes and behaviors. This research has revealed that, especially among men who already tend toward aggressive behavior, exposure to pornography increases sexually violent attitudes and behaviors (Hald et al., 2010; Malamuth et al., 2000; Vega & Malamuth, 2007). Use of pornography appears to promote attitudes that support violence against women, and these attitudes increase the likelihood that sexual aggression and coercion will occur (Hald et al., 2010).

One survey of college males (18 to 29 years old) suggests that pornography influences male viewers' sexual scripts, which they subsequently attempt to employ in their real-world interactions. The researchers found that greater exposure to pornography increased the likelihood that college men would view pornography during sexual encounters, ask their partners to re-create acts they had seen in the pornography and deliberately think about pornography to maintain arousal during sex. In addition, the study showed that, after controlling for relevant covariates, pornography consumption was significantly and negatively correlated with enjoyment of intimate behaviors such as cuddling, kissing and caressing with their sexual partners. This study did not include questions about sexually coercive behaviors, but the findings support the idea that frequent exposure to pornography leads men to adopt the sexual scripts pornography includes (Sun et al., 2014).

A survey of college fraternity members revealed that fraternity men's use of pornography was linked to acceptance of rape myths and decreased willingness to intervene to prevent a sexual assault. In addition, men who watched more mainstream pornography, sadomasochistic pornography and pornography depicting rape reported greater likelihood of sexually assaulting or raping a woman if they were certain they would not be caught or punished. The effects were especially strong for men who viewed sadomasochistic or rape pornography. As the researchers note, "this does not mean that all men who view pornography will commit rape, [but] it does raise concern about the increased risk that viewing mainstream pornography has for men's intent to commit sexual violence" (Foubert et al., 2011, p. 222).

A meta-analysis of non-experimental research on pornography effects confirmed that pornography consumption is a significant predictor of attitudes supporting violence against women among men who have not been convicted of any sex crime. The correlation between the use of sexually violent pornography and rape-supportive attitudes was stronger than that between non-violent pornography and rape-supportive attitudes; however, even consumption of non-violent pornography was significantly and positively correlated with holding attitudes likely to lead to sexual aggression (Hald et al., 2010).

Relatively few studies seem to have linked pornography use to sexually coercive behavior among men who have not been convicted of rape. However, one recent study of college men did make that link. More than one-third of college men surveyed for the study acknowledged coercing a date into oral sex or sexual intercourse after she had indicated that she was not interested; 8 percent of the men admitted to physically restraining a woman to force her to have sex. Men who were more frequent consumers of pornography were more likely to use sexual coercion with female partners. Men who had experienced harsh corporal punishment in their family of origin were more likely to engage in sexual victimization, but only if they were also frequent consumers of pornography (Simons et al., 2012).

Some especially disturbing research suggests that the use of pornography increases recidivism rates among convicted child molesters. One Canadian study found that frequent pornography use by high-risk offenders was a strong predictor of subsequent recidivism, and the use of pornography portraying deviant behavior increased the risk of future violent and sexually violent behavior. For those who watched deviant pornography, the odds of subsequent violent and sexually violent crime increased 185 to 233 percent, depending on which other variables were included in the model (Kingston et al., 2008).

The bottom line appears to be that exposure to pornography, which so consistently depicts women as objects to be used for men's sexual gratification regardless of the woman's desires or even her suffering, increases the likelihood that viewers will adopt attitudes and even behaviors consistent with those shown in the pornographic materials. As Foubert et al. (2011) note, increased exposure to pornography focuses attention on the impersonal, instant gratification aspects of sexual interaction, and denigrates the connection between intercourse and emotional intimacy:

> It is not surprising then that such men would be more likely to do something sexual with a woman who is unwilling if they have been habituated to a medium where the scripts reinforce that the desire of the woman is not important, that women are there to service men's needs at all times, and the women are merely objects to be penetrated.
>
> (Foubert et al., 2011, p. 225)

At one time it was fairly easy to draw clear distinctions between the portrayals of human sexual interaction found in pornography, especially sexually violent pornography, and those found in mainstream media. Like pornography, mainstream media might objectify women by focusing on appearance, rather than intellect, as their most important characteristics, and it might portray casual sexual relationships as normative. However, unlike pornography, mainstream media would not include graphic, close-up images of genitalia; nor was it likely to include scenes depicting sadomasochism, bondage and physical and emotional abuse as normal, acceptable aspects of a romantic relationship. The immense popularity of the *Fifty Shades of Grey* books and movie and the often sexually violent TV hit *Game of Thrones* raises the question of whether the latter distinction has begun to fade.

New Media as Sexual Health Educator

In the realm of entertainment media, there seems to be little good news regarding effects on sexual health or sexual behavior. The research fairly consistently supports the notion that exposure to media portrayals of sexual behavior has negative effects, namely encouraging earlier initiation of sexual intercourse, discouraging the use of contraceptives, increasing the likelihood that individuals will have multiple sexual partners and engage in other behaviors that increase their risk of contracting STDs; in relation to some types of media, particularly rap and heavy metal music and pornography, the negative impact extends to fostering attitudes and behaviors that lead to coercive and even criminal behavior in the form of sexual harassment, sexual assault and rape.

However, this discussion would be incomplete if it did not acknowledge some positive effects. First, there is some evidence that although lesbian, gay, bisexual and transgender characters remain uncommon in the media, representing just 4.4 percent of all characters on regularly scripted broadcast TV, that number represents an increase over previous years. During the 2012/2013 series, there were 48 sexual minority characters in regularly scripted roles in broadcast TV, and 56 regular and recurring LGBT characters in cable network programs (GLAAD, 2012). This increasing visibility of LGBT characters seems to be contributing to the growing acceptance of homosexuality (Bonds-Raacke et al., 2007; Calzo & Ward, 2009) and also may provide models and inspiration for LGBT individuals in the real world (Gomillion & Giuliano, 2011).

In addition, some research has suggested that the Internet has the potential to help fill the "sex education gap" that faces growing numbers of adolescents today, increasing the likelihood that they will be able to find accurate and useful information about contraceptives, STDs and other sexual health issues even as increasing numbers of schools have turned to "abstinence-only" sex education programs that often exclude such information. A recent Kaiser Family Foundation survey of teens showed that 28 percent say they obtain sexual or reproductive health information from the Internet – a higher percentage than those reporting getting such information from health care providers (21%) (Kaiser Family Foundation, 2014).

There are limitations, however, to the Internet's usefulness as a sexual health information source. One study of high school students suggested that teens may use the Internet for sexual health information but remain wary of its content and find it difficult to sort through the enormous amounts of sex-related information (including pornography) to find the information they need (Jones & Biddlecom, 2011a, 2011b). Another showed that undergraduates could use online resources to find accurate answers to sexual health questions, but the authors stressed that young people need to be educated about how to make the most effective use of online sexual health information resources (Buhi et al., 2009).

A series of focus group interviews with 14- to 19-year-old females showed that the teens were enthusiastic about the possibilities of obtaining sexual health information through social networking sites and text messages because it would make such information easily accessible. They were concerned, however, not only about the trustworthiness of the information they could find online but also about ensuring the protection of their privacy when searching for sexual health information. In addition, they wanted sexual health information to be provided in non-threatening ways; they did not want to be lectured to or intimidated (Selkie et al., 2011). A much larger study, involving an online survey of 5,542 Internet users aged 13 to 18, echoed the importance of privacy in youths' searching for sexual health information online. Although privacy and curiosity were the most important reasons the teens offered for seeking sexual health information online, sexual minority youth were also likely to report that they had no alternative sources from which to seek sexual health information (Mitchell et al., 2014).

A survey of 34 teenage boys and girls who had used the Teen Sexual Health Information Facebook page created by researchers at Creighton University showed that 58 percent said the site helped them learn more about STIs. Another 15 percent mentioned that the site provided good sexual health information in general, and 12 percent mentioned learning about specific STI testing locations. Half of the teens identified additional questions they would like the site to answer, such as providing information for pregnant teens and explaining how much the medications used to treat STIs would cost (Yager & O'Keefe, 2012).

The research on online sexual health information suggests – but has not yet confirmed – that the Internet, as well as mobile technologies such as texting, could have a positive impact on adolescents' and adults' sexual health, especially as more and more people carry smartphones that give them immediate access to the Internet wherever they are. However, for online sexual health information resources to be useful, individuals must recognize gaps in their knowledge and be willing and able to search for those answers online. Unfortunately, people may not always recognize their lack of knowledge about sexual health subjects. For instance, one study of Louisiana college students demonstrated that those who rated their previous sex education most highly had the *lowest* levels of actual sexual health knowledge (Synovitz et al., 2002). Another study of adolescents' knowledge about correct condom use revealed that misconceptions about condom use were common and that there was little relationship between perceived knowledge and actual knowledge (Crosby & Yarber, 2001).

The problem, therefore, may be that frequent exposure to portrayals of sexual behavior via the mass media may lead audiences to *believe* they are well informed about key sexual health issues, including the risks of unwanted pregnancy and STIs associated with unprotected sex, when in fact they are ill informed. If that is the case, they will have little motivation to seek additional sexual health information online, especially when doing so may lead to unwanted exposure to pornography. In addition, for teenagers, the fact that Google and other search engines now track search terms and subsequently display advertising related to those search terms means that teens conducting legitimate searches for sexual health information may find their Facebook news feeds and space around other "innocent" websites (e.g., shopping sites or email) surrounded by sex-related ads. Additional research will be needed to determine the circumstances under which individuals are able to make effective use of online sexual health information resources.

REFERENCES

Alan Guttmacher Institute. (2015). *Fact Sheet: Unintended Pregnancy in the United States*. Washington, DC: Alan Guttmacher Institute.

Alter, C. (2015, February 15). "50 Shades of Grey" Has Best Presidents Day Box Office Opening in History. *Time*. Retrieved March 9, 2015 from http://time.com/3710416/fifty-shades-box-office-opening/.

American Teens' Sexual and Reproductive Health. (2014, May). Retrieved March 10, 2015 from www.guttmacher.org/pubs/FB-ATSRH.html#10a.

Aubrey, J.S. (2007). Does Television Exposure Influence College-aged Women's Sexual Self-concept? *Media Psychology*, *10*(2), 157–181. http://doi.org/10.1080/15213260701375561.

Aubrey, J.S. & Frisby, C.M. (2011). Sexual Objectification in Music Videos: A Content Analysis Comparing Gender and Genre. *Mass Communication and Society*, *14*(4), 475–501. http://doi.org/10.1080/15205436.2010.513468.

Aubrey, J.S., Hopper, K.M. & Mbure, W.G. (2011). Check That Body! The Effects of Sexually Objectifying Music Videos on College Men's Sexual Beliefs. *Journal of Broadcasting & Electronic Media*, *55*(3), 360–379. http://doi.org/10.1080/08838151.2011.597469.

Beasley, B. & Collins Standley, T. (2002). Shirts vs. Skins: Clothing as an Indicator of Gender Role Stereotyping in Video Games. *Mass Communication and Society*, *5*(3), 279–293. http://doi.org/10.1207/S15327825MCS0503_3.

Beaumont-Thomas, B. (2015). Fifty Shades of Grey Protests Escalate. Retrieved March 9, 2015 from www.theguardian.com/film/2015/feb/10/fifty-shades-of-grey-protests-imax.

Bleakley, A., Romer, D. & Jamieson, P.E. (2014). Violent Film Characters' Portrayal of Alcohol, Sex, and Tobacco-related Behaviors. *Pediatrics*, *133*(1), 71–77. http://doi.org/10.1542/peds.2013-1922.

Bleakley, A., Hennessy, M., Fishbein, M. & Jordan, A. (2008). It Works Both Ways: The Relationship Between Exposure to Sexual Content in the Media and Adolescent Sexual Behavior. *Media Psychology*, *11*(4), 443–461. http://doi.org/10.1080/15213260802491986.

Bonds-Raacke, J.M., Cady, E.T., Schlegel, R., Harris, R.J. & Firebaugh, L. (2007). Remembering Gay/Lesbian Media Characters. *Journal of Homosexuality*, *53*(3), 19–34. http://doi.org/10.1300/J082v53n03_03.

Bosman, J. (2014, February 26). For "Fifty Shades of Grey," More Than 100 Million Sold. *New York Times*. Retrieved March 9, 2015 from www.nytimes.com/2014/02/27/business/media/for-fifty-shades-of-grey-more-than-100-million-sold.html.

Braithwaite, S.R., Coulson, G., Keddington, K. & Fincham, F.D. (2015). The Influence of Pornography on Sexual Scripts and Hooking up among Emerging Adults in College. *Archives of Sexual Behavior*, *44*(1), 111–123. http://doi.org/10.1007/s10508-014-0351-x.

Braun-Courville, D.K. & Rojas, M. (2009). Exposure to Sexually Explicit Web Sites and Adolescent Sexual Attitudes and Behaviors. *Journal of Adolescent Health*, *45*(2), 156–162. http://doi.org/10.1016/j.jadohealth.2008.12.004.

Bridges, A.J., Wosnitzer, R., Scharrer, E., Sun, C. & Liberman, R. (2010). Aggression and Sexual Behavior in Best-selling Pornography Videos: A Content Analysis Update. *Violence Against Women, 16*(10), 1065–1085. http://doi.org/10.1177/1077801210382866.

Brown, J.D. & L'Engle, K.L. (2009). X-rated Sexual Attitudes and Behaviors Associated With U.S. Early Adolescents' Exposure to Sexually Explicit Media. *Communication Research, 36*(1), 129–151. http://doi.org/10.1177/0093650208326465.

Brown, J.D., Halpern, C.T. & L'Engle, K.L. (2005). Mass Media as a Sexual Super Peer for Early Maturing Girls. *Journal of Adolescent Health, 36*(5), 420–427. http://doi.org/10.1016/j.jadohealth.2004.06.003.

Brown, J.D., L'Engle, K.L., Pardun, C.J., Guo, G., Kenneavy, K. & Jackson, C. (2006). Sexy Media Matter: Exposure to Sexual Content in Music, Movies, Television, and Magazines Predicts Black and White Adolescents' Sexual Behavior. *Pediatrics, 117*(4), 1018–1027. http://doi.org/10.1542/peds.2005-1406.

Bufkin, J. & Eschholz, S. (2000). Images of Sex and Rape: A Content Analysis of Popular Film. *Violence Against Women, 6*(12), 1317–1344. http://doi.org/10.1177/1077801200006012002.

Buhi, E.R., Daley, E.M., Fuhrmann, H.J. & Smith, S.A. (2009). An Observational Study of How Young People Search for Online Sexual Health Information. *Journal of American College Health, 58*(2), 101–111. http://doi.org/10.1080/07448480903221236.

Buhi, E.R., Daley, E.M., Oberne, A., Smith, S.A., Schneider, T. & Fuhrmann, H.J. (2010). Quality and Accuracy of Sexual Health Information Web Sites Visited by Young People. *Journal of Adolescent Health, 47*(2), 206–208. http://doi.org/10.1016/j.jadohealth.2010.01.002.

Calzo, J.P. & Ward, L.M. (2009). Media Exposure and Viewers' Attitudes Toward Homosexuality: Evidence for Mainstreaming or Resonance? *Journal of Broadcasting & Electronic Media, 53*(2), 280–299. http://doi.org/10.1080/08838150902908049.

Centers for Disease Control and Prevention. (2013). *Incidence, Prevalence, and Cost of Sexually Transmitted Infections in the United States*. Atlanta, GA. Retrieved March 10, 2015 from www.cdc.gov/std/stats/sti-estimates-fact-sheet-feb-2013.pdf.

Centers for Disease Control and Prevention. (2014a). *CDC Fact Sheet: Reported STDs in the United States – 2013 National Data for Chlamydia, Gonorrhea, and Syphilis*. Atlanta, GA. Retrieved March 10, 2015 from www.cdc.gov/nchhstp/newsroom/docs/std-trends-508.pdf.

Centers for Disease Control and Prevention. (2014b). *Genital HPV Infection – CDC Fact Sheet*. Atlanta, GA. Retrieved March 10, 2015 from www.cdc.gov/std/hpv/hpv-factsheet-march-2014.pdf.

Centers for Disease Control and Prevention. (2014c). *HIV in the United States: At a Glance*. Atlanta, GA. Retrieved March 10, 2015 from www.cdc.gov/hiv/pdf/statistics_basics_ataglance_factsheet.pdf.

Chambers, W.C. (2007). Oral Sex: Varied Behaviors and Perceptions in a College Population. *Journal of Sex Research, 44*(1), 28–42. http://doi.org/10.1080/00224490709336790.

Chandra, A., Martino, S.C., Collins, R.L., Elliott, M.N., Berry, S.H., Kanouse, D.E. & Miu, A. (2008). Does Watching Sex on Television Predict Teen Pregnancy? Findings From a National Longitudinal Survey of Youth. *Pediatrics, 122*(5), 1047–1054. http://doi.org/10.1542/peds.2007-3066.

Chen, X.-K., Wen, S.W., Fleming, N., Demissie, K., Rhoads, G.G. & Walker, M. (2007). Teenage Pregnancy and Adverse Birth Outcomes: A Large Population Based Retrospective Cohort Study. *International Journal of Epidemiology, 36*(2), 368–373. http://doi.org/10.1093/ije/dyl284.

Clarke, J. (2009). Women's Work, Worry and Fear: The Portrayal of Sexuality and Sexual

Health in US Magazines for Teenage and Middle-aged Women, 2000-2007. *Culture, Health & Sexuality, 11*(4), 415-429. http://doi.org/10.1080/13691050902780776.

Collins, R.L., Elliott, M.N., Berry, S.H., Kanouse, D.E., Kunkel, D., Hunter, S.B. & Miu, A. (2004). Watching Sex on Television Predicts Adolescent Initiation of Sexual Behavior. *Pediatrics, 114*(3), e280-289. http://doi.org/10.1542/peds.2003-1065-L.

Conrad, K., Dixon, T.L. & Zhang, Y. (2009). Controversial Rap Themes, Gender Portrayals and Skin Tone Distortion: A Content Analysis of Rap Music Videos. *Journal of Broadcasting & Electronic Media, 53*(1), 134-156. http://doi.org/10.1080/08838150802643795.

Crosby, R.A. & Yarber, W.L. (2001). Perceived Versus Actual Knowledge about Correct Condom Use among U.S. Adolescents: Results from a National Study. *Journal of Adolescent Health, 28*(5), 415-420. http://doi.org/10.1016/S1054-139X(00)00213-5.

Cross, K.A. (2014). Ethics for Cyborgs: On Real Harassment in an "Unreal" Place. *Loading…, 8*(13). Retrieved March 16, 2015 from http://journals.sfu.ca/loading/index.php/loading/article/view/140.

Cuklanz, L.M. (2000). *Rape on Prime Time: Television, Masculinity, and Sexual Violence.* Philadelphia: University of Pennsylvania Press.

DiClemente, R.J., Alexander, A.O., Braxton, N.D., Ricks, J.M. & Seth, P. (2013). African-American Men's Exposure to Music Videos and their Sexual Attitudes and Risk Behaviour. *Sexual Health, 10*(3), 279-281. http://doi.org/10.1071/SH12176.

Dill, K.E. (2009). Violent Video Games, Rape Myth Acceptance, and Negative Attitudes toward Women. *Violence against Women in Families and Relationships, 4,* 125-140.

DuRant, R.H., Neiberg, R., Champion, H., Rhodes, S.D. & Wolfson, M. (2008). Viewing Professional Wrestling on Television and Engaging in Violent and other Health Risk Behaviors. *Southern Medical Journal, 101*(2), 129-137. http://doi.org/10.1097/SMJ.0b013e31815d247d.

Eaton, L.A., Cain, D.N., Pope, H., Garcia, J. & Cherry, C. (2012). The Relationship between Pornography Use and Sexual Behaviours among At-risk HIV-negative Men Who Have Sex With Men. *Sexual Health, 9*(2), 166-170. http://doi.org/10.1071/SH10092.

Edwards, S. & Carne, C. (1998). Oral Sex and the Transmission of Viral STIs. *Sexually Transmitted Infections, 74*(1), 6-10. http://doi.org/10.1136/sti.74.1.6.

Eyal, K. & Finnerty, K. (2007). The Portrayal of Sexual Intercourse on Prime-time Programming. *Communication Research Reports, 24*(3), 225-233. http://doi.org/10.1080/08824090701439125.

Eyal, K., & Finnerty, K. (2009). The Portrayal of Sexual Intercourse on Television: How, Who, and With What Consequence? *Mass Communication and Society, 12*(2), 143-169. http://doi.org/10.1080/15205430802136713.

Fabes, R.A. & Strouse, J. (1987). Perceptions of Responsible and Irresponsible Models of Sexuality: A Correlational Study. *The Journal of Sex Research, 23*(1), 70-84. http://doi.org/10.1080/00224498709551342.

Fact Sheet: Contraceptve Use in the United States. (2014, June). Retrieved July 30, 2016 from www.guttmacher.org/pubs/fb_contr_use.html.

Foubert, J.D., Brosi, M.W. & Bannon, R.S. (2011). Pornography Viewing among Fraternity Men: Effects on Bystander Intervention, Rape Myth Acceptance and Behavioral Intent to Commit Sexual Assault. *Sexual Addiction & Compulsivity, 18*(4), 212-231. http://doi.org/10.1080/10720162.2011.625552.

GLAAD. (2012). *Where We Are on TV Report: 2012–2013 Season* (Text). Retrieved March 24, 2015 from www.glaad.org/publications/whereweareontv12.

Gomillion, S.C. & Giuliano, T.A. (2011). The Influence of Media Role Models on Gay, Lesbian, and Bisexual Identity. *Journal of Homosexuality, 58*(3), 330–354. http://doi.org/10.1080/00918369.2011.546729.

Gottfried, J.A., Vaala, S.E., Bleakley, A., Hennessy, M. & Jordan, A. (2013). Does the Effect of Exposure to TV Sex on Adolescent Sexual Behavior Vary by Genre? *Communication Research, 40*(1). http://doi.org/10.1177/0093650211415399.

Hald, G.M., Malamuth, N.M. & Yuen, C. (2010). Pornography and Attitudes Supporting Violence against Women: Revisiting the Relationship in Nonexperimental Studies. *Aggressive Behavior, 36*(1), 14–20. http://doi.org/10.1002/ab.20328.

Halpern-Felsher, B.L., Cornell, J.L., Kropp, R.Y. & Tschann, J.M. (2005). Oral Versus Vaginal Sex Among Adolescents: Perceptions, Attitudes, and Behavior. *Pediatrics, 115*(4), 845–851. http://doi.org/10.1542/peds.2004-2108.

Hamblin, J. (2014, March 29). How Not to Talk About the Culture of Sexual Assault. Retrieved March 10, 2015 from www.theatlantic.com/health/archive/2014/03/how-not-to-talk-about-the-culture-of-sexual-assault/359845/.

Harkness, E.L., Mullan, B.M. & Blaszczynski, A. (2015). Association between Pornography Use and Sexual Risk Behaviors in Adult Consumers: A Systematic Review. *Cyberpsychology, Behavior and Social Networking, 18*(2), 59–71. http://doi.org/10.1089/cyber.2014.0343.

Holley, P. (2015, February 23). College Student Accused of Rape Claims He Was Reenacting "Fifty Shades of Grey." *Washington Post.* Retrieved March 9, 2015 from www.washingtonpost.com/news/morning-mix/wp/2015/02/23/college-student-accused-of-rape-claims-he-was-reenacting-50-shades-of-grey/.

HPV and Cancer. (2012, March 15). Retrieved March 10, 2015 from www.cancer.gov/cancertopics/causes-prevention/risk-factors/infectious-agents/hpv-fact-sheet.

Hust, S.J.T., Brown, J.D. & L'Engle, K.L. (2008). Boys Will Be Boys and Girls Better Be Prepared: An Analysis of the Rare Sexual Health Messages in Young Adolescents' Media. *Mass Communication and Society, 11*(1), 3–23. http://doi.org/10.1080/15205430701668139.

Jones, J., Mosher, W., Daniels, K. et al. (2012). Current Contraceptive Use in the United States, 2006–2010, and Changes in Patterns of Use Since 1995. *National Health Statistics Reports, 60,* 1–25.

Jones, R.K. & Biddlecom, A.E. (2011a). Is the Internet Filling the Sexual Health Information Gap for Teens? An Exploratory Study. *Journal of Health Communication, 16*(2), 112–123. http://doi.org/10.1080/10810730.2010.535112.

Jones, R.K. & Biddlecom, A.E. (2011b). The More Things Change…: The Relative Importance of the Internet as a Source of Contraceptive Information for Teens. *Sexuality Research and Social Policy, 8*(1), 27–37. http://doi.org/10.1007/s13178-011-0039-0.

Kaestle, C.E., Halpern, C.T. & Brown, J.D. (2007). Music Videos, Pro Wrestling, and Acceptance of Date Rape among Middle School Males and Females: An Exploratory Analysis. *The Journal of Adolescent Health: Official Publication of the Society for Adolescent Medicine, 40*(2), 185–187. http://doi.org/10.1016/j.jadohealth.2006.08.010.

Kahlor, L. & Eastin, M.S. (2011). Television's Role in the Culture of Violence Toward Women: A Study of Television Viewing and the Cultivation of Rape Myth Acceptance in the United States. *Journal of Broadcasting & Electronic Media, 55*(2), 215–231. http://doi.org/10.1080/08838151.2011.566085.

Kaiser Family Foundation. (2014). *Sexual Health of Adolescents and Young Adults in the*

United States. Menlo Park, CA. Retrieved March 24, 2015 from http://kff.org/womens-health-policy/fact-sheet/sexual-health-of-adolescents-and-young-adults-in-the-united-states/.

Kelley, S.S., Borawski, E.A., Flocke, S.A. & Keen, K.J. (2003). The Role of Sequential and Concurrent Sexual Relationships in the Risk of Sexually Transmitted Diseases among Adolescents. *Journal of Adolescent Health, 32*(4), 296–305. http://doi.org/10.1016/S1054-139X(02)00710-3.

Kelly, M. (2010). Virginity Loss Narratives in "Teen Drama" Television Programs. *Journal of Sex Research, 47*(5), 479–489. http://doi.org/10.1080/00224490903132044.

Kingston, D.A., Fedoroff, P., Firestone, P., Curry, S. & Bradford, J.M. (2008). Pornography Use and Sexual Aggression: The Impact of Frequency and Type of Pornography Use on Recidivism among Sexual Offenders. *Aggressive Behavior, 34*(4), 341–351. http://doi.org/10.1002/ab.20250.

Kistler, M.E. & Lee, M.J. (2009). Does Exposure to Sexual Hip-Hop Music Videos Influence the Sexual Attitudes of College Students? *Mass Communication and Society, 13*(1), 67–86. http://doi.org/10.1080/15205430902865336.

Kitchens, C. (2014, March 20). It's Time to End "Rape Culture" Hysteria. *Time*. Retrieved March 10, 2015 from http://time.com/30545/its-time-to-end-rape-culture-hysteria/.

Klaassen, M.J.E. & Peter, J. (2014). Gender (In)equality in Internet Pornography: A Content Analysis of Popular Pornographic Internet Videos. *Journal of Sex Research*, 1–15. http://doi.org/10.1080/00224499.2014.976781.

Kunkel, D., Eyal, K., Finnerty, K., Biely, E., & Donnerstein, E. (2005). *Sex on TV 4*. Menlo Park, CA: Henry J. Kaiser Family Foundation. Retrieved March 17, 2015 from http://kff.org/other/event/sex-on-tv-4/.

Kunkel, D., Biely, E., Eyal, K., Cope-Farrar, K.M., Donnerstein, E. & Fandrich, R. (2003). *Sex on TV 3: A Biennial Report of the Kaiser Family Foundation*. Menlo Park, CA: Henry J. Kaiser Family Foundation.

Lau, M., Lin, H. & Flores, G. (2015). Clusters of Factors Identify a High Prevalence of Pregnancy Involvement among US Adolescent Males. *Maternal and Child Health Journal*. http://doi.org/10.1007/s10995-015-1685-2.

L'Engle, K.L., Brown, J.D. & Kenneavy, K. (2006). The Mass Media are an Important Context for Adolescents' Sexual Behavior. *Journal of Adolescent Health, 38*(3), 186–192. http://doi.org/10.1016/j.jadohealth.2005.03.020.

Lenhart, A., Madden, M., Smith, A. & Macgill, A.R. (2009). *Teens and Social Media: An Overview*. Washington, DC: Pew Internet and American Life. Retrieved March 19, 2015 from http://isites.harvard.edu/fs/docs/icb.topic786630.files/Teens%20Social%20Media%20and%20Health%20-%20NYPH%20Dept%20Pew%20Internet.pdf.

Malamuth, N.M., Addison, T. & Koss, M. (2000). Pornography and Sexual Aggression: Are There Reliable Effects and Can We Understand Them? *Annual Review of Sex Research, 11*, 26–91.

Martino, S.C., Collins, R.L., Elliott, M.N., Strachman, A., Kanouse, D.E. & Berry, S.H. (2006). Exposure to Degrading versus Nondegrading Music Lyrics and Sexual Behavior among Youth. *Pediatrics, 118*(2), e430–441. http://doi.org/10.1542/peds.2006-0131.

Maxwell, Z. (2014, March 27). Rape Culture Is Real. *Time*. Retrieved March 10, 2015 from http://time.com/40110/rape-culture-is-real/.

McNary, D. (2015, February 20). Box Office: "Fifty Shades" Still No. 1 Despite 70% Drop in Ticket Sales. Retrieved March 9, 2015 from http://variety.com/2015/film/news/box-office-fifty-shades-still-no-1-despite-70-drop-in-ticket-sales-1201437798/.

Ménard, A.D. & Kleinplatz, P.J. (2007). Twenty-one Moves Guaranteed to Make his Thighs go up in Flames: Depictions of "Great Sex" in Popular Magazines. *Sexuality & Culture*, *12*(1), 1–20. http://doi.org/10.1007/s12119-007-9013-7.

Mitchell, K.J., Ybarra, M.L., Korchmaros, J.D. & Kosciw, J.G. (2014). Accessing Sexual Health Information Online: Use, Motivations and Consequences for Youth with Different Sexual Orientations. *Health Education Research*, *29*(1), 147–157. http://doi.org/10.1093/her/cyt071.

Morgan, E.M. (2011). Associations between Young Adults' Use of Sexually Explicit Materials and Their Sexual Preferences, Behaviors, and Satisfaction. *The Journal of Sex Research*, *48*(6), 520–530. http://doi.org/10.1080/00224499.2010.543960.

Office of Adolescent Health. (2015, February 27). Reproductive Health: Teen Pregnancy and Childbearing. Retrieved March 10, 2015 from www.hhs.gov/ash/oah/.

O'Hara, R.E., Gibbons, F.X., Gerrard, M., Li, Z. & Sargent, J.D. (2012). Greater Exposure to Sexual Content in Popular Movies Predicts Earlier Sexual Debut and Increased Sexual Risk Taking. *Psychological Science*, *23*(9), 984–993. http://doi.org/10.1177/0956797611435529.

Ortiz, R.R. & Brooks, M.E. (2014). Getting What They Deserve? Consequences of Sexual Expression by Central Characters in Five Popular Television Teen Dramas in the United States. *Journal of Children and Media*, *8*(1), 40–52. http://doi.org/10.1080/17482798.2014.863477.

Pardun, C.J., L'Engle, K.L. & Brown, J.D. (2005). Linking Exposure to Outcomes: Early Adolescents' Consumption of Sexual Content in Six Media. *Mass Communication and Society*, *8*(2), 75–91. http://doi.org/10.1207/s15327825mcs0802_1.

Peter, J. & Valkenburg, P.M. (2011). The Influence of Sexually Explicit Internet Material on Sexual Risk Behavior: A Comparison of Adolescents and Adults. *Journal of Health Communication*, *16*(7), 750–765. http://doi.org/10.1080/10810730.2011.551996.

Reid-Brinkley, S.R. (2007). The Essence of Res(ex)pectability: Black Women's Negotiation of Black Femininity in Rap Music and Music Video. *Meridians: Feminism, Race, Transnationalism*, *8*(1), 236–260.

Reproductive Health – Data and Statistics. (2015, February 4). Retrieved March 9, 2015 from www.cdc.gov/reproductivehealth/data_stats/#Abortion.

Rosenberg, M.D., Gurvey, J., Adler, N., Dunlop, M.B. & Ellen, J. (1999). Concurrent Sex Partners and Risk for Sexually Transmitted Diseases. *Sexually Transmitted Diseases*, *26*(4), 208–212.

Saul, H. (2015, February 24). University Student Charged with Rape Claimed he was Re-enacting Fifty Shades of Grey Film. Retrieved March 9, 2015 from www.independent.co.uk/news/world/americas/university-student-charged-with-rape-claimed-he-was-reenacting-fifty-shades-of-grey-film-10066805.html.

Sedgh, G., Finer, L.B., Bankole, A., Eilers, M.A. & Singh, S. (2015). Adolescent Pregnancy, Birth, and Abortion Rates Across Countries: Levels and Recent Trends. *The Journal of Adolescent Health: Official Publication of the Society for Adolescent Medicine*, *56*(2), 223–230. http://doi.org/10.1016/j.jadohealth.2014.09.007.

Selkie, E.M., Benson, M. & Moreno, M. (2011). Adolescents' Views Regarding Uses of Social Networking Websites and Text Messaging for Adolescent Sexual Health Education. *American Journal of Health Education*, *42*(4), 205–212. http://doi.org/10.1080/19325037.2011.10599189.

Simons, L.G., Simons, R.L., Lei, M.-K. & Sutton, T.E. (2012). Exposure to Harsh Parenting and Pornography as Explanations for Males' Sexual Coercion and Females' Sexual Victimization. *Violence and Victims*, *27*(3), 378–395.

Solderman, A.K., Greenberg, B.S. & Linsangan, R. (1988). Television and Movie Behaviors of Pregnant and Non-pregnant Adolescents. *Journal of Adolescent Research*, 3(2), 153–170. http://doi.org/10.1177/074355488832004.

Steinberg, L. & Monahan, K.C. (2011). Adolescents' Exposure to Sexy Media Does Not Hasten the Initiation of Sexual Intercourse. *Developmental Psychology*, 47(2), 562–576. http://doi.org/10.1037/a0020613.

Steinhauer, J. (2014, December 8). UVA Furor Sparks Debate Over Existence of "Rape Culture." *New York Times*. Retrieved March 10, 2015 from www.nytimes.com/2014/12/09/us/fraternity-and-sorority-groups-call-for-uva-to-lift-ban-on-greek-life.html.

Strouse, J.S. & Buerkel-Rothfuss, N.L. (1987). Media Exposure and the Sexual Attitudes and Behaviors of College Students. *Journal of Sex Education and Therapy*, 13(2), 43–51. http://doi.org/10.1080/01614576.1987.11074908.

Sun, C., Bridges, A., Johnason, J. & Ezzell, M. (2014). Pornography and the Male Sexual Script: An Analysis of Consumption and Sexual Relations. *Archives of Sexual Behavior*. http://doi.org/10.1007/s10508-014-0391-2.

Synovitz, R.L, Hebert, E., Kelley, R.M. & Carlson, G. (2002). Sexual Knowledge of College Students in a Southern State: Relationship to Sexuality Education. *American Journal of Health Studies*, 17(4), 163.

Taylor, L.D. (2005). All for Him: Articles About Sex in American Lad Magazines. *Sex Roles*, 52(3–4), 153–163. http://doi.org/10.1007/s11199-005-1291-7.

Taylor, L.D. (2006). College Men, Their Magazines, and Sex. *Sex Roles*, 55(9–10), 693–702. http://doi.org/10.1007/s11199-006-9124-x.

Tolman, D.L., Kim, J.L., Schooler, D. & Sorsoli, C.L. (2007). Rethinking the Associations between Television Viewing and Adolescent Sexuality Development: Bringing Gender into Focus. *The Journal of Adolescent Health: Official Publication of the Society for Adolescent Medicine*, 40(1), 84.e9–e16. http://doi.org/10.1016/j.jadohealth.2006.08.002.

Vannier, S.A., Currie, A.B. & O'Sullivan, L.F. (2014). Schoolgirls and Soccer Moms: A Content Analysis of Free "Teen" and "MILF" Online Pornography. *Journal of Sex Research*, 51(3), 253–264. http://doi.org/10.1080/00224499.2013.829795.

Vega, V. & Malamuth, N.M. (2007). Predicting Sexual Aggression: The Role of Pornography in the Context of General and Specific Risk Factors. *Aggressive Behavior*, 33(2), 104–117. http://doi.org/10.1002/ab.20172.

Walsh-Childers, K., Gotthoffer, A. & Lepre, C.R. (2002). From "Just the Facts" to "Downright Salacious": Teens and Women's Magazine Coverage of Sex and Sexual Health. *Sexual Teens, Sexual Media: Investigating Media's Influence on Adolescent Sexuality*, 153–171.

Ward, L.M. (2003). Understanding the Role of Entertainment Media in the Sexual Socialization of American Youth: A Review of Empirical Research. *Developmental Review*, 23(3), 347–388. http://doi.org/10.1016/S0273-2297(03)00013-3.

Ward, L.M. & Friedman, K. (2006). Using TV as a Guide: Associations Between Television Viewing and Adolescents' Sexual Attitudes and Behavior. *Journal of Research on Adolescence*, 16(1), 133–156. http://doi.org/10.1111/j.1532-7795.2006.00125.x.

Ward, L.M., Epstein, M., Caruthers, A. & Merriwether, A. (2011). Men's Media Use, Sexual Cognitions, and Sexual Risk Behavior: Testing a Mediational Model. *Developmental Psychology*, 47(2), 592–602. http://doi.org/10.1037/a0022669.

Weitzer, R. & Kubrin, C.E. (2009). Misogyny in Rap Music: A Content Analysis of Prevalence and Meanings. *Men and Masculinities*, 12(1), 3–29. http://doi.org/10.1177/1097184X08327696.

Welsh, A. (2010). On the Perils of Living Dangerously in the Slasher Horror Film: Gender Differences in the Association Between Sexual Activity and Survival. *Sex Roles*, 62(11–12), 762–773. http://doi.org/10.1007/s11199-010-9762-x.

What Are the Key Statistics about Cervical Cancer? (2014, September 19). Retrieved March 10, 2015 from www.cancer.org/cancer/cervicalcancer/detailedguide/cervical-cancer-key-statistics.

White House Council on Women. (2014). *Rape and Sexual Assault: A Renewed Call to Action*. Retrieved March 10, 2015 from https://www.ncjrs.gov/App/AbstractDB/AbstractDBDetails.aspx?id=266766.

Whiteley, L.B., Mello, J., Hunt, O. & Brown, L.K. (2012). A Review of Sexual Health Web Sites for Adolescents. *Clinical Pediatrics*, 51(3), 209–213. http://doi.org/10.1177/0009922811423311.

Wingfield, N. (2014, October 15). Feminist Critics of Video Games Facing Threats in "GamerGate" Campaign. *New York Times*. Retrieved March 18, 2015 from www.nytimes.com/2014/10/16/technology/gamergate-women-video-game-threats-anita-sarkeesian.html.

Wingood, G.M., DiClemente, R.J., Harrington, K., Davies, S., Hook, E.W. & Oh, M.K. (2001). Exposure to X-rated Movies and Adolescents' Sexual and Contraceptive-related Attitudes and Behaviors. *Pediatrics*, 107(5), 1116–1119. http://doi.org/10.1542/peds.107.5.1116.

Wingood, G.M., DiClemente, R.J., Bernhardt, J.M., Harrington, K., Davies, S.L., Robillard, A. & Hook, E.W. (2003). A Prospective Study of Exposure to Rap Music Videos and African American Female Adolescents' Health. *American Journal of Public Health*, 93(3), 437–439. http://doi.org/10.2105/AJPH.93.3.437.

Wright, P.J. (2009). Sexual Socialization Messages in Mainstream Entertainment Mass Media: A Review and Synthesis. *Sexuality & Culture*, 13(4), 181–200.

Wright, P.J. (2011). Mass Media Effects on Youth Sexual Behavior Assessing the Claim for Causality. *Communication Yearbook*, 35, 343–386.

Wright, P.J. & Randall, A.K. (2012). Internet Pornography Exposure and Risky Sexual Behavior among Adult Males in the United States. *Computers in Human Behavior*, 28(4), 1410–1416. http://doi.org/10.1016/j.chb.2012.03.003.

Yager, A.M. & O'Keefe, C. (2012). Adolescent Use of Social Networking to Gain Sexual Health Information. *The Journal for Nurse Practitioners*, 8(4), 294–298. http://doi.org/10.1016/j.nurpra.2012.01.016.

Ybarra, M.L., Strasburger, V.C. & Mitchell, K.J. (2014). Sexual Media Exposure, Sexual Behavior, and Sexual Violence Victimization in Adolescence. *Clinical Pediatrics*, 53(13), 1239–1247. http://doi.org/10.1177/0009922814538700.

CHAPTER 10

THE MEAN AND SCARY MEDIA WORLD: THE IMPACT OF MEDIA VIOLENCE

Columbine High School. Virginia Tech. A movie theater in Aurora, Colorado. The Safeway grocery store in Tucson, Arizona. Sandy Hook Elementary School in Newtown, Connecticut. The Navy Yard in Washington, DC.

What these places have in common, of course, is that each was the site of a mass shooting in which a young man (two, in the case of Columbine) killed between six and 32 people and injured multiple other individuals who were targeted essentially at random. The majority of the victims were either strangers to the shooters or, if they were acquainted, were shot because of their location, not because of anything they had done.

The other commonality among these incidents is that, in every case, the shooters were discovered to have been avid fans of violent video games and, in the case of the Aurora movie theater shooting, of the Batman movie villain *The Joker*. And in every case, at least some of the media coverage of the shooting raised the issue of whether the shooters' consumption of violence-filled media content might have contributed to their shooting rampage[1] (Kain, 2013).

The question of how exposure to media violence via television, movies and video games relates to viewers' likelihood of engaging in real-world violence is among the most-studied topics in mass communication research. It is arguably one of the most important, given that that answer truly may life-or-death consequences.

VIOLENCE IN THE UNITED STATES

Half of American adults surveyed in a September 2014 poll said they believed that violent crime in the United States had increased over the past 20 years; another 15 percent said violent crime rates had remained the same ("What Is," 2014). This perception is wrong, according to the FBI data, which show that the rate of violent crimes reported declined by nearly half between 1993 and 2012. During that time period, violent crime rates declined from 747 violent incidents (murder, rape, aggravated assault, robberies) to 387 incidents per 100,000 people. Homicide reports have declined by 51 percent, forcible rape by 35 percent, robberies by 56 percent and aggravated assaults by 45 percent.

Data from the National Crime Victimization Surveys, sponsored by the Bureau of Justice Statistics, show even greater declines – 67 percent since 1993, including a 70 percent decline in sexual assaults, drops of 77 percent and 64 percent, respectively, in aggravated and simple assaults. The number of people who say they have been robbed declined by two-thirds during that 19-year period (Wolfers, 2014).

But what about trends in violence among adolescents and young adults, the groups most likely to commit crimes, including violent crimes (National Institute of Justice, 2014), and whose violent behaviors are most likely to be linked to violent media consumption? FBI data show that since 2008, arrest rates for violent crimes committed by individuals younger than age 18 have declined steadily. In 1994, law enforcement agencies reported 500 violent crime arrests for every 100,000 youth ten to 17 years old; by 2013, the rate had declined to fewer than 200 arrests per 100,000 youth (Butts, 2014).

And yet, homicide is the second most common cause of death among 15- to 24-year-olds in the United States, killing 8,500 young people each year. Suicide causes another 4,140 deaths, making it the third leading cause of death. Among 25- to 34-year-olds these rankings are reversed, with suicide second and homicide third as causes of death (Centers for Disease Control and Prevention, 2014). In addition, some critics have argued that the focus on declining homicide rates ignores an increase in gunshot *injuries*. Although fewer people *die* of gunshot wounds due to improved surgical treatment, this does not mean that fewer people suffer gunshot wounds. In 2002, 58,841 non-fatal gunshot injuries occurred in the United States, a rate of 20.5 injuries per 100,000 population. By 2011, however, both the number of injuries and the rate had grown – to 73,883, or 23.7 per 100,000 population; most of these injuries represented violent assaults rather than accidental shootings (Jena et al., 2014).

Data suggest that U.S. adolescents and young adults are no more or less likely to get into fights than are youth in other high-income countries (e.g., Canada, Western European countries). Among U.S. boys, nearly half (47.8%) reported involvement in a physical fight in the past year; fighting was more common among French (54%), Spanish (54.8%), and English youth (59.2%) and those from many other European countries. A quarter of U.S. girls reported physical fighting in the previous year, compared to 21.1 percent in France, 24.2 percent in Canada, 27.3 percent in Spain and 29.2 percent in England. However, U.S. adolescents were far more likely to report carrying weapons, especially guns, compared to their peers in other countries. Only 10 percent of boys from Belgium and France reported carrying a weapon in the past 30 days, compared to nearly a quarter (22%) of U.S. boys. Carrying a weapon was a strong predictor of having to receive medical treatment for an injury (Pickett et al., 2005).

Perhaps largely due to easy access to guns, American children and adolescents are far more likely to be the victims of violent crime than are children in other developed countries – "four times more likely to be killed by a gun than Canadian children, seven times more likely than Israeli children and an astonishing 65 times more likely than British children" (Kelly, 2014, p. vii). The problem is particularly serious among African American communities, given that African Americans constitute 13 percent of the population but 55 percent of all gun homicide victims.

Unfortunately, the Centers for Disease Control has done little research on either the causes or consequences of gun violence since 1996, when the agency initiated a self-imposed ban on gun-related research in response to a Congressional threat to eliminate CDC funding because some Congress members (and the National Rifle Association) believed the CDC was promoting gun control. Even after President Obama's 2013 executive order directing the CDC to resume gun violence research, which came in the wake of the Newtown shootings, the CDC has done little gun-related research, primarily because Republicans in the House of Representatives refuse to support any dedicated funding for gun violence studies. According to a January 2015 *New York Times* article, fear of retaliation by the NRA also has discouraged gun violence research by the National Institute of Justice and even some non-profit organizations (Frankel, 2015).

Violence unrelated to the use of guns also remains a problem. One recent study showed that 42 percent of young adult couples reported being involved in some sort of physical relationship violence; more than a quarter of the young adults surveyed said this violence resulted in an injury for them or their partner, including cuts, bruises or sprains. For two-thirds of the couples who reported any relationship violence, the previous year had included multiple violent incidents. Somewhat surprisingly, women were more likely to report having behaved violently toward their partners than to report that their male partners had been violent toward them (Berger et al., 2012). More recent data from the 2013 national Youth Risk Behavior Survey revealed that more than one-fifth of girls (20.9%) and 10.4 percent of boys had experienced dating violence (Vagi et al., 2015). In high-risk communities, dating violence is prevalent even among middle school students, with 77 percent of students who had dated reporting that they had verbally or emotionally abused a dating partner and nearly one-third (32%) reporting physical abuse of a partner. One in five acknowledged having threatened a partner, and 15 percent reported sexual abuse of a partner (Niolon et al., 2015).

WHAT LEADS TO VIOLENCE?

Researchers have identified numerous personal characteristics, life experiences and environmental factors that increase the likelihood of individuals engaging in violent behavior. For instance, one study examining the shared predictors of peer and dating violence showed that anger, family conflict and exposure to models of deviant behavior in school (e.g., perceiving higher numbers of peers who use marijuana or engage in fighting) were linked positively to both peer and dating violence for boys and girls. For girls, anxiety and exposure to models of deviance in the neighborhood were also predictors; for boys, heavy alcohol use predicted both peer and dating violence (Foshee et al., 2015).

As noted earlier, carrying a weapon is associated with a greater risk of injury requiring medical treatment (Pickett et al., 2005). In turn, the likelihood of carrying a gun is associated with the use of tobacco, alcohol and other drugs, feeling unsafe at school and having been threatened at school, as well as with many other types of risky behaviors, from riding with a drunk driver to depression and suicide ideation (Ruggles & Rajan, 2014). In addition, research suggests that the likelihood of carrying a gun is influenced not only by the number of peers who carry guns (Wilkinson et al., 2009) but by *perceptions* of peers' likelihood of carrying guns (Hemenway et al., 2011). One study of Boston adolescents showed that teens vastly overestimated the percentage of youth in their neighborhoods who carried guns; on average, teens estimated that nearly one-third (32.6%) of the youth in their neighborhoods carried guns, while the actual rate, based on teens' self-reported behavior during the past year, was about 5.5 percent. Teens who overestimated peer gun carrying by 15 percentage points or more were significantly more likely to have carried a gun themselves, as were those who reported that it was fairly or very easy to obtain a gun (Hemenway et al., 2011).

The most common reason adolescents give for carrying guns is self-protection (Wilkinson et al., 2009), and violent adolescents are at least 50 percent more likely to have been victimized than their non-violent peers. Among adolescents, violence also has been associated with alcohol and drug abuse, race, gender, sexual abuse within the family, and being raised in a single-parent family. Not surprisingly, having a violent parent increases the likelihood of adolescents behaving violently, as does gang membership, low literacy and poverty (Blum et al., 2003).

Having a violent parent may contribute to individuals becoming violent themselves in at least two ways. First, research suggests that adolescents' antisocial behavior is linked to having low levels of attachment to one's parents, and children who are abused by their parents or who witness family trauma are less likely to develop strong bonds with their parents (Sousa et al., 2011). The other mechanism, of course, is the same one that links many other parental behaviors – including negative behaviors such as smoking, use of smokeless tobacco, consumption of alcohol and other drugs, and positive behaviors such as exercise and reading, etc. – with those same behaviors among their children: modeling. That is, children are more likely to adopt behaviors their parents have modeled, in part because the parents' actions may make the behavior seem normal.

Social cognitive theory (Bryant & Oliver, 2009) posits that we may learn behavior not only from other real-world models, such as parents and peers, but also from mass media models. Herein lies a key underpinning of the argument that consumption of mass-mediated violence contributes to real-world violence and aggressive behavior, especially among children and adolescents. If we can learn how to behave by copying the models offered via mass media, then it is critical to understand what those media tell us about what to expect from other people we encounter in the world and how we should respond to them. Should we expect others to be respectable, law-abiding, trustworthy citizens? Or should we expect them to be lying, cheating, predatory criminals who threaten our own and our family members' safety? And when we are in conflict with or threatened by people, can we expect to find non-violent solutions? Or are we justified in shooting first and asking questions later?

MEDIA PORTRAYALS OF VIOLENCE

Television

Violence has long been a staple element of television programming. In fact, concern about the extent and potential impact of television violence stems from the earliest years of TV; the first Congressional hearings on television violence occurred in the early 1950s (Hoerrner, 1999). The violence depicted in these early shows would seem almost quaint to viewers today – bar fights and the occasional shoot-out among cowboys on *Bonanza, Gunsmoke, Have Gun – Will Travel* and *The Lone Ranger*, and car chases, fistfights and gunfire, when necessary, to subdue the bad guys in crime dramas such as *Dragnet, 77 Sunset Strip, Highway Patrol* and *The Untouchables*.

The Untouchables, in which Robert Stack portrayed implacable U.S. Treasury Department Prohibition Agent Eliot Ness, sparked substantial controversy over what critics called excessive violence in its depiction of Ness's battles against organized crime. ABC argued that the violence was required for an accurate portrayal of the real-life stories on which the series was based. However, the network's concern for historical accuracy did not prevent the series' writers from producing episodes in which Ness brought down mobsters who, in real life, had been arrested by other FBI agents (Kassel, n.d.).

Critics who were concerned about the violence portrayed in *The Untouchables* would no doubt be thoroughly horrified by many of the scenes included in prime-time television programming today. For instance, the CBS show *Stalker* showed a woman being burned alive within the first five minutes of the pilot episode. NBC's *Hannibal* follows the activities of cannibal Hannibal Lector. *American Horror Story*, from the cable TV channel FX, includes an episode focused on a murderous clown named Twisty. Human–zombie battles are required elements of every episode of *The Walking Dead* on AMC. Even the History Channel offers a wealth of blood and gore via its *Vikings* series ("14 Very, Very, VERY Violent TV Shows," n.d.). And HBO's medieval fantasy series *Game of Thrones* has sparked criticism worldwide for its inclusion not only of graphic warfare and numerous grisly murders but also for frequent sexual violence, including a fourth-season episode in which a scheming noblewoman, Cersei Lannister, is raped by her twin brother Jaime; the criticism was only heightened when the episode's director publicly defended the scene, saying that the rape became "consensual by the end" (Itzkoff, 2014, paragraph 7).

Certainly not every current television show or even every drama contains rampant violence, although violence in television programming certainly seems to have grown more graphic and more common; however, we cannot know for certain if TV violence is increasing because no comprehensive content analyses of television violence have been completed since the mid-1990s, although Signorielli (2003) investigated prime-time violence between 1993 and 2001. The National Television Violence Study (NTVS), the most comprehensive study ever of the frequency and context of violent incidents in entertainment programming, collected data on the content of television programs on 23 channels between October 1994 and June 1997 – nearly 10,000 hours of television content. The study included network and independent broadcast channels, public television, and basic and premium cable channel shows. The study showed that, in the third year of the study, 61 percent of all programs included depictions of violence. Within violent programming, only 16 percent showed long-term negative consequences, and 45 percent included "bad" characters who never faced punishment. Characters in 71 percent of Year Three violent scenes (down from 75 percent in Year Two) showed no remorse and received no criticism or penalty for their violent behavior. More than four in every ten violent scenes (42%) included humor (Wilson et al., 1997)

Much of the portrayal of violence was unrealistic, in that only 51 percent of violent interactions apparently caused pain (down from 58 percent in the first year), and more than one-third (34%) showed unreal-istically low levels of harm, although more than one in every four violent interactions (26%) involved the use of a gun. Across all three years of the study, "nearly 40% of the violent incidents on television are initiated by characters who possess qualities that make them attractive role models" (Wilson et al., 1997, p. 26).

The study showed that prime-time violence had increased in both broadcast and cable programs, with the average violent program includ-ing at least six instances of violence per hour. It is important to note here that each interaction may include multiple violent behaviors: punches, stabbing, shooting, etc. The most problematic depictions of violence, the authors concluded, are those that include five key elements: violent behavior by an attractive character; an apparent justification for the violence; a lack of punishment, criticism or remorse; little harm or negative consequences for the victims; and a realistic portrayal of the violent acts. The authors note, however, that for viewers younger than seven years old, who may not be able to distinguish between fantasy and realistic violence, cartoons offer the most common juxtaposition of these five elements – heroes using justified violence that results in few or no harmful consequences, either to the perpetrator or to the victim (Wilson et al., 1997).

Signorielli's (2003) update included only prime-time programming. Her study showed that the ratio of violent to non-violent prime-time programs remained stable over the nine years she examined, with about 60 percent of the programs in each year depicting some kind of violence. The frequency of violence ranged from 3.06 to 8.20 violent actions per program hour. In about one-third of the programs, violence was a signi-ficant or major plot element. In about a quarter of the shows, violence was depicted as at least somewhat humorous. The programs included fewer incidents of graphic or gratuitous violence than had been found in the NTVS. However, Signorielli (2003) concluded that the portrayals depicted violence in a "sanitized" way, in that it was not gory, characters rarely regretted or received punishment for their violent actions, and victims' suffering was rarely shown.

Given the frequent criticism that television in the current era is becom-ing more violent than ever (Bauder, 2013; Hanks, 2014), it is somewhat surprising that no recent studies have examined television violence in a comprehensive way. One recent study by the Parents Television Council

Figure 10.1: TV Violence May Be Increasing

investigated violence in basic cable and broadcast programs since the fall of 2012 and 2013; however, that study did not include all television programming or even all prime-time programming. Instead, it focused on seven of the most violent shows available on basic cable (FX's *American Horror Story, Sons of Anarchy* and *Justified;* AMC's *The Walking Dead* and *Breaking Bad,* BBC America's *Copper* and IFC's *Bullet in the Face*) and seven of the most violent broadcast TV shows (NBC's *Revolution, Blacklist* and *Law & Order: SVU;* CBS's *Criminal Minds* and *CSI;* CW's *Supernatural,* and Fox's *Sleepy Hollow* (Parents Television Council, 2013). While the shows were not chosen based on popularity, the list included three of the most-watched series of 2012/2013: *The Walking Dead,* with an average of 14.3 million viewers per week, *Criminal Minds,* with 12.6 million, and *CSI,* with 11.9 million viewers (Schneider, 2013). The researchers determined that all of the shows included incidents that qualified as "graphic," which should have meant that they would earn a rating of TV-MA. These incidents, which included not only gunfire and stabbings but torture, cannibalism, individuals being burned alive, rape, mutilation and dismemberment, occurred in programs labeled TV-14 with a V descriptor, which indicates that the program may include "intense" violence. However, none was labeled to warn audiences of the graphic nature of the portrayals.

Broadcast programs accounted for 37 percent of the graphic violence depicted and, in fact, "there was only a 6% difference between the amount of violence on cable shows compared to shows that aired on broadcast television" (Parents Television Council, 2013, p. 6).

Among the most disturbing of the study's findings were that graphic violence was most common during times when children were likely to be watching TV and that the ratings system did not work to warn parents when shows were likely to include graphic violence. Every three minutes, on average, a new gun or weapon appeared on screen, with guns representing 69 percent of the traditional weapons used and 62 percent of all weapons (including blunt objects, explosives and poison). The report concludes that "media violence is prevalent, graphic, and growing" (Parents Television Council, 2013, p. 17).

Movies

As appears to be true on television, violence has become more common and more graphic in popular movies. One study of 15 of the top-selling U.S. movies for every year from 1950 to 2006 showed that, overall, 89 percent of these films included some portrayal of violence. Over the entire period of the study, 31 percent of female characters initiated violence, while 28 percent were the victims of violence; among male characters, 42 percent initiated violence and 44 percent were violently assaulted. Male characters were consistently more likely than female characters to be involved in violence, but, over time, both male and female characters became significantly more likely to be involved in violence, with the percentage of male characters either initiating or receiving violence rising to more than 60 percent by 2006, while the percentage of female characters involved in violence rose to the mid-40s (Bleakley et al., 2012).

Another study, which used the same movie content database but followed movies through 2012, showed that among the 420 movies released since 1985, 94 percent included at least one five-minute segment containing violence. In those 396 films, coders identified 783 segments depicting gun violence. Analysis of the frequency of violent segments showed that not only did violence increase steadily from 1950 to 2012, but the rate of increase doubled; that is, movies not only became more violent but became increasingly violent increasingly quickly. Gun violence also increased significantly from 1985 to 2012, with the increase virtually all attributable to PG-13 movies. Gun violence decreased in G/PG films and remained stable in R-rated movies, but since 2009, the frequency of gun violence in PG-13-rated movies has been as high or higher than that in R-rated movies. "In 2012, the level of gun violence in PG-13 films exceeded the mean in R-rated films" (Bushman et al., 2013, p. 1017). The authors note that this increase may be exacerbating the "weapons effect," the finding that the mere presence of a weapon, or even exposure to words describing weapons, increases aggression; thus, the increasing inclusion of violence, especially gun violence, in movies may promote aggressive behavior among audiences.

Exposure to violent content is thus increasing for movie viewers of all ages. However, research suggests that, even without the dramatic increase in violent content in PG-13 films, many adolescents nonetheless would be exposed to extremely violent movies. Researchers who surveyed middle school students from Vermont and New Hampshire found that an average of 28 percent of the students had seen each of the 51 extremely violent movies identified among box-office hits released between 1988 and 1999. The most popular of the movies included in the list was *Scream*, a 1996 horror movie in which a masked killer terrorizes teenagers in a small town; two-thirds of the middle schoolers overall, including 40 percent of fifth-graders, had seen the movie. More than one in four students (27%) had seen *The General's Daughter*, which includes scenes depicting the gang rape of a female soldier and a male character blowing himself apart. One in five students (20%) had seen *Natural Born Killers*, in which Woody Harrelson and Juliette Lewis play psychopaths who become lovers and go on a murder spree during which they kill 52 people and are glamorized and celebrated by the tabloid media (Sargent et al., 2002).

The study showed that the likelihood of having seen one or more of the movies was highest among the oldest students (13- and 14-year-olds), boys, those whose parents had less education and those whose grades in school were poor (Sargent et al., 2002). These findings were echoed in a more recent survey examining exposure to 40 violent movies among a national sample of adolescents. That study revealed that each movie had reached, on average, 12.5 percent of children ten to 14 years old. Boys, older children, non-whites, those whose parents had less education and those doing poorly in school were most likely to have seen the violent movies. In particular, the survey revealed that among black male adolescents, more than 80 percent had seen three of the most popular violent movies (Worth et al., 2008).

Sargent et al. (2002) note that the film industry markets these very violent movies to teenagers, creating demand by advertising R-rated movies on MTV and showing previews before extremely popular PG and PG-13 movies are released, such as the *Star Wars* sequel *The Phantom Menace* (Sargent et al., 2002). The most recent Federal Trade Commission report on the marketing of violent media to children concluded that the movie industry does not specifically target children younger than 17 with advertising for R-rated movies. However, 18 of the 20 R-rated movies whose online marketing the FTC examined were advertised on websites for which people younger than age 17 constitute more than one-third and in some cases as much as half of the site's visitors. In addition, the FTC's "mystery shopper" program revealed that 40 percent of under-age youth were admitted to R-rated movies without adult supervision, and 70 percent were allowed to buy R-rated DVDs in retail stores. The FTC report also acknowledged that "ratings creep" has meant an increase in the likelihood of significantly violent movies receiving PG-13 rather than R ratings (Federal Trade Commission, 2007).

Video Games

The same FTC report concluded that the video game industry's internal marketing documents and ad placements showed that most game manufacturers were not deliberately marketing M-rated games (those intended only for people aged 17 and older) to younger audiences; they also noted that fewer ads for M-rated games now appear in teens' favorite television programs. As with television, however, online advertising often violated the video game industry's internally established standard prohibiting M-rated game advertising on websites where at least 45 percent of the audience is younger than 17; 80 percent of the M-rated games the FTC investigated were advertised on sites for which those aged 17 and younger constituted 45 percent or more of the audience. The report also noted that the standard, even when it is met, allows M-rated games to be advertised to a very substantial number of individuals for whom the industry itself has decided that the games are inappropriate. Although video game retailers had "substantially improved their enforcement of policies prohibiting children under 17 from purchasing M-rated games without parental permission" (Federal Trade Commission, 2007, p. iii), 42 percent of children in the "mystery shopper" survey were allowed to buy M-rated games.

One reason the FTC (along with parents and health experts) have been so concerned about adolescents' and younger children's access to M-rated games is that video games are often even more violent and gory than the worst of movies and television. For instance, one study examined a random sample of 37 of the 147 M-rated console games available in the United States in April 2004; the analysis examined both the types of content warnings assigned to each game by the Entertainment Software Rating Board (ESRB) and the actual content included in at least one hour of game play. Within this sample, 98 percent had ESRB content descriptors for violence; 55.6 percent had warnings for "blood and gore" and 8.3 percent warned consumers that the game contained "intense violence." The latter percentage was actually lower than the comparable figure when content descriptors for all 147 M-rated games were considered; overall, 15 percent of M-rated games had "intense violence" content warnings (Thompson et al., 2006). In addition, 81 percent of the games included content that *should* have warranted a content descriptor that was not assigned to the game.

The researchers found that when acts of violence, time spent planning violence and depiction of injuries were combined, more than one-third of game play time (36%) was directly related to violence. Even considering only the time during which game characters were actually *engaged* in violent acts, violence accounted for more than one-fifth of game play time (22%) and constituted as much as 62 percent of game play time for some games. Violence resulted in 145 character deaths per hour of game play on average, but ranged as high as 1,142 deaths per hour in a game called *Drakengard*, which follows a soldier named Caim, who combines his soul with a dragon's to gain the powers he needs to rescue his sister from evil Empire kidnappers ("Drakengard Review," n.d.; Thompson et al., 2006). All of the sampled games rewarded the player for injuring other characters, and 92 percent rewarded killing other characters.

The authors compared M-rated games to a sample of games rated T (indicating their appropriateness for teen players). Overall, M-rated games were more violent, showing more blood, more severe injuries and higher rates of human deaths than T-rated games. However, the difference appeared to stem from the fact that 23 percent of T-rated games do not include any portrayals of character deaths. Considering only the T-rated games that do include depictions of character deaths, the researchers found no significant difference in the rate of character deaths (Thompson et al., 2006).

Analysis of the violent content in T-rated games showed that 94 percent had ESRB content descriptors for violence, and more than one in four (26%) had content warnings for blood. Detailed analysis of 81 sample games revealed that 98 percent showed characters intentionally injuring or killing other characters, 90 percent rewarded players for injuring others and 69 percent rewarded killing other characters. Of the games that included violence, that action accounted for more than one-third (36%) of game play time on average. In addition, nearly half of the games (48%) included problematic content (violence, profanity, substance use, etc.) that would have warranted a content descriptor the game's rating did not include. For instance, the researchers identified sexual material in 22 of the 81 games, although only 16 had content descriptors for sexual themes, and nearly half of the games (46%) could have been considered to include sexual material if the definition was expanded to reflect the portrayal of characters with "pronounced cleavage, large breasts or provocative clothing" (Haninger & Thompson, 2004, p. 859).

The same team of researchers earlier examined the ESRB content descriptors for 672 console-based games rated E for "everyone" and available in April 2001, as well as examining a sample of 55 games. Even in these games, 64 percent included intentional violence that accounted, on average, for nearly one-third of game play time (30.7%), and 60 percent of the games either rewarded the player for injuring others or required such action to advance in the game. Thirty-two of the games had not received a content descriptor for violence, but violence was an element in 14 of these games. Among the action games, 21 of 22 included violence leading to characters' deaths, with an average of 2.3 character deaths per minute. The researchers concluded that even E-rated video games include significant amounts of violence, even though an E rating ostensibly means that the game includes no more than minimal violence (Thompson & Haninger, 2001).

More recent research has provided more detail about the types and context of violence video game players encounter. One study catalogued the "moral disengagement cues" in 17 of the most popular first-person shooter games (e.g., *Call of Duty*) in 2011. The findings showed that 100 percent of coded game segments included at least one distortion of consequences cue, such as the character using a weapon that enabled him to attack while distant from his target or having the target display no suffering, bleeding or pain reaction after being hit. In addition, 100 percent of the coded game segments included cues suggesting that the violence was morally justified (such as verbal aggression by the target or the target character having attacked first); all coded game segments included dehumanization cues, such as not showing the target's face, having enemies appear identical to each other or dehumanizing labeling of the target. The analysis demonstrated that first-person shooter games "tend to lack features that potentially make violence an irritating or distressful experience, such as killing for unjustified reasons, harming innocent victims, or showing victims' enduring physical and psychological pain" (Hartmann et al., 2014, p. 327).

Another study allowed researchers to account for the interactivity of games – the fact that no two players encounter exactly the same content; players who are highly skilled at a game will be exposed to different types of experiences than less skilled players. The results demonstrated that players who rated their skills more highly after playing a violent video game for 28 minutes were more likely than less skilled players to perpetrate violence, while lower skilled players were more often the targets of violence. More skilled players were somewhat more likely to observe gory consequences of the violence and also were more likely to see the violence up close rather than at a distance (Matthews & Weaver, 2013).

The inclusion of sexually violent content has been a particular focus of public concern about video games since the 1982 Atari game *Custer's Revenge*, the object of which was to prevent the General George Custer character from being hit by flying arrows until he reached the opposite end of the screen, enabling him to force sex on a captive Native American woman. As much outrage as that game produced (Yao et al., 2009), the crude animation never could have been mistaken for a realistic portrayal. The same could not be said of the content of a segment of *Grand Theft Auto V*, which gave players a first-person perspective view of the main character paying a prostitute for sex, which is graphically portrayed, and then knocking the woman unconscious or simply killing her outright. Inexplicably, the chief executive officer of Take-Two, which publishes the *Grand Theft Auto* game series, defended the scene as "beautiful art," albeit "gritty" (Allen, 2014).

Sexualization and objectification of women is common in video games. Female characters are more likely than their male counterparts to be scantily clad (Beasley & Collins Standley, 2002; Dietz, 1998; Dill et al., 2005). Content analyses of M-rated and T-rated video games available in 2004 did not identify any depictions of sexual violence, although female characters were more likely than male characters to be partially nude or in sexually revealing clothing or engaging in sexual behaviors (Downs & Smith, 2009; Haninger & Thompson, 2004; Thompson et al., 2006).

At least two substantial gaps exist in what we know about the violent content of video games. First, the most comprehensive analyses of violent content in video games appear to have been conducted prior to 2005, meaning that these analyses do not reflect changes in game content that have occurred over the past decade. In addition, and partly because the major studies of violent game content were conducted so long ago, the content analyses conducted thus far have involved console-based games – those played primarily either alone or with others in a single location, using a gaming console such as the Wii, Playstation and Xbox series. Today, however, gamers often play online games that may be accessed via a regular desktop or laptop computer or via an Internet-connected console. The availability of these games – at least some of which are free – is partly responsible for the 241 percent growth in the number of people in the United States who play video games for at least one hour per month – 135 million of them in 2011 (Macchiarella, n.d.). Some analysts predict that in 2016, the value of the online and mobile gaming markets will reach $46 million, representing 60 percent growth in only four years (Sluis, 2013). Worldwide, an estimated 23.4 million individuals were active monthly subscribers to at least one "massively multiplayer online game" (MMOG) such as the role-playing games *World of Warcraft* or *League of Legends*, or first-person shooter games such as *MAG* or *Firefair* ("MMO Gaming," n.d.). In 2014, the most popular online game worldwide, *League of Legends*, boasted 67 million individuals per month and 27 million people per day playing the game ("League of

Legends," 2014). Yet no research thus far has attempted to analyze what kinds of content online gamers are likely to encounter.

Music/Music Videos

Music and music videos represent another type of media content through which audiences may be exposed to violent images or ideas. Numerous researchers have assessed violence-related imagery in music videos, producing estimates of the frequency of violent content ranging from about 15 percent to more than one-third of all videos, depending on the specific study and the music genre (Baxter et al., 1985; Greeson & Williams, 1986; Rich et al., 1998; Smith & Boyson, 2002). In their review of the literature on music video violence, Smith and Boyson (2002) identify three trends in the content analyses of music videos: channel variations in the amount of violence, with MTV appearing to have the highest prevalence of violence-containing videos; channel variations in who is portrayed as an aggressor versus a victim; and variations by genre, with rap and rock music videos generally including the most violence. These two genres are not equivalent, however; 37 percent of rap videos contained physical aggression, compared to only 17 percent of rock videos (Smith & Boyson, 2002).

The context in which violence occurs in music videos is important, and the most recent analyses of music videos suggest cause for concern, in that portrayals of violence often feature attractive perpetrators (36%) but show little harm or pain to the victim. Nearly three-quarters (73%) of videos that included violence in this study showed the victim suffering no pain, and more than half (55%) depicted no harm to the victim. Violence was punished or not rewarded in only 40 percent of the videos (Smith & Boyson, 2002).

Surprisingly little research seems to have examined the prevalence of violent ideas and terms in music *lyrics*, although researchers have been interested in the impact of violent lyrics. The handful of studies that have specifically examined music lyrics have revealed dramatic increases in references to violence in rap music (Armstrong, 2001; Hunnicutt & Andrews, 2009). Herd (2009) assessed the level of violence in rap music, with 27 percent of songs released between 1979 and 1984 including references to violence, compared to 60 percent of songs released between 1994 and 1997; the number of mentions of violence per song increased

325

significantly as well, and the context also changed, with 45 percent of the songs in the latest period referencing violence in positive ways. During the later period, violence was more likely to be associated with masculinity, glamor and wealth, and with bragging or bravado. "Gangsta rap," perhaps not surprisingly, was the most violent subgenre; 93 percent of gangsta rap songs included references to violence. Similarly, Hunnicutt and Andrews (2009) found that rap song references to murder included themes such as the normalization of killing, vengeance and masculinity, and the maintenance of respect.

Other scholars have noted that rap music is particularly likely to include misogynistic lyrics, often depicting violence toward and sexual humiliation of women (Adams & Fuller, 2006), and a content analysis of the most popular songs from 2005, according to *Billboard* magazine, showed that rap songs were indeed the most likely to contain references to degrading sex. Songs that included references to degrading sex were also more likely than songs containing no reference to sexual activity to make reference to violence, drugs and weapons. Overall, the study demonstrated that references to degrading sex were more common than references to non-degrading sex, representing 65 percent versus 35 percent, respectively, of all songs that made any mention of sexual activity (Primack et al., 2008).

In summary, content analyses of television, movies, video games, music lyrics and music videos all suggest that media audiences are almost certain to be exposed to frequent portrayals of and references to violent behavior. The research suggests that these portrayals are becoming more frequent (e.g., more violent incidents/references per hour) and more graphic (more gory, sadistic and disturbing). The media world encountered by the average viewer/listener/player is one where violence is common, even normative, and that conclusion seems to inspire little argument.

MEDIA EFFECTS ON PRO-VIOLENCE/ANTISOCIAL ATTITUDES

However, the impact of all that media violence is a far more contentious issue. Numerous studies, drawing on cross-sectional surveys, experiments and longitudinal analyses, have provided evidence of a significant positive link between higher levels of exposure to various types of mediated violence and a variety of negative outcomes, including antisocial

326

attitudes, aggression and outright violent behavior (Bushman & Anderson, 2001; Coyne & Padilla-Walker, 2015; Funk et al., 2004; Huesmann, 2007; Paik & Comstock, 1994; Rowell et al., 2003; Uhlmann & Swanson, 2004). However, other researchers, sometimes examining some of the same studies, have concluded that although exposure to media violence may be positively correlated with hostile or aggressive attitudes and behaviors, the evidence does not support a causal relationship between media violence and real-world violence (Ferguson, 2007, 2015; Ferguson & Kilburn, 2009; Ferguson et al., 2009, 2013; Schwartz & Beaver, 2015).

In one review of the research, Huesmann (2007) distinguished between short-term effects of exposure to media violence, including priming, arousal and mimickry, and long-term effects. Priming refers to the idea that exposure to media violence activates specific emotional, cognitive or behavioral nodes within the brain's neural network; recently activated nodes respond more quickly to subsequent cues, increasing the likelihood that the individual will engage in behavior that is linked to those nodes. "When media violence primes aggressive concepts, aggression is more likely" (Huesmann, 2007, p. 3). Arousal refers to the idea that media portrayals of violence can lead to excitation transfer, so that the viewer perceives a subsequent provocation more strongly than he or she would otherwise or that media violence increases general arousal, leading to disinhibition of responses the viewer otherwise might suppress. In either case, the effect is to increase the likelihood of aggressive responses to a subsequent situation. Finally, mimicry refers to the fact that people, especially children, "have an innate tendency to mimic whomever they observe" (Huesmann, 2007, p. 3). Thus, those who watch violent acts are more likely, in the short term, to copy those behaviors.

In the long term, Huesmann (2007) explained, exposure to violent content may increase the likelihood of aggressive behavior through observational learning of ideas and behaviors, through desensitizing reactions to scenes or events that normally would provoke negative emotions or through enactive learning of aggressive reactions to any sort of conflict situation (or some combination of these three). Thus, exposure to media violence may increase audiences' tendency to attribute hostile intent to the actions of people in the real world as well as making aggressive behavior (to protect oneself or simply to gain advantage) seem normative. Desensitization refers to the process whereby we become habituated to images of gore or violence, such that they no longer cause a sense of discomfort; this desensitization then makes thinking about one's own violent or aggressive behavior less uncomfortable. Finally, enactive learning acknowledges that when individuals play violent video games they are not simply observing violent behavior; they are practicing violent behavior in the virtual sense, especially through first-person shooter games.

Television and Movies

Some researchers have documented significant positive effects of exposure to television and movie violence on subsequent attitudes toward aggression and desensitization to violence. For instance, one early paper described two experiments in which different age groups – eight- to ten-year-old children and college students – first watched either an excerpt from a violent crime drama or a video of an exciting volleyball game. The participants then watched films of real-life violence, with the children watching a fight between two pre-school children and the college students watching news reports of the 1968 Democratic National Convention riots. The children and male college students who had watched the violent programming displayed less emotion in reaction to the scenes of real aggression, compared to those who had previously watched the non-violent volleyball game; the difference was not significant for college women. In addition, the researchers found that self-reported time spent viewing violent television was linked to weaker responses to the real-life violence (Thomas et al., 1977).

Exposure to violent movies may desensitize viewers not only in terms of their own reaction to violence but also may lead to reduced concern about youth exposure to violence. In one study, researchers exposed a national sample of 1,000 parents of six- to 17-year-old children to three pairs of short movie scenes, which depicted either violence or sexual interactions. The parents then were asked the minimum age at which they believed it would be appropriate for children to see the movie from which the clips came. Parents who saw more violent clips were more willing to allow younger children to see the movie, and those who watched movies more often were desensitized to violence more quickly than were less frequent movie viewers. This desensitization may explain greater tolerance for children's exposure to violent content among both parents and those who rate movies, which could be contributing to the "ratings creep" described earlier (Romer et al., 2014).

In a more recent study, Anderson (1997) found that individuals exposed to a violent movie clip subsequently reported significantly higher levels of state hostility, a measure of how irritated or angry the individual feels at that specific time. In a second experiment the researchers controlled for trait hostility, which measures individuals' general or enduring tendencies to feel irritated or angry. The results showed that exposure to the violent movie clip increased state hostility. Individuals high in trait hostility also reported greater state hostility after watching the movie clip, but there was no significant interaction effect. Both low and high trait hostility individuals reported greater state hostility after watching the violent movie clip.

Researchers also have confirmed that watching violent videos primes or increases the accessibility of aggressive or hostile concepts (Bushman, 1998; Josephson, 1987). Bushman (1998) found that college students who watched a violent movie listed more aggressive words in a word–association task than did students who had watched a non-violent movie, even when the trigger words had no aggressive connotations. A second experiment described in the same paper tested how quickly students could determine whether a string of letters was a real word or a non-word. This study showed that those who had watched the violent video had significantly shorter reaction times for aggressive words, compared to those who watched the non-violent movie, but there was no difference in their reaction times for non-aggressive words. The results, Bushman concluded, "suggest that violent media prime cognitive-associative networks related to aggression" (1998, p. 537).

This priming effect may encourage individuals exposed to violent media content to be more likely to select violent content in the future. Researchers have found that, for male college students at least, priming aggressive concepts by having the students write stories using a list of aggressive words increased the likelihood that those students would subsequently express interest in seeing movies containing violence; the same effect did not occur for students who wrote their stories using prosocial or unrelated words that were inconsistent with violence (Langley et al., 1992). The results suggest that exposure to violent media content makes subsequent exposure to violent media content more salient and attractive to the individual, increasing the likelihood that, in the future, he or she will seek out additional violent media to consume.

Music and Music Videos

Fewer studies have examined the impact of music or music videos on attitudes related to violence. However, researchers have identified links between exposure to violence-related lyrics and music video images and aggressive cognitions and beliefs. For instance, one study used five separate experiments to test the impact of listening to songs with violent lyrics on college students' aggressive cognitions and hostility. The results showed that listening to violent songs increased the students' state hostility levels; in addition, when asked to fill in the missing letters for words that could be either violence-related or not (e.g., h_t could be either *hit* or *hat*), those who had listened to violent songs generated more violence-related word completions than did those who had listened to a song with non-violent lyrics (Anderson et al., 2003). Another study found that young African American men who watched violent rap music videos subsequently expressed greater acceptance of violence as a way of dealing with interpersonal conflicts and reported a higher probability that they would use violence in the future, compared with men who had watched a non-violent rap music video or no video at all (Johnson et al., 1995).

Due to concern about the misogynistic nature of many popular rap songs, much of the research on the impact of music has focused on how exposure to violent music lyrics and/or music videos influences attitudes related to sexual violence and violence toward women generally. In one study, St. Lawrence and Joyner (1991) tested the impact of listening to sexually violent heavy metal music, Christian heavy metal music or classical music. The study revealed that men who had listened to heavy metal music – regardless of the type of lyrics the song contained – expressed greater acceptance of sex role stereotypes and more negative attitudes toward women. In contrast, a German study demonstrated that men who listened to music with misogynous lyrics subsequently listed more negative characteristics of women and reported more vengeful feelings toward women than did men who had listened to songs with neutral lyrics. Interestingly, listening to songs with "men-hating" lyrics did not have similar effects on female participants (Fischer & Greitemeyer, 2006).

Watching violent music videos also has been shown to increase negative attitudes toward women in experimental studies. For instance, Peterson and Pfost (1989) assessed the impact of watching erotic and violent, erotic and non-violent, violent and non-erotic and non-violent, non-erotic music videos on undergraduate men's attitudes toward women. The researchers found that men who watched the non-erotic violent video reported significantly more adversarial sexual beliefs than did men in the other conditions; they also reported more anger, anxiety, frustration and offense. The authors concluded that violent rock videos "can foster in men a calloused and antagonistic, though not necessarily violent, orientation toward women" (Peterson & Pfost, 1989, p. 321). On the other hand, Kistler and Lee (2009) found that, in comparison to men who watched hip-hop videos with low sexual content, men who watched highly sexualized hip-hop videos subsequently reported not only more objectification of women and stereotypical gender attitudes but also greater rape myth acceptance.

A more recent study compared male undergraduates' endorsement of adversarial sexual beliefs and acceptance of interpersonal violence after watching three music videos by female artists; in one set of videos, each of the artists presented herself in a highly objectified and sexualized way, and in the other set, the same three artists appeared, but in non-objectified ways. The researchers found that watching the objectified videos primed adversarial beliefs, such as the idea that women use their sexuality to their advantage. Initially, the objectified videos appeared to increase acceptance of interpersonal violence, but this effect was mediated fully by adversarial sexual beliefs (Aubrey et al., 2011). Interestingly, although the videos used in this study were not overtly violent, they nonetheless prompted participants to think about women in more adversarial ways, which is important, because holding adversarial sexual beliefs has been linked to greater likelihood of sexual violence (Zinzow & Thompson, 2014).

Video Games

Researchers have also examined the impact of video games on attitudes related to violence, and these studies, in general, have confirmed that playing violent games is related to lower levels of empathy for others and more aggressive or hostile emotions and attitudes toward oneself and toward others (Anderson et al., 2004; Bartholow et al., 2005; Bushman & Anderson, 2002; Carnagey & Anderson, 2005; Funk et al., 2004; Uhlmann & Swanson, 2004). For instance, Funk et al. (2004) examined whether playing violent video games increased desensitization to violence among fourth- and fifth-graders from a Midwestern U.S. city. The results showed that greater time spent playing violent video games was associated with lower empathy scores and more pro-violence attitudes. The researchers noted that exposure to violent video games in early childhood may be particularly problematic in that these children are still developing their own internal moral reasoning structures; practicing acting without empathy or moral evaluation – both of which are rewarded in violent video game play – may interfere with the development of empathy and moral reasoning abilities.

Another correlational study used Amazon's Mechanical Turk to recruit men and women for a survey assessing the links between exposure to video games and hostile sexism and rape myth acceptance. The results confirmed that lifetime exposure to video games was linked to greater interpersonal aggression, greater hostile sexism and greater rape myth acceptance. The authors suggest that regular exposure to the stereotypical and objectifying portrayals of women within video games, along with being rewarded for aggressive and violent virtual behavior within the game, contributes to the development of cognitive schema that dehumanize women, making those who regularly play video games more likely to blame rape victims for their victimization (Fox & Potocki, 2015).

An experimental study showed that male and female college students who played the violent game *Doom*, in which players battle with virtual zombies, demons and other monsters, were subsequently more likely to automatically associate themselves with aggression, in comparison with students who had played a non-violent video game. However, there were no significant differences by game type in self-reported feelings of aggression. The study also showed that both automatic and self-reported aggressiveness were correlated positively with long-term exposure to violent games, "suggesting that violent media may exert their influence through multiple routes, some more amenable to conscious assent than others" (Uhlmann & Swanson, 2004, p. 49).

Another experimental study provided evidence that playing violent video games may change the way players interpret others' behavior in subsequent conflict situations. In this study, undergraduate students played one of four violent video games or one of four non-violent games, then read the beginnings of stories in which there might be interpersonal conflict and predicted what would happen next in the story, including what they believed the main character would do or say, think and feel. Those who had played the violent game predicted greater aggressiveness in the main character's reactions, compared to those who played the non-violent game. In response to a car accident, for instance, one of the students who had played the violent game predicted that the main character would shoot or stab the other driver. Another said the main character in a story about people going to a restaurant might think about setting fire to a tablecloth, and individuals who had played a violent game were significantly more likely to report that the main character would be angry. These effects held across gender, with women as likely as men to predict hostile, aggressive thoughts and feelings from the main characters in the stories they read, although men were more likely than women to predict that the characters would engage in aggressive behavior. Further analysis revealed a positive correlation between the level of violence in the game (even within violent games) and the participants' predictions of how hostile and aggressive the story characters' thoughts, feelings and behavior would be (Bushman & Anderson, 2002).

MEDIA EFFECTS ON BEHAVIOR

As the previous section demonstrates, researchers have identified links between exposure to violent content in television, movies, music and video games and an increased likelihood of developing antisocial and even hostile attitudes and emotions. The real focus of concern, however, centers around whether exposure to mass media violence causes aggressive and/or antisocial *behavior*. In other words, does consumption of violent content in the media world lead audience members to act in violent ways in the real world?

Researchers have identified connections between all types of media violence and violent behavior in the real world. As early as the mid-1970s, Rothenberg (1975) identified 50 studies examining the links between television violence exposure and aggressive behavior in the real world; these studies, discussed in 146 published journal articles and involving more than 10,000 children and adolescents, all supported the conclusion that viewing television violence increases subsequent aggressive behavior.

By 1982, Huesmann's analysis of the television violence literature, included in the National Institute of Mental Health's report on television and behavior, led him to conclude that "it should be difficult to find any researcher who does not believe that a significant positive relation exists between viewing television violence and subsequent aggressive behavior under most conditions" (Huesmann, 1982, p. 126). Data from laboratory studies, survey data and observational field studies – including several longitudinal studies – all documented a positive relationship between viewing television violence and increases in aggressive behavior. Huesmann (1982) cites two particularly interesting studies that examined the impact of television viewing on populations previously not exposed to TV. In both studies, the introduction of television led to increases in physical and verbal aggression among children; a key variable was the amount of TV the children viewed, with greater increases in aggressive behavior among children who watched more TV.

More than a decade later, a formal meta-analysis of television violence studies (Paik & Comstock, 1994) summarized the results of 217 studies linking consumption of television programming with subsequent aggressive behavior. The meta-analysis produced "a highly significant positive association for the magnitude of effect between exposure to portrayals of violence and antisocial behavior" (Paik & Comstock, 1994, p. 525). These studies measured aggressive behavior in a variety of ways, including the use of "aggression machines" to deliver an electric shock or some other annoying or unpleasant effect to a research collaborator, physical violence against an object, verbal aggression and mild physical violence toward another person. Some studies even included measures of criminal behavior, including assault; not surprisingly, studies in which the outcome variable was illegal activity produced smaller effect sizes. The researchers note that exposure to television violence had significant effects on aggressive behavior for every age group examined, including pre-school and elementary schoolchildren, adolescents, college students and adults, indicating that "the influence of violent television portrayals is not confined to childhood or early adolescence" (Paik & Comstock, 1994, p. 537). They conclude that "the findings obtained in the last decade and a half strengthen the evidence that television violence increases aggressive and antisocial behavior" (p. 538).

Although some studies have examined the impact of violent movies on subsequent aggressive behavior, there appears to have been no systematic review or meta-analysis of these studies. Nonetheless, it is worth mentioning some of the individual studies on the impact of movie violence. Meyer (1972) tested the impact of viewing violent or non-violent film segments (or no film) on male college students who had been angered by having the experimenter's accomplice administer electric shocks. Students watched a segment of news film in which South Vietnamese soldiers executed a North Vietnamese prisoner, a fictional movie segment showing a knife fight between two main characters, a non-violent movie, or nothing. Those who watched the violent film segments were further divided into three groups each, with some hearing a preliminary voice track or voice-over that provided justification for the violence, some hearing the voice track or voice-over suggesting that the violence was not justified, and some hearing no explanation. After the stimulus, the students had the opportunity to administer shocks to the accomplice. The results showed that those who saw either real or fictional violence that was presented without explanation or was presented as justified delivered more and more intense shocks to the experimenter's accomplice, compared to those who saw the non-violent film, or no film. In addition, these groups delivered more punishment than the students who had seen the news film or the fictional film with the voice track suggesting that the violence was not justified.

Another study examined the impact of viewing either violent or non-violent movies every night for a week. The participants in this study were Belgian secondary schoolboys living in an institution for juvenile delinquents. The boys lived in four separate cottages, and two cottages were assigned to each type of movie. The researchers observed the boys' behavior during the week before the movies, during the movie-watching week and during the week after the movies. The findings revealed that among the boys who had watched the violent movies, both impersonal and interpersonal physical aggression increased significantly more than among the boys who had watched the non-violent movies. The effects were not uniform across all residents of the cottages showing the violent movies; instead, the most significant effects were observed among the boys who were perceived by their peers as the most dominant and those who were the most and least popular within their cottages (Leyens et al., 1975).

Given the prominence of violence as a feature of modern movies and the fact that many adolescents are exposed to even extremely violent movies (Sargent et al., 2002; Worth et al., 2008), it is somewhat surprising that relatively few researchers seem to have examined the effects of these movies. Researchers may simply assume that exposure to television violence and exposure to movie violence have the same types of effects and, in the current media environment, it may be difficult to make the distinction, given that DVDs, digital downloads and online streaming services mean that adolescents may be far more likely to view movies in their own homes rather than in movie theaters ("Preferred Movie Watching Location," 2015).

Music videos represent another distinct type of (sometimes violent) media content individuals are likely to view in their own homes, whether via cable television channels such as BET or MTV, or online via YouTube, Yahoo Music, Vimeo or some other music video streaming site. Some correlational studies have suggested that watching MTV more often is positively related to children's self-reports of getting into physical fights with other children and with peers' and teachers' ratings of their levels of verbal, relational and physical aggression. A review of research on the effects of music and music videos on children's behavior concluded that music alone, even violent music, has significantly less effect than violent television or video games. However, music videos may affect viewers in the same way as other types of violent media images (Roberts et al., 2003).

On the other hand, at least one study did suggest that violent music lyrics – even without violent imagery – may increase aggressive behavior. In this intriguing study, college students were assigned to listen to music either with or without lyrics and with or without the accompanying music video; in the no-lyrics condition, the lyrics had been digitally edited out. After exposure to the music, the participants were given the chance to decide how much hot sauce to include in a "taste-test" sample, which they were told another participant would be required to consume entirely. Those who were exposed to violent lyrics – with or without the music video imagery – allocated more hot sauce to the next participant (Lennings & Warburton, 2011). The results were consistent with those of a German study, which revealed that men who had listened to misogynous song lyrics allocated more hot sauce to a female research confederate than to a male confederate; there was no difference when the song lyrics were neutral. Similar results were produced when the aggressive behavior involved having the research participant decide how long another student would be required to keep his or her hand in ice water; men who listened to misogynous lyrics assigned longer times to a female participant than to a male participant. In addition, both male and female participants who had listened to "men-hating" lyrics assigned more ice water exposure time to male participants, in comparison to those who had listened to neutral lyrics (Fischer & Greitemeyer, 2006).

In recent years, most of the research – and controversy – surrounding media effects on aggressive and violent behavior have focused on the impact of video games. Here, too, scholars disagree about whether the evidence shows that playing violent video games *causes* increased aggression. Ferguson and his colleagues (Ferguson, 2007, 2015; Ferguson & Kilburn, 2009; Ferguson et al., 2009) insist that exposure to violent media content, including playing violent games, has no significant effect on "serious acts of youth aggression or violence" (Ferguson, 2010b, p. 377). In fact, in some cases, Ferguson has argued, playing violent video games benefits players by improving their visual acuity and their perception and processing of and memory for visual information; video games, therefore, could be useful educational tools (Ferguson, 2010a). The research supporting the negative effects of violent video games, he concludes, is characterized by what he regards as invalid aggression measures, failure to account for third variables that might explain away the links between video game exposure and aggressive behavior, publication and citation biases in favor of findings that support a negative view of games, "small" effect sizes, a failure to specify the point at which aggressive behavior ceases to be positive and becomes "pathological," unstandardized use of aggression measures, a lack of correspondence between video game consumption and violent crime rates, and "low standards of evidence" (Ferguson, 2010a, p. 75).

Other researchers also have questioned whether playing violent video games contributes to violent crime. One research team conducted time series analyses to assess associations between rates of violent crime and video game sales, game release dates and keyword searches for video game guides; based on these comparisons, they concluded that there was no evidence of an association between sales of violent video games and serious real-world violence (Markey et al., 2014).

337

The vast majority of other researchers, however, appear to agree that playing violent video games does lead to increases in aggressive thoughts, attitudes and behaviors, at least for some segments of the population (Bushman & Anderson, 2002; Carnagey & Anderson, 2005; Engelhardt et al., 2011; Gentile et al., 2004, 2014; Lam et al., 2013; Lin, 2013). The most recent comprehensive meta-analysis assessed results from 136 papers involving more than 130,000 participants from both Western and Eastern countries, notable because many of the studies from Eastern countries reflect results from cultures that are far less violent than the United States. The analysis included 92 experimental comparisons, 82 cross-sectional comparisons and 34 longitudinal comparisons. Using these comparisons, the researchers found significant effects of video game exposure on increased aggressive behavior, regardless of the type of study, how conservative the analysis was or whether the studies were examining short- or long-term effects. In addition, the effects held across both Eastern and Western cultures (Anderson et al., 2010).

In addition to having significant effects on increased aggressive behavior, the meta-analysis also demonstrated significant relationships between exposure to violent video games and higher levels of aggressive thoughts. For longitudinal studies there was a significant effect of culture, with video game exposure producing larger effects in Western countries than in Eastern countries; however, different types of measures were used in the five longitudinal studies in Japan as compared to the three longitudinal studies from Western countries, making the cultural difference finding less definitive. Additional comparisons demonstrated consistent effects of violent video game exposure on emotion, empathy and prosocial behavior; greater exposure to violent games increased aggressive affect and reduced prosocial behavior and empathy. The authors conclude that "the newly available longitudinal studies provide further confirmation that playing violent video games is a causal risk factor for long-term harmful outcomes" (Anderson et al., 2010, p. 169).

The paper acknowledges that other researchers, notably Ferguson and Kilburn (2009), have published meta-analyses purporting to show no significant effects of video game play on subsequent aggressive behavior. The authors reject this analysis.

In sum, the only way one can "demonstrate" that the existing literature on violent video game effects does not show multiple causal harmful effects is to use an incredibly small subset of the existing literature, include some of the methodologically poorest studies, exclude many of the methodologically strongest studies, and misuse standard meta-analytic techniques.

(Anderson et al., 2010, p. 169)

In a commentary on the Anderson et al. (2010) study, long-time media violence researcher Rowell Huesmann compares the research on violent video games to that linking smoking to lung cancer and lead-based paint to mental retardation, noting that we view these relationships as public health problems, even though some people smoke without developing lung cancer or suffer no loss of mental capacity despite exposure to lead-based paint. He also notes, however, that the high quality of the meta-analysis will probably not change the views of those who prefer to believe that video games have no negative effects (Huesmann, 2010). After all, the U.S. Surgeon General's report concluding that exposure to television violence increases antisocial behavior was published in 1972. In that report, the Surgeon General stated that the data linking television violence and aggressive behavior were "sufficient to justify action" (Steinfeld, 1972, p. 27); and yet, more than 40 years later, it would be

Figure 10.2: Few Parents Restrict their Children's Access to Violent Media

difficult to argue that any government action has been effective in reducing Americans' exposure to violent content on television or in any other medium.

This may be due, in part, to public ambivalence about whether exposure to media violence increases aggressive behavior, as well as misunderstanding the distinction between aggression and violence. A 2007 Kaiser Family Foundation (KFF) survey showed that 81 percent of American parents believe exposure to media violence contributes to violent behavior in children "somewhat" (38%) or "a lot" (43%) (Rideout, 2007); however, more recent KFF research reveals that few parents enforce any rules restricting their children's exposure to media violence. Fewer than half of eight- to 18-year-olds in a 2010 Kaiser Family Foundation survey said their parents restrict the types of television shows they can watch, and only 28 percent said their parents restrict the amount of time they spend watching TV. Nearly two-thirds (64%) said the television is usually on during meals, and 45 percent said the TV is on all the time, whether or not anyone is watching. Less than one-third of the children (30%) said their parents have any rules about the types of video games they can play or how long they can spend playing games; among 15- to 18-year-olds, only 12 percent said their parents restricted the types of games they could play, and only 18 percent said their parents limited their video game time (Rideout et al., 2010).

Even so, two-thirds of parents in the 2004 KFF survey said they supported regulations that would limit the amount of sex and violence allowed in television shows during the early evening hours. Parents may be likely to support such regulations, even when they don't enforce rules restricting their own children's access to violent content, because they believe media violence mostly affects the behavior of other people's children. This third-person effect may reflect parents' belief that they themselves provide appropriate supervision of their children's media use, while others do not. Only 18 percent of parents acknowledged that they need to do more to monitor their children's media use; 16 percent said such monitoring was unnecessary, and 65 percent said they already closely monitor their children's media use – a figure that seems to be at odds with children's own reports about their parents' media monitoring (Rideout, 2007).

Anderson and Gentile (2008) argue that the media industries contribute to parents' and policy-makers' confusion about media violence effects in at least three ways. First, media companies aggressively promote the idea that no valid research supports negative effects of media violence; in some instances, this includes promoting and sometimes providing funding for "academicians without true expertise in media violence research. These 'experts' denounce as poorly conducted any research that finds harmful effects, but praise the occasional study with nonsignificant findings" (Anderson & Gentile, 2008, p. 283). In addition, some research suggests that even as evidence of the negative effects of violent media was mounting, news coverage of the issue grew weaker. Indeed, a recent study examining 30 years' worth of news coverage of the media violence issue showed that since 2001, the percentage of articles suggesting that media violence has negative effects has declined sharply – from 69.6 percent in 1997 to 2001 to 50 percent in articles published from 2002 to 2006 and even further, to 38.8 percent, in 2007 to 2011 articles. During the most recent period, only 5 percent of articles suggested that there was no link, but the majority of articles (56.2%) were neutral (Martins et al., 2013). News coverage, therefore, suggests that there is no consensus on the evidence, despite the fact that overwhelming percentages of researchers and pediatricians agree that exposure to media violence has negative effects (Bushman et al., 2014).

One further element of confusion is the difference between media violence exposure as a risk factor for future aggressive or violent behavior versus media violence exposure *causing* violent behavior in a specific individual. Violent behavior rarely results from a single cause; rather, it is the confluence of numerous factors that would lead an individual to behave in aggressive or violent ways. People sometimes argue, for instance, that media violence must have no effect because they themselves, or someone they know, had years of exposure to violent media and yet committed no violent crime. This sort of statement confuses "risk factor" with "guarantee" (Anderson & Gentile, 2008). Exposure to media violence is a risk factor for future involvement in aggressive and violent behavior, in the same way that smoking is a significant risk factor for lung cancer and heart disease. Not everyone who smokes, even for extended periods of time, develops lung cancer, but by 1999, 92 percent of respondents to a survey about smoking agreed that cigarette smoking is one cause of lung cancer (Pacheco, 2011). Communication researchers need to find ways of helping the public and policy-makers understand the relationship between media violence and aggressive or violent behavior in the same way.

NOTE

1 The investigations of several of these mass shooting incidents have demonstrated that the shooters were motivated, at least in part, by the desire for notoriety. Their names, therefore, will not be used in this chapter.

REFERENCES

14 Very, Very, VERY Violent TV Shows. (n.d.). Retrieved April 3, 2015 from www. tvguide.com/galleries/very-violent-tv-shows-1088287/.

Adams, T.M. & Fuller, D.B. (2006). The Words Have Changed but the Ideology Remains the Same: Misogynistic Lyrics in Rap Music. *Journal of Black Studies*, 36(6), 938–957. http://doi.org/10.1177/0021934704274072.

Allen, G. (2014, November 20). Grand Theft Auto V: Shocking Video of Prostitute Sex with Gamer in Controversial First-person Viewpoint. Retrieved April 7, 2015 from www.mirror.co.uk/news/uk-news/grand-theft-auto-v-shocking-4659247.

Anderson, C.A. (1997). Effects of Violent Movies and Trait Hostility on Hostile Feelings and Aggressive Thoughts. *Aggressive Behavior*, 23(3), 161–178. http://doi.org/10.1002/(SICI)1098-2337(1997)23:3161::AID-AB23.0.CO;2-P.

Anderson, C.A. & Gentile, D.A. (2008). Media Violence, Aggression and Public Policy. In *Beyond Common Sense: Psychological Science in the Courtroom*. Malden, MA: Blackwell. Retrieved from https://books.google.com/books?hl=en&lr=&id=G7lGt8UkU_AC&oi=fnd&pg=PA281&dq=Media+Violence,+Aggression,+and+Public+Policy&ots=IDU25TLAaf&sig=eIBlw3SRTZp97rgQW6Qz56oaFlI.

Anderson, C.A., Carnagey, N.L. & Eubanks, J. (2003). Exposure to Violent Media: The Effects of Songs with Violent Lyrics on Aggressive Thoughts and Feelings. *Journal of Personality and Social Psychology*, 84(5), 960.

Anderson, C.A., Carnagey, N.L., Flanagan, M., Benjamin, A.J., Eubanks, J. & Valentine, J.C. (2004). Violent Video Games: Specific Effects of Violent Content on Aggressive Thoughts and Behavior. *Advances in Experimental Social Psychology*, 36, 200–251.

Anderson, C A., Shibuya, A., Ihori, N., Swing, E.L., Bushman, B.J., Sakamoto, A. & Saleem, M. (2010). Violent Video Game Effects on Aggression, Empathy, and Prosocial Behavior in Eastern and Western Countries: A Meta-analytic Review. *Psychological Bulletin*, 136(2), 151–173. http://doi.org/10.1037/a0018251.

Armstrong, E.G. (2001). Gangsta Misogyny: A Content Analysis of the Portrayals of Violence against Women in Rap Music, 1987–1993. *Journal of Criminal Justice and Popular Culture*, 8(2), 96–126.

Aubrey, J.S., Hopper, K.M. & Mbure, W.G. (2011). Check That Body! The Effects of Sexually Objectifying Music Videos on College Men's Sexual Beliefs. *Journal of Broadcasting & Electronic Media*, 55(3), 360–379. http://doi.org/10.1080/08838151.2011.597469.

Bartholow, B.D., Sestir, M.A. & Davis, E.B. (2005). Correlates and Consequences of Exposure to Video Game Violence: Hostile Personality, Empathy, and Aggressive Behavior. *Personality and Social Psychology Bulletin*, 31(11), 1573–1586. http://doi.org/10.1177/0146167205277205.

Bauder, D. (2013, May 1). TV Violence Increasing, Growing Darker Post-Newtown, Study Finds. Retrieved April 3, 2015 from www.washingtontimes.com/news/2013/may/1/report-shows-persistence-of-violence-in-prime-time/.

Baxter, R.L., De Riemer, C., Landini, A., Leslie, L. & Singletary, M.W. (1985). A Content Analysis of Music Videos. *Journal of Broadcasting & Electronic Media*, 29(3), 333–340.

Beasley, B. & Collins Standley, T. (2002). Shirts vs. Skins: Clothing as an Indicator of Gender Role Stereotyping in Video Games. *Mass Communication & Society*, 5(3), 279–293.

Berger, A., Wildsmith, E., Manlove, J. & Steward-Streng, N. (2012). *Relationship Violence among Young Adult Couples* (No. 2012–14). Washington, DC: Child Trends. Retrieved April 1, 2015 from http://citeseerx.ist.psu.edu/viewdoc/download?doi=10.1.1.405.4990&rep=rep1&type=pdf.

Bleakley, A., Jamieson, P.E. & Romer, D. (2012). Trends of Sexual and Violent Content by Gender in Top-grossing U.S. Films, 1950–2006. *The Journal of Adolescent Health: Official Publication of the Society for Adolescent Medicine*, 51(1), 73–79. http://doi.org/10.1016/j.jadohealth.2012.02.006.

Blum, J., Ireland, M. & Blum, R.W. (2003). Gender Differences in Juvenile Violence: A Report from Add Health. *Journal of Adolescent Health*, 32(3), 234–240. http://doi.org/10.1016/S1054-139X(02)00448-2.

Bryant, J. & Oliver, M.B. (eds). (2009). Social Cognitive Theory of Mass Communication. In *Media Effects: Advances in Theory and Research* (3rd edn). New York: Taylor & Francis.

Bushman, B.J. (1998). Priming Effects of Media Violence on the Accessibility of Aggressive Constructs in Memory. *Personality and Social Psychology Bulletin*, 24(5), 537–545. http://doi.org/10.1177/0146167298245009.

Bushman, B.J. & Anderson, C.A. (2001). Media Violence and the American Public: Scientific Facts versus Media Misinformation. *American Psychologist*, 56(6–7), 477–489. http://doi.org/10.1037/0003-066X.56.6-7.477.

Bushman, B.J. & Anderson, C.A. (2002). Violent Video Games and Hostile Expectations: A Test of the General Aggression Model. *Personality and Social Psychology Bulletin*, 28(12), 1679–1686. http://doi.org/10.1177/014616702237649.

Bushman, B.J., Gollwitzer, M. & Cruz, C. (2014). There Is Broad Consensus: Media Researchers Agree That Violent Media Increase Aggression in Children, and Pediatricians and Parents Concur. *Psychology of Popular Media Culture*. http://doi.org/10.1037/ppm0000046.

Bushman, B.J., Jamieson, P.E., Weitz, I. & Romer, D. (2013). Gun Violence Trends in Movies. *Pediatrics*, 132(6), 1014–1018. http://doi.org/10.1542/peds.2013-1600.

Butts, J.A. (2014). *Violent Youth Arrests Continue to Fall Nationwide*. New York: John Jay College of Criminal Justice, City University of New York. Retrieved March 31, 2015 from www.njjn.org/uploads/digital-library/JohnJay_Violent-Youth-Arrests-Continue-to-Fall_November_2014.pdf.

Carnagey, N.L. & Anderson, C.A. (2005). The Effects of Reward and Punishment in Violent Video Games on Aggressive Affect, Cognition, and Behavior. *Psychological Science*, 16(11), 882–889. http://doi.org/10.1111/j.1467-9280.2005.01632.x.

Centers for Disease Control and Prevention. (2014, October 22). Key Data and Statistics. Retrieved April 1, 2015 from www.cdc.gov/injury/overview/data.html.

Coyne, S.M. & Padilla-Walker, L.M. (2015). Sex, Violence, & Rock n' Roll: Longitudinal Effects of Music on Aggression, Sex, and Prosocial Behavior during Adolescence. *Journal of Adolescence*, 41, 96–104. http://doi.org/10.1016/j.adolescence.2015.03.002.

Dietz, T.L. (1998). An Examination of Violence and Gender Role Portrayals in Video Games: Implications for Gender Socialization and Aggressive Behavior. *Sex Roles, 38*(5–6), 425–442.

Dill, K.E., Gentile, D.A., Richter, W.A. & Dill, J.C. (2005). Violence, Sex, Race and Age in Popular Video Games: A Content Analysis. In *Featuring Females: Feminist Analyses of the Media.* Washington, DC: American Psychological Association. Retrieved April 2, 2015 from www.researchgate.net/profile/Karen_Dill-Shackleford/publication/230800325_Violence_Sex_Race_and_Age_in_Popular_Video_Games_A_Content_Analysis/links/542ebdbb0cf29bbc126f4546.pdf.

Downs, E. & Smith, S.L. (2009). Keeping Abreast of Hypersexuality: A Video Game Character Content Analysis. *Sex Roles, 62*(11–12), 721–733. http://doi.org/10.1007/s11199-009-9637-1.

Drakengard Review. (n.d.). Retrieved April 7, 2015 from www.ign.com/games/drakengard/ps2-497011.

Engelhardt, C.R., Bartholow, B.D., Kerr, G.T. & Bushman, B.J. (2011). This is Your Brain on Violent Video Games: Neural Desensitization to Violence Predicts Increased Aggression Following Violent Video Game Exposure. *Journal of Experimental Social Psychology, 47*(5), 1033–1036. http://doi.org/10.1016/j.jesp.2011.03.027.

Federal Trade Commission. (2007). *Marketing Violent Entertainment to Children: A Fifth Follow-up Review of Industry Practices in the Motion Picture, Music Recording & Electronic Game Industries.* Washington, DC: Federal Trade Commission. Retrieved April 7, 2015 from www.ftc.gov/sites/default/files/documents/reports/marketing-violent-entertainment-children-fifth-follow-review-industry-practices-motion-picture-music/070412marketingviolentechildren.pdf.

Ferguson, C.J. (2007). The Good, The Bad and the Ugly: A Meta-analytic Review of Positive and Negative Effects of Violent Video Games. *Psychiatric Quarterly, 78*(4), 309–316. http://doi.org/10.1007/s11126-007-9056-9.

Ferguson, C.J. (2010a). Blazing Angels or Resident Evil? Can Violent Video Games Be a Force for Good? *Review of General Psychology, 14*(2), 68–81. http://doi.org/10.1037/a0018941.

Ferguson, C.J. (2010b). Video Games and Youth Violence: A Prospective Analysis in Adolescents. *Journal of Youth and Adolescence, 40*(4), 377–391. http://doi.org/10.1007/s10964-010-9610-x.

Ferguson, C.J. (2015). Does Media Violence Predict Societal Violence? It Depends on What You Look at and When. *Journal of Communication, 65*(1), E1–E22. http://doi.org/10.1111/jcom.12129.

Ferguson, C.J. & Kilburn, J. (2009). The Public Health Risks of Media Violence: A Meta-analytic Review. *The Journal of Pediatrics, 154*(5), 759–763. http://doi.org/10.1016/j.jpeds.2008.11.033.

Ferguson, C.J., San Miguel, C. & Hartley, R.D. (2009). A Multivariate Analysis of Youth Violence and Aggression: The Influence of Family, Peers, Depression, and Media Violence. *The Journal of Pediatrics, 155*(6), 904–908.e3. http://doi.org/10.1016/j.jpeds.2009.06.021.

Ferguson, C.J., Muñoz, M.E., Garza, A., & Galindo, M. (2013). Concurrent and Prospective Analyses of Peer, Television and Social Media Influences on Body Dissatisfaction, Eating Disorder Symptoms and Life Satisfaction in Adolescent Girls. *Journal of Youth and Adolescence, 43*(1), 1–14. http://doi.org/10.1007/s10964-012-9898-9.

Fischer, P. & Greitemeyer, T. (2006). Music and Aggression: The Impact of Sexual-aggressive Song Lyrics on Aggression-related Thoughts, Emotions, and Behavior

Toward the Same and the Opposite Sex. *Personality & Social Psychology Bulletin*, *32*(9), 1165–1176. http://doi.org/10.1177/0146167206288670.

Foshee, V.A., McNaughton Reyes, L., Tharp, A.T., Chang, L-Y., Ennett, S.T., Simon, T.R. & Suchindran, C. (2015). Shared Longitudinal Predictors of Physical Peer and Dating Violence. *The Journal of Adolescent Health: Official Publication of the Society for Adolescent Medicine*, *56*(1), 106–112. http://doi.org/10.1016/j.jadohealth.2014.08.003.

Fox, J. & Potocki, B. (2015). Lifetime Video Game Consumption, Interpersonal Aggression, Hostile Sexism, and Rape Myth Acceptance: A Cultivation Perspective. *Journal of Interpersonal Violence*. http://doi.org/10.1177/0886260515570747.

Frankel, T.C. (2015, January 14). Why the CDC Still Isn't Researching Gun Violence, Despite the Ban Being Lifted Two Years Ago. *Washington Post*. Retrieved April 1, 2015 from www.washingtonpost.com/news/storyline/wp/2015/01/14/why-the-cdc-still-isnt-researching-gun-violence-despite-the-ban-being-lifted-two-years-ago/.

Funk, J.B., Baldacci, H.B., Pasold, T. & Baumgardner, J. (2004). Violence Exposure in Real-life, Video Games, Television, Movies, and the Internet: Is There Desensitization? *Journal of Adolescence*, *27*(1), 23–39. http://doi.org/10.1016/j.adolescence.2003.10.005.

Gentile, D.A., Lynch, P.J., Linder, J.R. & Walsh, D.A. (2004). The Effects of Violent Video Game Habits on Adolescent Hostility, Aggressive Behaviors, and School Performance. *Journal of Adolescence*, *27*(1), 5–22. http://doi.org/10.1016/j.adolescence.2003.10.002.

Gentile, D.A., Li, D., Khoo, A., Prot, S. & Anderson, C.A. (2014). Mediators and Moderators of Long-term Effects of Violent Video Games on Aggressive Behavior: Practice, Thinking, and Action. *JAMA Pediatrics*, *168*(5), 450–457. http://doi.org/10.1001/jamapediatrics.2014.63.

Greeson, L.E. & Williams, R.A. (1986). Social Implications of Music Videos for Youth: An Analysis of the Content and Effects of MTV. *Youth & Society*, *18*(2), 177–189. http://doi.org/10.1177/0044118X86018002005.

Haninger, K. & Thompson, K.M. (2004). Content and Ratings of Teen-rated Video Games. *JAMA*, *291*(7), 856–865. http://doi.org/10.1001/jama.291.7.856.

Hanks, H. (2014, January 22). Is TV More Violent Than Ever? Retrieved April 3, 2015 from www.cnn.com/2014/01/20/showbiz/tv-violence/index.html.

Hartmann, T., Krakowiak, K.M. & Tsay-Vogel, M. (2014). How Violent Video Games Communicate Violence: A Literature Review and Content Analysis of Moral Disengagement Factors. *Communication Monographs*, *81*(3), 310–332. http://doi.org/10.1080/03637751.2014.922206.

Hemenway, D., Vriniotis, M., Johnson, R.M., Miller, M. & Azrael, D. (2011). Gun Carrying by High School Students in Boston, MA: Does Overestimation of Peer Gun Carrying Matter? *Journal of Adolescence*, *34*(5), 997–1003. http://doi.org/10.1016/j.adolescence.2010.11.008.

Herd, D. (2009). Changing Images of Violence in Rap Music Lyrics: 1979–1997. *Journal of Public Health Policy*, *30*(4), 395–406. http://doi.org/10.1057/jphp.2009.36.

Hoerrner, K.L. (1999). *The Forgotten Battles: Congressional Hearings on Television Violence in the 1950s*. Manship School of Mass Communication Mimeograph.

Huesmann, L.R. (1982). Television Violence and Aggressive Behavior. In *Television and Behavior: Ten Years of Scientific Progress and Implications for the Eighties* (Vol. 2, pp. 126–137). Retrieved April 15, 2015 from http://files.eric.ed.gov/fulltext/ED228979.pdf#page=136.

Huesmann, L.R. (2007). The Impact of Electronic Media Violence: Scientific Theory and Research. *The Journal of Adolescent Health: Official Publication of the Society for*

Adolescent Medicine, 41(6, Suppl. 1), S6–S13. http://doi.org/10.1016/j.jadohealth.2007.09.005.

Huesmann, L.R. (2010). Nailing the Coffin Shut on Doubts that Violent Video Games Stimulate Aggression: Comment on Anderson et al. (2010). *Psychological Bulletin, 136*(2), 179–181. http://doi.org/10.1037/a0018567.

Hunnicutt, G. & Andrews, K.H. (2009). Tragic Narratives in Popular Culture: Depictions of Homicide in Rap Music. *Sociological Forum, 24*(3), 611–630.

Itzkoff, D. (2014, May 2). For "Game of Thrones," Rising Unease Over Rape's Recurring Role. *New York Times*. Retrieved April 3, 2015 from www.nytimes.com/2014/05/03/arts/television/for-game-of-thrones-rising-unease-over-rapes-recurring-role.html.

Jena, A.B., Sun, E.C. & Prasad, V. (2014). Does the Declining Lethality of Gunshot Injuries Mask a Rising Epidemic of Gun Violence in the United States? *Journal of General Internal Medicine, 29*(7), 1065–1069. http://doi.org/10.1007/s11606-014-2779-z.

Johnson, J.D., Jackson, L.A. & Gatto, L. (1995). Violent Attitudes and Deferred Academic Aspirations: Deleterious Effects of Exposure to Rap Music. *Basic and Applied Social Psychology, 16*(1–2), 27–41. http://doi.org/10.1080/01973533.1995.9646099.

Josephson, W.L. (1987). Television Violence and Children's Aggression: Testing the Priming, Social Script, and Disinhibition Predictions. *Journal of Personality and Social Psychology, 53*(5), 882–890. http://doi.org/10.1037/0022-3514.53.5.882.

Kain, E. (2013, September 18). Do Games Like "Grand Theft Auto V" Cause Real-world Violence? Retrieved March 31, 2015 from www.forbes.com/sites/erikkain/2013/09/18/do-games-like-grand-theft-auto-v-cause-real-world-violence/.

Kassel, M.B. (n.d.). The Untouchables. Retrieved April 2, 2015 from www.emmytvlegends.org/interviews/shows/untouchables-the.

Kelly, R.L. (2014). *2014 Kelly Report: Gun Violence in America*. Washington, DC: Office of Congresswoman Robin Kelly. Retrieved April 1, 2015 from http://robinkelly.house.gov/sites/robinkelly.house.gov/files/wysiwyg_uploaded/KellyReport_1.pdf.

Kistler, M.E. & Lee, M.J. (2009). Does Exposure to Sexual Hip-Hop Music Videos Influence the Sexual Attitudes of College Students? *Mass Communication and Society, 13*(1), 67–86. http://doi.org/10.1080/15205430902865336.

Lam, L.T., Cheng, Z. & Liu, X. (2013). Violent Online Games Exposure and Cyberbullying/Victimization among Adolescents. *Cyberpsychology, Behavior and Social Networking, 16*(3), 159–165. http://doi.org/10.1089/cyber.2012.0087.

Langley, T., O'Neal, E.C., Craig, K.M. & Yost, E.A. (1992). Aggression-Consistent, -Inconsistent, and -Irrelevant Priming Effects on Selective Exposure to Media Violence. *Aggressive Behavior, 18*(5), 349–356. http://doi.org/10.1002/1098-2337(1992)18:5349::AID-AB2480180543.0.CO;2-A.

Lawrence, J. St. S. & Joyner, D.J. (1991). The Effects of Sexually Violent Rock Music on Males' Acceptance of Violence Against Women. *Psychology of Women Quarterly, 15*(1), 49–63. http://doi.org/10.1111/j.1471-6402.1991.tb00477.x.

League of Legends: Number of Players 2012–2014 (Fee-based). (2014, January 28). Retrieved April 7, 2015 from www.statista.com/statistics/329015/number-lol-players/.

Lennings, H.I.B. & Warburton, W.A. (2011). The Effect of Auditory versus Visual Violent Media Exposure on Aggressive Behaviour: The Role of Song Lyrics, Video Clips and Musical Tone. *Journal of Experimental Social Psychology, 47*(4), 794–799.

Leyens, J-P., Camino, L., Parke, R.D. & Berkowitz, L. (1975). Effects of Movie Violence on Aggression in a Field Setting as a Function of Group Dominance and

Cohesion. *Journal of Personality and Social Psychology, 32*(2), 346–360. http://doi.org/10.1037/0022-3514.32.2.346.

Lin, J.-H. (2013). Do Video Games Exert Stronger Effects on Aggression than Film? The Role of Media Interactivity and Identification on the Association of Violent Content and Aggressive Outcomes. *Computers in Human Behavior, 29*(3), 535–543. http://doi.org/10.1016/j.chb.2012.11.001.

Macchiarella, P. (n.d.). *Trends in Digital Gaming: Free-to-play, Social and Mobile Games.* Dallas, TX: Parks Associates.

Markey, P.M., Markey, C.N. & French, J.E. (2014). Violent Video Games and Real-world Violence: Rhetoric versus Data. *Psychology of Popular Media Culture,* n.p.g. http://doi.org/10.1037/ppm0000030.

Martins, N., Weaver, A.J., Yeshua-Katz, D., Lewis, N.H., Tyree, N.E. & Jensen, J.D. (2013). A Content Analysis of Print News Coverage of Media Violence and Aggression Research. *Journal of Communication, 63*(6), 1070–1087. http://doi.org/10.1111/jcom.12052.

Matthews, N.L. & Weaver, A.J. (2013). Skill Gap: Quantifying Violent Content in Video Game Play between Variably Skilled Users. *Mass Communication and Society, 16*(6), 829–846. http://doi.org/10.1080/15205436.2013.773043.

Meyer, T.P. (1972). Effects of Viewing Justified and Unjustified Real Film Violence on Aggressive Behavior. *Journal of Personality and Social Psychology, 23*(1), 21–29. http://doi.org/10.1037/h0032868.

MMO Gaming – Statistics & Facts. (n.d.). Retrieved April 7, 2015 from www.statista.com/topics/2290/mmo-gaming/.

National Institute of Justice. (2014, March 11). From Juvenile Delinquency to Young Adult Offending. Retrieved April 1, 2015 from www.nij.gov/topics/crime/Pages/delinquency-to-adult-offending.aspx.

Niolon, P.H., Vivolo-Kantor, A.M., Latzman, N.E., Valle, L.A., Kuoh, H., Burton, T. & Tharp, A.T. (2015). Prevalence of Teen Dating Violence and Co-occurring Risk Factors among Middle School Youth in High-risk Urban Communities. *The Journal of Adolescent Health: Official Publication of the Society for Adolescent Medicine, 56*(2, Suppl. 2), S5–S13. http://doi.org/10.1016/j.jadohealth.2014.07.019.

Pacheco, J. (2011). Trends – Public Opinion on Smoking and Anti-smoking Policies. *Public Opinion Quarterly, 75*(3), 576–592.

Paik, H. & Comstock, G. (1994). The Effects of Television Violence on Antisocial Behavior: A Meta-analysis. *Communication Research, 21*(4), 516–546. http://doi.org/10.1177/009365094021004004.

Parents Television Council. (2013). *Media Violence: An Examination of Violence, Graphic Violence and Gun Violence in the Media.* Los Angeles, CA: Parents Television Council. Retrieved April 3, 2015 from http://w2.parentstv.org/main/Research/Studies/CableViolence/vstudy_dec2013.pdf.

Peterson, D.L. & Pfost, K.S. (1989). Influence of Rock Videos on Attitudes of Violence against Women. *Psychological Reports, 64*(1), 319–322.

Pickett, W., Craig, W., Harel, Y., Cunningham, J., Simpson, K., Molcho, M. & Currie, C.E. (2005). Cross-national Study of Fighting and Weapon Carrying as Determinants of Adolescent Injury. *Pediatrics, 116*(6), e855–e863. http://doi.org/10.1542/peds.2005-0607.

Preferred Movie Watching Location: Theater vs. Home in the U.S. 2013. (2015). Retrieved April 16, 2015 from www.statista.com/statistics/299170/preferred-movie-watching-location-theater-home-usa/.

Primack, B.A., Gold, M.A., Schwarz, E.B. & Dalton, M.A. (2008). Degrading and

Non-degrading Sex in Popular Music: A Content Analysis. *Public Health Reports*, *123*(5), 593–600.

Rich, M., Woods, E.R., Goodman, E., Emans, S.J. & DuRant, R.H. (1998). Aggressors or Victims: Gender and Race in Music Video Violence. *Pediatrics*, *101*(4, Part 1), 669–674.

Rideout, V. (2007). *Parents, Media and Public Policy: A Kaiser Family Foundation Survey*. Menlo Park, CA: Henry J. Kaiser Family Foundation. Retrieved April 20, 2015 from https://kaiserfamilyfoundation.files.wordpress.com/2013/01/7638.pdf.

Rideout, V.J., Foehr, U.G. & Roberts, D.F. (2010). *Generation M2: Media in the Lives of 8- to 18-Year-Olds*. Menlo Park, CA. Retrieved April 16, 2015 from http://kff.org/other/report/generation-m2-media-in-the-lives-of-8-to-18-year-olds/.

Roberts, D.F., Christenson, P.G. & Gentile, D.A. (2003). The Effects of Violent Music on Children and Adolescents. *Media Violence and Children*, 153–170.

Romer, D., Jamieson, P.E., Bushman, B.J., Bleakley, A., Wang, A., Langleben, D. & Jamieson, K.H. (2014). Parental Desensitization to Violence and Sex in Movies. *Pediatrics*, *134*(5), 877–884. http://doi.org/10.1542/peds.2014-1167.

Rothenberg, M.B. (1975). Effect of Television Violence on Children and Youth. *JAMA*, *234*(10), 1043–1046.

Rowell, L., Moise-Titus, J., Podolski, C.-L. & Eron, L.D. (2003). Longitudinal Relations between Children's Exposure to TV Violence and their Aggressive and Violent Behavior in Young Adulthood: 1977–1992. *Developmental Psychology*, *39*(2), 201–221. http://doi.org/10.1037/0012-1649.39.2.201.

Ruggles, K.V. & Rajan, S. (2014). Gun Possession among American Youth: A Discovery-based Approach to Understand Gun Violence. *PloS ONE*, *9*(11), e111893. http://doi.org/10.1371/journal.pone.0111893.

Sargent, J.D., Heatherton, T.F., Ahrens, M.B., Dalton, M.A., Tickle, J.J. & Beach, M.L. (2002). Adolescent Exposure to Extremely Violent Movies. *Journal of Adolescent Health*, *31*(6), 449–454. http://doi.org/10.1016/S1054-139X(02)00399-3.

Schneider, M. (2013, June 10). America's Most Watched: The Top 25 Shows of the 2012–2013 TV Season. Retrieved April 3, 2015 from www.tvguide.com/news/most-watched-tv-shows-top-25-2012-2013-1066503/.

Schwartz, J.A. & Beaver, K.M. (2015). Revisiting the Association Between Television Viewing in Adolescence and Contact With the Criminal Justice System in Adulthood. *Journal of Interpersonal Violence*, 0886260515576970. http://doi.org/10.1177/0886260515576970.

Signorielli, N. (2003). Prime-time Violence 1993–2001: Has the Picture Really Changed? *Journal of Broadcasting & Electronic Media*, *47*(1), 36–57.

Sluis, A. (2013, August 30). Online Gaming is Set for Massive Growth in the Coming Years. Retrieved April 7, 2015 from http://wallblog.co.uk/2013/08/30/why-online-gaming-is-set-for-massive-growth-in-the-coming-years/.

Smith, S.L. & Boyson, A.R. (2002). Violence in Music Videos: Examining the Prevalence and Context of Physical Aggression. *Journal of Communication*, *52*(1), 61–83. http://doi.org/10.1111/j.1460-2466.2002.tb02533.x.

Sousa, C., Herrenkohl, T.I., Moylan, C.A., Tajima, E.A., Klika, J.B., Herrenkohl, R.C. & Russo, M.J. (2011). Longitudinal Study on the Effects of Child Abuse and Children's Exposure to Domestic Violence, Parent–Child Attachments, and Antisocial Behavior in Adolescence. *Journal of Interpersonal Violence*, *26*(1), 111–136. http://doi.org/10.1177/0886260510362883.

Steinfeld, J. Statement in Hearings before Subcommittee on Communications of Committee on Commerce, Pub. L. No. Serial No. 92–52 § U.S. Senate Subcommittee on Communications of Committee on Commerce. (1972). Washington, DC: U.S. Government Printing Office.

Thomas, M.H., Horton, R.W., Lippincott, E.C. & Drabman, R.S. (1977). Desensitization to Portrayals of Real-life Aggression as a Function of Television Violence. *Journal of Personality and Social Psychology*, 35(6), 450–458. http://doi.org/10.1037/0022-3514.35.6.450.

Thompson, K.M. & Haninger, K. (2001). Violence in E-rated Video Games. *JAMA*, 286(5), 591–598.

Thompson, K.M., Tepichin, K. & Haninger, K. (2006). Content and Ratings of Mature-rated Video Games. *Archives of Pediatrics & Adolescent Medicine*, 160(4), 402–410. http://doi.org/10.1001/archpedi.160.4.402.

Uhlmann, E. & Swanson, J. (2004). Exposure to Violent Video Games Increases Automatic Aggressiveness. *Journal of Adolescence*, 27(1), 41–52. http://doi.org/10.1016/j.adolescence.2003.10.004.

Vagi, K.J., O'Malley Olsen, E., Basile, K.C. & Vivolo-Kantor, A.M. (2015). Teen Dating Violence (Physical and Sexual) among US High School Students: Findings From the 2013 National Youth Risk Behavior Survey. *JAMA Pediatrics*. http://doi.org/10.1001/jamapediatrics.2014.3577.

Wilkinson, D.L., McBryde, M.S., Williams, B., Bloom, S. & Bell, K. (2009). Peers and Gun Use Among Urban Adolescent Males: An Examination of Social Embeddedness. *Journal of Contemporary Criminal Justice*, 25(1), 20–44. http://doi.org/10.1177/1043986208328449.

Wilson, B.J., Kunkel, D., Linz, D., Potter, J., Donnerstein, E., Smith, S. & Gray, T. (1997). Television Violence and its Context: University of California, Santa Barbara Study. *National Television Violence Study*, 1, 3–268.

Wolfers, J. (2014, September 16). Perceptions Haven't Caught Up to Decline in Crime. *New York Times*. Retrieved March 31, 2015 from www.nytimes.com/2014/09/17/upshot/perceptions-havent-caught-up-to-decline-in-crime.html.

Worth, K.A., Chambers, J.G., Nassau, D.H., Rakhra, B.K. & Sargent, J.D. (2008). Exposure of US Adolescents to Extremely Violent Movies. *Pediatrics*, 122(2), 306–312. http://doi.org/10.1542/peds.2007-1096.

Yao, M.Z., Mahood, C. & Linz, D. (2009). Sexual Priming, Gender Stereotyping, and Likelihood to Sexually Harass: Examining the Cognitive Effects of Playing a Sexually-explicit Video Game. *Sex Roles*, 62(1–2), 77–88. http://doi.org/10.1007/s11199-009-9695-4.

YouGov | What is America's Most Dangerous City? (2014, September). Retrieved March 31, 2015 from https://today.yougov.com/news/2014/09/15/what-is-americas-most-dangerous-city/.

Zinzow, H.M. & Thompson, M. (2014). A Longitudinal Study of Risk Factors for Repeated Sexual Coercion and Assault in U.S. College Men. *Archives of Sexual Behavior*, 44(1), 213–222. http://doi.org/10.1007/s10508-013-0243-5.

Chapter 11

REPORTING ON HEALTH FOR BETTER OR WORSE: NEWS MEDIA EFFECTS ON KNOWLEDGE, BELIEFS AND BEHAVIORS

In the early part of the twentieth century in the United States, nearly every child contracted measles before his or her fifteenth birthday. Of every 1,000 cases between 1912 and 1916, 26 people died, accounting for 6,000 measles-related deaths, on average, each year. By the 1950s, both nutrition and disease treatment had improved, but measles was no less common, infecting three to four million people each year in the United States, killing 400 to 500 and leading to 48,000 hospitalizations. About 4,000 cases each year resulted in encephalitis, a swelling of the brain that can lead to deafness and intellectual disability (Centers for Disease Control and Prevention, 2014, 2015b; Pearce, 2015).

In 1963, however, the U.S. government licensed the first measles vaccine. By the late 1960s and early 1970s, state laws required all children to be vaccinated against measles before they started school (Pearce, 2015). The average number of annual measles cases dropped from 530,217 (with 440 deaths) between 1953 and 1962 (Roush et al., 2007) to 3,411 cases and three deaths in 1988 (Centers for Disease Control and Prevention, 1989).

From 1989 to 1991, the United States experienced a measles outbreak: 55,000 cases leading to 123 deaths and 11,000 hospitalizations (Pearce, 2015) and costing the country $100 million in direct medical costs ("The Measles Epidemic," 1991); some of those infected during this outbreak had been vaccinated, which prompted the initiation of requirements for a "booster" vaccine. As parents, pediatricians and schools adopted this two-vaccine regimen, the incidence of U.S. measles infections dropped so low that, by 2000, the CDC declared that measles had been eliminated in the United States, although it remained common in other countries, especially in the developing world (Pearce, 2015).

However, in February 1998, the highly respected journal *The Lancet* published a paper by a team of British researchers, led by physician Andrew Wakefield. The article described case histories of 12 children and linked the development of "behavioral problems" among eight of the children with MMR (measles, mumps, rubella) vaccination. In essence, the article suggested that receiving the MMR vaccine could cause autism in children (Ziv, 2015).

Few scientists ever thought Wakefield's theory to be worth considering seriously, and by 2010 researchers and journalists had determined that Wakefield's article was a fraud based on manipulated and even falsified data. An investigative journalist provided evidence that Wakefield and his colleagues had created the findings as a money-making scheme related to a lawsuit against the vaccine manufacturer (Deer, 2011a, 2011b). In February 2010, *The Lancet* retracted Wakefield's original paper after the British General Medical Council (GMC) found him guilty of dishonesty and other ethics violations (Dyer, 2010); later in 2010, the GMC revoked Wakefield's medical license (Brainard, 2013).

By the time Wakefield's claims had been debunked and his article retracted, however, the damage had largely been done already. Parents had begun to worry that vaccination was not safe. By 2009, data from the U.S. National Immunization Survey showed that 60.2 percent of parents with children aged 24 to 35 months had had their children vaccinated as recommended and on time; more than a quarter (25.8%) had delayed their children's vaccinations, 8.2 percent had refused the vaccinations outright and 5.8 percent had delayed and refused vaccinations. Parents who delayed or refused vaccinations were significantly less likely to agree that vaccinations were safe for their children (Smith et al., 2011). By the 2013/2014 school year, fewer than 90 percent of children in eight states had received appropriate doses of the MMR vaccine; in Colorado, only 81.7 percent of kindergarteners had received the recommended MMR vaccination (Seither et al., 2014).

Worse yet, low vaccination rates have contributed to the worst measles outbreaks in the United States in 20 years. In 2014, there were

668 cases in 27 states, and between December 28, 2014, and April 24, 2015, the CDC already had identified 147 measles cases in seven states, all linked to an outbreak that began at California's Disneyland (Centers for Disease Control and Prevention, 2015c, 2015d). Fortunately, no deaths had been reported as a result of the outbreak, at least up until April 2015 (Clemmons et al., 2015).

Of course, few parents would have read Wakefield's original *Lancet* article; and yet 29 percent of 1,000 adults participating in a November 2012 YouGov.com survey said they believe autism is linked to vaccination. During a Congressional hearing that same month, a number of Congress members expressed similar beliefs (Berinsky, 2012). Where would people have learned about the alleged link between vaccination and autism, and why would they continue to see the claim as credible, despite overwhelming scientific consensus to the contrary?

The answer, scholars and journalism critics argue, is news coverage that has continued to present "balanced" coverage of the controversy, implying that scientists disagree about the validity of the autism–vaccination link when, in fact, no credible scientific research has supported Wakefield's theory and his own data have been proven unreliable at best (Brainard, 2013; Clarke, 2008; Dixon & Clarke, 2013; Smith et al., 2008; Speers & Lewis, 2004). The entire episode illustrates the power news media can have in influencing public awareness of, beliefs about and behavioral responses to health research and health claims – whether empirically supported or not.

Unlike some of the media effects discussed earlier (e.g., media violence, tobacco and alcohol advertising), news coverage can influence individual health behaviors in both positive and negative ways, depending on the specific topic. For instance, recent data suggest that Americans' consumption of carbonated beverages – especially "diet" sodas like Diet Coke and Diet Pepsi – is on the decline, largely due to increased consumer concerns about possible links between artificial sweeteners and cancer, and recent news coverage of research suggesting that consumption of diet soda leads to *more*, not less, weight gain (Esterl, 2014). News coverage of the recent measles outbreaks in the United States also may have pushed some anti-vaccination parents to agree to have their children immunized; sales of the Merck measles vaccine grew rapidly as news of the outbreak spread, peaking at levels four times the normal rates in February 2015 (Koons & Armstrong, 2015).

This chapter summarizes the research on what health topics news media are most likely to cover, how those topics are covered and what effects researchers believe news coverage has on individual health behaviors. The focus here is on individual change, such as a woman choosing to reduce or eliminate consumption of diet sodas after reading, hearing or viewing a news story (or several news stories) linking diet sodas to obesity risks. A later chapter will examine news media's potential to influence health behaviors indirectly through influences on either corporate or government policy affecting the health environment; for instance, news coverage of research on sugar-sweetened beverages may prompt a school board to ban on-campus sales of such beverages, thereby decreasing children's access to and consumption of such drinks.

WHY HEALTH NEWS COVERAGE IS IMPORTANT

Understanding the content and effects of health news is important because a substantial body of research demonstrates that consumers obtain a significant portion of their health information from news media (Brodie et al., 2003; Gaglio et al., 2012; Geana et al., 2011; Hesse et al., 2005; Hesse et al., 2010; Kakai et al., 2003; Murphy et al., 2010; Tu, 2011). For instance, Brodie and colleagues (2003) found that approximately 40 percent of American adults follow health news closely, and those who pay close attention to health stories are more knowledgeable about health topics. Among respondents to the first Health Information National Trends Survey (HINTS), 71 percent report putting "a lot" or "some" trust in the health information they received from television; the comparable percentages for trust in magazine and newspaper health information were 67 percent and 63 percent, respectively (Hesse et al., 2005).

Not surprisingly, consumers put much greater trust in the information they receive from health professionals than in what they learn from the media (Hesse et al., 2005; Rains, 2007). However, research by the Center for Studying Health System Change showed that between 2001 and 2007, the percentages of people who reported seeking health information from mass media sources increased significantly, jumping from 23 to 32.7 percent who said they sought health information from books, magazines and newspapers, and from 11.3 to 15.3 percent of people who reported seeking health information from radio and television. During the same period of time, the percentages of people who said they sought health information via the Internet doubled, from 16 to 32 percent. The authors of this report point out that these sources are not mutually exclusive, given that one may access newspapers, magazines, television and radio reports and even books online, or one may first hear about a health topic in one medium and later seek out more information on that topic from another (Tu & Cohen, 2008). Thus, despite the fact that relatively few people fully trust the health information they find in news media, they remain important health information sources.

THE CONTENT OF HEALTH NEWS

For a number of reasons, it is somewhat difficult to draw broad conclusions about what news media report about health. The vast majority of health news content analyses do not address health news in the broad sense but rather examine in detail journalists' coverage of specific health issues, such as vaccination safety, HIV/AIDS, cancer, heart disease, mental health and so on. Nonetheless, a few studies have provided broader overviews of what news organizations tell their audiences about health.

The most current analysis of health news content was conducted by the Kaiser Family Foundation, in conjunction with the Pew Research Center's Project for Excellence in Journalism, and examined health news coverage in all media during the first six months of 2009, at the height of the debate over passage of the Affordable Care Act (ACA). The study, which included analysis of 1,568 health stories from the front pages of small, medium and large market newspapers, broadcast TV morning and evening news programs, cable TV, radio news and talk shows, and online news sources, revealed that health stories accounted for 4.9 percent of the total newshole during January to June 2009 in the 55 news outlets examined, ranking eighth, behind the economy, government agencies, foreign stories, U.S. foreign affairs, business, crime and politics. Health issues increased their share of the total newshole by more than one-third (36%) compared to an earlier analysis that had examined news coverage from January 2007 to June 2008. During April, May and June 2009, the percentage of all news devoted to health was even higher (7.4%, 6.9% and 6.7%, respectively); health policy and the health care system and public health concerns (especially swine flu and a salmonella outbreak attributed to contaminated peanut butter) contributed significantly to this increase, collectively accounting for 75.9 percent of all health news stories (Kaiser Family Foundation & Pew Research Center's Project for Excellence in Journalism, 2009).

The remaining quarter of all health news stories dealt with specific diseases and health conditions, with cancer gaining the most coverage (5.9% of all health stories), followed by mental health (2.5%) and diabetes/obesity (1.9%). The coverage of cancer actually had decreased overall from the earlier study, when cancer stories accounted for one in every ten health stories, and attention to obesity/diabetes also had dropped (from 5.2% of all stories). These declines likely reflect the dramatic increase in attention to health policy issues as a result of the debate over health care reform. In the earlier KFF/Pew study, stories

Figure 11.1: Stories about Specific Diseases Account for a High Proportion of Health News

355

about health policy and the health care system had accounted for only 27.4 percent of all health stories, in comparison to 40.2 percent in the 2009 study (Kaiser Family Foundation & Pew Research Center's Project for Excellence in Journalism, 2008, 2009).

Comparing across different media sectors, the broadcast networks' evening newscasts devoted the most space to health (7.7% of the newshole), while cable news devoted the least (3.6%); the *PBS NewsHour* was second, followed by network morning news shows and newspapers (6.8%, 5.8% and 5.6%, respectively). Commercial broadcast networks focused primarily on specific diseases and health conditions, with cancer, heart disease and mental health receiving the most attention, followed by diabetes/obesity, autism and Alzheimer's disease. The evening newscasts were the least likely of any media sector to provide coverage of health policy and the U.S. health care system, despite the prominence of the health care reform debate.

The morning network news shows devoted the greatest share of their health airtime to public health issues, primarily the H1N1 flu outbreak. Such issues accounted for 44.3 percent of all health airtime on the morning shows, while nearly one-third of the airtime (32.3%) was devoted to specific diseases and conditions; nearly one-tenth of all health airtime (9.9%) was spent on cancer-related stories. Stories about health policy and the U.S. health care system accounted for less than a quarter (23.4%) of all health airtime during the morning news shows, but there were significant variations across networks, with ABC's *Good Morning America* providing more than half of the airtime on this topic, twice as much as NBC's *Today* show and almost 3.5 times as much as CBS's *Early Show* (Kaiser Family Foundation & Pew Research Center's Project for Excellence in Journalism, 2009).

On PBS, on the other hand, health policy issues accounted for more than half (58%) of all health story airtime. In particular, PBS stories addressed the issue of health care costs. About a quarter of PBS stories (25.8%) dealt with public health concerns, especially the H1N1 flu outbreak, with only 16.2 percent of its health coverage time devoted to specific diseases and conditions. As with the other television channels, cancer received more attention than any other specific disease or condition (Kaiser Family Foundation & Pew Research Center's Project for Excellence in Journalism, 2009).

The study examined only the front pages of newspapers, which means that the study percentages likely reflect much more "breaking news" content than if all health stories throughout the newspaper had been examined. Front-page health stories were most likely to address health policy or health care system stories (39.5% of all health content); however, newspapers also devoted substantial space to public health concerns (31.5%) and specific diseases and conditions (28.9%). Health stories were more likely to be categorized as the "lead" story – the most prominent story in any given edition – than were any of the other news genres, with more than one in every five stories (21.8%) rated as the lead story (Kaiser Family Foundation & Pew Research Center's Project for Excellence in Journalism, 2009).

News radio – National Public Radio's *Morning Edition* and radio headline news – provided nearly equal attention to the three categories of health stories, devoting 35.5 percent of health airtime to health care system and policy stories, 34 percent to stories about specific diseases and conditions, and 30.5 percent to stories about public health concerns. In contrast, cable news shows paid relatively little attention to specific diseases and conditions, which accounted for only 12.4 percent of health airtime overall. Instead, almost half of the health airtime addressed health policy and health care system issues (47.6%), while the remaining 40 percent of airtime dealt with public health concerns; 81.1 percent of public health coverage was related to the H1N1 outbreak. Among the relatively few stories about specific diseases, cancer was again the dominant issue (Kaiser Family Foundation & Pew Research Center's Project for Excellence in Journalism, 2009).

The KFF/Pew study did not examine health coverage in local TV news, but a somewhat earlier study, examining health stories aired between December 2004 and June 2005, provided a look at how local news stations cover health. The researchers coded health stories from the morning, noon, evening and late evening newscasts on seven stations, all from the Midwest (Chicago, Indianapolis, South Bend and Terre Haute). Overall, during the study time period, the local stations aired 50.3 hours of health news stories, with an average story length of less than one minute (57.46 seconds). Nearly half of the stories (46%) dealt with specific diseases and conditions, with cancer the most common topic, followed by heart disease, the flu, obesity, diabetes and eye disorders. "Healthy living" advice was the focus of nearly one in four (24.8%) local TV health stories. Overall, the researchers determined that more news stories dealt with cancer than any other single topic, accounting for more than one in every ten stories (12.2%); cancer stories were nearly twice as common as the next most frequently covered topic, nutrition (6.2%), and more than twice as common as heart disease stories (5.5%). The coding revealed that local TV health stories were almost equally likely to focus on prevention (20.3%) and treatment (20.4%), while health policy was addressed in about one in every ten stories (9.5%) (Wang & Gantz, 2010).

News organizations often report on medical research, but researchers have found that the highest quality studies are not necessarily the most likely to be covered. For instance, one study examined news stories about 75 "clinically oriented" articles from the five medical journals with the highest impact factor score. (Impact factor is a measure of the likelihood that a journal's articles will be cited by other researchers.) The study revealed that randomized clinical trials, which generally are regarded as the best type of study, were less likely to be covered than were observational studies. In addition, observational studies that were covered by the news media had smaller sample sizes and were more likely to be cross-sectional (rather than longitudinal) than were observational studies that did not receive news attention. The researchers conclude, therefore, that "newspapers preferentially cover medical research with weaker methodology" (Selvaraj et al., 2014, p. 5).

In terms of news attention to specific diseases, researchers have found that the number of deaths caused by specific diseases influences the likelihood of news coverage, although death rates are not the only important determinant of coverage. For instance, one study analyzed newspaper coverage of cancer, heart disease, AIDS, diabetes, Alzheimer's disease and arthritis from 1977 to 1997; the data showed that frequency of coverage was positively related to mortality rates for these diseases, but incidence and prevalence trends have less impact on newspapers' attention to the diseases (Adelman & Verbrugge, 2000). Another study, which examined both print and broadcast health stories published or aired between 1980 and 1998, produced similar results in terms of the relationship between number of deaths and number of news stories – except in the case of HIV/AIDS. The data also revealed that news media pay less attention to diseases that disproportionately affect African Americans in comparison to whites. In addition, and perhaps not surprisingly, the amount of attention news media give to a disease varies according to the number of advocacy groups associated with that disease, particularly when a greater proportion of a disease's advocacy groups engage in political lobbying (Armstrong et al., 2006).

Many researchers have examined news coverage of specific diseases and health conditions, from heart disease and cancer to HIV/AIDS, obesity and eating disorders, mental illness and many others; it would be virtually impossible to review and summarize all of those studies. However, it is worth examining in more detail news coverage of the two leading causes of death in the United States: heart disease and cancer (Centers for Disease Control and Prevention, 2015a).

Cancer

Analyses of cancer coverage have shown that certain types of cancer garner disproportionate attention in the news media, in comparison to cancer incidence rates. For instance, analysis of a sample of cancer stories aired or published by local and national newspapers, television and magazines in 2002 and 2003 revealed that incidence rates for various types of cancer were more strongly correlated with the number of news stories than were mortality rates; however, comparison of either incidence or mortality rates with frequency of news coverage revealed under-reporting on lung cancer and over-representation of stories about breast cancer (Slater et al., 2008).

The over-representation of breast cancer within cancer news coverage has been documented by numerous researchers (Cohen et al., 2008; Gantz & Wang, 2009; Jensen et al., 2010; Gerlach et al., 1997; Stryker et al., 2007). For instance, a study of cancer stories aired by local TV news stations in the Midwest revealed that more than one in four cancer stories (25.1%) dealt with breast cancer, making these stories almost twice as common as those about colorectal cancer, which was the next most common topic, and three times as common as prostate cancer stories. Stories about brain cancer ranked fourth in terms of frequency, followed by lung or bronchial cancer stories (Gantz & Wang, 2009). In reality, however, the incidence rates for breast and prostate cancer are quite similar. The American Cancer Society (ACS) predicted 234,190 new cases of breast cancer and 220,800 new cases of prostate cancer in 2015, although the number of breast cancer deaths (40,730) was projected to be somewhat higher than those from prostate cancer (27,540) (American Cancer Society, 2015). Prostate cancer is more common than colorectal cancers (with 132,700 new cases and 49,700 deaths for 2015); colorectal cancer, while less common than breast or prostate cancer, is more deadly. It is also worth noting that brain cancer is less common than many other types of cancers that received substantially less coverage; for instance, while the ACS predicted 22,850 new brain cancer diagnoses in 2015, their data predicted 138,710 urinary system cancers, 80,900 cases of lymphoma, 54,270 cases of leukemia, 80,100 skin cancers (not including basal or squamous cell cancers), 64,860 endocrine system cancers and 48,960 pancreatic cancers (American Cancer Society, 2015).

Gantz and Wang (2009) also found that nearly a quarter of cancer stories did not address any specific type of cancer; rather, they were about cancer in general. In terms of the central topic of the stories, half dealt with either prevention (25.9%) or treatment (24.4%). Nearly one in five (19.7%) did not address any specific topic, but about one in every seven stories (14.5%) focused on early detection. About one in every seven stories was also about fundraising for cancer-related charities; as the researchers note, so much attention to fundraising:

> may decrease air time for stories on available treatment regimes, the side-effects of existing and new therapies, as well as prognoses and the likelihood of cure, all of which have been identified as key information needs of cancer patients and those close to them.
>
> (Gantz & Wang, 2009, p. 70)

Across all types of cancers, Slater et al. (2008) found that television stories were most likely to focus on death (29.5 percent of all TV cancer stories), magazine stories were most likely to discuss detection and diagnosis (26.3 percent of magazine stories) and newspaper stories most commonly focused on cancer treatment (17.4 percent of all stories.) For four of the five most commonly covered cancer types (breast, colon, prostate, lung and brain cancer), there was more coverage of treatment and causes than of prevention and detection or diagnosis. However, a quarter of the lung cancer stories dealt with detection and diagnosis, while nearly one-third (30.6%) were focused on death.

Similarly, a study of cancer stories in the 50 highest circulation U.S. newspapers revealed that cancer stories focus consistently on treatment more often than prevention or diagnosis; in addition, when prevention is covered, the stories tend to attribute cancer incidence to lifestyle factors such as smoking and diet (45.9 percent of stories mentioning a risk factor), followed by demographic characteristics such as sex or race (39.5%), genetics or heredity (22.3%); occupational or environmental risks were mentioned in about one in every five stories that included any risk factor, a dramatic decline from coverage during the late 1970s and early 1980s, when researchers found that more than half of all stories that discussed a risk factor for cancer mentioned environmental or occupational risks (Freimuth et al., 1984; Jensen et al., 2010).

Heart Disease

Given that heart disease is the leading cause of death in the United States, one might expect that researchers would have been keenly interested in the quantity and quality of heart disease information news media provide for their audiences. Surprisingly, relatively few researchers appear to have given concentrated attention to this topic; in a recent review of the literature on print media coverage of heart disease and gender, Clarke (2010) concluded that we know little about how the news media portray heart disease and its impact on women; she also identified no studies of the portrayal of gender and heart disease in television news content.

The existing analyses of heart disease content generally have examined magazine coverage, frequently with a particular focus on how women's magazines portray women's heart disease risk. For instance, Edy (2010) conducted a textual analysis of heart disease-related information in *Good Housekeeping* magazine articles published from 1997 to 2007. She found that the articles often focused on the risks to young women (younger than age 40), although heart disease risk increases significantly with age; thus, the content overemphasized the risks to women who were, in fact, at low risk of heart disease. The articles all mentioned high blood pressure as a risk factor, but only briefly. High cholesterol and diet in general were the most prominently mentioned risk factors. Astonishingly, although nearly all the articles mentioned smoking as a risk factor, they provided no advice about how to quit.

In an earlier study, Clarke and Binns (2006) found that magazines framed heart disease as a medical issue, paying less attention to either lifestyle factors or social/structural contributors to heart disease. Medical care was portrayed as uniformly good and a source of hope,

361

although heart disease also was portrayed as an individual responsibility. Further qualitative analysis of this same dataset suggested that heart disease was portrayed quite differently in relation to men versus women. For men, the magazines portrayed heart disease "as an element of, or even a badge of, manhood" (Clarke et al., 2007, p. 22). Men could be expected to receive aggressive and successful treatment for heart disease, and both the disease itself and treatment were described in battle terms; men were portrayed as being in control, able to conquer heart disease and return to a healthy lifestyle. Most articles portrayed women as the caretakers in heart disease, rather than as those likely to suffer from the disease. On the other hand, women often were portrayed as being ignorant of their own heart disease risk, and of falling victim to both doctors' lack of knowledge about women's heart disease risks and researchers' failure to devote enough time to studying heart disease in women. Female heart disease sufferers often were portrayed as being embarrassed, and treatment was described in less optimistic terms than was true for men.

In addition to analyses of coverage of specific diseases, another important research topic is how news sources cover the benefits and risks of medical interventions. This research suggests that news media may not provide audiences with the information they most need to make informed treatment, diet and lifestyle change decisions. Researchers have found that news coverage often falls into one of two categories that the late *Washington Post* science reporter Vic Cohn called "new hope" or "no hope" (Cohn, 1988). These stories overemphasize both relative risks and relative benefits, and fail to discuss alternative explanations for medical research findings (Woloshin et al., 2009). In addition, researchers have demonstrated that news coverage tends to emphasize benefits over risks in coverage of screening tests (Moriarty & Stryker, 2008; Schwartz & Woloshin, 2002), genetics research (Bubela & Caulfield, 2004) and drugs (Cassels et al., 2003; Moynihan et al., 2000). Some health news stories include dangerously inaccurate information (Pribble et al., 2006).

An analysis of the first 500 news story reviews published by Health-NewsReview.org, a U.S. organization dedicated to providing independent expert reviews of health news stories, showed that journalists often failed to provide adequate information about "costs, the quality of the evidence, the existence of alternative options, and the absolute magnitude of potential benefits and harms" (Schwitzer, 2009, p. 700). A more recent article on all HNR reviews from 2005 through 2013 demonstrated that, although coverage had improved on some of the criteria, news stories were least likely to provide adequate information about the risks and costs of medical interventions (Walsh-Childers et al., in press).

One other important theme in research on news coverage of health is the focus of most stories on individual responsibility for health problems. Although public health officials generally acknowledge that socio-economic factors and the social environment play critical roles in determining an individual's health (Wilkinson & Marmot, 2003), news coverage generally attributes health problems to failures of individual behavior and places responsibility for improving health on the individual. For instance, Kim and Willis (2007) analyzed television and newspaper stories about obesity from January 1995 to August 2004 and found that the stories were more than twice as likely to mention individual responsibility for obesity as they were to discuss societal causes. During the study period, there was a rapid increase in mentions of societal causes for obesity, particularly in references to food industry practices, especially in newspapers; however, overall, individual change was more likely than societal changes to be discussed as the solution to obesity.

Similarly, a content analysis of newspaper articles about type 2 diabetes revealed that the stories usually blamed behavioral factors, including obesity. Strategies for reducing the incidence of diabetes focused on individual behavior change and medical solutions. Of the articles that mentioned any approach to preventing or treating diabetes, nearly six in ten stories (58.4%) mentioned individual behavior changes, including better diet (46.3%), increased exercise (38.1%) and weight loss (23.2%). More than half (53.9%) mentioned drug treatment or biotechnology (e.g., bariatric surgery). In contrast, only 5.6 percent mentioned school-based prevention strategies such as requiring physical education classes and reducing the availability of unhealthy foods on school grounds. Of the 698 articles examined, only 17 "described food policy strategies such as taxing junk food, food labeling, trans fats regulations, voluntary food industry changes, and food marketing regulations" (Gollust & Lantz, 2009, p. 1094).

Behavioral explanations also dominated in newspaper coverage of racial and ethnic health disparities. The researchers identified 3,823 newspaper articles about racial/ethnic health disparities published from 1996 through 2005 and catalogued in the Lexis/Nexis database. Of those articles, the majority (69.6%) did not discuss either a cause or a solution for racial/ethnic health disparities; discussion of causes (85.9%) was more common than mention of solutions (46%). Within the articles that mentioned a cause, behavioral factors were most likely to be mentioned. In discussing solutions, the articles were twice as likely to mention behavioral changes (48.1%) as to mention societal-level policy change (23.2%). The authors note that although individual behavior continued to dominate the news discourse on racial/ethnic health disparities, the stories also paid significant attention to societal-level causes and solutions (Kim et al., 2010).

News media also focus on individual behavior, rather than societal causes, in their coverage of crime and violence, a category that accounts for a significant percentage of the newshole in many news outlets. For instance, Rodgers and Thorsen (2001) analyzed all of the stories in 29 randomly selected issues of the *Los Angeles Times* between August 1997 and July 1998 and found that nearly one-third of all stories (32%) were about crime and violence. Only 16 percent of the crime stories were coded as "issue stories," those that provided a context for crime and violence and might help readers better understand the causes and impact of crime in their communities. The event-focused stories framed crime as the result of bad people choosing bad behavior. "The inference waiting to be made is that there can be no solutions – except to punish – and prevention is not at all part of the picture" (Rodgers & Thorsen, 2001, p. 178).

The problem with focusing on individual responsibility for causing – and solving – health problems is that it encourages audiences to blame the victims and discourages support for societal-level solutions that are, according to public health experts, far more likely to lead to long-term resolution of the issues. As Dorfman and colleagues (2005, p. 327) argue:

> Without a sense of the forces that brought the people in the story to this point, viewers are likely to distance themselves from the "victims" portrayed, assume that those portrayed in the story brought it on themselves, look to them to work harder to solve their own problem or accept the consequences of their behavior. Watching

episodic stories, viewers gain no insight into the larger social and political circumstances that contribute to the individual problem.

WHAT INFLUENCES HEALTH NEWS COVERAGE

As problematic as the focus on individual behavior may be to public health advocates, it is hardly surprising that journalists take this approach. Dorfman and colleagues call individualism the "first language of America" (2005, p. 327), and journalists, like other citizens, tend to reflect this dominant value in their reporting.

The patterns of health news coverage also are influenced by a variety of characteristics of health journalists and of the environments in which they work. For instance, a survey of 468 health-focused reporters, editors and producers showed that while 70 percent of the journalists had at least a Bachelor's degree, only 8 percent had majored in life sciences. More than 90 percent of health journalists are white and non-Hispanic, and more than two-thirds (67%) are women. While journalists from national news outlets said they most often get their story ideas from scientific journals, local journalists are more likely to rely on sources for story ideas. Broadcast and wire service journalists are more likely than print reporters to say their story ideas initially come from sources, and in general, the survey showed that print journalists identify a broader range of story idea sources (Viswanath et al., 2008).

The journalists surveyed reported using a variety of well-defined criteria to determine whether to continue pursuing a story once an initial idea has been presented. Across all types of reporters (national and local, print and broadcast), the primary criterion was "potential for public impact," mentioned by nearly all broadcast journalists (98.2%) and the vast majority of print journalists (89.3%). Broadcast journalists were significantly more likely than print journalists to say they needed new information or some new development to justify pursuing a story (92.4% vs. 75%, respectively). Local journalists, not surprisingly, were more likely to say that there needs to be a local angle to make the story worth pursuing; broadcast journalists also prioritized the local angle, and this same pattern also applied to the need for a human interest angle on the story (Viswanath et al., 2008).

Additional analysis of the same survey responses showed that female journalists were significantly more likely than male journalists to prioritize educating the public to make informed health decisions, disseminating new information accurately, influencing individual health behavior and promoting public health literacy. White respondents were less likely than minority journalists to emphasize their role in influencing the public's health behaviors. Men and minority journalists were more likely than women and whites to say they focus on the economic impact of a health issue; women were more likely than men to frame their stories around the need to change personal behavior, controversial new information and human interest. In general, the researchers found that female health journalists are more oriented toward social issues and public health, viewing journalism as a potential catalyst of positive social change (McCauley et al., 2013).

Some aspects of the journalists' background and job circumstances were also important predictors of their approach to health stories. Occupational autonomy – the journalist's perception of his or her freedom to determine what to emphasize in a story – was also a key determinant; those who said they had little autonomy were half as likely as journalists with autonomy to ascribe importance to any of the story goals. Journalists with a Master's degree or higher, somewhat surprisingly, were about half as likely as those with a Bachelor's degree or lower to prioritize educating the public to make informed health decisions. Better educated journalists were more likely to focus on economic impacts as a health story angle, but less likely to prioritize the pursuit of controversial new information or to emphasize the need for a human interest angle in health stories. More veteran journalists (16 or more years on the job) placed less importance on entertaining the audience (Wallington et al., 2010).

Organizational characteristics also influence health journalists' priorities. In comparison to journalists working for publicly traded corporations, those who worked for privately owned organizations were 3.5 times as likely to prioritize educating audiences to make informed health decisions and almost 2.5 times as likely to emphasize entertaining their audiences through their health stories. Journalists working for chain-owned news outlets were less likely than non-chain outlets to prioritize audience education and entertainment (Wallington et al., 2010).

While characteristics of individual journalists and the organizations for whom they report may influence which stories and story angles receive emphasis, the current trend toward downsizing in newsrooms

(Guskin, 2013; Matsa, 2013) threatens the quality of health reporting in several ways. First, health journalists have not been excluded from lay-offs and buy-outs. In a 2009 survey of Association of Health Care Journalists members, 40 percent said the number of health reporters in their organization had declined since they were hired, and 39 percent believed their own positions were at least somewhat likely to be cut within the next few years. About a quarter of journalists said staffing declines represent the most important threat to quality health journalism because the remaining journalists have less time to spend on each story and less opportunity to take time off for training. Other threats to quality health journalism, according to the AHCJ members, include increased demand for "quick hit," "news you can use" and hyper-local stories, which tend to crowd out the production of more challenging and time-consuming in-depth, enterprise and policy-related stories (Schwitzer, 2009). At the same time, drug and device manufacturers and health facilities have ramped up their marketing and public relations efforts, reducing the likelihood that news organizations will keep "unfiltered public relations and advertising messages" out of health news stories (Schwitzer, 2009, p. 2).

The AHCJ members reflected these concerns in their evaluations of the quality of health journalism today, with 36 percent of those who completed the 2009 survey rating coverage of health disparities as poor. At least one in four of the respondents rated as poor coverage of health care as a business (25%), health care quality and performance (26%) and health policy (27%); nearly one-third (30%) rated coverage of the politics of health care as poor. There was a tendency, however, to view these problems as existing primarily in other news outlets; only 15 percent said coverage at their own organization had deteriorated, while more than 40 percent said the quality of health journalism had improved in their own organization over the past several years (Schwitzer, 2009).

Severe staffing cuts at news organizations also threaten quality health reporting by reducing staff experience levels; because senior staffers draw higher salaries, they are often targeted for buy-out offers (Calderone, 2013). Compared to more veteran reporters, less experienced journalists use as sources fewer scientists or researchers not affiliated with either the government or with the industry about which they are writing, and more patient or advocacy organization representatives; reliance on industry and advocacy organization sources may reduce the likelihood that the journalist's sources will raise questions about the benefits, costs and potential risks of medical interventions.

THE EFFECTS OF HEALTH NEWS COVERAGE

Given that the public's capacity for awareness of and concern about issues is not unlimited, one of the primary functions of news media in U.S. society is to focus public attention on certain topics, problems, people and places. In other words, many developments can occur in the health realm without the public's knowledge, including disease outbreaks, failures in the health delivery system, changes in preferred treatment approaches, and shifts in scientific understanding of a health condition or disease. For the majority of the public, awareness of these events depends almost entirely on journalists deciding that they are important enough to warrant a story (although, in the age of social media, this may be changing somewhat). Most people first hear about new developments in health through a news story. For instance, one early study of the impact of news media use on knowledge and attitudes about AIDS showed that people who read a newspaper and watched TV news every day were more likely to believe that they knew a lot about AIDS. In addition, those who relied on newspapers as their major news source were more knowledgeable about AIDS, while those who relied on TV news, at least to some extent, were more likely to give incorrect answers to AIDS knowledge questions (Stroman & Seltzer, 1989). More recently, researchers have found that while overall exposure to news content was unrelated to knowing about the link between the human papillomavirus and cervical cancer, exposure to health-related media content was a positive predictor of HPV knowledge (Kelly et al., 2009).

In addition, a study sponsored by the Kaiser Family Foundation and the Harvard School of Public Health revealed that individuals who report following health news closely give more accurate answers when questioned about health-related stories (Brodie et al., 2003). Another study revealed that individuals who pay more attention to health news had greater knowledge of cancer risks linked to food consumption and smoking – topics frequently covered by the news media; however, attention to health news was not linked to greater knowledge about less often covered behaviors that can reduce one's cancer risks, including increased exercise, limiting alcohol consumption and protecting oneself from excessive sun exposure (Stryker et al., 2008).

Of course, these cross-sectional findings do not necessarily mean that people learn about health issues from news coverage; it is quite likely that those who are already more knowledgeable about health tend to pay more attention to health news. However, some studies have indeed confirmed that news coverage of health issues increases knowledge of those issues. For instance, Wanta and Elliott (1995) found that news coverage of basketball star "Magic" Johnson's announcement that he was HIV-positive did not significantly reduce the HIV/AIDS knowledge gap between low- and high-education groups; the gap remained consistent before and after Johnson's announcement. However, HIV/AIDS knowledge among both groups increased substantially between the two waves of the study, confirming that news about the basketball star provided both groups with information about the disease.

In addition to increasing public awareness of and knowledge about health issues, research suggests that news coverage also can influence the public's estimations of the incidence and importance of particular health problems. "This ability to influence the salience of topics on the public agenda has come to be called the agenda-setting role of the news media" (McCombs & Reynolds, 2002, p. 1). Although agenda-setting theory originated in research on the news media's role in political communication, it applies equally well to health journalism.

For instance, as noted earlier, the news media under-report certain types of cancers and over-report others. This distorted picture of cancer incidence carries over into public estimates of the frequency of certain cancer diagnoses, in that individuals who report greater news consumption are more likely than those who paid less attention to the news to overestimate breast cancer incidence rates and underestimate bladder and kidney cancer incidence, mirroring patterns seen in news coverage of these cancers (Jensen et al., 2014). In addition, because cancer coverage, especially in TV news, often suggests that cancer causes lurk around every corner, exposure to this coverage seems to promote fatalistic beliefs about cancer prevention (Niederdeppe et al., 2010, 2014).

When controversies arise among cancer experts, however, news coverage may increase the public's confusion rather than helping them to feel more confident about their health decisions. For instance, researchers found that news coverage of new guidelines for mammography use, announced by the U.S. Preventive Services Task Force in 2009, confused women more than helping them understand when they should begin having mammograms. This was particularly true for women in the "disputed" age group – those aged 40 to 49 years who, under the previous guidelines, would have been encouraged to have mammograms, and among women who had never had a mammogram or who had not had one during the preceding two years (Squiers et al., 2011).

Other researchers compared Massachusetts newspapers' coverage of cancer and eastern equine encephalitis (EEE), a mosquito-borne disease, and found that cancer stories emphasized progress, while EEE stories tended to focus on new cases of the disease. A survey of adults subsequently showed that more than half perceived EEE as being at least as much of a threat as cancer, and attention to health media was associated with both a greater likelihood of seeing EEE as threatening and perceiving the risk of EEE and the risk of cancer as similar (Ackerson & Viswanath, 2010).

In addition, an earlier time series analysis revealed that variations in public opinion about the importance of illegal drug use between 1985 and 1994 could be reliably predicted by the extent of news media reporting on the drug abuse "crisis." Public opinion also contributed to greater news attention, but was a much weaker predictor (Fan, 1996). Another study documented the effects of news coverage on adolescents' beliefs about marijuana use, showing that aggregate news coverage of the reasons people should not use marijuana predicted population-level variations in adolescent personal disapproval of marijuana use but not the drug's perceived harmfulness (Stryker, 2003). Adolescents' attitudes toward cigarette smoking also have been linked to newspaper coverage of tobacco issues (Clegg-Smith et al., 2008).

News coverage also can influence public fears about disease epidemics. For instance, early in the U.S. experience with HIV/AIDS, researchers found that the shift in public opinion about AIDS, from the belief that the disease was confined to high-risk groups to the realization that all population groups could be at risk, followed a similar shift in emphasis with news coverage of the disease (Fan & McAvoy, 1989). In a later study, Hertog and Fan (1995) found that shifts in press coverage of the possibility of "casual" transmission of HIV – through mosquito bites, sneezing and use of public toilets – were strong predictors of changes in public belief that HIV could be transmitted casually. Additional analyses confirmed that news coverage influenced public opinion, rather than vice versa.

Researchers also have documented an impact of news coverage on the stigma associated with individuals with mental illness. For instance, one study showed that individuals who read a news story describing a mass shooting by an individual described as having a serious mental illness subsequently reported more negative attitudes toward mentally ill people. Compared to individuals who read the same story with no indication that the shooter was mentally ill, those who read the story linking the shooting with mental illness were less willing to work with or live near someone with a serious mental illness and rated these individuals as far more dangerous than the general population (McGinty et al., 2014).

BEHAVIORAL EFFECTS

Although the impacts of news coverage on knowledge and beliefs are important in their own right, what health professionals and officials are most concerned about is how the public's exposure to news coverage influences their health behavior. It is clear that news coverage can have significant effects on a variety of health behaviors, including what may be an important first step for many individuals, namely seeking additional information beyond that included in the news story. One research team, for example, found a significant positive correlation between the volume of cancer news coverage and reported cancer information seeking, but only among those who said they paid close attention to health news and those who had a family history of cancer (Niederdeppe et al., 2008). Another study showed that news coverage about celebrities being diagnosed with or dying from cancer stimulated cancer information seeking more frequently among highly educated individuals compared to those with less education, in part because those with more education already knew more about health and were more involved in their communities (Niederdeppe, 2008). Conflict-oriented health news stories, such as those related to the controversy over the U.S. Preventive Services Task Force's 2009 recommendations regarding mammography, also promote information searching (Weeks et al., 2012).

In addition to encouraging audiences to seek out additional information about cancer, news coverage can encourage individuals to participate in cancer screening. For instance, Yanovitzky and Blitz (2000) found that the volume of media coverage of mammography in one month was a statistically significant predictor of mammogram use by women aged 40 and older in the subsequent month, even after controlling for physicians' advice to women. Coverage of celebrities' cancer diagnoses also has been found to increase use of cancer screening, both in the United States (Brown & Potosky, 1990; Fink et al., 1978; Lane et al., 1989) and in other Western countries (Casey et al., 2013; Chapman et al., 2005; Kelaher et al., 2008; Marlow et al., 2012). Some researchers have found that media coverage of celebrities' cancer diagnoses can be especially influential among low-income individuals and those who do not have regular access to a doctor (Marlow et al., 2012; Yanovitzky & Blitz, 2000).

While news coverage that encourages cancer screening and other diagnostic tests can be helpful, it also can encourage overuse of such tests. For instance, one team of researchers compared the number of positive and negative tests for Group A streptococcal disease (strep throat) during two consecutive December through February periods in a single pediatric emergency department. During the first year, 55 children were tested. During the second year – after a spate of news coverage about strep throat – 1,000 children were tested; however, there was no statistically significant difference in the percentage of positive tests. Thus, the increased testing was likely a result of the media coverage rather than an outbreak of strep throat in the community (Sharma et al., 2003).

News coverage also can encourage the public to engage in disease prevention behaviors other than screening tests. For instance, a study that examined the public's response to basketball star Earvin "Magic" Johnson's announcement that he was HIV-positive showed that exposure to print news coverage was linked to increased intentions to avoid high-risk sexual behaviors. The researchers found that although news coverage increased knowledge about Johnson's diagnosis, the link with intentions to avoid high-risk sexual behavior operated primarily through involvement, or a sense of identification, with Johnson.

> The positive influence resulted from the favorable emotional attachment that the public had to Johnson ... for those who were most exposed to Johnson through the media, the positively valenced

involvement that the exposure produced had a significant influence on adolescents and young adults.

(Brown & Basil, 1995, p. 364)

Researchers also have found that news coverage is linked to rates of smoking cessation at the population level; however, news coverage seems to have little effect on individuals' decisions to *start* smoking, only on their attempts to quit. Pierce and Gilpin (2001) compared the number of articles about smoking and health published in major magazines between 1950 and 1990 to the percentage of former smokers (1965 through 1992) who had quit for at least three months. "The incidence of successful smoking cessation followed a pattern remarkably similar to the level of media coverage, particularly among middle aged smokers" (Pierce & Gilpin, 2001, p. 150); however, this relationship disappeared during periods when health advocacy groups were disagreeing about whether certain cigarettes were "safer" than others.

Some evidence suggests that news coverage also influences adolescents' marijuana use, or abstinence from use. Stryker (2003) found that news coverage of marijuana was associated with increases in the percentage of teens who reported that they did not use the drug. Stories focusing on the negative consequences of pot use led to increases in reported abstinence and, conversely, stories that discussed positive uses of marijuana led to decreased abstinence; however, stories emphasizing pot's negative consequences had a greater impact. Personal disapproval of marijuana use mediated this relationship, but perceived harmfulness of marijuana use was not a significant mediator. The authors note that news coverage does not necessarily directly affect adolescents' attitudes and behavior regarding marijuana; rather, news coverage may influence overall societal disapproval of marijuana, which, in turn, discourages adolescents from using marijuana. Of course, the reverse also could be true, in that news coverage of apparent societal approval of marijuana use (for instance, the legalization of recreational marijuana in Colorado, Alaska and Oregon) could lead to increased use among adolescents.

In addition to affecting information seeking, use of screening and diagnostic tests and preventive health behaviors, news coverage also can have dramatic effects on the public's decisions about medical treatment. For instance, researchers found that after former First Lady Nancy Reagan chose to undergo a mastectomy rather than breast-conserving lumpectomy for breast cancer, many women decided to follow Mrs. Reagan's example. White women's likelihood of choosing lumpectomy dropped 25 percent in the last quarter of 1987 and first quarter of 1988, immediately after Mrs. Reagan's mastectomy, compared to the rates of lumpectomy use during the third quarter of 1987. There was no similar effect for non-white women (Nattinger et al., 1998).

News coverage also influences the public's use of drug treatments. For instance, in July 2002, the Women's Health Initiative announced findings linking the use of hormone replacement therapy (estrogen plus progestin) with an increased risk of breast cancer, heart disease and stroke. The findings received substantial media coverage, and at least two studies have linked exposure to news reports about the study to women's decisions to discontinue taking hormone replacement therapy (HRT). Haas and colleagues (2007) found that the use of HRT declined among women in all areas, even those with little potential exposure to news coverage of the study findings. However, in areas with more coverage of the WHI findings (at least three articles per month), the percentage of postmenopausal women who self-reported HRT use dropped from 45 to 27 percent, while, among women whose potential exposure was less than one article per month, HRT use dropped from 43 to 31 percent.

Similarly, a survey of postmenopausal North Carolina women who previously had used HRT showed that 52 percent reported making changes in their HRT use after hearing or reading about the WHI results via media reports. Women who had been using estrogen alone were almost equally likely to have changed their behavior, even though the WHI study results that caused so much concern involved women using estrogen plus progestin (Mcintosh & Blalock, 2005). The study also showed that women who changed their HRT use after the story broke trusted their physicians less than women who made no changes; however, it is not clear whether the coverage negatively influenced women's trust in their doctors or if the news had a greater impact on women who already trusted their doctors less.

In some cases, however, news coverage of the risks associated with specific drugs seems, counterintuitively, to increase their use. For instance, a study that used time series analysis to compare news coverage of opioid drug use and abuse with the number of deaths due to such drugs revealed that the volume of news coverage was a significant predictor of drug overdose deaths between 1999 and 2006. Increased news reporting preceded increases in drug deaths, suggesting that news coverage was contributing to the number of drug deaths, rather than the other way around. Furthermore, the volume of news coverage of specific medications was strongly correlated with overdose deaths from those drugs. The authors suggest that some articles "amounted to inadvertent endorsements of prescription drug abuse" because the stories opened with positive descriptions of the effects of the drug, while harms associated with the drug's use were included only later in the story (Dasgupta et al., 2009, p. 5).

As the measles discussion that opened this chapter suggests, news coverage also can influence parental decisions about vaccination. For instance, in one study, news coverage and family recommendations tied for fourth place as the most important influences on parents' decisions about vaccinations for their teenage children. Health providers' recommendations were most important, but nearly one-third of parents surveyed (31%) said news reports influenced their decisions about which vaccinations their teens should have (Dorell et al., 2013).

On the other hand, at least one study questioned the impact of news coverage of the MMR–autism link on parents' vaccination decisions. This study showed that MMR vaccination declined soon after the publication of the original article suggesting the link to autism but before there was any significant news coverage of the controversy. The authors suggest that while news coverage may have raised parents' concerns about the vaccine's safety, for most, reassurance from health providers was enough to persuade parents to complete their children's scheduled vaccinations (Smith et al., 2008).

Perhaps the most thoroughly documented effect of news coverage on health-related behavior has raised enough concern to warrant its own label: suicide contagion. The term refers to the fact that news coverage of suicide has been found to increase the incidence of subsequent "copycat" suicides within the news outlet's coverage area. Teenagers may be especially vulnerable. For instance, Phillips and Carstensen (1986) examined suicides before and after national TV news reports about 38 suicides that received attention from 1973 to 1979. The study revealed that teen suicides were more frequent than normal in the seven days after a TV story about suicide, and the more networks that carried a suicide story, the greater the subsequent increase in teen suicides. The effect was greater for teen suicides than for those by adults. One particularly disturbing finding was that general information or feature stories about suicides produced the same impact on teen suicide as did stories about a specific individual killing himself or herself.

More recently, Stack used logistic regression analysis to examine findings from studies linking non-fiction stories about suicide to subsequent suicide incidence. The analysis revealed that copycat suicides were more likely following non-fiction reporting about celebrity suicides than after stories about private individuals who killed themselves. Studies related to TV stories were less likely to confirm the copycat effect; copycat suicides were 99 percent less likely when the stories emphasized negative definitions of suicide. Studies examining effects on female suicide attempts were more likely to show a copycat effect (Stack, 2000, 2005).

Evidence of media suicide contagion is sufficiently strong that several organizations have issued guidelines for journalists to use in reporting on this issue. A review of guidelines from multiple countries showed that most emphasize that journalists should avoid glamorizing or sensationalizing suicide or the person who has committed or attempted suicide; exclude, as much as possible, specific information about the suicide method the individual has used or attempted to use; provide information that can help vulnerable audience members find assistance or support; and be cautious in dealing with family members or other survivors who may be at risk themselves in the wake of a suicide. Several of the guidelines also note that journalists who cover suicides may themselves be vulnerable in the aftermath (Pirkis et al., 2006).

An evaluation of the impact of the U.S. guidelines, published in 2001 through the joint efforts of the Centers for Disease Control and Prevention and several private foundations, showed that in the following year (2002–2003), newspapers did not consistently follow the guidelines. Although only 21 percent of the suicide stories analyzed included images, nearly three-quarters of the images (74%) met the suicide guidelines criteria for inappropriate photos, including showing the suicidal person, grieving family members or friends, or the site at which the suicide occurred. More than half of the stories included detailed information about the suicide method (56%) or the location (58%). Only 1 percent provided information about warning signs or risk factors for suicide, and only 4 percent mentioned whether the individual had been depressed. Although one- to two-thirds of individuals who completed suicides have alcohol in their systems, only 2 percent of the stories mentioned alcohol. Perhaps most disturbingly, only 6 percent of the stories provided any sort of suicide prevention resources or information. The authors note that many journalists likely are unaware of either the guidelines or of the suicide contagion phenomenon; further education of journalists may help reduce this unintended and highly negative effect (Tatum et al., 2010).

SUMMARY

Most journalists who cover health issues view their role as simply providing information, although some are more likely than others to acknowledge the intent to encourage audience members to make better health choices. Whatever journalists' intentions, however, their stories can have both positive and negative impacts. While news coverage often raises awareness of and increases knowledge about health issues, research also indicates that sensationalized and sometimes inaccurate coverage may do more harm than good. In addition, health journalism tends to overemphasize individual responsibility for poor health choices and outcomes, providing substantially less attention to the societal or environmental factors that contribute to disease, injury and ill-health. News coverage can spur audience members to take action to reduce their own or their family members' risks of certain diseases but also can raise unwarranted concerns and, in some cases, even encourage people to engage in risk behaviors such as illicit drug use.

It is worth noting that journalists themselves recognize many of the flaws in their reporting on health (Schwitzer, 2009) and that, in response, many of those who specialize in health reporting have attempted to improve their own and their colleagues' health coverage through participation in the Association of Health Care Journalists (AHCJ) training programs. Founded in 1998, AHCJ sponsors an annual national conference and multiple regional training workshops aimed at helping journalists do a better job of covering health (Association of Health Care Journalists, 2015a). In addition, the organization regularly publishes resource guides, which have addressed such issues as covering health care quality, multicultural health issues, medical research, nursing homes, the CDC, obesity and hospitals. In addition, the AHCJ website offers journalists resources on covering health care reform,

377

aging, oral health, insurance and the social determinants of health (Association of Health Care Journalists, 2015b). While some of these resources are available to AHCJ members only, others are available to anyone interested in the topic, all in an effort to increase the percentage of health journalism that impacts the public in positive rather than negative ways.

REFERENCES

Ackerson, L.K. & Viswanath, K. (2010). Media Attention and Public Perceptions of Cancer and Eastern Equine Encephalitis. *Journal of Community Health*, 35(4), 409–416. http://doi.org/10.1007/s10900-010-9257-2.

Adelman, R.C. & Verbrugge, L.M. (2000). Death Makes News: The Social Impact of Disease on Newspaper Coverage. *Journal of Health and Social Behavior*, 41(3), 347–367. http://doi.org/10.2307/2676325.

American Cancer Society. (2015). *Cancer Facts & Figures 2015*. Atlanta: American Cancer Society. Retrieved April 30, 2015 from www.cancer.org/acs/groups/content/@editorial/documents/document/acspc-044552.pdf.

Armstrong, E.M., Carpenter, D.P. & Hojnacki, M. (2006). Whose Deaths Matter? Mortality, Advocacy, and Attention to Disease in the Mass Media. *Journal of Health Politics, Policy and Law*, 31(4), 729–772. http://doi.org/10.1215/03616878-2006-002.

Association of Health Care Journalists. (2015a). History of AHCJ. Retrieved May 13, 2015 from http://healthjournalism.org/about-history.php.

Association of Health Care Journalists. (2015b). Resources. Retrieved May 13, 2015 from http://healthjournalism.org/resources-jump.php.

Berinsky, A. (2012, December 5). Public Support For Vaccination Remains Strong. Retrieved April 29, 2015 from https://today.yougov.com/news/2012/12/05/public-support-vaccination-remains-strong/.

Brainard, C. (2013, June). Sticking With the Truth: How "Balanced" Coverage Helped Sustain the Bogus Claim that Childhood Vaccines Can Cause Autism. Retrieved April 28, 2015 from www.cjr.org/feature/sticking_with_the_truth.php.

Brodie, M., Hamel, E.C., Altman, D.E., Blendon, R.J. & Benson, J.M. (2003). Health News and the American Public, 1996–2002. *Journal of Health Politics, Policy and Law*, 28(5), 927–950. http://doi.org/10.1215/03616878-28-5-927.

Brown, M.L. & Potosky, A.L. (1990). The Presidential Effect: The Public Health Response to Media Coverage About Ronald Reagan's Colon Cancer Episode. *Public Opinion Quarterly*, 54(3), 317–329. http://doi.org/10.1086/269209.

Brown, W.J. & Basil, M.D. (1995). Media Celebrities and Public Health: Responses to "Magic" Johnson's HIV Disclosure and Its Impact on AIDS Risk and High-risk Behaviors. *Health Communication*, 7(4), 345–370. http://doi.org/10.1207/s15327027hc0704_4.

Bubela, T.M. & Caulfield, T.A. (2004). Do the Print Media "Hype" Genetic Research? A Comparison of Newspaper Stories and Peer-reviewed Research Papers. *Canadian Medical Association Journal*, 170(9), 1399–1407. http://doi.org/10.1503/cmaj.1030762.

Calderone, M. (2013, January 24). New York Times Buyouts Push Veteran Journalists To The Exits. *The Huffington Post*. Retrieved January 5, 2015 from www.huffingtonpost.com/2013/01/24/new-york-times-buyouts-veteran-editors-leave_n_2544574.html.

Casey, G.M., Morris, B., Burnell, M., Parberry, A., Singh, N. & Rosenthal, A.N. (2013). Celebrities and Screening: A Measurable Impact on High-grade Cervical Neoplasia Diagnosis from the "Jade Goody Effect" in the UK. *British Journal of Cancer, 109*(5), 1192–1197. http://doi.org/10.1038/bjc.2013.444.

Cassels, A., Hughes, M.A., Cole, C., Mintzes, B., Lexchin, J. & McCormack, J.P. (2003). Drugs in the News: An Analysis of Canadian Newspaper Coverage of New Prescription Drugs. *CMAJ: Canadian Medical Association Journal = Journal de l'Association Medicale Canadienne, 168*(9), 1133–1137.

Centers for Disease Control and Prevention. (1989). Current Trends Measles – United States, 1988. *MMWR Weekly, 38*(35), 601–605.

Centers for Disease Control and Prevention. (2014, November 3). Measles History. Retrieved April 28, 2015 from www.cdc.gov/measles/about/history.html.

Centers for Disease Control and Prevention. (2015a, February 6). Leading Causes of Death. Retrieved May 4, 2015 from www.cdc.gov/nchs/fastats/leading-causes-of-death.htm.

Centers for Disease Control and Prevention. (2015b, February 17). Complications of Measles. Retrieved May 4, 2015 from www.cdc.gov/measles/about/complications.html.

Centers for Disease Control and Prevention. (2015c, April 27). Measles cases and outbreaks. Retrieved May 4, 2015 from www.cdc.gov/measles/cases-outbreaks.html.

Centers for Disease Control and Prevention. (2015d, April 27). U.S. Multi-state Measles Outbreak 2014–2015. Retrieved May 4, 2015 from www.cdc.gov/measles/multi-state-outbreak.html.

Chapman, S., McLeod, K., Wakefield, M. & Holding, S. (2005). Impact of News of Celebrity Illness on Breast Cancer Screening: Kylie Minogue's Breast Cancer Diagnosis. *The Medical Journal of Australia, 183*(5), 247–250.

Clarke, C.E. (2008). A Question of Balance: The Autism-Vaccine Controversy in the British and American Elite Press. *Science Communication, 30*(1), 77–107. http://doi.org/10.1177/1075547008320262.

Clarke, J. (2010). Heart Disease and Gender in Mass Print Media. *Maturitas, 65*(3), 215–218. http://doi.org/10.1016/j.maturitas.2009.11.019.

Clarke, J.N. & Binns, J. (2006). The Portrayal of Heart Disease in Mass Print Magazines, 1991–2001. *Health Communication, 19*(1), 39–48. http://doi.org/10.1207/s15327027hc1901_5.

Clarke, J., van Amerom, G. & Binns, J. (2007). Gender and Heart Disease in Mass Print Media: 1991, 1996, 2001. *Women & Health, 45*(1), 17–35. http://doi.org/10.1300/J013v45n01_02.

Clegg-Smith, K., Wakefield, M., Terry-McElrath, Y., Chaloupka, F., Flay, B., Johnston, L. & Siebel, C. (2008). Relation between Newspaper Coverage of Tobacco Issues and Smoking Attitudes and Behaviour among American Teens. *Tobacco Control, 17*(1), 17–24.

Clemmons, N.S., Gastanaduy, P.A., Fiebelkorn, A.P., Redd, S.B. & Wallace, G.S. (2015). Measles – United States, January 4–April 2, 2015. *MMWR. Morbidity and Mortality Weekly Report, 64*(14), 373–376.

Cohen, E.L., Caburnay, C.A., Luke, D.A., Rodgers, S., Cameron, G.T. & Kreuter, M.W. (2008). Cancer Coverage in General-audience and Black Newspapers. *Health Communication, 23*(5), 427–435. http://doi.org/10.1080/10410230802342176.

Cohn, V. (1988). *News & Numbers: A Guide to Reporting Statistical Claims and Controversies in Health and Other Fields* (1st edn). Ames: Iowa State Press.

Dasgupta, N., Mandl, K.D. & Brownstein, J.S. (2009). Breaking the News or Fueling the Epidemic? Temporal Association between News Media Report Volume and Opioid-related Mortality. *PloS ONE*, *4*(11), e7758. http://doi.org/10.1371/journal.pone.0007758;.

Deer, B. (2011a). How the Case against the MMR Vaccine was Fixed. *BMJ*, *342*. http://doi.org/10.1136/bmj.c5347.

Deer, B. (2011b). Secrets of the MMR Scare. How the Vaccine Crisis was Meant to Make Money. *BMJ (Clinical Research Edn)*, *342*, c5258.

Dixon, G.N. & Clarke, C.E. (2013). Heightening Uncertainty around Certain Science Media Coverage, False Balance, and the Autism–Vaccine Controversy. *Science Communication*, *35*(3), 358–382.

Dorell, C., Yankey, D., Kennedy, A. & Stokley, S. (2013). Factors that Influence Parental Vaccination Decisions for Adolescents, 13 to 17 Years Old: National Immunization Survey-Teen, 2010. *Clinical Pediatrics*, *52*(2), 162–170. http://doi.org/10.1177/0009922812468208.

Dorfman, L., Wallack, L. & Woodruff, K. (2005). More Than a Message: Framing Public Health Advocacy to Change Corporate Practices. *Health Education & Behavior*, *32*(3), 320–336. http://doi.org/10.1177/1090198105275046.

Dyer, C. (2010). Lancet Retracts Wakefield's MMR Paper. *BMJ (Clinical Research Edn)*, *340*, c696.

Edy, C.M. (2010). Women's Magazine Coverage of Heart Disease Risk Factors: Good Housekeeping Magazine, 1997 to 2007. *Women & Health*, *50*(2), 176–194. http://doi.org/10.1080/03630241003705029.

Esterl, M. (2014, March 31). The Diet Soda Business is in Freefall. *Wall Street Journal*. Retrieved May 4, 2015 from www.wsj.com/articles/SB10001424052702304157204579473772336022200.

Fan, D.P. (1996). News Media Framing Sets Public Opinion that Drugs is the Country's Most Important Problem. *Substance Use & Misuse*, *31*(10), 1413–1421.

Fan, D.P. & McAvoy, G. (1989). Predictions of Public Opinion on the Spread of AIDS: Introduction of New Computer Methodologies. *The Journal of Sex Research*, *26*(2), 159–187. http://doi.org/10.1080/00224498909551504.

Fink, R., Roeser, R., Venet, W., Strax, P., Venet, L. & Lacher, M. (1978). Effects of News Events on Response to a Breast Cancer Screening Program. *Public Health Reports*, *93*(4), 318–327.

Freimuth, V.S., Greenberg, R.H., DeWitt, J. & Romano, R.M. (1984). Covering Cancer: Newspapers and the Public Interest. *Journal of Communication*, *34*(1), 62–73. http://doi.org/10.1111/j.1460-2466.1984.tb02985.x.

Gantz, W. & Wang, Z.W. (2009). Coverage of Cancer in Local Television News. *Journal of Cancer Education*, *24*(1), 65–72. http://doi.org/10.1080/08858190802664727.

Geana, M.V., Kimminau, K.S. & Greiner, K.A. (2011). Sources of health information in a multiethnic, underserved, urban community: Does ethnicity matter? *Journal of Health Communication*, *16*(6), 583–594.

Gollust, S.E. & Lantz, P.M. (2009). Communicating Population Health: Print News Media Coverage of Type 2 Diabetes. *Social Science & Medicine*, *69*(7), 1091–1098. http://doi.org/10.1016/j.socscimed.2009.07.009.

Guskin, E. (2013, June 25). Newspaper Newsrooms Suffer Large Staffing Decreases | Pew Research Center.

Haas, J.S., Miglioretti, D.L., Geller, B., Buist, D.S.M., Nelson, D.E., Kerlikowske, K. & Ballard-Barbash, R. (2007). Average Household Exposure to Newspaper Coverage about the Harmful Effects of Hormone Therapy and Population-based Declines in Hormone Therapy Use. *Journal of General Internal Medicine, 22*(1), 68–73. http://doi.org/10.1007/s11606-007-0122-7.

Hertog, J.K. & Fan, D.P. (1995). The Impact of Press Coverage on Social Beliefs: The Case of HIV Transmission. *Communication Research, 22*(5), 545–574. http://doi.org/10.1177/009365095022005002.

Hesse, B.W., Moser, R.P. & Rutten, L.J. (2010). Surveys of Physicians and Electronic Health Information. *The New England Journal of Medicine, 362*(9), 859–860. http://doi.org/10.1056/NEJMc0909595.

Hesse, B.W., Nelson, D.E., Kreps, G.L., Croyle, R.T., Arora, N.K., Rimer, B.K. & Viswanath, K. (2005). Trust and Sources of Health Information: The Impact of the Internet and its Implications for Health Care Providers: Findings from the First Health Information National Trends Survey. *Archives of Internal Medicine, 165*(22), 2618–2624. http://doi.org/10.1001/archinte.165.22.2618.

Jensen, J.D., Moriarty, C.M., Hurley, R.J. & Stryker, J.E. (2010). Making Sense of Cancer News Coverage Trends: A Comparison of Three Comprehensive Content Analyses. *Journal of Health Communication, 15*(2), 136–151. http://doi.org/10.1080/10810730903528025.

Jensen, J.D., Scherr, C.L., Brown, N., Jones, C., Christy, K. & Hurley, R.J. (2014). Public Estimates of Cancer Frequency: Cancer Incidence Perceptions Mirror Distorted Media Depictions. *Journal of Health Communication, 19*(5), 609–624. http://doi.org/10.1080/10810730.2013.837551.

Kaiser Family Foundation & Pew Research Center's Project for Excellence in Journalism. (2008). *Health News Coverage in the U.S. Media: January 2007– June 2008.* Menlo Park, CA: Kaiser Family Foundation & Pew Research Center. Retrieved April 30, 2015 from https://kaiserfamilyfoundation.files.wordpress.com/2013/01/7839.pdf.

Kaiser Family Foundation & Pew Research Center's Project for Excellence in Journalism. (2009). *Health News Coverage in the U.S. Media: January–June 2009.* Menlo Park, CA: Kaiser Family Foundation & Pew Research Center. Retrieved April 29, 2015 from www.journalism.org/files/legacy/health_coverage_2009_0.pdf.

Kakai, H., Maskarinec, G., Shumay, D.M., Tatsumura, Y. & Tasaki, K. (2003). Ethnic differences in choices of health information by cancer patients using complementary and alternative medicine: an exploratory study with correspondence analysis. *Social Science & Medicine, 56*(4), 851–862.

Karen, K., Gerlach, M., Christina Marino, M. & Laurie Hoffman-Goetz, M. (1997). Cancer Coverage in Women's Magazines: What Information are Women Receiving? *Journal of Cancer Education, 12*(4), 240–244. http://doi.org/10.1080/08858199709528496.

Kelaher, M., Cawson, J., Miller, J., Kavanagh, A., Dunt, D. & Studdert, D.M. (2008). Use of Breast Cancer Screening and Treatment Services by Australian Women Aged 25-44 Years Following Kylie Minogue's Breast Cancer Diagnosis. *International Journal of Epidemiology, 37*(6), 1326–1332. http://doi.org/10.1093/ije/dyn090.

Kelly, B.J., Leader, A.E., Mittermaier, D.J., Hornik, R.C. & Cappella, J.N. (2009). The HPV Vaccine and the Media: How Has the Topic Been Covered and What are the Effects on Knowledge about the Virus and Cervical Cancer? *Patient Education and Counseling, 77*(2), 308–313. http://doi.org/10.1016/j.pec.2009.03.018.

Kim, A.E., Kumanyika, S., Shive, D., Igweatu, U. & Kim, S.-H. (2010). Coverage and Framing of Racial and Ethnic Health Disparities in US Newspapers, 1996-2005. *American Journal of Public Health, 100*(S1), S224–S231. http://doi.org/10.2105/AJPH.2009.171678.

Kim, S.-H. & Willis, A.L. (2007). Talking about Obesity: News Framing of Who is Responsible for Causing and Fixing the Problem. *Journal of Health Communication*, 12(4), 359–376.

Koons, D. & Armstrong, C. (2015, April 28). Merck Measles Vaccine Sales Surged as California Outbreak Grew. Retrieved April 29, 2015 from www.bloomberg.com/news/articles/2015-04-28/merck-measles-vaccine-sales-surged-as-california-outbreak-grew.

Lane, D.S., Polednak, A.P. & Burg, M.A. (1989). The Impact of Media Coverage of Nancy Reagan's Experience on Breast Cancer Screening. *American Journal of Public Health*, 79(11), 1551–1552.

Marlow, L.A.V., Sangha, A., Patnick, J. & Waller, J. (2012). The Jade Goody Effect: Whose Cervical Screening Decisions were Influenced by her Story? *Journal of Medical Screening*, 19(4), 184–188. http://doi.org/10.1258/jms.2012.012095.

Matsa, K. (2013, August 8). Local TV Newsrooms in 2012: Bigger Budgets, Smaller Staffs | Pew Research Center.

McCauley, M.P., Blake, K.D., Meissner, H.I. & Viswanath, K. (2013). The Social Group Influences of US Health Journalists and their Impact on the Newsmaking Process. *Health Education Research*, 28(2), 339–351. http://doi.org/10.1093/her/cys086.

McCombs, M.E. & Reynolds, A. (2002). News Influence on our Pictures of the World. In J. Bryant, D. Zillmann & M.B. Oliver (eds), *Media Effects: Advances in Theory and Research* (pp. 1–18). Abingdon and New York: Routledge.

McGinty, E.E., Webster, D.W., Jarlenski, M. & Barry, C.L. (2014). News Media Framing of Serious Mental Illness and Gun Violence in the United States, 1997–2012. *American Journal of Public Health*, 104(3), 406–413. http://doi.org/10.2105/AJPH.2013.301557.

Mcintosh, J. & Blalock, S.J. (2005). Effects of Media Coverage of Women's Health Initiative Study on Attitudes and Behavior of Women Receiving Hormone Replacement Therapy. *American Journal of Health-System Pharmacy*, 62(1), 69.

Moriarty, C.M. & Stryker, J.E. (2008). Prevention and Screening Efficacy Messages in Newspaper Accounts of Cancer. *Health Education Research*, 23(3), 487–498. http://doi.org/10.1093/her/cyl163.

Moynihan, R., Bero, L., Ross-Degnan, D., Henry, D., Lee, K., Watkins, J. & Soumerai, S.B. (2000). Coverage by the News Media of the Benefits and Risks of Medications. *New England Journal of Medicine*, 342(22), 1645–1650. http://doi.org/10.1056/NEJM200006013422206.

Murphy, M.W., Iqbal, S., Sanchez, C.A. & Quinlisk, M.P. (2010). Postdisaster health communication and information sources: the Iowa flood scenario. *Disaster Medicine and Public Health Preparedness*, 4(02), 129–134.

Nattinger, A.B., Hoffmann, R.G., Howell-Pelz, A. & Goodwin, J.S. (1998). Effect of Nancy Reagan's Mastectomy on Choice of Surgery for Breast Cancer by US Women. *JAMA*, 279(10), 762–766.

Niederdeppe, J. (2008). Beyond Knowledge Gaps: Examining Socioeconomic Differences in Response to Cancer News. *Human Communication Research*, 34(3), 423–447. http://doi.org/10.1111/j.1468-2958.2008.00327.x.

Niederdeppe, J., Frosch, D.L. & Hornik, R.C. (2008). Cancer News Coverage and Information Seeking. *Journal of Health Communication*, 13(2), 181–199.

Niederdeppe, J., Fowler, E.F., Goldstein, K. & Pribble, J. (2010). Does Local Television News Coverage Cultivate Fatalistic Beliefs about Cancer Prevention? *Journal of Communication*, 60(2), 230–253.

Niederdeppe, J., Lee, T., Robbins, R., Kim, H.K., Kresovich, A., Kirshenblat, D. & Fowler, E.F. (2014). Content and Effects of News Stories about Uncertain Cancer Causes and Preventive Behaviors. *Health Communication*, 29(4), 332–346. http://doi.org/10.1080/10410236.2012.755603.

Pearce, M. (2015, February 5). The History of Measles: A Scourge for Centuries. *Los Angeles Times*. Retrieved April 28, 2015 from www.latimes.com/local/california/la-na-measles-timeline-20150205-story.html#page=1.

Phillips, D.P. & Carstensen, L.L. (1986). Clustering of Teenage Suicides after Television News Stories about Suicide. *The New England Journal of Medicine*, 315(11), 685–689. http://doi.org/10.1056/NEJM198609113151106.

Pierce, J.P. & Gilpin, E.A. (2001). News Media Coverage of Smoking and Health is Associated with Changes in Population Rates of Smoking Cessation but not Initiation. *Tobacco Control*, 10(2), 145–153.

Pirkis, J., Warwick, R., Beautrais, A., Burgess, P. & Skehan, J. (2006). Media Guidelines on the Reporting of Suicide. *Crisis: The Journal of Crisis Intervention and Suicide Prevention*, 27(2), 82–87. http://doi.org/10.1027/0227-5910.27.2.82.

Pribble, J.M., Goldstein, K.M., Fowler, E.F., Greenberg, M.J., Noel, S.K. & Howell, J.D. (2006). Medical News for the Public to Use? What's on Local TV News. *The American Journal of Managed Care*, 12(3), 170–176.

Rains, S.A. (2007). Perceptions of Traditional Information Sources and Use of the World Wide Web to Seek Health Information: Findings From the Health Information National Trends Survey. *Journal of Health Communication*, 12(7), 667–680. http://doi.org/10.1080/10810730701619992.

Rodgers, S. & Thorsen, E. (2001). The Reporting of Crime and Violence in the Los Angeles Times: Is There a Public Health Perspective? *Journal of Health Communication*, 6(2), 169–182. http://doi.org/10.1080/10810730120636.

Roush, S.W., Murphy, T.V. & Vaccine-Preventable Disease Table Working Group. (2007). Historical Comparisons of Morbidity and Mortality for Vaccine-preventable Diseases in the United States. *JAMA*, 298(18), 2155–2163.

Schwartz, L.M. & Woloshin, S. (2002). News Media Coverage of Screening Mammography for Women in their 40s and Tamoxifen for Primary Prevention of Breast Cancer. *JAMA: The Journal of the American Medical Association*, 287(23), 3136–3142.

Schwitzer, G. (2009). *The State of Health Journalism in the US*. Henry J. Kaiser Family Foundation, Menlo Park, CA. Retrieved January 25, 2015 from https://kaiserfamilyfoundation.files.wordpress.com/2013/01/7858.pdf.

Seither, R., Masalovich, S., Knighton, C.L., Mellerson, J., Singleton, J.A., Greby, S.M. & Centers for Disease Control and Prevention (CDC). (2014). Vaccination Coverage among Children in Kindergarten – United States, 2013-14 School Year. *MMWR. Morbidity and Mortality Weekly Report*, 63(41), 913–920.

Selvaraj, S., Borkar, D.S. & Prasad, V. (2014). Media Coverage of Medical Journals: Do the Best Articles Make the News? *PLoS ONE*, 9(1), e85355. http://doi.org/10.1371/journal.pone.0085355.

Sharma, V., Dowd, M.D., Swanson, D.S., Slaughter, A.J. & Simon, S.D. (2003). Influence of the News Media on Diagnostic Testing in the Emergency Department. *Archives of Pediatrics & Adolescent Medicine*, 157(3), 257.

Slater, M.D., Long, M., Bettinghaus, E.P. & Reineke, J.B. (2008). News Coverage of Cancer in the United States: A National Sample of Newspapers, Television, and Magazines. *Journal of Health Communication*, 13(6), 523–537. http://doi.org/10.1080/10810730802279571.

Smith, M.J., Ellenberg, S.S., Bell, L.M. & Rubin, D.M. (2008). Media Coverage of the Measles-Mumps-Rubella Vaccine and Autism Controversy and Its Relationship to MMR Immunization Rates in the United States. *Pediatrics, 121*(4), e836–e843. http://doi.org/10.1542/peds.2007-1760.

Smith, P.J., Humiston, S.G., Marcuse, E.K., Zhao, Z., Dorell, C.G., Howes, C. & Hibbs, B. (2011). Parental Delay or Refusal of Vaccine Doses, Childhood Vaccination Coverage at 24 Months of Age, and the Health Belief Model. *Public Health Reports, 126*(Suppl 2), 135–146.

Speers, T. & Lewis, J. (2004). Journalists and Jabs: Media Coverage of the MMR Vaccine. *Communication & Medicine, 1*(2), 171–181.

Squiers, L.B., Holden, D.J., Dolina, S.E., Kim, A.E., Bann, C.M. & Renaud, J.M. (2011). The Public's Response to the U.S. Preventive Services Task Force's 2009 Recommendations on Mammography Screening. *American Journal of Preventive Medicine, 40*(5), 497–504. http://doi.org/10.1016/j.amepre.2010.12.027.

Stack, S. (2000). Media Impacts on Suicide: A Quantitative Review of 293 Findings. *Social Science Quarterly, 81*(4), 957–971.

Stack, S. (2005). Suicide in the Media: A Quantitative Review of Studies Based on Nonfictional Stories. *Suicide and Life-Threatening Behavior, 35*(2), 121–133. http://doi.org/10.1521/suli.35.2.121.62877.

Stroman, C.A. & Seltzer, R. (1989). Mass Media Use and Knowledge of AIDS. *Journalism Quarterly, 66*(4), 881–887.

Stryker, J.E. (2003). Articles Media and Marijuana: A Longitudinal Analysis of News Media Effects on Adolescents' Marijuana Use and Related Outcomes, 1977–1999. *Journal of Health Communication, 8*(4), 305–328.

Stryker, J.E., Emmons, K.M. & Viswanath, K. (2007). Uncovering Differences across the Cancer Control Continuum: A Comparison of Ethnic and Mainstream Cancer Newspaper Stories. *Preventive Medicine, 44*(1), 20–25. http://doi.org/10.1016/j.ypmed.2006.07.012.

Stryker, J.E., Moriarty, C.M. & Jensen, J.D. (2008). Effects of Newspaper Coverage on Public Knowledge About Modifiable Cancer Risks. *Health Communication, 23*(4), 380–390. http://doi.org/10.1080/10410230802229894.

Tatum, P.T., Canetto, S.S. & Slater, M.D. (2010). Suicide Coverage in U.S. Newspapers Following the Publication of the Media Guidelines. *Suicide and Life-Threatening Behavior, 40*(5), 524–534. http://doi.org/10.1521/suli.2010.40.5.524.

The Measles Epidemic. The Problems, Barriers, and Recommendations. The National Vaccine Advisory Committee. (1991). *JAMA, 266*(11), 1547–1552.

Tu, H.T. (2011). *Surprising Decline in Consumers Seeking Health Information.* Washington, DC: Center for Studying Health System Change.

Tu, H.T. & Cohen, G.R. (2008). *Striking Jump in Consumers Seeking Health Care Information* (No. 20). Washington, DC: Center for Studying Health System Change. Retrieved May 4, 2015 from www.amcp.org/WorkArea/DownloadAsset.aspx?id=12579.

Viswanath, K., Blake, K.D., Meissner, H.I., Saiontz, N.G., Mull, C., Freeman, C.S. & Croyle, R.T. (2008). Occupational Practices and the Making of Health News: A National Survey of US Health and Medical Science Journalists. *Journal of Health Communication, 13*(8), 759–777.

Wallington, S.F., Blake, K., Taylor-Clark, K. & Viswanath, K. (2010). Antecedents to Agenda Setting and Framing in Health News: An Examination of Priority, Angle, Source, and Resource Usage from a National Survey of US Health Reporters and Editors. *Journal of Health Communication, 15*(1), 76–94.

Walsh-Childers, K., Braddock, J., Rabaza, C. & Schwitzer, G. (in press). One step forward, one step back: Changes in news coverage of medical interventions. *Health Communication*.

Wang, Z. & Gantz, W. (2010). Health Content in Local Television News: A Current Appraisal. *Health Communication*, 25(3), 230–237. http://doi.org/10.1080/10410231003698903.

Wanta, W. & Elliott, W.R. (1995). Did the "Magic" Work? Knowledge of HIV/AIDS and the Knowledge Gap Hypothesis. *Journalism & Mass Communication Quarterly*, 72(2), 312–321. http://doi.org/10.1177/107769909507200205.

Weeks, B.E., Friedenberg, L.M., Southwell, B.G. & Slater, J.S. (2012). Behavioral Consequences of Conflict-oriented Health News Coverage: The 2009 Mammography Guideline Controversy and Online Information Seeking. *Health Communication*, 27(2), 158–166. http://doi.org/10.1080/10410236.2011.571757.

Wilkinson, R.G. & Marmot, M.G. (2003). *Social Determinants of Health: The Solid Facts.* Geneva: World Health Organization.

Woloshin, S., Schwartz, L.M. & Kramer, B.S. (2009). Promoting Healthy Skepticism in the News: Helping Journalists Get it Right. *Journal of the National Cancer Institute*, 101(23), 1596–1599. http://doi.org/10.1093/jnci/djp409.

Yanovitzky, I. & Blitz, C.L. (2000). Effect of Media Coverage and Physician Advice on Utilization of Breast Cancer Screening by Women 40 Years and Older. *Journal of Health Communication*, 5(2), 117–134. http://doi.org/10.1080/108107300406857.

Ziv, S. (2015, February 10). Andrew Wakefield, Father of the Anti-vaccine Movement, Responds to the Current Measles Outbreak for the First Time. Retrieved April 28, 2015 from www.newsweek.com/2015/02/20/andrew-wakefield-father-anti-vaccine-movement-sticks-his-story-305836.html.

CHAPTER 12

PEER-TO-PEER HEALTH: THE GOOD AND BAD NEWS ABOUT FACEBOOK, INSTAGRAM, BLOGS AND OTHER SOCIAL MEDIA

In June 2009, during the last week of school, a 13-year-old Ruskin, FL, girl named Hope Witsell made a mistake. She used a cell phone to take a photo of her breasts and "sexted" them to a boy named Alex, in whom she was interested romantically. Another girl who was friends with Alex – and who considered Hope a rival for her boyfriend – borrowed Alex's phone on the school bus. When she found the image Hope had sent, she forwarded the text to other students, who then forwarded it to others. By the end of the day, Hope's photo had reached students throughout her middle school and at the high school nearby. For the rest of the school year, Hope's friends had to surround her in the school hallways when she walked between classes, attempting to shield her from the taunts of "whore" and "slut" and from students who would shove Hope into the lockers (Meacham, 2009).

Shortly after the end of the year, school officials learned about the photo and called Hope's parents. They briefly took her to counseling, but after three weeks the counselor told the Witsells that their daughter wasn't benefitting from the counseling because she did not want to be there. Hope also faced a week-long suspension when school began again in the fall, but the summer break meant she would not be subjected to the taunts and slurs or physical abuse she had endured at school (Meacham, 2009).

Being physically separated from her bullies, however, did not end Hope's torment. Children from the middle school continued to taunt and insult her via MySpace, where they wrote horrible comments about her on pages called "Shields Middle School Burn Book" and the "Hope Hater Page." By the time Hope returned to school the following year, the bullying had intensified. She wrote about the bullying in her journal, but never told her parents ("How a Cell Phone," 2010).

On Friday, September 11, 2009, Hope met with the middle school's social worker, to whom she was referred after another adult saw worrisome cuts on Hope's legs. The counselor had Hope sign a "no harm contract," in which she promised to tell an adult if she was thinking about harming herself. On Saturday, Hope's parents went to work at the post office, came home to cook and share a seafood meal with Hope, and spent a few hours watching television. They invited Hope to watch with them, but she declined, preferring to stay in her room, writing in her journal (Meacham, 2009).

One of the entries read, "I'm done for sure now. I can feel it in my stomach. I'm going to try and strangle myself. I hope it works" (Meacham, 2009, para. 65).

The next time Hope's mother went to her room to check on her daughter before going to bed, she found that Hope had killed herself. She attempted CPR while her husband called 911, but it was too late. The honor roll student who had dreamed of attending the University of Florida and then setting up her own landscaping and nursery business had given up hope of overcoming her sexting mistake.

Although Hope Witsell's suicide is often cited as the second case in which a teenager's sexting led ultimately to suicide, it also illustrates one element of the darker side of the Internet, especially the now ubiquitous and heavily used social networking sites like Facebook, Twitter, Instagram, Snapchat and askFM. These social networking sites, which now play a central role in the lives of many teens and young adults, facilitate cyberbullying, a type of victimization estimated to affect at least one in every five youths at least once in their lives (Tokunaga, 2010).

Cyberbullying clearly has negative health effects, but categorizing the overall health impacts of social media, including social networking sites, blogs, forums and online discussion groups, is somewhat complicated by the wide variety of content creators, the content they produce, and the nature of the interactions between content producers and content consumers. Chapter 2 already has dealt with the research on the effects of consumer use of the Internet for health information seeking. For the most part, that research addresses the content, use and effects of government, organizational and corporate websites that provide health information intended for consumer use. This chapter, in contrast, will focus on content produced by individuals who may or may not intend to encourage those who consume their content to make health decisions based on that content.

We will begin with what the research tells us about consumers' use of social media in relation to health. According to the Pew Research Center's 2009 study on the social life of health information, consumers frequently access "user-generated" health information (as distinguished from health information provided by a government agency, health advocacy group, hospital, etc.); of the 57 percent of American adults who look for health information online, a group the Pew Center calls "e-patients," 41 percent have read another consumer's commentary or recounting of his or her experience with a health or medical issue via a blog, a website or an online news group, and almost one in four (24%) have checked online rankings or reviews of health professionals and health facilities. On the other hand, only a small percentage of consumers create health content online, with 6 percent of e-patients saying they have posted health-related comments or information, or asked health questions. Use of social networking sites for health information acquisition is relatively common. Pew's 2009 survey showed that 41 percent of e-patients had read another individual's online discussion of his or her health or medical issues; younger adults (aged 18–49) are more likely than older adults to have read such commentaries (Fox & Jones, 2009).

More than one-third of all adults (37%) and almost two-thirds (60%) of e-patients use social media in health-related ways, including obtaining information and advice, giving and receiving emotional or social support and so on (Fox & Jones, 2009). In particular, 23 percent of individuals with a chronic condition (e.g., cancer, heart disease, diabetes) and nearly one-third (32%) of those with multiple chronic conditions reported searching for others who share their health concerns; this compares to 15 percent of individuals with no chronic conditions who report similar searches. Looking online for people with similar health concerns also seems to be common among caregivers for those with a chronic condition and among people dealing with a medical crisis or with some sort of significant health change or issue, such as pregnancy, quitting smoking, and gaining or losing weight (Fox, 2011).

A Pew Research Center national survey showed that 13 percent of adults say they have received online information or support regarding a health issue from friends and family, and 5 percent have interacted online with other patients. The survey respondents cited health professionals as the most important sources of information when they are looking for an accurate diagnosis of a medical problem, information about drugs and treatment alternatives, and recommendations for other doctors or medical facilities; however, they are more likely to value information from family, friends and fellow patients when they need emotional support or a practical solution for an everyday health issue (Fox, 2011).

The Pew study showed that online interaction with fellow patients and caregivers is especially important for people who have or care for someone with a rare disease. "Patients say they will confide to others in these extended networks in ways that are sometimes hard to confide to their closest family members and friends" (Fox, 2011, p. 9). A survey of individuals who participate in six PatientsLikeMe communities showed that 42 percent agreed that using the site had helped them connect with another patient who could help them understand what they were likely to experience while undergoing specific treatments for their condition (Wicks et al., 2010). Other researchers have found that people with diseases that can be embarrassing, such as irritable bowel syndrome, use online communities to challenge the stigmas associated with their disease (Frohlich & Zmyslinski-Seelig, 2014; Frohlich, in press).

It is important to note, however, that social media can have health impacts even when the site is being used for other purposes, such as entertainment and maintaining contact with friends. For instance, recent research suggests that teenagers have become disenchanted with Facebook as the site has become more popular with adults and as they have tired of over-sharing and the social tensions online interactions sometimes create; nonetheless, in 2012, "94% of teen social media users said they had a Facebook profile, and 81% said that Facebook is the profile they use most often" (Madden, 2013, para. 5). Teens' social media use is hardly limited to Facebook, however. Among all teens 13 to 17 years old, 52 percent use Instagram, 41 percent use Snapchat, 33 percent use Twitter and Google+, 24 percent use Vine, and 14 percent use Tumblr. Nearly three-quarters of teens (71%) use more than one social networking site. The Pew Research Center's most recent data suggest that social media use varies according to socioeconomic background; teens from lower income families use Facebook more than do their more affluent peers, while those from better-off families use Snapchat and Twitter. Whichever social media and other online sites teens are using, nearly one in four (24%) report that they are online "almost constantly," and more than half (56%) say they access the Internet several times a day (Lenhart, 2015).

Facebook also dominates social media use among adults, with 71 to 77 percent of adults who use the Internet reporting use of Facebook; even among older adults (65+), more than half (56%) use Facebook (Anderson, 2015; Duggan et al., 2015). YouTube is the second most important social media site, with 63 percent of online adults reporting use of the site in 2014 (Anderson, 2015). LinkedIn and Pinterest tie for a fairly distant third, with 28 percent of all online adults reporting use of each site, followed closely by Instagram (26%) and Twitter (23%). Like teens, increasing numbers of adults are using multiple sites, with more than half of all online adults (52%) reporting that they use two or more social media sites. Facebook tends to dominate social media time, with 70 percent of adults with a Facebook profile reporting that they visit the site daily and 45 percent checking Facebook several times a day (Duggan et al., 2015).

Video-sharing sites such as YouTube and Vimeo are also playing increasingly important roles in peer-to-peer information exchange. According to the Pew Research Center, in 2013, 72 percent of adults reported that they had used a video-sharing site, reflecting a more than 100 percent increase since 2006. Nearly one-third of online adults (31%) posted a video online in 2013. Of course, most of these videos are not necessarily health-related; the most common subjects for individuals' uploaded videos are family members and friends engaging in common-place activities, the individual himself or herself or another person doing something funny, events the individual attended, and pets or other animals. Just under one-third of Internet users (30%) have posted "tutorial" videos, which cover a wide range of subjects (Anderson, 2015).

THE HEALTH IMPACTS OF SOCIAL MEDIA USE

The increasingly common use of social media by both youth and adults has led many scholars to investigate the potential health impacts of these sites. This research has produced evidence that social media use can have both positive and negative impacts on multiple dimensions of health, including social (or interpersonal), emotional and physical health. Hettler's (1976) model distinguishes between emotional health and social/interpersonal health, with the interpersonal dimension focusing on the "interdependence between others and nature" (Hettler, 1976, p. 1) and addressing issues of friendship, personal relationships and community involvement. Research in this area deals with the impact of social media on loneliness, friendships and intimate relationships.

LONELINESS

Increased use of electronic media and electronic forms of communication is well documented across all age groups. One key question, however, is whether that increased electronic communication supplements or replaces face-to-face communication. In other words, does reading about and interacting with people online increase interpersonal communication overall, or does the time we spend keeping up with friends and family online use up time we would otherwise spend in face-to-face communication with them?

Some critics argue that, especially among young adults and youth, communication via text, instant message and other electronic means increases the frequency of communication with family members and friends but decreases the quality of that communication. They argue that children who spend more time communicating via screens and emoticons, rather than interacting face-to-face with other people, have difficulty understanding body language cues through which the majority of human communication actually occurs and therefore have more trouble understanding emotion and developing strong relationships, potentially leading to more loneliness (Johnson, 2014; Tardanico, n.d.; Uhls et al., 2014).

Some researchers indeed have found that increased Internet use is associated with loneliness (Bonetti et al., 2010; Kraut et al., 1998; Teppers et al., 2014). However, the direction of that relationship has been less clear, with some research suggesting that people who self-report being lonely can compensate for weaker offline relationships by interacting with others online (Bonetti et al., 2010); among older adults, online communication can decrease loneliness and increase social contact (Cotton et al., 2013). Other researchers, however, have suggested that Facebook use increases loneliness when adolescents use the site for social skills compensation, rather than for making new friends or learning more about them (Teppers et al., 2014). Research with adults also suggests that time spent simply browsing online also is associated with increased loneliness (Stepanikova et al., 2010).

A recent meta-analysis of the research on Facebook use and loneliness attempted to determine whether lonely people are simply drawn to using Facebook more than non-lonely people, or whether Facebook use actually increases loneliness. Based on analysis of eight studies linking Facebook use to loneliness, the researchers concluded that although all of the studies identified positive relationships between Facebook use and loneliness, the data better supported the conclusion that lonely people spend more time on Facebook, rather than Facebook use increasing loneliness. They argue that "lonely individuals who are shy and have low social support may turn to Facebook to compensate for their lack of social skills and/or social networks" that would provide face-to-face interactions (Song et al., 2014, p. 450).

FRIENDSHIPS

As the research on loneliness might suggest, studies of the impact of social media on friendships also have produced mixed findings. Early studies of Internet use showed that the more time adolescents and adults spent in online communication, the fewer friends they had, the less time they spent with friends offline and the less socially connected they felt (Kraut et al., 1998; Mesch, 2001; Nie, 2001; Nie et al., 2008). More recently, however, researchers have begun to find the opposite effect – that online communication actually can strengthen and improve relationships with real-world friends. When Kraut and his colleagues followed up their study of (initially negative) effects of online communication two years later, they found strikingly different results; online communication actually improved Internet users' social connectedness, although the impact was more significant for those who were already extroverted than for more introverted individuals (Kraut et al., 2002).

In a more recent study, researchers studying electronically mediated communication among 11- to 15-year-olds in 30 countries from Europe and North America found that the more time adolescents spent communicating with friends over the telephone, through text messages and online, the more at ease they felt talking about their concerns with opposite-sex friends (Boniel-Nissim et al., 2015). In addition, Valkenburg and colleagues have found that instant messaging has positive effects on the quality of adolescent friendships, primarily because it increases teens' likelihood of sharing personal information with their friends (Valkenburg & Peter, 2007, 2009b). Similarly, Quinn and Oldmeadow (2013) found that, among younger children (aged 9–13), intensity of social networking site usage was linked to a stronger sense of belonging to one's friendship network, but only among boys. The authors argue that this gender difference likely occurs because girls of this age are already more adept than boys at self-disclosure in the offline world, so the opportunity to practice self-disclosure online, thereby building a greater sense of belonging and intimacy, provides more benefit for boys.

Researchers also have examined the links between the intensity of college students' Facebook usage (a measure that includes daily time spent on Facebook and its integration into the individual's daily activities) and three types of social capital representing maintenance of connections with the individual's "weak tie" Facebook friends (bridging), their close friend networks (bonding) and their previous communities, such as friends from high school (maintenance). The study showed that Facebook use was linked significantly to all three types of social capital; the strongest link was to bridging social capital, leading the authors to conclude that Facebook use might help college students build and strengthen "weak ties" to individuals who might be helpful to them in their courses and their employment pursuits (Ellison et al., 2007).

One explanation for this shift from negative to positive effects lies in the growth of social networking sites as the primary sites for online communication. Valkenburg and Peter (2009a) argue that early studies of online communication dealt almost exclusively with interactions between strangers because relatively few people were involved in online communities; thus, online communication took time away from communication with offline friends. However, since the advent of social networking sites, most online communication involves interactions with existing networks of friends and acquaintances, whether or not those people are in regular contact in the offline world (such as at work or school). Thus, as long as adolescents are using online communication to interact with existing friends, that communication generally produces positive results (Valkenburg & Peter, 2009b; Wang & Wellman, 2010); however, research continues to show that individuals who prefer online communication because they are uncomfortable with face-to-face communication often do not succeed in using online communication to make new friends (Valkenburg & Peter, 2011).

ROMANTIC RELATIONSHIPS

While the use of social media and online communication in general may have positive effects on the maintenance of interpersonal relationships with offline friends and family members, some evidence suggests that those positive effects do not extend to romantic relationships. In fact, some researchers have found that social media use increases romantic jealousy, thereby decreasing relationship satisfaction (Clayton, 2014; Clayton et al., 2013; Muise et al., 2009; Utz et al., 2015). In large part, this may be due to the fact that Facebook can make the individual aware of interactions his or her romantic partner has had with those who could be perceived as romantic rivals or threats. The interactions themselves are not necessarily new; romantic partners have always known, in a vague sense, that their spouse, boyfriend or girlfriend might be attracted to someone else whom they met through school, work or other activities. However, before the advent of social media, the partner's interactions with these other individuals were more likely to remain hidden (Muise et al., 2009).

Even imagining a scenario in which the person's romantic partner has no photos of the couple on his or her Facebook profile elicited jealousy, as did imagining that the romantic partner had privacy settings on these photos such that only he or she could see the couple photos. The authors of this experimental study reasoned that having no couple photos or having the photos set to be visible only to the profile owner signals to the romantic partner that the individual either does not acknowledge that there is a relationship or is attempting to hide that relationship from others. Women experienced all of these negative emotions – jealousy, anger, hurt and disgust – to a greater extent than did men (Muscanell et al., 2013).

Women tend to be more likely than men to become jealous due to their partner's activity on Facebook; interestingly, one study showed that men are aware of this gender difference but women are not (McAndrew & Shah, 2013). Romantic jealousy may be a particular problem for individuals who score highly on a "Facebook intrusion" scale, indicating that the individual thinks about Facebook even when not using it, may have conflicts with others about his or her Facebook use, or feels distress when he or she cannot access Facebook. "Facebook intrusion may translate into hypervigilance for relationship threats, jealousy-related suspicions, and surveillance behaviors in a person's romantic relationship" (Elphinston & Noller, 2011, p. 632).

Social media-related jealousy also seems to depend, to some extent, on the individual's attachment style. Those who report "anxious attachment styles," characterized by doubting one's worthiness for love, worrying that one's romantic partners cannot be depended upon and fear of rejection, are more likely to engage in "Facebook surveillance" or "creeping," meaning they monitor their partners' Facebook profiles for evidence of infidelity or rejection and feel more jealousy. On the other hand, Facebook surveillance and jealousy are less common among those with avoidant attachment styles, who tend to maintain emotional distance and control in relationships. However, Facebook surveillance was also common among individuals who felt secure in and passionate about their relationships, suggesting that, in some cases, checking the partner's page may simply represent a way of being "close" to him or her (Fox & Warber, 2014; Marshall et al., 2013).

Use of social media for relationship maintenance is especially important and common for individuals involved in long-distance romantic relationships. A study of Facebook use among people involved in both geographically close and long-distance romantic relationships showed, not surprisingly, that those in long-distance relationships were more likely than those in physically close relationships to use Facebook to communicate with the partner, to say "I love you," and for other relationship maintenance behaviors. They were also more likely to use Facebook to gauge their partner's involvement in or commitment to the relationship, and they experienced more social media-related jealousy than those who could see their partner face-to-face more regularly (Billedo et al., 2015).

The results of this social media surveillance and jealousy can be quite significant. Analysis of survey data from married couples revealed that greater use of social networking sites is associated with lower perceived marriage quality and happiness and greater likelihood of reporting problems in the relationship and consideration of divorce. In this same paper, analysis of state-level divorce data showed that, controlling for many other relevant factors, the increased diffusion of Facebook in the United States was correlated with increasing divorce rates (Valenzuela et al., 2014). Clayton and colleagues (2013) found that high levels of Facebook use were related to increased romantic partner conflict over Facebook, to emotional and physical "cheating" on one's partner and, ultimately, to break-ups and even divorce. This was primarily true for individuals in a relationship that had been going on for three years or less, suggesting that "Facebook may be a threat to relationships that are not fully matured" (Clayton et al., 2013, p. 719). Similarly, Twitter use can also lead to romantic relationship conflict, ultimately resulting in cheating, break-ups and divorce; Clayton (2014) found that the length of the romantic relationship did not affect the connection between Twitter use and negative relationship outcomes.

Even after romantic relationships have ended, social media use related to that relationship can be problematic. In one study of 411 college students, 67.3 percent reported at least sometimes engaging in "covert provocation" of a former romantic partner through Facebook; this behavior included updating one's status to make the ex-partner jealous, taunting

Figure 12.1: More Women Than Men Experience Social Media Jealousy

the partner through wall posts or posting of poetry or music lyrics and attempting to find photos of the ex- with his or her new partner. Less commonly, about one in five (18%) of the respondents acknowledged using Facebook to publicly harass the ex-partner or to vent about him or her. More than half (50.9%) acknowledged engaging in behaviors the researchers labeled "cyber obsessional pursuit," meaning that they "persistently pursued" the ex-partner to re-establish the relationship, even after the partner had made it clear that he or she was not interested (Lyndon et al., 2011).

When a relationship ends, those who engage in more Facebook monitoring of the ex-partner report greater distress over the break-up (Lukacs & Quan-Haase, 2015), as well as more negative feelings, more sexual desire for the ex-partner, more longing to renew the relationship and less personal growth (Marshall, 2012). Remaining "friends" with the ex-partner on Facebook was related to less negative feelings and longing, but also to lower personal growth, in comparison to individuals who discontinued their Facebook friendship with their ex-partner (Marshall, 2012). Other researchers have found that individuals who accepted former partners' Facebook friend requests reported greater trait anxiety and depression than those who did not; men were more depressed than women when they "met" former partners through Facebook, regardless of how the relationship had ended (Tsai et al., 2015).

EMOTIONAL HEALTH

Although issues of romantic attachment, friendships and loneliness all have emotional consequences, researchers also have identified connections between social media use and emotional health outside the context of relationships. The research focuses on three areas: social media or Internet addiction, cyberbullying and depression.

Addiction

The term "Internet addiction" may sound rather like the kind of overly negative and fearful reaction that often accompanies the introduction of many technological changes, but researchers have, in fact, identified it as a new clinical disorder that is similar, in some ways, to compulsive gambling. A 1996 survey of 596 Internet-using adults revealed that those who met the criteria for Internet dependency reported spending, on average, 38.5 hours online each week, *excluding* academic or work-related use, compared to 4.9 hours per week among those who were not Internet dependent. Non-dependent users primarily gathered information and used email when they were online, whereas individuals classified as Internet dependent spent much of their time in chat rooms and multi-user dungeons or "MUDs", both of which could be considered precursors of today's social networking sites and online games in that they facilitate real-time multi-way communication. Internet-dependent users were more likely than their non-dependent peers to use the Internet to meet and socialize with others (Young, 1998).

Virtually all of the Internet-dependent individuals in the study reported that their Internet use resulted in "moderate" (40%) or "severe" (58%) negative impacts on their academic performance and their offline relationships (45 percent "moderate," 53 percent "severe"). In addition, large majorities said that their Internet use had moderate or severe impacts on their financial well-being (90%) and their occupational performance (85%). In some cases, the individuals reported that their Internet use led them to avoid important activities; one mother reported being so wrapped up in her online activities that she sometimes forgot to pick her children up from school, prepare dinner for them or put them to bed. More than half of these individuals described themselves as "completely hooked" on Internet use, to the point that they did not even attempt to reduce the number of hours they spent online (Young, 1998).

A more recent study of "pathological" Internet use among college students confirmed that slightly fewer than one in ten students (8.1%) qualified as "pathological users"; these individuals reported spending four times as many hours online for personal/entertainment reasons as did students whose Internet use was not problematic. Men were more likely than women to meet the criteria for pathological use, and problematic users were significantly more likely to go online to play games, download software, use online communication tools and to surf websites. As in the earlier study, they were also more likely to report using the Internet to meet new people, to access adults-only sites (e.g., pornography), to seek emotional support, to communicate with people who shared their interests, to play games and gamble, to simply kill time and for relaxation. Problematic users were more likely than their peers to agree that the Internet made it easier for them to make friends and that they go online to escape real-world pressure (Morahan-Martin & Schumacher, 2000).

Perhaps not surprisingly, given the early research linking problematic Internet use to motivations related to meeting people and socializing, researchers have found that the use of social networking sites like Facebook, Instagram or Twitter also can be problematic for some people. For instance, in one study of college students, Kittinger and colleagues (2012) found that the number of times individuals visited Facebook each day was a significant predictor of higher scores on the Internet Addiction Test, even after controlling for other demographic and computer use variables. A systematic review of problematic social networking site (SNS) usage suggests that it is more common among people who are narcissistic and neurotic; the potential for SNS use to become an addiction appears to be higher among those who use the sites to feel included or for a sense of belonging to a social group. In particular, introverts who use SNS to compensate for having few offline relationships and low self-esteem seem likely to be at risk; on the other hand, high levels of extraversion also may be related to problematic use of social networking sites because these individuals tend to feel a stronger need to remain connected with and to socialize with their friends online (Kuss & Griffiths, 2011).

Over the past decade, health experts have become increasingly concerned about problematic involvement in online gaming, particularly involvement in massively multiplayer online role-playing games, or MMORPGs, such as *World of Warcraft, Guild Wars 2, Total Domination* or *TERA* (Kuss et al., 2012). The prevalence of online gaming addiction appears to vary worldwide, from less than 1 percent in Germany to nearly half of South Korean teenagers (Kuss, 2013). In the United States, about 8 percent of eight- to 18-year-olds met the criteria for pathological game playing, based on responses to a 2009 Harris poll (Gentile, 2009). A systematic review of the literature identified a number of risk factors that increase the likelihood of online gaming addiction, including introversion, neuroticism and impulsivity; motivations for online gaming related to dysfunctional coping abilities, socializing and personal satisfaction; and game characteristics that encourage continued play, including rewarding extensive game play with adult content, access to rarely shown items and scenes cut from the "normal" version of the game. Individuals classified as being addicted to online gaming were more likely than their peers to have symptoms of generalized anxiety and panic disorders, social phobias and depression; in addition, online gaming addiction has been associated with numerous interpersonal, occupational and physiological consequences, including the failure of real-life relationships, increased stress, aggression and maladaptive coping behaviors, sleep disorders, and numerous other negative outcomes (Kuss & Griffiths, 2012).

Cyberbullying

As the story included at the beginning of this chapter indicates, even those who maintain "normal" Internet use patterns may be subject to the negative consequences of cyberbullying. The prevalence of cyberbullying varies from one study to another, but some researchers have found that more than half of all adolescents reported cyberbullying victimization. Among middle and high school students in one study, nearly half (49.5%) say they have been the victims of online bullying, which includes the use of email, social networking sites, online games and other websites and text messages to threaten, humiliate or socially

Figure 12.2: Nearly Half of Teens Report Being Cyberbullied

exclude someone else. In addition, more than one-third (33.7%) of the students acknowledged having cyberbullied someone else (Mishna et al., 2010). However, in a study of 500 undergraduates at a New England university, 56.1 percent recalled cyberbullying victimization, including nearly three in every four women (72.1%) and more than one in four men (27.9%). In addition, 89 percent of the students in this study had a friend who had been cyberbullied (Hoff & Mitchell, 2009).

Somewhat surprisingly, one-third of the middle and high school students who had been victims said it was a friend who had cyberbullied them (Mishna et al., 2010); more than one in five (22%) had been cyberbullied by another student at their school, and a little more than one in every ten reported cyberbullying by strangers (13%), someone from another school (11%) or an unidentified person (11%). Consistent with those findings, among the undergraduates Hoff and Mitchell surveyed (2009), 91 percent said the cyberbullying was related to relationship issues, including break-ups, envy, intolerance and ganging up on or isolating the victim from a social group.

The severity of victims' reactions to cyberbullying also vary from one study to another. Among students in Mishna et al.'s study (2010), one in five (21%) said the online harassment did not bother them. The most commonly reported negative reaction was anger (16%), followed by embarrassment (8%), sadness (7%) and fear (5%). However, Hoff and Mitchell (2009) found that those who had been cyberbullied rated the emotional effects higher than the midpoint for scales measuring anger, powerlessness, sadness and fear. Students were especially likely to experience distress when they were unable to identify their tormenter. The authors note that the potential for cyberbullies to remain anonymous creates a distinction between cyberbullying and traditional bullying.

A recent systematic review of research on cyberbullying among adolescents concluded that symptoms of depression are more common among teens who have been cyberbullied. Emotional distress was especially common when the cyberbully was an adult, when it included publication of a picture of the victim and when the harassment included offline aggressive acts such as phone calls or the bully coming to the victim's home (Bottino et al., 2015).

Mishna and colleagues (2010) also asked their participants about cyberbullying others. Among the study's respondents who admitted cyberbullying, the most common reason was to be funny (25%); others said cyberbullying someone else made them feel powerful (9%), popular (6%) or superior to others (4%). Cyberbullies rarely (16%) felt guilty about what they had done.

The systematic review of cyberbullying among adolescents concluded that both cyberbullies and their victims often have been involved in traditional face-to-face bullying. The victims often reported psychosomatic problems, including headaches, stomach aches and sleep problems, had more emotional problems and difficulty in social relationships, and were more likely to say they did not feel safe at school. Cyberbullies reported many of these same problems, in addition to behavior problems, smoking, alcohol abuse and infrequent prosocial behavior. Unfortunately, due to the cross-sectional nature of many of these studies, it is difficult to know whether cyberbullying is a cause or an effect of these characteristics, or if both relate to some other factor (Bottino et al., 2015).

In some cases, however, the direction of the relationship was clearer, and more worrying. Bottino et al.'s review (2015) showed that victims may be more likely to abuse drugs and alcohol to deal with the anxiety and other negative emotions provoked by cyberbullying. In addition, cyberbullying victimization predicted suicidal thoughts and suicide attempts; cybervictims were almost twice as likely as their non-harassed peers to report attempting suicide. However, the authors stress that cyberbullying alone is not likely to drive a young person to suicide, but it "may exacerbate an adolescent's instability and hopelessness at a time when they are already struggling with stressful life circumstances" (Bottino et al., 2015, p. 472).

Depression

As the previous section demonstrates, being the victim of online harassment can increase an individual's risk of depression. However, research has shown that even those who do not experience victimization online can end up feeling more bleak and depressed as a result of their online activities. On the other hand, interacting with others online can provide an emotional boost.

In 2011, a paper in the journal *Pediatrics* warned pediatricians that their older patients might be at risk of "Facebook depression," which they defined as "depression that develops when preteens and teens spend a great deal of time on social media sites, such as Facebook, and then begin to exhibit classic symptoms of depression" (O'Keeffe & Clarke-Pearson, 2011, p. 802). The existence of such a social media-related phenomenon has been studied subsequently among young adults (Chen, 2013; Davila et al., 2012; Jelenchick et al., 2013; Kross et al., 2013; Lup et al., 2015; Simoncic, 2012), teenagers (Nesi & Prinstein, 2015) and older adults (Cotten et al., 2012, 2013; Heo et al., 2015). The results of these studies have been somewhat contradictory.

Kross and his colleagues (2013) studied young adults who responded to text messages over a two-week period to report on their moment-to-moment emotional states and their overall life satisfaction. The researchers found that more frequent use of Facebook during the two-week period was associated with declines in both current well-being ratings and overall life satisfaction, and these effects did not disappear when the researchers controlled for the size and perceived supportiveness of people's Facebook networks, their reasons for using Facebook, their gender, and emotional characteristics such as loneliness, depression and self-esteem. Offline interactions with others did not have the same impact.

Similarly, Chen and Lee (2013) found that Facebook interaction was related to greater psychological distress among college students. In particular, students who spent more time on Facebook experienced a greater degree of "communication overload," which tended to reduce their reported self-esteem, and lower self-esteem was associated with greater psychological distress. One explanation for this finding may be that because Facebook users are more likely to post positive messages and pictures about themselves, Facebook encourages users to view others as being happier and enjoying life more fully, especially in relation to Facebook friends outside their circle of real-world contacts. Chou and Edge (2011) found that the longer individuals had been using Facebook, the stronger was their belief that others were happier; this effect was stronger among those whose Facebook friends lists included more people whom they did not personally know. The effect was lessened among those who spent more time in offline relationships with friends.

Facebook is not the only social networking site that has raised concern. Lup and colleagues (2015) examined the relationship between depression and use of the photo-sharing site Instagram among 117 young adults. The findings suggested that the impact of Instagram use depends on who users "follow" on the site. For those who followed more strangers rather than friends, more frequent Instagram use was associated with negative social comparison and more depression; however, the reverse was true for those who followed fewer strangers and used the site more for interacting with friends.

Similarly, an earlier (pre-Facebook) study that examined Internet use more generally showed that individuals who reported using the Internet to communicate with friends and family had lower depression scores six months later. However, among those who went online to meet new people and to interact with others in groups, those who had initially reported high or medium levels of social support became more depressed after six months. No such change occurred among those who initially reported low levels of social support. The authors suggest that the increased depression among those who initially had higher levels of social support may occur because the more time they spend interacting with new acquaintances online, the less time they spend with offline family members and friends (Bessière et al., 2008).

On the other hand, a 2011 study of university students' Facebook use revealed no association between daily time spent on Facebook and likelihood of reporting depression (Jelenchick et al., 2013). Another researcher who surveyed 245 undergraduate students similarly found no association between Facebook use and depression overall; in fact, among female students who scored high in neuroticism, greater Facebook use was associated with lower levels of depression (Simoncic, 2012).

In another pair of studies involving surveys of nearly 700 college students, researchers found that the quality of social networking interactions, rather than either total time spent or frequency of checking social media, influenced depressive symptoms. When people reported that their social media interactions were more negative, they were more likely to report feeling down immediately after their social media use and during a follow-up survey three weeks later. This seemed to be particularly true among individuals prone to "depressive rumination," meaning that they spent time thinking about their negative social media interactions, making them feel even worse (Davila et al., 2012).

Research by a team of European researchers suggests that another key factor in social media impact is the types of activities in which users engage when they are using Facebook (and potentially other social media platforms). These researchers studied German teenagers' use of Facebook and found that active participation, including posting status updates and chatting with friends, tended to improve teens' perceived life satisfaction. However, engaging primarily in passive following of others' posts led to lower life satisfaction ratings. Overall time spent on Facebook had no effect, perhaps because this measure would have effectively combined all types of Facebook activities, such that the effects of active activities and passive activities would cancel each other out (Wenninger et al., 2014).

Using technology for social comparison also seems to have negative effects on users. A study of 619 U.S. adolescents revealed that those who spent more time using Facebook, Instagram and cell phone messages to compare themselves to others and seek interpersonal feedback reported higher levels of depression a year later. The effect was especially strong among girls who rated themselves low in popularity, and the impact of technology use for social comparison held, even after controlling for offline reassurance seeking and baseline depression (Nesi & Prinstein, 2015).

The bottom line seems to be that whether online interactions will increase or decrease users' likelihood of feeling depressed depends significantly on the kinds of activities they engage in online, with whom they interact online, and the extent to which online interactions are balanced with real-world interactions with friends and family members. Overall, it seems that people who have good social support networks in the offline world and who do not allow the time they spend online to supplant their offline relationships can benefit from their online relationships. However, those who have difficulty interacting successfully with others face-to-face and attempt to build social lives primarily with people they meet online are at greater risk of suffering from Internet-related depression.

Physical Health

One significant impact of the peer-to-peer communication and user-generated content that define Web 2.0 is that it enhances individuals' ability to find and interact with others who share their health concerns. For the most part, researchers have concluded that the "virtual communities" that develop around specific diseases or health conditions provide primarily information and emotional support, rather than having significant effects on participants' physical health outcomes (Eysenbach et al., 2004; Ilioudi et al., 2012).

A few recent studies, however, have provided evidence that interacting with other patients online can produce positive changes in health behaviors. For instance, one study surveyed people involved in six specific disease communities on the PatientsLikeMe website, which enables members to share data about their disease symptoms, treatments and treatment outcomes in an effort to benefit others with the same disease. The survey results showed that 41 percent of HIV patients using the site said the interactions led them to engage in fewer risky behaviors. In addition, more than one in five mood disorder patients surveyed (22%) reported that their use of PatientsLikeMe had reduced their need for inpatient care (Wicks et al., 2010). In addition, studies of participants in the PatientsLikeMe community suggested that the information patients provide on the site might offer health officials a new and less expensive source of data about "off-label" uses of prescription drugs, leading to more efficient long-term evaluation of drug effectiveness and side effects (Frost et al., 2011; Wicks et al., 2011).

The evidence suggests, therefore, that patients who interact with each other (or with health experts) online may experience positive physical health outcomes. However, whether peer-to-peer sharing of health information has positive effects, negative effects or no effects will depend on what health information individuals share. In some cases, individuals may support each other in engaging in unhealthy behaviors, leading to negative health outcomes.

Eating Disorders

In most cases, we expect that individuals who have a health problem want to be cured, or at least treated successfully to eliminate or reduce that health problem. However, among some individuals with serious eating disorders, including anorexia and bulimia, that does not necessarily hold true; these individuals, in some cases, regard self-starvation as a lifestyle choice or "a means of demonstrating their willpower and freedom from what they regard as base corporeal requirements" (Tierney, 2006, p. 182), rather than a health problem from which they seek recovery. Some individuals with eating disorders express this anti-recovery viewpoint through the creation of or participation in pro-anorexia or pro-bulimia websites, blogs and forums; experts disagree about whether these sites are intended merely to provide support for individuals struggling with but not ready to recover from eating disorders or if they are meant to encourage the adoption and maintenance of self-starvation behaviors (Tierney, 2006).

Whatever their intention, the research suggests that exposure to this sort of content may promote the adoption of a drive for thinness among women and drive for muscularity among men. For instance, a study of 300 male and female college students showed that drive for muscularity among men and drive for thinness among women were both positively correlated with the internalization of pro-anorexia website content, a measure based on responses to questions such as "I like to browse websites that support anorexia" and "I like to browse websites that support anorexia in order to get motivated to lose weight." Among men, internalization of the pro-anorexia website content was the only significant predictor of drive for muscularity in a model that also included the internalization of general media content (e.g., wanting to look like thin or muscular celebrities in the mass media), friends' influence in weight and diet concerns or friends' encouragement to view pro-anorexia websites. Among women, the internalization of pro-anorexia website content was also the strongest predictor of drive for thinness, but general friend influences and general media internalization were also significant predictors (Juarez et al., 2012). Of course, this was a cross-sectional study, so the results do not necessarily mean that accessing pro-anorexia websites increased men's or women's acceptance of unhealthy attitudes toward muscularity and thinness.

Another cross-sectional study revealed that heavy users of pro-eating disorder websites had lower quality of life scores and reported more disordered eating behaviors (Peebles et al., 2012). In another study, healthy women were exposed to pro-eating disorder websites, health/exercise websites or tourism sites during two 45-minute sessions. In the following week, those who had visited the pro-ED websites reported a significant decrease in weekly calorie intake, with 60 percent of these women cutting their calories by at least 2,500; on average, caloric consumption dropped 2,470 calories, compared to a drop of 176 calories among those who visited the health/exercise websites. In addition, women who had visited the pro-ED websites acknowledged using techniques they had seen on the sites to help them reduce their food consumption. Follow-up data collected three weeks after the initial week of the study revealed that about a quarter of the women from the pro-ED website group were still using weight control tips they had seen on the websites (Jett et al., 2010).

Another experimental study showed that college women exposed to a prototype pro-anorexia website reported greater increases in negative emotions and larger declines in social self-esteem and appearance self-efficacy than did women who had been randomly assigned to view a fashion website using average-sized models or a home décor website. The pro-anorexia group were also more likely to compare themselves to the images they had seen, to rate themselves as overweight, and reported a lower likelihood of overeating and a greater likelihood of exercising, self-induced vomiting and thinking about their weight (Bardone-Cone & Cass, 2007).

More recently, researchers have begun to assess the impact of social media, which enable like-minded individuals to share ideas and information and offer each other social support without creating a specific website. Most of the research thus far has focused on quantitative and qualitative analyses of these interactions (Brotsky & Giles, 2007; Gavin, Rodham & Poyer, 2008; Mulveen & Hepworth, 2006; Riley et al., 2009; Syed-Abdul et al., 2013; Yom-Tov et al., 2012), rather than attempting to address the impacts such forums and social media groups have on participants. One study of members of a French "pro-anorexia" online community revealed that participation was motivated by a desire for rapid weight loss or to maintain weight loss but also by the desire for social support and a sense of belonging. The participants reported that other forum members offered tips for avoiding eating, decreasing hunger, avoiding weight gain and losing weight, using techniques that included vomiting, fasting, severe food restrictions and drinking excessive amounts of fluids (Rodgers et al., 2012).

At least one other study of such forums showed that they encourage both healthy and unhealthy behaviors and that participants report adopting many of the unhealthy behaviors:

> Forum members most frequently reported learning new information about how to use thinspiration (63%), how to effectively hide eating behaviors from family and/or friends (60%), how to fast (57%), use diet pills (47%), use diuretics and laxatives (45%), vomit (23%), use alcohol or drugs to inhibit appetite (22%), and how to engage in self-harm behaviors (22%).
>
> (Ransom et al., 2010, p. 165)

Unfortunately, forum members actually adopted many of these behaviors, with substantial numbers reporting using new weight loss methods, techniques for hiding their eating disordered behaviors, using thinspiration and vomiting. More than two-thirds reported reading posts between other members encouraging use of these behaviors, while 44 percent said they had personally received feedback encouraging them to try these techniques. On the other hand, 83 percent reported reading posts that encouraged recovery, 78 percent had read posts encouraging healthy eating, and more than three-quarters had seen posts encouraging people to accept their current body weight, size or image, or to speak with a professional about their eating behaviors. Participants also reported receiving direct encouragement for these positive behaviors (Ransom et al., 2010).

Substance Use

As earlier chapters have described, the Internet has become a powerful tool for marketing tobacco and alcohol, and both substances are commonly referenced or pictured in social media posts (Brockman et al., 2012; Egan & Moreno, 2011; Freeman, 2012; Hoffman et al., 2014). Increasingly, researchers are finding that these posts may play a significant role in the maintenance and escalation of substance use behaviors. For instance, one study of 2,153 U.S. 18- to 24-year-olds revealed that the density of online networks (the extent to which individuals connected to the main participant also know each other) was positively related to alcohol use among men, while the total number of peer ties (links among the five people with whom the person most often interacts online) and the emotional closeness of those ties were related to increased alcohol use for men and women. Network density was not related to drug use, but there was a positive association between drug use and the number of online network members with whom the individual also interacted offline; drug use was also positively related to discussing drugs with one's network ties and perceiving those individuals to be accepting of drug use (Cook et al., 2012).

Studies of Dutch and Australian youth also support the idea that online interactions influence substance use. A study of Dutch adolescents showed that more frequent electronic media communication, including talking on the phone, texting and using instant messaging, was correlated strongly with the increased use of alcohol and also positively correlated with the use of tobacco and marijuana (Gommans et al., 2015). In addition, a study that combined a survey of Australian college students with analysis of their Facebook profiles showed that those whose photos and texts presented alcohol use as a more important aspect of their identity scored higher on a measure of problematic alcohol use. In addition, the total number of Facebook friends the individual had was related significantly to alcohol abuse measures (Ridout et al., 2012).

Stoddard and her colleagues argue that social network postings can promote pro-alcohol and drug use norms among young people, and these perceived norms play a significant role in increasing substance use behaviors (Stoddard et al., 2012). In a study of 18- to 24-year-olds, they found that the more alcohol content the young adults said they or their friends had posted on their social networking profiles, the higher their reported levels of alcohol use. On the other hand, the more online peer support participants received (from people they knew only online), the lower their alcohol consumption. There was no significant relationship between references to online norms related to alcohol and drug use and marijuana use.

At least one experimental study has supported the idea that exposure to pro-alcohol Facebook profiles can encourage teens to adopt pro-alcohol attitudes. In this study, teens 13 to 15 years old were randomly assigned to view fabricated Facebook profiles for four older high school students, which included either three who were shown drinking alcohol and one who was not, or three non-drinkers and one drinker. Comments posted to the profiles were manipulated to match the individual's apparent drinking status (e.g., "You were so drunk last night"). Teens assigned to the pro-alcohol profile condition subsequently reported greater willingness to drink alcohol, more favorable ratings of the alcohol-using Facebook profiles, less vulnerability to the consequences of alcohol use and greater agreement that alcohol use is normal for high school students. The researchers concluded that "alcohol use descriptive norms, via the social networking site Facebook, influences risk cognitions related to alcohol use," increasing the likelihood that teens who "see" their peers and older friends using alcohol via their Facebook posts will be encouraged to copy this behavior (Litt & Stock, 2011, p. 5).

Sexual Health

Much of the research on social media in relation to sexual health focuses on the potential for efforts to use social media as a health promotion tool for reaching the target audience. For instance, a systematic review of research on the use of social media to foster positive health outcomes among teens and young adults identified 23 studies that addressed high-risk sexual behaviors (Yonker et al., 2015). However, researchers also have identified a number of ways in which social media use may contribute to or exacerbate sexual risk behaviors, especially among adolescents and homosexual men. For instance, an analysis of teenagers' profiles on a teen dating website called MyLol.net showed that about one in six of the profiles contained content related to sexual behavior; girls were more likely than boys to include such content in their profiles (Pujazon-Zazik et al., 2012). Researchers examining 500 publicly available MySpace pages found that references to sex were even more common, appearing on one of every four (24%) pages; again, females were more likely than males to include sexual content (Moreno et al., 2009).

The display of sexual content on social media sites can have an impact on teens' and young adults' sexual risk behaviors and attitudes. For instance, an experimental study demonstrated that after viewing sexually suggestive Facebook photos, college students believed that more of their peers had unprotected sex and engaged in sex with strangers, compared to students who had not seen the photos. In addition, those who saw the sexual photos reported greater willingness to engage in unprotected or casual sex themselves. In a separate study, the same team of researchers found that after browsing a set of peer Facebook photos that included little sexually suggestive content, youth rated their peers as less likely to have unprotected sex and were also more likely to report plans to use a condom when they had sex (Young & Jordan, 2013).

Researchers also have identified significant correlations between teens' actual involvement in sexual risk behaviors and their perceptions of their Facebook friends' risky sex practices. Teens who perceived that their Facebook friends have had multiple partners and one-night stands, had used alcohol or drugs during sex and had more sexual experience in general were more likely to have engaged in these same practices themselves. However, teens' perceptions of their friends' behaviors were not

411

always accurate; the study revealed no significant correlations between friends' perceived and actual behaviors for discussing condom use with partners, age at first intercourse, having had a one-night stand or having been diagnosed with a sexually transmitted disease. Teens tend to over-estimate the frequency of their online friends' involvement in risky behaviors and to underestimate their likelihood of taking actions to protect their sexual health (Black et al., 2013). This finding may simply mean that teens tend to assume that their peers are engaging in the same behaviors as they are; however, the perception that sexual risk behaviors are normative among their friends also may increase the likeli-hood that teens will take these same sexual health risks.

A study linking the use of media technologies and sexual risk behaviors among African American teens revealed that both more frequent cell phone use and more frequent Internet use were linked to sexual sensation seeking. In addition, teens who went online more often were more likely to have engaged in oral, vaginal and/or anal sex (Whiteley et al., 2011). Another study of African American youth showed that 6 percent reported meeting sexual partners via the Internet, and finding sex partners online was associated with higher risks of alcohol and drug use during sex, unprotected vaginal and anal sex, higher numbers of anal and vaginal sex partners, and greater sexual sensation seeking (Whiteley et al., 2012). Researchers who surveyed teen clients of a Florida public health clinic found similar results, with 15 percent saying they had met someone online with whom they later had sex. These teens were more likely than those who had not met sex partners online to be gay or bisexual, and having online sex partners also was correlated with being younger than age 14 at first intercourse, using alcohol during or immediately before sex and having more lifetime sex partners (Buhi et al., 2013).

Social media use has been linked to sexual risk behavior among adults as well. For instance, one study of black men who have sex with other men found that these men spent an average of 34 hours per week accessing social media. More than half (53%) said they had used the Internet to arrange sexual hook-ups at least once in the preceding three months; the average number of Internet-facilitated sexual encounters was ten. In addition, social media users and those who connected with sexual partners online engaged in riskier sexual behavior (Broaddus et al., 2015). Other researchers have reported similar findings among African American (White et al., 2012) and Latino men who have sex with men (Young et al., 2013). In addition, a recent study of clients at a sexually transmitted infection clinic revealed that women and both homosexual and straight men who met sex partners online engaged in riskier sexual behaviors than individuals who did not have sex with people they met online (Brown et al., 2015). It is important to note, however, that these correlations do not necessarily mean that use of the Internet or social media increases risky sexual behavior; it is at least equally likely that using social media and other online tools to find sex partners is simply a characteristic of individuals who are already prone to risky sexual behavior.

In addition to concerns about the Internet's role in facilitating consensual sexual risk behaviors, parents, health officials and others often have expressed concerns about whether the Internet puts children and adolescents at greater risk of sexual victimization (Bates, 2013; Bourg, 2015). Some evidence suggests that concerns about Internet use putting young people at severe risk of sexual victimization by predators appear to be overblown. Ybarra and Mitchell (2008) found that 15 percent of ten- to 15-year-olds who used the Internet had received an unwanted sexual solicitation in the previous year; 4 percent of youth said that solicitation had come through a social networking site. On the other hand, a more recent study that compared the use of social networking sites by middle school, high school and college students and by adults who had committed a sexual offense revealed that both students and sexual offenders reported frequently visiting social networking sites; offenders preferred MySpace, whereas students generally used Facebook. The sexual offenders also reported visiting teen chat rooms, and more than half of those who did so hid their real name and age from those with whom they chatted. Most said they would initiate discussion of sex in the first chat session with someone (Dowdell et al., 2011). A survey of law enforcement personnel in 2006 revealed that individuals who committed sex crimes against minors used social networking sites to initiate sexual relationships, to communicate with their victims, to gather information about the victim, to contact the victim's friends and to post pictures of or information about the victim (Mitchell et al., 2010).

Suicide

Of all possible health impacts of the Internet, perhaps the most concerning is the notion that some aspects of Internet use may put vulnerable

413

individuals at increased risk of taking their own lives. Unfortunately, research suggests that such concerns are not unfounded. First, those considering suicide can find a wealth of information online, and many of these sites are not intended to discourage suicide. In fact, one analysis of 240 websites identified through a search of suicide-related terms categorized half of the sites as pro-suicide (Biddle et al., 2008), although another study that examined suicide-related sites identified only 11 percent as pro-suicide (Recupero et al., 2008).

Some research also suggests that online interactions may increase the risk of suicide. Gaining information about suicide through online forums has been linked to increased suicidal ideation (Dunlop et al., 2011) and, in some cases, to suicide attempts that imitate methods the individual learned about online (Biddle et al., 2012). One study of adolescents showed that, controlling for other suicide risk factors, youth who had visited a pro-suicide website were seven times more likely to report thinking about killing themselves; they were also 11 times more likely to have considered hurting themselves in a non-fatal way (Mitchell et al., 2014). The use of pro-suicide websites and setting up an online "suicide pact," in which two individuals agree to kill themselves at the same time and place, also puts individuals at significantly increased risk of attempting or completing a suicide (Durkee et al., 2011).

Cyberbullying also may increase an individual's risk of suicide. A recent meta-analysis confirmed that cyberbullying is more strongly linked to suicidal ideation among children and adolescents than is traditional face-to-face bullying (van Geel et al., 2014). In part, this may be true because cyberbullying is not limited by the requirement for face-to-face interaction as is traditional bullying; the cyberbully can, as Tokunaga (2010) puts it, follow the victim home from school. At least one study has shown that, among high school girls, being the victim of cyberbullying was linked significantly to increased depression and, in turn, to suicide attempts. The study also revealed that having cyberbullied others was a direct predictor of suicide attempts among high school boys (Bauman et al., 2013).

Despite the potential for negative effects, however, it is important to note that the Web also can play a positive role in preventing suicide. Numerous suicide prevention and public health organizations provide online resources aimed at helping those who are considering suicide find assistance and treatment to recover their interest in life. Social media forums can help family members and friends keep tabs on those suffering from depression, potentially increasing the likelihood that someone will recognize the signs that a loved one may be considering suicide in time to intervene. In addition, as noted earlier, for many individuals, interacting with family members and friends online helps reduce loneliness and depression, thereby decreasing the likelihood of suicide (Alao et al., 2006; Robert et al., 2015).

<h2 style="text-align:center">SUMMARY</h2>

Using the matrix discussed at the beginning of this book to classify the impacts of individuals' online peer-to-peer interactions is no simple matter. While the research discussed here is focused entirely on effects on individual attitudes, behaviors and emotional reactions, the research evidence supports claims for both positive and negative effects. In general, online interactions with family and friends with whom individuals have offline relationships appear to have primarily positive effects. However, there are exceptions, such as when online interactions constitute cyberbullying, when they interfere with romantic relationships and when individuals develop such an obsession with online gaming that it interferes with normal daily activities. In addition, when individuals spend too much time online interacting with those with whom they have no offline relationships, the result seems to be greater loneliness and depression. On the other hand, when those online "strangers" share experiences of an embarrassing, stigmatizing or rare disease, these peer-to-peer interactions can offer valuable information and social and emotional support that may not be available in the offline world. Peer-to-peer interactions can connect young people with geographically distant family members and friends who can help them navigate the challenges adolescence inevitably brings. However, online forums also can facilitate risky sexual hook-ups and may increase the chances of teenagers and other vulnerable individuals falling prey to sexual predators who use online interactions to groom potential victims.

The research also addresses online interactions whose effects vary in terms of the intentions of the originator of the communication. Most people who post lovely vacation photos, wedding photos, new baby photos or status updates about the happy moments in their lives do so with no intention of making others envious or depressed. Even those who create and maintain pro-suicide or pro-eating disorders blogs, forums and social media pages probably see themselves as "helping" those who visit their online content; nonetheless, it often does appear to be the intent of such individuals to "help" people engage in unquestionably unhealthy, even deadly, behavior. Finally, it seems clear that, for some individuals, there can be "too much of a good thing"; too much time spent online, regardless of the purpose or content of those interactions, has negative health effects when online interactions begin to interfere with school, work, family needs and offline relationships in general.

REFERENCES

Alao, A.O., Soderberg, M., Pohl, E.L. & Alao, A.L. (2006). Cybersuicide: Review of the Role of the Internet on Suicide. *CyberPsychology & Behavior, 9*(4), 489–493. http://doi.org/10.1089/cpb.2006.9.489.

Anderson, M. (2015, February 12). 5 Facts about Online Video, for YouTube's 10th Birthday. Retrieved May 21, 2015 from www.pewresearch.org/fact-tank/2015/02/12/5-facts-about-online-video-for-youtubes-10th-birthday/.

Bardone-Cone, A.M. & Cass, K.M. (2007). What Does Viewing a Pro-anorexia Website Do? An Experimental Examination of Website Exposure and Moderating Effects. *International Journal of Eating Disorders, 40*(6), 537–548.

Bates, L. (2013, February 13). Next Generation of Social Media "Exposing Girls to Sexual Abuse." Retrieved June 6, 2015 from www.independent.co.uk/news/media/online/next-generation-of-social-media-exposing-girls-to-sexual-abuse-8493945.html.

Bauman, S., Toomey, R.B. & Walker, J.L. (2013). Associations among Bullying, Cyberbullying, and Suicide in High School Students. *Journal of Adolescence, 36*(2), 341–350. http://doi.org/10.1016/j.adolescence.2012.12.001.

Bessière, K., Kiesler, S., Kraut, R. & Boneva, B.S. (2008). Effects of Internet Use and Social Resources on Changes in Depression. *Information, Communication & Society, 11*(1), 47–70. http://doi.org/10.1080/13691180701858851.

Biddle, L., Donovan, J., Hawton, K. & Kapur, N. (2008). Suicide and the Internet. *BMJ: British Medical Journal, 336*(7648), 800–802.

Biddle, L., Gunnell, D., Owen-Smith, A., Potokar, J., Longson, D., Hawton, K. & Donovan, J. (2012). Information Sources Used by the Suicidal to Inform Choice of Method. *Journal of Affective Disorders, 136*(3), 702–709. http://doi.org/10.1016/j.jad.2011.10.004.

Billedo, C.J., Kerkhof, P. & Finkenauer, C. (2015). The Use of Social Networking Sites for Relationship Maintenance in Long-distance and Geographically Close Romantic Relationships. *Cyberpsychology, Behavior, and Social Networking, 18*(3), 152–157.

Black, S.R., Schmiege, S. & Bull, S. (2013). Actual versus Perceived Peer Sexual Risk Behavior in Online Youth Social Networks. *Translational Behavioral Medicine, 3*(3), 312–319. http://doi.org/10.1007/s13142-013-0227-y.

Bonetti, L., Campbell, M.A. & Gilmore, L. (2010). The Relationship of Loneliness and Social Anxiety with Children's and Adolescents' Online Communication. *Cyberpsychology, Behavior and Social Networking, 13*(3), 279–285.

Boniel-Nissim, M., Lenzi, M., Zsiros, E., de Matos, M.G., Gommans, R., Harel-Fisch, Y. & van der Sluijs, W. (2015). International Trends in Electronic Media Communication among 11- to 15-year-olds in 30 Countries from 2002 to 2010: Association with Ease of Communication with Friends of the Opposite Sex. *European Journal of Public Health*, 25(Suppl 2), 41–45. http://doi.org/10.1093/eurpub/ckv025.

Bottino, S.M.B., Bottino, C.M.C., Regina, C.G., Correia, A.V.L. & Ribeiro, W.S. (2015). Cyberbullying and Adolescent Mental Health: Systematic Review. *Cadernos De Saúde Pública*, 31(3), 463–475.

Bourg, A. (2015, March 9). Reports of Online Sexual Abuse of Children Rising. Retrieved June 6, 2015 from www.abc2news.com/news/state/reports-of-online-sexual-abuse-of-children-rising.

Broaddus, M.R., DiFranceisco, W.J., Kelly, J.A., St. Lawrence, J.S., Amirkhanian, Y.A. & Dickson-Gomez, J.D. (2015). Social Media Use and High-risk Sexual Behavior among Black Men Who Have Sex with Men: A Three-city Study. *AIDS and Behavior*. http://doi.org/10.1007/s10461-014-0980-z.

Brockman, L.N., Pumper, M.A., Christakis, D.A. & Moreno, M.A. (2012). Hookah's New Popularity among US College Students: A Pilot Study of the Characteristics of Hookah Smokers and their Facebook Displays. *BMJ Open*, 2(6). http://doi.org/10.1136/bmjopen-2012-001709.

Brotsky, S.R. & Giles, D. (2007). Inside the "Pro-ana" Community: A Covert Online Participant Observation. *Eating Disorders*, 15(2), 93–109. http://doi.org/10.1080/10640260701190600.

Brown, M.J., Pugsley, R. & Cohen, S.A. (2015). Meeting Sex Partners Through the Internet, Risky Sexual Behavior, and HIV Testing among Sexually Transmitted Infections Clinic Patients. *Archives of Sexual Behavior*, 44(2), 509–519. http://doi.org/10.1007/s10508-014-0463-3.

Buhi, E.R., Klinkenberger, N., McFarlane, M., Kachur, R., Daley, E.M., Baldwin, J. & Rietmeijer, C. (2013). Evaluating the Internet as a Sexually Transmitted Disease Risk Environment for Teens: Findings From the Communication, Health, and Teens Study. *Sexually Transmitted Diseases*, 40(7), 528–533. http://doi.org/10.1097/OLQ.0b013e31829413f7.

Chen, W. & Lee, K.H. (2013). Sharing, Liking, Commenting, and Distressed? The Pathway Between Facebook Interaction and Psychological Distress. *Cyberpsychology, Behavior & Social Networking*, 16(10), 728–734. http://doi.org/10.1089/cyber.2012.0272.

Chou, H.-T.G. & Edge, N. (2011). "They Are Happier and Having Better Lives than I Am": The Impact of Using Facebook on Perceptions of Others' Lives. *Cyberpsychology, Behavior, and Social Networking*, 15(2), 117–121. http://doi.org/10.1089/cyber.2011.0324.

Clayton, R.B. (2014). The Third Wheel: The Impact of Twitter Use on Relationship Infidelity and Divorce. *Cyberpsychology, Behavior, and Social Networking*, 17(7), 425–430. http://doi.org/10.1089/cyber.2013.0570.

Clayton, R.B., Nagurney, A. & Smith, J.R. (2013). Cheating, Breakup, and Divorce: Is Facebook Use to Blame? *Cyberpsychology, Behavior, and Social Networking*, 16(10), 717–720. http://doi.org/10.1089/cyber.2012.0424.

Cook, S.H., Bauermeister, J.A., Gordon-Messer, D. & Zimmerman, M.A. (2012). Online Network Influences on Emerging Adults' Alcohol and Drug Use. *Journal of Youth and Adolescence*, 42(11), 1674–1686. http://doi.org/10.1007/s10964-012-9869-1.

Cotten, S.R., Anderson, W.A. & McCullough, B.M. (2013). Impact of Internet Use on Loneliness and Contact with Others among Older Adults: Cross-sectional Analysis. *Journal of Medical Internet Research, 15*(2), e39. http://doi.org/10.2196/jmir.2306.

Cotten, S.R., Ford, G., Ford, S. & Hale, T.M. (2012). Internet Use and Depression among Older Adults. *Computers in Human Behavior, 28*(2), 496–499. http://doi.org/10.1016/j.chb.2011.10.021.

Davila, J., Hershenberg, R., Feinstein, B.A., Gorman, K., Bhatia, V. & Starr, L.R. (2012). Frequency and Quality of Social Networking among Young Adults: Associations with Depressive Symptoms, Rumination, and Corumination. *Psychology of Popular Media Culture, 1*(2), 72–86. http://doi.org/10.1037/a0027512.

Dowdell, E.B., Burgess, A.W. & Flores, J.R. (2011). Online Social Networking Patterns among Adolescents, Young Adults, and Sexual Offenders. *AJN The American Journal of Nursing, 111*(7), 28–36.

Duggan, M., Ellison, N.B., Lampe, C., Lenhart, A. & Madden, M. (2015, January 9). Social Media Update 2014. Retrieved May 20, 2015 from www.pewinternet.org/2015/01/09/social-media-update-2014/.

Dunlop, S.M., More, E. & Romer, D. (2011). Where Do Youth Learn about Suicides on the Internet, and What Influence Does this Have on Suicidal Ideation? *Journal of Child Psychology and Psychiatry, and Allied Disciplines, 52*(10), 1073–1080. http://doi.org/10.1111/j.1469-7610.2011.02416.x.

Durkee, T., Hadlaczky, G., Westerlund, M. & Carli, V. (2011). Internet Pathways in Suicidality: A Review of the Evidence. *International Journal of Environmental Research and Public Health, 8*(10), 3938–3952. http://doi.org/10.3390/ijerph8103938.

Egan, K.G. & Moreno, M.A. (2011). Alcohol References on Undergraduate Males' Facebook Profiles. *American Journal of Men's Health*, 1557988310394341. http://doi.org/10.1177/1557988310394341.

Ellison, N.B., Steinfield, C. & Lampe, C. (2007). The Benefits of Facebook "Friends": Social Capital and College Students' Use of Online Social Network Sites. *Journal of Computer-Mediated Communication, 12*(4), 1143–1168. http://doi.org/10.1111/j.1083-6101.2007.00367.x.

Elphinston, R.A. & Noller, P. (2011). Time to Face It! Facebook Intrusion and the Implications for Romantic Jealousy and Relationship Satisfaction. *Cyberpsychology, Behavior and Social Networking, 14*(11), 631–635. http://doi.org/10.1089/cyber.2010.0318.

Eysenbach, G., Powell, J., Englesakis, M., Rizo, C. & Stern, A. (2004). Health Related Virtual Communities and Electronic Support Groups: Systematic Review of the Effects of Online Peer to Peer Interactions. *BMJ, 328*(7449), 1166. http://doi.org/10.1136/bmj.328.7449.1166.

Fox, J. & Warber, K.M. (2014). Social Networking Sites in Romantic Relationships: Attachment, Uncertainty, and Partner Surveillance on Facebook. *Cyberpsychology, Behavior, and Social Networking, 17*(1), 3–7.

Fox, S. (2011). *Peer-to-peer Health Care*. Washington, DC. Retrieved May 19, 2015 from www.pewinternet.org/2011/02/28/peer-to-peer-health-care-2/.

Fox, S. & Jones, S. (2009). *The Social Life of Health Information*. Washington, DC: Pew Internet & American Life Project, 2009–2012.

Freeman, B. (2012). New Media and Tobacco Control. *Tobacco Control, 21*(2), 139–144. http://doi.org/10.1136/tobaccocontrol-2011-050193.

Frohlich, D.O. & Zmyslinski-Seelig, A.N. (2014). How Uncover Ostomy Challenges Ostomy Stigma, and Encourages Others to Do the Same. *New Media & Society*, 1461444814541943. http://doi.org/10.1177/1461444814541943.

Frohlich, D.O. (in press). The Social Construction of Inflammatory Bowel Disease Using Social Media Technologies. *Health Communication*.

Frost, J., Okun, S., Vaughan, T., Heywood, J. & Wicks, P. (2011). Patient-reported Outcomes as a Source of Evidence in Off-label Prescribing: Analysis of Data From PatientsLikeMe. *Journal of Medical Internet Research*, 13(1). http://doi.org/10.2196/jmir.1643.

Gavin, J., Rodham, K. & Poyer, H. (2008). The Presentation of "Pro-anorexia" in Online Group Interactions. *Qualitative Health Research*, 18(3), 325–333. http://doi.org/10.1177/1049732307311640.

Gentile, D. (2009). Pathological Video-game Use among Youth Ages 8 to 18: A National Study. *Psychological Science*, 20(5), 594–602. http://doi.org/10.1111/j.1467-9280.2009.02340.x.

Gommans, R., Stevens, G.W.J.M., Finne, E., Cillessen, A.H.N., Boniel-Nissim, M. & Bogt, T.F.M. (2015). Frequent Electronic Media Communication with Friends is Associated with Higher Adolescent Substance Use. *International Journal of Public Health*, 60(2), 167–177. http://doi.org/10.1007/s00038-014-0624-0.

Heo, J., Chun, S., Lee, S., Lee, K.H. & Kim, J. (2015). Internet Use and Well-being in Older Adults. *Cyberpsychology, Behavior, and Social Networking*, 18(5), 268–272. http://doi.org/10.1089/cyber.2014.0549.

Hettler, B. (1976). *Six Dimensions of Wellness*. National Wellness Institute (www. Nwi. Org), and www.Hettler.Com/sixdimen.Htm.

Hoff, D.L. & Mitchell, S.N. (2009). Cyberbullying: Causes, Effects, and Remedies. *Journal of Educational Administration*, 47(5), 652–665. http://doi.org/10.1108/09578230910981107.

Hoffman, E.W., Pinkleton, B.E., Weintraub Austin, E. & Reyes-Velázquez, W. (2014). Exploring College Students' Use of General and Alcohol-related Social Media and their Associations with Alcohol-related Behaviors. *Journal of American College Health*, 62(5), 328–335. http://doi.org/10.1080/07448481.2014.902837.

How a Cell Phone Picture Led to Girl's Suicide. (2010, October 7). Retrieved May 14, 2015 from www.cnn.com/2010/LIVING/10/07/hope.witsells.story/.

Ilioudi, S., Lazakidou, A.A., Glezakos, N. & Tsironi, M. (2012). Health-related Virtual Communities and Social Networking Services. In A.A. Lazakidou (ed.), *Virtual Communities, Social Networks and Collaboration* (pp. 1–13). New York: Springer. Retrieved June 4, 2015 from http://link.springer.com/chapter/10.1007/978-1-4614-3634-8_1.

Jelenchick, L.A., Eickhoff, J.C. & Moreno, M.A. (2013). "Facebook Depression?" Social Networking Site Use and Depression in Older Adolescents. *Journal of Adolescent Health*, 52(1), 128–130. http://doi.org/10.1016/j.jadohealth.2012.05.008.

Jett, S., LaPorte, D.J. & Wanchisn, J. (2010). Impact of Exposure to Pro-eating Disorder Websites on Eating Behaviour in College Women. *European Eating Disorders Review*, 18(5), 410–416.

Johnson, C. (2014, August 29). Face Time vs. Screen Time: The Technological Impact on Communication. Retrieved May 21, 2015 from http://national.deseretnews.com/article/2235/face-time-vs-screen-time-the-technological-impact-on-communication.html.

Juarez, L., Soto, E. & Pritchard, M.E. (2012). Drive for Muscularity and Drive for Thinness: The Impact of Pro-anorexia Websites. *Eating Disorders*, 20(2), 99–112. http://doi.org/10.1080/10640266.2012.653944.

Kittinger, R., Correia, C.J. & Irons, J.G. (2012). Relationship between Facebook Use and Problematic Internet Use among College Students. *Cyberpsychology, Behavior, and Social Networking*, 15(6), 324–327. http://doi.org/10.1089/cyber.2010.0410.

Kraut, R., Kiesler, S., Boneva, B., Cummings, J., Helgeson, V. & Crawford, A. (2002). Internet Paradox Revisited. *Journal of Social Issues, 58*(1), 49–74. http://doi. org/10.1111/1540-4560.00248.

Kraut, R., Patterson, M., Lundmark, V., Kiesler, S., Mukophadhyay, T. & Scherlis, W. (1998). Internet Paradox: A Social Technology That Reduces Social Involvement and Psychological Well-being? *American Psychologist, 53*(9), 1017.

Kross, E., Verduyn, P., Demiralp, E., Park, J., Lee, D.S., Lin, N. & Ybarra, O. (2013). Facebook Use Predicts Declines in Subjective Well-being in Young Adults. *PLoS ONE, 8*(8), e69841. http://doi.org/10.1371/journal.pone.0069841.

Kuss, D.J. (2013). Internet Gaming Addiction: Current Perspectives. *Psychology Research and Behavior Management, 6,* 125–137. http://doi.org/10.2147/PRBM.S39476.

Kuss, D.J. & Griffiths, M.D. (2011). Online Social Networking and Addiction – A Review of the Psychological Literature. *International Journal of Environmental Research and Public Health, 8*(9), 3528–3552. http://doi.org/10.3390/ijerph8093528.

Kuss, D. & Griffiths, M. (2012). Internet Gaming Addiction: A Systematic Review of Empirical Research. *International Journal of Mental Health & Addiction, 10*(2), 278–296. http://doi.org/10.1007/s11469-011-9318-5.

Kuss, D.J., Louws, J. & Wiers, R.W. (2012). Online Gaming Addiction? Motives Predict Addictive Play Behavior in Massively Multiplayer Online Role-playing Games. *Cyberpsychology, Behavior and Social Networking, 15*(9), 480–485. http://doi. org/10.1089/cyber.2012.0034.

Lenhart, A. (2015). *Teens, Social Media & Technology Overview 2015.* Washington, DC: Pew Internet & American Life Project. Retrieved May 20, 2015 from www. pewinternet.org/files/2015/04/PI_TeensandTech_Update2015_0409151.pdf.

Litt, D.M. & Stock, M.L. (2011). Adolescent Alcohol-related Risk Cognitions: The Roles of Social Norms and Social Networking Sites. *Psychology of Addictive Behaviors, 25*(4), 708–713. http://doi.org/10.1037/a0024226.

Lukacs, V. & Quan-Haase, A. (2015). Romantic Breakups on Facebook: New Scales for Studying Post-breakup Behaviors, Digital Distress, and Surveillance. *Information, Communication & Society, 18*(5), 492–508. http://doi.org/10.1080/1369118X.2 015.1008540.

Lup, K., Trub, L. & Rosenthal, L. (2015). Instagram #Instasad?: Exploring Associations Among Instagram Use, Depressive Symptoms, Negative Social Comparison, and Strangers Followed. *Cyberpsychology, Behavior and Social Networking, 18*(5), 247–252. http://doi.org/10.1089/cyber.2014.0560.

Lyndon, A., Bonds-Raacke, J. & Cratty, A.D. (2011). College Students' Facebook Stalking of Ex-partners. *Cyberpsychology, Behavior, and Social Networking, 14*(12), 711–716. http://doi.org/10.1089/cyber.2010.0588.

Madden, M. (2013, August 15). Teens Haven't Abandoned Facebook (Yet). Retrieved May 20, 2015 from www.pewinternet.org/2013/08/15/teens-havent-abandoned-facebook-yet/.

Marshall, T.C. (2012). Facebook Surveillance of Former Romantic Partners: Associations with PostBreakup Recovery and Personal Growth. *Cyberpsychology, Behavior, and Social Networking, 15*(10), 521–526. http://doi.org/10.1089/cyber.2012.0125.

Marshall, T.C., Bejanyan, K., Di Castro, G. & Lee, R.A. (2013). Attachment Styles as Predictors of Facebook-related Jealousy and Surveillance in Romantic Relationships. *Personal Relationships, 20*(1), 1–22. http://doi.org/10.1111/j.1475-6811.2011.01393.x.

McAndrew, F.T. & Shah, S.S. (2013). Sex Differences in Jealousy over Facebook Activity. *Computers in Human Behavior, 29*(6), 2603–2606. http://doi.org/10.1016/j. chb.2013.06.030.

Meacham, A. (2009, November 27). Sexting-related Bullying Cited in Hillsborough Teen's Suicide. Retrieved May 14, 2015 from www.tampabay.com/news/human interest/sexting-related-bullying-cited-in-hillsborough-teens-suicide/1054895.

Mesch, G.S. (2001). Social Relationships and Internet Use among Adolescents in Israel. *Social Science Quarterly, 82*(2), 329–339. http://doi.org/10.1111/0038-4941.00026.

Mishna, F., Cook, C., Gadalla, T., Daciuk, J. & Solomon, S. (2010). Cyber Bullying Behaviors among Middle and High School Students. *The American Journal of Orthopsychiatry, 80*(3), 362–374. http://doi.org/10.1111/j.1939-0025.2010.01040.x.

Mitchell, K.J., Finkelhor, D., Jones, L.M. & Wolak, J. (2010). Use of Social Networking Sites in Online Sex Crimes Against Minors: An Examination of National Incidence and Means of Utilization. *Journal of Adolescent Health, 47*(2), 183–190. http://doi.org/10.1016/j.jadohealth.2010.01.007.

Mitchell, K.J., Wells, M., Priebe, G. & Ybarra, M.L. (2014). Exposure to Websites that Encourage Self-harm and Suicide: Prevalence Rates and Association with Actual Thoughts of Self-harm and Thoughts of Suicide in the United States. *Journal of Adolescence, 37*(8), 1335–1344. http://doi.org/10.1016/j.adolescence.2014.09.011.

Morahan-Martin, J. & Schumacher, P. (2000). Incidence and Correlates of Pathological Internet Use among College Students. *Computers in Human Behavior, 16*(1), 13–29. http://doi.org/10.1016/S0747-5632(99)00049-7.

Moreno, M.A., Parks, M.R., Zimmerman, F.J., Brito, T.E. & Christakis, D.A. (2009). Display of Health Risk Behaviors on Myspace by Adolescents: Prevalence and Associations. *Archives of Pediatrics & Adolescent Medicine, 163*(1), 27–34. http://doi.org/10.1001/archpediatrics.2008.528.

Muise, A., Christofides, E. & Desmarais, S. (2009). More Information Than You Ever Wanted: Does Facebook Bring Out the Green-eyed Monster of Jealousy? *Cyber-Psychology & Behavior, 12*(4), 441–444. http://doi.org/10.1089/cpb.2008.0263.

Mulveen, R. & Hepworth, J. (2006). An Interpretative Phenomenological Analysis of Participation in a Pro-anorexia Internet Site and Its Relationship with Disordered Eating. *Journal of Health Psychology, 11*(2), 283–296. http://doi.org/10.1177/1359105306061187.

Muscanell, N.L., Guadagno, R.E., Rice, L. & Murphy, S. (2013). Don't it Make My Brown Eyes Green? An Analysis of Facebook Use and Romantic Jealousy. *Cyberpsychology, Behavior and Social Networking, 16*(4), 237–242. http://doi.org/10.1089/cyber.2012.0411.

Nesi, J. & Prinstein, M.J. (2015). Using Social Media for Social Comparison and Feedback-seeking: Gender and Popularity Moderate Associations with Depressive Symptoms. *Journal of Abnormal Child Psychology.* http://doi.org/10.1007/s10802-015-0020-0.

Nie, N.H. (2001). Sociability, Interpersonal Relations, and the Internet Reconciling Conflicting Findings. *American Behavioral Scientist, 45*(3), 420–435. http://doi.org/10.1177/00027640121957277.

Nie, N.H., Hillygus, D.S. & Erbring, L. (2008). Internet Use, Interpersonal Relations, and Sociability. In B. Wellman & C. Haythornthwaite (eds), *The Internet in Everyday Life* (pp. 215–243). Malden, MA: John Wiley & Sons. Retrieved May 22, 2015 from https://books.google.com/books?hl=en&lr=&id=v-UR_2QRFpwC&oi=fnd&pg=PA215&dq=related:u0JyMtfvqGUJ:scholar.google.com/&ots=KZ9st8IIN9&sig=3JpLWQzaisClFHtFr20SlCdD6Mo#v=onepage&q=243&f=false.

O'Keeffe, G.S. & Clarke-Pearson, K. (2011). The Impact of Social Media on Children, Adolescents, and Families. *Pediatrics, 127*(4), 800–804. http://doi.org/10.1542/peds.2011-0054.

Peebles, R., Wilson, J.L., Litt, I.F., Hardy, K.K., Lock, J.D., Mann, J.R. & Borzekowski, D.L.G. (2012). Disordered Eating in a Digital Age: Eating Behaviors, Health, and Quality of Life in Users of Websites with Pro-eating Disorder Content. *Journal of Medical Internet Research, 14*(5), e148. http://doi.org/10.2196/jmir.2023.

Pujazon-Zazik, M.A., Manasse, S.M. & Orrell-Valente, J.K. (2012). Adolescents' Self-presentation on a Teen Dating Web Site: A Risk-content Analysis. *Journal of Adolescent Health, 50*(5), 517–520. http://doi.org/10.1016/j.jadohealth.2011.11.015.

Quinn, S. & Oldmeadow, J.A. (2013). Is the Igeneration a "We" Generation? Social Networking Use among 9- to 13-year-olds and Belonging. *The British Journal of Developmental Psychology, 31*(Part 1), 136–142. http://doi.org/10.1111/bjdp. 12007.

Ransom, D.C., La Guardia, J.G., Woody, E.Z. & Boyd, J.L. (2010). Interpersonal Interactions on Online Forums Addressing Eating Concerns. *International Journal of Eating Disorders, 43*(2), 161–170. http://doi.org/10.1002/eat.20629.

Recupero, P.R., Harms, S.E. & Noble, J.M. (2008). Googling Suicide: Surfing for Suicide Information on the Internet. *The Journal of Clinical Psychiatry, 69*, 878–88.

Ridout, B., Campbell, A. & Ellis, L. (2012). "Off Your Face(book)": Alcohol in Online Social Identity Construction and its Relation to Problem Drinking in University Students. *Drug and Alcohol Review, 31*(1), 20–26. http://doi.org/10.1111/j.1465-3362.2010.00277.x.

Riley, S., Rodham, K. & Gavin, J. (2009). Doing Weight: Pro-ana and Recovery Identities in Cyberspace. *Journal of Community & Applied Social Psychology, 19*(5), 348–359. http://doi.org/10.1002/casp. 1022.

Robert, A., Suelves, J.M., Armayones, M. & Ashley, S. (2015). Internet Use and Suicidal Behaviors: Internet as a Threat or Opportunity? *Telemedicine and E-Health, 21*(4), 306–311. http://doi.org/10.1089/tmj.2014.0129.

Rodgers, R.F., Skowron, S. & Chabrol, H. (2012). Disordered Eating and Group Membership among Members of a Pro-anorexic Online Community. *European Eating Disorders Review: The Journal of the Eating Disorders Association, 20*(1), 9–12. http://doi.org/10.1002/erv.1096.

Simoncic, T.E. (2012). *Facebook Depression Revisited: The Absence of an Association between Facebook Use and Depressive Symptoms.* University of Michigan. Retrieved June 3, 2015 from http://deepblue.lib.umich.edu/handle/2027.42/91787.

Song, H., Zmyslinski-Seelig, A., Kim, J., Drent, A., Victor, A., Omori, K. & Allen, M. (2014). Does Facebook Make You Lonely?: A Meta Analysis. *Computers in Human Behavior, 36*, 446–452. http://doi.org/10.1016/j.chb.2014.04.011.

Stepanikova, I., Nie, N.H. & He, X. (2010). Time on the Internet at Home, Loneliness, and Life Satisfaction: Evidence from Panel Time-diary Data. *Computers in Human Behavior, 26*(3), 329–338. http://doi.org/10.1016/j.chb.2009.11.002.

Stoddard, S.A., Bauermeister, J.A., Gordon-Messer, D., Johns, M. & Zimmerman, M.A. (2012). Permissive Norms and Young Adults' Alcohol and Marijuana Use: The Role of Online Communities. *Journal of Studies on Alcohol and Drugs, 73*(6), 968.

Syed-Abdul, S., Fernandez-Luque, L., Jian, W.-S., Li, Y.-C., Crain, S., Hsu, M.-H. & Liou, D.-M. (2013). Misleading Health-related Information Promoted Through Video-based Social Media: Anorexia on YouTube. *Journal of Medical Internet Research, 15*(2), e30. http://doi.org/10.2196/jmir.2237.

Tardanico, S. (n.d.). Is Social Media Sabotaging Real Communication? Retrieved May 21, 2015 from www.forbes.com/sites/susantardanico/2012/04/30/is-social-media-sabotaging-real-communication/.

Teppers, E., Luyckx, K., Klimstra, T.A. & Goossens, L. (2014). Loneliness and Facebook

Motives in Adolescence: A Longitudinal Inquiry into Directionality of Effect. *Journal of Adolescence, 37*(5), 691–699. http://doi.org/10.1016/j.adolescence.2013.11.003.

Tierney, S. (2006). The Dangers and Draw of Online Communication: Pro-anorexia Websites and their Implications for Users, Practitioners, and Researchers. *Eating Disorders, 14*(3), 181–190. http://doi.org/10.1080/10640260600638865.

Tokunaga, R.S. (2010). Following You Home from School: A Critical Review and Synthesis of Research on Cyberbullying Victimization. *Computers in Human Behavior, 26*(3), 277–287. http://doi.org/10.1016/j.chb.2009.11.014.

Tsai, C.-W., Shen, P.-D. & Chiang, Y.-C. (2015). Meeting Ex-partners on Facebook: Users' Anxiety and Severity of Depression. *Behaviour & Information Technology, 34*(7), 668–677. http://doi.org/10.1080/0144929X.2014.981585.

Uhls, Y.T., Michikyan, M., Morris, J., Garcia, D., Small, G.W., Zgourou, E. & Greenfield, P.M. (2014). Five Days at Outdoor Education Camp without Screens Improves Preteen Skills with Nonverbal Emotion Cues. *Computers in Human Behavior, 39*, 387–392. http://doi.org/10.1016/j.chb.2014.05.036.

Utz, S., Muscanell, N. & Khalid, C. (2015). Snapchat Elicits More Jealousy than Facebook: A Comparison of Snapchat and Facebook Use. *Cyberpsychology, Behavior and Social Networking, 18*(3), 141–146. http://doi.org/10.1089/cyber.2014.0479.

Valenzuela, S., Halpern, D. & Katz, J.E. (2014). Social Network Sites, Marriage Wellbeing and Divorce: Survey and State-level Evidence from the United States. *Computers in Human Behavior, 36*, 94–101. http://doi.org/10.1016/j.chb.2014.03.034.

Valkenburg, P.M. & Peter, J. (2007). Preadolescents' and Adolescents' Online Communication and their Closeness to Friends. *Developmental Psychology, 43*(2), 267.

Valkenburg, P.M. & Peter, J. (2009a). Social Consequences of the Internet for Adolescents: A Decade of Research. *Current Directions in Psychological Science, 18*(1), 1–5.

Valkenburg, P.M. & Peter, J. (2009b). The Effects of Instant Messaging on the Quality of Adolescents' Existing Friendships: A Longitudinal Study. *Journal of Communication, 59*(1), 79–97.

Valkenburg, P.M. & Peter, J. (2011). Online Communication among Adolescents: An Integrated Model of its Attraction, Opportunities, and Risks. *Journal of Adolescent Health, 48*(2), 121–127.

van Geel, M., Vedder, P. & Tanilon, J. (2014). Relationship between Peer Victimization, Cyberbullying, and Suicide in Children and Adolescents: A Meta-analysis. *JAMA Pediatrics, 168*(5), 435–442. http://doi.org/10.1001/jamapediatrics.2013.4143.

Wang, H. & Wellman, B. (2010). Social Connectivity in America: Changes in Adult Friendship Network Size From 2002 to 2007. *American Behavioral Scientist, 53*(8), 1148–1169. http://doi.org/10.1177/0002764209356247.

Wenninger, H., Krasnova, H. & Buxmann, P. (2014). ACTIVITY MATTERS: INVESTIGATING THE INFLUENCE OF FACEBOOK ON LIFE SATISFACTION OF TEENAGE USERS. *ECIS 2014 Proceedings.* Retrieved June 3, 2015 from http://aisel.aisnet.org/ecis2014/proceedings/track01/13.

White, J.M., Mimiaga, M.J., Reisner, S.L. & Mayer, K.H. (2012). HIV Sexual Risk Behavior among Black Men Who Meet Other Men on the Internet for Sex. *Journal of Urban Health, 90*(3), 464–481. http://doi.org/10.1007/s11524-012-9701-y.

Whiteley, L.B., Brown, L.K., Swenson, R.R., Romer, D., DiClemente, R.J.P., Salazar, L.F., & Valois, R.F. (2011). African American Adolescents and New Media: Associations with HIV/STI Risk Behavior and Psychosocial Variables. *Ethnicity & Disease, 21*(2), 216–222.

Whiteley, L.B., Brown, L.K., Swenson, R.R., Valois, R.F., Vanable, P.A., Carey, M.P. & Romer, D. (2012). African American Adolescents Meeting Sex Partners Online:

Closing the Digital Research Divide in STI/HIV Prevention. *The Journal of Primary Prevention*, *33*(1), 13–18. http://doi.org/10.1007/s10935-012-0262-3.

Wicks, P., Vaughan, T.E., Massagli, M.P. & Heywood, J. (2011). Accelerated Clinical Discovery Using Self-reported Patient Data Collected Online and a Patient-matching Algorithm. *Nature Biotechnology*, *29*(5), 411–414. http://doi.org/10.1038/nbt.1837.

Wicks, P., Massagli, M., Frost, J., Brownstein, C., Okun, S., Vaughan, T. & Heywood, J. (2010). Sharing Health Data for Better Outcomes on PatientsLikeMe. *Journal of Medical Internet Research*, *12*(2), e19. http://doi.org/10.2196/jmir.1549.

Ybarra, M.L. & Mitchell, K.J. (2008). How Risky Are Social Networking Sites? A Comparison of Places Online Where Youth Sexual Solicitation and Harassment Occurs. *Pediatrics*, *121*(2), e350–357. http://doi.org/10.1542/peds.2007-0693.

Yom-Tov, E., Fernandez-Luque, L., Weber, I. & Crain, S.P. (2012). Pro-anorexia and Pro-recovery Photo Sharing: A Tale of Two Warring Tribes. *Journal of Medical Internet Research*, *14*(6). http://doi.org/10.2196/jmir.2239.

Yonker, L.M., Zan, S., Scirica, C.V., Jethwani, K. & Kinane, T.B. (2015). "Friending" Teens: Systematic Review of Social Media in Adolescent and Young Adult Health Care. *Journal of Medical Internet Research*, *17*(1), e4. http://doi.org/10.2196/jmir.3692.

Young, K.S. (1998). Internet Addiction: The Emergence of a New Clinical Disorder. *Cyberpsychology & Behavior*, *1*(3), 237–244. http://doi.org/10.1089/cpb.1998.1.237.

Young, S.D. & Jordan, A.H. (2013). The Influence of Social Networking Photos on Social Norms and Sexual Health Behaviors. *Cyberpsychology, Behavior and Social Networking*, *16*(4), 243–247. http://doi.org/10.1089/cyber.2012.0080.

Young, S.D., Szekeres, G. & Coates, T. (2013). Sexual Risk and HIV Prevention Behaviors among African-American and Latino MSM Social Networking Users. *International Journal of STD & AIDS*, 0956462413478875. http://doi.org/10.1177/0956462413478875.

Part II

Media Effects on Health Policy

INTRODUCTION

Every chapter in this book thus far has dealt with the potential for exposure to mass media content to influence individual health behavior. These questions, revolving around whether and how mass media might improve (or interfere with) our health knowledge, promote healthy (or unhealthy) attitudes and encourage us to take better care of ourselves (or to engage in risky behavior), have dominated health-related media effects research. This is probably not surprising in the United States, given the centrality of individualism in our culture (Dutta-Bergman, 2005; Jeffery, 1989).

However, public health experts have long recognized that although individuals do have the capacity to make behavioral choices that either benefit or threaten their health, many social, structural and policy circumstances limit some people's access to the full range of choices. These social/structural determinants of health, including gender, race or ethnicity, income, education, social class and occupation, create material and psychosocial circumstances that are often critical factors in determining health behavior. Both corporate and government policies can change the health environment in ways that may have more important impacts on health than any individual behaviors could have (Lynch et al., 2000).

Consider, for example, a young man who began smoking regularly at age 16. Now in his early twenties, he has recognized the health risks of smoking and wants to quit. He will, of course, have to cope with the physiological symptoms of addiction, regardless of where he lives or works. However, if his employer allows smoking in the workplace, he may be surrounded by others who smoke, creating constant physical, visual and social cues that will make quitting more difficult. If he works in a bar or restaurant that allows smoking, he may have to cope with those cues, as well as with the second-hand smoke, even if none of his co-workers smoke. He can use nicotine replacement products to help him quit, but if he has no insurance or if his insurance does not cover smoking cessation assistance, this will cost him between $3.50 and $6 per day, depending on the specific product (e.g., gum, lozenges, nasal spray, patches) he uses (National Cancer Institute, n.d.). A lack of insurance also will make it more difficult for the would-be quitter to seek the advice and support of health professionals. Of course, regardless of where he works or what sort of insurance he has, he is likely to encounter advertising, some of it specifically designed to discourage smokers from quitting, but if he lives in a low-income or predominantly African American or Latino neighborhood, he is more likely to see billboards, point-of-sale and print advertising for tobacco (Barbeau et al., 2005; Laws et al., 2002; Luke et al., 2000). This disproportionate exposure to advertising would also likely have played a role in the young man's decision to start smoking in the first place.

The point here is that many characteristics of the health environment can increase or decrease the challenges individuals face as they attempt to engage in healthy behavior. And just as mass media can influence individual behavior, they also can affect corporate and government decisions that change the health environment. These effects have received less scholarly attention, but they are nonetheless important to discuss. Part II, therefore, will address research on three key (and related) topics: how news coverage of health influences policy, how political issue advertising affects policy, and the use of media advocacy techniques to influence both government and corporate policy.

References

Barbeau, E.M., Wolin, K.Y., Naumova, E.N. & Balbach, E. (2005). Tobacco Advertising in Communities: Associations with Race and Class. *Preventive Medicine*, 40(1), 16–22. http://doi.org/10.1016/j.ypmed.2004.04.056.

Dutta-Bergman, M.J. (2005). Theory and Practice in Health Communication Campaigns: A Critical Interrogation. *Health Communication*, *18*(2), 103–122. http://doi.org/10.1207/s15327027hc1802_1.

Jeffery, R.W. (1989). Risk Behaviors and Health: Contrasting Individual and Population Perspectives. *American Psychologist*, *44*(9), 1194–1202. http://doi.org/10.1037/b0003-066X.44.9.1194.

Laws, M.B., Whitman, J., Bowser, D.M. & Krech, L. (2002). Tobacco Availability and Point of Sale Marketing in Demographically Contrasting Districts of Massachusetts. *Tobacco Control*, *11*(Suppl. 2), ii71–ii73. http://doi.org/10.1136/tc.11.suppl_2.ii71.

Luke, D., Esmundo, E. & Bloom, Y. (2000). Smoke Signs: Patterns of Tobacco Billboard Advertising in a Metropolitan Region. *Tobacco Control*, *9*(1), 16–23. http://doi.org/10.1136/tc.9.1.16.

Lynch, J.W., Smith, G.D., Kaplan, G.A. & House, J.S. (2000). Income Inequality and Mortality: Importance to Health of Individual Income, Psychosocial Environment, or Material Conditions. *BMJ: British Medical Journal*, *320*(7243), 1200–1204.

National Cancer Institute. (n.d.). Dispelling Myths about Nicotine Replacement Therapy. National Cancer Institute. Retrieved June 10, 2015 from http://smokefree.gov/sites/default/files/pdf/mythsaboutNRTfactsheet.pdf.

CHAPTER 13

HOW HEALTH NEWS CAN AFFECT NON-NEWS CONSUMERS: NEWS MEDIA AND HEALTH POLICY

In April 2011, Health News Florida (HNF), an online news site focused on health business and health policy in the state, published a story noting that although the Florida Department of Health operated a website enabling consumers to check health professionals' backgrounds for complaints about illegal or incompetent behavior, that website often listed health licensees as "clear/active" even after they had been convicted of felonies requiring imprisonment or probation. The story explained that, using Google and publicly available state databases, HNF had easily identified nine health professionals (dentists and allied mental health professionals) who had been convicted of crimes, including drug-related crimes, sex crimes with minors, tax evasion and theft; none of the convictions was mentioned in the state database. State officials were generally "flying blind" on crimes by health professionals because Florida law required background checks only for doctors, nurses and a few other types of health profession-als, excluding dentists, psychologists and clinical social workers, among others (Gentry, 2011a). About a month later, Health News Florida reported that two dozen Florida doctors who had "lost their Drug Enforcement Administration (DEA) licenses as part of a federal crackdown on pain clinics still have clear Florida medical licenses" (Davis, 2011, para. 1). The state's consumer website still listed them as having clean records, even though the DEA had released the doctors' names to the media in February in conjunction with announcements about its "Operation Pill Nation" investigation of South Florida pain clinics (Davis, 2011).

Health News Florida
Journalism for a Healthy State

Live Radio · News Information & All Night Jazz

Home   HNF Stories   Ongoing Coverage ▾   NPR Health   News Staff   Search

Health Dept. flying blind on crime

By CAROL GENTRY · APR 21, 2011

SHARE
Twitter
Facebook
Google+
Email

After three years in a federal pen, dentist David Goldston is back in practice in Polk City.

He'll have to fix a lot of teeth to pay off $2 million in tax-fraud penalties, but at least he doesn't have to worry about losing his state dental license. He didn't get even a slap on the wrist from the Department of Health or Board of Dentistry.

In fact, there is no indication that they are even aware of Goldston's federal conviction.

Figure 13.1: HNF Story Revealed Risks to Patients (http://health.wusf.usf.edu)

Two months later, in July, the state's Surgeon General explained that the Department of Health (DoH) had introduced several common-sense steps to ensure that health professionals would be subject to emergency suspensions of their medical licenses within days, rather than months, after being arrested in connection with their medical practices. The changes included designating a DoH official to contact law enforcement agencies, including the DEA and the State Attorney's Office, on a regular basis to seek information about arrests of health professionals. As a result of the changes, the DoH had issued 20 emergency suspensions in June 2011, compared to only four in June 2010 (Gentry, 2011b).

Not all news stories about the shortcomings of health policy have such clear and immediate effects as those illustrated in the case of Health News Florida's "Flying Blind" report. However, the U.S. public does expect news media to serve as a "watchdog," meaning that journalists scrutinize the way in which government officials do their jobs (Dimock et al., 2013). In general, the media system in the United States operates in accordance with the social responsibility theory of the press, meaning that news organizations are expected to provide the public with information and debate on issues of public importance; to keep the public informed about the activities of government so that they are capable of self-governance; to ensure that government actions do not trample on individual liberties; to benefit the economic system by connecting buyers to sellers via advertising; to entertain; and to be financially independent of special interest groups. Government is not expected to interfere with media activities – except when media organizations are deemed to have failed to perform these functions so as to serve the public good, in which case government is justified in intervening to ensure adequate performance (Siebert, 1956).

This chapter focuses on the circumstances under which news coverage influences health policy and the mechanisms through which that influence occurs. This issue is important because, as noted in the introduction to Part II, policy is a key element in the health environment. Health news can have a direct impact on individual health decisions only when the individual is exposed to the story either directly or indirectly, understands its recommendations *and* has the capability to act on those recommendations. However, news that influences health policy can affect individuals who were never exposed to that coverage.

Given that providing information the public needs to understand government policy and actions is one of the news media's most critical roles, one might expect that substantial amounts of health news coverage would address health policy in some way. However, the research suggests that relatively little health news focuses directly on policy issues. The most recent comprehensive report on health news coverage, produced jointly by the Kaiser Family Foundation and the Pew Research Center's Project for Excellence in Journalism, showed that at the beginning of President Barack Obama's first term in early 2009, health news represented 4.5 percent of all news, a 36 percent increase over a previous analysis from January 2007 through the first six months of 2008. Given President Obama's focus on reforming the health care system, this increase is probably not surprising. In addition, during early 2009, health policy and the health care system received more attention than any other health topic, representing 40.2 percent of all space devoted to health news. Again, this focus on health policy represented a significant change from the earlier study, when health policy received the *least* attention of any health topic (Kaiser Family Foundation & Pew Research Center's Project for Excellence in Journalism, 2009).

The study also showed, however, that attention to health policy was not consistent across all types of news outlets. The PBS *NewsHour* provided the most coverage of health policy, devoting 58 percent of its health newshole to health policy and the health care system. However, on the major networks' evening newscasts, only one in every five health stories dealt with health policy, although overall the networks paid more attention to health than any other outlet type; specific diseases, such as cancer, heart disease and mental health, were the focus of more than half of the networks' health stories. In newspapers, coverage was more evenly split, with health policy stories accounting for 39.5 percent of the health newshole, followed by public health issues (31.6%, primarily the H1N1 flu outbreak) and specific diseases and conditions (28.9%). The networks' morning news programs focused primarily on public health issues, again dominated by the H1N1 flu outbreak, followed by specific diseases and conditions, which were the focus of one-third of all coverage. Less than a quarter of morning news show health stories (23.4%) discussed health policy issues, and more than half of that coverage (56.7%) came from ABC's *Good Morning America* (Kaiser Family Foundation & Pew Research Center's Project for Excellence in Journalism, 2009).

Since that report was released, there has been no comprehensive analysis of health news coverage in the United States. However, a more recent study, which examined only local TV news health coverage, showed that only 16.9 percent of the stories dealt with health policy change (Lee et al., 2013). Another study specifically examined coverage of the Patient Protection and Affordable Care Act (sometimes called "Obamacare") during the first stage of the law's implementation in October 2013. The researchers identified 1,286 local TV news stories mentioning the ACA across the 210 media markets they examined. Four in every ten stories dealt only with the political fight surrounding the ACA, including stories about the federal government shut-down aimed at defunding or delaying the law. New health insurance options were the focus of 46 percent of the stories, and 12 percent mentioned both the new products and the political conflict. Of the stories dealing with new health insurance products, half were coded as optimistic or encouraging, while 26 percent were negative or discouraging. However, news stories airing in states that were running their own health insurance exchanges were significantly more positive than stories aired in states relying on the federal exchange or federal–state partnerships (Gollust et al., 2014); this may reflect the fact that many of the states using the federal exchange (e.g., Florida, Texas, Alabama, Georgia) had refused to set up state exchanges because political leaders opposed the law.

Other analyses have examined news coverage of specific health policy issues, such as local land use actions designed to restrict fast-food restaurants (Nixon et al., 2015), the Health Security Act of 1993 proposed by then-President Bill Clinton (Dorfman et al., 1996), anti-obesity legislation (Ries et al., 2011), tobacco control regulations (Menashe & Siegel, 1998) and HPV vaccine mandates (Casciotti et al., 2014). Some of these studies have shown that when news media cover broad health care system policy proposals, they tend to focus on only limited aspects of the proposals and fail to provide in-depth explanations of these complex proposals. For instance, an analysis of 316 TV news stories about the introduction of the Health Security Act showed that 57 percent of the stories dealt with political interest groups' support of or opposition to the legislation. The content of the stories tended to focus on how the cost of the plan would be covered, who would be eligible to benefit and what types of preventive services would be covered; less attention went to coverage of long-term care, changes in Medicare and Medicaid, and the plan's mechanisms for lowering health care costs. The authors concluded that local TV news "provided superficial coverage framed largely in terms of the risks and costs of reform to specific stakeholders" (Dorfman et al., 1996, p. 1201).

One of the most recent studies examined news coverage of fast-food-related land use policies proposed in 77 communities nationwide between January 2001 and June 2013. The proposals included policies restricting chain businesses or restaurants in certain areas, restricting drive-through businesses including restaurants, specifically restricting fast-food restaurants, or some combination of these types of measures. The researchers concluded that when the policies were based on improving nutrition in the area, they were likely to receive negative coverage. In stories dealing with nutrition-focused proposals, 41 percent of the arguments included in news stories supported the proposal, compared to 58 percent of the arguments offered in support of policies for the same types of restrictions but with some other justification, such as maintaining the "small-town charm" of an area, protecting the local economy or improving quality of life. Even when the land use policies proposed were very similar, those that were introduced with a focus on improving nutrition in the area received more negative coverage and greater opposition in general (Nixon et al., 2015).

433

A study comparing U.S., Canadian and United Kingdom newspaper coverage of policy and legislative efforts to combat obesity revealed that, across the three nations, coverage attributed obesity to poor behavioral choices, including poor eating habits (56.7%) and lack of exercise (23.1%); less than a quarter of the stories (22.2%) mentioned environmental factors that contribute to obesity. Coverage differed from one country to the next in terms of which group was held responsible for reducing obesity. The highest percentage of Canadian newspapers stories (29.2%) mentioned government action, followed by discussion of personal behavior change (20.2%). In the United States, news stories addressed the need for food industry change (38.4%) and governmental action (19.8%, including regulation and educational initiatives), with only 12.8 percent of stories focused on individual behavior change. In the United Kingdom, discussions of individual behavior change were even less common (10.7%), while 23 percent of stories mentioned governmental actions and more than one-third (34.2%) called on industry to solve the problem. While these statistics may suggest that news coverage promotes the need for government and/or industry action to create a healthier environment, the authors conclude that the news stories primarily suggest government action to encourage individual behavior change. Still, they note, "there appears to be a growing recognition that environmental factors that constrain or promote healthier choices are critical – and are appropriate targets of government policy interventions" (Ries et al., 2011, p. 85).

Another recent study examined newspaper stories about the HPV vaccine in states requiring HPV vaccination. The research, which examined stories from the *Washington Post*, the *Houston Chronicle*, *The* (Norfolk) *Virginian-Pilot* and the *Richmond Times Dispatch*, revealed that more than two-thirds of the stories (69%) dealt with government and state activities, making this the most common topic for stories about the vaccine; in comparison, only 57 percent focused on providing information about characteristics of the vaccine or cervical cancer. Within the 63 news items (45 stories and 18 opinion pieces) that dealt with the vaccine mandate and legislative action, only five mentioned Pap testing as an alternative to vaccination. The authors noted that the tendency to provide minimal context for discussions of HPV vaccination mandates "may lead to conclusions that vaccine mandates are vital to cancer prevention" (Casciotti et al., 2014, p. 78); however, the stories also typically framed government involvement in the issue as problematic, motivated by pharmaceutical companies' desire for profits and representing interference with parental autonomy, "again framing policy and family as competing, rather than complementary, public health strategies" (Casciotti et al., 2014, pp. 78–79).

How News Coverage Influences Health Policy

Understanding how the news media cover health policy-relevant issues is only important, of course, if that coverage is likely to influence those who set health policy. Several mechanisms exist through which that may occur. First, news coverage may directly inform health policy-makers about the issues, although there appears to be no recent research assessing that impact, in the United States, at least. An early study of American political and economic leaders, including Congress members, White House staff and political party officials, found that these individuals acknowledged using the mass media as valuable sources of information (Weiss, 1974). The *New York Times* was the most commonly cited information source across all groups, and the *Wall Street Journal* also was read widely by these political and economic elites. Not surprisingly, among federal elected and appointed officials, the *Washington Post* was the most widely read; 92 percent of the political and economic leaders from Washington, DC, read the *Post*. Similarly, Grau (1976) found that more than half of the news media items cited in the Congressional Record were from the *Post* or the *Times*. Unfortunately, no recent research is available to determine which news outlets, if any, currently reach state and national legislators or other policy-makers, or to what extent those policy-makers use news media content to inform their understanding of health issues.

There is more evidence, however, that news coverage of health policy issues influences public opinion, which, in turn, may influence policy-makers' decisions. As discussed in Chapter 11, the news media are important sources of health information for the general public (Geana et al., 2011; Brodie et al., 2003; Hesse et al., 2005; Kakai et al., 2003; Murphy et al., 2010; Gaglio et al., 2012). In addition to providing information about personal health issues, however, news coverage also can influence public attitudes toward health policy in at least three ways. First, news coverage of a health policy issue can help put that issue on the public's agenda by signaling that the issue is important and should receive attention from policy-makers; this is known as the agenda-setting function of the media (McCombs & Shaw, 1972, 1993). Researchers have demonstrated that news coverage indeed can elevate to public consciousness and concern a health issue about which the public was previously unaware or relatively unconcerned. For instance, Cook et al. (1983) took advantage of having advance knowledge of a TV station's investigative report on home health care fraud to test the impact of the programs on area residents' concern about home health care. Their analysis showed that people who had watched the TV news report "saw home health care as a more important program, saw government help for the program as more important, and saw fraud and abuse as a larger problem within the program," while these same beliefs did not change among individuals who had not seen the program (Cook et al., 1983, p. 24).

A time series analysis of changing public opinion about the importance of illegal drug use as a problem facing the United States showed that public views were driven primarily by the news media describing drug abuse as a crisis. Public opinion about the drug issue was a very weak predictor of news coverage, demonstrating that the news media's impact on audiences was substantially greater than audiences' impact on news coverage (Fan, 1996). Similarly, Nielsen and Bonn (2008) used data from the General Social Surveys from 1975 to 2004 to examine the links between exposure to news media and support for increased spending to address drug addiction. The results showed that both TV viewing and newspaper reading were associated with the belief that the government spends too little on the drug addiction problem. Individuals who consumed both types of news daily were most likely to believe that more money should be devoted to solving the drug addiction problem, and these results held even after controlling for which president was in office, and for both drug use statistics and the amount of actual drug control spending during that time period.

Second, news coverage about policies can increase not only awareness of the issue but knowledge about the specific policy proposals. For instance, Barabas and Jerit (2009) compared public knowledge about health policy proposals introduced by then-President Bill Clinton in 1997, including two that had received little or no media coverage and two that had received significant coverage. Using responses to polls conducted by Princeton Survey Research Associates, the researchers determined that no more than 20 percent of respondents gave correct answers to questions about the policy proposals that had not received media attention; however, 71 percent offered correct answers to a proposal that had been covered in nine stories within the sources the researchers examined, and nearly 80 percent of respondents knew about the proposal that had received the most attention (18 stories). Additional analyses revealed that knowledge levels increased by nearly 11 percentage points for issues that had received both television and print news coverage. The researchers concluded that "breadth of coverage and the prominence of a story are equally powerful predictors of knowledge and are more important than demographic characteristics or indicators of socioeconomic status" (Barabas & Jerit, 2009, p. 86).

In addition to putting health issues on the public agenda, news coverage can influence public beliefs about who is to blame for causing a health problem and about which policy options offer appropriate solutions. This occurs through the process known as "framing," which refers to the fact that in producing news stories, journalists "select some aspects of a perceived reality and make them more salient in a communicating text, in such a way as to promote a particular problem definition, causal interpretation, moral evaluation, and/or treatment recommendation" (Entman, 1993, p. 52). The comparison of obesity framing in Canadian, U.S. and U.K. news media, discussed earlier, provides a good example of this idea. Although the study did not examine the impact of news framing on public attitudes toward obesity, the results suggest that, by framing government action as needed primarily as a way of encouraging individual behavior change to reduce obesity, news coverage would reinforce the idea that individuals' poor health choices and behaviors, rather than food industry practices, are primarily responsible for the obesity epidemic (Ries et al., 2011).

An experimental study examined the impact of another common framing technique in news coverage of health issues: the use of "real patient" stories to add human interest to stories about medical technology advances. The study showed that participants were more likely to view medical advances positively when they were exposed to TV news stories that included video and personal information about specific patients who had benefitted from the technologies, in comparison to stories that focused only on the medical development with no patient exemplar included. In addition to seeing the human interest-framed technologies as offering more benefits to society and to individuals, participants expressed greater support for government and private research funding for these medical advances. The researchers noted that while human interest framing increases viewer involvement in and potentially learning from health news stories, it also could decrease the audience's critical consideration of the medical development being covered. This is problematic because informed decision-making about public policy related to medical advances requires that the public appreciate not only the benefits but also the risks these new technologies may pose (Hong, 2012).

Researchers have confirmed that when news stories personalize health issues by presenting them in the context of their impacts on individuals rather than societal effects, audiences are more likely to view individuals as responsible for causing and solving the health problem and therefore will be less supportive of public policy changes aimed at reducing those health issues. On the other hand, when news stories focus on how health problems affect society as a whole, audiences are more likely to attribute responsibility to society. For instance, a study of framing effects in news stories about obesity, diabetes, immigrant health and smoking by Major (2009) found that this was especially true when the news story focused on the societal costs of lung cancer and obesity, rather than on how society would benefit from reductions in these diseases.

Another study, however, found that audiences exposed to "public health model" reporting, which emphasizes social determinants of health, were no more likely than those who read a traditional news story to agree that society is responsible for causing or solving health problems, including diabetes, obesity, smoking and immigrant health issues. However, those exposed to the public health-oriented story were more likely than those who read the traditional story to support public policy changes to reduce these health issues. Interestingly, participants who read the public health-framed story also reported greater intentions to adopt healthier behaviors themselves (Coleman et al., 2011).

Other researchers have found that news story framing of health issues may not affect all audiences in the same ways. An experimental study examining public responses to a news story about the causes of type 2 diabetes revealed that political preferences influenced individuals' responses to the story and to proposed government intervention to reduce type 2 diabetes. Regardless of whether the story they read emphasized genetics, behavioral choices or social determinants as causes of diabetes, Democrats were more likely than Republicans or Independents to agree that social determinants play a key role in the development of type 2 diabetes. Individuals who read the story emphasizing social determinants subsequently expressed greater support for bans on trans-fats; however, there were no differences across story condition in support for banning fast-food sales in public schools, government investment in parks, government subsidies to promote healthy food consumption, taxes on unhealthy foods, government providing financial incentives to encourage grocery store development in "food deserts," or government regulation of fast-food advertising. There was, however, a significant interaction effect between exposure to the social determinants story and political affiliation. Compared to Democrats who read a story with no information about what causes type 2 diabetes, Democrats exposed to the social determinants story expressed greater support for government policy changes; however, the reverse was true for Republicans, with those who read the social determinants story expressing *less* support for policy changes than those who read the control story (Gollust et al., 2009).

Evidence also suggests that people's emotional reactions to news stories influence their support for policies relevant to the subject of the story. For instance, a comparison of people's reactions to stories about accidental and crime-related injuries showed that when the stories specifically mentioned the role alcohol played in the injury, respondents were angrier, but less fearful; the reverse was true when there was no discussion of alcohol. Anger increased respondents' likelihood of blaming individuals and also increased support for stricter enforcement of existing laws regulating individual behavior, as well as support for laws aimed at altering social contexts that might contribute to alcohol-related crimes and accidents. "Fear heightened support for the development of new laws intended to influence social context, but had no impact on support for enforcement of existing laws" (Goodall et al., 2013, p. 387). A related study showed that exposure to news stories that mentioned alcohol's role in accidental and crime-related injuries increased concern about societal-level risks, leading to greater support for alcohol control policies (Slater et al., 2012).

Perhaps not surprisingly, when news stories include discussion of potential policy solutions to a problem, readers tend to be more supportive of those policies. For instance, McGinty and colleagues (2013) found in an experimental study that news coverage of a mass shooting not only increased negative attitudes toward people with serious mental illness but also increased public support for policies to limit gun access for people with serious mental illnesses and to ban sales of large-capacity magazines. Support for the large-capacity magazine ban was strongest when the story specifically included discussion of that policy; this version of the story also produced significantly higher support for limiting access to guns among those who are seriously mentally ill. Interestingly, participants who read the mass shooting story with specific discussion of a policy to limit gun access to the mentally ill were no more supportive of this policy than individuals in the control group who did not read a news story. However, they were more supportive of banning large-capacity magazines.

Research also suggests that media framing influenced public opinion on the two most significant health care reform efforts of the past 30 years in the United States: then-President Bill Clinton's attempt to provide universal health coverage through the Health Security Act and President Barack Obama's Patient Protection and Affordable Care Act. First, a study linking public opinion data with content analysis of Health Security Act coverage in 22 daily newspapers nationwide showed that media coverage accounted for 54 percent of the variance in public opinion about the health reform proposal. As news coverage increasingly reflected opponents' framing of the proposal, focusing on allegations that it would increase government bureaucracy, raise health care costs, lead to declines in employment and reduce individuals' ability to choose their own doctors, public opinion about the proposal also grew more negative.

> In contrast, positive coverage mostly focused on individual access. There was little discussion of other perspectives, such as the advantages of a universal coverage system for society and such benefits appealing to America's middle class as catastrophic illness coverage, security, and portability.
>
> (Huebner et al., 1997, p. 267)

The authors conclude that the media helped kill the Health Security Act by inflicting a "'death of a thousand cuts'" through a steady stream of negative stories. Thus, although public support for the concept of universal health coverage remained strong, opponents of Clinton's proposal were able to persuade the public that the president's plan was too badly flawed to be acceptable (Huebner et al., 1997).

More recently, researchers assessed the relationships between information sources people used to learn about the Affordable Care Act (ACA) and their opinions of the law and its provisions. In surveys of Indiana adults, they found that people who reported learning about the legislation from national TV news programs had more favorable attitudes toward the ACA in general and its specific provisions (Shue et al., 2014).

HEALTH NEWS AND POLICY-MAKERS

There is significant evidence, then, that health news coverage and framing can have significant effects on public support for health policy change. To the extent that policy-makers attempt to develop and maintain public policies that are popular with their constituents and to address health problems that concern significant proportions of their constituents, then, news agenda-setting and framing should influence health policy development. Otten (1992) argues that this influence occurs not only indirectly, through news media's effects on public opinion, but also directly, by increasing policy-makers' awareness of and even outrage over health problems. He cites, for instance, the *Wall Street Journal*'s 1987 Pulitzer Prize-winning story documenting how excessive workloads and poor training among laboratory technicians led to inaccurate readings of Pap smears; the result was that many women were misinformed about whether they had cervical cancer. The article, he says, led to Congressional passage in 1988 of the Clinical Laboratory Improvement Amendments, which set minimum standards for lab technicians' training, evaluation and workloads.

As this anecdote suggests, investigative reporting that uncovers flaws in the health care system can influence policy as well as public opinion. Cook et al. (1983) collaborated with a team of investigative reporters to assess the impact of an "NBC News Magazine with David Brinkley" story about fraud and abuse, including overbilling, use of poor-quality equipment, mistreatment of patients and failure to provide needed care, in the federally funded home health care program. A week before the story aired, the researchers interviewed 57 government and interest

441

group policy-makers, including officials from the Chicago Mayor's Office of Senior Citizens, the Illinois Department of Aging, Illinois state senators and representatives, and other state officials, along with high-ranking officers with interest groups such as the American Association of Retired Persons, the Illinois Health Care Association and Advocates for the Handicapped. Within two weeks after the story aired, 51 of these individuals completed a follow-up telephone survey. Government policy-makers who had either watched the program or had heard about it were much more likely to agree that policy action was needed to curb fraud and abuse in home health care than were their peers who had no exposure to the program. There was no significant difference among interest group leaders who had or had not been exposed to the program, possibly because they already may have been aware of the issue before the program aired. The follow-up survey also showed that exposure to the program increased not only government policy-makers' perceptions of the importance of the home health fraud but also their assessments of the public's view of its importance.

In another study, researchers from this same group examined the impact of investigative reporting on the public's and policy-makers' opinions about toxic waste (Protess et al., 1987). The investigative story, in this case, was a three-part television report showing that the University of Chicago was storing hazardous chemicals and radioactive waste underneath campus buildings, including classrooms, in violation of standards and regulations from the Chicago Fire Department, U.S. Environmental Protection Agency, U.S. Occupational Safety and Health Administration and U.S. Department of Energy. The series implicated failures in these agencies, as well as the university, for allowing the violations to continue. In addition to surveying members of the public, the researchers surveyed 40 policy-makers, including state legislators, officials with state and federal environmental protection agencies, Chicago City Council members, university officials, and lobbyists from public interest groups and waste disposal companies.

After the stories aired, 31 of the 40 policy leaders completed follow-up interviews. The study results showed no significant impact on public opinion. However, after the series ran, policy elites reported lower performance evaluations of three of the four government agencies mentioned in the stories as having responsibility for ensuring safe disposal of toxic wastes. Policy leaders exposed to the series were significantly more likely to say they would spend more time in the coming months dealing with toxic waste disposal issues. In addition, the morning after the first story ran, the Chicago Fire Department inspected buildings where the university was storing chemical wastes and issued citations for failure to comply with 20 safety regulations. Circumstances suggested that the inspection likely was prompted as much by the fire department's interactions with the reporter developing the story as it was by the airing of the story. In addition, there was no evidence that the series led to the introduction of legislation, regulation or budgetary changes to deal with the issue of toxic waste, leading the researchers to conclude that the story's impact had been limited to the specific problem of toxic waste disposal at the University of Chicago (Protess et al., 1987).

In a review of these two cases, as well as two others involving stories about police brutality and the handling of sexual assault cases, the researchers concluded that government responses to investigative reporting depend on a number of factors, including:

> the timing of the publication in relation to political exigencies, the extent of journalistic collaboration with policymakers, the level of general public and interest group pressures, and the availability of cost-effective solutions to the problems disclosed.
>
> (Protess et al., 1987, p. 182)

A case study investigation of the impact of newspaper coverage of health issues also suggested a number of factors that may determine whether news coverage does or does not affect health policy. This study, which examined two series published by the *Atlanta Journal-Constitution* and one each produced by the *Orlando Sentinel* and the (Montgomery) *Alabama Journal*, revealed that only the *Alabama Journal*'s series on infant mortality had clear policy effects. Reporters, editors and policy-makers familiar with the other three series (two *Journal-Constitution* series dealing with access to health care and the *Sentinel*'s series about abuses in mental health treatment of adolescents) agreed the series raised awareness and concern about the problems among both the public and policy-makers but ultimately did not lead to specific legislative or regulatory impacts. On the other hand, journalists and policy-makers in Alabama agreed that the *Journal*'s series on infant mortality, including distribution of series reprints and continued editorializing on the issue, "helped convince state legislators that Alabama citizens wanted something done about the infant mortality problem" and that "Alabama could achieve a great deal of progress on infant mortality without spending very much state money" (Walsh-Childers, 1994b, p. 93). Ultimately, the legislature agreed to participate in a federal matching funds program that would cover much of the cost of expanding Medicaid to cover an additional 30,000 pregnant women and their babies.

Comparison of the series' impact suggested that newspaper coverage was most likely to influence health policy when the health experts agree on recognized solutions, when the policy action needed could occur at the state or local level, and when private citizens' groups and policy officials already are working for specific policy changes. In addition, factors related to the newspapers may have played a role. The *Alabama Journal* and the *Atlanta Journal-Constitution* are both "hometown" newspapers for their state's legislators, increasing the likelihood of exposure to the series. In addition, both newspapers published series reprints that could be distributed by advocacy groups. In the case of the *Journal*, which had a daily circulation of about 20,000 at the time the series ran, publishing 50,000 to 60,000 reprints significantly multiplied its reach throughout the state. However, neither being located in the state capitol nor publishing series reprints seemed to increase the impact of the *Journal-Constitution*'s two series. Two factors unique to the *Alabama Journal* may have had a greater impact: continued editorializing following the publication of the initial series and national recognition. Winning the 1988 Pulitzer Prize for general news for the infant mortality series brought a national spotlight and some political embarrassment to Alabama officials and put infant mortality back on the public's agenda (Walsh-Childers, 1994a, 1994b).

Yanovitzky (2002; Yanovitzky & Bennett, 1999) examined the media-policy connection to explain how news coverage of drunk driving influenced policy-makers' actions at the national level. He tested the association between news coverage of drunk driving and subsequent policy attention and actions. Policy attention was operationalized as the number of Congressional hearings on the issue and the number of drunk driving-related bills introduced in the U.S. Congress between 1978 and 1995. Policy action was defined as the amount of federal funding appropriated toward reducing drunk driving and the adoption of anti-drunk driving laws within the 50 states and the District of Columbia between 1978 and 1995. Using time series analysis, he demonstrated that both the volume and the framing of news coverage (focusing on deterrence versus education) did indeed increase policymakers' attention to the problem, with increases in coverage leading not only to more Congressional hearings but also to more rapid introduction of anti-drunk driving legislation. The results also revealed a strong positive association between news coverage and policy actions. "Specifically, the results suggest that the increased volume of DD-related policy actions between 1981 and 1984 was largely driven by increased media attention to the problem" (Yanovitzky, 2002, p. 444).

The research described thus far demonstrates that news coverage of health can have significant effects on the development and implementation of health policy. It also suggests some circumstances that may determine whether specific instances or periods of news media attention to a problem lead to policy actions, including the extent to which news media provide sustained attention to the issue (Walsh-Childers, 1994b), the degree of collaboration, and interaction between journalists and policymakers (Protess et al., 1987), and the existence, involvement and level of consensus among citizen interest groups (Protess et al., 1987; Walsh-Childers, 1994b). In addition, the likelihood of news coverage influencing policy action "is also a function of the extent to which media framing of public problems serves policy-makers' interests or the interests they represent" (Yanovitzky, 2002, p. 445). In other words, when news framing of an issue coincides with policy-makers' existing views of the problem, they are more likely to move from attention (e.g., convening hearings, setting up study panels) to action (introducing and passing legislation).

Unfortunately, since the publication of Yanovitzky's (2002) most recent article, there seems to have been little research addressing this issue. Much work, therefore, remains to be done to produce a complete understanding of the ways in which news coverage can change the health environment through influences on health policy.

SUMMARY

Research relating health news coverage to health policy development is far less extensive than that linking news coverage to individuals' health beliefs and behaviors. Nonetheless, the existing research suggests that

445

news coverage can influence health policy development by raising public awareness of health problems, by suggesting (or excluding) specific explanations for the cause of the health problem and by focusing greater attention on some potential solutions than on others. In this way, news coverage can push health issues higher up the public's agenda and increase their likelihood of viewing specific solutions as the correct approach. In turn, increasing public concern about a health issue and public demand for solutions can encourage policy-makers to take action. In addition, both coverage itself and interactions with journalists reporting on the issue may encourage policy-makers to take action on an issue, especially when news framing of the issue and/or the solution fits within the policy-makers' pre-existing stances, when health experts agree on the correct approach and when advocacy groups are active in pushing for specific policy approaches.

REFERENCES

Barabas, J. & Jerit, J. (2009). Estimating the Causal Effects of Media Coverage on Policy-specific Knowledge. *American Journal of Political Science, 53*(1), 73–89. http://doi.org/10.1111/j.1540-5907.2008.00358.x.

Brodie, M., Hamel, E.C., Altman, D.E., Blendon, R.J. & Benson, J.M. (2003). Health News and the American Public, 1996–2002. *Journal of Health Politics, Policy and Law, 28*(5), 927–950. http://doi.org/10.1215/03616878-28-5-927.

Casciotti, D.M., Smith, K.C., Andon, L., Vernick, J., Tsui, A. & Klassen, A.C. (2014). Print News Coverage of School-based Human Papillomavirus Vaccine Mandates. *The Journal of School Health, 84*(2), 71–81. http://doi.org/10.1111/josh.12126.

Coleman, R., Thorson, E. & Wilkins, L. (2011). Testing the Effect of Framing and Sourcing in Health News Stories. *Journal of Health Communication, 16*(9), 941–954. http://doi.org/10.1080/10810730.2011.561918.

Cook, F.L., Tyler, T.R., Goetz, E.G., Gordon, M.T., Protess, D., Leff, D.R. & Molotch, H.L. (1983). Media and Agenda Setting: Effects on the Public, Interest Group Leaders, Policy Makers, and Policy. *Public Opinion Quarterly, 47*(1), 16–35.

Davis, B. (2011, May 18). Doctors Lose DEA Licenses in Pill-mill Crackdown, but Are Still Active. Retrieved June 18, 2015 from http://health.wusf.usf.edu/post/doctors-lose-dea-licenses-pill-mill-crackdown-are-still-active.

Dimock, M., Doherty, C. & Tyson, A. (2013). *Amid Criticism, Support for Media's "Watchdog" Role Stands Out.* Washington, DC: Pew Research Center for the People & The Press. Retrieved June 18, 2015 from www.people-press.org/2013/08/08/amid-criticism-support-for-medias-watchdog-role-stands-out/.

Dorfman, L., Schauffler, H.H., Wilkerson, J. & Feinson, J. (1996). Local Television News Coverage of President Clinton's Introduction of the Health Security Act. *JAMA, 275*(15), 1201–1205.

Entman, R.M. (1993). Framing: Towards Clarification of a Fractured Paradigm. *McQuail's Reader in Mass Communication Theory,* 51–58.

Fan, D.P. (1996). News Media Framing Sets Public Opinion That Drugs is the Country's Most Important Problem. *Substance Use & Misuse*, *31*(10), 1413–1421.

Gaglio, B., Glasgow, R.E. & Bull, S.S. (2012). Do Patient Preferences for Health Information Vary by Health Literacy or Numeracy? A Qualitative Assessment. *Journal of Health Communication*, *17* (Suppl. 3), 109–121. http://doi.org/10.1080/10810730.2012.712616;.

Geana, M.V., Kimminau, K.S. & Greiner, K.A. (2011). Sources of Health Information in a Multiethnic, Underserved, Urban Community: Does Ethnicity Matter? *Journal of Health Communication*, *16*(6), 583–594. http://doi.org/10.1080/10810730.2011.551992;.

Gentry, C. (2011a, April 21). Health Dept. Flying Blind on Crime. Retrieved June 18, 2015 from http://health.wusf.usf.edu/post/health-dept-flying-blind-crime.

Gentry, C. (2011b, July 25). Surgeon General Speeds Up "Emergency" Suspensions. Retrieved June 18, 2015 from http://health.wusf.usf.edu/post/surgeon-general-speeds-emergency-suspensions.

Gollust, S.E., Lantz, P.M. & Ubel, P.A. (2009). The Polarizing Effect of News Media Messages about the Social Determinants of Health. *American Journal of Public Health*, *99*(12), 2160–2167. http://doi.org/10.2105/AJPH.2009.161414.

Gollust, S.E., Barry, C.L., Niederdeppe, J., Baum, L. & Fowler, E.F. (2014). First Impressions: Geographic Variation in Media Messages during the First Phase of ACA Implementation. *Journal of Health Politics, Policy and Law*, *39*(6), 1253–1262. http://doi.org/10.1215/03616878-2813756.

Goodall, C.E., Slater, M.D. & Myers, T.A. (2013). Fear and Anger Responses to Local News Coverage of Alcohol-related Crimes, Accidents, and Injuries: Explaining News Effects on Policy Support Using a Representative Sample of Messages and People. *Journal of Communication*, *63*(2), 373–392. http://doi.org/10.1111/jcom.12020.

Grau, C.H. (1976). What Publications Are Most Frequently Quoted in the Congressional Record. *Journalism & Mass Communication Quarterly*, *53*(4), 716–719. http://doi.org/10.1177/107769907605300416.

Hesse, B.W., Nelson, D.E., Kreps, G.L., Croyle, R.T., Arora, N.K., Rimer, B.K. & Viswanath, K. (2005). Trust and Sources of Health Information: The Impact of the Internet and its Implications for Health Care Providers: Findings from the First Health Information National Trends Survey. *Archives of Internal Medicine*, *165*(22), 2618–2624. http://doi.org/10.1001/archinte.165.22.2618.

Hong, H. (2012). The Effects of Human Interest Framing in Television News Coverage of Medical Advances. *Health Communication*, (ahead-of-print), 1–9.

Huebner, J., Fan, D.P. & Finnegan, J., Jr. (1997). "Death of a Thousand Cuts": The Impact of Media Coverage on Public Opinion About Clinton's Health Security Act. *Journal of Health Communication*, *2*(4), 253–270. http://doi.org/10.1080/108107397127581.

Kaiser Family Foundation & Pew Research Center's Project for Excellence in Journalism. (2009). *Health News Coverage in the U.S. Media: January–June 2009*. Menlo Park, CA: Kaiser Family Foundation & Pew Research Center. Retrieved April 29, 2015 from www.journalism.org/files/legacy/health_coverage_2009_0.pdf.

Kakai, H., Maskarinec, G., Shumay, D.M., Tatsumura, Y. & Tasaki, K. (2003). Ethnic Differences in Choices of Health Information by Cancer Patients Using Complementary and Alternative Medicine: An Exploratory Study with Correspondence Analysis. *Social Science & Medicine (1982)*, *56*(4), 851–862.

Lee, H., Lee, Y., Park, S.-A., Willis, E. & Cameron, G.T. (2013). What Are Americans Seeing? Examining the Message Frames of Local Television Health News Stories.

Health Communication, *28*(8), 846–852. http://doi.org/10.1080/10410236.2012.743 842.

Major, L.H. (2009). Break It To Me Harshly: The Effects of Intersecting News Frames in Lung Cancer and Obesity Coverage. *Journal of Health Communication*, *14*(2), 174–188.

McCombs, M.E. & Shaw, D.L. (1972). The Agenda-setting Function of Mass Media. *Public Opinion Quarterly*, *36*(2), 176–187.

McCombs, M.E. & Shaw, D.L. (1993). The Evolution of Agenda-setting Research – Twenty-five years in the Marketplace of Ideas. *Journal of Communication*, *43*(2), 58.

McGinty, E.E., Webster, D.W. & Barry, C.L. (2013). Effects of News Media Messages about Mass Shootings on Attitudes toward Persons with Serious Mental Illness and Public Support for Gun Control Policies. *The American Journal of Psychiatry*, *170*(5), 494–501. http://doi.org/10.1176/appi.ajp. 2013.13010014.

Menashe, C.L. & Siegel, M. (1998). The Power of a Frame: An Analysis of Newspaper Coverage of Tobacco Issues – United States, 1985–1996. *Journal of Health Communication*, *3*(4), 307–325. http://doi.org/10.1080/108107398127139.

Murphy, M.W., Iqbal, S., Sanchez, C.A. & Quinlisk, M.P. (2010). Postdisaster Health Communication and Information Sources: The Iowa Flood Scenario. *Disaster Medicine and Public Health Preparedness*, *4*(2), 129–134.

Nielsen, A.L. & Bonn, S. (2008). Media Exposure and Attitudes Toward Drug Addiction Spending, 1975–2004. *Deviant Behavior*, *29*(8), 726–752. http://doi.org/10.1080/01639620701839492.

Nixon, L., Mejia, P., Dorfman, L., Cheyne, A., Young, S., Friedman, L.C. & Wooten, H. (2015). Fast-food Fights: News Coverage of Local Efforts to Improve Food Environments Through Land-use Regulations, 2001–2013 [corrected]. *American Journal of Public Health*, *105*(3), 490–496. http://doi.org/10.2105/AJPH.2014.302368.

Otten, A.L. (1992). The Influence of the Mass Media on Health Policy. *Health Affairs*, *11*(4), 111–118. http://doi.org/10.1377/hlthaff.11.4.111.

Protess, D.L., Cook, F.L., Curtin, T.R., Gordon, M.T., Leff, D.R., McCombs, M.E. & Miller, P. (1987). The Impact of Investigative Reporting on Public Opinion and Policymaking Targeting Toxic Waste. *Public Opinion Quarterly*, *51*(2), 166–185. http://doi.org/10.1086/269027.

Ries, N.M., Rachul, C. & Caulfield, T. (2011). Newspaper Reporting on Legislative and Policy Interventions to Address Obesity: United States, Canada, and the United Kingdom. *Journal of Public Health Policy*, *32*(1), 73–90. http://doi.org/10.1057/jphp. 2010.39.

Shue, C.K., McGeary, K.A., Reid, I., Khubchandani, J. & Fan, M. (2014). Health Care Reform: Understanding Individuals' Attitudes and Information Sources. *BioMed Research International*, *2014*. http://doi.org/10.1155/2014/813851.

Siebert, F.S. (1956). *Four Theories of the Press: The Authoritarian, Libertarian, Social Responsibility, and Soviet Communist Concepts of what the Press Should Be and Do*. University of Illinois Press.

Slater, M.D., Hayes, A.F., Goodall, C.E. & Ewoldsen, D.R. (2012). Increasing Support for Alcohol-control Enforcement through News Coverage of Alcohol's Role in Injuries and Crime. *Journal of Studies on Alcohol and Drugs*, *73*(2), 311–315.

Walsh-Childers, K. (1994a). "A Death in the Family" – A Case Study of Newspaper Influence on Health Policy Development. *Journalism & Mass Communication Quarterly*, *71*(4), 820–829. http://doi.org/10.1177/107769909407100406.

Walsh-Childers, K. (1994b). Newspaper Influence on Health Policy Development. *Newspaper Research Journal*, *15*(3), 89.

Weiss, C.H. (1974). What America's Leaders Read. *Public Opinion Quarterly, 38*(1), 1–22.

Yanovitzky, I. (2002). Effects of News Coverage on Policy Attention and Actions: A Closer Look Into the Media–Policy Connection. *Communication Research, 29*(4), 422–451. http://doi.org/10.1177/0093650202029004003.

Yanovitzky, I. & Bennett, C. (1999). Media Attention, Institutional Response, and Health Behavior Change The Case of Drunk Driving, 1978–1996. *Communication Research, 26*(4), 429–453. http://doi.org/10.1177/009365099026004004.

CHAPTER 14

FOCUSING THE SPOTLIGHT
ON PROBLEMS UPSTREAM:
MEDIA ADVOCACY TO
INFLUENCE POLICY

In November 2014, voters in Berkeley, CA made their city the first in the nation to impose a tax on the distribution of sugar-sweetened beverages like Coca-Cola, Pepsi, Gatorade, Arizona Green Tea and Starbucks Frappuccino. In May 2015, Berkeley City Council members announced that, in the first month in which the tax was collected, the city took in $116,000, at the rate of one cent per ounce of qualifying beverages distributed. Although the ballot measure allows the city to spend the money on whatever it wants, Berkeley has convened a panel of education and health experts to advise the council on how best to spend the proceeds, which are intended to be used to reduce consumption of sugar-sweetened beverages (SSBs) and to deal with the public health effects of consumption, which can include obesity and diabetes (Lochner, 2015).

Although Berkeley was the first city in the nation to succeed in passing the so-called "soda tax," it was far from the first to attempt such a policy change. Thirty previous city and state soda tax measures had failed, the failures including a 2014 proposal levying two cents per ounce on SSBs distributed in nearby San Francisco (Knight, 2014). So why did Berkeley's measure succeed where so many others had failed?

The answer, of course, includes numerous factors, including the size and demographic characteristics of the cities, the specific nature of the tax proposals, and the political strategies and funding of pro- and anti-tax groups. However, one element that seems to have contributed to Berkeley's success was the way in which its pro-tax coalition used the media in concert with community organizing. The coalition used

Figure 14.1: The 2014 Media Advocacy Campaign for Local "Soda Tax"

analyses of news coverage of previous soda tax efforts to inform their strategies, which included early recruitment of people from low-income and minority groups who, in other cities, had been drawn into the soda tax opposition camps. In addition, noting that the beverage industry had defeated previous measures in large part due to "unprecedented spending on advertising including TV, billboards and direct mail" (Quintero, 2014, para. 13), the Berkeley organizers decided to make that spending part of the debate. By using "Berkeley vs. Big Soda" as its campaign slogan, the pro-tax coalition framed the debate as a David-and-Goliath contest that put the beverage industry's flood of direct mail advertising against the tax in a negative light; the coalition effectively framed the beverage industry's extensive advertising as an attempt to "buy" the community's vote (Quintero, 2014).

Previous failed soda tax efforts also taught the Berkeley coalition the value of embedding their message in the values important to their community; in Berkeley, this led to media messages reminding the community of its "long tradition of supporting public health measures, as well as putting people's health before profit" (Quintero, 2014, para. 16). The coalition also identified spokespeople willing to tell the community, through the media, about the health impacts of SSBs, such as a respected community member who spoke about losing his son to diabetes. Letters-to-the-editor and opinion columns sent to the local news media also helped the coalition get their message out.

It remains to be seen whether Berkeley's success on the soda tax will stand as a fluke, possible only in a quirky, ultra-liberal college town, or whether it will inspire and instruct other coalitions in other cities (or even states) to pass taxes or other policy efforts that reduce consumption of unhealthy beverages. In either case, Berkeley vs. Big Soda illustrates a number of key principals of a strategy known as "media advocacy," which is a type of public health campaign that uses mass media, along with community organizing, to influence health behaviors through public policy change. Media advocacy thus represents the *intentional* use of media, primarily news coverage but also sometimes paid advertising, to change the health environment in which people operate through changes in government or corporate *policy* (e.g., public policies such as taxes on smoking, alcohol and unhealthy beverages, or bans on the use of trans-fats, corporate practices such as providing health insurance options that reward employees for engaging in healthy behaviors, offering healthier options in fast-food "value meals" or removing known carcinogens from the products they sell).

WHAT IS MEDIA ADVOCACY?

Traditional public health campaigns often target the "information gap" between individuals who engage in healthy behavior and those who do not. The assumption here is that people who behave in unhealthy ways do so because they do not understand how their unhealthy behaviors lead to negative outcomes or perhaps because they are not sufficiently motivated to adopt healthier behaviors. Thus, traditional health campaigns use mass media to increase awareness and understanding of healthier behaviors and/or to increase individuals' motivation to adopt or maintain those behaviors. These campaigns assume that people have the resources they need (e.g., healthy living environments, access to health care, adequate income) to engage in healthier behaviors if only they would make the right choices (Wallack, 1994).

Like traditional health campaigns, media advocacy campaigns use mass media in intentional ways to bring about better health outcomes. However, media advocacy focuses not on the "information gap" but on the "'power gap,' where health problems are viewed as a lack of power to define the problem and create social change" (Wallack, 1994, p. 422). Media advocacy campaigns are intended to narrow this power gap by focusing attention on determinants of health that often exist outside the individual's control, including food and housing security, quality education, and access to health care, in addition to marketing that promotes unhealthy products like tobacco, alcohol and low-nutrient food and beverages. Media advocacy, then, is the "strategic use of mass media to advance a social or policy initiative" (Wallack, 1994, p. 424) that will improve the health environment and remove barriers to healthier behavior. "Media advocacy attempts to reframe and shape public discussion to increase support for and advance healthy public policies" (Wallack, 1994, p. 424).

Although media advocates sometimes use paid advertising to stimulate public discussion of policy changes, the primary tool of media advocacy is news coverage of the issue. The challenge, however, is that news media, like traditional public health campaigns, usually present health problems as resulting from deficits or failures at the individual level and focus on individual behavior change as the solution to these health problems. Media advocates therefore must attempt to change the framing of health problems in two ways. First, media advocacy attempts to frame for *access* to news coverage, meaning they must gain journalists' attention and persuade them that the topic is worthy of coverage. This may, at times, require humanizing the issue through telling the story of individuals' health struggles, even though the goal of media advocacy is to shift attention *away* from individuals and toward the needed policy change.

To shift the focus to policy change, media advocates attempt to frame the issue for *content* after they have obtained the journalists' attention. "*Framing for content* means telling the story from the policy advocacy perspective, emphasizing root causes or 'upstream' conditions" (Wallack & Dorfman, 1996, p. 299);[1] news coverage that focuses on the social or environmental determinants of the health problem, rather than on individual behavior, is more likely to promote policy change as the appropriate solution. However, framing for content can be more challenging because a focus on corporate or government decisions that contribute to poor health outcomes often conflicts with the dominant view of individuals as bearing full responsibility for their own health decisions (Wallack & Dorfman, 1996).

MEDIA ADVOCACY EFFECTIVENESS

Public health advocates have been using media advocacy approaches for more than two decades at least, which should provide ample opportunity to determine whether these campaigns are actually effective. However, measuring the effectiveness of any given media advocacy campaign is challenging, for several reasons. First, media advocacy generally occurs in the context of community organizing that involves recruiting members of a community to work with health professionals to define and solve community-specific health problems. In addition, media advocacy is often aimed at producing complex changes in public policy, and as such, media advocacy efforts may continue for longer periods of time than is the norm for traditional media campaigns aimed at individual behavior change. Stead and colleagues argue that "the traditional biomedical approach to evaluations, with the randomized controlled trial as its gold standard, has limited relevance for the analysis of complex health promotion interventions" (Stead et al., 2002, p. 354).

Evaluating the impact of media advocacy also requires specifying the outcome variable of interest, with at least four types of relevant outcomes – news coverage, public opinion related to the policy change being sought, policy change itself and the health outcomes resulting from that policy change. In addition, there may be value in determining the extent to which the media advocacy initiative "enhanced the community's capacity to control the determinants of its health" and to what extent the campaign "enhanced the capacity of the media advocacy organization[s]" (Stead et al., 2002, p. 357). Although these last two impacts are certainly worth evaluating, this chapter focuses on the relatively limited research assessing media advocacy's impacts on news coverage, public opinion, policy change and health outcomes.

MEDIA ADVOCACY AND NEWS COVERAGE

As noted above, the primary mechanism through which media advocates attempt to influence public opinion and public or corporate policy is news coverage. Research suggests that media advocacy efforts sometimes, but not always, influence news coverage. For instance, analysis of the media advocacy impact of the quasi-experimental Stanford Five-City Project showed that the media advocacy campaign influenced news coverage in one of the treatment communities (Salinas) but not in the other (Monterey). During the five-year media advocacy campaign, the researchers found that coverage of cardiovascular disease increased in the *Salinas Californian* but changed little in the *Monterey Peninsula Herald*. In both cities, CVD-related articles published during the media advocacy campaign were more likely to include photographs and more likely to appear higher on the page, in comparison to articles in the reference city newspaper. During the campaign, the *Californian*'s CVD-related articles were more likely to emphasize prevention rather than treatment, but the framing effect did not appear in the *Monterey Peninsula Herald*. In addition, the ratio of staff-written to wire stories on CVD increased in the *Californian* but not in the *Herald*. The researchers noted that the Five-City Project had a stronger presence in Salinas than in Monterey, and the Salinas newspaper had agreed to publish a regular column related to the campaign while the Monterey newspaper did not (Schooler et al., 1996). It is worth noting that the analysis in this study did not differentiate between policy-related stories and prevention stories focused on individual behavior change.

In another study comparing treatment and control communities, media advocacy was used as part of an effort to increase public support for policies related to drinking and driving, under-age alcohol consumption, "responsible" alcohol sales by retailers and alcohol access. Analysis of news coverage linked to the media advocacy activities showed that such coverage increased in the intervention communities but not in the comparison communities. The data showed that increased coverage appeared in both community newspapers and television reports; this finding is important due to the different demographic characteristics of newspaper versus television audiences (Holder & Treno, 1997).

In addition to these quasi-experimental studies, a number of case study analyses have demonstrated that media advocacy efforts can successfully influence both the amount and the framing of news coverage related to health issues. For instance, a study of a Canadian media advocacy intervention to influence public and policy-maker awareness of food insecurity showed that the advocates' strategy succeeded in that every media story generated by the campaign included the intended message, which was that poverty should be considered a public health problem. In addition, most stories communicated that food insecurity was common among Canadians and that many members of "mainstream society" were ignorant about poverty's impacts. Perhaps most impressively, the researchers concluded that "Not one media story in our dataset was off-message" (Rock et al., 2011, p. 954).

Media advocacy efforts also have been successful in influencing newspaper coverage of policy and environmental factors that encourage (or discourage) physical activity. Researchers working with a community-based participatory research project to increase physical activity examined news coverage of the issue in their intervention county, where the campaign included media advocacy and community education activities, and in a comparison community that was geographically and demographically similar. The newspaper in the intervention county published significantly more articles about safety, policy and community initiatives related to physical activity and devoted more stories to issues about sidewalk availability and other recreational resources. In addition, stories about physical activity and health were more prominent in the intervention county (Granner et al., 2010).

Several studies have shown that media advocacy efforts can influence news coverage of tobacco control issues. For instance, one study compared local newspaper stories and editorials related to tobacco control policies in the 17 states participating in the American Stop Smoking Intervention Study (ASSIST) versus coverage in states not participating. In each participating state, ASSIST staff developed statewide networks of local community representatives to interact with journalists to promote positive coverage of tobacco control policy. Analysis of articles published between 1994 and 1998 showed that, compared to newspapers in non-ASSIST states, ASSIST state newspapers published more tobacco control articles overall and more articles dealing with specific tobacco control policies, such as bans on indoor smoking, restrictions on youth access, economic disincentives for smoking, and restrictions on advertising and promotion of tobacco. Although the results were not definitive, the data did show significant differences between ASSIST and non-ASSIST states' news coverage, controlling for pre-existing differences between the states in a measure of commitment to tobacco control (Stillman et al., 2001).

Niederdeppe and colleagues (2007) analyzed coverage of tobacco control issues in Florida before and after implementation of the Florida Tobacco Control Program's (FTCP) media advocacy activities, which began in 1999. The analysis examined overall coverage and coverage of the efforts of Students Working Against Tobacco (SWAT), a statewide anti-tobacco organization for youth. The data showed that while overall coverage of the FTCP campaign between July 1999 and December 2001 was actually lower than before the media advocacy efforts began, the percentage of stories focused on SWAT increased. The researchers reasoned that the decline in overall coverage likely resulted from the fact that the initiation of the FTCP in 1998 and the Florida budget crisis in 1999 (which led to a decline in FTCP funding) had produced high levels of coverage. The results suggested "that media advocacy was successful in promoting news coverage of SWAT activities," in comparison to other aspects of the FTCP (Niederdeppe et al., 2007, p. 50).

Media advocacy also proved successful in promoting news coverage of under-age drinking as a societal problem, rather than a failing of individual behavior, in a study of a Louisiana coalition's efforts to gain passage of new laws to combat youth alcohol abuse. Analysis of news coverage in the Baton Rouge *Advocate* and the New Orleans *Times-Picayune* showed that use of the terms "under-age drinking" or "under-age drinker" was more common in stories emphasizing societal responsibility and policy, while stories focused on individual behavior were more likely to discuss "teen drinking" or "teenage drinking." Examining trends in references to "under-age" drinking or drinkers "clearly shows the increased activity in late 1997 corresponding to the launching of a coalition mobilized to increase public awareness of underage drinking problems" (Harwood et al., 2005, p. 252). This increased media coverage of under-age drinking as a societal problem continued through mid-2002.

MEDIA ADVOCACY'S POLICY IMPACT

The research suggests, then, that media advocacy can be successful not only in increasing news media attention to a public health issue but also in focusing media attention on policy change, rather than on individual behavior change, as the appropriate solution to those health problems. The more important question, of course, is whether media advocacy's impact on news coverage translates into a greater likelihood of policymakers adopting the desired policy changes. The evidence on this point is also mixed; some media advocacy-driven news coverage leads to the desired policy change, while in other cases, policy efforts fail even when the news coverage is supportive. For instance, Harwood et al.'s (2005) analysis examined the correlation between intensity of news coverage and passage or failure of 13 related bills introduced in the Louisiana legislature during the study period; each of the bills dealt with one of four policy goals, including banning minors (18 to 20 years old) from entering bars, increasing taxes on alcohol, "zero tolerance" laws setting lower allowable blood alcohol content (BAC) levels for drivers aged 16 to 20, and laws requiring retailers to collect information about the purchaser of every beer keg to enable identification and punishment of adults who purchase kegs subsequently found to have been used by under-age individuals. Analysis of media attention in connection with each of the 13 bills showed that heightened media attention was associated with *failure* of the bills; when laws were enacted, passage usually occurred when there was little or no media attention. The only exception was the passage of Louisiana's "zero tolerance" law, a measure the state had to pass to remain eligible for federal highway funding (Harwood et al., 2005).

In other instances, however, increased media advocacy-driven news coverage seems to help public health advocates win the passage of health-promoting policy changes. The success of the Berkeley, CA, soda tax coalition, mentioned at the beginning of this chapter, offers one example. Another comes from Niederdeppe et al.'s (2007) analysis of the impact of news coverage on the passage of tobacco control policies to reduce teen smoking in Florida. The researchers determined that a one-unit increase in public exposure to news coverage of Students Working Against Tobacco (SWAT) "was associated with a 94% increase in the odds of counties enacting policy change" (Niederdeppe et al., 2007, p. 49), typically consisting of the passage of tobacco product placement ordinances requiring retailers to put tobacco products behind checkout counters, where they are less visible to youth. Wallack and Dorfman (2001) argue that public health proponents have used media advocacy to support numerous tobacco control policy changes, including increased excise taxes on tobacco, vending machine bans and giving the Food and Drug Administration the power to regulate tobacco.

Media advocacy also was used successfully in the California Violence Prevention Initiative, a five-year comprehensive campaign to reduce youth violence. The first three years of the initiative focused on winning the passage of a ban on the manufacture and sales of "Saturday night specials" – small, inexpensive, low-quality handguns that are easily concealed and often popular with youth. When the initiative began, statistics showed that 80 percent of SNS guns made in the United States came from six Southern California companies and that the guns were "disproportionately involved in violent crime" (Wallack, 1999, p. 845). Media advocacy for the initiative included organizing a 1997 "Caravan for the Junk-Gun Ban" to encourage state legislators to vote for a proposed ban on SNS manufacturing and sales:

> The caravan received print and television news coverage, and, in nearly every case, the coverage reflected the advocates' frame: Personal stories of tragedy were used to highlight the call for a junk-gun ban. Statistics and media bites from the caravan participants appeared in the coverage, whereas the perspective of the opposition was virtually absent. Copies of the newspaper stories were sent to the legislators.
>
> (Wallack, 1999, p. 854)

The California legislature passed the SNS ban, but in September, then-Governor Pete Wilson vetoed the measure. Nonetheless, within a year of the veto, 67 cities and six counties had approved handgun limitation ordinances. Subsequent court decisions upheld these measures (Wallack, 1999). In 1999, the state enacted manufacturing safety standards for handguns; four years later, five of the six original California manufacturers of SNS handguns had declared bankruptcy ("Design Safety," 2013). By March 2013, seven other states had adopted "junk-gun" bans (Eichelberger, 2013).

Other successful media advocacy efforts aimed at public policy change have helped win the passage of national legislation to reduce childhood lead poisoning and to improve the availability of accessible public transportation for individuals with disabilities through the Americans with Disabilities Act of 1990. Disability activists also used media advocacy to change Medicare policy to provide more funding for attendants, enabling more individuals with disabilities to avoid nursing home placement. Media advocacy also helped a coalition of public housing residents, the Henry Horner Mothers Guild, when it sued the Chicago Housing Authority, demanding that the city meet the same maintenance and upkeep standards as other area landlords (Wallack & Dorfman, 2001).

MEDIA ADVOCACY AND CORPORATE POLICY

In some cases, the change public health advocates want does not require public policy change; in these cases, media advocacy efforts are aimed at corporate decision-makers rather than at city councils, state legislatures, or local, state or federal agencies. Here, too, research suggests that media advocates have found success by influencing news coverage of the conflict. For instance, the Dangerous Promises campaign pressured alcohol companies to discontinue advertising that associates alcohol use with sexual success. The coalition argued that while sexist alcohol advertising does not cause domestic violence, advertising messages can contribute to domestic and sexual violence when they treat both alcohol and women as commodities, suggest that women who drink (or who serve drinks to men) are offering themselves for sex, or juxtapose images linking alcohol, violence and sex. Although the advertising problem related primarily to beer and hard liquor advertising, the Wine Institute was the first to change its code of ethics to include many of the requirements suggested by the Dangerous Promises coalition. In Los Angeles and San Francisco, the coalition attempted to buy billboard space for counter-advertisements with slogans like "Hey Bud – Stop Using Our Cans to Sell Yours" and "Bloodweiser, King of Tears – Selling Violence Against Women." When area billboard companies refused to run the counter-ads, the coalition generated significant news media attention to the conflict and the campaign's concerns and goals. The negative publicity created pressure for the alcohol industry groups to change their advertising content, and a year after the intensive media advocacy campaign began, none of the alcohol advertising billboards in San Diego County included images of women. By 1995, the Distilled Spirits Council of the United States (DISCUS) had adopted a code of advertising ethics that reflected all three of the coalition's suggested tenets, including prohibiting ads that depict alcohol as improving sexual prowess, those that associate alcohol with abusive or violent relationships, or ads that degrade or objectify women or minority group members (Woodruff, 1996).

Another successful use of media advocacy in relation to alcohol marketing led to significant changes in the marketing of a fortified wine called Cisco (Jernigan & Wright, 1996). The 20 percent alcohol drink, sold during the early 1990s in bottles similar to wine coolers and often placed near them in stores, came in multiple fruit flavors popular with young people. Cisco's strength led many young people to call it "liquid crack," a label media advocates used to demonstrate how dangerous the product could be. They also noted that one bottle of Cisco packed the punch of five shots of vodka and that, for a 100-pound individual, drinking two bottles of Cisco in an hour could lead to alcohol poisoning ("Surgeon General," 1991). The campaign ultimately led Cisco's manufacturer, Canandaigua Wine Co., to change the drink's packaging and placement, making it more like other fortified wines and less like wine coolers ("Cisco wine," 1991).

Community coalitions also succeeded in using media advocacy to influence beer marketing in the six Sea World marine parks. After Anheuser-Busch, then the world's largest beer manufacturer, bought the Sea World properties, it initially introduced marketing practices that included beer-branded key chains, stuffed animals and candies wrapped to look like beer cans. Media coverage, generated by a community coalition in San Diego that accused Anheuser-Busch of "turning Sea World into 'Beer World,'" persuaded the company to discontinue sales of these items (Jernigan & Wright, 1996, p. 313), although the parks continued to offer free daily beer tastings up until 2009 (Garcia, 2009).

Another example of media advocacy influencing corporate policy without government action comes from the Smokefree Movies campaign, based at the University of California-San Francisco. This campaign, aimed at reducing adolescents' exposure to portrayals of smoking in movies, used paid advertising in the entertainment magazine *Variety*, as well as gaining news coverage of the role movies play in encouraging adolescent smoking. The campaign's impact has not been evaluated formally, but in May 2007, the Motion Picture Association of American announced that it would revise the movie rating system to include smoking as a factor that might lead to an R rating (Abroms & Maibach, 2008). And in March 2015, Walt Disney Studios Chairman Bob Iger announced that he would prohibit smoking in all Disney movies with a PG-13 or lower rating, unless the smoking was "historically pertinent" for the film (Kelley, 2015, para. 1).

MEDIA ADVOCACY AND HEALTH OUTCOMES

Media advocates focus on policy change rather than motivating individual behavior change directly, but in many cases the long-term goal is to reduce the number of individuals engaging in unhealthy behaviors and/or to increase the number engaging in healthy behaviors. Most often, success in achieving the policy goal has the desired effect. However, it is important to note that advocates must choose policy goals carefully to ensure that achievement of the goals will, in fact, translate into better health outcomes.

The media advocacy campaign to encourage the passage of tobacco control ordinances in Florida provides a case in point. In that case, analysis revealed that media advocacy efforts led to increased coverage of Students Working Against Tobacco, and counties where exposure to SWAT stories was greater were significantly more likely to pass tobacco product placement ordinances (TPPOs), meaning tobacco products would be available only behind retail store counters. Unfortunately, although smoking rates were lower in counties with TPPOs, the difference was not statistically significant, suggesting that TPPOs are not an effective method of reducing youth smoking. Niederdeppe and colleagues (2007) note that tobacco manufacturers usually do not oppose restrictions on youth access to cigarettes, perhaps because such ordinances help frame tobacco use as an adult practice, unacceptable only for youth; in effect, this may make smoking even more attractive to teens who wish to seem more grown up. In addition, focusing on attempts to reduce youth access to tobacco may draw attention away from the need for comprehensive tobacco use reduction among adults as well as youth. In any case, the message for those planning to use media advocacy for non-tobacco-related issues is to make certain the policy goal being pursued has been shown to be effective in supporting the desired health outcomes.

MEDIA ADVOCACY CAN WORK BOTH WAYS

The term "media advocacy," as it is commonly used, refers to "strategic use of mass media to advance a social or policy initiative" (Wallack, 1994, p. 424); whether the media advocates want changes in government policy or in corporate practices, they believe the change will improve health outcomes. Unfortunately, however, the policy changes some organizations pursue may be misguided, even to the point of endangering the health of individuals or entire population groups. For instance, according to its website, the association Vaccination Liberation includes in its mission the "repeal of all compulsory vaccination laws nationwide" ("Vaccination Liberation," n.d., para. 1). Similarly, the International Medical Council on Vaccination describes itself as a group of "qualified medical professionals" whose goals include legislative guarantees of the right to refuse vaccination ("About," 2011). Both groups are involved in efforts to influence media coverage of the vaccination issue, both to encourage elimination of vaccine mandates and to encourage individual parents to forgo immunization of their children. While it is difficult to know whether either group has employed formal media advocacy campaigns, it is clear that their goals conflict with the recommendations of both the American Academy of Pediatrics (2015) and the Centers for Disease Control's Advisory Committee on Immunization Practices ("General Recommendations on Immunization," 2011). Thus, from the perspective of some of the most widely respected health organizations in the United States, the successful achievement of these groups' policy goals would have very negative health effects.

It is also worth noting that organizations may share health outcome goals (e.g., fewer adolescent pregnancies or fewer gun injuries and deaths) while advocating dramatically different policy goals for achieving those outcomes (e.g., abstinence-only school sex education curricula vs. school-based distribution of condoms or other contraceptives; stricter controls on access to firearms vs. allowing or even encouraging possession of concealed weapons in churches, schools and workplaces). It is essential that media advocates and the journalists with whom they work rigorously investigate the policy changes being proposed to ensure, as far as possible, that successful media advocacy campaigns result in *better* health environments for those affected, rather than exacerbating existing health problems.

NOTE

1 The reference to "upstream" conditions reflects a metaphor often used by public health practitioners. They argue that emphasizing individual behavior change to solve health problems is like waiting until people begin drowning in a river and then rescuing them by throwing life preservers or encouraging the victims to swim. Focusing on public policy, in contrast, requires the health advocate to go "upstream" to identify – and correct – the conditions that cause victims to fall into the river in the first place.

References

About. (2011, January 4). Retrieved July 2, 2015 from www.vaccinationcouncil.org/about/.

Abroms, L.C. & Maibach, E.W. (2008). The Effectiveness of Mass Communication to Change Public Behavior. *Annual Review of Public Health, 29*(1), 219–234. http://doi.org/10.1146/annurev.publhealth.29.020907.090824.

American Academy of Pediatrics. (2015, January 23). American Academy of Pediatrics Urges Parents to Vaccinate Children to Protect Against Measles. Retrieved July 2, 2015 from https://www.aap.org/en-us/about-the-aap/aap-press-room/pages/American-Academy-of-Pediatrics-Urges-Parents-to-Vaccinate-Children-to-Protect-Against-Measles.aspx.

Cisco Wine To Get New Packaging. (1991, February 9). *Washington Post.* Washington, DC. Retrieved July 1, 2015 from www.washingtonpost.com/archive/politics/1991/02/09/cisco-wine-to-get-new-packaging/1647bfaf-e3ba-44ff-af08-b02aeeeabfd5/.

Design Safety Standards Policy Summary. (2013, December 1). Retrieved July 1, 2015 from http://smartgunlaws.org/gun-design-safety-standards-policy-summary/.

Eichelberger, E. (2013, March 5). Dem Bill Would Ban "Saturday Night Specials." Retrieved July 1, 2015 from www.motherjones.com/mojo/2013/03/luis-gutierrez-junk-gun-ban-saturday-night-special.

Garcia, J. (2009, January 6). It's Last Call for Long-standing Tradition of Free Beer Tasting at SeaWorld Orlando, Companies Other Parks. Retrieved July 1, 2015 from http://articles.orlandosentinel.com/2009-01-06/news/busch06_1_busch-seaworld-orlando-anheuser.

General Recommendations on Immunization. (2011, January 28). Retrieved July 2, 2015 from www.cdc.gov/mmwr/preview/mmwrhtml/rr6002a1.htm.

Granner, M.L., Sharpe, P.A., Burroughs, E.L., Fields, R. & Hallenbeck, J. (2010). Newspaper Content Analysis in Evaluation of a Community-based Participatory Project to Increase Physical Activity. *Health Education Research, 25*(4), 656–667. http://doi.org/10.1093/her/cyp049.

Harwood, E.M., Witson, J.C., Fan, D.P. & Wagenaar, A.C. (2005). Media Advocacy and Underage Drinking Policies: A Study of Louisiana News Media From 1994 Through 2003. *Health Promotion Practice, 6*(3), 246–257. http://doi.org/10.1177/1524839905276079.

Holder, H.D. & Treno, A.J. (1997). Media Advocacy in Community Prevention: News as a Means to Advance Policy Change. *Addiction, 92*(6s1), 189–200.

Jernigan, D.H. & Wright, P.A. (1996). Media Advocacy: Lessons from Community Experiences. *Journal of Public Health Policy, 17*(3), 306–330.

Kelley, S. (2015, March 12). Disney CEO to "Absolutely Prohibit" Smoking in Films Made for Kids. Retrieved July 1, 2015 from http://variety.com/2015/film/news/disney-ceo-to-absolutely-prohibit-smoking-in-films-made-for-kids-1201451616/.

Knight, H. (2014, November 7). Why Berkeley Passed a Soda Tax and S.F. Didn't. Retrieved June 23, 2015 from www.sfgate.com/bayarea/article/Why-Berkeley-passed-a-soda-tax-and-S-F-didn-t-5879757.php.

Lochner, T. (2015, May 19). Berkeley Soda Tax: First Month's Take, $116,000. Retrieved June 23, 2015 from www.mercurynews.com/my-town/ci_28141086/berkeley-soda-tax-first-months-take-116-000.

Niederdeppe, J., Farrelly, M.C. & Wenter, D. (2007). Media Advocacy, Tobacco Control Policy Change and Teen Smoking in Florida. *Tobacco Control, 16*(1), 47–52. http://doi.org/10.1136/tc.2005.015289.

Quintero, F. (2014, December 15). 5 Lessons in Media Advocacy from Battles with Big Soda. Retrieved June 22, 2015 from www.bmsg.org/blog/5-media-advocacy-lessons-from-big-soda-battles.

Rock, M.J., McIntyre, L., Persaud, S.A. & Thomas, K.L. (2011). A Media Advocacy Intervention Linking Health Disparities and Food Insecurity. *Health Education Research*, 26(6), 948–960. http://doi.org/10.1093/her/cyr043.

Schooler, C., Sundar, S.S. & Flora, J. (1996). Effects of the Stanford Five-City Project Media Advocacy Program. *Health Education & Behavior*, 23(3), 346–364. http://doi.org/10.1177/109019819602300306.

Stead, M., Hastings, G. & Eadie, D. (2002). The Challenge of Evaluating Complex Interventions: A Framework for Evaluating Media Advocacy. *Health Education Research*, 17(3), 351–364. http://doi.org/10.1093/her/17.3.351.

Stillman, F.A., Cronin, K.A., Evans, W.D. & Ulasevich, A. (2001). Can Media Advocacy Influence Newspaper Coverage of Tobacco: Measuring the Effectiveness of the American Stop Smoking Intervention Study's (ASSIST) Media Advocacy Strategies. *Tobacco Control*, 10(2), 137–144. http://doi.org/10.1136/tc.10.2.137.

Surgeon General Calls Potent Wine a Threat. (1991, January 10). *New York Times*. New York City. Retrieved July 1, 2015 from www.nytimes.com/1991/01/10/us/surgeon-general-calls-potent-wine-a-threat.html.

Vaccination Liberation. (n.d.). Retrieved July 2, 2015 from www.vaclib.org/.

Wallack, L. (1994). Media Advocacy: A Strategy for Empowering People and Communities. *Journal of Public Health Policy*, 15(4), 420–436.

Wallack, L. (1999). The California Violence Prevention Initiative: Advancing Policy to Ban Saturday Night Specials. *Health Education & Behavior*, 26(6), 841–857. http://doi.org/10.1177/109019819902600607.

Wallack, L. & Dorfman, L. (1996). Media Advocacy: A Strategy for Advancing Policy and Promoting Health. *Health Education & Behavior*, 23(3), 293–317.

Wallack, L. & Dorfman, L. (2001). Putting Policy into Health Communication. In *Public Communication Campaigns* (3rd edn, pp. 389–399). Thousand Oaks, CA. Retrieved July 1, 2015 from https://books.google.com/books?hl=en&lr=&id=Dft0AwAAQBAJ&oi=fnd&pg=PA389&dq=Putting+policy+into+health+communication:+the+role+of+media+advocacy.&ots=H5n_QWMk6J&sig=XsEZn3tx-LQbwUAR-ubSDl6oIbU.

Woodruff, K. (1996). Alcohol Advertising and Violence Against Women: A Media Advocacy Case Study. *Health Education & Behavior*, 23(3), 330–345. http://doi.org/10.1177/109019819602300305.

CHAPTER 15

BIG SPENDERS IN THE MARKETPLACE OF IDEAS: POLITICAL ISSUE ADVERTISING EFFECTS ON HEALTH POLICY

In January 2014, the Florida Supreme Court ruled in favor of proponents of a state constitutional amendment that would have made the use and distribution of medical marijuana legal in the state. In a split decision, the court rejected the initiative opponents' claim that the amendment's wording included too many loopholes and would enable anyone willing to fake a "debilitating" medical condition to obtain marijuana. At the time of the state Supreme Court ruling, polls showed the amendment was likely to pass with the required 60 percent of the vote. The *Miami Herald* reported that a recent Public Policy Polling survey had shown that 65 percent of voters were likely to vote in favor of the amendment; other polls put support for the measure as high as 82 percent (Caputo & Klas, 2014).

Later surveys, taken during the spring and summer of 2014, suggested that as many as 90 percent of Floridians supported the legalization of medical marijuana in general, but by October, different surveys, focusing on the specific language of the proposed amendment, produced widely varying estimates of support. A poll sponsored by the University of North Florida suggested that 67 percent of voters approved of the measure, but a *Miami Herald*/University of Florida survey concluded that the amendment was likely to fail, with only 48 percent of voter support (Pollick, 2014).

In the final two months before the election, both proponents and opponents of the amendment turned to advertising, most of it on television, to win voters to their side. Ad spending was not balanced, however. The primary opposition group, Drug Free Florida, outspent United For Care, which had gotten the amendment onto the ballot, by a ratio of 10-to-1, pouring most of its $6.34 million war chest into advertising; $5.5 million of the money came from Republican casino owner Sheldon Adelson, a Las Vegas, NV, resident whom *Forbes* magazine identified as the tenth richest person in the world (Pollick, 2014). His donation allowed Drug Free Florida to spend $5 million on "Vote No on 2" ads, such as one stating, "They don't call it the Drug-Dealer Protection Act, but they should" (Pollick, 2014, para. 17). The ad claimed that the amendment would allow felons, including drug dealers, to dispense medical marijuana with no medical training; in reality, the amendment required the Florida Department of Health to develop regulations regarding caregivers, patients, doctors, retailers and growers.

United For Care had far less money for advertising, having spent much of the $4 million it had raised getting the proposal onto the ballot (Pollick, 2014). Instead of focusing on expensive television ad buys, United For Care turned to digital banner and video advertising carefully targeted to people deemed to be the measure's most likely supporters and those most likely to be persuadable. In particular, they targeted senior citizens likely to be open to the pro-medical marijuana arguments, based on data modeling by United For Care's media strategy consultants. The digital advertising was effective, according to a post-election day survey. Among those who saw the online ads, 65 percent voted in favor of Amendment 2; among those who did not see the ads, only 53 percent voted for the measure. Among seniors, who represented one-third of those who recalled seeing the online ads, 65 percent voted in favor of the amendment. ("Digital Advertising," 2014).

Figure 15.1: Don't Let It Go To Pot Campaign Billboard

Ultimately, however, the measure failed. Despite its effectiveness, the digital advertising, even combined with some pro-amendment spending for television ads, could not overcome the torrent of "No on 2" television ads. "Yes" votes on Amendment 2 fell two percentage points short of the 60 percent approval required for passage (Pollick, 2014).

Florida's battle over the legalization of medical marijuana illustrates another way in which mass media may be used intentionally in the attempt to change (or maintain) health policy. Political issue advertising has become a major element now used by health advocates and their opponents to gain leverage in the policy process. In some cases, as in the case of Florida's Amendment 2, this advertising plays a direct role in determining policy through building voter support for or opposition to health-related ballot initiatives. In other cases, issue advertising may attempt to influence local, state or federal policy-makers by building public opinion in support of (or opposition to) a specific health policy and/or by encouraging constituents to contact their representatives in an attempt to influence their votes. Such ads also may serve to signal an interest group's "willingness to reward legislators who help it and punish those who don't" (Hall & Anderson, 2012, p. 222). Increasingly, nonprofit political and advocacy groups use messages carefully crafted as "issue" ads to influence political office election outcomes, a particularly disturbing practice because such groups are not required to identify their donors; in the wake of the U.S. Supreme Court's Citizens United case, these donors may include not only individuals but also corporations and unions, and there are no limits on the amounts of money they can contribute (Bogardus, 2012).

How Much Health Issue Advertising?

First, it is important to define issue advertising and to distinguish it (to the extent possible) from advertising for products or for political candidates. Simply put, issue advertising is meant to sell ideas rather than products or services. It may overlap, to some extent, with image advertising, the purpose of which is to improve audience members' opinions of a corporation or organization. However, the primary purpose of issue advertising is to sway audience members toward a particular viewpoint on a public policy issue.

During election periods (and sometimes between them), however, the line between issue advertising and campaign advertising can be blurred because issue advertising can include references to specific political leaders. Thus, organizations may use issue advertising to reward their political allies by praising them for their contribution to a popular political action, such as voting for legislation widely supported among the target audience; conversely, organizations may attempt to punish (and ultimately defeat) their political enemies by linking them to unpopular political decisions. So long as the ads steer clear of statements that clearly urge support for or opposition to a candidate for public office, especially in the run-up to an election, they are considered to be issue advertising (Baye, 2014). For instance, a *Huffington Post* review of national nonprofit organizations' issue advertising between the 2012 election and mid-2013 showed that 63 percent named a candidate up for re-election in 2014 (Blumenthal, 2013).

Two studies of legislative issue advertising in the Washington, DC, media during the 107th and 108th Congresses (2001 through 2002 and 2003 through 2004, respectively) showed a phenomenal increase in issue advertising between these two sessions. The studies, conducted by the Annenberg Public Policy Center, revealed that during the 107th Congress, organizations spent $105 million on television and print advertising in the Washington area alone. During the 108th Congress, that total had nearly quadrupled, to $404 million; spending on television ads alone rose from $41 million for the 107th Congress to $225 million for the 108th Congress (Falk, 2003, 2005). In both analyses, health care issues ranked second in terms of spending. It is worth noting that in both analyses, the health category excluded advertising on some health topics. For the analysis of 107th Congress ad spending, the health category excluded advertising related to abortion/family planning ($6.05 million) and tobacco ($1.53 million); the analysis for the 108th Congress excluded spending for ads related to tort reform ($5.09 million), gun control ($3.02 million), substance abuse ($1.06 million) and abortion ($700,000).

A Kaiser Family Foundation (KFF) study of health-related political advertising and insurance advertising during the first nine-and-a-half months of 2014 suggests that spending on health issue advertising has continued to rise. The study, which included local TV ads in 210 markets and ads from 90 national broadcast and cable networks, showed that health-related political advertising expenditures totaled $303 million; in comparison, spending for health insurance advertising, whether or not it mentioned the ACA, totaled $482 million. Of the 592,092 political issue ads, about 45 percent dealt with something other than the ACA. Of the ads that were about the ACA, only 8 percent praised the program; fully half of the political ads were anti-"Obamacare" spots (DiJulio et al., 2014).

The study showed that health-related political issue ads accounted for more than one in every four (26%) political spots identified in the study. Perhaps not surprisingly, all Republican ads mentioning the ACA were negative, as were 22 percent of Democrats' ads that mentioned the ACA. Among Democrats, health-related political spots were much more likely to mention Medicare (46%), usually in the context of accusing Republicans of trying to restructure Medicare and/or require seniors to pay more for prescription drugs. Among Republicans, 84 percent mentioned the ACA in a negative way, while 16 percent mentioned Medicare. Americans For Prosperity, a right-wing group co-founded by conservative billionaires David and Charles Koch, paid for 7 percent of the anti-ACA ads, including two ads attacking then-Democratic gubernatorial candidate Charlie Crist; the two ads, which cost an estimated $2.3 million and $2.7 million, respectively, aired about 9,000 times in total (DiJulio et al., 2014).

None of these studies examined the increasingly important category of online issue advertising. During the 2009 Congressional debate over the ACA, pro-health reform groups took advantage of the viral spread of the term "death panels" (coined by former vice presidential candidate Sarah Palin) to target online advertising to individuals searching for that phrase or related terms on Google. The ads linked audiences to web pages providing pro-health care reform information. In September 2009, the *Los Angeles Times* quoted Google's director of political advertising noting that in one week, 97 organizations had sought to buy Google search ads related to the health care reform debate (Wallsten, 2009). Unfortunately, no one yet appears to have published any analyses of political issue advertising via the Internet.

HEALTH ISSUE ADS' IMPACT ON PUBLIC OPINION AND INVOLVEMENT

Regardless of the medium in which it appears, health issue advertising is generally intended to influence public opinion, citizens' behavior and, ultimately, policy decisions. In the case of ballot initiatives, such as the

Florida medical marijuana legalization proposal, voters themselves may be the policy decision-makers; thus, organizations on both sides of the issue will attempt to influence their attitudes and their votes on the issue. For instance, during the November 2014 election in which Florida voters failed to support medical marijuana legalization, voters in Oregon and Alaska voted to legalize recreational marijuana use. In Oregon, pro-legalization advocates raised about $4 million, compared to less than $200,000 for opponents, enabling proponents to develop a significant advertising campaign while opponents "largely had to rely on a word-of-mouth campaign" (Crombie, 2014, para. 12). In California, physicians successfully fought Proposition 45, which would have required drug testing for doctors, and health insurance-backed groups defeated Proposition 46, which would have required special approval for insurance rate increases; collectively, opponents of the two measures spent almost $60 million on TV advertising, outspending proponents of the measures by seven to one (Whyte, 2014). Opposition from food companies such as Pepsi and Monsanto helped defeat Colorado and Oregon measures requiring labeling of genetically modified foods. In Oregon, opponents spent more than $21 million, compared to supporters' $8 million, making the measure the costliest in the state's history (Brence, 2014). In Colorado, supporters of GMO labeling had raised less than $500,000, but the opposing campaign had spent $6.8 million by mid-October and had $4.1 million left in its coffers. Monsanto Company alone contributed $4.7 million to the anti-labeling campaign (Kuntz, 2014).

However, advertising spending did not always determine the outcome of these ballot initiatives. Monsanto and other agribusiness companies spent more than $7.9 million fighting a Maui County, Hawaii, ban on growing genetically modified plants; although opponents had spent less than $80,000, the measure passed (Chao, 2014; Kerr, 2014).

Even when citizens themselves do not make the policy decisions, interest groups still seek to influence public opinion and citizen behavior as a first step toward affecting the actions of legislators. In most cases, the organizations sponsoring issue ads cannot reach every single citizen; even if they did, most organizations recognize that some citizens already may hold strongly entrenched opinions that conflict with the organization's position on the issue, while others are simply not interested enough in the issue to take action. Thus, advertising to these individuals likely would be a waste of resources. Hall and Anderson (2012)

471

argue that most advocacy organizations target their advertising to people who are already supporters of their position or who are, at least, open to persuasion – especially those who are concerned about the topic and more likely to be politically involved, including voting, writing letters to the editor and participating in other political activities. For instance, an analysis of ads related to the 2003 Medicare Prescription Drug and Modernization Act (MMA) showed that the average number of TV ads that ran in each state was positively related to the number of prescriptions written for people aged 65 and older in that state. Both proponents and opponents of the bill, which provided a prescription drug benefit for Medicare recipients, focused their advertising efforts on states with the greatest numbers of senior citizens (Hall & Anderson, 2012).

The extent to which a company or interest group has a presence in a particular location also affects which audiences they will target with issue advertising. For instance, unions are more likely to focus their advertising campaigns in areas where they have many or larger chapters; corporations tend to focus on locations where they have headquarters offices or manufacturing facilities. "In such areas, issue ads should prove more effective in that a subset of citizens will have a predisposition – perhaps a self-interested incentive – to contact their representatives" (Hall & Anderson, 2012, p. 228). Data on issue advertising on the MMA support this contention, in that the concentration of MMA issue ads was higher in states with greater numbers of sites associated with the organizations sponsoring MMA ads.

Interviews with representatives from interest groups involved in lobbying for or against then-President Bill Clinton's health care reform proposal also confirmed that organizations advertised more heavily in areas in which they had greater numbers of members, employees, retirees, stockholders and others with a connection to the organization, especially when those individuals lived in what were considered key congressional districts. In addition, they bought advertising space or time in media most likely to reach "involved" Americans, including those who were registered to vote, who attended meetings, who wrote letters to the newspapers or to public officials, and/or who made political contributions (Goldstein, 1999).

These targeted advertising strategies do have an impact on public involvement in health care issue debates, as illustrated by the success of the "Harry and Louise" ad campaign sponsored by the Health Insurance

Association of American (HIAA) during the 1993/1994 debate over the Clinton health care reform proposal. The now iconic ads featured a middle-aged suburban couple shown sitting at their kitchen table "sometime in the future," after the hypothetical passage of the Health Security Act, glumly comparing their current health insurance coverage to the plan they had before. Through the voice-over, the ads argued that the passage of the Health Security Act would limit Americans' health insurance coverage options to those selected by "government bureaucrats." With melancholy music playing in the background, Louise complains, "Having choices we don't like is no choice at all." Unlike most political ads of the time, the campaign used the story-telling techniques more common in ads for coffee, laundry detergent and other consumer products (Goldsteen et al., 2001).

The $14 million "Harry and Louise" campaign was part of a systematic strategy by the HIAA to turn public opinion against the "health alliances" proposed by the HSA, which HIAA members believed would exclude them from providing health insurance to most citizens (Goldsteen et al., 2001). The HIAA had reason to be concerned, given that health care reform had been a major provision of Clinton's successful campaign for the presidency, and polls at the time showed that the majority of Americans, even those who had good health insurance themselves, were concerned about the number of uninsured Americans. During the early 1990s, strong majorities of the public supported the development of a system that would provide health insurance coverage to all Americans, regardless of age or income (Jacobs, 1993).

Through the "Harry and Louise" ads, the HIAA promoted seven separate messages:

1) Government involvement in health care would limit the number of health plan choices available to consumers.
2) While everyone wants universal coverage, government involvement would limit health care spending, meaning that consumers might not be able to get all the health services they need.
3) Insurance companies can ensure coverage of people who change jobs or lose their jobs without government involvement.
4) The HSA would increase the number of government employees, increase costs and coerce the public to make health choices they might not want.

5) Not everyone is equally deserving of health insurance coverage at the same cost, and the HSA would force deserving citizens to pay more to cover the expenses of the undeserving.

6) People who already have good insurance coverage deserve to have better coverage, making taxes on health benefits "unfair."

7) "Better" health care reform means "private insurance, no government-run health care, no government-imposed spending limits, and no tax on benefits" (Goldsteen et al., 2001, p. 1330).

The HIAA reported that nearly half a million people called the 800 number included at the end of the "Harry and Louise" ads, asking for more information or offering comments and personal stories about their health care experiences. Of those, the HIAA estimated that 45,000 made calls to Congress members or wrote letters, either to their representatives or to the media (West et al., 1996).

Researchers disagree, however, about how much impact the "Harry and Louise" campaign actually had on public opinion regarding health care reform. Some argue that the ads weakened public support for universal health care and increased concerns about government control of health care (Goldsteen et al., 2001), while others contend that the impact was indirect, operating through the ads' influence on news coverage and Congress members' perceptions of public opinion (Jamieson et al., 1995; West et al., 1996).

One study of changes in public opinion about health care reform during and after the "Harry and Louise" campaign suggests that, in fact, the campaign may have influenced public opinion, at least in Oklahoma. The researchers argue that there were two phases of the campaign, which initially suggested agreement with the goal of universal health care but questioned the specifics of the plan. In the later phase, the campaign questioned the assumption that everyone deserves health care. Analysis of data from monthly public opinion surveys in Oklahoma showed that, during the year before the "Harry and Louise" campaign began, the public generally supported universal health coverage, and that support seemed to be growing. It continued to grow in the first half of the campaign, during which the ads suggested that universal health coverage was an accepted goal. However, after the ads began to include messages questioning the idea that everyone had a right to health care, "support dropped to the pre-broadcast level and remained at that level for the remainder of the survey period" (Golds-teen et al., 2001, p. 1339).

Survey data suggested the same pattern in public opinion regarding the importance of a state health system providing health insurance for those without private coverage; during the first phase of the "Harry and Louise" campaign support increased, but after the turning point in the campaign it dropped, eventually declining to pre-campaign levels. Okla-homa citizens' support for limitations on health coverage based on an individual's behavior (e.g., smoking, drug abuse, being overweight) or resources (being unemployed, being on welfare) declined during the early part of the "Harry and Louise" campaign; however, as the cam-paign went on, support for these limitations increased again, returning to pre-campaign levels. The authors acknowledge that they cannot say definitively that the "Harry and Louise" campaign caused these changes in public opinion. They did not track other political advertising or measure the effects of changes in news coverage of health care reform; nonetheless, they argue that the consistency of the associations between the campaign's messages and changes in public opinion "are highly sug-gestive of a campaign effect" (Goldsteen et al., 2001, p. 1346).

More recently, issue advertising about the Affordable Care Act (ACA or "Obamacare") appears to have played a role in widespread public dis-approval of the law – despite the fact that most Americans support all major provisions of the law except the individual mandate requiring people to buy insurance or pay a penalty (Brodie et al., 2010; "Results," 2012). According to a survey by the Kaiser Family Foundation in July 2015, 43 percent of American adults now hold a favorable view of the law, an increase of ten percentage points since the law's lowest point, in November 2013. Disapproval of the law also has dropped recently, with 40 percent of adults polled in July 2015 reporting negative views of the law; 62 percent of Americans said they approved of the recent Supreme Court decision to uphold individual health insurance subsidies in all states ("Kaiser Health Tracking Poll," 2015).

Nonetheless, substantial segments of the population – especially Republicans – still disapprove of the law and believe it should be repealed or dramatically scaled back. In March 2015, five years after the ACA's passage, 46 percent of American adults, but only 16 percent of Republicans, said the government should move forward with imple-menting the law or even expand it. Among Republicans, however, 13 percent said the law should be scaled back, and 61 percent favored wholesale repeal (DiJulio et al., 2015).

Although little scholarly research has examined directly the impact of issue advertising on attitudes toward the ACA, some have blamed the huge imbalance of negative versus positive advertising about the ACA for continued opposition to the law (Dalen et al., 2015). Between the law's passage in March 2010 and April 2015, opponents of the law spent $418 million on anti-ACA ads, compared with only $27 million spent promoting the law. Opponents had outspent advocates by a ratio of 15-to-1, and anti-"Obamacare" ad campaigns were continuing to be developed (Reston, 2015).

Given the overwhelming prominence of anti- versus pro-ACA ads, it is somewhat surprising that a September 2014 poll of registered voters showed that nearly a quarter (23%) reported seeing equal numbers of pro- and anti-ACA ads. One in five, however, said they had seen more negative than positive ads, while only 7 percent said they had seen more ads supporting the ACA than ads criticizing the law. Nearly half of those polled, however, didn't remember seeing any ads mentioning the ACA (47%). Voters were more likely to report seeing anti-ACA ads when they lived in states that had competitive Senate races in fall 2014. However, the poll results suggested that opposition to the ACA was not the primary factor influencing greater Republican enthusiasm for voting in 2014; only 3 percent of voters mentioned the ACA as the primary reason they were planning to vote (Hamel et al., 2014), suggesting that perhaps the anti-ACA advertising has had less effect on public opinion than might have been anticipated.

One study of health care reform issue advertisements suggests that these ads influenced the audiences' perceptions of the importance of health care reform relative to other public issues (e.g., the economy, the budget deficit, terrorism). In addition, the issue ads influenced perceptions of political actors, with pro-health reform ads linked to more positive evaluations of the job President Obama was doing on health care. The pro-health reform issue ads had the greatest effects on Republicans with low political knowledge, who were more likely to express support after exposure to these ads. However, the ads had no significant effects on Democrats, regardless of knowledge level, or on high-knowledge Republicans. The authors note, however, that in this naturalistic experiment, the anti-health reform ads did not include harsh attacks either on

President Obama or on health care reform. Nonetheless, the researchers concluded that "issue ads could influence the policy-making process indirectly by influencing the importance of health care as a policy issue" (Bergan & Risner, 2012, p. 536).

ISSUE ADVERTISING AND NEWS COVERAGE

Some scholars have argued that, rather than directly influencing public opinion, issue advertising's primary effect is indirect, channeled through news coverage of the issue. Several researchers have concluded, for instance, that the "Harry and Louise" ads garnered huge amounts of news media attention, and it was the news coverage, rather than the ads themselves, that led the Clinton administration and members of Congress to believe that the ads were turning public opinion against the HSA proposals (Jamieson et al., 1995; West et al., 1996). In one interview, Ben Goddard, head of the media consulting firm that developed the "Harry and Louise" ads, said the advertising was targeted to Washington, DC, and New York, where it would most effectively reach Congress members themselves and the major media organizations covering the health care reform debate. This strategy worked, with most major newspapers and television networks running stories about the "Harry and Louise" ads, including a front-page story in the *New York Times*. Ironically, the Clinton administration's effort to discredit the ads worked against them because it provided the sort of conflict the news media are most likely to cover (West et al., 1996).

Research by the Annenberg Center for Public Policy concluded that the "Harry and Louise" ads were not effective in communicating to the public their specific messages about problems with the Clinton health care reform plan. Analysis of data from surveys in which individuals were asked if they had seen any health care reform-related ads showed no significant relationships between having seen the ads and "believing the Clinton program would increase taxes, create another large and inefficient government bureaucracy, cost too much, limit choice of doctors or hospitals or pay for legal abortions" (West et al., 1996, p. 55). Even in the study of Oklahoma citizens' changing views on the health care system, Goldsteen et al. (2001) found that neither having cable television nor living in the state's major media markets, which would have increased exposure to the "Harry and Louise" campaign, was associated with public opinion change. However, legislators *believed* the ads were effective and that the public was turning against the HSA's major provisions; ultimately, this led to the failure of the HSA (Jamieson et al., 1995).

In addition to the direct and indirect routes of influence described by other researchers, Brodie (2001) suggests an additional mechanism through which the "Harry and Louise" campaign (and political advertising in general) may affect public policy debates: by framing discussion of the policy around specific issues.

> In effect, the ads tell everyone involved what is important to talk about and focus on, serving as an agenda setter for the policy discussion and political debate; this then enters the public arena and frames the way the public hears discussion about the issue. This framing of the issue then helps to define and influence public opinion on the topic.
>
> (Brodie, 2001, p. 1356)

This framing effect may represent the most important long-term impact of the "Harry and Louise" campaign because it has influenced the way other interest groups have responded to health policy proposals since the failure of the HSA. Brodie (2001) notes that public debate about the 1999 Patients' Bill of Rights legislation initially focused on whether the bill would increase the cost of health insurance; however, public support for the Patients' Bill of Rights was most affected by the suggestion that the passage of the bill might cause employers to drop insurance coverage for their workers. Opponents of the bill subsequently launched ads that focused on this idea: not that health insurance premiums would increase but that increased costs would lead employers to discontinue covering their workers.

Advertising criticizing the Patients' Bill of Rights seems to have affected the tone of news coverage of that bill. Rabinowitz (2010) analyzed newspaper coverage of managed care regulation in five states that were the target of July 1999 advertising campaigns sponsored by the Health Benefits Coalition, the Business Roundtable and the American Association of Health Plans (AAHP); collectively, these groups spent more than $7 million on advertising and public relations campaigns designed to increase opposition to the bill in Michigan, Minnesota,

Ohio, Texas and Washington, each of which had Republican senators running for re-election in 2000. The analysis compared coverage to that of newspapers in five states matched to the "treatment" for similarity in terms of geographic proximity, state size, state demographic and health sector characteristics and political variables.

The data showed that news coverage in the states targeted by the advertising campaigns was more critical of the Patients' Bill of Rights, with 13 percent of comparison state stories and 28 percent of treatment state stories deemed negative toward managed care regulation. In the states where the ad campaigns ran, news coverage was more likely to mention possible negative outcomes of the Patients' Bill of Rights, including increasing health insurance premiums and the number of people without insurance. The differences in coverage on these specific issues, which were mentioned in the ads, were statistically significant. News stories in treatment states were also more likely than those in comparison states to make references to increases in government bur-eaucracy, but the differences on this issue, which was not specifically addressed in the anti-Bill of Rights ads, were not statistically significant (Rabinowitz, 2010).

The frames used in news coverage also differed among states targeted by the ad campaigns versus those not included in the campaigns. In states where the ads ran, newspapers were twice as likely to use a "worker as victim" frame, focusing on how the passage of the bill might nega-tively affect working people, while comparison state newspaper stories were significantly more likely to include a "HMO enrollee as victim" frame. The messages included in the ads were more likely to be men-tioned in news coverage in states running the ad campaigns. "Readers were exposed to different perspectives and arguments about managed care regulation depending on whether the newspapers they read were published in states that were targeted by extensive political advertising campaigns" (Rabinowitz, 2010, p. 787).

Using a similar strategy, Rabinowitz's dissertation (2012) examined the impact of issue advertising on newspaper coverage of the Affordable Care Act in four states (Arkansas, Connecticut, Maine and Nebraska) in which an alliance of national medical societies ran an anti-ACA ad cam-paign during December 2009; news coverage of the bill in these states was compared to coverage in four states matched to the "treatment" states in terms of demographic, political and health-related characteristics but where the ad campaign did not run. The results showed no statistically significant difference in coverage or framing of the ACA debate, regardless of whether the ad campaign did or did not run in that state. He argues that the most likely explanation for this finding is that the physician group's ads simply ran too late in the debate, when media framing of the issue already had been set.

Issue Advertising and Election Outcomes

As noted earlier, federal and state laws in the United States make a distinction between "issue advertising," in which organizations may argue about the merits of a particular policy, and "campaign advertising," which is intended to encourage citizens to vote for or against a candidate for political office. Issue ads, which are supposed to be focused on informing or persuading the public about policy issues, can mention office holders, but only in the context of encouraging citizens to express their views about the policy issue to that official; these ads are not supposed to encourage or discourage votes for an individual (Baye, 2014; Blumenthal, 2013). Nonetheless, many nonprofit groups have used issue advertising in their attempts to influence public opinion about political leaders who currently hold office and who may be up for re-election. The difference may be important because nonprofit organizations and political parties need not disclose who donated the money to pay for issue advertising, meaning that the public never know which corporations, individuals or other organizations are paying for issue ads (Kotch, 2014; Mears, 2012). For instance, a *Huffington Post* analysis of issue advertising that mentioned individual Congress members between the 2012 election and June 2013 revealed that nearly two-thirds "targeted a candidate up for reelection in 2014" (Blumenthal, 2013, para. 4).

Although some political communication specialists express skepticism about the impact of political advertising (Liasson, 2012), there is evidence that campaign advertising – which may include "issue ads" that single out specific politicians for blame or praise – does have an effect. For instance, a study that examined the impact of exposure to Republican- and Democrat-sponsored campaign ads during the 2004 presidential and Senate elections showed that seeing Democratic ads led to more favorable evaluations of Democratic presidential candidate John Kerry, while seeing more Republican ads lowered evaluations of Kerry. There was no impact, however, on evaluations of then-President George Bush (Franz & Ridout, 2007). The same pattern held in voter choices for Senate candidates, with greater exposure to Democratic ads associated with a greater preference for Democratic candidates and more exposure to Republican ads linked to support for Republican candidates. The data, the researchers conclude, "provide strong evidence that ads influence people's evaluations of candidates and their candidate preferences" (Franz & Ridout, 2007, p. 476).

Unfortunately, little research appears to have addressed the impact of health-related issue advertising on election outcomes. As noted earlier, a Kaiser Family Foundation poll suggested that concerns about the Affordable Care Act had relatively little impact on enthusiasm for voting in the fall 2014 mid-term elections. However, an analysis of the 14 states with competitive Senate races in 2014 showed that these states tended to be more politically conservative than the United States as a whole, and, of course, conservatives tend to oppose the Affordable Care Act. Blendon and Benson (2014) note that in at least two polls conducted during the 2014 campaign season, voters named health care as the third most important issue influencing their congressional candidate preferences, and when asked to identify the specific health care issue that most concerned them, nearly half (48%) mentioned the ACA. Among those most likely to vote, only 41 percent agreed that the federal government should ensure that all Americans have access to health care. In addition, voters were more likely to say they would vote *against* a candidate who supported the ACA (40%) than to say they would vote *for* a candidate because he or she supported the ACA (Blendon & Benson, 2014).

These results, combined with the Kaiser Family Foundation data showing the dominance of anti-ACA advertising over pro-ACA advertising during the 2014 election cycle, suggest that political and issue advertising related to the ACA may well have affected the outcome of the November 2014 elections, in which Republicans maintained control of the House of Representatives and gained control of the Senate. The election outcome may have impacts on other aspects of health policy, but since the election, most analysts seem to have concluded that the ACA itself would not change dramatically, despite pledges by some Republican leaders that they would repeal the law once they controlled both houses of Congress. First, sweeping changes to the law are unlikely as long as President Obama remains in office because he could veto any major overhauls of the bill. In addition, recent Kaiser Health Tracking polls show that majorities of Americans now support improving the law rather than repealing it (DiJulio et al., 2015). Growing support for most aspects of the law would make continued attempts to repeal it politically dangerous (Kirsch, 2014).

ISSUE ADVERTISING'S EFFECTS ON POLICY

Regardless of effects on public opinion, voting, news coverage and election outcomes, arguably the most important question is whether policymakers ultimately make decisions consistent with the positions advocated in the issue ads. The research evidence suggests that issue ads indeed do increase the likelihood that the policy advocated in the ads will win legislative approval. In her study of legislative issue spending during the 107th Congress, Falk (2003) found that the side that spent the most money on issue advertising prevailed on ten of 15 issues, while advocates who were outspent prevailed on only two issues. Among the issues for which greater spending proved effective were four health policy issues:

> Much more money was spent on alternatives to a drug benefit under Medicare, and no drug benefit was added to Medicare. More money was spent to protect drug companies' patents, and legislation to prevent drug companies from easily extending patents failed. More money was spent to prevent reimportation of drugs, and legislation that would have allowed this practice failed. More was spent to oppose a patients' bill of rights, and none was passed.
>
> (Falk, 2003, p. 41)

Perhaps the most disturbing element of Falk's findings in studies of issue advertising for both the 107th and the 108th Congresses was that, during both sessions, corporate interests outspent citizen groups dramatically, and thus corporate interests were more likely to be upheld in the final policy decisions. During the 107th Congress, on ten of the policy issues examined, there was a dramatic imbalance in the spending on issue advertising; even for the least imbalanced issue in terms of spending (a Medicare prescription drug benefit), opponents outspent proponents by three-to-one. "Because exposure to information and argumentation can influence thinking and decision making, those with more money may have more influence" (Falk, 2003, p. 44).

During the 108th Congress, the data showed a pattern of significantly unbalanced issue ad spending for 94 percent of the 52 issues examined. Among the issues on which the most money was spent for advertising, "those that had significantly unbalanced issue ad spending were more often than not decided in favor of the side that spent more on ads" (Falk et al., 2006, p. 159). The data suggest, then, that "[w]henever there is a well-funded position in a policy debate, it is likely that it can dictate, at least to some extent, the terms of the debate" (Brodie, 2001, p. 1359), thus giving those with more money to spend on advertising a better chance of winning the outcome that side seeks.

In his dissertation examining issue advertising related to the Affordable Care Act, Rabinowitz offers an intriguing potential solution to the problem of imbalance in issue advertising. He proposes a "marketplace of ideas" tax, to be levied on all political advertisements and used to create a "marketplace of ideas trust fund." This endowment would provide funding that could subsidize the cost of political ads reflecting alternative and under-represented viewpoints. "Indeed, it may be fair to distribute the cost of improving viewpoint diversity to each speaker in direct proportion to how loudly he is speaking" (Rabinowitz, 2012, p. 76). Not surprisingly, the logistics of determining which viewpoints are under-represented but also worthy of being included in the public discourse would be daunting. However, the discussion raises an important point about the need to ensure that citizens have the opportunity to hear multiple perspectives on any policy issue, and not only those whose corporate or organizational backers have the resources to buy millions of dollars' worth of advertising space and time.

SUMMARY

In the current U.S. political system, health policy debates generate millions of dollars of spending on both legitimate issue advertising and political advertising that invokes health policy concerns on behalf of, or in opposition to, political candidates. This advertising appears to influence public opinion and, in turn, to have an impact on citizens' voting decisions, whether those votes directly determine a policy decision, such as in the case of ballot initiatives, or indirectly, through voters' candidate choices and interactions with elected officials. In addition to having some direct effects on public opinion, issue advertising may influence public opinion indirectly through its effects on news coverage of health policy debates; advertising content appears to play a significant role in determining which frames journalists use – and which they exclude – in writing about health policy questions. Finally, there is evidence that issue advertising affects legislative outcomes, whether that occurs because the advertising sways public opinion, because it makes policy decision-makers *perceive* a particular policy position to be more popular with their constituents, or because it signals to legislators that those sponsoring the advertising will reward those who side with them and/or punish those who vote against them.

Of course, on many issues, whether this effect on health policy appears helpful or harmful depends on one's view of the policy's likely health outcome. Those who view restrictions on abortion rights as threatening women's reproductive health, for instance, will view ads promoting such restrictions as harmful, while anti-abortion advocates likely will see the promotion of such policies as protecting the lives of unborn children. Gun rights advocates see advertising that encourages the passage of concealed carry limitations or other gun access restrictions as dangerous, not only to citizens' rights under the Second Amendment but to their ability to protect themselves and their family members from harm; gun control advocates, on the other hand, will view such advertising as helping to promote greater public safety by reducing the number of guns in circulation or limiting the venues to which they may be brought.

If issue advertising primarily reflected these differing citizen viewpoints about health policy, its overall effect might be deemed positive, in that greater issue advertising expenditures would suggest that a larger percentage of the population favored the health policy (or lack of policy) touted in those ads. Unfortunately, however, in what seems to be a majority of cases, the contest does not pit one group of citizens with a particular health perspective against another group of citizens who value different health outcomes. Instead, issue advertising imbalances seem to occur most often when a policy that may have substantial positive health effects for the population triggers a flood of counter-advertising by corporate interests (and sometimes health professional organizations) aiming to protect their profit margins or income potential.

In many of these cases, public health interests may not have the resources to compete successfully in the policy debate, leading to negative health outcomes or, at the least, slowing health progress.

Jacobs (2001) argues that, under most circumstances, wealthy corporations and other organizations will be unable to "manipulate" public opinion on the issues because such manipulation depends on the public receiving "unified and monolithic information" favoring one position and on the public holding ambiguous or malleable opinions on the issue at the outset. "Public attitudes that are least susceptible to manipulation tend to be fundamental policy preferences (such as support for Medicare or spending on health care), which do not regularly change in a statistically significant manner" (Jacobs, 2001, p. 1363).

On the other hand, Jacobs acknowledges that public dependence on mass media for the information they use in forming policy-relevant attitudes means that media, including both news coverage and issue advertising, can "heighten the public's awareness of the uncertainty and risks of altering the status quo, which in turn invites cynicism and distrust about the uses of government and erodes support for policy reform" (Jacobs, 2001, p. 1365). Thus, unless media messages overwhelmingly support policy change, even conflicting messages may be more likely to lead to public wariness about the proposed policy change; in other words, it may be easier for groups to win public support for maintaining the status quo than it is to gain public support for change, no matter how much that change would improve population health.

REFERENCES

Baye, R. (2014, March 7). Issue Ad or Political Ad? You Be the Judge. Retrieved July 20, 2015 from www.publicintegrity.org/2014/03/07/14331/issue-ad-or-political-ad-you-be-judge.

Bergan, D. & Risner, G. (2012). Issue Ads and the Health Reform Debate. *Journal of Health Politics, Policy and Law, 37*(3), 513–549. http://doi.org/10.1215/03616878-1573103.

Blendon, R.J. & Benson, J.M. (2014). Voters and the Affordable Care Act in the 2014 Election. *New England Journal of Medicine, 371*(20), e31. http://doi.org/10.1056/NEJMsr1412118.

Blumenthal, P. (2013, June 21). Issue Ads Show 2014 Election Savvy As They Sidestep Campaign Laws. Retrieved July 14, 2015 from www.huffingtonpost.com/2013/06/21/issue-ads-2014-election_n_3474425.html.

Bogardus, K. (2012, September 30). "Dark Money" Flowing Back to Issue Ads [Text]. Retrieved July 6, 2015 from http://thehill.com/homenews/campaign/259283-campaigns-dark-money-starts-flowing-back-to-issue-ads.

Brence, M. (2014, December 11). Measure 92 Supporters Concede Defeat on Oregon GMO Labeling - For Now. Retrieved July 9, 2015 from www.oregonlive.com/politics/index.ssf/2014/12/measure_92_supporters_concede.html.

Brodie, M. (2001). Impact of Issue Advertisements and the Legacy of Harry and Louise. *Journal of Health Politics, Policy and Law, 26*(6), 1353–1360.

Brodie, M., Altman, D., Deane, C., Buscho, S. & Hamel, E. (2010). Liking the Pieces, Not the Package: Contradictions in Public Opinion during Health Reform. *Health Affairs, 29*(6), 1125–1130. http://doi.org/10.1377/hlthaff.2010.0434.

Caputo, M. & Klas, M.E. (2014, January 27). Medical Marijuana Headed to Florida Ballot after Supreme Court's 4–3 Decision. Retrieved July 3, 2015 from www.miamiherald.com/news/politics-government/article1959660.html.

Chao, E. (2014, November 6). Monsanto Plans Challenge to Approved Ban on GMOs. Retrieved July 9, 2015 from www.mauinews.com/page/content.detail/id/591761/Monsanto-plans-challenge-to-approved-ban-on-GMOs.html?nav=5161.

Crombie, N. (2014, November 4). Measure 91 Would Legalize Recreational Marijuana: Oregon Election Results 2014. Retrieved July 9, 2015 from www.oregonlive.com/politics/index.ssf/2014/11/measure_91_would_legalize_mari.html.

Dalen, J.E., Waterbrook, K. & Alpert, J.S. (2015). Why Do So Many Americans Oppose the Affordable Care Act? *The American Journal of Medicine.* http://doi.org/10.1016/j.amjmed.2015.01.032.

Digital Advertising Had Significant Impact on Medical Marijuana Vote in Florida. (2014, December 18). Retrieved July 3, 2015 from www.prnewswire.com/news-releases/digital-advertising-had-significant-impact-on-medical-marijuana-vote-in-florida-300011731.html.

DiJulio, B., Firth, J. & Brodie, M. (2015, March). Kaiser Health Tracking Poll: March 2015. Retrieved July 14, 2015 from http://kff.org/health-costs/poll-finding/kaiser-health-tracking-poll-march-2015/.

DiJulio, B., Norton, M., Brodie, M., Wilner, E. & West, M. (2014, October 30). ACA Advertising in 2014 - Insurance and Political Ads. Retrieved July 6, 2015 from http://kff.org/health-reform/report/aca-advertising-in-2014-insurance-and-political-ads/.

Falk, E. (2003). *Legislative Issue Advertising in the 107th Congress: A Report.* Annenberg Public Policy Center of the University of Pennsylvania. Retrieved July 8, 2015 from http://cdn.annenbergpublicpolicycenter.org/wp-content/uploads/2003_APPC_IssueAds107th2.pdf.

Falk, E. (2005). *Legislative Issue Advertising in the 108th Congress.* Washington, DC.

Falk, E., Grizard, E. & McDonald, G. (2006). Legislative Issue Advertising in the 108th Congress: Pluralism or Peril? *The Harvard International Journal of Press/Politics, 11*(4), 148–164. http://doi.org/10.1177/1081180X06293080.

Franz, M.M., & Ridout, T.N. (2007). Does Political Advertising Persuade? *Political Behavior, 29*(4), 465–491. http://doi.org/10.1007/s11109-007-9032-y.

Goldsteen, R.L., Goldsteen, K., Swan, J.H. & Clemeña, W. (2001). Harry and Louise and Health Care Reform: Romancing Public Opinion. *Journal of Health Politics, Policy and Law, 26*(6), 1325–1352.

Goldstein, K.M. (1999). *Interest Groups, Lobbying, and Participation in America.* Cambridge University Press. Retrieved July 10, 2015 from https://books.google.com/books?hl=en&lr=&id=raPgCM53hUsC&oi=fnd&pg=PR8&dq=%22interest+groups,+lobbying+and+participation+in+America%22&ots=mknEm47i5-&sig=kxeOHVoeZb2RE3SBLPF-zlJkS4g.

Hall, R.L. & Anderson, R. (2012). Issue Advertising and Legislative Advocacy in Health Politics. *Interest Group Politics*, 221–242.

Hamel, L., Firth, J. & Brodie, M. (2014, September 9). Kaiser Health Tracking Poll: August–September 2014. Retrieved July 6, 2015 from http://kff.org/health-reform/poll-finding/kaiser-health-tracking-poll-august-september-2014/.

Jacobs, L.R. (1993). Health Reform Impasse: The Politics of American Ambivalence toward Government. *Journal of Health Politics, Policy and Law*, 18(3), 629–655. http://doi.org/10.1215/03616878-18-3-629.

Jacobs, L.R. (2001). Manipulators and Manipulation: Public Opinion in a Representative Democracy. *Journal of Health Politics, Policy and Law*, 26(6), 1361–1374.

Jamieson, K.H., Cappella, J.N. & Moyers, B.D. (1995). *Media in the Middle: Fairness and Accuracy in the 1994 Health Care Reform Debate*. Princeton, NJ: Films for the Humanities & Sciences.

Kaiser Health Tracking Poll: The Public's Views on the ACA. (2015). Retrieved July 14, 2015 from http://kff.org/interactive/tracking-opinions-aca/.

Kerr, K. (2014, October 28). Pro-GMO Companies Spend $8 Million to Fight Maui Initiative. Retrieved July 9, 2015 from www.hawaiinewsnow.com/story/27106705/pro-gmo-companies-spend-8-million-to-fight-maui-initiative.

Kirsch, R. (2014, November 3). Why the GOP Won't Touch Obamacare. Retrieved July 14, 2015 from www.politico.com/magazine/story/2014/11/why-the-gop-wont-touch-obamacare-112460.html.

Kotch, A. (2014, December 19). How Are Charitable Nonprofits Getting Away with Election-season Political Ads? Retrieved July 14, 2015 from www.southernstudies.org/2014/12/how-are-charitable-nonprofits-getting-away-with-el.html.

Kuntz, K. (2014, October 20). The $11 Million Ad Campaign against GMO Labeling. Retrieved July 9, 2015 from www.9news.com/story/news/politics/2014/10/20/colorado-gmo-labeling-bill-campaign/17627351/.

Liasson, M. (2012, October 26). Do Political Ads Actually Work? Retrieved July 14, 2015 from www.npr.org/sections/itsallpolitics/2012/10/26/163652827/nine-states-near-unlimited-cash-a-flurry-of-ads.

Mears, B. (2012, January 23). Where the Money Is: A Campaign Spending Primer – CNNPolitics.com. Retrieved July 14, 2015 from www.cnn.com/2012/01/23/politics/campaign-spending-primer/index.html.

Pollick, M. (2014, November 4). Florida Voters Reject Medical Marijuana. Retrieved July 3, 2015 from http://politics.heraldtribune.com/2014/11/04/florida-voters-reject-medical-marijuana/.

Rabinowitz, A. (2010). Media Framing and Political Advertising in the Patients' Bill of Rights Debate. *Journal of Health Politics, Policy and Law*, 35(5), 771–795. http://doi.org/10.1215/03616878-2010-027.

Rabinowitz, A. (2012, December 13). *The Fourth Branch of Government: The Role of Interest Groups, the Media, and Political Advertisements in Contemporary Health Policy Debates*. Harvard University. Retrieved July 14, 2015 from http://dash.harvard.edu/handle/1/10056541.

Reston, M. (2015, May 20). $10-million Ad Campaign Joins "Avalanche" of Anti-Obamacare Ads. *Los Angeles Times*. Retrieved July 14, 2015 from www.latimes.com/nation/politics/politicsnow/la-pn-new-10-million-ad-campaign-avalanche-obamacare-ads-20140520-story.html#page=1.

Results of the New York Times/CBS News Poll. (2012, March 27). Retrieved July 14, 2015 from www.nytimes.com/interactive/2012/03/27/us/03272012_polling_doc.html.

Wallsten, P. (2009, September 4). Healthcare Debate Gives Internet Advertising a Huge Shot in the Arm. *Los Angeles Times*. Retrieved July 9, 2015 from http://articles.latimes.com/2009/sep/04/nation/na-health-internet4.

West, D.M., Heith, D. & Goodwin, C. (1996). Harry and Louise Go To Washington: Political Advertising and Health Care Reform. *Journal of Health Politics, Policy and Law, 21*(1), 35–68.

Whyte, L.E. (2014, November 6). Ballot Measure Backers Spend Big, Win Big. Retrieved July 3, 2015 from www.publicintegrity.org/2014/11/06/16229/ballot-measure-backers-spend-big-win-big.

CHAPTER 16

MEDIA EFFECTS ON HEALTH: WHAT WE STILL NEED TO KNOW

As the previous chapters have demonstrated, researchers have published thousands, probably hundreds of thousands, of books, papers and reports examining the myriad ways in which mass media technologies and content can and do affect our health, both directly through impacts on our own health-related knowledge, beliefs, expectations, attitudes and behaviors, and indirectly through media effects on health policy. And yet, in spite of all the information and insights those scholars have provided, there is still much we do not fully understand about how interacting with mass media influences individual and public health.

Fifty years from now, regardless of how many more media health effects studies have been conducted and published, that last statement will remain true. New media technologies, new types of content and new patterns of interacting with those technologies and that content are developing every day and will continue to do so. New health issues arise or gain prominence every year. For example, in January 2015, CNN's chief medical correspondent, Dr. Sanjay Gupta, published his list of "America's 9 Biggest Health Issues" for the coming year. It included brief discussions of such issues as the shortage of doctors in the United States, deadly hospital errors and infections, antibiotic resistance, food deserts, the cost and expected increased incidence of Alzheimer's disease, the likely shortage of caregivers for our aging population, the absence of an acceptable work–life balance in the lives of most American adults, and the growing use of "do-it-yourself" health care applications and technology (Gupta, 2015). Each of these issues has appeared, to a greater or lesser extent, in some type of media content, primarily news, and, of course, DIY health apps and technology could be considered health-related media in their own right. Yet none has been addressed to any significant extent in the preceding chapters, not because the issues are unimportant but because other issues have garnered the majority of attention from media effects researchers.

My point here is that the need to investigate both positive and negative, intended and unintended effects of media use will continue. Some important questions, based on the preponderance of research, have been settled. Exposure to cigarette advertising does increase the likelihood of smoking initiation among young people; the same relationship almost certainly exists for alcohol advertising and the initiation of alcohol use. Consumption of violent media content increases the likelihood of aggressive and even violent behavior among some children and adolescents. News media attention to health issues significantly influences public ratings of the importance of those health issues. And yet, there is more work to be done if we are to understand more completely who is most vulnerable to these and other media effects and how best to enhance media's positive health effects and reduce or even eliminate negative health effects.

The purpose of this chapter, therefore, is not to list every important research question that remains to be answered in relation to media effects on health; that is an impossible task. Rather, the chapter examines some general observations one can make about gaps in the existing research and suggests some additional specific issues that would be useful to investigate.

UPDATED AND NEW CONTENT ANALYSES

Several types of media health content need either new and more comprehensive or updated content analysis. For instance, although some researchers have examined advertising for e-cigarettes, additional study will be needed to track the methods e-cigarette manufacturers and marketers are using to promote these products; in particular, it will be important to document the use of techniques likely to appeal to children and adolescents. In addition, we need to know whether e-cigarettes are being promoted primarily as tools for smoking cessation or if manufacturers are encouraging audiences to view e-cigarettes as something new non-smokers should try or as products that will enable existing smokers to maintain their habit in situations that do not allow the use of traditional cigarettes.

A more complete understanding of the impact of media portrayals of substance use, including illegal drugs, will require updated content analysis of entertainment content. The most recent comprehensive analysis of portrayals of substance use in television examined programs that ran during fall 1998 and winter 1999. Some more recent studies have examined portrayals of alcohol and tobacco use, but little research has examined portrayals of illicit drug use. Little research has assessed the use of tobacco, alcohol or illegal drugs in video games, and we know relatively little about the inclusion of substance use content in social media. In particular, it will be important to keep track of trends in substance use content in new social media platforms as each new platform (e.g., Pinterest, Instagram, Tumblr) gains popularity among young people.

Similarly, we need updated and comprehensive analyses of the portrayals of violence in entertainment media, especially given the apparent increase in the graphic nature of that content and in the inclusion of sexual violence in "mainstream" media (Saraiya, 2015). In addition, most of the published studies of violent content in video games appear to have been published before the rise of online games, such as *World of Warcraft*; given the immense popularity of these games, it seems crucial that we know how violence is portrayed in these games. Music continues to play an important role in the lives of adolescents and young people, so updated studies on the inclusion of violent lyrics in music also will be needed. The rise of streaming music services such as Spotify, which suggest songs to users based on other music they have selected, may be especially important to study. Logically, once an individual using one of these services has chosen several songs that include violent lyrics, the services could be expected to recommend additional songs including violent lyrics. Researchers should know whether such streaming services have the effect of further concentrating certain individuals' exposure to music that glorifies violent behavior.

Little recent research has examined the portrayals of food and eating habits in entertainment programming; updated research will be needed if we are to understand how non-advertising content influences beliefs, attitudes and behavior related to food and nutrition. Some sources estimate that there are two million food blogs in the world (Bernard,

2014), and one researcher has even cautioned that frequently posting photos of one's meals to Facebook, Instagram or Pinterest may signal that the individual has a significant mental health issue related to food (Kingkade, 2013). The practice of posting photos of food one has cooked or is about to be served at a restaurant is so common that it has developed its own Internet meme; non-food posters have created numerous creative ways of advising friends to *stop* posting pictures of their food. To understand whether and under what circumstances entertainment portrayals and social media sharing related to food has positive or negative effects, on either those who view the content or on those who create it, we first will need a more systematic analysis of what is on the media menus.

In general, we will need to keep track of all sorts of health-related content available online and via social media in particular, including portrayals of thinness, muscularity and other body image-related content, sex, sexual health and sexual violence, violence in general, substance use, exercise and fitness, as well as social media sharing of information related to diseases such as cancer, heart disease, diabetes, mental illness, etc. To document and analyze such content effectively, health communication scholars will need to learn to harness the social media analytic techniques businesses and organizations now use to follow social media conversations about their industries and issues. While that may be a challenge, the realm of "big data" also may offer important new opportunities for understanding the kinds of health-related information people encounter online, whether from "official" sources such as government agencies, from corporate entities focused primarily on improving their profits, from not-for-profit health advocacy organizations or from their online peers. Already, health organizations have begun using text-mining techniques for identifying and following infectious disease outbreaks (Brownstein et al., 2009; Collier, 2012). Creative scholars should be able to use similar techniques to learn about how other diseases and health issues are being discussed online.

Finally, it will be important to continue to document news coverage of health and health policy issues as public reliance on traditional news sources such as newspapers and television declines or shifts to emerging pathways; for instance, the links provided in social media such as Facebook and Twitter (Anderson & Caumont, 2014). As Schwitzer (2009) has noted, continuing declines in the number of trained and experienced health journalists, along with the rise of public relations and marketing efforts by health product manufacturers and health service providers, are threatening news organizations' ability to keep biased, potentially inaccurate and even dangerously misleading health content out of health news stories. On the other hand, it seems reasonable to expect that health promotion organizations will become increasingly effective in using media advocacy techniques to influence health news coverage in positive ways. Researchers will need to follow these developments if we are to understand the role news channels play in informing and influencing both individual health behavior and health policy in the future.

UNDERSTANDING HOW PEOPLE USE MEDIA HEALTH CONTENT

The next major area in which significant gaps in our knowledge exist involves the way people use media resources for health information, especially in regard to the newer media forms such as online content, social media, information accessed via mobile devices and that are made available – or tailored to the individual – in response to his or her use of personal fitness trackers such as the Fitbit or Jawbone. One in five smartphone owners now has a health application (or "app") on their phone, most often to help them with exercise, diet or weight management issues, and yet we know relatively little about what people actually do with this information or whether and to what extent the use of these apps helps people improve their health behaviors. Some researchers have examined the quality of health information provided by some of these apps (e.g., Azar et al., 2013; Bender et al., 2013; Boulos et al., 2014; Cowan et al., 2012; Rosser & Eccleston, 2011; West et al., 2012), but because new apps arrive nearly every day and existing apps are updated on a fairly regular basis, it is indeed a challenge to form any definitive conclusions about the benefits – and potential risks – their use offers.

Although numerous researchers have assessed the quality and usability of online health information, usually within specific health topics (e.g., heart disease, diabetes, child health), it appears that no one has yet investigated the impact of information search tailoring on the types of health information an individual is likely to reach. The point here is that Google and other general search engines, which are the starting point for most health information searches, now commonly tailor the results they return in accordance with algorithms intended to ensure that the

493

results offered "fit" the individual conducting the search. It remains to be seen what effect this will have. For instance, if a teenager's previous searches for health information suggest that he or she frequently accesses blogs produced by other users, rather than more authoritative sources such as government websites, does the algorithm tend to put consumer-generated blogs higher on the list of search results? Or if a woman searching for information about the seasonal flu has, in the past, frequently accessed anti-vaccination sites, will she be more likely to see links to sites questioning the value and safety of flu vaccination? To the extent that this happens, search engines designed to tailor search results to individuals' preferences could unintentionally increase the knowledge gap by returning links to more authoritative and credible sites for those who have tended to use such sites in the past, while individuals who have, for whatever reason, frequently visited websites of more dubious scientific quality may be directed to more of the same when they search for information.

We also will need additional study of the impact of search-based tailoring of online advertising to specific users, known as behavioral targeting. It is already indisputable that accessing information related to particular topics (e.g., vacations, sports, specific consumer items) subsequently affects the advertising to which Internet users are exposed (Rusmevichientong & Williamson, 2006). So, for instance, if one searches online for information about weight loss, nearly every subsequent ad-supported page one visits – whether it's Facebook or a news site or Amazon.com – is likely to include advertising for some type of weight loss product, book, program, etc. This may have the effect of dramatically increasing exposure to potentially unhealthy sites, such as those promoting tobacco products or online pornography, after just one search for a related topic or one visit to this sort of site. In fact, such ads may be targeted to Internet users based on apparently unrelated searches or on social media profile information; for example, pornography websites may target users whose Facebook profiles indicate that they are high school or young adult males.

We also need to know more about the specific factors that increase or decrease Internet users' reactions to the health information they find online. In the course of a typical health information search, how exactly do people decide which links to click on and which to bypass? How do online health information seekers deal with conflicting information they may find online, or with conflicts between what they learn online and what health professionals have told them? One review of the literature relating health literacy to the use of online health information showed that health literacy does play a key role in users' perceptions of online health information quality, their trust in the information they find and their use of recommended quality evaluation criteria; those with lower education and less skill in using online information were more likely to search for information that confirmed their pre-existing beliefs about a health topic, rather than attempting to find the best possible information about that issue (Diviani et al., 2015). Future research will be needed to determine the implications of these differences, as well as to identify best practices for improving individuals' online health literacy skills.

A closely related topic is the question of how individuals are using social media for health communication. A recent review of the literature identified numerous gaps in the literature, including several that relate to consumers' use of social media for health information. The researchers concluded that additional study is needed to help us understand more clearly how specific population groups, such as those with particular health concerns and members of minority and cultural groups, use health information from social media and what role social media play in communication between health professionals and their patients. In addition, further study is needed to examine peer-to-peer communication around health issues. The review also stressed that the methodological quality of many of the existing studies was low, primarily because many were exploratory. Thus, going forward, we will need to ensure that more rigorous methods are used in studies of the health uses of social media (Moorhead et al., 2013).

In general, more research is needed on the development and impact of what scholars have begun to call "media health literacy," which refers to users' ability to recognize and evaluate critically the health messages found in media (Levin-Zamir et al., 2011). Although scholars are paying increasing attention to eHealth literacy, which refers specifically to skills in using digital information and technologies to improve their own health (Norman, 2011), we also continue to need better understanding of what influences people's ability to recognize and respond appropriately to intended and unintended health messages in all forms of media, digital or otherwise. In addition, researchers have questioned the validity

495

of the most commonly used eHealth literacy measure, the eHEALS (van der Vaart et al., 2011), suggesting that additional research will be needed to ensure that we understand fully how access to and use of digital health resources influences health outcomes.

HEALTH MEDIA EFFECTS: INDIVIDUALS

Despite the thousands of studies that have examined how media consumption affects individuals' health-related knowledge, attitudes and behaviors, some interesting gaps remain. One such gap stems from the fact that the vast majority of studies of the impact of media content, including violence, tobacco and alcohol advertising, portrayals of body image and sex and nutrition and fitness content, have focused on children and adolescents. To be sure, some research – especially that related to media portrayals of substance use and abuse, body image and sex – has extended to research with young adults, in part because college students provide an easily accessible source of research participants.

To some extent, however, it is as if researchers have assumed that once an individual reaches adulthood (age 25 or older, perhaps), he or she is no longer vulnerable to the influence of media messages related to many risky behaviors. These assumptions could be correct. Factors unrelated to media consumption could explain all significant variations in adults' attitudes and behaviors related to violence, substance use, sex, diet and exercise, or media effects could stem entirely from media exposure during childhood through early adulthood.

However, research has linked media exposure to some types of adult health-related attitudes and behaviors, such as parental decisions regarding vaccination (Kelly et al., 2009) and sexual risk behaviors among pornography users (Harkness, Mullan et al., 2015). In addition, of course, all mass media health promotion campaigns aimed at adults are premised on the notion that exposure to mediated health messages will influence adults' health knowledge, attitudes and/or behavior. If we believe that media messages intended to change adults' attitudes and behaviors can significantly affect their health, then questions related to how media messages may unintentionally influence adults' health attitudes and behaviors are also worthy of future study.

In particular, research is needed to examine potential impacts of adults' exposure to advertising for tobacco products, including e-cigarettes, for alcohol and, in states that have legalized either medicinal or recreational use, for marijuana. Although only a handful of states thus far permit recreational use of marijuana and advertising for both recreational and medical marijuana is banned or tightly controlled, it seems reasonable to assume that pot advertising will develop as marijuana sellers learn to negotiate the challenges posed by marketing a product that remains illegal according to federal law (Klara, 2014). How that advertising will affect rates of marijuana use among adults and youth will be an important topic, as will the potential growth of media portrayals of marijuana as a "normal" element of adult social activities. A 2014 report from the Rocky Mountain High Intensity Drug Trafficking Area already has demonstrated the impact marijuana legalization in Colorado has had concerning health impacts, with traffic fatalities related to drivers who were under the influence of marijuana increasing 100 percent from 2007 to 2012. The agency reported that most impaired driving arrests in the state now involve marijuana; in 25 to 40 percent of such arrests, marijuana is the only drug causing the impairment. In addition, marijuana-related emergency room visits increased 57 percent between 2011 and 2013, while hospitalizations involving marijuana use increased 82 percent (Rocky Mountain High Intensity Drug Trafficking Area, 2014). These and other trends demonstrate that the health impacts of marijuana legalization – and its promotion through media – are likely to be considerable.

Media portrayals and advertising of e-cigarettes also demand continued study to ensure that we know not only what messages the media are sending about e-cigarettes but how those messages affect e-cigarette use. Although some research suggests that "vaping" helps existing smokers reduce or eliminate their use of traditional cigarettes (e.g., Brown et al., 2014), a recent study among younger teens showed that those who had ever used e-cigarettes were more likely to start smoking traditional cigarettes within the next year (Leventhal et al., 2015), suggesting that vaping may lead to smoking, with all its attendant health consequences. Given the rapid increases in e-cigarette use, which more than tripled among middle and high school students between 2013 and 2014, continued study of the media's role in encouraging e-cigarette use is critical.

Substantial numbers of adults, especially men, play video games, with a Pew Research Center survey indicating that 60 percent of 30- to

49-year-olds, 40 percent of those aged 50 to 64 and a quarter (25%) of adults aged 65 and older reported playing video games in 2008 (Lenhart et al., 2008), and more recent research from the Entertainment Software Association revealing that women aged 18 and older now constitute the largest single demographic group for games, accounting for 33 percent of the gaming population (Entertainment Software Association, 2015). For many adults, especially women, this reflects the growth of casual mobile and social games such as Words With Friends, Candy Crush, Cookie Jam and Bubble Witch Saga; however, research suggests that a significant segment of older adults spend time, sometimes daily, sometimes daily, playing online games, with adventure/puzzle games such as Myst and Riven being the most popular (Pearce, 2008). It seems likely that adult use of computer games will continue to increase, given that larger segments of the population now will have grown up playing console, mobile and online games; thus, the study of the health impacts of these games on adult players is warranted.

The growing numbers of adult gamers, both male and female, points to another area that will require additional study, which is the impact of exposure to media violence, including not only video games but also television and movies. As Chapter 10 notes, there appears to be a trend toward increasingly graphic violence, including sexual violence, in prime-time television, and, of course, streaming services such as Netflix, Hulu and Amazon make violent movies (and television) available on demand. Few studies have examined the impact of exposure to media violence on adult viewers. However, researchers have documented a relationship between the use of violent pornography and men's attitudes toward sexual violence, as discussed in Chapter 9. In addition, some research has linked the rate of domestic violence incidents reported to police to the timing of NFL football broadcasts (Adubato, 2015; Gantz & Wang, 2006; Sachs & Chu, 2000), and a Spanish study identified significant "copycat" effects during the week immediately following news reports of intimate partner murders (Vives-Cases et al., 2009). This research suggests that adults may be vulnerable to the effects of exposure to media violence just as children and adolescents are; therefore, research examining these potential effects is clearly needed.

One final understudied area of potential individual-level media effects concerns the notion that mass media may be contributing to the medicalization of society, encouraging unwarranted trust that all medical interventions are safe, effective and beneficial, that there exists (or should exist) a "pill for every ill." The concept of medicalization refers to the tendency to treat previously accepted conditions (e.g., male baldness, erectile dysfunction, loss of sexual desire among older women, adult "attention deficit disorder") as medical problems that can and should be "fixed" through the application of drugs or some other medical treatment. Social scientists have been studying the phenomenon since the 1970s, at least, but Conrad (2005) argues that the primary drivers of medicalization have shifted from the medical profession and special interest groups to biotechnology, consumers and managed care.

Biotechnology's effect on medicalization stems, to a significant degree, from the tremendous growth of direct-to-consumer advertising of prescription drugs and, increasingly, of medical devices and genetic testing (Conrad, 2005); the research described in Chapter 5 certainly supports this contention. Others contend that advertising for over-the-counter (OTC) drugs, a topic that has received far less research attention, also may tend to mislead consumers about the safety of these drugs, especially those the FDA has approved for transition from prescription to OTC status. Faerber and Kreling (2012) found, for instance, that ads for OTC drugs were less likely than DTC ads for prescription drugs to include specific side effect and risk information, and a more recent study identified more potentially misleading claims in ads for OTC drugs, compared to those for prescription drugs, most likely because DTC advertising for prescription drugs is subject to much more rigorous FDA regulation (Faerber & Kreling, 2014). Scholars will need to continue to explore the possibility that OTC advertising, which has received far less research attention than DTC advertising for prescription drugs (DeLorme et al., 2010), contributes to the public's tendency to assume that any lapse or interruption in an individual's perceived physical and mental health should be treated and can be treated with no significant risk of harm.

In addition to the marketing efforts of biotechnology companies, Conrad (2005) identified consumers themselves as significant drivers of the trend toward medicalization. "Individuals as consumers rather than patients help shape the scope, and sometimes the demand for, medical treatments" (Conrad, 2005, p. 9). If that is the case, then we should investigate the potential for media portrayals of health care and as sources of health information to contribute to that demand. This is especially true because consumer expectations about medical care play a role in medical overtreatment, defined as the utilization of tests and treatments that provide no medically valuable information or benefit to the patient. Overtreatment, by some estimates, accounts for as much as one-third of all health care spending in the United States (Orszag, 2008); in addition, it leads to poorer health outcomes for patients subjected to unnecessary tests and treatments (Brownlee, 2010; Hadler et al., 2012; Welch & Black, 2010; Welch et al., 2011).

MEDIA EFFECTS ON PUBLIC OPINION AND HEALTH POLICY

No doubt there are many other important questions to be answered about the unintended effects of media use on individuals' knowledge of and beliefs about health and on their health behavior. However, arguably, an even more important gap to be filled lies in our understanding of the role media play in influencing health policy, including corporate policies, because these policies can have effects that extend far beyond the users of any media channel. This final section, then, outlines several areas that seem particularly important to examine in relation to media's potential influence on health policy development and implementation.

One key area is the impact of news coverage on public opinion about and public support for health policy. Although previous research has assessed how coverage and framing of specific issues (e.g., drug abuse, the Medicare prescription drug benefit) influenced public attitudes toward relevant policies, we also need examinations of the extent to which news coverage and framing of health care, in a more general sense, influences health policy preferences. For instance, research suggests that although the public supports government investment in comparative effectiveness research to determine which interventions are most useful for specific medical problems, consumers generally oppose the use of comparative effectiveness data to limit the types of treatments health insurance will cover (Gerber et al., 2010). One question worth pursuing, then, is whether this skepticism about the uses of comparative effectiveness research may be influenced by news coverage that tends to emphasize (but not fully explain) the benefits of medical testing and treatment, without providing comparable information about the risks and costs (Schwitzer, 2008; Walsh-Childers et al., 2014). News coverage of medical interventions may tend to bolster the idea that all treatments and tests have value, increasing consumers' reluctance to accept limitations on the availability of these interventions, no matter how poorly they compare to other available options.

Another question that remains to be answered relates to the interaction between news coverage of health and consumers' pre-existing political and social beliefs, and how those interactions influence policy support. For instance, although journalists are often encouraged to pay greater attention to the social determinants of health, at least one study suggests that Republicans and Democrats diverged in their reactions to a story focusing on the social determinants of diabetes, with Republicans expressing less support for policies intended to address social influences on diabetes when they had read a social determinants-framed story. Rather than encouraging audiences uniformly to understand the role social, economic and environmental conditions play in individuals' health, the study suggests that stories focusing on the social determinants of health may trigger resistance to public health policy change among individuals (including both consumers and policy-makers) who prioritize personal responsibility (Gollust et al., 2009). Additional research is needed to broaden our understanding of how news outlets and many other types of media (e.g., talk radio, partisan websites, social media interactions) may be contributing to political polarization about health issues.

In the United States, little research seems to have addressed the potential direct impact of media on policy-makers at the local, state or national levels, and thus this represents another gap in the literature. We need updated research showing where policy-makers at all levels get their information about health and health policy, and how those information sources influence policy-makers' support for or opposition to specific health policy proposals. At the national level, policy-makers may rely very little on information they receive directly from news channels; however, there may be a greater impact on state and local-level health policy-makers. In addition, it would be valuable to know how the staff members who summarize information about health issues for state or national policy-makers make use of media sources. Certainly there are instances in which news coverage of a health issue influences policy-makers' attention to that issue, even at the national level, as illustrated by the recent case in which the Federal Centers for Medicare & Medicaid Services launched an investigation of death rates among infant heart surgery patients at a Florida hospital after several news organizations, including CNN and Florida television stations and newspapers, reported on the hospital's unusually high rate of infant deaths and complications (Cohen & Bonifield, 2015); ultimately, the hospital closed its pediatric heart surgery program (Sonawane, 2015). Additional research is needed to determine what types of media reports draw the attention of policy-makers and how news coverage influences the outcome of these cases.

A related question – and one that appears to have received virtually no research attention – is the extent to which entertainment media may influence public opinion about health policy. Both the health care system (e.g., *The Doctors*, ABC's *Grey's Anatomy*) and the world of politics (HBO's *Veep*, *House of Cards* from Netflix) are frequently the focus of entertainment programming, and it seems reasonable to assume that viewers may be exposed to ideas relevant to health policy from both types of shows. Even programming that does not specifically deal with either health or policy, such as the wildly successful *Breaking Bad* – about a high school chemistry teacher turned methamphetamine manufacturer/ dealer – can offer messages about health policy. We need to understand more about how exposure to such content influences the public's views about policies that may be discussed or touched upon in these shows, especially those with very large and often long-term audiences.

We also need a much better understanding of the role social media interactions play in influencing public and policy-maker views about health policy, and this will include social media effects on health-related corporate decisions. A recent *New York Times* article, focusing on ride-rental company Uber's use of its social media networks to fight some cities' attempts to regulate Uber's operations, noted that "[m]any tech firms now recognize the organizing power of their user networks, and are weaponizing their apps to achieve political ends" (Walker, 2015, para. 4). Certainly, political candidates have begun to recognize the value of social media as channels for organizing supporters and for spreading their views, and health-related organizations such as Planned Parenthood have used social media networks to defend themselves when threatened with de-funding by the Susan G. Komen for the Cure organization (Perry, 2012). More recently, however, some argued that Planned Parenthood was losing the social media war when undercover videos related to the organization's system for dealing with fetal tissue from abortions led to large protests and Congressional calls to withdraw federal funding for the organization (Richardson, 2015). These incidents reveal the very significant potential social media may have to draw larger numbers of consumers into the political process. By making it far easier for citizens to hear about others' views and to express their own views on policy issues, social media may become major channels of influence on health policy development. Whether that influence ultimately benefits or harms the public good may depend on the ability of public health advocates to match the social media use skills of wealthier organizations and corporations more focused on profits than health.

A related area that demands significant research attention is how digital advertising will influence health policy development and implementation. Chapter 15 offered some evidence that organizations have already begun to use digital advertising in their attempts to influence election outcomes and ballot initiatives that affect health policy. It seems almost certain that this trend will intensify as digital media become increasingly dominant as the channels through which most people receive most of their information. Health advocates interested in using digital channels to promote health policy progress will need research documenting the circumstances and characteristics that make digital advertising successful.

A FINAL COMMENT

Although no human being is immune to health concerns, there may be places on Earth in which media never or almost never have any significant influence on either individual health or health policy. For most of the world, however, and certainly in the United States, media have a ubiquitous presence in our lives, from birth – perhaps even before birth (Graven & Browne, 2008) – until death. Video tributes, usually including photos of the deceased individual and music reflecting his or her personality, are now considered "part of the essential steps that funeral directors need to take in order to personalize services" ("Video Tributes," n.d., para. 1), and it is now common for an individual's Facebook profile to remain available – and even active – after the profile owner has died (Oremus, 2015). We live our lives surrounded by media in various forms, and interaction with those media messages can have both positive and negative effects on our health. That reality is unlikely to disappear, no matter how much change the media industries or the health care system experiences. Given that reality, it makes sense for us to understand as much as we possibly can about when and how media help people live better, healthier lives and when media interactions cause harm.

Although media messages can promote better health outcomes, much of the research discussed in this book focuses on the potential for media to cause negative health effects. Most often, the negative health impacts of mass media represent unintentional side effects of the media content creators' efforts to accomplish some other goal – to sell a product, to entertain an audience, or simply to provide information about an individual, a group, a community or some specific health issue. But the fact that negative media health effects are not intended does not absolve media professionals of responsibility for those damaging effects. Thus, in addition to understanding when and how media messages cause harm, future research should focus on finding ways to encourage (or pressure) media organizations to take responsibility for the damage they cause and to develop new approaches to reaching their goals without harming the societies they serve.

REFERENCES

Adubato, B. (2015). The Promise of Violence Televised, Professional Football Games and Domestic Violence. *Journal of Sport & Social Issues*, 0193723515594209. http://doi.org/10.1177/0193723515594209.

Anderson, M. & Caumont, A. (2014, September 24). How Social Media is Reshaping News. Retrieved August 1, 2015 from www.pewresearch.org/fact-tank/2014/09/24/how-social-media-is-reshaping-news/.

Azar, K.M.J., Lesser, L.I., Laing, B.Y., Stephens, J., Aurora, M.S., Burke, L.E. & Palaniappan, L.P. (2013). Mobile Applications for Weight Management: Theory-based Content Analysis. *American Journal of Preventive Medicine*, 45(5), 583–589. http://doi.org/10.1016/j.amepre.2013.07.005.

Bender, J.L., Yue, R.Y.K., To, M.J., Deacken, L. & Jadad, A.R. (2013). A Lot of Action, But Not in the Right Direction: Systematic Review and Content Analysis of Smartphone Applications for the Prevention, Detection, and Management of Cancer. *Journal of Medical Internet Research*, 15(12), e287. http://doi.org/10.2196/jmir.2661.

Bernard, E. (2014, September 10). Food Blogs: Computers & The Kitchen. Retrieved July 31, 2015 from http://htekidsnews.com/food-blogs-how-your-computer-gets-you-in-the-kitchen/.

Boulos, M.N.K., Brewer, A.C., Karimkhani, C., Buller, D.B. & Dellavalle, R.P. (2014). Mobile Medical and Health Apps: State of the Art, Concerns, Regulatory Control and Certification. *Online Journal of Public Health Informatics*, 5(3), 229. http://doi.org/10.5210/ojphi.v5i3.4814.

Brown, J., Beard, E., Kotz, D., Michie, S. & West, R. (2014). Real-world Effectiveness of E-cigarettes When Used to Aid Smoking Cessation: A Cross-sectional Population Study. *Addiction, 109*(9), 1531–1540. http://doi.org/10.1111/add.12623.

Brownlee, S. (2010). *Overtreated: Why Too Much Medicine is Making Us Sicker and Poorer.* New York: Bloomsbury USA.

Brownstein, J.S., Freifeld, C.C. & Madoff, L.C. (2009). Digital Disease Detection – Harnessing the Web for Public Health Surveillance. *New England Journal of Medicine, 360*(21), 2153–2157. http://doi.org/10.1056/NEJMp0900702.

Cohen, E. & Bonifield, J. (2015, June 8). CNN Report on Surgery Death Rates of Babies Spurs Probe – CNN.com. Retrieved August 23, 2015 from www.cnn.com/2015/06/05/health/st-marys-medical-center-investigation/index.html.

Collier, N. (2012). Uncovering Text Mining: A Survey of Current Work on Web-based Epidemic Intelligence. *Global Public Health, 7*(7), 731–749. http://doi.org/10.1080/17441692.2012.699975.

Conrad, P. (2005). The Shifting Engines of Medicalization. *Journal of Health and Social Behavior, 46*(1), 3–14. http://doi.org/10.1177/002214650504600102.

Cowan, L.T., Wagenen, S.A.V., Brown, B.A., Hedin, R.J., Seino-Stephan, Y., Hall, P.C. & West, J.H. (2012). Apps of Steel: Are Exercise Apps Providing Consumers With Realistic Expectations? A Content Analysis of Exercise Apps for Presence of Behavior Change Theory. *Health Education & Behavior*, 1090198112452126. http://doi.org/10.1177/1090198112452126.

DeLorme, D.E., Huh, J., Reid, L.N. & An, S. (2010). The State of Public Research on Over-the-counter Drug Advertising. *International Journal of Pharmaceutical and Healthcare Marketing, 4*(3), 208–231. http://doi.org/10.1108/17506121011076156.

Diviani, N., van den Putte, B., Giani, S. & van Weert, J.C. (2015). Low Health Literacy and Evaluation of Online Health Information: A Systematic Review of the Literature. *Journal of Medical Internet Research, 17*(5). http://doi.org/10.2196/jmir.4018.

Entertainment Software Association. (2015). *Essential Facts About the Computer and Video Game Industry: 2015 Sales, Demographic and Usage Data.* Washington, DC: Entertainment Software Association. Retrieved August 21, 2015 from www.theesa.com/wp-content/uploads/2015/04/ESA-Essential-Facts-2015.pdf.

Faerber, A.E. & Kreling, D.H. (2012). Now You See It. Now You Don't: Fair Balance and Adequate Provision in Advertisements for Drugs Before and After the Switch from Prescription to Over-the-counter. *Health Communication, 27*(1), 66–74. http://doi.org/10.1080/10410236.2011.569001.

Faerber, A.E. & Kreling, D.H. (2014). Content Analysis of False and Misleading Claims in Television Advertising for Prescription and Nonprescription Drugs. *Journal of General Internal Medicine, 29*(1), 110–118. http://doi.org/10.1007/s11606-013-2604-0.

Gantz, W. & Wang, Z. (2006). Televised NFL Games, the Family, and Domestic Violence. In *Handbook of Sports and Media* (pp. 365–382). Abingdon and New York: Routledge.

Gerber, A.S., Patashnik, E.M., Doherty, D. & Dowling, C. (2010). The Public Wants Information, not Board Mandates, from Comparative Effectiveness Research. *Health Affairs, 29*(10), 1872–1881.

Gollust, S.E., Lantz, P.M. & Ubel, P.A. (2009). The Polarizing Effect of News Media Messages about the Social Determinants of Health. *Journal Information, 99*(12), 2160–2167.

Graven, S.N. & Browne, J.V. (2008). Auditory Development in the Fetus and Infant. *Newborn and Infant Nursing Reviews, 8*(4), 187–193. http://doi.org/10.1053/j.nainr.2008.10.010.

Gupta, S. (2015, January 5). America's 9 Biggest Health Issues. Retrieved July 30, 2015 from www.cnn.com/2015/01/02/opinion/gupta-health-challenges-2015/index.html.

Hadler, N.M., Brownlee, S. & Lenzer, J. (2012). *Worried Sick: A Prescription for Health in an Overtreated America*. Chapel Hill, NC: The University of North Carolina Press.

Harkness, E.L., Mullan, B.M. & Blaszczynski, A. (2015). Association between Pornography Use and Sexual Risk Behaviors in Adult Consumers: A Systematic Review. *Cyberpsychology, Behavior and Social Networking, 18*(2), 59–71. http://doi.org/10.1089/cyber.2014.0343.

Kelly, B.J., Leader, A.E., Mittermaier, D.J., Hornik, R.C. & Cappella, J.N. (2009). The HPV Vaccine and the Media: How Has the Topic Been Covered and What are the Effects on Knowledge about the Virus and Cervical Cancer? *Patient Education and Counseling, 77*(2), 308–313. http://doi.org/10.1016/j.pec.2009.03.018.

Kingkade, T. (2013, May 7). Instagramming Your Food May Signal Bigger Problem, Researcher Says. Retrieved July 31, 2015 from www.huffingtonpost.com/2013/05/07/instagramming-food-problem-foodstagramming_n_3230129.html.

Klara, R. (2014, July 27). Who Will Become the Starbucks of Pot? Retrieved August 22, 2015 from www.adweek.com/news/advertising-branding/who-will-become-starbucks-pot-159145.

Lenhart, Jones, S. & Macgill, A. (2008, December 7). Adults and Video Games. Retrieved August 21, 2015 from www.pewinternet.org/2008/12/07/adults-and-video-games/.

Leventhal, A.M., Strong, D.R., Kirkpatrick, M.G. et al. (2015). Association of Electronic Cigarette Use with Initiation of Combustible Tobacco Product Smoking in Early Adolescence. *JAMA, 314*(7), 700–707. http://doi.org/10.1001/jama.2015.8950.

Levin-Zamir, D., Lemish, D. & Gofin, R. (2011). Media Health Literacy (MHL): Development and Measurement of the Concept among Adolescents. *Health Education Research, 26*(2), 323–335. http://doi.org/10.1093/her/cyr007.

Moorhead, S.A., Hazlett, D.E., Harrison, L., Carroll, J.K., Irwin, A. & Hoving, C. (2013). A New Dimension of Health Care: Systematic Review of the Uses, Benefits, and Limitations of Social Media for Health Communication. *Journal of Medical Internet Research, 15*(4). http://doi.org/10.2196/jmir.1933.

Norman, C. (2011). eHealth Literacy 2.0: Problems and Opportunities With an Evolving Concept. *Journal of Medical Internet Research, 13*(4), e25.

Oremus, W. (2015, February 12). Dying on Facebook Just Got a Little Less Awkward. Retrieved August 23, 2015 from www.slate.com/blogs/future_tense/2015/02/12/facebook_legacy_contact_who_manages_account_when_you_die.html.

Orszag, P. (2008). Opportunities to Increase Efficiency in Health Care, § Committee on Finance. Washington, DC: Congressional Budget Office. Retrieved July 8, 2015 from www.cbo.gov/sites/default/files/cbofiles/ftpdocs/93xx/doc9384/06-16-health summit.pdf.

Pearce, C. (2008). The Truth About Baby Boomer Gamers: A Study of Over-forty Computer Game Players. *Games and Culture, 3*(2), 142–174. http://doi.org/10.1177/1555412008314132.

Perry, S. (2012, May 27). Planned Parenthood's Social-media Magic. Retrieved August 23, 2015 from https://philanthropy.com/article/Planned-Parenthood-s/156541/.

Richardson, V. (2015, August 21). Planned Parenthood Losing Social-media War Sparked by Undercover Videos. Retrieved August 23, 2015 from www.washington-times.com/news/2015/aug/21/planned-parenthood-losing-social-media-war-sparked/.

Rocky Mountain High Intensity Drug Trafficking Area. (2014). *The Legalization of Marijuana in Colorado: The Impact.* Denver, CO: Rocky Mountain High Intensity Drug Trafficking Area. Retrieved August 22, 2015 from www.in.gov/ipac/files/August_2014_Legalization_of_MJ_in_Colorado_the_Impact(1).pdf.

Rosser, B.A. & Eccleston, C. (2011). Smartphone Applications for Pain Management. *Journal of Telemedicine and Telecare, 17*(6), 308–312. http://doi.org/10.1258/jtt.2011.101102.

Rusmevichientong, P. & Williamson, D.P. (2006). An Adaptive Algorithm for Selecting Profitable Keywords for Search-based Advertising Services. In *Proceedings of the 7th ACM Conference on Electronic Commerce* (pp. 260–269). ACM. Retrieved August 11, 2015 from http://dl.acm.org/citation.cfm?id=1134736.

Sachs, C.J. & Chu, L.D. (2000). The Association Between Professional Football Games and Domestic Violence in Los Angeles County. *Journal of Interpersonal Violence, 15*(11), 1192–1201. http://doi.org/10.1177/088626000015011006.

Saraiya, S. (2015, June 25). The Truth about TV's Rape Obsession: How We Struggle with the Broken Myths of Masculinity, on Screen and Off. Retrieved July 31, 2015 from www.salon.com/2015/06/25/the_truth_about_tvs_rape_obsession_how_we_struggle_with_the_broken_myths_of_masculinity_on_screen_and_off/.

Schwitzer, G. (2008). How Do US Journalists Cover Treatments, Tests, Products, and Procedures? An Evaluation of 500 Stories. *PLoS Medicine, 5*(5), e95.

Schwitzer, G. (2009). *The State of Health Journalism in the US.* Henry J. Kaiser Family Foundation, Menlo Park, CA. Retrieved January 5, 2015 from https://kaiserfamilyfoundation.files.wordpress.com/2013/01/7858.pdf.

Sonawane, V. (2015, August 18). Florida Hospital Closes Open Heart Surgery Program After Report of High Infant Mortality Rate. Retrieved August 23, 2015 from www.ibtimes.com/florida-hospital-closes-open-heart-surgery-program-after-report-high-infant-mortality-2057732.

van der Vaart, R., van Deursen, A.J., Drossaert, C.H., Taal, E., van Dijk, J.A. & van de Laar, M.A. (2011). Does the eHealth Literacy Scale (eHEALS) Measure What it Intends to Measure? Validation of a Dutch Version of the eHEALS in Two Adult Populations. *Journal of Medical Internet Research, 13*(4), e86.

Video Tributes. (n.d.). Retrieved August 23, 2015 from www.funeralfuturist.com/funeral-technologies/memorial-video-tributes/.

Vives-Cases, C., Torrubiano-Domínguez, J. & Alvarez-Dardet, C. (2009). The Effect of Television News Items on Intimate Partner Violence Murders. *European Journal of Public Health, 19*(6), 592–596. http://doi.org/10.1093/eurpub/ckp086.

Walker, E.T. (2015, August 6). The Uber-ization of Activism. *New York Times.* Retrieved August 23, 2015 from www.nytimes.com/2015/08/07/opinion/the-uber-ization-of-activism.html.

Walsh-Childers, K., Braddock, J., Rabaza, C. & Schwitzer, G. (2014). One Step Forward, One Step Back: Changes in News Coverage of Medical Interventions. Presented at the Association for Education in Journalism & Mass Communication, Montreal, Canada.

Welch, H.G. & Black, W.C. (2010). Overdiagnosis in Cancer. *Journal of the National Cancer Institute, 102*(9), 605–613.

Welch, H.G., Schwartz, L. & Woloshin, S. (2011). *Overdiagnosed: Making People Sick in the Pursuit of Health.* Boston, MA: Beacon Press.

West, J.H., Hall, P.C., Hanson, C.L., Barnes, M.D., Giraud-Carrier, C. & Barrett, J. (2012). There's an App for That: Content Analysis of Paid Health and Fitness Apps. *Journal of Medical Internet Research, 14*(3), e72. http://doi.org/10.2196/jmir.1977.

INDEX

Page numbers in **bold** denote figures.